ALASKA

D1285413

Welcome to Alaska

Alaska is America's last frontier, with landscapes that stretch out seemingly to infinity. From the lush rain forests of Southeast to the vast, flat tundra in the north, you can stare in awe at calving glaciers, volcanic valleys, jagged sea cliffs, the northern lights, and more. Here you can kayak to icebergs, fly over the highest peak in North America, and spot wildlife from eagles to whales. This book was produced in the middle of the COVID-19 pandemic. As you plan your upcoming travels to Alaska, please confirm that places are still open and let us know when we need to make updates by writing to us at editors@fodors.com.

TOP REASONS TO GO

★ **Denali National Park:** Whether you're flightseeing, rafting, or on foot, this national park is a must.

★ **Cruising:** Nothing beats the panoramic glacier views from an Inside Passage cruise.

★ **Outdoor Adventures:** Fishing the Kenai and hiking Harding Icefield are just the start.

★ **Bears:** When the salmon run, the brown bears of Katmai spring into action.

★ **Crafts:** Aleut weaving and Iñupiaq ivory carvings represent Alaska Native traditions.

Contents

MAPS

Chapter 1

EXPERIENCE ALASKA

20 ULTIMATE EXPERIENCES

Alaska offers terrific experiences that should be on every traveler's list. Here are Fodor's top picks for a memorable trip.

1 Juneau and Mendenhall Glacier

Alaska's capital city has a vibrant downtown filled with charming shops, restaurants, and bars, but it's also known for its proximity to the most easily accessible glacier in the state, Mendenhall Glacier. (Ch. 4)

2 Bear-Spotting

Magnificent brown bears are found all over southern and interior Alaska, but Kodiak Island and Katmai National Park are the most popular spots for a sighting. (Ch. 5, 8)

3 Cruising the Inside Passage

This network of waterways in southeastern Alaska is one of the most-traveled routes for cruise ships, taking passengers past glaciers and to small towns. (Ch. 4)

4 Kayaking and Rafting

With 365,000 miles of streams and rivers, there are plenty of opportunities for water adventures, whether it's calm kayaking or class IV white-water rafting. (Ch. 5)

5 Gold Rush History

The discovery of gold created modern Alaska, bringing thousands north to establish towns like Skagway and Dawson City, which still offer gold-panning tours today. (Ch. 4, 7)

6 Whale-Watching

A variety of cetaceans, from gray whales to humpbacks to orcas, are found in Alaskan waters. Prince William Sound and the Inside Passage are prime spots for watching. (Ch. 4, 5)

7 Anchorage

Alaska's most populous city is also its most thriving urban center, with impressive cuisine and nightlife, not to mention gorgeous urban trails for hiking and biking. (Ch. 3)

8 Denali National Park

Home to North America's tallest mountain, Denali is Alaska's most famous park and yet remains surprisingly pristine, with plenty of moose, bears, caribou, and wolves. (Ch. 6)

9 Native Culture

With 229 federally recognized tribes, Alaska has a thriving Native culture, from Anchorage's Alaska Native Heritage Center to Ketchikan's Saxman Totem Park. (Ch. 3, 4)

10 Flightseeing Tours

Not everywhere in Alaska is accessible by road, but small bush planes offer amazing views and unparalleled access to some of the state's most wondrous spots. (Ch. 5)

11 Fishing

From Ketchikan to Homer, Alaska is perhaps the best place for fishing in the world. Try your hand at nabbing a salmon or halibut or fly-fishing via a chartered boat. (Ch. 4)

12 The Midnight Sun

In summer, some Alaskan regions see nearly 24 hours of sunlight. Take advantage by seeing a midnight baseball game in Fairbanks or attending various festivals. (Ch. 7)

13 Fairbanks

Home to the University of Alaska, the state's second largest city is a young, hip college town with plenty of art, culture, breweries, and outdoor activities. (Ch. 7)

14 Glacier-Trekking

Alaska is home to nearly 100,000 glaciers, like Mendenhall and Matanuska, and a guided glacier trek is the perfect way to explore these otherworldly giants up close. (Ch. 5)

15 Dog sledding

Mushing is one of Alaska's most popular sports, thanks to the famed Iditarod race from Anchorage to Nome. In the offseason, you can visit dog sled camps across the state. (Ch. 8)

16 Seafood

Dining in Alaska is all about the freshly caught seafood, from Copper River red salmon and halibut cheeks to Dungeness and king crabs. (Ch. 4, 5, 7)

17 Wildlife

Wildlife abounds all over Alaska, from bears, moose, caribou, and wolves in Denali to bison, bald eagles, and Dall sheep in various parks and reserves. (Ch. 6)

18 Kenai Fjords National Park

To experience Alaska's coastline at its best, visit Kenai Fjords and its impressive array of glaciers and sea life, including orcas, otters, and dolphins. (Ch. 5)

19 The Northern Lights

Seeing the stunning colors of the aurora borealis is an unforgettable experience. Visit northern Alaska between October and March for your best chance. (Ch. 8)

20 Alaska's Railroads

The best way to see Alaska's towering mountains and wide-open vistas is from the windows of a train, like the famed White Pass & Yukon Railway. (Ch. 4)

WHAT'S WHERE

1 Anchorage. Containing nearly half the state's population, Anchorage is Alaska's biggest city. The restaurants, art and history museums, numerous espresso stands, and performing arts have earned the city the sobriquet "Seattle of the North." Alaskans often deride the place as "Los Anchorage," but the occasional moose ambling down a street hints at the wilderness nearby.

2 Juneau, the Inside Passage, and Southeast Alaska. Southeast Alaska (or "the Panhandle") includes the state capital (Juneau) and Lynn Canal (the Inside Passage). The region is speckled with small towns and villages, most accessible only by boat or plane. Haines and Skagway are the only towns along the water route that have roads to "the Outside," while the Inside Passage ties together almost all the populated places in the region. Here fjords snake between the mountains, timbered slopes plunge to rocky shores, and marine life abounds.

3 The Kenai Peninsula and Southcentral Alaska. This region offers great fishing, hiking, rafting,

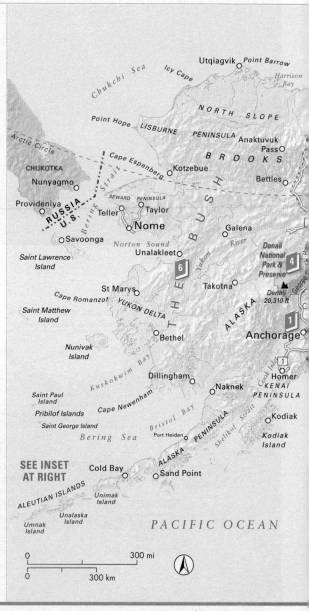

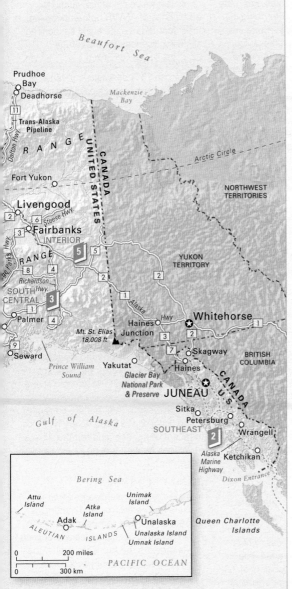

kayaking, and wildlife viewing. Visit Seward and Homer on the Kenai Peninsula and dip your paddle into marine wilderness. Kodiak, in the Gulf of Alaska, is known for its green-carpeted mountains and brown bears. Charter outfits take you to remote areas and choice fishing spots.

4 Denali National Park & Preserve. Home to Denali—the highest peak in North America—Denali National Park & Preserve comprises 6 million acres of Alaska's best wildlife, scenery, and adventures.

5 Fairbanks, the Yukon, and the Interior. Bound by the Brooks Range to the north and the Alaska Range to the south, the Interior is home to a vast expanse of pristine backcountry. Fairbanks is the largest city in this immense region that includes Canada's Yukon Territory; it's also a gateway to the towns of the Arctic.

6 The Bush. Iñupiat people share the tundra with the Prudhoe Bay oil fields, brown bears roam Katmai National Park, and prospectors still pan for gold. Except for the Dalton Highway and a few short roads near Nome, the region is essentially roadless. Traveling here requires planning; the reward is true adventure.

Alaska Today

POLITICS

Alaska's politics and policies seem as wild as its vast, untamed acres. From the Iditarod to cabin building, everything in Alaska is steeped in politics—there are more politicians per capita than police officers. The largest state in the nation comes with a seemingly limitless supply of natural resources, and with them come conflict and controversy. Alaska's politics are thus saddled with numerous fiscal and environmental responsibilities, none of which are easily met. Before it entered statehood in 1959, Alaska had been reviled as Seward's Folly; and for nearly 50 years of statehood, it was often overlooked in the political media. Since then, certain instances have kept Alaska politics in the limelight: then-governor Sarah Palin was tapped to be the 2008 presidential running mate, current senator Lisa Murkowski continues to be an occasional swing vote in the Senate, and an increasing demand for Alaska oil continues to shape climate change policy.

Gas and mining corporations have enormous influence on public policy in Alaska, but not without pushback from environmentalists and subsistence advocates. There are ongoing and highly publicized battles over proposed mines and offshore oil drilling. Also in the media spotlight is the Arctic National Wildlife Refuge (ANWR), 19.2 million roadless acres supporting 45 species of land and marine mammals, 36 species of fish, and 180 species of birds. ANWR is in the northeast corner of the state and has been dubbed the Last Great Wilderness. The only way to get there is by bush plane. In 2015, then-president Barack Obama proposed new protections for parts of ANWR to Congress, which sparked much national and statewide debate. Area 1002, which consists of 1.5 million acres along the refuge's coastal plain, is thought to contain a large supply of oil that the state would like to explore. Then-president Donald Trump, in one of his last moves in office, auctioned off patches of ANWR before incoming President Biden once again suspended all drilling licenses for the refuge.

ECONOMICS

More than 75% of Alaska's revenue is derived from oil extraction. The state is also the nation's leader in commercial fishing but ranks dead last in numbers of farms and farm products. There is very little manufacturing in the state. Thus the cost of manufactured goods, produce, and other foodstuffs is considerably higher than in other states.

Because Alaska is predominantly composed of rural villages, thousands of miles from any distribution center, the cost of living is relatively high. In some cities in the Bush, for instance, one can expect to pay $10 for a gallon of milk.

The Permanent Fund Dividend (PFD) is a sacred check that Alaskans receive once a year, and for many in the Bush it can be a lifesaver. In 1977 the fund was created to receive 25% of Alaska's oil royalty income. It was designed to maintain a state income even after the reserves had been tapped out. Residents receive a check every October in amounts that vary from year to year, but are currently in the ballpark of $1,200. Every bit helps; in recent years, rural and remote Alaska have seen heating fuel go as high as $12 per gallon.

CLIMATE CHANGE

In Alaska few people disagree that the glaciers and permafrost are melting; it's just a fact. Warmer temperatures mean new economic opportunities and financial challenges. As the Arctic ice melts, the region is becoming more accessible, which means there is greater possibility for more oil and gas exploration.

However, as temperatures rise, so does the ocean. Newtok's 375 residents are some of the state's first climate refugees, with residents moving to a new townsite nine miles upriver at a cost of $100 million. The village of Kivalina, a remote whaling community of almost 400 inhabitants, is also under immediate threat as the water rises and the coast erodes. Relocation is essential, but the cost is high both financially and for these people's history and way of life.

Many Native tribes in the Arctic region have begun to adapt to the changes that global warming has impressed upon them. Their hunting patterns have adjusted to new migration times and routes. Unfortunately permafrost, the frozen ground they live upon, is also melting. Towns and villages are sinking, traditional underground food storage is untenable, and the cost of relocation could rise into the billions of dollars. Groups like the Army Corps of Engineers, social artists, and political and environmental activists are scrambling to save the villages, the people, and their cultures.

THE ARTS

Visitors are often surprised to find that Alaska is filled with an impressive number of talented contemporary artists. Not only do some of the world's foremost artists, writers, and photographers reside in Alaska, there is equal talent found among those whose work never sees the Outside. For many Alaskans the long, dark winter is a great time to hunker down, season their craft, and prepare to sell their wares in the summer at galleries, museums, and theaters all over the state. In summer, weekend outdoor markets are also an excellent place to find local and Alaska Native talent. Look for the "Made in Alaska" sticker or the silver hand symbol for authenticity.

SPORTS

In a state full of renegades and thrill seekers, it is no wonder that the biggest sporting event of the year occasionally requires a racer to permanently relinquish feeling in a finger or foot. The Iditarod Trail Sled Dog Race, a 1,049-mile-long trek, is by far the most popular sporting event in Alaska. It began in 1973 in homage to the brave souls who ventured to Nome in 1925 to take medicine to villagers struck with one of the worst outbreaks of diphtheria ever recorded. Nowadays, more than 50 racers and their packs of canines converge on the ice and snow on the first Saturday in March to race from Anchorage to Nome. The sport is not without controversy; high-profile mushers have come under scrutiny since several groups have made allegations of animal cruelty.

Although Alaskans from all over the state are passionate about their dog mushers, the most popular sport is basketball. Even as far north as Utqiaġvik (where it is most popular), one can find basketball courts both inside and outside. The most popular urban team sport is ice hockey.

What to Eat and Drink in Alaska

BLACK COD

Black cod may be overshadowed by more famous Alaskan seafood like salmon and halibut, but it's still one of the most delicious fresh fishes you can sample here. So oily it's also known as butterfish, black cod is a rich and succulent choice found on many menus throughout the state.

BLUEBERRIES

Berry-picking here is a serious business. People compete with each other for the best spots during the short growing season for the chance to sample fresh, sweet berries. If you can't go berry-picking, look for options like gooseberry pie, wild berry cobbler, and blueberry French toast on menus.

BEER

The craft beer craze has made it to Alaska, and now dozens of microbreweries scattered across the state provide ample tasting opportunities for beer lovers. Try creations that make use of the native bounty, like beers brewed with spruce tips, an Alaska specialty since Captain Cook's first voyage here.

SALMON

Sampling salmon, perhaps Alaska's most famous food, is an essential experience. Throughout the summer, five types of salmon (king, coho, sockeye, chum, and pink) fill Alaska's rivers, beckoning commercial and amateur fishers alike. Many consider Copper River salmon to be some of the best in the world, and there's nothing like trying it fresh. Have it grilled simply and alongside fresh local vegetables. Or try smoked salmon, a quintessential Alaska snack.

CRABS

Whether it's Dungeness, snow, or king, you'll find crab in any seaside Alaska town, freshly caught from places like the Aleutian Islands. Get ready to crack open a crab leg and dip the succulent meat in melted butter, one of the most memorable, and tastiest, Alaska culinary experiences. Be sure to wear a bib, or at least have plenty of napkins.

HALIBUT CHEEKS

Another favorite of amateur fishers (Ketchikan in particular has some excellent waters for halibut fishing), fresh-caught halibut should also be on your must-eat list, and halibut cheeks are a delicate, sweet treat. Cut from the head of the fish, the cheeks are small, oval-shaped, and often compared to scallops in appearance and texture. Try them breaded or sautéed with garlic and butter.

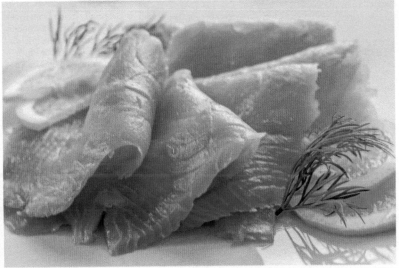

Traditional Alaskan smoked salmon

REINDEER

These domesticated cousins of caribou were first brought over from Siberia and have since become a popular Alaskan protein. Reindeer store their fat on the outside of their muscles, which results in a lean cut free from the marbling found in other red meats. Pair a side of reindeer sausage with breakfast or savor reindeer meatloaf or burgers at dinner.

SOURDOUGH BREAD

A favorite of those who came to Alaska in search of riches during the Klondike gold rush, sourdough bread is created with naturally occurring fermentation instead of baker's yeast. During the gold rush, yeast and baking soda were difficult to find, and so a legend was born (sourdough also keeps a lot longer than regular bread). Today items like sourdough pancakes and pastries help keep the gold rush spirit alive on menus throughout the state.

KELP

Kelp has been on the menu for Native people along Alaska's southern coast for centuries. Luckily for gourmands, interest has been sparked again and local companies, such as Barnacle Foods, are harvesting and selling it in a variety of forms, including kelp pickles, salsa, and spice mix. Pick some up from an Alaskan grocery store.

AKUTAQ

Don't leave Alaska without experiencing its rich indigenous culture and sampling foods eaten here for centuries. Sometimes called Alaskan ice cream, akutaq is a dessert traditionally made from whipped animal fat and berries. Today, the dish is often made with Crisco, sugar, and berries.

What to Buy in Alaska

ULU KNIFE

Originally made from rock, slate, or jade with a wooden or bone handle, the ulu is a curved, all-purpose knife originally used by Alaska Natives for everything from making clothes to cutting food to building boats. Today, it's a fun gift with an interesting history as well as a great kitchen tool, often paired with a bowl for dicing and mincing.

XTRATUFS

These dependable rubber boots are quintessential Alaska, owned by nearly every local in a coastal town. Preferred because of their comfort and ability to withstand brutal Alaska weather, XTRATUFS have become a veritable rite-of-passage for Alaskans. In recent years, the boot-maker has paired with Homer-based company Salmon Sisters, releasing more fashionable XTRATUFS with colorful, patterned interiors.

SMOKED SALMON

You can't head home without bringing back some of Alaska's most famous seafood. Caught fresh and then filleted, brined, and smoked with a variety of methods, smoked salmon is especially delicious when paired with crackers and/or cheese. It often needs to be kept refrigerated, so be sure to check the package before you put it in your luggage.

HANDCRAFTED BOWLS

Birch logs that arrive at the Great Alaskan Bowl Company undergo a 22-step process of shaping, sanding, oiling, and drying until they turn into beautiful objets d'art that ripple with streaks of dark and light grain unique to each piece.

QIVIUT HATS

Alaskans excel at inventing ways to keep warm, and the qiviut hat is one of their most beloved creations. Qiviut is the undercoat of a musk ox that yields a yarn finer than cashmere and eight times warmer than wool. Find hand-knit hats in places like the Oomingmak Musk Ox Producers' Co-operative.

JADE

Alaska's state gem, jade has long been used by Alaska Native people for tools, jewelry, and weapons. There's lots of it to go around—including an entire jade mountain on Alaska's Seward Peninsula—so jade carvings and jewelry can be found in gift shops across the state.

The Kobuk tea company in Anchorage

TEA

Alaskans can get pretty experimental with their tea. Popular varieties include wild rose and tea made from chaga, an antioxidant-packed fungus that grows on birch trees throughout the north. Anchorage-based The Kobuk has been leading this tea brigade for more than 50 years, and at their eclectic downtown store, you can buy all manner of local and international goods; be sure to take home some of their signature Samovar Tea.

GOLD

Alaska's other most famous precious metal is what sent thousands careening north during the Yukon gold rush. Today, you can easily buy this prized Alaska gold or find some yourself on a gold-panning tour. Once you get home, you'll be able to relive the thrill of those first Klondikers as you show off your Alaska gold.

CHRISTMAS DECORATIONS

It may be July, but that won't stop shoppers from buying Christmas ornaments at the Santa Claus House in North Pole, Alaska. Fifteen minutes south of Fairbanks, the town is decorated for the holidays year-round and offers plenty of items to put you in the holiday spirit. You can even tell your kids that their gifts really did come from the North Pole.

NATIVE CRAFTS

The Alaska Native culture is reflected in its abundance of craft traditions, from totem poles to intricate baskets and detailed carvings. Many of these reflect traditions passed down across countless generations. Each indigenous group is noted for particular skills and visual-art styles.

Best Outdoor Adventures in Alaska

**VIEW THE NORTHERN LIGHTS
FROM CHENA HOT SPRINGS**
Located 60 miles northeast of Fairbanks, Chena Hot Springs experiences nearly 24 hours of darkness in mid-winter, making it an ideal place to view aurora borealis displays.

CAMP IN DENALI NATIONAL PARK
Alaska's most popular national park, Denali's wilderness stretches as far as the imagination, and you shouldn't settle for seeing it from a tour bus. Grab your backpack and a bear-proof food container and head out for a multiday backcountry adventure. Shuttle buses allow you to start your hike anywhere along the 92-mile Denali Park Road.

EXPLORE KATMAI NATIONAL PARK
Accessible only by plane, Katmai, known as the land of ten thousand smokes, features a dynamic combination of volcanic activity and coastal brown bears. Float trips, hiking, and kayaking are popular activities, all with a high chance of spotting one of the park's 2,200 bears.

TREK ON MENDENHALL GLACIER
The cruise-ship industry has turned downtown Juneau into a thriving summer tourism destination. Get away from the crowds and board a helicopter for Mendenhall Glacier. A litany of tour options are available, including landings next to glittering blue glacial lakes and dog sledding tours.

TAKE A FLIGHTSEEING TOUR OVER DENALI
Even if you are lucky enough to glimpse "the High One" from within Denali National Park, there's still nothing like seeing Denali up close. Charter a flightseeing tour out of Healy or Talkeetna and get so close to the continent's highest peak that you can practically feel the ice beneath your feet.

BACKPACK IN THE ARCTIC NATIONAL WILDLIFE REFUGE
Meant for those who find a Denali backpacking trip too easy, the Arctic National Wildlife Refuge (known in conservation circles simply as "the Refuge") is a remote, protected body of more than 19 million acres in the northeast corner of the state. It is perhaps best known for the Porcupine Caribou herd, which numbers more than 210,000 animals. An eclectic mix of ecosystems, mountain ranges, plants, and wildlife make this distant but magical piece of the planet an unforgettable sight. If disappearing alone into the largest protected region above the Arctic Circle isn't to your taste, outfitters offer rafting, hiking, and backpacking tours.

KAYAK IN GLACIER BAY NATIONAL PARK
Millions have traveled to Glacier Bay to see this incredible park forged by ice, and there is no better way to explore it than from your very own kayak. Guided tours and personal rentals are offered by park concessionaires and get you as close to the glaciers as possible.

HIKE THE CHILKOOT TRAIL
Originating just north of Skagway, the Chilkoot Trail became famous as the starting point for the Klondike gold rush. Today the well-maintained trail crosses the Canadian border and stretches 33 miles. Guided hikes are available, or you can set out on your own.

Best Wildlife Experiences in Alaska

THE BIG 5 IN DENALI NATIONAL PARK

Denali gives you the best chance to spot the "Big 5" of Alaska animals. Bears, moose, wolves, caribou, and Dall sheep all live throughout the park in various regions, and sightings happen often. Always be on the lookout (even if you're on a bus tour), and be sure to keep your distance.

BALD EAGLES IN HAINES

These majestic birds can be found all over the state, lounging everywhere from the docks of Juneau to the northern villages of the Bush. But the world's largest gathering of bald eagles occurs in Southeast Alaska each winter, along the Chilkat River near Haines. Here they build some of the biggest nests in the world, the largest one recorded to date weighing almost 3 tons.

HUMPBACK AND ORCA WHALES IN JUNEAU

Whale-watching tours are offered from many coastal towns, but the best leave from Juneau. Here huge humpback whales move in pods, traveling and feeding together. The finale occurs when every whale rockets to the surface for air. You can also often spot majestic orcas traveling with their young.

OTTERS AND SEALS IN GLACIER BAY

Whether you're sailing through Glacier Bay National Park on a large cruise ship or kayaking on a guided tour, keep your eyes out for the many animals that inhabit this area. Otters and harbor seals are often found on the rocky shores, hanging out on ice floes, or swimming in the waters.

IDITAROD TRAIL SLED DOG RACE

The original Iditarod was a relay of dog teams getting medication to Nome during a diphtheria outbreak in 1925. Today the Iditarod commemorates the history and culture of dog mushing in Alaska. The race begins in early March in Anchorage, with the top runners reaching Nome eight to ten days later.

SALMON IN KETCHIKAN

The Southeast town of Ketchikan is often referred to as the salmon capital of the world. Head out on a fishing boat to try your luck catching one yourself. Every summer, salmon return to where they were born to spawn and die; seeing them fill the rivers is morbid, but part of the circle of life.

BROWN BEARS ON KODIAK ISLAND

Brown bears, or grizzlies, are found throughout the state, from Admiralty Island near Juneau to Katmai National Park. But one of the most accessible places is Kodiak National Wildlife Refuge. Spot them most easily in July and August, feeding along the salmon-filled streams.

BELUGA WHALES AND DOLPHINS IN TURNAGAIN ARM

Turnagain Arm, a waterway in the northwestern part of the Gulf of Alaska, is known for its large tidal ranges (it has the second-highest tides in North America). Driving along it through Cook Inlet is one of the most scenic road trips in the country. As you head from Anchorage to the Kenai Peninsula, be on constant lookout for the beluga whales and dolphins that regularly swim through these waters; Beluga Point is a popular stop for a photo-op.

CARIBOU IN ARCTIC NATIONAL WILDLIFE REFUGE

Sometimes called the nomads of the north, caribou are long-distance wandering mammals. Within the Arctic National Wildlife Refuge, you'll find the Porcupine Caribou herd, one of the greatest remaining groups of caribou in the world; the herd has ranged between 100,000 and 210,000 over the past decades. Glimpsing these majestic creatures en masse is an unforgettable experience.

Alaska Cruises 101

Alaska is one of cruising's showcase destinations. From traditional loop cruises of the Inside Passage to one-way trips between the Inside Passage and the Gulf of Alaska, traveling by boat allows you to glimpse gorgeous glaciers and visit charming small towns, all places that are otherwise difficult to reach on your own.

WHEN TO GO
Cruise season runs from mid-May to late September. The most popular sailing dates are from late June through August, when warm days are plentiful, wildlife is most visible, and crowds (and prices) are at their peak. In spring, wildflowers are abundant and early fall brings the splendor of autumn colors. Cruising in these low and shoulder seasons will give you discounted fares, better availability of ships and certain cabins, and ports almost completely free of tourists. However, some excursions and establishments may not be open for the season in May or already closed for the season in September.

CRUISE ITINERARIES
Cruise ships typically follow one of two itineraries in Alaska: round-trip Inside Passage loops and one-way Inside Passage–Gulf of Alaska routes. Itineraries are usually seven days, although some lines offer longer trips. The most popular ports of call you'll most likely visit on your cruise are Juneau, Skagway, Ketchikan, and Sitka. Many itineraries also take you through Glacier Bay National Park and to some of Alaska's largest glaciers, like Hubbard Glacier.

Smaller ships typically sail from Juneau or other ports, stopping at the popular towns as well as smaller, less visited villages. Some expedition vessels focus on remote beaches and fjords with few, if any, port calls.

Most cruise lines also offer shore excursions you can book before you board. These activities best capture what a particular port is most known for and are usually associated with local guides and companies. Not all excursions are available at all times of the year, so double-check your dates if you have anything on your must-do list.

LAND TOURS
Most cruise lines offer the option of independent, hosted, or fully escorted land tours before or after your cruise. Typical land tours can take you to Anchorage, Denali National Park, and/or Fairbanks, and many include a ride aboard the Alaska Railroad. Some cruise lines also offer tours into the Yukon.

BOOKING YOUR CRUISE
As a rule, the majority of cruisers plan their trips four to six months ahead of time. It follows, then, that a four-to-six month window should give you the best pick of sail dates, ships, itineraries, cabins, and flights to the port city. If you're looking for a standard itinerary and aren't choosy about the vessel or dates, you could wait for a last-minute discount, but they are harder to find than in the past.

Many shore excursions offer the chance to trek on a glacier.

WHAT'S INCLUDED

Cruise fares typically include accommodation, onboard meals and snacks, and most onboard activities. Not normally included are airfare, shore excursions, tips, soft drinks, alcoholic drinks, specialty dining, or spa treatments. Many cruise lines offer an option to add unlimited alcohol to your trip for an extra cost. Note that because single cabins for solo travelers are nonexistent on cruise ships, those traveling alone may pay twice the advertised per-person rate for a double cabin. Some cruise lines will find roommates of the same sex for singles so that each can travel at the regular per-person rate.

ABOARD THE SHIP

While you'll probably be out and about when your ship docks at a port of call, many itineraries include at least one full day at sea. Regardless of the cruise line, there are always numerous activities to keep you occupied while onboard. There are usually several different restaurants and bars, as well as a spa and several pools (yes, sometimes it does get warm enough to swim in Alaska). There's nightly entertainment, ranging from talent shows to live performances, and most cruise lines also offer classes, games, and entertainment throughout the day. As a rule, the larger the ship, the more activities are available.

SMALL-SHIP CRUISING

Compact expedition-type vessels bring you right up to the shoreline to skirt the face of a glacier and pull through narrow channels where big ships don't fit. You'll see more wildlife and call into smaller ports, as well as some of the better-known towns. Enrichment talks—conducted by naturalists, Alaska Natives, and other experts—are the norm. Small-ship cruising can be pricey, as fares tend to be all-inclusive, but have few onboard charges, and, given the size of the ship, fewer opportunities for spending time onboard.

MOST POPULAR CRUISE LINES

Nearly every major cruise line offers multiple itineraries and ships in Alaska, but some of the most popular are Princess Cruises, Holland America, Norwegian Cruise Line, Celebrity Cruises, and Royal Caribbean.

Best Shore Excursions in Alaska

SNORKELING IN KETCHIKAN

With a wet suit and guide, you can spend an hour spying on the cool marine species—including sunflower and blood starfish, sea urchins, and sea cucumbers—that inhabit the calm tide pools and submerged rock walls around Mountain Point.

HELICOPTER GLACIER TREKKING IN JUNEAU

The Juneau Icefield is home to massive glaciers with awesome bright blue crevasses and can be your landing pad when you take a scenic helicopter tour from Juneau. No experience is required, but you'll need to be in decent physical condition as you strap on mountaineering spikes and other glacier gear and explore two miles or more of steep, uneven, and visually surreal terrain. Some treks even teach you the basics of ice-wall climbing.

ROCK CLIMBING IN SKAGWAY

If you're looking for a physical challenge in the remote Alaska wilderness, the Klondike Rock Climbing and Rappelling Adventure in Skagway definitely qualifies. After a short hike to the base of granite cliffs in the region's renowned White Pass, you'll learn the proper techniques of rock climbing and rappelling from experienced guides. There are multiple climbing routes to choose from—from easy to very difficult. The payoff is twofold: the awesome views of the Skagway River and surrounding wilderness as well as the exhilaration of rappelling back down to the base.

FISHING IN SITKA

If you love to fish, Sitka is the place to go, thanks to its location on the open ocean; anglers can catch any of five species of Pacific salmon, including prized king salmon, as well as halibut. Opt for a half-day excursion focused on trolling or mooching for salmon or book a full day to also anchor and jig for halibut. Any fish you catch can be processed, frozen, and shipped home for you to enjoy.

ATV TOUR IN KETCHIKAN

Keep your foot on the gas pedal and your eyes on the trail as you navigate an ATV over 10 miles of backcountry rain forest. There's a chance to spot local wildlife—from eagles to deer and bears—as you race over rugged terrain. Enjoy the adrenaline rush of navigating sharp curves, then swap the steering wheel for the passenger seat and enjoy the views of the Tongass National Forest (the largest in the country), Behm Canal, and the Inside Passage, where your ship is docked.

WHALE-WATCHING IN THE ICY STRAIT

Humpbacks or orcas—do you have a favorite? It doesn't really matter because during a whale-watching excursion in the Icy Strait, you're likely to see both. How many and how close depends on the month, the weather, and however the whales are feeling that day. But spending three or four hours watching these magnificent creatures surface, splash,

Glacier trekking on the Juneau Icefield

spout, bubble-feed, and even breach out of the water from any distance is pretty amazing. Sea lions, dolphins, and even bears are bonus species you might see, so bring your binoculars and have your camera ready.

MISTY FIORDS FLIGHTSEEING TOUR IN KETCHIKAN

During a Misty Fiords Flightseeing tour, you'll soar above the huge granite cliffs, cascading waterfalls, and unspoiled wilderness of this two million-acre National Monument area located on postcard-perfect Rudyerd Bay. Depending on the tour you book, you might even land on a secluded lake, where you can soak in the serenity by stepping onto the pontoon.

DOG SLEDDING ON MENDENHALL GLACIER IN JUNEAU

If you've always wanted to get behind a sled of ready-to-run Alaska huskies and yell mush, book an authentic dog sled adventure—even in the middle of summer—by helicoptering from Juneau to a dog sled camp on the icy-blue Mendenhall Glacier. There, you'll meet dozens of resident canines who love to run (as well as their irresistibly cute puppies) and even take the reins yourself to guide your dog team on an exhilarating sled adventure across the snow pack.

WHITE PASS TRAIN AND MOUNTAIN BIKING IN SKAGWAY

Don't let the sedate train ride from Skagway on the vintage White Pass & Yukon Route Railroad fool you. Once you've enjoyed the stunning scenery of the Skagway Valley and arrive

at White Pass Summit, it will be time to put on your helmet, straddle your mountain bike, and ride back down—descending almost 3,000 thrilling feet over 15 miles along the Klondike Highway.

BEAR-WATCHING AND FLIGHTSEEING IN KETCHIKAN

Soar high above the wild landscape around Ketchikan in a floatplane before landing on a lake at one of several locations where Alaska black bears (and occasionally brown bears) congregate: Neets Bay (home to the highest black bear population per square mile in North America), Prince of Wales Island (the third-largest island in the United States and a known bear habitat), or Misty Fiords.

Alaska's History

THE FIRST PEOPLE

No one knows for sure when humans first began living in the northwest corner of the North American continent. How and when they arrived is still a subject of debate. One popular theory is that 12,000 years ago humans followed the eastern migration of Ice Age mammals over the Bering Land Bridge, a 600-mile-wide stretch of land that connected present-day Alaska to Siberia. To date, the oldest human remains found in Alaska are 11,500 years old, the second-oldest Ice Age remains to be found in the world. Found in Central Alaska near the Tanana River, the remains of a three-year-old girl are thought to be those of an Athabascan ancestral relative.

No matter when humans first arrived, by 1750, there were only 57,300 Native peoples living in Russian Alaska, including Aleuts, Alutiit, Yupiit, Iñupiat, Athabascans, Tlingits, and Haidas; many had been killed by disease and Russian traders. Notably, according to the U.S. Census, today there are more than 120,000 American Indians and Alaska Natives living in the state.

RUSSIANS IN ALASKA

It wasn't until 1741 that Danish navigator Vitus Bering, under Russian rule, made the Alaska region known to his fellow European explorers. Bering died before he could ever explore the continent further or return to Russia.

Politically speaking, Russia then imposed itself on Alaska to varying degrees. It was the arrival of the promyshlenniki, or fur hunters, that had the biggest impact on Alaska Native cultures. By most accounts, the hunters were illiterate, quarrelsome, hard-drinking, and virtually out of control. They penetrated the Aleutian chain and made themselves masters of the islands and their inhabitants, the Aleuts. Several times the Natives

revolted; their attempts were squelched, and they were brutalized. By 1790 the small fur traders were replaced by large Russian companies. Siberian fur trader Alexander Andreyevich Baranov became manager of a fur-trading company and director of a settlement on Kodiak Island in 1791. He essentially governed all Russian activities in North America until 1818, when he was ordered back to Russia. Word was spreading to the Russian government that foreigners, particularly Americans, were gaining a disproportionate share of the Alaska market. The Russian Navy was ordered to assume control of Alaska, and by 1821 it had barred all foreign ships from entering Alaska waters. Russia created new policies forbidding any trade with non-Russians and requiring that the colonies be supplied solely by Russian ships.

The 1853 Crimean War between Imperial Russia and Britain and France put a great financial burden on Russia. It fiscally behooved the country to sell Russian Alaska. In 1867, under a treaty signed by U.S. Secretary of State William H. Seward, Alaska was sold to the United States for $7.2 million. On October 18, 1867, the territory officially changed hands. Newspapers around the nation hailed the purchase of Alaska as "Seward's Folly." Within 30 years, however, one of the biggest gold strikes in the world would bring hundreds of thousands of people to this U.S. territory.

THE GOLD RUSH

The great Klondike gold discoveries of 1896 gained national (and worldwide) attention. Due to the depression of 1893, the need for food, money, and hope sparked a gold fever unmatched in history. Men and women alike clamored for information about Alaska, not realizing that the Klondike was in the Yukon Territory of Canada. Perhaps if they'd known their geography, Alaska would never have become the state that it is now.

The most popular route for the gold stampeders was to go entirely by water. It wasn't cheaper, but it was far easier than taking the inland route. They would start in either San Francisco or Seattle, buy passage on a steamship, and disembark more than 1,000 nautical miles later in Skagway, Alaska. No gold was in Skagway, but overnight it became a city of 20,000 miners. Gold-seekers used it as a place to negotiate and get ready for the only part of their journey that would be traversed on foot. The Chilkoot Trail was 35 challenging miles that were too rugged for packhorses. The hardest part of the journey was the climb to the summit, Chilkoot Pass. This climb was known as the Golden Staircase, a ¾-mile hike on a 45-degree incline. Chilkoot Pass was the gateway to Canada and the point at which the Canadian government required each person entering the territory to have at least a year's supply (approximately 1 ton) of food. This is partially why it took most stampeders one to three months to travel this 35-mile stretch. At the base of the Golden Staircase, stampeders had everything they were taking over the pass weighed and were charged $1 per pound. Once into Canada, they built boats and floated the remaining 600 miles to Dawson City, where the gold rush was taking place. By 1899 the Yukon gold rush was over, however, and the population of Skagway shrank dramatically.

Alaska experienced its own gold strike in Nome, on the Seward Peninsula, in 1898. The fever didn't actually hit until 1900, but, because it did, gold mining all over Alaska began to get more national attention.

WORLD WAR II

In 1942, after the United States entered the war, the War Production Board deemed gold mining nonessential to the war effort and forced gold mining all over the country to come to a halt. Despite this, World War II was financially beneficial to parts of Alaska. Numerous bases and ports were strategically built around the state, and the Alaska Highway was created to help deliver supplies to them.

The only time Alaska had any direct involvement with the war was in June 1942, when the Japanese attacked Attu and Kiska Islands in the Aleutian chain. The attack has been recorded in history as an "incident," but it had a great impact on many lives; a few hundred casualties occurred due to friendly fire. Nearly a thousand Alaska Native inhabitants were relocated and many died in the process.

STATEHOOD

On January 3, 1959, "Seward's Folly" became the 49th state in the nation—more than 100 years after Seward first visited. Soon, a mass of investors, bold entrepreneurs, tourists, and land grabbers began to arrive. It's still a new state, far from direct scrutiny by the rest of the nation. With a constantly growing, competitive industry of oil and other natural resources, Alaska has made an identity for itself that resembles that of no other state. It boasts the second-highest production of gas and oil in the country, is twice the size of the second-largest state, and has millions of lakes, minimal pollution, and endless possibilities.

What to Read and Watch Before Your Trip

BALTO
This 1995 animated classic captures the spirit of adventure and heroism in Alaska dog-sledding with a very fictionalized tale of the sled dog who led the journey to deliver medicine to Nome, Alaska, during the 1925 diphtheria outbreak (the inspiration for the Iditarod).

BETWEEN EARTH AND SKY
From melting permafrost to depleting salmon stocks to whole villages falling into the sea, Paul Allen Hunton's documentary examines Alaska's role on the front lines of the fight against climate change and what we can do to make this region habitable for the generations to follow.

BLONDE INDIAN
BY ERNESTINE HAYES
A real and at times sobering examination of the Alaska Native population since the arrival of Europeans, Ernestine Hayes's memoir is required reading for those wishing to confront the recent struggles and issues of the state.

THE CALL OF THE WILD
BY JACK LONDON
Inspired by Jack London's time in the Yukon, this 1903 adventure novel follows a husky named Buck who is kidnapped from his home in California and sent north to become a sled dog.

CLASSIC
It's hard to believe Christopher Guest didn't produce this endearing documentary about the Nenana Ice Classic, the state's annual ice-melt guessing game.

DEADLIEST CATCH
This popular television series highlights the dangers faced by the fishing crews based in Dutch Harbor, Alaska, as they search for king crabs on the Bering Sea.

GRIZZLY MAN
In this acclaimed documentary, Werner Herzog examines the life of Timothy Treadwell, a self-proclaimed grizzly bear expert who spent several summers in the Alaska Bush communing with multiple bears before being killed by a grizzly in 2003.

HYPERBOREAL
BY JOAN NAVIYUK KANE
Written in both English and the writer's native Iñupiaq, Hyperboreal is a collection of poetry that captures the beauty of Alaska's far north.

INTO THE WILD
BY JON KRAKAUER
Arguably the most controversial and divisive story to come out of the state in the last 25 years, Jon Krakauer's book (and the subsequent 2007 film adaptation) examines the life and travels of Chris McCandless, whose adventures hitchhiking to Alaska and living in Denali National Park eventually led to his demise.

NORTHERN EXPOSURE
A fish-out-of-water tale of a New York City doctor who finds himself in a quirky small town in Alaska, this television show aired for six seasons in the 1990s and was inspired by the equally quirky town of Talkeetna, Alaska.

ORDINARY WOLVES
BY SETH KANTNER
A heartbreaking and beautiful novel from the far north, Seth Kantner's story follows the life of Cutuk Hawcly, who, like Kantner, is raised in a sod igloo in Alaska's Arctic region.

THE SNOW CHILD BY EOWYN IVEY
Set in the 1920s, The Snow Child is the story of a childless homesteading couple whose lives are turned upside down by the sudden appearance of a mysterious little girl who seems capable of surviving alone in the harsh wilderness.

Chapter 2

TRAVEL SMART
ALASKA

Updated by
Amy Fletcher

★ **CAPITAL:**
Juneau

👥 **POPULATION:**
731,545

💬 **LANGUAGE:**
English

$ **CURRENCY:**
U.S. Dollar

☎ **AREA CODES:**
907, 250

⚠ **EMERGENCIES:**
911

🚗 **DRIVING:**
On the right side of the road

⚡ **ELECTRICITY:**
120-240 v/60 cycles;
plugs have two or three
rectangular prongs

🕐 **TIME:**
4 hours behind New York
(5 hours in parts of the
Aleutian Islands)

🌐 **WEB RESOURCES:**
www.travelalaska.com
www.alaskamagazine.com
www.alaskanative.net
www.alaskageographic.org

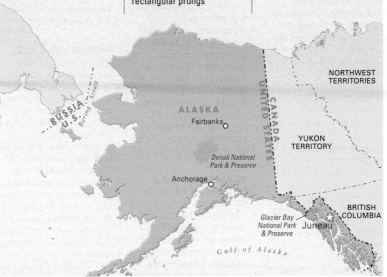

Need to Know

As one of the most popular destinations in the United States, there are numerous things to see and do in Alaska, and visiting can be overwhelming for a first-time visitor. Here are some key tips to help you navigate your trip, whether it's your first time visiting or your twentieth.

IT CAN BE COLD, EVEN IN THE MIDDLE OF THE SUMMER.

While some places in Alaska's interior can hit the high 80s during the summer, odds are you won't be wearing shorts and T-shirts most of the time. On overcast days or along coastal regions, the temperature rarely cracks 70 degrees. Combine that with a little bit of wind (not uncommon near the water or in the mountains) and things can get downright chilly. Be prepared with plenty of warm layers, including hats and gloves. Also, always be prepared for rain, as sudden storms are common year-round. On the flip side, you should always pack sunscreen, even if the temperature is cool. Sunglasses are also essential, especially when visiting glaciers.

RESPECTING WILDLIFE IS CRUCIAL.

Alaska is indeed as untamed as you might imagine, and sightings of wild animals are common, especially in national and state parks and reserves. Be respectful of any animals you encounter, and be sure to keep your distance as much as possible. If you spot a bear, make your presence known by talking, singing, or clapping (bears don't like noise). If you encounter a bear at close range, don't run. Make yourself as big as possible and talk in a normal voice. If a brown bear attacks you, play dead. If a black bear attacks you, you are better off fighting back with anything you can find.

DON'T GET OVERCONFIDENT ABOUT YOUR HIKING SKILLS.

Travelers lacking outdoor experience need to take precautions when venturing away from the beaten path in national and state parks. Hiking and camping in Alaska can be an amazing experience, but also challenging and sometimes dangerous. If you lack backcountry experience, hire a guide or go on a guided group tour.

BE PREPARED FOR A LOT OF SUN, OR NONE AT ALL.

The light (or lack thereof) is one of Alaska's most dynamic characteristics. Because of its location on the Earth's axis, during summer, parts of Alaska see nearly 24 hours of daylight (the farther north you go, the more sunlight you get). However, in winter, this means some places have several months of total darkness (luckily this makes for some amazing northern lights viewing). Once again, the farther north you go, the more darkness you get.

ALCOHOL MIGHT BE HARD TO FIND.

The drinking age in Alaska is 21, but keep in mind that alcoholism is a devastating problem in many areas, and because of this, many Bush communities do not sell it and some do not allow it at all. Check the rules before flying into a Bush community with alcohol, as it is possible to be charged with illegally importing it. In addition, while there are now many craft breweries throughout Alaska, state law dictates that an individual can only be served 36 ounces of beer per brewery per day (no such law exists for bars).

WEED IS LEGAL HERE.

Recreational marijuana became legal in Alaska for people 21 or older in 2014. Many dispensaries have opened since then, and visitors are allowed to buy and carry up to one ounce of marijuana at a time. Like with cigarettes, it is still illegal to smoke in most indoor public places and all national parks. Unlike cigarettes, it is still illegal to consume marijuana on public streets (you'll get a $100 fine if you're caught doing so).

THERE ARE TWO STATE HOLIDAYS.

In addition to standard national holidays, Alaska also celebrates Alaska Day on October 18th and Seward's Day on the last Monday in March. Some businesses and government offices might be closed on these days, while others (especially museums and national parks) might be more crowded than usual.

IN SUMMER, MOSQUITOES ARE EVERYWHERE.

Alaskan summers are infamous for their mosquitoes. If traveling in the summer, be sure to bring insect repellent; mosquito coils may helpful if you are camping or staying in remote cabins. Head nets can also be a wise purchase.

THERE'S NO SALES TAX (KIND OF).

Alaska does not impose a state sales tax, but individual cities and boroughs (except for Anchorage) have their own taxes.

OUTSIDE OF CITY CENTERS, CELL PHONE SERVICE ISN'T ALWAYS RELIABLE.

It can be easy to take access to a cell phone network for granted in the Lower 48, but you'll quickly learn this isn't always the case in Alaska, where remote stretches of highway or treks into the mountains will often take you out of the range of service. Make sure you have physical backups of directions, itinerary numbers, and anything else you might need before you leave.

DON'T EXPECT TO SEE EVERYTHING.

Alaska's scenery and wildlife is varied and spectacular, but it's also unpredictable so be wary of unrealistic expectations. Weather, uncooperative animals, and other factors will likely prevent you from seeing everything on your checklist. It's possible you won't see bears or moose during your trip at all or that Denali itself will be covered in clouds. Helicopter and small plane tours are often canceled or postponed due to high wind speeds. Don't let this get you down; the challenge will make the wildlife and views you are lucky enough to experience all the more special.

SEAFOOD IS PLENTIFUL, BUT EXPENSIVE.

Alaska is renowned for its natural resources, but the majority of Alaska's commercially harvested fish is exported. The seafood that remains in the state is mostly marketed to visitors (locals are perfectly happy to go out and catch their own) and priced accordingly.

YOU'LL HAVE A HARD TIME FINDING WILD GAME.

While seafood is attainable, Alaska's wild game, like elk and caribou, is not so easily sampled. Specific laws forbid its commercial sale; the closest you can get is domesticated reindeer. There's no good way around this restriction (although a rising farm-to-table movement means an increasing number of restaurants offer exotic

Alaska-raised meats, like yak). Your best bet is to make some friends around the campfire and hope to be offered a sample.

WHEN CAMPING OR HIKING, ALWAYS FILTER UNTREATED WATER.

Alaska has a reputation as a pristine landscape, but no matter how clean your water source may seem, always filter untreated water before drinking it. It may be time-consuming, but nothing ruins a trip faster than a nasty case of giardiasis.

PLACES CAN BE MUCH MORE DIFFICULT TO REACH THAN YOU THINK.

Most of Alaska's hidden gems are located far from the main highway system, which sometimes means they are completely inaccessible via cars or buses. In addition, many smaller communities and towns don't have runways big enough for standard domestic airplanes. Instead, small bush planes or Alaska state ferries are the best ways to reach these out-of-the-way places. Be aware that ferry service doesn't run every day, and anyone with a fear of flying won't be thrilled by the small planes that typically transfer passengers to these towns. Also keep in mind that except for Skagway and Haines, none of the major cities and towns in southeast Alaska (including the state capital of Juneau) are accessible by roads; they can only be reached via plane, cruise ship, or ferry.

Getting Here and Around

Air

Alaska Airlines is the state's flagship carrier, with year-round service from its Seattle hub to Anchorage, Fairbanks, Juneau, Ketchikan, and Sitka. The airline and its subsidiary, Horizon Air, offer direct flights from Anchorage to a handful of American cities year-round, including Chicago, Las Vegas, Los Angeles, and Portland. Alaska Airlines flies to many other North American cities via Seattle or Portland. Other airlines that fly to and from the Lower 48 include American, Delta, JetBlue, and United. Note, however, that few offer nonstop flights; any nonstop flights to Alaska you do find will most likely be in the summer.

Air travel within Alaska is quite expensive, particularly to Bush destinations where flying is the only option. There are also air taxis that fly between towns or backcountry locations and smaller planes that can take you everywhere from the top of Denali to famed glaciers; these often won't fly in poor weather.

AIRPORTS

Anchorage's Ted Stevens International Airport is Alaska's main hub. There are also major airports in Fairbanks, Juneau, and Ketchikan. Sixteen other airports throughout the state also accommodate jet planes.

Boat/Ferry

The ferries of the Alaska Marine Highway System will take you through some of the state's most beautiful regions. These are meant for longer-haul trips, so you can reserve cabins in advance, or even camp out with tents and sleeping bags. The Inside Passage route, the most popular, stretches from Bellingham, Washington, all the way to Skagway and Haines (taking roughly 36 hours).

Bus

Traveling by bus in Alaska can be more economical than traveling by train or by air, but don't count on it being your main mode of travel. Interior Alaska Bus Line, Denali Overland Transportation, and Green Tortoise are some of the most popular bus companies. Keep in mind that buses aren't an option in most of Southeast Alaska.

Car

The Alaska Highway begins in British Columbia and stretches 1,442 miles through the Canadian Yukon. The two-lane highway is paved for its entire length and is open year-round. Highway services are available about every 50 to 100 miles, but there are stretches where gas stations are sparser or open limited hours and areas where cell phone service is nonexistent, so planning ahead is crucial. The rest of the state's roads are found almost exclusively in the Southcentral and Interior regions. They lie mainly between Anchorage, Fairbanks, and the Canadian border.

Rental cars are plentiful in Alaska, and renting a car can be a good way to see the Interior, but note that many destinations (including major cities and towns in the Inside Passage, like Juneau) cannot be reached by car from Anchorage and the Interior. Be advised that most rental outfits don't allow you to drive on some of unpaved roads, such as the Denali Highway, the Haul Road to Prudhoe Bay, and the McCarthy Road. If your plans include any sketchy routes, make sure your rental agreement covers those areas.

Gas prices in the Anchorage area are usually higher than those in the Lower 48, and you can expect to pay even more in Juneau and Ketchikan, and far more in remote villages off the road network, where fuel must be flown in. Driving in Alaska is much less rigorous than it used to be, although it still presents some unusual obstacles. Frost damage can create potholes that require slower driving. Moose often wander onto roads and highways. If you encounter one, pull off to the side and wait for the moose to cross. Flying gravel is a hazard along the Alaska and Dalton Highways, especially in summer. A bug screen will help keep gravel and kamikaze insects off the windshield, and some travelers use clear, hard plastic guards to cover their headlights.

🚢 Cruise

Cruising the Inside Passage has become one of the most popular ways to see the state (not to mention one of the most popular cruise ship routes in the world). Nearly all the major cruise ship lines run trips (ranging from 5 days to 2 weeks) from May through September, taking travelers past glaciers and stopping in ports of call like Haines, Skagway, Juneau, and Ketchikan.

🚕 Taxi

Taxis within cities and larger towns are relatively dependable, although it's still better to call ahead for a car rather than hailing one on the street. Except for in the Bush communities, cabs can be ordered in advance for most towns in Alaska. Some popular cab companies are Alaska Yellow Cabs based in Anchorage, Arctic Taxi in Fairbanks, Alaska Cab in Kenai, and Kodiak City Cab in Kodiak.

Uber and Lyft were only legally allowed in Alaska in 2017. Since then, major cities like Anchorage and Fairbanks have seen ridership spike, but it's best to depend on taxis in smaller towns.

Train

The state-owned Alaska Railroad has service connecting Seward, Anchorage, Talkeetna, Denali National Park, and Fairbanks, as well as additional service connecting Anchorage with Whittier, Portage Glacier, and Spencer Glacier. The Alaska Railroad offers one of the last flagstop trains in North America, the Hurricane Turn, which you can hop on and off at will as you travel through roadless backcountry between Talkeetna and Hurricane Gulch. Traveling by train isn't as economical as traveling by bus, but it's a wonderful way to see the scenery.

Gray Line Alaska offers two- to seven-en-day packages that include luxury train travel from Anchorage to Fairbanks or vice versa, with at least a day of exploring in Denali National Park. For a scenic and historic five-hour trip between Skagway and Fraser, British Columbia, take the White Pass & Yukon Route, which follows the treacherous path taken by prospectors during the Klondike gold rush of 1897–98.

Essentials

🏃 Activities

Sadly, no major league sports team calls Alaska home just yet. Basketball is the most popular sport in the state, with ice hockey following close behind (college ice hockey gets the most attention). The biggest sport event is the Iditarod Trail Sled Dog Race, a 1,149-mile-long trek that sees over 100 racers and their packs of canines race from Anchorage to Nome.

Nature is Alaska's greatest tourism draw, with eight national parks and multiple state parks and reserves for visitors to explore. Chances are you'll find something here that gets your adrenaline pumping, whether you're a hiker, biker, mountain climber, bird-watcher, kayaker, fisher, rafter, or all of the above.

🍽 Dining

Alaska is best known for its seafood, particularly king salmon, halibut, king crab, and shrimp. At the open-air (and often all-you-can-eat) salmon bakes in Juneau, Denali National Park, and Fairbanks, you can expect excellent grilled salmon and halibut. Anchorage has the greatest diversity of restaurants, including sophisticated fine dining, noisy brewpubs, fresh sushi, and a wide variety of international cuisines. Note that many small towns have only one or two eateries; it's not rare for establishments in these small towns not to accept credit cards.

📍 Holidays

In addition to the standard nationwide holidays, Alaska celebrates two state-wide holidays: Alaska Day (October 18), celebrating the transfer of the state's ownership from Russia to the United States; and Seward's Day (last Monday in March), which marks the signing of the treaty that authorized the transfer. In 2017, Alaska officially renamed Columbus Day as Indigenous Peoples Day, celebrated on the second Monday of October, and many communities, particularly in Southeast Alaska, observe Elizabeth Peratrovich Day (February 16) in honor of the Tlingit civil rights hero. Although these are not major holidays, some businesses and government offices may be closed.

🛏 Lodging

Off-season hotel rates are often much lower, but most travelers prefer to visit Alaska in summer, when days are long and temperatures are mild. During the shoulder season (early May and late September) travelers may find slightly lower rates, but some businesses and attractions may be closed.

Alaskan hotels and motels are similar in quality to those in the Lower 48; you'll find many well-known chains in Anchorage and Fairbanks. Nearly every town (with the exception of Bush villages) has at least one B&B, and dozens of choices are available in larger cities. Westmark Hotels is a regional chain, owned by cruise-tour operator Holland America, with hotels in Anchorage, Fairbanks, Sitka, and Skagway, as well as near the entrance to Denali National

Park, plus Dawson City in Canada's Yukon Territory. Princess Tours owns a luxury hotel in Fairbanks and lodges outside Denali National Park, in Denali State Park, near Wrangell–St. Elias National Park, and on the Kenai Peninsula. The most unique way to stay in Alaska is at a wilderness lodge; most stays include all meals and a variety of outings (and can be quite expensive).

🌟 Nightlife

Even in its major cities, nightlife in Alaska is mostly just bars and pubs, but the state has become known for some excellent microbreweries, including Denali Brewing, Skagway Brewing, and Broken Tooth Brewing (Moose's Tooth). There's also a growing number of Alaska distilleries that serve craft cocktails in the evenings (there's a two-drink limit), including the Anchorage Distillery and the Amalga Distillery in Juneau.

🎭 Performing Arts

Anchorage and Fairbanks have some decent performing arts selections, with everything from theater to opera available. Juneau also has a blossoming contemporary art scene, but the best art in the state comes from the rich and varied Alaska Native cultures in each region, reflected in the abundance of art traditions.

🛍 Shopping

Alaska is not quite the place for Fifth Avenue–level shopping, but you will find some gorgeous Native art and crafts. Everything from intricate Aleut baskets and Athabascan birch-bark statues to Iñupiat ivory carvings and Tlingit masks are for sale.

➕ Safety

Cities in Alaska are generally safe and welcoming; as always, be sure to use common sense. The biggest dangers in the state are in the great outdoors, so be smart, responsible, and travel with a guide if you are not prepared for the realities of camping and the wilderness. Female solo travelers should feel safe, especially when traveling in tour groups. Cities like Anchorage and Fairbanks are LGBTQ-friendly, although not quite as much as their Lower 48 counterparts. While travelers should have no reason to feel unsafe, most other towns do not have openly gay communities, and LGBTQ travelers should especially exercise discretion in rural communities.

💲 Tipping

In addition to tipping servers, bartenders, taxi drivers, and baggage handlers, tipping others who provide personalized service is common in Alaska. Tour-bus drivers who offer a particularly informative trip generally receive a tip from passengers at the end of the tour. Fishing guides are commonly tipped 15%–20%, and gratuities may also be given to pilots following a particularly good flightseeing trip.

Essentials

🗓 When to Go

Mid-May through August is the height of cruise season and when all operators and businesses are open. Crowds (and mosquitoes) are high, but so are the temperature and sunshine in many areas (thanks to that midnight sun).

Not all of Alaska has the fierce winters that people expect (the Southeast and Southcentral regions are actually quite mild), but no matter where you go, expect that many, if not nearly all, operators and businesses will be closed for the season. And of course, during the winter some towns do experience frigid temperatures and nearly 24 hours of darkness.

Fall can be quite lovely in some regions of Alaska, with temperatures and sunshine still high in September and October (though in Southeast you can expect steady rain). Most operators will start to close up shop sometime in September, with the majority closing for the season by late September. October is the most affordable time to go that may still give you pleasant weather, but you won't have as many options for restaurants and hotels. April can be an equally lovely and affordable time to visit, but most operators and seasonal shops don't re-open for the season until the beginning of May.

📍 Visitor Information

The Alaska Travel Industry Association (a partnership between the state and private businesses) publishes the *Alaska Vacation Planner,* a free, comprehensive information source for statewide travel year-round (order online at *www.travelalaska.com/planners/planner.aspx*). Alaska's regional tourism councils also distribute vacation planners highlighting their local attractions.

Get details on Alaska's vast public lands from Alaska Public Lands Information Centers in Ketchikan, Tok, Anchorage, and Fairbanks.

The **Alaska Department of Fish and Game** has tips on wildlife viewing, news on conservation issues, and information about fishing and hunting licenses and regulations. **Alaska Geographic** has links to sites with information on the state's public lands, national parks, forests, and wildlife refuges, as well as an online bookstore, where you can find maps and books about the Alaskan experience. **Alaska Magazine** posts some of its feature stories online and maintains an extensive statewide events calendar. The **Alaska Native Heritage Center** has information on Alaska's Native tribes, as well as links to other cultural and tourism websites.

What to Pack

WATERPROOF OR WATER-RESISTANT FOOTWEAR

Wherever your Alaskan travels take you, it's a good bet you'll encounter plenty of moisture. Even if most of your trip is spent on concrete, you'll still need to avoid wet feet. A cursory glance at any local and their brown-booted uniform (called XtraTufs) serves as a reminder of the importance of dry feet here. If you don't feel like purchasing and packing a big pair of boots, at least make sure your hiking shoes are water resistant.

SUNSCREEN AND HAT

While locals may wear their sunburned arms and ears like badges of honor, a nasty burn can torpedo the best-laid plans. You'll probably be wearing long sleeves so you won't need too much, but bring along a small container of sunscreen to protect the most sensitive areas. This is especially true if you plan on spending time on the water. Water will reflect the sun and can burn twice as fast.

BUG NET AND BUG SPRAY

The scourges of the Alaskan wilderness are the mosquitoes, no-see-ums, horseflies, white sox, and other six-legged pests that populate the state. For those who plan on backpacking or camping, a bug net is essential. Bug nets and spray take up very little space, but could very well be the most important items you bring.

WOOL OR SIMILAR CLOTHING

Packing clothes for Alaska can be difficult. More times than not, it's necessary to pack for all four seasons. You can mitigate this by leaving your cotton clothing at home and instead packing wool, polyester, or similar materials that wick away water and retain heat when wet. Layering these items along with a waterproof outer shell will make you as prepared as possible for any weather.

RAIN JACKETS, RAIN PANTS, AND WATERPROOF CASES

Wool and similar materials are all well and good, but they don't do much in a driving rainstorm. Don't scrimp on your rain gear. Bring battle-tested gear that either has stitched seams and nylon fabric or is rubberized. Rubberized gear doesn't breathe as well as lighter shells, but you'll be glad you have it if the rain starts pouring. Also consider bringing an OtterBox or similar item to protect your phone and other electronics.

BINOCULARS

For most visitors, a trip to Alaska isn't complete without wildlife sightings. But these encounters aren't always right outside your window or along the trail. Whether you're scanning the tundra for grizzlies or the water for whales, a quality, sturdy, and waterproof pair of binoculars are worth their weight in gold. If you'll be on the water, consider attaching a small flotation device to the straps just in case.

BEAR SPRAY AND BEAR-PROOF CONTAINERS

This is a tricky one, as airplane companies are understandably hesitant to allow cans of concentrated mace in an enclosed environment traveling at 30,000 feet. Bear spray is also a semi-expensive purchase (expect to pay around $50). But think of it as traveler's insurance. Whether you plan on backpacking or just doing some hiking, the entire state is bear country. And while bear attacks are relatively rare, bear spray is statistically the safest deterrent. If nothing else, you can always purchase some when you arrive. If you're planning on camping, you will definitely need bear-proof containers for your food.

Great Itineraries

The Best of the Inside Passage

The Inside Passage is the second-longest and-deepest fjord in the world, and a ride on the ferry up the Passage during summer months offers fantastic views of waterfalls and sharp peaks cascading into the ocean; it can be a great way to spot orcas and humpback whales.

DAY 1: JUNEAU

Kick off your journey in Juneau, where you'll have to arrive by plane or boat, as there aren't any roads to it. Stay at Alaska's Capital Inn, a bed-and-breakfast far away from the cruise-ship traffic. Be sure to book in advance, as this place is popular with returning visitors.

Once you're settled into your quarters, take a ride on the Mt. Roberts Tramway, which takes you on a beautiful six-minute ride up the side of Mt. Roberts. Once you reach the top, you can spend a few hours hiking on the nearby trails, learning about the history and culture of the Tlingit people, and spotting bald eagles. Afterward, head into downtown Juneau and peruse the shops and galleries, many of which specialize in original local art.

Finish the day with dinner at Tracy's King Crab Shack by enjoying some—what else—Alaskan king crab. An after-dinner drink at the touristy but famed Red Dog Saloon (one of Juneau's most historic bars since its opening in 1890) is another must, unless you'd rather hang out with the locals, in which case you can continue up the street to The Narrows or the Imperial Saloon.

DAY 2: MENDENHALL GLACIER
(Excursion takes approximately 5 hours)

One of Juneau's most popular attractions, Mendenhall Glacier, is nestled right up against the town. Whether you arrive by boat or plane, you can't miss it as you approach the capital city. The glacier sits at the back of icy blue Mendenhall Lake. Several companies lead bus tours to the glacier, but Alaska Boat & Kayak Rental Shop offers shuttle service from downtown Juneau as well as kayak rentals. Kayak across the lake and up close to icebergs that have calved off the glacier, or hit the trails and hike up to the waterfalls.

Grab lunch before checking out of the inn. Board an afternoon or early-evening flight to Gustavus on Alaska Seaplanes.

DAYS 3 AND 4: GLACIER BAY NATIONAL PARK
(25 minutes by plane from Juneau; 4½ hours by ferry)

Located at the northern tip of the Inside Passage, Glacier Bay National Park is one of the country's most awe-inspiring national treasures. Stay at Glacier Bay Lodge, the only accommodation located inside the park. The lodge can arrange a daylong boat excursion that will take you past hundreds of lush green islands and straight up to the calving glaciers. Some excursions allow you to disembark and kayak around the glaciers for a couple of hours.

Or take a kayaking adventure like none you've ever had before. Experienced guides can be hired for multiday excursions that paddle all the way to the calving glaciers. Regardless of how far you paddle, the experience is incredibly

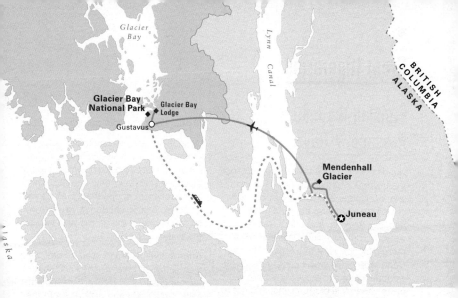

rewarding. Though the lodge does rent solo kayaks, unless you are a very experienced sea kayaker, we recommend taking a tour.

Whichever way you decide to explore the park, you'll find great comfort in the hot meals and comfy beds at the end of the day. If you're only spending one night at the park, get up early on the day of your departure and set out on any of a number of great hikes that begin at the lodge. If you have time, consider tacking on a few extra days.

DAY 5: RETURN TO JUNEAU
(4½ hours by ferry from Glacier Bay)

The ferry departs Gustavus at different times depending on the day of the week, but it's usually before 3 pm.

Stay at the Silverbow Inn, in the heart of downtown. If you get back from Gustavus in time, drive or take the bus to Douglas Island and take a walk along Sandy Beach. If you're visiting between September and May, try to catch a show at Perseverance Theatre, renowned for its great set designs and talented casts.

DAY 6: HIKING AROUND JUNEAU

On your last day in Juneau, get out and see some of the countryside. One of the locals' favorite hikes is Perseverance Trail. To get here, follow Gold Street until it turns into 8th Street. Follow 8th until it dead-ends at Basin Road. Take a left and keep walking until you get to the trail. This 3-mile trail (one way) takes about three to four hours to hike.

After your hike, grab lunch at any of the many eateries around downtown Juneau, like Twisted Fish Company. Then immerse yourself in history at the Alaska State Museum, view the contemporary Southeast Alaska Native art at Sealaska Heritage, or take one last stroll along the waterfront.

DAY 7: TAKE OFF FOR HOME
Head to the airport for your flight back.

Great Itineraries

Cruising the Inside Passage, 7 Days

Hands down, the best way to experience the Inside Passage is by boat. For visitors and locals, the ferry is the number one choice for traversing the fjord; it's economical, relaxing, and offers tremendous views. To optimize your time and cover more distance, fly some legs of the trip. Don't worry, this won't compromise your sightseeing: a bird's-eye view from your plane window is breathtaking, and not to be missed.

DAYS 1 AND 2: KETCHIKAN

Fly directly into Ketchikan and stay at the Black Bear Inn, an elegant, affordable waterfront B&B. It's highly regarded, so be sure to book well in advance.

Get settled in and take a day trip on a catamaran by Allen Marine to the awe-inspiring Misty Fjords National Monument. The Ketchikan area is known for its salmon fishing, so if you're interested in catching your own dinner, book a day trip that includes fishing.

On your second day, acquaint yourself with the beautiful town of Ketchikan. This charming community is known for its contemporary and traditional Native art. Spend a few hours walking through the town's totem pole parks, Totem Bight, Potlatch, and Saxman Totem. Stop in at the Soho Coho gallery, owned by well-known Alaskan artist Ray Troll, where you'll find an array of locally made collectibles. And don't miss the Ketchikan Area Arts and Humanities Council's Main Street Gallery.

DAY 3: WRANGELL
(6 hours by ferry from Ketchikan)

Wrangell is less touristy than many of the towns along the Inside Passage. It's an excellent place to get away from the hectic cruise-ship foot traffic and the T-shirt and knickknack shops that go along with it. Check in at Stikine Inn downtown and try to get one of the rooms with views of the water.

After you've unloaded at your hotel, take a stroll through the galleries and shops featuring wares by local artists and artisans. Grab lunch and walk down to the Petroglyph Beach State Historic Site and see ancient art chiseled on the rocks. No one knows who created these carvings or how long ago; they're curious, original, and intriguing.

For the latter part of the afternoon, take a jet-boat ride with Breakaway Adventures and soak in the nearby Chief Shakes Hot Springs.

DAY 4: PETERSBURG
(3-hour ferry ride from Wrangell)

Petersburg's Scandinavian heritage is evident from the moment you arrive. The Norwegian-style homes and boat docks set it apart from other Alaskan towns. Book a room in Scandia House and then spend the day glacier viewing and whale watching with Tongass Kayak Adventures. Just 25 miles outside of town is LeConte Glacier, the continent's southernmost tidewater glacier and Petersburg's biggest draw.

DAY 5: JUNEAU
(8-hour ferry ride from Petersburg)

Most of the ferries from Petersburg to Juneau depart in the wee hours. You can book a cabin, or do as most Alaskans do and just curl up with your blanket on a deck chair under the heat lamps.

Once you're in Juneau, check into your room at Alaska's Capital Inn. Grab breakfast at the Rookery and then take a helicopter ride with Temsco Helicopters to the Juneau Icefield. Spend an exciting afternoon dogsledding across the ice like the great Iditarod mushers do.

Once you're back in town, head to The Hangar on the Wharf for dinner, where you can sample local brews and gaze out the huge windows at the mountains across the channel.

DAY 6: HAINES
(4½-hour ferry ride from Juneau)

Check into the Hotel Hälsingland, the old Victorian officers' bunkers of Ft. Seward, then head over to Mountain Market. This popular hangout is a health-food market–deli–coffee shop. Grab some things for a packed lunch, then rent a bike from Sockeye Cycle and spend an afternoon on the well-groomed trails that meander through the rain forest.

Get back to your hotel in time to visit the Kroschel Wildlife Center (be sure to make reservations in advance). Afterward, have a libation at the Fogcutter and rub elbows with the locals. Don't lose track of time, though: Southeast bars stay open until the wee hours of the morning, and you'll need to catch the ferry or flight back to Juneau the next day for your trip home.

DAY 7: HEAD HOME
Travel back to Juneau and depart for home.

Great Itineraries

Anchorage and Denali, 8 days

Like all of Alaska, the Southcentral region is very spread out and the topography is diverse. But unlike in other regions, there are loads of ways to get around, and each mode of transport offers a different kind of experience.

DAY 1: ARRIVE IN ANCHORAGE

As soon as you land in Anchorage, you'll probably want to rent a car in preparation for an early departure the next day. Decompress after your flight at the tasteful Copper Whale Inn; it's a stone's throw from the Tony Knowles Coastal Trail and its great eateries and shops. For a leisurely stroll, walk along the Coastal Trail to Westchester Lagoon, or hike the entire 9 miles past Earthquake Park to Kincaid Park.

For dinner, Simon & Seafort's is within walking distance of the inn and has great food and a fantastic view across the water to Mt. Susitna (the "Sleeping Lady"). Humpy's Great Alaskan Alehouse is a fun bar with live music and surprisingly good pub grub.

DAY 2: KAYAKING IN WHITTIER
(1½-hour drive from Anchorage)

Fuel up with an early breakfast at the inn, and then go pick up some picnic fixings for your day trip. Drive down the scenic Seward Highway and turn off toward Whittier. Before reaching Whittier, pull over at the Portage Glacier turnoff, where you can see the glacier and the iceberg-filled lake right from your car. Continue on to the Anton Anderson Memorial Tunnel, the longest highway tunnel in North America that's shared with trains.

Kayaking on Prince William Sound is wonderful, and the knowledgeable guides at Alaska Sea Kayakers provide the gear and know-how to make it an experience of a lifetime.

At the end of the day, head back to Anchorage and return the car. Have dinner at Glacier Brewhouse; be sure to sample a pint or two of the local craft beer. If you're not too tired, check out the nightlife at Bernie's Bungalow Lounge.

DAY 3: TALKEETNA
(7-hour train trip from Anchorage)

Board the morning train with the Alaska Railroad and enjoy the seven-hour scenic ride to Talkeetna, a small Alaska town where artists, pilots, and mountaineers congregate. It's where climbers preparing to ascend Denali hang out before they're flown to base camp. Book a room at Susitna River Lodge and take a chartered flight over the summit (weather permitting) with Talkeetna Air Taxi. Spend the rest of the afternoon walking on a glacier.

Take a before- or after-dinner stroll through this tiny town, and check out the artwork that residents create during the quiet, cold winter months. *Denali Brewing Company and BrewPub* is a nice dinner option and a good place to soak in the bustling summer scene.

DAYS 4–6: DENALI NATIONAL PARK
(5-hour train trip from Talkeetna)

For more than 25 years, Camp Denali has been family-owned and-operated. It offers three-, four-, or seven-night stays. A shuttle will pick you up at the train station and deliver you to rustic wilderness cabins deep within Denali National Park. Knowledgeable naturalists offer daily guided outings; evening programs focus on the natural and cultural history of Denali.

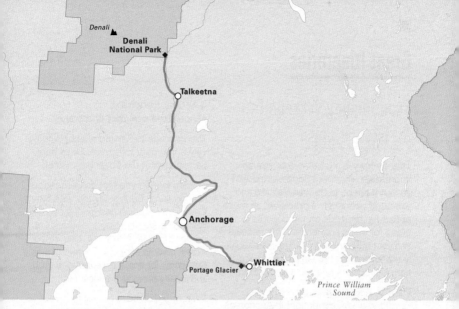

Denali National Park is a 6 million–acre Arctic wonderland that teems with wildlife. On any given day you may see grizzlies, wolves, caribou, and moose. The weather around Denali is fickle, so there's never a guarantee of seeing the mountain's peaks, though that hardly matters as you explore the glaciers, forests, and vividly colored tundra. On day two in the park, take advantage of Camp Denali's outstanding off-trail wild-life-watching expedition. Fill the rest of your time here with canoeing on Wonder Lake, biking, or a flightseeing tour around the mountain.

DAY 7: ANCHORAGE
(8-hour train trip from Denali)

Take the afternoon train back to Anchor-age and arrive in time for a late dinner. Check into one of our recommended hotels, and get ready for your flight the next day.

DAY 8: FLY HOME

Pack your bags and check out of the hotel. It's time to go to the airport and fly home.

Mighty Denali

Denali has the highest peak in North America and it is an awesome sight—if you can see it. In the summer, the 20,310-foot peak has its own weather system. It can be sunny and warm down below, but it might be shrouded in cloud at the summit. It's often easier to see it from Anchorage, 140 miles away. Though the views may be blocked, it's still worth trying to catch a glimpse up close. If you're not going to climb it or fly over it, a ride on the Denali Park Shuttle is the closest you will get to the High One. When you get to the Eielson Visitor Center at Mile 66, if the sky is clear and the mountain is out, continue on to Wonder Lake (approximately 88 more miles). It's a fantastic treat to catch Denali's peak reflecting in the water.

Great Itineraries

Experiencing Wrangell–St. Elias, 9 days

This itinerary is a great way to see an impressive amount of Southcentral Alaska, but it needs to be well planned and executed with relative precision, as much of this trip depends on the departure times for trains and ferries. One mistake and your itinerary can change dramatically—which doesn't mean a ruined vacation, just not the one you'd planned on.

DAY 1: ANCHORAGE

For this trip, you'll overnight in Anchorage and catch the train out early the next morning. Make the most of your time here by booking a room at the Hotel Captain Cook. Put on your hiking shoes and grab the Flattop Mountain Shuttle to the popular trailhead at the edge of the city, where the Chugach Mountains range begins. The hour-long hike to the top can be strenuous, but from the summit you can see the entire city of Anchorage, the bay, and, on a clear day, the Alaska Range and even Denali. Should you opt to explore only the easier portion of the trail, you'll still enjoy excellent views. If you still have energy after Flattop, check out the Powerline Trail; it's the left-hand path at the trailhead. These trails are used year-round, for hiking in the summer and snowshoeing, skiing, and snowmachining in the winter. You'll understand why Anchoragites refer to their city as a great base camp.

After an afternoon of hiking in Anchorage's backyard, 49th State Brewing is a nice option for dinner.

DAY 2: SEWARD
(4-hour train ride from Anchorage)

The train ride to Seward offers stunning views that motorists miss. Once here, get situated at the Edgewater Hotel.

Seward is renowned for its tremendous sea kayaking. Book a day trip with Sunny Cove. Their experienced guides can take you past pods of orcas, sea otters, and groups of seals. Afterward, dine at the locals' favorite hangout, Seward Brewing Company, for some excellent pub grub and locally brewed libations.

DAY 3: VALDEZ
(3-hour bus ride from Seward; 6-hour ferry trip from Whittier)

Book an early-morning bus to Whittier, where you'll connect immediately with the ferry for a six-hour trip to Valdez. Know that as the weather gets colder, ferries run less frequently, so be sure to plan ahead.

Arrange a room at the Valdez Harbor Inn and rent a car with Valdez-U-Drive; be sure to request an SUV or a high-clearance vehicle for the drive to McCarthy, just outside Wrangell–St. Elias National Park. If you arrived late and want to linger in Valdez, spend the next day on a day trip to Worthington Glacier State Recreation Site. Dine at the Alaska Halibut House, and be sure to try the fresh catch.

DAYS 4–7: WRANGELL–ST. ELIAS NATIONAL PARK & PRESERVE
(5-hour drive from Valdez)

You've got some driving to do and one of the most gorgeous mountains in the state to see, so you'll want to get an early start. On the road, take care to fill the gas tank at every opportunity; gas stations here are few and far between. Summer is the only time that road construction can get done, so be prepared for delays.

Anchorage

Whittier

Valdez

Seward

Wrangell–St. Elias
National Park
and Preserve

U.S.A.

Arrange your accommodations with Kennicott Glacier Lodge. After you've arrived, and if you still have energy, the lodge can help you book a tour of the mining ghost towns of Kennicott and McCarthy to explore the abandoned mines. The menu at the lodge is terrific, but there is also fine dining and a good-time saloon a few miles down the road at the McCarthy Lodge.

In the days to follow, get out and enjoy the park. Contact Wrangell Outfitters for a horseback-riding adventure into the heart of the preserve. The front desk at the lodge can also arrange glacier trekking, flightseeing, rafting, and alpine hiking. And the kitchen will pack you a picnic lunch.

DAY 8: WHITTIER AND ANCHORAGE CONNECTIONS
(6 hours by ferry from Valdez to Whittier; 2-hour train ride from Whittier to Anchorage)

It's another early-morning departure. Take your car back and catch the 7 am ferry to Whittier. You'll only have a couple of hours to spare before you catch the train to Anchorage, but Whittier is small and easy to explore.

An Icy Kennicott Hike

Kennicott Glacier extends 27 miles from where it originates at Mt. Blackburn to its terminus at the Kennicott River—just a short scenic hike from Kennicott Glacier Lodge. You can walk right out onto the glacier, but using crampons on the ice is always a good idea, and a guide can ensure you don't get lost or make a wrong turn into a deep crevasse.

Once you're in Anchorage, if you're flying out the next day, book your stay at The Lakefront Anchorage, near the airport and right on the shore of Lake Spenard. Take a cab to Moose's Tooth Pub & Pizzeria; it's the best pizza in the state. If you're up for it, check out Kinley's Restaurant afterward for dessert and some wine.

DAY 9: HEAD HOME
Say goodbye to Alaska and start your journey home.

Contacts

✈ Air

AIRPORTS Fairbanks International Airport. (*FAI*). ☎ *907/474–2500* ⊕ *www.dot.state.ak.us/faiiap.* **Juneau International Airport.** (*JNU*). ☎ *907/789–7821* ⊕ *www.juneau.org/airport.* **Ketchikan Airport.** (*KTN*). ☎ *907/225–6800* ⊕ *www.borough.ketchikan.ak.us/130/Airport.* **Ted Stevens Anchorage International Airport.** (*ANC*). ☎ *907/266–2525* ⊕ *www.dot.alaska.gov/anc.*

AIR TAXIS AND SMALL PLANE COMPANIES Alaska Seaplanes. ✉ *Juneau* ☎ *907/789–3331* ⊕ *www.flyalaskaseaplanes.com.* **Bering Air.** ☎ *800/478–5422 Nome reservations, 800/478–3943 Kotzebue reservations* ⊕ *www.beringair.com.* **Grant Aviation.** ☎ *888/359–4726* ⊕ *www.flygrant.com.* **Ravn Alaska.** ☎ *907/266–8394, 800/866–8394* ⊕ *www.flyravn.com.* **Warbelow's Air Ventures.** ☎ *907/474–0518* ⊕ *www.warbelows.com.*

⛴ Boat/Ferry

Alaska Marine Highway. ☎ *907/465–3941, 800/642–0066* ⊕ *www.dot.state.ak.us/amhs.* **Inter-Island Ferry Authority.** ☎ *907/225–4848 Ketchikan Terminal, 907/530–4848 Hollis Terminal, 866/308–4848* ⊕ *www.interislandferry.com.*

🚌 Bus

BUS INFORMATION Alaska Park Connection. ☎ *800/266–8625* ⊕ *www.alaskacoach.com.* **Alaska/Yukon Trails.** ☎ *907/452–3337* ⊕ *www.alaskashuttle.com.* **Denali Overland Transportation.** ☎ *907/733–2384* ⊕ *www.denalioverland.com.* **Green Tortoise.** ☎ *415/722–0471* ⊕ *www.greentortoise.com.* **Interior Alaska Bus Line.** ☎ *800/770–6652* ⊕ *www.interioralaskabusline.com.*

🚆 Train

CONTACTS Alaska Railroad. ☎ *800/544–0552* ⊕ *www.alaskarailroad.com.* **Gray Line Alaska.** ☎ *907/264–7950 in Anchorage, 888/425–1737* ⊕ *www.graylinealaska.com.* **White Pass & Yukon Route.** ☎ *800/343–7373* ⊕ *www.wpyr.com.*

📍 Visitor Information

CONTACTS Alaska Department of Fish and Game. ☎ *907/465–4100 Juneau* ⊕ *www.state.ak.us/adfg.* **Alaska Division of Parks.** ☎ *907/269–8700* ⊕ *www.alaskastateparks.org.* **Alaska Geographic.** ⊕ *www.alaskageographic.org.* **Alaska Magazine.** ⊕ *www.alaskamagazine.com.* **Alaska Native Heritage Center.** ⊕ *www.alaskanative.net.* **Alaska Public Lands Information Centers.** ☎ *907/644–3680 in Anchorage, 907/459–3730 in Fairbanks, 907/228–6220 in Ketchikan, 907/883–5667 in Tok* ⊕ *www.alaskacenters.gov.* **Alaska Travel Industry Association.** ⊕ *www.alaskatia.org.* **Kenai Chamber of Commerce & Visitor Center.** ☎ *907/283–1991* ⊕ *www.visitkenai.com.* **Kenai Peninsula Tourism Marketing Council.** ☎ *907/262–5229* ⊕ *www.kenaipeninsula.org.* **Southeast Alaska Discovery Center.** ☎ *907/228–6220* ⊕ *www.fs.usda.gov/recarea/tongass.* **Southwest Alaska Municipal Conference.** ☎ *907/562–7380* ⊕ *swamc.org.* **Yukon Department of Tourism & Culture.** ☎ *800/661–0494* ⊕ *www.travelyukon.com.* **Juneau Convention & Visitors Bureau.** ✉ *800 Glacier Ave., Suite 201, Juneau* ☎ *907/586–2201, 888/581–2201* ⊕ *www.traveljuneau.com.*

Chapter 3

ANCHORAGE

3

Updated by
J. Besl

👁 Sights
★★★☆☆

🍴 Restaurants
★★★★☆

🛏 Hotels
★★★★☆

🛍 Shopping
★★★☆☆

🍸 Nightlife
★★★☆☆

WELCOME TO ANCHORAGE

TOP REASONS TO GO

★ **Fishing:** Anglers can cast for huge king salmon or feisty silvers while wading among reflections of skyscrapers at Ship Creek.

★ **Winter celebrations:** Beginning in late February, locals celebrate the two-week Fur Rendezvous Festival. Events, from the blanket toss to the Running of the Reindeer—Alaska's spin on the classic Pamplona tradition—lead up to the start of the Iditarod Trail Sled Dog Race in early March.

★ **Shopping:** Shops and vendors at the Saturday and Sunday markets sell everything from kid-friendly tchotchkes to elegant Alaska Native crafts and locally produced foods.

★ **Hiking and biking:** Laced with more than 120 miles of paved urban trails, Anchorage is a paradise for hikers and bicyclists. The 50-km (31-mile) Moose Loop—incorporating most of the core urban trails—uncannily resembles the shape of a moose when viewed from above.

1 Downtown. The city's cultural center has a festive atmosphere on summer afternoons, with flowers hung from street lamps and the smell of grilled onions and reindeer hot dogs in the air along 4th Avenue.

2 Midtown. Some 3 miles east of the airport, Midtown is a commercial district with an assortment of restaurants, shopping centers, and large hotels.

3 Spenard. Sandwiched between the airport and Midtown, Spenard is one of Anchorage's oldest neighborhoods, yet also one of its up-and-comers.

4 Greater Anchorage. This is a massive city—nearly the size of Delaware—and gems are tucked into all its corners. You can rent a bike Downtown and head west along the 11-mile Tony Knowles Coastal Trail past tidal marshes and inlet views to 1,400-acre Kincaid Park.

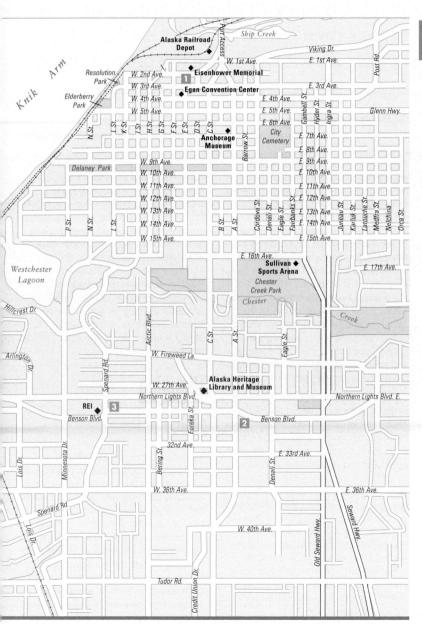

By far Alaska's largest and most sophisticated city, Anchorage is situated in a truly spectacular location and is the state's medical, financial, and banking center, as well as home to the executive offices of most of the Alaska Native corporations.

The city has nearly 300,000 people, accounting for roughly 40% of the state's population. The relative affluence of this white-collar city—with a sprinkling of olive drab from nearby military bases—fosters an ever-growing range of restaurants, shops, and first-rate entertainment. The permanently snow-covered peaks and volcanoes of the Alaska Range lie to the west of the city while part of the craggy Chugach Range is within the eastern edge of the municipality; the Talkeetna and Kenai Ranges are visible to the north and south. Two arms of Cook Inlet embrace the town's western and southern borders, and on clear days Denali looms on the northern horizon.

Dena'ina Athabascan people have lived in this area for more than 1,000 years. Their fish camps once dotted the shores of Cook Inlet, only a short distance from Downtown Anchorage. And yet Anchorage is a young city, incorporated in only 1915. Nearly everything has been built since the 1970s—an Anchorage home dating from the 1950s basically merits historic status. The city got its start with the construction of the federally built Alaska Railroad, completed in 1917, and traces of its railroad heritage remain today. The city's architecture is far from memorable—though it has its quirky and charming moments—but the surrounding mountains make up for it.

Boom and bust periods followed major events: an influx of military bases during World War II; a massive buildup of Arctic missile-warning stations during the Cold War; reconstruction following the devastating Good Friday earthquake of 1964; and in the late 1960s the biggest jackpot of all—the discovery of oil at Prudhoe Bay and the construction of the Trans-Alaska Pipeline. It is no surprise that Anchorage then positioned itself as the perfect home for the pipeline administrators and support industries, and it continues to attract a large share of the state's oil-tax dollars.

Planning

When to Go

You'll find plenty to do year-round in Anchorage, though most visitors (particularly first-timers) might be happiest from late May through early September, when the days are longer—up to 19 hours, 21 minutes during the summer solstice—and the temperatures warmer. If you choose one of the shoulder seasons, go with fall. Though there's a greater chance of rain, the snow has not yet arrived on trails, except in the highest mountain passes, and there's an excellent chance of warm, sunny days, cool nights, and dazzling color changes in the trees and tundra. But if you do choose fall, pack a few extra layers as a just-in-case for early snow (or be prepared to visit one of Anchorage's many gear shops): the city's earliest measurable dose of snow fell on September 20, 1947.

Of the snow-free months, May is typically the driest, while August and September are the wettest. July is the warmest month, with an average temperature of 58.4°F; May is the coolest at 46.6°F. But don't be fooled by statistics. Late-May temperatures can exceed 70°F, and "hot" July and August days sometimes break 80°F. Of course, rainy low-pressure systems from the Gulf of Alaska can skulk in at any time, bringing wet and cool weather.

With such vagaries, do as the locals do: come prepared to go with the flow. That means packing light rain jackets and layers as well as tank tops and sunblock, and allowing for some flexibility with your plans.

Getting Here and Around

AIR

Ted Stevens Anchorage International Airport is 6 miles from Downtown Anchorage on International Airport Road. Several carriers, including Ravn Alaska, connect Anchorage with smaller Alaska communities. Floatplane operators and helicopters serve the area from Lake Hood, which is adjacent to and part of Anchorage International Airport. A number of smaller air taxis and air-charter operations are at Merrill Field, 2 miles east of Downtown on 5th Avenue.

Taxis queue up at the lower level of the airport terminals outside the baggage-claim areas. They are on a meter system; it costs about $20, not including tip, for a ride Downtown. Most of the larger hotels provide free airport shuttle services.

AIRPORTS Ted Stevens Anchorage International Airport. ✉ *5000 W. International Airport Rd., West Anchorage* ☎ *907/266–2526* ⊕ *www.ancairport.com.*

BUS TRAVEL

The municipal People Mover bus system covers the high-traffic areas of Anchorage, with most routes originating Downtown. A one-way fare is $2 for rides anywhere in the city; day passes good for unlimited rides are $5. Route 40 connects Downtown and the airport and runs late on weeknights.

■ TIP→ **Get schedules and information from the central bus depot at 6th Avenue and G Street.**

CONTACTS People Mover. ☎ *907/343–6543* ⊕ *www.peoplemover.org.*

CAR

The Glenn Highway enters Anchorage from the north and becomes 5th Avenue near Merrill Field; this route will lead you directly into Downtown. Gambell Street leads out of town to the south, becoming New Seward Highway at about 20th Avenue. South of town, it becomes the Seward Highway. Yes, that means there's only one road in and one road out of Anchorage. If you bring your RV or rent one on arrival, know that parking an RV Downtown on weekdays can be challenging; there's a big parking lot on 3rd Avenue between C and E Streets that's your best bet. Parking is usually not a problem in other parts of town. You can find an up-to-date parking map on the Anchorage Downtown Partnership website (*www.anchoragedowntown.org*; click on "Downtown Parking" under the "Services & Programs" tab).

TAXI

If you need a taxi, call a company to organize a pickup; it's not common to hail one. Prices are $2.75 for a pickup, plus an additional $2.50 for each mile. Allow 20 minutes for arrival of the cab during morning and evening rush hours. Alaska Yellow Cab has taxis with wheelchair lifts.

CONTACTS Alaska Yellow Cab.
☎ *907/222–2222* ⊕ *www.alaskayel-lowdispatch.com.*

TRAIN

From mid-May through mid-September, the Alaska Railroad runs daily between Anchorage and Seward; daily between Anchorage and Fairbanks via Talkeetna and Denali National Park and Preserve; and daily between Anchorage and Whittier, Portage, Spencer, and Grandview. Winter service is available once each month from Anchorage to Talkeetna, and there is a weekly round-trip from Anchorage to Fairbanks and back. Call for schedule and fare information.

The Alaska Railroad trains have glass-dome observation cars in summer and onboard guides year-round, and they make the trip between Anchorage and Fairbanks and Anchorage and Seward while hooked up to the same engines as the cruise-line cars. Alaska Railroad's website has details.

CONTACT Alaska Railroad. ☎ *907/265–2494, 800/544–0552* ⊕ *www.alaskarail-road.com.*

Restaurants

Anchorage's dining scene has, to the relief of repeat visitors and, even more so, locals, been on the rise for the past several years. Established (and still highly recommended) restaurants like Jens' and The Marx Bros. Café have been joined by the likes of the small-plate and wine-focused Crush Bistro & Bottle Shops and the Pacific Rim cuisine–focused Ginger. No matter the restaurant, the local catch is a frequent star. Beware: eating salmon or halibut in-state may ruin you for fish served in the Lower 48. Anchorage also offers up plenty of worldly flavors thanks to the city's diversity; it actually has the most diverse schools in the country after New York City. And nobody should leave Anchorage without trying the local fast-food specialty:

a reindeer sausage from the carts along 4th Avenue (in summer).

Hotels

Most of the major chains are represented in Anchorage, and there are some strong independent hotels as well. Anchorage is also home to many bed-and-breakfasts. New chain hotels have clustered in Mid-town in recent years, but consider staying Downtown if you're traveling without a car. Reservations at least a week ahead are a must for the major hotels, especially during the summer months.

Hotel and restaurant reviews have been shortened. For full information, visit Fodors.com. Restaurant prices are per person for a main course at dinner or if dinner is not served, at lunch. Hotel prices are for two people in a standard double room in high season.

What It Costs			
$	$$	$$$	$$$$
RESTAURANTS			
under $14	$14–$22	$23–$30	over $30
HOTELS			
under $100	$100–$200	$201–$300	over $300

Tours

Tour Anchorage and the surrounding mountains and glaciers of Southcentral Alaska by land or by air with one of the many sightseeing companies in the region. The Downtown Log Cabin Visitor Center and adjacent Visitor Information Center have brochures for Anchorage bus tours.

Any air-taxi company can arrange for a flightseeing trip over Anchorage and environs. The fee is determined by the length of time you are airborne, the number of passengers, and the size of the plane.

Anchorage Trolley Tours

This one-hour city tour starts and ends at the Log Cabin Visitor Information Center, taking guests on a 15-mile loop through Anchorage's original neighborhoods and past landmarks like the Alaska Railroad terminal and Lake Hood, the busiest floatplane base in the world. A two-hour extended tour allows for folks to disembark at certain stops for photos. ⊠ 546 W 4th Ave., Downtown ☎ 907/276–5603, 888/917–8687 ⊕ www.alaskatrolley.com ⬚ From $20.

Gray Line Alaska

Part of the international Gray Line brand, this company arranges Alaska tours by road or rail. Guests can add a host of options to their vacation packages, including city tours, float trips, jetboat excursions, and dogsled demonstrations across the state. ☎ 907/264–7950, 888/425–1737 ⊕ www.graylinealaska. com ⬚ From $399.

Rust's Flying Service

If you want to land on a glacier in full view of Denali, check with Rust's. Among the city's most established flight-seeing operations, Rust's regularly flies guests from its Anchorage base to back-country lodges and bear-viewing platforms. There are also flightseeing tours of Prince William Sound and Denali National Park and Preserve. ⊠ 4525 Enstrom Cir. ☎ 907/243–1595, 800/544–2299 ⊕ www. flyrusts.com ⬚ From $110.

Health and Safety

Though most areas populated by tourists are safe to wander, Anchorage is a city, so it's best just to stay aware as you walk around town. That definitely holds true if you choose to hike any local trails—even those within the city limits. Before Anchorage was a paved city, it was wild. Many locals have stories of surprise visits

by a moose or bear during a morning bathrobe run to get the newspaper. Moose and other animals walk the trails, too. If traveling into the Chugach Mountains, be sure to purchase bear spray at any outdoor retailer in advance. As you walk along, make some noise, either by singing or talking to a friend to help ward off the animals. The award for the biggest pest of all goes to the mosquito. Bring repellent with you for all hiking excursions.

Visitor Information

Alaska sees nearly 2 million visitors each summer and, of that total, more than 40% spend at least one night in Anchorage. The tourist-friendly city offers a wealth of information and services to help visitors along the way. In addition to the Log Cabin Visitor Information Center Downtown, there are two visitor information centers in Ted Stevens Anchorage International Airport: one in the north terminal (open mid-May through September) and one in the south terminal in the C Concourse baggage-claim area (open year-round).

Alaska Department of Fish and Game

Visit the state website to purchase permits and licenses, plus find helpful information like hunting seasons and fishing lakes across the state. ⊠ 333 Raspberry Rd., Midtown ☎ 907/267–2218 ⊕ www. adfg.alaska.gov.

Alaska Public Lands Information Center

Stop here for information on all of Alaska's public lands, including national and state parks, national forests, and wildlife refuges. You can plan a hiking, sea-kayaking, bear-viewing, or fishing trip; purchase state and national park passes; find out about public-use cabins; learn about Alaska's plants and animals; or head to the theater for films highlighting different parts of the state. The bookstore also sells maps and nature books. Guided walks to historic Downtown sights depart daily throughout the summer at 11 am and 3:15 pm. The center is housed in a federal facility, meaning a security screening is required to enter. ⊠ *605 W. 4th Ave., at F St., Suite 105, Downtown* ☎ *907/644–3661, 866/869–6887* ⊕ *www. alaskacenters.gov/visitors-centers/ anchorage.*

Downtown Log Cabin Visitor Center and Visitor Information Center

Housed in a rustic log cabin, the center's sod roof is festooned with huge hanging baskets of flowers. Anchorage is a major stopping point for cargo jets en route to Asia, and a signpost out front marks the mileage to many international destinations. After a stop in the cabin, step out the back door to the more spacious visitor center stocked with brochures. There are also two visitor information centers in Ted Stevens Anchorage International Airport, one in the north terminal and one in the south terminal in the C Concourse baggage-claim area. ⊠ *4th Ave. and F St., Downtown* ☎ *907/257–2363, 800/478– 1255 to order visitor guides* ⊕ *www. anchorage.net.*

Activities

Few American cities feel as connected to the outdoors as Anchorage. From the in-town Tony Knowles Coastal Trail to a nearly endless supply of trails and other outdoor adventures in the Chugach National Forest and on nearby waterways, Anchorage is an outdoor-lover's playground. And that doesn't just hold true for the warmer months; a nearby ski resort offers downhill delights, and there's plenty of dog mushing, ice-skating, and other wintry sports to try. Up for some spectator sports instead? Anchorage doesn't disappoint: summer league baseball, the start of the Iditarod, and even shoulder-to-shoulder "combat" fishing await you.

BASEBALL
Mulcahy Stadium

BASEBALL & SOFTBALL | Two summer baseball teams made up of college students—the Bucs and the Glacier Pilots—play at Mulcahy Stadium, right off the Chester Creek Trail. With tickets only $5, it's an excellent option for a summer evening in town. The games can get intense—many athletes have gone on to play in the major leagues—but the setting is relaxed, with innings played under evening sunshine amid sweeping views of the Chugach Mountains. The short season lasts from June through July. ⊠ *E. 16th Ave. at Cordova St., Downtown* ⊕ *www.alaskabaseballleague.org.*

BICYCLING

Anchorage has more than 120 miles of paved bicycle trails, and several streets have marked bike lanes. Although busy during the day, Downtown streets are uncrowded and safe for cyclists in the evening.

Alaskabike

BIKING | Serious gearheads can book multiday touring packages through this company to explore Southcentral, the Interior, the Yukon Territory, and nearby scenic highways. Another option is the all-inclusive multisport tour, which features biking, hiking, canoeing, sea kayaking, and a glacier cruise. ⊠ *Anchorage* ☎ *907/245–2175* ⊕ *www.alaskabike.com.*

Alaska Pablo's Bicycle Rentals

BIKING | Rates start at $15 at this shop perched just two blocks uphill from the ocean and the Tony Knowles Coastal Trail. Treat yourself to a post-ride reward at the hot dog stand out front, run by the owner's twin brother. ⊠ *415 L St., Downtown* ☎ *907/272–1600* ⊕ *www.pablobicyclerentals.com.*

Downtown Bicycle Rental

BIKING | With an inventory of more than 170 bikes of all types, Downtown Bicycle Rental also rents trailers, clip-in pedals, and shoes. The minimum rental rate is $18 for three hours, which includes free lock, helmet, panniers, and trail map. In winter, fat bikes and studded-tire bikes are available for $35 per day. Rent a bike rack to expand your adventures around the region. Owner Peter Roberts offers once-a-day shuttle van rides to the Flattop trailhead in summer for both hikers and bikers. ⊠ *333 W. 4th Ave., Downtown* ☎ *907/279–3334* ⊕ *www. alaska-bike-rentals.com.*

Lifetime Adventures

BIKING | Just 30 miles northeast of Anchorage, Lifetime Adventures operates out of the state park campground at Eklutna Lake, renting out bikes, trailers, and kayaks. You can choose the popular Paddle & Pedal package, where you paddle in one direction and pedal your way back, or take a guided bike tour along the lake with a picnic lunch. ⊠ *Anchorage* ☎ *907/746–4644* ⊕ *www.lifetimeadventures.net.*

BIRD-WATCHING

Popular bird-watching places include the Tony Knowles Coastal Trail, which provides access to Westchester Lagoon and nearby tide flats, along with Potter Marsh on the south end of Anchorage.

Anchorage Audubon Society

BIRD WATCHING | The Anchorage chapter of the National Audubon Society offers downloadable birding checklists on their website and can refer you to local birders who will advise you on the best bird-watching spots. The society also hosts bird-watching field trips and events, like the Potter Marsh-a-Thon Birding Smackdown in early summer. ⊠ *Anchorage* ⊕ *www.anchorageaudubon.org.*

Wilderness Birding Adventures

BIRD WATCHING | With a staff of naturalist guides, Homer-based Wilderness Birding Adventures offers backcountry birding, wildlife, and natural-history trips to remote parts of Alaska, as well as village-based, birding-focused trips to some of the state's birding hot spots. ☎ *907/299–3937* ⊕ *www.wildernessbirding.com.*

CANOEING, CRUISING, AND KAYAKING

Local lakes and lagoons, such as Westchester Lagoon, Goose Lake, and Jewel Lake, have favorable conditions for canoeing and kayaking. More adventurous paddlers should head to Whittier or Seward for sea kayaking.

Alaska Raft and Kayak

CANOEING & ROWING | Rent or buy from a flotilla's worth of small boats, including kayaks, canoes, paddleboards, and one-man fishing pontoons. And if your trip was wilder than expected, the store also repairs boats of all styles and sizes. ⊠ *401 W. Tudor Rd., Midtown* ☎ *907/561–7238, 800/606–5950* ⊕ *www. alaskaraftandkayak.com.*

Kenai Fjords Tours

BOATING | Give your arms a rest, soak up glacier views, and spot the abundant wildlife of Kenai Fjords National Park from a cruise boat. Kenai Fjords Tours offers day-trip packages to the national park from late March through September, and can help arrange coach and train between Anchorage and Seward. ⊠ *509 W. 4th Ave., Downtown* ☎ *800/808–8068* ⊕ *www.kenaifjords.com.*

DOG MUSHING

Fur Rondy Festival

LOCAL SPORTS | **FAMILY** | World-championship dog-mushing races are run in February, with three consecutive 25-mile heats through Downtown Anchorage, out into the foothills, and back. People line the route with cups of coffee in hand to cheer on their favorite mushers. The

3

Anchorage PLANNING

three-day races are part of the annual Fur Rendezvous Festival, known locally as Fur Rondy, one of the largest winter festivals in the United States. Other cabin fever–kicking attractions include the running of the reindeer (yes, just like Pamplona but with far less furious reindeer), a snow-sculpture competition, Alaska Native blanket toss (a holdover from earlier days when dozens of people would launch a hunter high into the air, trampoline-style, in an effort to spot distant seals, walrus, and whales), a carnival, and even snowshoe softball. Fur Rondy events start in late February, culminating ten days later with the ceremonial Iditarod start on 4th Avenue in early March. ⊠ *Anchorage* ⊕ *www. furrondy.net.*

Iditarod Trail Sled Dog Race

LOCAL SPORTS | The 1,049-mile Iditarod Trail Sled Dog Race commemorates the delivery of serum to Nome by dog mushers during the diphtheria epidemic of 1925. In early March, dog teams leave the mushing hub of Willow, about 70 miles northeast of Anchorage, and wind through the Alaska Range, across the Interior, out to the Bering Sea coast, and on to Nome. Depending on weather and trail conditions, winners can complete the race in less than nine days. ⊠ *Anchorage* ☎ *907/376–5155 Iditarod trail headquarters* ⊕ *www.iditarod.com.*

FISHING

More than 30 local lakes and streams are stocked with catchable game fish. You must have a valid Alaska sportfishing license to fish in the state. Fishing licenses can be purchased at any Fred Meyer or Carr's/Safeway grocery or local sporting goods store or bought online prior to arrival (*www.admin.adfg.state. ak.us/buyonlin*).

Nonresidents can buy an annual license or a 1-, 3-, 7-, or 14-day permit. A separate king salmon stamp is required to fish for the big guys.

Rainbow trout, arctic char, landlocked salmon, Dolly Varden, grayling, and northern pike are among the species found in waters like Jewel Lake in South Anchorage and Mirror and Fire Lakes near Eagle River. Coho salmon return to Ship Creek (Downtown) in mid-July, and king salmon are caught there between late May and early July. Campbell Creek and Bird Creek just south of town are also good spots for coho (silver) salmon. Anywhere in Alaska there are fish, it's possible there are also bears, so stay aware.

Alaska Department of Fish and Game

FISHING | Contact the Alaska Department of Fish and Game for licensing information. For information about Anchorage-area lakes, go to the website; click on "Sport" under the Fishing menu, the Southcentral portion of the "Fisheries by Area" map, and then Anchorage. ⊠ *Anchorage* ☎ *907/267– 2218* ⊕ *www.adfg.alaska.gov.*

The Bait Shack

FISHING | You don't have to leave Downtown to fish for salmon—they come right through Ship Creek. Dustin Slinker, the friendly owner of The Bait Shack, will tell you exactly where to fish to land a salmon; first-timers are welcome. He'll also fillet and vacuum-pack your catch. Daily rentals last for 24 hours and include a rod, reel, waders, tackle box, landing net, and even a nonresident fishing license. Dustin rents gear for up to two weeks if your plans expand beyond the Bait Shack's backyard, but Ship Creek offers urban fishing among locals—a markedly different experience from pricey fishing charters. ⊠ *212 W. Whitney Rd., Downtown* ☎ *907/522–3474* ⊕ *www.thebaitshackak.com.*

Slam'n Salm'n Derby

FISHING | Each June, locals fish for king salmon on Ship Creek to raise money for a range of nonprofits. If you're not into fishing, the crowded combat fishing is just as entertaining to observe from the bridge. ⊠ *211 W. Ship Creek Ave., Downtown* ⊕ *www.anchorage.net/events/ salmon-derby.*

FLIGHTSEEING

This area is the state's air-travel hub. Plenty of flightseeing services operating out of city airports and floatplane bases can take you on spectacular tours of **Denali,** the **Chugach Range, Prince William Sound, Kenai Fjords National Park,** and the **Harding Icefield.** Anchorage hosts the greatest number and variety of services, including companies operating fixed-wing aircraft, floatplanes, and helicopters.

★ Rust's Flying Service

AIR EXCURSIONS | An Anchorage company in business since 1963, Rust's will take you on narrated flightseeing tours of Denali, Knik Glacier, and Prince William Sound. Rust's also offers bear-viewing flights to several destinations, including Katmai National Park and Preserve and the Bristol Bay region, and can arrange multiday fishing and hiking trips to various backcountry locations. ✉ *4525 Enstrom Circle, West Anchorage* ☎ *907/243–1595, 800/544–2299* ⊕ *www. flyrusts.com.*

GOLF

Anchorage is Alaska's golfing capital, with several public courses. They won't compare to offerings in Phoenix or San Diego, but there are tee times up until 10 pm on long summer days, and at some courses the mountain views put the sights of most other courses to shame.

Anchorage Golf Course

GOLF | Overlooking the Anchorage Bowl, this challenging course has 18 holes, a pro shop, restaurant, and bar, as well as great views. ✉ *3651 O'Malley Rd., South Anchorage* ☎ *907/522–3363* ⊕ *www. anchoragegolfcourse.com* ⛳ *$49* ⛳ *18 holes, 6600 yards, par 72* ⛳ *Facilities: driving range, putting green, pitching area, golf carts, pull carts, rental clubs, pro shop, golf academy/lessons, restaurant, bar.*

Moose Run Golf Course

GOLF | Moose Run offers two 18-hole, scenic courses; the Creek Course boasts the longest layout in the state and is more challenging than the Hill Course. Though open to the public, the course is on military land and military discounts are available. Moose Run has an unusual hazard: moose and bears live in the nearby woods. Keep your eyes peeled, and if an animal ambles onto the green, by all means let it play through. ✉ *27000 Arctic Valley Rd., East Anchorage* ☎ *907/428–0056* ⊕ *www.mooserungolfcourse.com* ⛳ *$49* ⛳ *18 holes, 7324/5183 yards, par 72* ⛳ *Facilities: driving range, putting green, pitching area, golf carts, pull carts, rental clubs, pro shop, golf lessons, restaurant.*

HIKING

Hiking is king in Anchorage all year long thanks to Chugach State Park, which provides nearly 500,000 acres of exploration right in the city's backyard. You'll find Alaskans from all walks of life hiking in summer, even at midnight. Winter and spring are easily tackled with snow spikes, and nearly every resident has their favorite mountain berry patch when fall arrives.

Crow Pass

HIKING & WALKING | This 23-mile trek— formerly part of the Iditarod Trail—is a popular overnight hiking trail for Anchorage residents (and yes, there's a trail marathon every July). Hikers can leave from the Crow Pass trailhead in Girdwood or the Eagle River Nature Center in Eagle River. There are marked campsites throughout, as well as rental yurts near Eagle River and a public-use cabin three miles uphill from Girdwood. Reservations are required for both. Prepare to get wet at river crossings, and plan your transport—it's a 70-mile drive between trailheads. ✉ *Eagle River Trailhead, 32750 Eagle River Rd.* ⛳ *$5 daily parking fee.*

Iditarod Trail History

Since 1973, mushers and their sled-dog teams have raced 1,000 miles across Alaska in the Iditarod Trail Sled Dog Race, one of the longest sled-dog races in the world.

After a ceremonial start in Downtown Anchorage on the first Saturday in March, dog teams wind through Alaska, battling almost every imaginable winter challenge. Iditarod mushers and dogs endure extreme cold, deep snow, gale-force winds, whiteouts, river overflow, and moose attacks, not to mention fraying tempers. Less than 10 days later, the front-runners in the "Last Great Race" cross under the burled-wood arch finish line in Nome, on the Bering Sea coast.

Race Revival

The Iditarod's origins can be traced to two events: an early-1900s long-distance race called the All-Alaska Sweepstakes and the delivery of a lifesaving serum to Nome by dog mushers during a diphtheria outbreak in 1925.

Fascinated with the trail's history, Alaskan sled-dog enthusiasts Dorothy Page and Joe Redington Sr. staged the first race in 1967 to celebrate the role of mushing in Alaska's history. Only 50 miles long and with a purse of $25,000—no small amount at that time—it attracted the best of Alaska's competitive mushers. Enthusiasm waned in 1969, however, when the available winnings fell to $1,000. Instead of giving up, Redington expanded the race.

In 1973, after three years without a race, he organized a 1,000-mile race from Anchorage to Nome, with a then-outrageous purse of $50,000. Critics scoffed, but 34 racers entered. First place went to a little-known musher named Dick Wilmarth, who finished in 20 days. Redington then billed the Iditarod as a 1,049-mile race to symbolize Alaska, the 49th state.

The Race Begins

The race actually begins in Willow, a 70-mile drive north of Anchorage. The first few hundred miles take mushers and dogs through wooded lowlands and hills, including the aptly named Moose Alley.

Teams then cross the Alaska Range and enter Interior Alaska, with Athabascan villages and gold-rush ghost towns, including one called Iditarod. Next, the trail follows the frozen Yukon River, then cuts over to the Bering Sea coast for the final 220-mile "sprint" to Nome. It was here, in 1985, that Libby Riddles drove her team into a blinding blizzard en route to a victory that made her the first woman to win the race. After that, Susan Butcher won the race four times. Lance Mackey holds the record for most consecutive wins, with his back-to-backs from 2007 to 2010. Mitch Seavey and his son Dallas traded the title from 2012 to 2017, setting the speed record three times. Currently, Mitch has the fastest time ever, finishing in 8 days, 3 hours, and 40 minutes in 2017. With five wins by the age of 34, Dallas is tied for most victories with the "King of the Iditarod," Rick Swenson.

Sled dogs start the Iditarod in Willow and stop here, at the Finger Lake Checkpoint, 194 miles into the 1,150-mile trek.

⭐ Flattop Mountain

HIKING & WALKING | Alaska's most popular peak, this manageable 3-mile round-trip escalates in difficulty, gaining nearly 1,500 feet from the parking lot. But whether you reach the flagpole at the summit or simply stroll the 0.3-mile wheelchair-accessible loop at the base, you'll be treated to astounding views of the Anchorage Bowl and Cook Inlet. Downtown Bicycle Rental runs a once-daily shuttle from late May to late September originating from its shop on 4th Avenue. ⊠ *Glen Alps Trailhead, Glen Alps Rd.* ⌧ *$5 parking fee.*

Thunderbird Falls

HIKING & WALKING | A reasonable 2-mile round-trip hike with easy road access, Thunderbird Falls is the simplest hike near Anchorage. The wide trail skirts the rim of Eklutna Canyon before culminating in a wooden viewing platform to take in Thunderbird Falls. Hikers can also scramble downhill to reach the pools below the 200-foot falls, which frequently freeze, offering winter ice-climbing. ⊠ *Mile 25.2 of Glenn Hwy.* ⌧ *$5 daily parking fee.*

ICE-SKATING

Ice-skating is a favorite wintertime activity in Anchorage, with several indoor ice arenas, outdoor hockey rinks, and local ponds opening when temperatures drop. Though Alaska's early winters and cold temperatures often allow for pond skating as early as mid-November, check with a visitor center or the city's parks and recreation department before stepping out onto pond ice. Pond skating possibilities include **Cheney Lake, Goose Lake, Potter Marsh, Jewel Lake,** and **Cuddy Family Midtown Park.**

Ben Boeke Ice Arena

ICE SKATING | Ben Boeke Ice Arena is a city-run indoor ice arena with open skating and skate rentals September to mid-March. ⊠ *334 E. 16th Ave., Midtown* ☎ *907/274–5715* ⊕ *www.benboeke.com.*

Dimond Ice Chalet

ICE SKATING | An indoor ice rink at Dimond Mall, the Dimond Ice Chalet is open to the public daily. ⊠ *800 E. Dimond Blvd., South Anchorage* ☎ *907/344–1212.*

Westchester Lagoon

ICE SKATING | In winter, Westchester Lagoon, 1 mile south of Downtown, is a favorite outdoor family skating area, with smooth ice, mountain views, and piles of firewood next to the warming barrels. ⊠ *15th Ave. and U St.* ⊕ *www.muni.org/ departments/parks.*

RUNNING AND WALKING

Alaska Run for Women

RUNNING | A number of popular running events are held annually in Anchorage, including the five-mile Alaska Run for Women in early June, which raises money for the fight against breast cancer. ⊠ *Anchorage* ⊕ *www.akrfw.org.*

Mayor's Marathon

RUNNING | Thousands of runners participate in the Mayor's Marathon, which features six races folded into one weekend: a marathon, marathon relay, half-marathon, half-marathon relay, 5K, and 1-mile youth run. The marathon is held annually on the Saturday closest to the summer solstice (June 21). ⊠ *Anchorage* ⊕ *www. mayorsmarathon.com.*

Skinny Raven

RUNNING | This bright downtown shoe shop is the running hub of Anchorage. Meet locals at the popular and low-key Tuesday night pub runs, held year-round in rain, sun, or snowstorm. Organized races occur nearly every month, including the Shamrock Shuffle in March and Turkey Trot in November. ⊠ *800 H St., Downtown* ☎ *907/274–7222* ⊕ *www. skinnyraven.com.*

SKIING

Cross-country skiing is extremely popular in Anchorage. Locals ski or skate-ski on trails in town at Kincaid Park or Hillside and farther away at Girdwood Valley, Turnagain Pass, and Chugach State Park.

Downhill skiing is convenient to Downtown. A number of cross-country ski events are held annually in Anchorage.

Alaska Mountaineering & Hiking

SKIING & SNOWBOARDING | The locally owned outdoors shop Alaska Mountaineering & Hiking has a highly experienced staff and plenty of cross-country skis for sale or rent. ⊠ *2633 Spenard Rd., Spenard* ☎ *907/272–1811* ⊕ *www.alaskamountaineering.com.*

Hilltop Ski Area

SKIING & SNOWBOARDING | FAMILY | Conveniently located on the eastern edge of town, Hilltop Ski Area is a beginner-friendly slope and a favorite for families. Skis and snowboards are available to rent. ⊠ *Abbott Rd. near Hillside Dr., East Anchorage* ☎ *907/346–2167 ski hotline* ⊕ *www.hilltopskiarea.org* ✉ *$34 lift passes.*

Kincaid Park

SKIING & SNOWBOARDING | On 1,400 acres of rolling, timbered hills and bordered on the west by Cook Inlet, Kincaid Park is a scenic treasure with maintained trails groomed for classic and skate-skiing. National cross-country skiing events (including U.S. Olympic team qualifying events) are sometimes held along the 60 km (37 miles) of interwoven trails—including 20 km (12 miles) that are lighted for night skiing. The park is open year-round: for skiing in winter; and for mountain biking, hiking, and other outdoor activities in summer. Keep an eye out for moose. ⊠ *Main entrance at far west end of Raspberry Rd., 9401 W. Raspberry Rd., Southwest Anchorage.*

Nordic Skiing Association of Anchorage

SKIING & SNOWBOARDING | The city's ski authority plans events all winter long. Elite skiers carve through the heart of the city during the 50K Tour of Anchorage in early March. The Ski for Women—a Super Bowl Sunday tradition—draws a colorful cavalcade of costumed skiers to Kincaid Park. And, believe it or not, ski jumping takes place 12 months of the year at Hilltop Ski Area. Check out the website's calendar for monthly events. ✉ *Anchorage* ☎ *907/276–7609* ⊕ *www. anchoragenordicski.com.*

Downtown

Anchorage's main hub holds the majority of its sights and restaurants, and the streets are lined with art galleries and shops.

Downtown is pedestrian- and bike-friendly, and its flower-lined streets are easily explored on foot. Several businesses rent out bicycles. The area is confined to the south by the Delaney Park Strip, Anchorage's 14-block backyard, where you'll find kite-flying, pickup soccer games, and free yoga every Wednesday in the summer (check *www.thealaskaclub.com* for times). Fourth Avenue remains the beating heart of the city, lined with reindeer sausage carts by day and crowded bars by night, and Downtown thrives all year long (especially during First Friday Art Walks). The grid plan was laid out by the Army Corps of Engineers, and streets and avenues run exactly east–west and north–south, with numbers in the first direction and letters of the alphabet or Alaska place-names (Barrow, Cordova, Denali, etc.) in the other. The only aberration is the absence of a J Street—a concession, some say, to the city's early Swedish settlers, who had difficulty pronouncing the letter. You'll need a car for longer stays or expeditions and to reach some of the city's better restaurants without relying on taxis. In the snow-free months a network of paved trails provides good avenues for in-city travel for bicyclists and walkers.

Outside Downtown, Anchorage is composed of widely scattered neighborhoods largely hidden by busy thoroughfares. And although there's no shortage of excellent restaurants Downtown, many of the town's best places are found in bland strip malls. Also, you're never more than a block or two from a good espresso stand or coffeehouse.

 Sights

Alaska Railroad Historic Depot

TRAIN/TRAIN STATION | Totem poles and a locomotive built in 1907 are outside this station, the headquarters of the Alaska Railroad since 1915. Photographs and plaques inside explain the history of the railroad, which brought an influx of people into the city during the early 1900s. During February's Fur Rendezvous Festival, model-train buffs set up their displays here. ✉ *411 W. 1st Ave., Downtown* ☎ *907/265–2494, 800/544–0552* ⊕ *www.alaskarailroad.com* ⊗ *Closed Sun. mid-Sept.–mid-May.*

★ Anchorage Museum

HISTORY MUSEUM | **FAMILY** | This striking, contemporary building with first-rate exhibits is an essential stop for visitors who want to celebrate the history of the North. The star of the museum is the Smithsonian Arctic Studies Center, which features more than 600 objects from Alaska Native cultures and short films that teach visitors about modern-day Native life. Wander the *Art of the North* galleries, filled with works that showcase Alaska landscape, history, and beauty. The *Alaska* exhibition shares Alaska's diversity and history with a knock-out eye for design. Cap the visit in the 9,000-square-foot, kid-focused Discovery Center, which includes a planetarium. Curated exhibitions rotate regularly and frequently spotlight Arctic issues, Northern design, and the unique perspective of life at these latitudes. In addition, the gift shop is one of Anchorage's best places to buy Alaska Native art and other souvenirs. ✉ *625 C St., Downtown* ☎ *907/929–9200* ⊕ *www.anchoragemuseum.org* ☑ *$20* ⊗ *Closed Mon.*

One of Alaska's best museums, the Anchorage Museum focuses on the history of the state, including several essential exhibits on Alaska Native cultures.

Historic City Hall

GOVERNMENT BUILDING | Offices of Visit Anchorage now occupy this 1936 building. A few exhibits and historic photos are right inside the lobby. Out front, take a look at the marble sculpture dedicated to William Seward, the secretary of state who engineered the purchase of Alaska from Russia. ⊠ *524 W. 4th Ave., Downtown* ☉ *Closed weekends.*

International Gallery of Contemporary Art

ART GALLERY | Anchorage's premier fine-arts gallery, the International Gallery of Contemporary Art has changing exhibits monthly and features some of Alaska's most forward-thinking work. ⊠ *427 D St., Downtown* ☎ *907/279–1116* ⊕ *www.igcaalaska.org* ☉ *Closed Sun.–Tues.*

Oscar Anderson House Museum

HISTORIC HOME | City butcher Oscar Anderson built Anchorage's first permanent frame house in 1915, at a time when most of Anchorage consisted of tents. Visits are by guided 45-minute tours only. ⊠ *420 M St., in Elderberry Park, Downtown* ☎ *907/274–2284* ⊕ *www.oscarandersonhousemuseum.org* ✉ *$10* ☉ *Closed Sun. and Oct.–May.*

★ Point Woronzof

CITY PARK | **FAMILY** | Perched between the airport and the coast, this city park provides an entertaining hodgepodge of nature and noise—you can enjoy beautiful views of Mt. Susitna while trans-Pacific cargo jets periodically roar overhead. Walk down to the beach and head east for a picture-perfect view of the city skyline framed against the Chugach Mountains. Just off the Tony Knowles Coastal Trail, expect food carts and ice cream trucks as your reward if you make the 5-mile bike ride from Downtown. ⊠ *9700 Point Woronzoff Rd., near end of Northern Lights Blvd., Anchorage.*

Resolution Park

CITY PARK | This tiny park has a cantilevered viewing platform dominated by a monument to Captain Cook, whose explorations in 1778 led to the naming of Cook Inlet and many other geographic features in Alaska. Mt. Susitna, known as the Sleeping Lady, is the prominent low mountain to the northwest, and Mts. Spurr and Redoubt, active volcanoes, are just south of Mt. Susitna. Denali, Mt. Foraker, and other peaks of the Alaska Range are often visible from more than 100 miles away. ✉ *3rd Ave. at L St., Downtown.*

Ship Creek

DAM | **FAMILY** | The creek is dammed right Downtown, with a footbridge across the dam and access from either bank. There's a waterfall; salmon running upstream from June through August; anglers; and, above it all, Downtown Anchorage. Farther upstream (follow Whitney Road and turn left on Post Road) is the William Jack Hernandez Sport Fish Hatchery—during the runs you can see salmon in the clear shallow water as they try to leap up the falls. Look for the wheelchair-accessible fishing platform on the trail directly north of the Comfort Inn. ✉ *Ship Creek Ave., Downtown* ⏲ *Fishery closed weekends Nov.–Mar.*

★ **Tony Knowles Coastal Trail**

TRAIL | Strollers, runners, bikers, dog walkers, and in-line skaters cram this recreation trail on sunny summer evenings, particularly around Westchester Lagoon. In winter, cross-country skiers take to it by storm. The trail begins off 2nd Avenue, west of Christensen Drive, and curls along Cook Inlet for approximately 11 miles to Kincaid Park, beyond the airport. In summer you might spot beluga whales offshore in Cook Inlet. Access points are on the waterfront at the ends of 2nd and 5th Avenues and at Westchester Lagoon near the end of 15th Avenue. When you get to the high points in the trail, look north; Denali is visible on clear days. ✉ *Anchorage.*

First Friday Arts Walk

The Anchorage First Friday Arts Walk is a popular monthly (and year-round) event, with dozens of galleries, coffee shops, and restaurants offering a chance to sample hors d'oeuvres while looking over the latest works by regional artists. The *Anchorage Press* prints a "First Friday" guide the first Thursday of every month.

🍴 Restaurants

The Bubbly Mermaid Oyster Bar

$$ | **SEAFOOD** | This tiny seafood joint easily offers the quirkiest dining experience in Downtown: almost the entire room is taken up by a boat-prow bar. At the helm, owner Apollo Naff has created a convivial environment where fellow diners become fast friends over plates of Alaska oysters and other briny bites, such as crab cake po'boys, seafood chowder, and seared scallops in umami sauce. **Known for:** menu items inspired by chef's Tijuana roots; Alaska oysters; nautical ambiance. [$] *Average main: $19* ✉ *417 D St., Downtown* ☎ *619/665–2852.*

Club Paris

$$$$ | **STEAKHOUSE** | Alaska's oldest steak house has barely changed since opening in 1957. The restaurant, with its dark wood and old-fashioned feel, serves tender, flavorful steaks of all kinds, along with a large seafood selection. **Known for:** classic martinis; four-inch-thick filet mignon; homemade desserts. [$] *Average main: $32* ✉ *417 W. 5th Ave., Downtown* ☎ *907/277–6332* 🌐 *www.clubparisrestaurant.com* ⏲ *No lunch weekends.*

Anchorage

★ Crow's Nest Restaurant

$$$$ | EUROPEAN | An absolute must for epicures and adventurous eaters, Crow's Nest uses inspired combinations to highlight, but never overpower, the freshest ingredients Alaska has to offer. Located on the top floor of the Hotel Captain Cook, this is also the best restaurant view in Anchorage, spanning the Chugach Mountains to the east, the Alaska Range to the north and west, and the city 20 stories below. **Known for:** 10,000-bottle wine cellar; unforgettable views and atmosphere; excellent steaks and seafood. $ *Average main: $45 ⊠ Hotel Captain Cook, 939 W. 5th Ave., 20th fl., Downtown ☎ 907/276–2217 ⊕ www. captaincook.com/dining/crows-nest ⊗ Closed Sun. and Mon. No lunch.*

★ Crush Bistro & Bottle Shops

$$$ | ECLECTIC | The combination of shared small plates and an international wine list makes this Anchorage's most conversation-friendly dining venue. Although it's more fun to share, diners who prefer a plate of their own can also opt for inventive entrees ranging from southern fried game hen to shawarma-spiced lamb chops. **Known for:** expansive next-door bottle shop; monthly wine tastings; charcuterie plates. $ *Average main: $28 ⊠ 328 G St., Downtown ☎ 907/865–9198 ⊕ www.crushak.com ⊗ Closed Sun. and Mon.*

Fire Island Rustic Bakeshop

$ | BAKERY | FAMILY | The scones and sandwiches at Fire Island draw bustling morning crowds. There are three locations across the city, but the original is embedded in a cozy neighborhood just blocks from Downtown, and makes a perfect destination for a leisurely morning muffin run. **Known for:** a different menu every day; busy open kitchen; hearty handcrafted breads. $ *Average main: $7 ⊠ 1343 G St., at 14th Ave., Downtown ☎ 907/569–0001 ⊕ www.fireislandbread. com ⊗ Closed Sun.–Tues. No dinner.*

Ginger

$$$ | ASIAN | Beautifully crafted Pacific Rim dishes like Panang curry and spicy ahi tuna are a mainstay at Ginger, where the menu offers food that will please both adventurous and more traditional diners. Decorated in beautiful woods and warm tones, the interior perfectly complements the menu. **Known for:** artful plates in an artful setting; hip happy hour menu; plenty of vegetarian options. $ *Average main: $27 ⊠ 425 W. 5th Ave., Downtown ☎ 907/929–3680 ⊕ www.gingeralaska.com ⊗ Closed Mon. and Tues.*

Glacier BrewHouse

$$$ | AMERICAN | The scent of hops permeates the cavernous, wood-beam BrewHouse, where at least a dozen beers are brewed on the premises. Locals mingle with visitors in this noisy, always-busy heart-of-town restaurant, and dinner selections range from chili-lime shrimp to fettuccine jambalaya and fresh seafood (in season). **Known for:** hefty imperial beers; wood-grilled rib eyes; can't-miss dessert menu. $ *Average main: $25 ⊠ 737 W. 5th Ave., Downtown ☎ 907/274–2739 ⊕ www. glacierbrewhouse.com.*

★ The Marx Bros. Café

$$$$ | AMERICAN | Inside a small frame house built in 1916, this nationally recognized 14-table restaurant opened in 1979 and is still going strong thanks to a regularly rotating menu that highlights classic Alaska ingredients. The wine list encompasses more than 700 international choices. **Known for:** exceptionally deep wine cellar; homemade butter pecan ice cream; table-made Caesar salads. $ *Average main: $47 ⊠ 627 W. 3rd Ave., Downtown ☎ 907/278–2133 ⊕ www.marxcafe.com ⊗ Closed Sun. and Mon. No lunch.*

New Sagaya's City Market

$ | ECLECTIC | Stop at either the Downtown or Midtown New Sagaya's grocery stores for quick lunches, healthy to-go food (perfect for hiking or camping), and Kaladi Brothers coffee. The in-house bakery and deli, L'Aroma, makes specialty breads, sandwiches, California-style pizzas, and a wide range of snack-worthy pastries. **Known for:** fresh seafood counter; outdoor seating; Asian ingredients galore. $ *Average main: $9* ✉ *900 W. 13th Ave., Downtown* ☎ *907/274–6173* 🌐 *www.newsagaya.com.*

Orso

$$$ | **ITALIAN** | The menu at Orso ("bear" in Italian) has gradually shifted from its Mediterranean roots, adding Alaska touches like baked seafood mac and cheese to the selection of traditional pastas, fresh seafood, and locally famous desserts. Be sure to ask about the daily specials. **Known for:** gluten-free options; light bites at happy hour; fresh takes on Italian standards. $ *Average main: $30* ✉ *737 W. 5th Ave., at G St., Downtown* ☎ *907/222–3232* 🌐 *www.orsoalaska.com* 🕒 *No lunch.*

Simon & Seafort's Saloon & Grill

$$$$ | **SEAFOOD** | Windows overlooking Cook Inlet vistas, along with the high ceilings and a classic brass-and-wood interior, have long made this an Anchorage favorite. The menu includes prime rib and other steak-house classics, but the main attraction is fresh Alaska seafood. **Known for:** enormous steaks; king crab dishes; happy hour food menu with an ocean view. $ *Average main: $36* ✉ *420 L St., Downtown* ☎ *907/274–3502* 🌐 *www.simonandseaforts.com.*

★ Snow City Cafe

$$ | **ECLECTIC** | On summer days, Snow City attracts some serious crowds—and for good reason. This modern but unassuming café, convenient to many of the Downtown hotels, serves one of Anchorage's best (and yet reasonably priced) breakfasts all day long. **Known for:** long waits unless you go early or make a reservation; inventive eggs Benedict with king crab and salmon; vegan and gluten-free options galore. $ *Average main: $15* ✉ *1034 W. 4th Ave., Downtown* ☎ *907/272–2489* 🌐 *www.snowcitycafe.com* 🕒 *No dinner.*

Tequila 61

$$ | **MODERN MEXICAN** | Whether you're at the cozy cocktail bar or on the wraparound lounge couches, this atmospheric fusion restaurant brings upscale Mexican flavors to the far north (the "61" in the name references the city's latitude). Though known for its tacos—including a duck confit option—the restaurant also prepares rib eyes, shrimp ceviche, and chipotle-glazed king crab. **Known for:** horchata cornbread; gourmet taco Tuesday; mezcal cocktails. $ *Average main: $19* ✉ *445 W 4th Ave., Downtown* ☎ *907/274–7678* 🌐 *www.tequila61.com* 🕒 *Closed Sun. and Mon. No lunch.*

Wild Scoops

$ | **ECLECTIC** | **FAMILY** | Step inside this Downtown microcreamery for Alaska-inspired ice cream flavors like almond birch brittle and rhubarb crumble. The homemade, small-batch ice cream options rotate constantly, emphasizing local ingredients like honey, blueberries, sea salt, and even beer. **Known for:** the favorite ice cream of Alaskan locals; vegan options; fresh, innovative ingredients. $ *Average main: $5* ✉ *429 E St., Downtown* ☎ *907/744-7295* 🌐 *www.wildscoops.com.*

🛏 Hotels

Anchorage Marriott Downtown

$$$$ | **HOTEL** | One of Anchorage's biggest lodgings, the brightly decorated Marriott appeals to business travelers, tourists, and corporate clients. **Pros:** near Downtown's best restaurants; great views; modern, up-to-date facilities. **Cons:** extra charge for Wi-Fi; cruise-ship crowds at times in summer; pricey valet parking. $ *Rooms from: $359* ✉ *820 W. 7th Ave., Downtown* ☎ *907/279–8000, 800/228–9290* 🌐 *www.marriott.com/ancdt* 🍴 *No Meals* 🛏 *392 rooms.*

Comfort Inn Downtown Ship Creek

$$$ | HOTEL | FAMILY | The namesake Ship Creek gurgles past this popular family hotel, which is a short walk northeast of the Alaska Railroad Historic Depot and practically on top of the creek's parallel paved walking trail. **Pros:** summertime salmon fishing in the creek out back; free parking; pet-friendly rooms. **Cons:** train noise; walk into Downtown is an uphill climb; close to an industrial part of town. $ *Rooms from: $249* ✉ *111 Ship Creek Ave., Downtown* ☎ *907/277–6887, 800/424–6423* ⊕ *www.choicehotels.com/ ak006* ❍❍ *Free Breakfast* ⇨ *100 rooms.*

Copper Whale Inn

$$$ | B&B/INN | This location offers the best of both worlds: it's walkable to everything worth seeing in Downtown, but it's on the quiet end of 5th Avenue, right next to a small park and the 11-mile Coastal Trail. **Pros:** beautiful private gardens; bike rentals in the front yard; convenient Downtown location. **Cons:** no airport shuttle; some rooms are small; occasional city street noise. $ *Rooms from: $229* ✉ *440 L St., Downtown* ☎ *907/258–7999* ⊕ *www.copperwhale. com* ⇨ *14 rooms* ❍❍ *Free Breakfast.*

Historic Anchorage Hotel

$$$ | HOTEL | Part of the Anchorage landscape since 1916, experienced travelers call this little building the most charming hotel in town. **Pros:** complimentary breakfast in the hotel's former saloon; excellent staff; on the National Register of Historic Places. **Cons:** no airport shuttle; some rooms are small; street noise affects some rooms. $ *Rooms from: $209* ✉ *330 E St., Downtown* ☎ *907/272–4553, 800/544–0988* ⊕ *www. historicanchoragehotel.com* ⇨ *26 rooms* ❍❍ *Free Breakfast.*

★ Hotel Captain Cook

$$$ | HOTEL | Recalling Captain Cook's voyages to Alaska and the South Pacific, dark teak paneling lines the hotel's interior, and a nautical theme continues into the guest rooms. **Pros:** destination hotel for visiting dignitaries, including President Obama in 2015; very well-trained and accommodating staff; excellent on-site pub and top-floor restaurant. **Cons:** lots of lobby traffic; 24-hour valet parking passes cost $36; no airport shuttle. $ *Rooms from: $275* ✉ *939 W. 5th Ave., Downtown* ☎ *907/276–6000, 800/843–1950* ⊕ *www.captaincook.com* ⇨ *642 rooms* ❍❍ *No Meals.*

Oscar Gill House

$$ | B&B/INN | Originally built by Gill in the settlement of Knik (north of Anchorage) in 1913, this historic home has been transformed into a comfortable B&B in a quiet neighborhood along the Delaney Park Strip, with Downtown attractions a short walk away. **Pros:** very hospitable owners; great breakfast; cozy home with some old Anchorage history. **Cons:** no king-size beds; shared bath in two of the rooms; no elevator to second floor. $ *Rooms from: $135* ✉ *1344 W. 10th Ave., Downtown* ☎ *907/570–2145, 907/351–6047* ⊕ *www. oscargill.com* ❍❍ *Free Breakfast* ⇨ *3 rooms, 1 with bath.*

Sheraton Anchorage Hotel & Spa

$$$$ | HOTEL | The 16-story Sheraton is one of the city's best hotels, with rooms that are sleek (but not sterile) and accented with comfy beds and postcard views. **Pros:** impressive amenities, including on-site dining and spa; tasteful, modern rooms; great views from the upper floors. **Cons:** extra charge for Wi-Fi; fees for parking; several blocks from most Downtown businesses. $ *Rooms from: $399* ✉ *401 E. 6th Ave., Downtown* ☎ *907/276–8700, 800/325–3535* ⊕ *www.sheratonanchorage.com* ❍❍ *No Meals* ⇨ *370 rooms.*

♈ Nightlife

Anchorage does not shut down when it gets dark—well, that is when it actually does get dark (it's still light at 3 am in the summer!). Bars here—and throughout Alaska—open early (in the morning) and close as late as 3 am on weekends. The listings in the *Anchorage Daily News* entertainment section, published on Friday, and in the free weekly *Anchorage Press* cover concerts, theater performances, movies, and a roundup of nightspots featuring live music.

BARS AND NIGHTCLUBS

Bernie's Bungalow Lounge

DANCE CLUBS | This low-key lounge pulls in plenty of twentysomethings looking to dance, drink, and tackle the late-night menu served on the equally expansive outdoor patio. On weekends there is usually a good local DJ upstairs and a mediocre live band outside. ⊠ *626 D St., Downtown* ☎ *907/276–8808* ⊕ *www. bernieslounge.com.*

Club Paris

BARS | Lots of old-timers favor the dark bar of Club Paris. This is your spot if you like a stiff, no-nonsense drink. ⊠ *417 W. 5th Ave., Downtown* ☎ *907/277–6332* ⊕ *www.clubparisrestaurant.com.*

49th State Brewing Company

BARS | The rustic interior here is all stone, wood, and antlers, but the real attraction is the sun-soaked two-story rooftop deck where, on clear days, you can see Denali hovering over the northern horizon. The menu of pizzas and hearty bar bites emphasizes all things Alaska, including giant burgers appropriately named for noteworthy peaks. Beers are brewed on-site using local ingredients like Sitka spruce tips and Talkeetna birch syrup. The restaurant also hosts a range of events in its on-site theater, including improv comedy and trivia nights. ⊠ *717 W. 3rd Ave., Downtown* ☎ *907/277–7727* ⊕ *www.49statebrewing.com.*

Mad Myrna's

DANCE CLUBS | Alaska's premier gay bar offers dozens of LGBTQ+ community events. Though housed in an unassuming beige building, the glittery interior offers weekly karaoke, DJ sets on the dance floor, lounge-y couches, a cozy patio, and a kitchen menu only overshadowed by the cocktail list. The main event is the all-inclusive drag show every Friday and Saturday night that rivals anything in the Lower 48. The entrance for Myrna's is in the alley between 5th and 6th Avenues. ⊠ *530 E. 5th Ave., Downtown* ☎ *907/276–9762* ⊕ *www.madmyrnas.net.*

Simon & Seafort's Saloon & Grill

BARS | A trendy place for the dressy crowd, the bar at Simon & Seafort's Saloon & Grill has stunning views of Cook Inlet, a special single-malt-Scotch menu, and tempting cocktails. The lavender martini is a highlight. Take advantage of the two happy hours each day, including a late-night stretch starting at 9 pm. ⊠ *420 L St., Downtown* ☎ *907/274–3502* ⊕ *www.simonandseaforts.com.*

Williwaw

GATHERING PLACES | This central three-story entertainment hub tries to be everything for everybody, and mostly succeeds. With a rooftop bar, coffee shop, pinball arcade, not-so-secret speakeasy, and concert venue, there's always something going on here. Check the online schedule for events like movie nights, DJs, trivia, and dance parties. ⊠ *609 F St., Downtown* ☎ *907/868–2000* ⊕ *www. williwawsocial.com.*

LIVE MUSIC

See the "Play" section in Friday editions of the *Alaska Dispatch News* for complete listings of upcoming concerts and other performances, or get the same entertainment information online (*www.adn.com*).

Humpy's Great Alaskan Alehouse

LIVE MUSIC | One of Anchorage's biggest bars, Humpy's Great Alaskan Alehouse serves up rock, blues, and folk several nights a week, along with dozens of microbrews (more than 40 beers are on tap) and surprisingly tasty pub grub. Check the website calendar for the full spread of bands, open mics, and trivia nights. You can grab one of Humpy's delicious halibut burgers on your way out of town—the company has a satellite restaurant in Terminal B of the Anchorage airport. ✉ *610 W. 6th Ave., Downtown* ☎ *907/276–2337* ⊕ *www.humpys.com.*

Live After Five

LIVE MUSIC | The city's bigger bands get the summer spotlight at Town Square Park. Designed for the after-work crowd, these Thursday evening shows start at 5:30 pm and feature a beer garden from Humpy's Great Alaskan Alehouse. ✉ *Town Square Park, 5th and F St., Downtown* ⊕ *www.anchoragedowntown.org.*

Performing Arts

Alaska Center for the Performing Arts

ARTS CENTERS | Four theaters make up the Alaska Center for the Performing Arts, which is home to 10 resident performing arts companies—including Alaska Dance Theatre, Anchorage Opera, and the Anchorage Symphony Orchestra. The center also showcases traveling production companies. The lobby box office sells tickets to the productions and is a good all-around source of cultural information. Take a look inside to learn more about upcoming events, or relax amid the blossoms in the adjacent flower-filled Town Square Park on a sunny afternoon. ✉ *621 W. 6th Ave., at G St., Downtown* ☎ *907/263–2787* ⊕ *www.alaskapac.org.*

Music in the Park

MUSIC | FAMILY | On summertime Wednesdays, open-air concerts are presented at noon in Peratrovich Park (also known as Old City Hall Park). Come back with the family on Mondays at noon, when music is geared to the little ones. ✉ *500 W. 4th Ave., at E St., Downtown* ⊕ *www.anchoragedowntown.org.*

Shopping

CLOTHING

Circular

WOMEN'S CLOTHING | Score eco-conscious dresses, weekend wear, and accessories at this forward-thinking women's clothing boutique. ✉ *320 W. 6th Ave., Downtown* ☎ *907/274–2472* ⊕ *www.circularboutique.com.*

David Green Master Furrier

MIXED CLOTHING | Although furs may not be to everyone's taste or ethics, a number of Alaska fur companies have stores and factories in Anchorage. One of the city's largest and best-known furriers is David Green Master Furrier, whose family has been in the fur business in Alaska since 1922. ✉ *130 W. 4th Ave., Downtown* ☎ *907/277–9595* ⊕ *www.davidgreenfur.com.*

Laura Wright Alaskan Parkys

MIXED CLOTHING | Started in 1947 in Fairbanks by Laura Wright, this family business is now owned by Wright's granddaughter, Sheila Ezelle, who sells distinctive Alaskan Iñupiat "parkys" (parkas) for both summer and winter. Visitors can find her booth at Alaska Native craft markets in Anchorage or place an order over the phone. ✉ *Downtown* ☎ *907/274–4215.*

CRAFTS

Oomingmak

CRAFTS | The Alaska Native–owned cooperative Oomingmak sells items made of qiviut, the ubersoft and warm undercoat of musk ox, from inside one of the few small houses remaining in Downtown. Scarves, shawls, hats, and tunics are knitted in traditional patterns by women in villages across Alaska. ✉ *604 H St., Downtown* ☎ *907/272–9225, 888/360–9665* ⊕ *www.qiviut.com.*

Sevigny Studio

CRAFTS | Find Alaska-made crafts for every budget—from glasswork to jewelry to notecards—at this bright, welcoming studio, owned by painter and printmaker Katie Sevigny. ✉ *312 G St., Downtown* ☎ *907/258–2787* ⊕ *www. sevignystudio.com.*

FOOD

The Kobuk

OTHER SPECIALTY STORE | One of Alaska's most popular tea companies, the Kobuk serves up a variety of classic and unique teas, including their signature Samovar tea (a samovar is a traditional Russian container used to brew tea). Pastries, coffee, fine china, and other gifts are also for sale. ✉ *504 W. 5th Ave., Anchorage* ☎ *907/272–3626* ⊕ *www.kobukcoffee.com.*

Midtown

Once you're done wandering the shops and handful of notable attractions Downtown, consider heading south to Midtown. The neighborhood has some of Anchorage's best restaurants and plenty of gear stores to help prep your out-of-town adventures. Midtown is sandwiched between high-traffic thruways, but these are lined with diverse shops proffering everything from high-quality brews to artisan ice cream to secondhand camp stoves. It's also a good neighborhood to stay in if you'd rather be slightly outside the main tourist fray. In this functional section of Anchorage, however, don't expect much in the way of sightseeing.

◉ Sights

UAA Planetarium and Visualization Theater

OTHER ATTRACTION | FAMILY | Kick back in this plush 60-seat auditorium as professors from the University of Alaska Anchorage add live commentary to Northern-focused science and education films, including several titles produced by the university itself in hard-to-reach

Alaska destinations. The theater offers Friday night double features during the academic year. ✉ *3101 Science Cir., Midtown* ☎ *907/786–1838* ⊕ *www.uaa. alaska.edu/planetarium* 🎟 *$10.*

Restaurants

Altura Bistro

$$$$ | MODERN AMERICAN | Yet another upscale eatery tucked into an Anchorage strip mall, the colorful plating at Altura makes up for its beige location. The inventive menu here features items like red king crab mac and cheese, prawns and grits, and caviar nachos *(yes, really)*. **Known for:** Wagyu rib eye and filet mignon; artful plating; slew of dessert wines. $ *Average main: $42* ✉ *4240 Old Seward Hwy., Midtown* ☎ *907/561–2373* ⊕ *www.facebook.com/AlturaAK* ☾ *Closed Mon. and Tues.*

Jens'

$$$$ | EUROPEAN | Don't let the Midtown strip mall that houses Jens' put you off: this is a true fine-dining establishment. The late chef-owner Jens Haagen Hansen's culinary legacy has led to the frequently changing menu that includes Alaska salmon, halibut, and rockfish. **Known for:** light bites at the wine bar; "almost world famous" pepper steaks; Danish lunch specials. $ *Average main: $35* ✉ *701 W. 36th Ave., at Arctic Blvd., Midtown* ☎ *907/561–5367* ⊕ *www. jensrestaurant.com* ☾ *Closed Jan., Sun., and Mon.*

★ Kinley's Restaurant & Bar

$$$ | AMERICAN | The dining room here offers a range of meat and seafood entrees, while the lounge's separate menu feels suitable for a romantic date or a girls' night out. Kinley's also has a special knack for finding wines that taste luxe, but don't break the bank. **Known for:** Midtown's mightiest wine list; seafood specials; casual yet classy atmosphere. $ *Average main: $26* ✉ *3230 Seward Hwy., Midtown* ☎ *907/644–8953* ⊕ *www.kinleysrestaurant.com* ☾ *Closed Sun. and Mon.*

Moose's Tooth Pub & Pizzeria

$$ | **PIZZA** | **FAMILY** | Always the top pick when local newspapers rate Anchorage pizzerias, Moose's Tooth is packed all week, despite the ample seating (it can hold up to 300 guests). The reason for the popularity is obvious: handcrafted beers from the on-site brewery, and a seemingly endless roster of pizzas topped with inventive options like jalapeños, cream cheese, shrimp, and lime. **Known for:** Alaska's best pizza; energetic outdoor waiting area; house-made brews, root beer, and cream soda. $ *Average main: $20* ⊠ *3300 Old Seward Hwy., Midtown* ☎ *907/258–2537* ⊕ *moosestooth.net.*

Hotels

Embassy Suites Anchorage

$$$$ | **HOTEL** | You'll find a long list of amenities at this upscale Anchorage hotel, including a hot cooked-to-order breakfast and an evening manager's reception featuring complimentary cocktails and snacks. **Pros:** great breakfast; top-of-the-line facilities; freebies at manager's reception. **Cons:** only some rooms have a (distant) mountain view; neighborhood is a high-traffic area; no sights within walking distance. $ *Rooms from: $329* ⊠ *600 E. Benson Blvd., Midtown* ☎ *907/332–7000, 800/362–2779* ⊕ *www.embassysuites.hilton.com* ⇨ *169 suites* ¶⊙¶ *Free Breakfast.*

SpringHill Suites Anchorage Midtown

$$$ | **HOTEL** | Spacious one-room suites have separate living and sleeping areas, with either a king bed or two double beds, plus a pullout sofa, microwave, mini-refrigerator, and flat-screen TV. **Pros:** nice pool; complimentary parking; 24-hour airport shuttle. **Cons:** most restaurants within easy walking distance are national chains; small laundry facilities for such a large hotel; very cookie-cutter decor. $ *Rooms*

from: $239 ⊠ *3401 A St., Midtown* ☎ *907/562–3247* ⊕ *www.marriott.com/ancsh* ¶⊙¶ *Free Breakfast* ⇨ *102 suites.*

Shopping

Alaska Fur Exchange

CRAFTS | In a large Midtown store, Alaska Fur Exchange sells both furs and Alaska Native artwork. ⊠ *4417 Old Seward Hwy., Midtown* ☎ *907/563–3877* ⊕ *www.alaskafurexchange.com.*

APU Outdoor Programs

SPORTING GOODS | The secluded liberal arts campus at Alaska Pacific University features a gear room offering low-cost equipment rentals to the public. Pick up items for overnight getaways or in-town adventures, including paddleboards, tents, kayaks, camp stoves, and avalanche gear. Items are limited, so call in advance. ⊠ *Atwood Center, 4101 University Dr., Midtown* ☎ *907/564–8614* ⊕ *www.alaskapacific.edu/equipment.*

REI

SPORTING GOODS | If you get to Alaska and discover you've left some critical camping or outdoor recreation gear behind, REI rents camping, skiing, and paddling equipment. It also gives regular seminars on season-specific outdoor topics. The salespeople are very knowledgeable about local conditions and activities and the gear required to get you out and back safely. ⊠ *500 E. Northern Lights Blvd., Spenard* ☎ *907/272–4565* ⊕ *www.rei.com/anchorage.*

Summit Spice & Tea Company

FOOD | This shop and tearoom blends its own teas and spices, and also sells a range of Alaska-made groceries from spruce tip jelly to kelp-and-cayenne chocolate bars. ⊠ *3030 Denali St., Midtown* ☎ *907/375–1975* ⊕ *www.summitspiceandtea.com.*

Spenard

The spirit of Spenard is captured by its winding namesake road—an anomaly in this meticulously gridlike city. The quieter neighborhood lies just west of Midtown and is known for its artsy vibe, some of the city's most notable casual restaurants, a good farmers' market, and Anchorage's largest independent bookstore, Title Wave.

Sights

Alaska Aviation Museum

OTHER MUSEUM | FAMILY | The state's unique aviation history is presented here with more than 25 vintage aircraft, a flight simulator, a theater, and an observation deck along the world's busiest seaplane base. Highlights include a Stearman C2B, the first plane to land on Denali back in the early 1930s, a recently restored 1931 Fairchild Pilgrim aircraft, and a well-done exhibit on the Battle of Attu, the only North American land battle of World War II. You may see volunteers busily restoring an aircraft and docents eager to talk about their bush pilot experiences. A free shuttle to and from Anchorage Airport is available, as is luggage storage. ✉ *4721 Aircraft Dr., West Anchorage* ☎ *907/248–5325* 🌐 *www.alaskaairmuseum.org* 🎟 *$17.*

Restaurants

Gwennie's Old Alaska Restaurant

$ | AMERICAN | Historic photos, mounted animals, and state memorabilia adorn this old family favorite near the airport. Lunch is available, but the restaurant is best known for its old-fashioned all-day breakfasts, which include menu items like reindeer sausage and crab omelets. **Known for:** endless entertainment from the wall decor; sourdough pancakes; generous portions. [$] *Average main: $12* ✉ *4333 Spenard Rd., Spenard* ☎ *907/243–2090* 🌐 *www.gwenniesrestaurant.com* 🕒 *No dinner.*

Spenard Food Truck Carnival

Food truck fans can count on the Spenard Food Truck Carnival, which occurs throughout the summer on Thursday and every other Saturday in the parking lot at Chilkoot Charlie's (2435 Spenard Road). There are typically up to 10 food trucks featuring everything from fresh Alaska fish tacos to barbecue.

Organic Oasis

$$ | CAFÉ | Part eatery and part community center and event space, this café offers plenty of healthy (or, at least, healthy-sounding) fare, including fresh-squeezed juices, smoothies, organic sandwiches, fresh vegan soups, and tempeh burgers. While vegans and vegetarian visitors to Anchorage should definitely make a beeline to Organic, omnivores are not left out in the cold: the menu also includes Thai chicken wraps, grass-fed burgers, and lamb. **Known for:** inventive juice bar; live music throughout the week; house-baked breads and buns. [$] *Average main: $15* ✉ *2610 Spenard Rd., Spenard* ☎ *907/277–7882* 🌐 *www.organicoasis.com* 🕒 *No dinner Sun.*

Spenard Roadhouse

$$ | AMERICAN | The amusing assortment of wall art here pays homage to the roadhouses that dot the state, but Spenard Roadhouse is by no means just a place to grab a quick meal while traveling. The warm and inviting restaurant offers creative comfort food, plus an unforgettable weekend brunch menu; the cocktails alone are worth the journey. **Known for:** house-infused vodkas and bourbon flights; bacon of the month; tater tots the locals love. [$] *Average main: $17* ✉ *1049 W. Northern Lights Blvd., Spenard* ☎ *907/770–7623* 🌐 *www.spenardroadhouse.com.*

Yak and Yeti Himalayan Restaurant
$ | **INDIAN** | Savor the flavors of India, Nepal, and Tibet in this cozy, homey restaurant owned by Lobsang Dorjee, a Tibetan who grew up in India, and his wife, lifelong Alaskan Suzanne Hull. Yak and Yeti delivers authenticity and depth, balancing the familiar—pork vindaloo, palak paneer, samosas—with the unexpected, such as *lhasa momos,* a type of Tibetan dumpling. **Known for:** cost-conscious entrées; hefty vegetarian options; cozy mugs of chai. [$] *Average main: $12* ✉ *3301 Spenard Rd., Spenard* ☎ *907/743–8078* 🌐 *www.yakandyetialaska.com* 🕒 *Closed Sun.*

Hotels

Courtyard by Marriott Anchorage Airport
$$$$ | **HOTEL** | Business travelers pack this modern hotel thanks to its well-designed lobby, comfortable accommodations, and proximity to the airport. **Pros:** close to airport; complimentary airport shuttle; free Wi-Fi. **Cons:** not close to attractions; business traveler focus; fee for breakfast. [$] *Rooms from: $329* ✉ *4901 Spenard Rd., Spenard* ☎ *907/245–0322* 🌐 *www.marriott.com/anccy* 🛏 *154 rooms* 🍴 *No Meals.*

Hampton Inn by Hilton
$$$ | **HOTEL** | Midway between the airport and Downtown, the Hampton has all the standard features of a good hotel, and a few that are better than average, such as designer furnishings, an indoor swimming pool, and a whirlpool. **Pros:** breakfast included; free Wi-Fi; great beds. **Cons:** basic chain-hotel ambience; some rooms near the pool can be noisy and smell of chlorine; surrounded by chain restaurants. [$] *Rooms from: $229* ✉ *4301 Credit Union Dr., Spenard* ☎ *907/550–7000, 800/426–7866* 🌐 *www.hamptoninn.com* 🛏 *101 rooms* 🍴 *Free Breakfast.*

The Lakefront Anchorage
$$$$ | **HOTEL** | Perched on the shore of Lake Spenard, this Anchorage favorite is one of the city's best spots to watch planes come and go from the hotel's private dock. **Pros:** pet-friendly (it's even home to the Iditarod mushers each February); shuttles available to airport and downtown; old Alaska hunting-lodge feel. **Cons:** distant from Downtown attractions; noise from airplanes on Lake Hood; no complimentary breakfast. [$] *Rooms from: $369* ✉ *4800 Spenard Rd., Spenard* ☎ *907/243–2300, 800/544–0553* 🌐 *www.millenniumhotels.com/anchorage* 🛏 *248 rooms* 🍴 *No Meals.*

Nightlife

Chilkoot Charlie's
DANCE CLUBS | A rambling timber building with sawdust floors, loud music, weekend DJs, and rowdy customers, Chilkoot Charlie's is where young Alaskans go to get crazy. The legendary bar has many unusual nooks and crannies, including a room filled with Russian artifacts and a reconstructed version of Alaska's infamous Birdhouse Bar. ✉ *2435 Spenard Rd., Spenard* ☎ *907/272–1010* 🌐 *www.koots.com.*

Performing Arts

Bear Tooth Theatrepub
FILM | Catch the latest foreign films, indie flicks, and off-the-wall art pieces at this second-run theater with a back-corner bar. Place an order at the counter outside and runners will deliver your nachos, pizzas, and garlic-cilantro fries from the attached Southwestern grill directly to your seat. Throughout the year, the Bear Tooth also clears out the movie seats to host nationally touring music acts. ✉ *1230 W. 27th Ave., Spenard* ☎ *907/276–4200* 🌐 *beartooththeatre.net.*

Shopping

BOOKS

Title Wave Books

BOOKS | Easily the largest independent bookstore in Alaska, Title Wave Books fills a 25,000-square-foot space in the Northern Lights Center. The shelves are filled with nearly half a million used books, CDs, and DVDs across more than 1,600 categories, including a large section of Alaska-focused books. The staff is very knowledgeable, and the store hosts regular game nights and children's story times. Anyone can bring in used books and trade them for store credit. ⊠ *1360 W. Northern Lights Blvd., Spenard* ☏ *907/278–9283, 888/598–9283* ⊕ *www. wavebooks.com.*

The Writer's Block

BOOKS | Alaska authors line the shelves at this cozy literary café, a neighborhood gathering place that's both a bookstore and coffee shop. The busy events calendar showcases local artists of all stripes, including spoken word performances, art openings, and book launches. ⊠ *3956 Spenard Rd., Spenard* ☏ *907/929–2665* ⊕ *www.writersblockak.com.*

GIFTS

Dos Manos

SOUVENIRS | This laid-back gallery features individually screen-printed T-shirts, leather satchels, silver jewelry, and affordable wall art displayed along a sweeping three-story spiral staircase. Most items don't say "Alaska" on them, but everything here is handmade in the state by established and emerging artists. ⊠ *1317 W. Northern Lights, Suite 3, Spenard* ☏ *907/569–6800.*

SPORTS AND OUTDOOR EQUIPMENT

Alaska Mountaineering & Hiking

SPORTING GOODS | This Alaskan-owned store is the go-to specialist for any gear having to do with, yep, mountaineering or hiking. Whether you're setting out on a series of day hikes or you're planning a serious climb, the knowledgeable staff can help you choose the right equipment for the task. Take the time to chat up the staff and you may hear some amazing Denali stories. ⊠ *2633 Spenard Rd., Spenard* ☏ *907/272–1811* ⊕ *www.alaska-mountaineering.com.*

Greater Anchorage

Anchorage has swelled since its start as a tent city just over a century ago. Although the hub of activity is still centered Downtown, some of the city's largest and best attractions as well as a number of newer and noteworthy restaurants are situated throughout Greater Anchorage, which can look a bit sprawly and prosaic in places but also extends into the scenic Chugach foothills to the east.

Sights

Alaska Botanical Garden

GARDEN | **FAMILY** | The garden showcases perennials hardy enough to make it in Southcentral Alaska in several large display gardens, a pergola-enclosed herb garden, and a rock garden amid 110 acres of mixed boreal forest. There's a 1-mile nature trail loop to Campbell Creek, with views of the Chugach Range and a wildflower trail between the display gardens. Interpretive signs guide visitors and identify plants along the trail. Docent tours are available upon request, and events occur throughout the year. ⊠ *4601 Campbell Airstrip Rd., off Tudor Rd. (park at Benny Benson School), East Anchorage* ☏ *907/770–3692* ⊕ *www.alaskabg. org* ◪ *$12* ⊘ *Closed Sun. and Mon. mid-May–mid-Sept.*

★ Alaska Native Heritage Center

INDIGENOUS SIGHT | **FAMILY** | On a 26-acre site facing the Chugach Mountains, this facility provides an introduction to Alaska Native peoples. The spacious Gathering Place has interpretive displays, artifacts, photographs, demonstrations, Alaska

Just outside of the city center, Potter Marsh is a beautiful place to bird-watch and to catch the sunrise.

Native dances, storytelling, and films, along with a gift shop selling crafts and artwork. Step outside for a stroll around the adjacent lake, where seven village exhibits represent 11 cultural groups through traditional structures and exhibitions. As you enter the homes in these villages, you can visit with the hosts, hear their stories, and try some of the tools, games, and utensils used in the past. ⊠ *8800 Heritage Center Dr., (Glenn Hwy. at Muldoon Rd.), East Anchorage* ☎ *907/330–8000, 855/330–8085* ⊕ *www.alaskanative.net* ✉ *$29* ⊘ *Closed mid-Sept.–mid-May.*

Alaska Zoo

ZOO | FAMILY | Roam the trails and visit with the polar bears, caribou, brown and black bears, seals, tigers, snow leopards, moose, wolves, lynx, and a large array of birds that call the Alaska Zoo home. The zoo provides a wide array of programs included with admission, such as zookeeper talks and toddler story times, that concentrate on promoting the conservation of arctic and subarctic animal species. Throughout the summer for an additional fee you can join daily two-hour tours that include behind-the-scenes stops. The zoo is located in the foothills on the edge of town, but a summer-only shuttle leaves from the Downtown Visitor Center at 4th Avenue and E Street every hour. ⊠ *4731 O'Malley Rd., 2 miles east of New Seward Hwy., South Anchorage* ☎ *907/346–2133* ⊕ *www. alaskazoo.org* ✉ *$17.*

Potter Marsh

BODY OF WATER | FAMILY | Sandhill cranes, trumpeter swans, and other migratory birds, as well as the occasional moose or beaver, frequent this marsh about 10 miles south of Downtown on the Seward Highway. An elevated boardwalk makes viewing easy, and in summer there are salmon runs in the creek beneath the bridge. An old railroad service building just south of the marsh operates as a state park office. ⊠ *Seward Hwy., South Anchorage.*

🍴 Restaurants

Kincaid Grill

$$$$ | **AMERICAN** | This out-of-the-way restaurant provides a respite after a summertime hike or wintertime ski in nearby Kincaid Park. Meals are artistically presented, and the diverse and creative menu, with a focus on Alaska regional cuisine, seafood, and game meats, changes seasonally. **Known for:** long list at the wine bar; shrimp grits and seafood gumbo; chocolate bourbon soufflé. [$] *Average main: $33* ✉ *6700 Jewel Lake Rd., South Anchorage* ☎ *907/243–0507* 🌐 *www.kincaidgrill.com* 🕑 *Closed Sun. and Mon. No lunch.*

Peanut Farm Sports Bar & Grill

$$ | **AMERICAN** | What started as a creekside log cabin is now a 70-screen sports bar with room for athletic fans of every stripe, from hockey (of course) to mushing and beyond. There's also an outdoor deck, pool tables, and a large and varied menu of tasty bar favorites. **Known for:** fireside seating in an original log cabin building; best wings in the city; patio on the bank of Campbell Creek. [$] *Average main: $18* ✉ *5227 Old Seward Hwy., South Anchorage* ☎ *907/563–3283* 🌐 *www.wemustbenuts.com.*

South Restaurant + Coffeehouse

$$ | **AMERICAN** | Perched on the edge of the city, South's expansive menu and bright airy space make it a destination brunch spot in Anchorage. The menu offers fresh Alaska spins on brunch classics like halibut tacos and salmon BLTs as well as a wide range of salads, sandwiches, and tapas. **Known for:** plenty of vegan and gluten-free options; destination brunch spot; cocktails on the firepit patio. [$] *Average main: $18* ✉ *11124 Old Seward Hwy., South Anchorage* ☎ *907/770–9200* 🌐 *www.southak.com.*

🛏 Hotels

Camai Bed and Breakfast

$$ | **B&B/INN** | At this elegant B&B, Anchorage's oldest, two of the suites have private entries and plenty of space for families, and all suites have private baths and in-room satellite televisions. **Pros:** lovely deck and hot tub; some suites have private exterior entrances; very experienced hosts. **Cons:** relatively long way from Downtown restaurants; only continental breakfast in winter; located in a neighborhood cul-de-sac. [$] *Rooms from: $140* ✉ *3838 Westminster Way, East Anchorage* ☎ *907/333–2219* 🌐 *www.camaibnb.com* 🛏 *3 suites* 🍴 *Free Breakfast.*

Dimond Center Hotel

$$$$ | **HOTEL** | **FAMILY** | For the price, the Dimond Center Hotel offers a shocking number of perks: every room has a 72-inch soaking tub, huge flat-screen television, microwave, and mini-refrigerator—not to mention the generous breakfast buffet, with waffles and biscuits and gravy. **Pros:** no fee for parking; Alaska Native corporation–owned; airport shuttle and free Wi-Fi. **Cons:** surrounded by national chain stores; 5 miles from Downtown; shares a parking lot with the city's largest mall. [$] *Rooms from: $369* ✉ *700 E. Dimond Blvd., South Anchorage* ☎ *907/770–5000, 866/770–5002* 🌐 *www.dimondcenterhotel.com* 🛏 *109 rooms* 🍴 *Free Breakfast.*

🍸 Nightlife

Anchorage Brewing Company

BARS | Arguably the most artistic brewery in the entire state, ABC's inventive beers skew toward the sour. Grab a glass in the high-ceiling tasting room and wander freely among the brewery's towering wood casks, or carry your pint outside to the cozy patio with a firepit. ✉ *148 W. 91st Ave., South Anchorage* ☎ *907/677–2739* 🌐 *www.anchoragebrewing.company.*

🛍 Shopping

★ Anchorage Market and Festival

MARKET | On weekends from mid-May to mid-September, the Anchorage Market and Festival opens for business in the south parking lot of the Dimond Center mall. Dozens of vendors offer Alaskan-made crafts, international imports, and deliciously fattening food. Stock up on birch candy and salmon jerky to snack on while traveling or as perfect made-in-Alaska gifts for friends back home. ✉ Dimond Center, 800 E. Dimond Blvd., Downtown ☎ 907/272–5634 ⊕ www.anchoragemarkets.com.

Mountain View Sports Fly Shop

SPORTING GOODS | If you're looking for brand names like Pendleton, Simms, and Filson, this locally owned store is your place. It is pretty much fly-fishing central in Anchorage, and you can find expert advice and guidance for your prospective fishing and hunting adventures. There's also an excellent book section that covers all sorts of outdoor activities in Alaska. ✉ 11124 Old Seward Hwy., Midtown ☎ 907/222–6633 ⊕ www.mtviewsports.com.

Side Trips from Anchorage

A ski resort, summer vacation spot, and home to an eclectic collection of locals, the town of Girdwood sits in a deep valley and is surrounded by tall mountains on three sides and, on the fourth, Turnagain Arm, one of the most photogenic sites in Southcentral Alaska.

Girdwood

40 miles southeast of Anchorage.

Originally called Glacier City, Girdwood got its start as a gold-mining town. The town was renamed for James Girdwood, an Irish linen merchant who had four gold claims. But the name wasn't the only thing that changed over the years; the town itself was moved 2½ miles from its original site after the 1964 earthquake.

Today Girdwood's main attraction is the Alyeska Ski Resort, the largest ski area in Alaska. Besides enjoying the obvious winter attractions, you can hike up the mountain, rent a bike, or visit several upscale restaurants and gift shops. Girdwood is wetter than Anchorage; it often rains or snows here while the sun shines to the north.

GETTING HERE AND AROUND

Though it's only 40 miles from Ted Stevens Anchorage International Airport, consider allowing extra time if you make the drive to Girdwood. The drive down the New Seward Highway is stunning; look out for beluga whales and Dall sheep. Other options include a ride on the Alaska Railroad's Coastal Classic or Glacier Discovery trains (*907/265–2494, 800/544–0552 www.alaskarailroad.com*). Once in Girdwood, you can get pretty much anywhere on the fare-free bus routes provided by Glacier Valley Transit (*www.glaciervalleytransit.com*).

WHEN TO GO

Though Girdwood is best known for its winter ski activities, there's plenty to do year-round. The town's restaurants remain popular with locals—snow or no snow—and the area offers some of Anchorage's best hiking trails, fishing, and much more.

Sights

Girdwood Center for Visual Arts

ART GALLERY | Though you'll go to Girdwood to ski or hike, you'll find yourself spending time perusing the crafts and artwork at this nonprofit co-op gallery. With pieces from more than 30 artists on display, there's plenty to look at—and you might end up taking care of any gift needs (from the trip or for the holidays) in one fell swoop. ⊠ *194 Olympic Mountain Loop, Girdwood* ☎ *907/783–3209* ⊕ *www.gcvaonline.org* ⊘ *Closed Tues. and Wed. in winter.*

Activities

Alaska Backcountry Access

ADVENTURE TOURS | This outfitter takes people out of town for jet-boat rides up the Twentymile River, summertime snowmobiling near Godwin Glacier, and kayak trips past icebergs on aptly named Glacier Lake. Winter excursions include snowmobile outings across Southcentral Alaska. ⊠ *Girdwood* ☎ *907/783–3600* ⊕ *www.akback.com.*

Alyeska Resort

SKIING & SNOWBOARDING | Alaska's largest and best-known downhill ski resort encompasses more than 1,600 skiable acres of terrain for all skill levels, where snowfall averages nearly 670 inches annually. Alyeska features a day lodge, hotel, restaurants, six lifts, a tram, a vertical drop of 2,500 feet, and 76 named trails for all abilities—including North America's longest continuous double black run. The tram is also open in summer ($35), providing access to Seven Glaciers restaurant and ridgeline hiking trails. Brave the stout hike up the mountain, and you can ride the tram down for free. Ski and snowboard rentals are available, and local guides teach classes on the mountain. Summertime thrill-seekers can take the lift up and head down the mountain on full-suspension mountain bike rentals. ⊠ *1000 Arlberg Ave., Girdwood* ☎ *907/754–2111, 800/880–3880* ⊕ *www.alyeskaresort.com* ⊿ *$89 lift passes.*

Chugach Powder Guides

SKIING & SNOWBOARDING | This helicopter and Sno-Cat skiing operation focuses on backcountry skiing and snowboarding in the interior Chugach Range, the Seward area, and the Talkeetna Mountains. Set itineraries and private charters are both available. ⊠ *Girdwood* ☎ *907/783–4354* ⊕ *www.chugachpowderguides.com.*

Winner Creek

HIKING & WALKING | An excellent outdoor option in Girdwood, Winner Creek is 45 minutes south of Anchorage. Leaving from the Hotel Alyeska's backyard, this gradual, well-maintained trail cuts through the country's northernmost rain forest. The simple 3-mile hike spans boggy boardwalks and wooden bridges before ending at gushing Glacier Creek. ⊠ *Trailhead behind Hotel Alyeska, 1000 Arlberg Ave., Girdwood.*

Restaurants

The Bake Shop

$ | AMERICAN | Order at the counter at this old-time, family-owned Girdwood favorite. Skiers and snowboarders drop by for a quick lunch or garden-fresh pizzas in winter, while summertime early birds enjoy cups of coffee and fluffy omelets on the flower-filled patio. **Known for:** bottomless soups perfect for cold ski days; sourdough pancakes; legendary sweet rolls. $ *Average main: $11* ⊠ *194 Olympic Mountain Loop, Girdwood* ☎ *907/783–2831* ⊕ *www.thebakeshop.com* ⊘ *Closed Tues. and Wed. in winter.*

Double Musky Inn

$$$$ | SOUTHERN | Anchorage residents say eating at this beloved spot is well worth the one-hour drive south to Girdwood and the inevitable wait for dinner. The interior is completely covered with tacky art and Mardi Gras souvenirs, but the windows frame views of huge Sitka spruce trees and the diverse menu mixes hearty Cajun-style meals with such favorites as garlic seafood pasta, rack of lamb, French pepper steak, and shrimp étouffée. **Known for:** gorgeous views; tasty Cajun creations; gooey, chocolate-rice pie. *Average main: $42 ⊠ Mile 0.3, Crow Creek Rd., Girdwood ☎ 907/783–2822 ⊕ www.doublemusky-inn.com ⊗ Closed Mon., Tues., and late Oct.–mid-Dec. No lunch.*

★ Seven Glaciers

$$$$ | EUROPEAN | This refined yet relaxing mountaintop restaurant is perched 2,300 feet up Mt. Alyeska, accessed by a 60-passenger aerial tram (free with dinner reservations, otherwise $29 round-trip). The forward-thinking prix fixe menu capitalizes on local produce and seafood, highlighted in dishes such as scallop bisque with smoked salmon mousse. **Known for:** unforgettable panoramic mountain views; 32-page wine menu; Alaska-grown ingredients and top-tier seafood. *Average main: $88 ⊠ Hotel Alyeska, 1000 Arlberg Rd., Girdwood ☎ 907/754–2237 ⊕ www.alyeskaresort. com/seven ⊗ No lunch.*

🛏 Hotels

Carriage House Accomodations

$$ | B&B/INN | This Girdwood inn is across from the Double Musky restaurant and close to Alyeska Resort's downhill ski slopes. **Pros:** very nice breakfast spread; elegant furnishings; gazebo-enclosed hot tub. **Cons:** restaurant traffic may be bothersome; location a bit remote for some; shared kitchen and dining room in the inn. *Rooms from: $175 ⊠ 388 Crow Creek Rd., Girdwood ☎ 907/250–1279 ⊕ www.carriagehouseaccommodations. com ⬎ 4 rooms, 3 cottages ❍ Free Breakfast.*

★ The Hotel Alyeska

$$$$ | HOTEL | Most rooms have stunning views of the Chugach Mountains and the lush forests surrounding this large and luxurious hotel at the base of Alyeska Ski Resort. **Pros:** frequent ski-and-stay packages in winter; great views; top-notch service. **Cons:** public traffic in lobby; some rooms are on the small side; car needed from Anchorage. *Rooms from: $429 ⊠ 1000 Arlberg Ave., Girdwood ☎ 907/754–2111, 800/880–3880 ⊕ www. alyeskaresort.com/hotel ⬎ 327 rooms ❍ No Meals.*

Nightlife

Girdwood Brewing Company

BARS | Tall windows frame the Chugach Mountains and old skis fence the patio at this airy brewery, opened by twin brothers, head brewers, and noted powder hounds Rory and Brett Marenco. Like all Anchorage breweries, Girdwood Brewing Company closes by 8 pm, so make sure to end your adventures on the nearby tides, trails, and mountaintops early enough to grab a pint. *⊠ 2700 Alyeska Hwy., Girdwood ☎ 907/783–2739 ⊕ www.girdwoodbrewing.com.*

Sitzmark Bar & Grill

LIVE MUSIC | Guests can ski straight to the back patio and firepit at this rollicking bar and grill. The Sitz hosts an event nearly every winter night under its spiral-painted ceiling, from game nights and trivia to nationally touring music acts. The bar closes each spring and fall as The Hotel Alyeska shifts between mountain bike and ski seasons; call to confirm hours before visiting. *⊠ 100 Olympic Cir., Anchorage ☎ 907/754–2256 ⊕ www. alyeskaresort.com/sitzmark.*

Chapter 4

JUNEAU, THE INSIDE PASSAGE, AND SOUTHEAST ALASKA

Updated by
Amy Fletcher

4

 Sights
★★★★★

 Restaurants
★★★★☆

 Hotels
★★★★☆

 Shopping
★★★★☆

 Nightlife
★★★☆☆

WELCOME TO JUNEAU, THE INSIDE PASSAGE, AND SOUTHEAST ALASKA

TOP REASONS TO GO

★ **Native art and culture:** Home of the Tlingit, Haida, and Tsimshian, Southeast Alaska is passionate about preserving and perpetuating Native cultures. Native art forms include totem poles, weavings, and masks.

★ **Rivers of ice:** Visitors relish the opportunity to walk on Southeast's accessible glaciers or to admire them on flight-seeing or kayak trips.

★ **Tongass National Forest:** America's largest national forest is home to bears, bald eagles, Sitka black-tailed deer, wolves, and marine mammals.

★ **Fishing nirvana:** This is an angler's paradise. The region's healthy populations of salmon and halibut—as well as the wealth of charter boats and fishing lodges—make this a premier fishing destination.

★ **Taking the ferry:** The Alaska Marine Highway is the primary means of transportation here. It's a low-cost, high-adventure alternative to cruising, and an easy way to spend time talking with Alaskans.

As remote as it is, Southeast Alaska shares a few traits with heavily populated regions. It has skyscrapers (the towering peaks of the Coast Range), traffic jams (try to swim through a salmon creek midsummer), and sprawl (the rain forests cover hundreds of thousands of acres).

1 **Ketchikan.** A town famous for its colorful totem poles, rainy skies, steep streets, and lush island setting.

2 **Misty Fjords National Monument.** A wilderness area filled with gorgeous fjords and coastal scenery.

3 **Metlakatla.** A quiet Inside Passage Tsimshian community.

4 **Prince of Wales Island.** The largest island in Southeast Alaska.

5 **Wrangell.** A fishing and timber community on North America's largest undammed river.

6 **Petersburg.** A hard-to-access town that will reward you with fishing and Nordic influence.

7 **Sitka.** A vibrant arts community with excellent parks and kayaking.

8 **Juneau.** Alaska's charming capital and home to famed Mendenhall Glacier.

9 **Juneau's Nearby Villages.** Native communities that offer insight into the area's Indigenous cultures.

10 **Admiralty Island.** The home of Southeast's largest population of brown bears.

11 **Tracy Arm.** A narrow fjord that leads to Sawyer Glacier.

12 **Glacier Bay National Park and Preserve.** The continent's largest (and most stunning) collection of tidewater glaciers.

13 **Gustavus.** The gateway to Glacier Bay National Park.

14 **Haines.** A small town known for fishing and an eagle preserve.

15 **Skagway.** A famed gold-rush town with gorgeous scenery and an incredible railway.

The communities of Southeast Alaska occupy a small fraction of this dramatic landscape, dotting mountainsides and natural harbors every hundred miles like far-flung pebbles. Ketchikan in the south, Sitka in the middle, and Juneau in the north are among the most visited locales.

In between, layers of mist-covered mountains and stretches of quiet forest remind visitors of what Southeast residents know and respect: this is nature's domain. West of Haines in the far northern reaches lies Glacier Bay National Park and Preserve, with its soaring glaciers, and the entire region provides habitats for bears, mountain goats, wolves, whales, and eagles. This is a world of steep-shouldered islands, cliff-rimmed fjords, snowcapped peaks, and majestic glaciers. Even in the biggest population centers, such as Juneau, man-made structures seem to sit lightly on the land, invariably dwarfed by their surroundings. Lush stands of spruce, hemlock, and cedar blanket thousands of islands. The region's myriad bays, coves, lakes, and swift, icy rivers provide some of the continent's best fishing grounds. Many of Southeast's wildest and most pristine landscapes are within Tongass National Forest, which comprises nearly 17 million acres—almost three-quarters of the Panhandle's land.

Southeast lacks only one thing: connecting roads. The lack of pavement between the area's communities presents obvious challenges to four-wheeled transport. To help remedy this, the state created the Alaska Marine Highway System, a network of passenger and vehicle ferries, some of which have staterooms, observation decks, video theaters, arcades, cafeterias, and heated, glass-enclosed solariums.

Southeast's natural beauty and abundance of wildlife have made it a popular cruise destination. About 25 big ships ply the Inside Passage during the height of summer. Smaller ships (some locally owned) also cruise through. Regular air service to Southeast is available from Seattle and other parts of Alaska, primarily Anchorage.

Southeast Alaska Natives—the Tlingit (*klink*-it), Haida, and Tsimshian (*sim*-shee-ann)—have lived in the region for thousands of years. Because ancestral knowledge of their traditions was once in danger of being lost, there's an ever-growing focus on revitalizing and perpetuating Native ways of life and promoting cross-cultural understanding. Efforts are under way in many towns to teach the often tricky-to-master Native languages in schools, and there's now an emphasis on cultural tourism, particularly in Hoonah at Icy Strait Point and in Juneau.

Southeast Natives, like their coastal neighbors in British Columbia, have rich traditions of Northwest Coast art, including carved poles, masks, textiles, baskets, and ceremonial objects. These traditions continue to evolve through the work of contemporary artists. In most villages and towns there's been a push to help residents learn these art forms and keep them alive for generations to come.

Alaska's diverse population is one of its great strengths. Residents—some from other states, some who can trace their ancestors back to the gold-rush days, and some whose ancestors have lived here "since time immemorial"—are an adventurous bunch. The rough-and-tumble spirit of Southeast often combines with a worldly sophistication: those who fish for a living might also be artists, Forest Service workers may run a B&B on the side, and homemakers may be Native or Filipino dance performers.

The Southeast Panhandle stretches some 500 miles from Yakutat at its northernmost point to Ketchikan and Metlakatla at its southern end. At its widest point, the region measures only 140 miles, and in the upper Panhandle just south of Yakutat, at 30 miles across, it is downright skinny by Alaska standards. Most of the Panhandle consists of a sliver of mainland buffered on the west by islands and on the east by the imposing peaks of the Coast Mountains. Those numerous coastal islands—more than 1,000 throughout the Inside Passage—collectively constitute the Alexander Archipelago. Most of them present mountainous terrain with lush covers of timber, though large clear-cuts are also common.

Most communities are on islands rather than on the mainland. The principal exceptions are Juneau, Haines, and Skagway, plus the hamlets of Gustavus and Hyder. Island outposts include Ketchikan, Wrangell, Petersburg, Sitka, and the villages of Craig, Pelican, Metlakatla, Kake, Angoon, and Hoonah. Bordering Alaska just east of the Panhandle lies the Canadian province of British Columbia.

MAJOR TOWNS AND REGIONS

Ketchikan and Around. The self-proclaimed "Salmon Capital of the World," Ketchikan is the doorway to Southeast. Be sure to check out the area's charter-fishing opportunities and wealth of local art. Ketchikan is a jumping-off point for Misty FjordsNational Monument and visits to the Tsimshian community of Metlakatla.

Wrangell and Petersburg. These towns provide access to the magnificent Stikine River. Wrangell, which welcomes some of the smaller cruise ships, is the primary hub for those who want to travel to the Anan Wildlife Observatory to see both brown and black bears fishing for salmon. Petersburg has a vibrant fishing community as well as stellar access to whale watching and hiking.

Sitka. With its mixed history of Tlingit, Russian, and American rule, Sitka is known for its vibrant art community, excellent parks (including Sitka National Historical Park), and many outdoor activities. It's a must-see for anyone traveling in Southeast and a must-paddle for kayakers of all experience levels.

Juneau and Around. Cruise passengers flock by the hundreds of thousands to take in the state capital's historic charm, artsy community, and natural beauty, including world-famous Mendenhall Glacier. But with a number of hotels and bed-and-breakfasts, Juneau also welcomes independent travelers. The city is the access point for surrounding attractions, including Admiralty Island National Monument, home to Southeast's largest population of brown bears, and is a growing hub for Alaska Native and Northwest Coast art.

Glacier Bay National Park and Preserve. Southeast's signature attraction, Glacier Bay is home to the continent's largest collection of tidewater glaciers, which are incredible to see. The park's remote, undeveloped location—Gustavus, the closest town, isn't really a town at

4

Juneau, the Inside Passage, and Southeast Alaska

all—ensures that travelers in search of quiet repose will not be disappointed.

Haines and Skagway. The northern outposts of the Inside Passage, these two towns seem to have it all. Haines, on stunning Chilkat Peninsula, is home to fishermen, helicopter-skiing guides, and eagle aficionados who flock to the nearby Chilkat Bald Eagle Preserve. Just down the road in Klukwan, a village 22 miles outside Haines, visitors can learn more about Tlingit culture. Skagway has gorgeous scenery, an incredible railway, and a boisterous gold-rush history.

Planning

When to Go

The best time to visit is May through August, when the weather is at its mildest, rain is less frequent, daylight hours are longest, wildlife is most abundant, and festivals and visitor-oriented activities are in full swing. But remember: Southeast sits in a rain forest, so rain can rule the day. There's a reason why XtraTuf waterproof boots are nicknamed "Southeast sneakers." Summertime high temperatures hover around the low to mid-60s, with far warmer days interspersed throughout. Shoulder-season temperatures are cooler, and the region is less crowded. Bring rain gear, layered clothing, sturdy footwear, a hat, and binoculars.

Allow yourself at least a week here. Plenty of adventures await ambitious independent travelers who plan ahead and ride state ferries.

If strolling through downtown shopping districts and museum-hopping is your idea of a perfect afternoon, journey to Ketchikan, Juneau, Skagway, Sitka, or Petersburg. For an immersive experience in a peaceful, remote location, consider booking a multiple-night stay at one of Southeast's remote fly-in lodges.

FESTIVALS

Alaska Folk Festival

The magic of this free, weeklong music festival is its inclusivity: every performer, regardless of his or her level of professionalism, is given 15 minutes on stage, with the exception of the featured guest artists, who play two one-hour sets. Held each April, Folk Fest draws singers, banjo masters, and fiddlers from all over the state and beyond. Past guest artists have included folk singer Nanci Griffith and western swing band Hot Club of Cowtown. Almost as fun as the festival itself is the after-hours bar scene that blossoms around it. Most local bars host performances and jam sessions; on the weekend the music continues into the wee hours. ⊠ *Centennial Hall, 101 Egan Dr., Juneau* ☎ *907/463–3316* ⊕ *www.akfolkfest.org.*

Celebration

More than 2,000 Native dancers gather in Juneau every even-numbered year in June to celebrate their heritage and the continued vitality of Alaska Native cultures. First held in 1982, this four-day cultural festival brings together tribal groups from all over the state, and includes a parade through the streets of Juneau for which participants don traditional, often very elaborate, handmade regalia. There's also a juried art show, Native fashion show, toddler regalia review, food contests, and a Native artist market. All events are open to the public, but the dance performances require a purchased ticket. ⊠ *1 Sealaska Plaza, Juneau* ☎ *907/463–4844* ⊕ *www.sealaskaheritage.org/institute/celebration* 🎟 *$18 one-day pass.*

Great Alaska Craft Beer and Homebrew Festival

This wildly popular festival in Haines, known locally as Beerfest, offers a five-course gourmet brewers' dinner, beer-tasting sessions, a home-brew competition, and live music. Tickets, which sell out quickly, go on sale in early February. ⊠ *296 Fair Dr., Haines*

☎ 907/766–2476 ⊕ www.seakfair.org/events/beer-fest.

Juneau Jazz & Classics

Performers from all over the world head to Juneau each May to celebrate music from Bach to Brubeck. Taj Mahal, Arlo Guthrie, Booker T. Jones, and the Manhattan Transfer are among past guests. First held in 1987, the festival runs for more than two weeks, showcasing jazz and classics along with blues, rock, and soul. Many events require tickets, but others—such as lunch-hour concerts at the State Office Building and jazz jams at a local bar called Lucky Lady—are free. In this spirit of accessibility, visiting musicians also perform in Juneau schools. ⊠ 350 Whittier St., Suite 105, Juneau ☎ 907/463–3378 ⊕ www.jazzandclassics.org.

Little Norway Festival

Enthusiasm for Petersburg's Norwegian heritage, expressed by rowdy locals dressed in horned helmets and fur vests, make this event one to catch. The festival has been held annually since 1958 on the weekend closest to May 17, *Syttende Mai*, or Norwegian Constitution Day. You won't find better Norwegian folk dancing or beer-batter halibut outside Norway. ⊠ Petersburg ☎ 907/772–4636 ⊕ www.petersburg.org.

Sitka Summer Music Festival

Now under the artistic direction of world-renowned cellist Zuill Bailey, this monthlong celebration in June attracts musicians from as far away as Europe and Asia for concerts and special events. Most performances are held at the Sitka Historical Society and Museum. ⊠ 104 Jeff Davis St., Sitka ☎ 907/747–6774 ⊕ www.sitkamusicfestival.org.

Sitka WhaleFest

Hosted by the Sitka Sound Science Center, this four-day festival and scientific symposium is held around town in early November, when the whales are plentiful (as many as 80) and tourists are not. Events include lectures, concerts, races, and cruises. ⊠ 834 Lincoln St., Suite 22, Sitka ☎ 907/747–8878 ⊕ www.sitka-whalefest.org.

Southeast Alaska State Fair

From a logging show to a fiddle contest, the Southeast Alaska State Fair provides a slice-of-life introduction to the state's eclectic pastimes. Music is a highlight, and there are also kids' activities, tons of food options, and impressive crafts. ⊠ 296 Fair Dr., Haines ☎ 907/766–2476 ⊕ www.seakfair.org ⌚ From $10 per day.

Getting Here and Around

AIR

Alaska Airlines and Delta Airlines operate several flights daily from Seattle to Juneau, Ketchikan, and Sitka (Alaska's flights are year-round, Delta's are seasonal); connections are also available to Wrangell, Petersburg, and Glacier Bay. Alaska Airlines also flies from Juneau to Anchorage, from which connections are available to much of the rest of the state.

FERRY TRAVEL

The Alaska Marine Highway System operates stateroom-equipped vehicle and passenger ferries from Bellingham, Washington, and from Prince Rupert, British Columbia. Popular among budget-minded travelers and those seeking an alternative to cruise-ship travel, the ferry system allows passengers to create their own itineraries. In Southeast the vessels call at Metlakatla, Ketchikan, Wrangell, Petersburg, Kake, Sitka, Angoon, Tenakee, Hoonah, Juneau, Gustavus, Pelican, Haines, Skagway, and Yakutat—and it's possible to take the ferry all the way to Southcentral and Southwest Alaska.

■ TIP➔ In summer, ferry staterooms sell out before sailing time; reserve months ahead. There are common areas on the ferries where you can throw down a sleeping bag or sit in a recliner seat.

If you are planning to take a car on the ferry, early reservations for vehicle space are also highly recommended. This is particularly true for recreational vehicles. Ferry travel is also an ideal way for bicyclists to hop from town to town. There is a fee of $15 to $50 (depending on your route) to bring a bicycle aboard. A separate ferry, operated by the Inter-Island Ferry Authority, runs between Ketchikan and Hollis (on Prince of Wales Island).

CONTACTS Alaska Marine Highway. ✉ *13485 Glacier Hwy., Juneau* ☎ *907/465–3941, 800/642–0066* ⊕ *dot. alaska.gov/amhs.***B.C. Ferries.** ☎ *888/223–3779* ⊕ *www.bcferries.com.***Inter-Island Ferry Authority.** ☎ *907/225–4848, 866/308–4848* ⊕ *www.interislandferry. com.*

FLIGHTSEEING

There's no better way to view Southeast's twisting channels, towering mountains, and gleaming glaciers than from one of the region's many small-aircraft flights.

Several services offer daily flights between Southeast's larger towns—Juneau, Haines, Skagway, Ketchikan, Sitka, Petersburg, and Wrangell—in addition to the bevy of helicopter flightseeing services that specialize in short, scenic flights.

Flying between destinations in Southeast—while significantly more expensive—is an experience you won't forget. If your itinerary includes an extra day or two in Southeast (particularly in Juneau), consider flying to and from a neighboring community. Round-trip tickets from Juneau to Skagway, for instance, start at around $300, about the same as a one-hour flightseeing trip in and around Juneau. **Alaska Seaplanes** offers wheeled plane and floatplane access to 14 destinations around Juneau, as well as charter services (*907/789–3331, www.flyalaska-seaplanes.com*).

Another floatplane service offering access to remote cabins and freshwater fishing destinations is Ketchikan-based **Southeast Aviation** (*888/359–6478, www. southeastaviation.com*).

Health and Safety

Southeast Alaska is, as we've mentioned, wet. Make sure you bring rain gear. No sense catching cold on vacation. Also, if you're new to catching seafood, consider hiring a guide to help you find the safest spots—Alaska's waters are powerful. Don't rent a boat and go out solo—even in a skiff—if you don't have boating experience. Shifts in weather and tides, along with other factors, can turn a pleasant kayaking experience into something far less fun.

Money Matters

Most towns—especially ones frequented by cruise ships—have plenty of ATMs, but it doesn't hurt to have some cash in your wallet, especially if you're visiting some of the smaller places on Prince of Wales Island.

Restaurants

From scallops to king salmon, fresh seafood dominates menus in Southeast. Juneau, Sitka, Skagway, and Ketchikan have all variety of global eateries, along with some notable restaurants serving more sophisticated, contemporary fare. Many towns also have good greasy spoons or roadhouses where you can get a serving of local gossip along with your breakfast or slice of pie.

Hotels

Lodging choices along the Inside Passage include centrally located hotels, all-inclusive fishing lodges, and a wide range of B&Bs. Southeast isn't known for its fancy hotels, so travelers accustomed to luxurious accommodations may be more comfortable in one of the region's high-end B&Bs, which also provide the opportunity to meet fellow travelers, enjoy a homemade breakfast, and learn about the area from local business owners. Fishing lodges on Prince of Wales Island and in other locales are another great alternative. These accommodations can be pricey, but rates drop from mid-September to mid-May. Budget travelers will find hostels and no-frills motel options in many of the larger towns.

CONTACTS Alaska Travelers Accommodations. ⊠ *Ketchikan* ☎ *907/247–7117* ⊕ *www.alaskatravelers.com.*

CABINS

Alaska State Parks and the U.S. Forest Service have cabins for rent.

Alaska State Parks

Near Ketchikan and Juneau, the park system has a small number of cabins for which reservations can be made up to six months in advance. **Pros:** wildlife viewing; scenic locations; private. **Cons:** often remote; no electricity or running water; preparation time can be extensive. Ⓢ *Rooms from: $60* ⊕ *www.dnr.alaska. gov/parks.*

U.S. Forest Service

At $45 to $75 per night, Forest Service cabins make for a cheap and charming escape, but they're popular; reserve in person, by mail, or online—up to six months in advance of your planned arrival date—with the National Recreation Reservation System *(www.reserveamerica. com).* Most cabins are reached by floatplane or boat, but some are accessible by road. **Pros:** private; scenic location; wildlife viewing. **Cons:** preparation time

can be extensive; no electricity or running water; often remote. Ⓢ *Rooms from: $45* ☎ *877/444–6777* ⊕ *www.recreation.gov.*

EQUIPMENT RENTALS

A few local outfitters rent cabin supplies. Alaska Wilderness Outfitting, part of Experience One Charters in Ketchikan, rents supplies such as cooking utensils, Coleman stoves, coolers, knives, and hot pads. Sitka Alaska Outfitters in Sitka can outfit you with a complete camping package that includes everything from sleeping pads to bear spray.

CONTACTS Experience One Charters. ⊠ *3857 Fairview Ave., Ketchikan* ☎ *907/225–2343* ⊕ *www.latitude56.com.* **Sitka Alaska Outfitters.** ⊠ *105 B Monastery St., Sitka* ☎ *907/966–2301* ⊕ *www. sitkaalaskaoutfitters.com.*

Restaurant and hotel reviews have been shortened. For full information, visit Fodors.com. Restaurant prices are the average cost of a main course at dinner or, if dinner is not served, at lunch. Hotel prices are the lowest cost of a standard double room in high season.

What It Costs			
$	$$	$$$	$$$$
RESTAURANTS			
under $14	$14–$22	$23–$30	over $30
HOTELS			
under $100	$100–$200	$201–$300	over $300

Tours

Alaska Tour & Travel

This operator offers shore excursions in Juneau, Ketchikan, Sitka, and Skagway, as well as customized tour packages throughout Southcentral and Southeast Alaska, including to most of the major national parks. Specific trips combine cruises through Southeast with an over-ground portion that includes bus travel to and lodging in Denali National Park. ✉ *3900 Arctic Blvd., Suite 304, Anchorage* ☎ *907/245–0200, 800/208–0200* ⊕ *www.alaskatravel.com* ✉ *From $800.*

Alaska Tours

This organization helps individuals and groups plan trips from Southeast to the Northwest and everything in between. ✉ *600 Barrow St., Suite 200, Anchorage* ☎ *907/277–3000, 866/317–3325* ⊕ *www.alaskatours.com* ✉ *Call for pricing.*

Viking Travel, Inc.

This reservations service can help you with your Alaska Marine Highway trip or other Alaska vacation plans. The agency has special airfares that are booked in conjunction with ferry itineraries. They also offers day tours from Ketchikan, Juneau, Skagway, Wrangell, and Petersburg. ✉ *101 N. Nordic Dr., Petersburg* ☎ *907/772–3818, 800/327–2571* ⊕ *www.alaskaferry.com* ✉ *From $160 (shore excursions) and $2175 (packages).*

Visitor Information

Visitor information centers are generally open mid-May through August, daily from 8 to 5, with additional hours when cruise ships are in port; between September and mid-May they're typically open weekdays from 8 to 5.

Ketchikan

Ketchikan is famous for its colorful totem poles, rainy skies, steep–as–San Francisco streets, and lush island setting. Some 13,900 people call the town home, and, in the summer, cruise ships crowd the shoreline, floatplanes depart noisily for Misty Fjords National Monument, and salmon-laden commercial fishing boats motor through Tongass Narrows. In the last decade Ketchikan's rowdy, blue-collar heritage of logging and fishing has been softened by the loss of many timber-industry jobs and the dramatic rise of cruise-ship tourism, but visitors can still glimpse the rugged frontier spirit that once permeated this hardscrabble cannery town. Art lovers should make a beeline for Ketchikan: the art community here is very active.

The town is at the base of 3,000-foot Deer Mountain, near the southeastern corner of Revillagigedo (locals shorten it to Revilla) Island. Prior to the arrival of white miners and fishermen in 1885, the Tlingit used the site at the mouth of Ketchikan Creek as a summer fish camp (the town's name comes from the Tlingit place name for the creek, Kichx̱áan). Gold discoveries just before the turn of the 20th century brought more immigrants, and valuable timber and commercial fishing resources spurred new industries. By the 1930s the town bragged that it was the "salmon-canning capital of the world." You will still find some of Southeast's best salmon fishing around here.

Ketchikan is the first bite of Alaska that many travelers taste. Despite its imposing backdrop, hillside homes, and many staircases, the town is relatively easy to walk through. Favorite downtown stops include Creek Street, a narrow boardwalk filled with locally owned shops, and the Southeast Alaska Discovery Center, where you can learn about the Tongass National Forest from local rangers. A bit farther away you'll find the Totem Heritage Center. Out of town (but included on most bus tours) are two longtime favorites: Totem Bight State Historical Park to the north and Saxman Totem Park to the south.

GETTING HERE AND AROUND

Ketchikan is a regular cruise-ship and ferry stop, and Alaska Airlines serves the town from Seattle. A three-minute ride on the Gateway Borough Ferry ($6) will get you from the airport to town, and there's a water taxi (cost varies) that serves waterfront marinas and piers.

If you're traveling out of town on the highway in either direction, you won't go far before you run out of road. The North Tongass Highway ends about 18 miles from downtown, at Settler's Cove Campground. The South Tongass Highway terminates about 13 miles from town. Side roads soon end at campgrounds and at trailheads, viewing points, lakes, boat-launching ramps, and private property.

Buses serve Ketchikan and outlying areas, and during the cruise-ship season (from May to September) a free shuttle bus travels a circular route from Berth 4. Notable stops include the Southeast Alaska Discovery Center, Creek Street, and the Totem Heritage Center.

ESSENTIALS

VISITOR INFORMATION Ketchikan Visitors Bureau. ⊠ *131 Front St., Ketchikan* ☎ *907/225–6166, 800/770–3300* ⊕ *www. visit-ketchikan.com.* **U.S. Forest Service.** ⊠ *648 Mission St., Ketchikan* ☎ *907/225– 3101* ⊕ *www.fs.fed.us/r10/tongass.*

 Sights

Alaska Rainforest Sanctuary

FOREST | The word "rainforest" may not immediately spring to mind when you picture Southeast Alaska, but as you walk amidst the giant cedars, hemlocks, and spruces at the Alaska Rainforest Sanctuary, the term will come into vivid focus, encompassing not just the trees but the interconnected web of plants and animals that live with them. The only way to experience the sanctuary is via a short, easy hike led by a naturalist guide; while on the trail, you'll keep an eye out for wildflowers, berries, bears, eagles, deer, and Herring Creek salmon. Located 8 miles outside Ketchikan, the tour is offered in all weather; sturdy shoes and a waterproof jacket are highly recommended. ⊠ *116 Wood Rd, Ketchikan* ☎ *907/225–8400* ⊕ *www. kawanti.com/activities/rainforest-sanctuary-totem-park-eagles* ⊠ *From $106 for guided naturalist tour.*

Creek Street

STREET | This was once Ketchikan's red-light district. During Prohibition, Creek Street was home to numerous speakeasies, and in the early 1900s more than 30 houses of prostitution operated here. Today the small, colorful houses, built on stilts over the creek waters, have been restored as interesting shops. When the fish are running, the Creek Street footbridge makes a stellar viewing platform for salmon and trout, as well as the sea lions and other animals that eat them. ⊠ *Ketchikan* ⊕ *creekstreetketchikan.com.*

Potlatch Totem Park

INDIGENOUS SIGHT | Walk along the waterfront and several forested paths to view striking examples of the monumental art form of totem pole carving, which is indigenous to Northwest Coast tribes. In addition to the totems, highlights include a carving shed where you can watch artists continue the work of their ancestors, a tribal house, and a large gift shop showcasing a wide range of authentic Native art. Also on the property are an antique car museum and antique firearm museum. Located adjacent to Totem Bight State Historical Park, Potlatch Park is 10 minutes north of town. ⊠ *9809 Totem Bight Rd., Ketchikan* ☎ *907/225–4445* ⊠ *Free.*

The Rock

PUBLIC ART | Ketchikan is known for its public art, and this bronze monument by local artist Dave Rubin provides a striking introduction. *The Rock* (2010) depicts seven life-size figures representative of Ketchikan's history: a Tlingit drummer, a logger, a miner, a fisherman, an aviator, a pioneer woman, and Tlingit chief George Johnson (the sculpture's only specific portrayal). The piece is located on the waterfront next to the Ketchikan Visitors Bureau. For a complete listing of Ketchikan's public art, galleries, museums, and cultural organizations, pick up a copy of *Art Lives Here,* the bureau's free guide. ⊠ *Front and Mill Sts., on boardwalk, Ketchikan.*

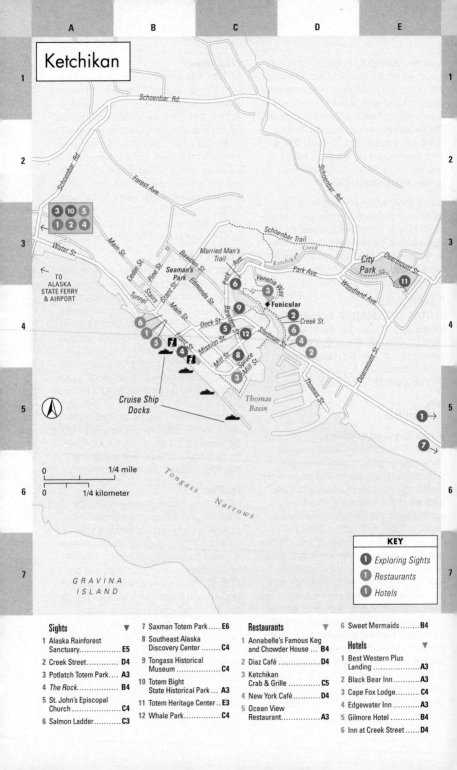

Ketchikan

TO ALASKA STATE FERRY & AIRPORT

Cruise Ship Docks

Thomas Basin

Tongass Narrows

GRAVINA ISLAND

City Park

0 ——— 1/4 mile
0 ——— 1/4 kilometer

KEY

1 Exploring Sights

1 Restaurants

1 Hotels

St. John's Episcopal Church

CHURCH | Completed in 1904 and Ketchikan's oldest house of worship, St. John's has an interior constructed of red cedar cut in the Native-operated sawmill in nearby Saxman. When cruise ships are in town, a docent is on hand to answer questions. ⊠ *503 Mission St., Ketchikan* ☎ *907/225–3680.*

Salmon Ladder

VIEWPOINT | Get out your camera and set it for high speed at the fish ladder, a series of pools arranged like steps that allow fish to travel upstream around a dam or falls. When the salmon start running, from June onward, thousands of fish leap the falls or take the easier fish-ladder route. They spawn in Ketchikan Creek's waters farther upstream. Many can also be seen in the creek's eddies above and below the falls. The falls, fish ladder, and a large carving of a jumping salmon are just off Park Avenue on Married Man's Trail. The trail was once used by married men for discreet access to the red-light district on Creek Street. ⊠ *Married Man's Trail, off Park Ave, Ketchikan.*

Saxman Totem Park

INDIGENOUS SIGHT | A 2½-mile paved walking path and bike trail parallels the road from Ketchikan to Saxman Native Village, named for a missionary who drowned while helping Native Alaskans establish a new settlement in the area in 1886. A totem park dominates the center of Saxman, with poles representing human- and animal-inspired figures, including bears, ravens, whales, and eagles. Saxman's Beaver Clan tribal house, which features a painted house screen by master carvers Nathan Jackson and Lee Wallace, is said to be the largest in Alaska. Carvers still create totem poles and totemic art objects in the adjacent carver's shed. You can visit the totem park on your own (on foot or by taxi, bicycle, or city bus), but to visit the tribal house and theater you must take a tour; book

Wet Yet Wonderful

Southeast gets a lot of rain, but that's to be expected—this is a rain forest, after all. If you plan to spend a week, be prepared for showers on at least a few days. Hard-core Southeast residents throw on slickers and rubber boots and shrug the rain off (leave your umbrella behind if you don't want to be pegged as a tourist). Their attitude is philosophical: without the rain, there would be no forests, no lakes, no streams running with salmon and trout, and no healthy populations of bears, moose, deer, mountain goats, and wolves.

through Cape Fox Lodge. ⊠ *S. Tongass Hwy., 2 miles south of town, Ketchikan* ⊕ *www.capefoxlodge.com* 🖅 *$5.*

Southeast Alaska Discovery Center

VISITOR CENTER | **FAMILY** | This impressive public lands interpretive center contains exhibits—including one on the rain forest—that focus on the resources, Native cultures, and ecosystems of Southeast. The U.S. Forest Service and other federal agencies provide information on Alaska's public lands, and a large gift shop sells natural-history books, maps, and videos about the region's sights. America the Beautiful–National Park and Federal Recreational Land Passes are accepted and sold. ⊠ *50 Main St., Ketchikan* ☎ *907/228–6220* ⊕ *www.alaskacenters. gov/visitors-centers/ketchikan* 🖅 *$5 May–Sept., free Oct.–Apr.* ⊘ *Closed Sat.– Thurs. in Oct.–Apr.*

Tongass Historical Museum

HISTORY MUSEUM | Native artifacts and pioneer relics revisit the mining and fishing eras at this museum in the same building as the library. Exhibits include a

The Aquaculture Debate

Life Cycle of an Alaskan Salmon

Five species of wild Pacific salmon are found in Alaska waters. All are anadromous (they spend part or all of their adult lives in saltwater but depart to freshwater streams and rivers to spawn), and all five species have at least two common names: pink (humpback) salmon, chum (dog) salmon, coho (silver) salmon, sockeye (red) salmon, and chinook (king) salmon. The smallest of these five, the pink salmon, has an average weight of only about 3 or 4 pounds, while king salmon can often tip the scales at more than 25 pounds. King salmon is generally considered the most flavorful, but sockeye and coho are also very highly regarded. Pink and chum salmon are the mainstay of canneries.

After spending a year or more in the ocean (the length of time varies among the species), Pacific salmon return to their native streams to spawn and die. The annual summertime return of adult salmon is a major event in Alaska, both for the animals (including bears) that depend on this bounty and for thousands of commercial fishers and sport anglers.

Farmed or Wild?

Alaska has long been famous for its seafood, and one of the first acts following statehood in 1959 was to protect fisheries from overharvesting. Today the stocks of salmon and other fish remain healthy, and careful management ensures that they will remain so in the future. In the 1980s and 1990s, aquaculture—fish farming—grew into an enormous international business, particularly in Norway, Chile, the United Kingdom, and British Columbia. Leery of the consequences to wild salmon, Alaska has never allowed any salmon aquaculture.

Pen-raised fish are affordable, available year-round, and of a consistent quality, but controversy surrounds the practice of fish farming. Many people believe it has a disastrous impact on the environment, citing such issues as disease, pollution from the waste of huge concentrations of fish, and the potential escape and infiltration of nonnative species, such as Atlantic salmon.

The Employment Question

On the other side of the debate, there are those who believe that fish farming is helping to protect Earth's valuable—and decreasing—populations of salmon. Proponents of fish farms point out that the practice also offers revenue and more jobs. Offshore fish farming in the United States is a highly incendiary topic of debate; those supporting it believe that if the farms are placed in deep ocean pockets, the pollution from and medication given to the pen-raised fish will be scattered better by strong currents. Many environmentalists beg to differ, hoping to establish stringent guidelines before opening the ocean to fish-farming corporations.

One Alaska bumper sticker says: "Friends don't let friends eat farmed salmon." Just across the border, in British Columbia, many people find employment as fish-farm workers. No matter which side you agree with in the aquaculture debate, be sure to enjoy a plate of delicious wild salmon during your visit to Alaska—perhaps from one you've hooked yourself.

big, brilliantly polished lens from Tree Point Lighthouse, well-presented Native tools and artwork, and photography collections. Other exhibits are temporary, but always include Tlingit items. ⊠ *629 Dock St., Ketchikan* ☎ *907/225–5600* ⊕ *www.ketchikan-museums.org* ⊠ *$6* ⊗ *Closed Oct.–Apr.*

★ **Totem Bight State Historical Park**
INDIGENOUS SIGHT | About a quarter of the Ketchikan bus tours include this park that contains many totem poles and has a hand-hewn Native clan house. Totem Bight sits on a scenic spit of land facing the waters of Tongass Narrows. Master Native carvers crafted the first replica poles here as part of a U.S. Forest Service program that began in the late 1930s. The tools the carvers used were handmade in the Native style, and modern paints were employed to re-create colors originally made using natural substances from clamshells to lichen. The clan house, open daily in summer, was built to resemble a type that might have held several related families. Note the raven painting on the front: each eye contains a small face. Try to save time for a stop at nearby Potlatch Totem Park as well. ⊠ *N. Tongass Hwy., about 10 miles north of town, Ketchikan* ☎ *907/247–8574 Ketchikan Ranger Station* ⊕ *dnr.alaska.gov/parks/units/totembgh.htm* ⊠ *Free.*

Totem Heritage Center
INDIGENOUS SIGHT | Gathered from Tlingit and Haida village sites, many of the Native totems in the center's collection are well over a century old—a rare age for cedar carvings, which are eventually lost to decay in Southeast's exceedingly wet climate. Other work by Tlingit, Haida, and Tsimshian artists is also on display inside the facility, and outside stand several more poles carved in the three decades since it opened. The center offers guided tours and hosts classes, workshops, and seminars related to Northwest Coast Native art and culture. ⊠ *601 Deermount St., Ketchikan* ☎ *907/225–5900* ⊕ *www.ketchikanmuseums.org* ⊠ *$6* ⊗ *Closed Sun. and Mon.*

Whale Park
CITY PARK | This small park on a traffic island across from St. John's Episcopal Church is the site of the Chief Kyan totem pole, now in its third incarnation. The current replica was erected in 1993 and then restored and re-raised in 2005. The original was carved in the 1890s, but over the decades it deteriorated and it was replaced in the 1960s. The 1960s edition is housed in the Totem Heritage Center. ⊠ *Mission and Bawden Sts., Ketchikan.*

🏃 Activities

BICYCLING
Ketchikan Kayak Company
BIKING | In addition to its popular kayak excursions, this small local company offers guided "eco-tours" on battery-powered electric bikes—a growing trend in Southeast. Paved trails lead the way to Tongass Forest, where riders dismount and continue into the woods on foot with their local guides, who provide information about the area's flora and fauna. The 4-hour tour, limited to 10 people, is suitable for all levels of ability. Those with a bit more time on their hands should consider the 7-hour bike-hike-kayak combo, a more peaceful introduction to life in Ketchikan than downtown can provide. ⊠ *540 Water St,, Ketchikan* ☎ *907/225–1272* ⊕ *www.ketchikankayakco.com* ⊠ *From $139.*

CANOPY TOURS
Kawanti Adventures
ZIP LINING | Featuring a series of zip lines, aerial boardwalks, and suspension bridges, this course at the Alaska Rainforest Sanctuary, 8½ miles south of town, provides an up-close view of the coastal forests. The longest of the tour's eight zip lines stretches more than 800 feet and whisks you along some 130 feet off the ground. The same outfit also offers off-road adventure kart expeditions and partners with Taquan Air for flightseeing tours. Book online (discounts are available) or through your cruise line. ⊠ *116*

Wood Rd., Ketchikan ☎ *907/225–8400* ⊕ *www.kawanti.com/activities/ziplines* 🖃 *From $200.*

Southeast Exposure

ZIP LINING | A rain-forest zip line and ropes course is offered through Southeast Exposure, a well-known kayaking outfit in the area. ✉ *37 Potter Rd., Ketchikan* ☎ *907/225–8829* ⊕ *www.southeastexposure.com* 🖃 *From $90 (kayaking) and $125 (zip-lining).*

DRIVING TOURS
Adventure Kart Expedition

FOUR-WHEELING | FAMILY | There's no faster route to feeling like a kid on a first go-kart outing than spending a few hours in one of Adventure Kart Expedition's cool little off-road vehicles. After choosing a helmet, you'll get a quick lesson in the how-tos of driving one of the vehicles. Then you, and the people in the lineup of ATVs you'll race along with, will put pedal to metal (literally) as you zip down old backcountry timber trails. Wear old clothes: there's no way you're coming back from this one clean. Depending on the weather, the trails will either be dusty or mud-filled; but they're always fun. Kids can ride along if they meet the height and weight requirements (50 inches and 40 pounds) and have an adult participating with them. ✉ *Whipple Creek, Ketchikan* ☎ *907/225–8400* ⊕ *www.kawanti.com/activities/adventure-kart-expedition* 🖃 *From $230.*

FISHING
Bering Sea Crab Fishermen's Tour

FISHING | FAMILY | This popular tour builds on the success of the Discovery Channel program *Deadliest Catch,* allowing visitors to ride on a Bering Sea crab boat featured in the show, the *Aleutian Ballad,* in the company of experienced commercial fishermen. The three-hour trip includes wildlife viewing, a live touch tank with sea creatures (released unharmed at the end of the tour), eagle feeding, details about Alaskan fish, and plenty of stories about life on the water. The tour takes

Totem Pole Parks

Most totem poles in Ketchikan's two biggest totem pole parks, Saxman and Totem Bight, are replicas of ones brought in from outlying villages as part of a federal project during the late 1930s. To see magnificent older poles, in various stages of decomposition, visit the Totem Heritage Center. This unique art tradition continues to be practiced today: contemporary poles from all three of the region's tribes—Tlingit, Haida, and Tsimshian—can be seen in front of the Ketchikan Indian Community Building *(2960 Tongass Ave.).*

place in protected waters and is suitable for kids. ✉ *Cruise ship dock, Ketchikan* ☎ *907/821–2722, 888/239–3816* ⊕ *www.alaskacrabtour.com* 🖃 *From $205.*

Ketchikan Visitors Bureau

FISHING | Sportfishing for salmon and trout is excellent in the Ketchikan area, in both saltwater and freshwater lakes and streams. The visitor bureau has information about the many local boat owners who offer charter and guide services. ✉ *50 Front St., Ketchikan* ☎ *907/225–6166, 800/770–3300* ⊕ *www.visit-ketchikan.com.*

HARBOR AND AIR TOURS
Alaska Travel Adventures

CANOEING & ROWING | This company's backcountry Jeep trips are fun, as are the 20-person canoe outings perfect for people just dipping their toes into (very) soft adventure travel. ✉ *63 Ward Lake Rd., Ketchikan* ☎ *800/323–5757, 907/247–5295* ⊕ *www.alaskatraveladventures.com* 🖃 *$102 (canoe outings), $164 (Jeep trips).*

Allen Marine Tours

BOATING | One of Southeast's best-known tour operators, Allen Marine conducts Misty Fjords National Monument catamaran tours throughout the summer. The company also offers half-day wildlife viewing tours. ✉ *5 Salmon Landing, Ketchikan* ☎ *907/225–8100, 877/686–8100* ⊕ *www.allenmarinetours.com.*

Southeast Aviation

AIR EXCURSIONS | Head out on a floatplane to tour the glaciers and mountains of Misty Fjords National Monument (90 minutes) or take a short trip over Revillagigedo Island (30 minutes). Charters are also available. ✉ *1249 Tongass Ave., Ketchikan* ☎ *907/225–2900, 888/359–6478* ⊕ *www. southeastaviation.com* 🖙 *From $139.*

HIKING

Get details on hiking around Ketchikan from the Southeast Alaska Discovery Center and Ketchikan Visitors Bureau.

Deer Mountain

HIKING & WALKING | The 3-mile trail from downtown to the 3,000-foot summit of Deer Mountain will repay your efforts with a spectacular panorama of the city below and the wilderness behind. The trail officially begins at the corner of Nordstrom Drive and Ketchikan Lake Road, but consider starting on the paved, 1½-mile scenic walk on the corner of Fair and Deermount Streets. Pass through dense forests before emerging into the alpine country. A shelter cabin near the summit provides a place to warm up. ✉ *Fair and Deermount Sts., Ketchikan* ⊕ *www.fs.usda.gov/activity/tongass/ recreation/hiking.*

Ward Lake Recreation Area

HIKING & WALKING | About 6 miles north of town, this recreation area has hikes next to lakes and streams and beneath towering spruce and hemlock trees; it also has several covered picnic spots and a pleasant campground. An easy 1.3-mile nature trail circles the lake, which is popular for steelhead and salmon fishing. ✉ *Ward Lake, Ketchikan* ☎ *907/225–2148 Ketchikan Ranger District* ⊕ *www.fs.usda.gov/detail/r10/specialplaces.*

LOCAL INTEREST

Great Alaskan Lumberjack Show

LOCAL SPORTS | FAMILY | The show consists of a 60-minute lumberjack competition providing a Disneyesque taste of old-time woodsman skills, including ax throwing, bucksawing, springboard chopping, log-rolling duels, and a 50-foot speed climb. It's a little hokey, but it's good fun (and kids will love it). Shows take place in a covered, heated grandstand and are presented rain or shine all summer. ✉ *420 Spruce Mill Way, Ketchikan* ☎ *907/225–9050, 888/320–9049* ⊕ *www. alaskanlumberjackshow.com* 🖙 *$40.*

SEA KAYAKING

Southeast Exposure

KAYAKING | This outfit conducts a 3½-hour guided Eagle Islands sea-kayak tour and a 4½-hour Tatoosh Islands sea-kayak tour in Behm Canal. ✉ *37 Potter Rd., Ketchikan* ☎ *907/225–8829* ⊕ *www.southeastexposure.com* 🖙 *From $90.*

★ Southeast Sea Kayaks

KAYAKING | Paddle across the Tongass Narrows in this company's 2½-hour introductory tour or venture farther afield on one of its guided multinight trips to Misty Fjords. Travelers with just one day to spend on a Ketchikan adventure should consider the five-hour combination tour of kayaking through Orcas Cove and flightseeing Misty Fjords National Monument. It's hard to beat a day that includes a transfer from a boat to a floatplane. ✉ *540 Water St., Ketchikan* ☎ *907/225–1258, 800/287–1607* ⊕ *www. kayakketchikan.com* 🖙 *From $139.*

Walking Around Ketchikan

The **Ketchikan Visitors Bureau**, on the docks that parallel Front Street, is a good starting point for a stroll through town. Next to the bureau you can't miss local artist Dave Rubin's **The Rock**, a bronze sculpture depicting seven figures associated with Ketchikan's past. Continuing down Front Street with the water on your right, take a left on Mill Street to visit the **Southeast Alaska Discovery Center**, where you can learn about the region's wild places. A little farther up Mill Street is minuscule **Whale Park**, whose centerpiece, Israel Shotridge's Chief Kyan totem pole, commemorates the Tlingit leader who sold the land that evolved into Ketchikan. From here you can follow Stedman Street across the bridge to **Thomas Street**, which overlooks one of Ketchikan's four harbors. Following Deermount Street uphill for several blocks, you'll come across the **Totem Heritage Center** and its collection of ancient totem poles. From here, Park Avenue runs parallel to Ketchikan Creek, heading downhill to the fish ladder and the salmon carving next to the Falls at Salmon Falls Resort. Glance uphill from the falls to see historic **Grant Street Trestle**, where the road becomes a steep plank bridge supported by pilings. It's about a 10-minute walk down Park Avenue from the hatchery.

From the fish ladder, a boardwalk path follows Ketchikan Creek and leads to trendy **Creek Street.** For a good side trip, take the short funicular ($2) to **Cape Fox Lodge** to get a great view of the harbor. Back on the Creek Street boardwalk is **Dolly's House**, a brothel in days gone by. Retrace your steps up the boardwalk and cross the **Creek Street Footbridge**; you may see salmon during summertime runs. Just in front of you is the Chief Johnson totem pole (Johnson, the chief depicted in *The Rock*, was a Tlingit leader). Nearby is the **Tongass Historical Museum**, with relics of the early days of mining and fishing. A left turn onto Bawden Street will take you past **St. John's Church.**

SNORKELING

★ Snorkel Alaska

SNORKELING | While signing up to go snorkeling in Alaska may seem like little more than a novelty, it takes just a few seconds in the waters off Ketchikan to understand that you're about to have an incredibly special experience. (Don't worry, you'll be given a wet suit to keep you warm.) Experienced guides provide both novice and experienced snorkelers the necessary information to quickly become comfortable and begin underwater gazing at giant sunflower stars, bright blood stars, sea cucumbers, and more. ✉ *4031 S Tongass Hwy., Ketchikan* ☎ *907/247–7782* 🌐 *www.snorkelalaska.com* 🎫 *$140.*

🍴 Restaurants

Annabelle's Famous Keg and Chowder House

$$ | **SEAFOOD** | An unpretentious Victorian-style restaurant on the Gilmore Hotel's ground floor, Annabelle's serves pastas, steamer clams and other seafood dishes, and several kinds of chowder. Prime rib on Friday and Saturday evenings is a favorite, and the lounge, which has a jukebox, has a friendly vibe. **Known for:** relaxed atmosphere; wide selection of seafood chowder; excellent Alaskan crab. [$] *Average main: $20* ✉ *326 Front St., Ketchikan* ☎ *907/225–6009* 🌐 *www.annabellesketchikan.com.*

Diaz Café

$ | **ASIAN** | Take a break from salmon saturation at this Old Town Ketchikan spot on historic Stedman Street. The café serves hearty Filipino cuisine beloved both of locals and cruise-ship staffers hungry for a taste of home, and the linoleum-and-tile 1950s interior is a wonderful time warp. **Known for:** retro decor; Filipino classics like lumpia and chicken adobo; local vibe. [$] *Average main: $10* ✉ *335 Stedman St., Ketchikan* ☎ *907/225–2257* 🌐 *diazcafe.business.site* 🕑 *Closed Sun. and Mon.*

Ketchikan Crab & Grille

$$ | **SEAFOOD** | Located at the end of the docks, this downtown grill owned by a former Floridian is the place to come to sample Alaska's famous king crab and enjoy a beer in the sun (if you're lucky) at one of the outdoor tables. If crab legs aren't your thing, try the Dungeness crab mac and cheese, the crab-topped fries, or the blackened halibut salad. **Known for:** Dungeness crab mac and cheese; Alaskan king crab legs; scenic outdoor seating. [$] *Average main: $17* ✉ *5 Salmon Landing, Ketchikan* ☎ *907/247–2866* 🌐 *www.facebook.com/KetchikanCrabAndGrille.*

New York Café

$$ | **AMERICAN** | The 1920s-era roots of this space adjacent to the New York Hotel come through in the antique bar and fixtures, creating a casual yet elegant place to enjoy a meal while staring out the plate-glass windows at life on busy Stedman Street, or admiring the mural by local artist Ray Troll that spans one wall. The menu includes reasonably priced seafood, salads, and burgers, along with Mediterranean-influenced fare. **Known for:** great fish-and-chips; old-fashioned charm; local beer on tap. [$] *Average main: $18* ✉ *211 Stedman St., Ketchikan* ☎ *907/247–2326* 🌐 *newyorkcafe.net* 🕑 *Closed Mon.*

Ocean View Restaurant

$$ | **MEXICAN** | A favorite with locals, the Ocean View serves decent burgers, steaks, pasta, pizzas, and seafood, but the main draws are the authentic and very filling Mexican dishes. Three tables in the back look out to the Tongass Narrows. **Known for:** pretty views; gigantic menu; authentic fajitas. [$] *Average main: $20* ✉ *1831 Tongass Ave., Ketchikan* ☎ *907/225–7566* 🌐 *www.oceanviewmex.com.*

Sweet Mermaids

$ | **BAKERY** | A tiny coffee shop and bakery, Sweet Mermaids is a great choice for breakfast. If you're here for lunch, try the salmon chowder—the perfect antidote for a rainy afternoon. **Known for:** sunny, enthusiastic staff; bagels with cream cheese and lox; homemade cinnamon rolls. [$] *Average main: $8* ✉ *340 Front St., Ketchikan* ☎ *907/225–3287* 🕑 *No dinner.*

🛏 Hotels

Best Western Plus Landing

$$ | **HOTEL** | Named for the state ferry landing directly across the road, this Best Western property has large, comfortable rooms decorated with mission-style furniture, and although the hotel is more than a mile from downtown, there's no need for a car; a free shuttle provides transport around town. **Pros:** free shuttle around town; near ferry; underground parking. **Cons:** bland room decor; pricey given the location and amenities; some road noise. [$] *Rooms from: $195* ✉ *3434 Tongass Ave., Ketchikan* ☎ *907/225–5166, 800/428–8304* 🌐 *www.landinghotel.com* 🛏 *107 rooms* 🍴 *No Meals.*

Black Bear Inn

$$$ | **B&B/INN** | The views of the Tongass Narrows from inside this waterfront B&B are remarkable, and the three suites all have plush furniture, comfortable beds, and porches or balconies. **Pros:** gracious local hosts; free parking; a phenomenal backyard space. **Cons:** some road noise;

outside downtown; rental car recommended. $ *Rooms from: $264* ✉ *5528 N. Tongass Hwy., Ketchikan* ☎ *907/225–4343* ⊕ *www.stayinalaska.com* ⇆ *3 suites* ❖ *Free Breakfast.*

Cape Fox Lodge

$$$ | HOTEL | With scenic views of the town and Thomas Basin from 135 feet above Creek Street, Cape Fox Lodge is cozy yet luxurious, and offers spacious rooms with traditional tribal colors and watercolors of Alaska birds. **Pros:** all rooms have views; beautiful site overlooking town; on-site artwork by master carvers. **Cons:** few amenities; hotel has a bit of a conference-property feel; rooms are rather plain. $ *Rooms from: $230* ✉ *800 Venetia Way, Ketchikan* ☎ *907/225–8001, 866/225–8001 reservations* ⊕ *www.capefoxlodge.com* ⇆ *72 rooms* ❖ *No Meals.*

Edgewater Inn

$$ | HOTEL | A modern lodge 3 miles from the center of town, the Edgewater Inn's waterside rooms, including three spacious suites, are decorated with simple furniture and have balconies overlooking the Tongass Narrows—a good place to watch seals, otters, and eagles. **Pros:** freezer available for fish storage; great views of Tongass in selected rooms; courtesy van service anywhere in town. **Cons:** not all rooms have good views; inconvenient location; some rooms are small. $ *Rooms from: $143* ✉ *4871 N. Tongass Hwy., Ketchikan* ☎ *907/247–2600, 888/686–2600* ⊕ *www.ketchikanedgewaterinn.com* ❖ *Free Breakfast* ⇆ *44 rooms.*

Gilmore Hotel

$$ | HOTEL | Crammed between the large buildings along Front Street, the Gilmore is a rustic historic property best suited for travelers who value character over modern amenities. **Pros:** some rooms view marina; handy location; has plenty of historic character. **Cons:** bar and street noise can be annoying; not handicapped accessible; rooms could use renovation.

$ *Rooms from: $154* ✉ *326 Front St., Ketchikan* ☎ *907/225–9423, 800/275–9423* ⊕ *www.wyndhamhotels.com* ⇆ *38 rooms* ❖ *No Meals.*

★ Inn at Creek Street

$$ | HOTEL | More than a century old, this quaint hotel's delightfully old-school hotel rooms are on the small side, but they have character in spades: one-of-a-kind antique furnishings, cozy quilts on the queen beds, and tile floors with pedestal sinks in the bathrooms. **Pros:** standard rooms are reasonably priced; loft suites have jetted tubs; adjacent to the New York Café. **Cons:** small rooms; fills up quickly; steep staircase and no elevator. $ *Rooms from: $154* ✉ *207 Stedman St., Ketchikan* ☎ *907/225–0246, 866/225–0246* ⊕ *www.creekstreet.com* ⇆ *8 rooms* ❖ *No Meals.*

🍸 Nightlife

Ketchikan is a bit of a party town, especially when crews stumble off fishing boats with cash in hand. You won't have trouble finding something going on at several downtown bars.

The Asylum Bar

BARS | With 30 beers on tap, including many regional varieties, this downtown favorite has four indoor and outdoor spaces and free Wi-Fi. Hungry patrons can order food from the Burger Queen and have it delivered to their table. ✉ *522 Water St., Ketchikan* ☎ *907/220–0809* ⊕ *www.theasylumbar.com.*

Fat Stan's Sports Bar

BARS | Young locals pack into lively, informal Fat Stan's, a cute spot with a decent selection of beers, wines, and spirits. You can snack on pizza as you sip. ✉ *330 Spruce Mill Way, Ketchikan* ☎ *907/247–9463.*

Ketchikan's beautiful waterfront is decked out with multicolor homes and shops.

🛍 Shopping

Crazy Wolf Studio

ART GALLERIES | Authentic Northwest Coast art is the specialty at this crowded gallery run by local Tsimshian artist Ken Decker and his wife. Decker's work includes dance paddles, drums, and bentwood boxes featuring formline ravens, eagles, bears, and salmon. ✉ 633 Mission St., Ketchikan ☎ 907/225–9653 ⊕ www.crazywolfstudio.com.

Main Street Gallery

ART GALLERIES | The gallery, a light and cheery space run by the Ketchikan Area Arts and Humanities Council, showcases established artists and rising stars. It's well worth a visit. ✉ 330 Main St., Ketchikan ☎ 907/225–2211 ⊕ www.ketchikanarts.org/galleries/main-street-gallery.

Parnassus Books

BOOKS | A book lover's bookstore with creaky floors and cozy quarters, Parnassus stocks many Alaskan titles. ✉ 105 Stedman St., Ketchikan ☎ 907/225–7690.

Scanlon Gallery

ART GALLERIES | In business since 1972, Scanlon carries the prints of well-known Alaska artists, including Byron Birdsall, John Fehringer, Barbara Lavallee, Rie Muñoz, and Jon Van Zyle. The gallery also exhibits jewelry, glasswork, and pottery. ✉ 318 Mission St., Ketchikan ☎ 907/247–4730 ⊕ www.scanlongallery.com.

Soho Coho Art Gallery

ART GALLERIES | Design, art, clothing, and collectibles can all be found at stylish Soho Coho. Also here are T-shirts featuring the work of owner Ray Troll—best known for his wacky fish art—and works by other Southeast artists. ✉ 5 Creek St., Ketchikan ☎ 907/225–5954, 800/888–4070 ⊕ www.trollart.com.

Misty Fjords National Monument

40 miles east of Ketchikan by air.

Pristine wilderness areas can be accessed from Ketchikan, most notably Misty Fjords National Monument and Prince of Wales Island. Both are somewhat remote, but tour companies abound to guide you to them.

Sights

Ketchikan Visitors Bureau

VISITOR CENTER | Most visitors to Misty Fjords arrive on day trips via floatplane from Ketchikan or onboard catamarans. Taquan Air *(www.taquanair.com)* and Allen Marine *(www.allenmarinetours. com)* are among the top local providers in each category; the bureau can provide a full list. ⊠ *131 Front St., Ketchikan* ☎ *800/770–3300* ⊕ *www.visit-ketchikan. com.*

★ Misty Fjords National Monument

NATURE SIGHT | Cliff-faced fjords, tall mountains, waterfalls, and islands with spectacular coastal scenery draw visitors to this wilderness area just east of Ketchikan. Most arrive on day trips via floatplane or aboard a catamaran. Both methods have their advantages: air travel reveals Misty Fjord's enormous scope, while trips by sea afford more intimate vistas. You can also kayak here, but it's a long paddle from Ketchikan. For a more manageable trip, consider having a boat drop you off within the monument. Traveling on these waters can be an almost mystical experience, with the green forests reflected in the many fjords' waters. You may find yourself in the company of a whale, see a bear along the shore fishing for salmon, or even pull in your own salmon. The 15 cabins the Forest Service manages here can be booked through the federal Recreation.gov website *(www.recreation.*

gov). ⊠ *Ketchikan* ☎ *907/225–2148 Ketchikan-Misty Fiords Ranger District* ⊕ *www.fs.usda.gov/visit/destination/ misty-fjords-national-monument.*

★ Salmon Glacier

NATURE SIGHT | A spectacular unpaved road from Hyder into Canada winds 17 miles to remote Salmon Glacier, one of the few glaciers accessible by road in Southeast Alaska and the fifth biggest glacier in North America. In summer, take Granduc Mine Road (also referred to as Salmon Glacier Road), which climbs several thousand feet to a viewing area. Be prepared for potholes, steep drop-offs, and incredible vistas along the way. The District of Stewart BC website provides a helpful downloadable Auto Tour Brochure of the route. ⊕ *www. districtofstewart.com/parks-recreation/ parks-sport-fields-trails.*

Metlakatla

12 miles south of Ketchikan.

The village of Metlakatla is on Annette Island, a dozen miles by sea from busy Ketchikan but a world away culturally. A visit to this quiet community offers the chance to learn about life in a small Inside Passage Native community.

In most Southeast Native villages, the people are of Tlingit or Haida heritage, but most residents of Metlakatla are Tsimshian; the village's name (*Maxłax-aała)*translates roughly from the Tsimshian language as "peaceful saltwater passage." They moved to the island from British Columbia in 1887 with William Duncan, an Anglican missionary from England. The town grew rapidly and soon contained dozens of buildings, including a cannery, a sawmill, and a church that could seat 1,000 people. Congress declared Annette Island a federal Indian reservation in 1891, and it remains the only reservation in Alaska today. Every year on August 7, locals celebrate

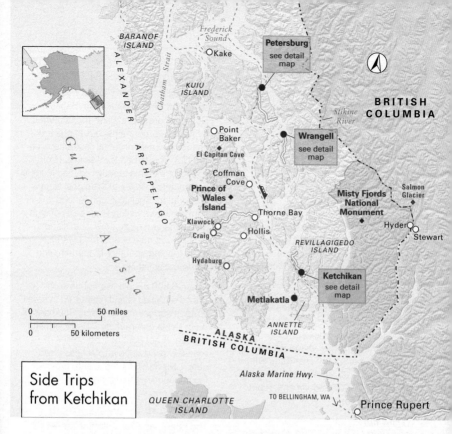

Side Trips from Ketchikan

Metlakatla's founding with a parade, foot races, food stands, and fireworks.

Though tiny with a population of only 1,650, Metlakatla has in recent years become a leader in the region due to their commitment to keeping Tsimshian traditions—including language and art—alive and to maintaining a community where this important work can thrive. This includes a more locally integrated, structured approach to managing tourism: while the community welcomes visitors and has several tour options that can be booked through cruise lines or independently, you must apply for a visitor's permit if you wish to stay for more than 24 hours.

GETTING HERE AND AROUND

Alaska Marine Highway System ferries connect Ketchikan and Metlakatla by sea, and Taquan Air provides flights.

Tours operated by Allen Marine include a Wildlife Safari boat trip from Ketchikan with a one-hour stop on the island for an Alaskan-style beach bonfire. Local taxis can take you to other Annette Island sights, including Yellow Hill and the old Air Force base.

AIRPLANE CONTACTS Taquan Air. ⊠ *4085 Tongass Ave., Ketchikan* ☎ *907/225–8800, 800/770–8800 toll free* ⊕ *www. taquanair.com.*

FERRY CONTACTS Alaska Marine Highway System. ⊠ *Wrangell* ☎ *907/465–3941, 800/642–0066* ⊕ *www.dot.state.ak.us/amhs.*

ESSENTIALS

TOUR INFORMATION Allen Marine Tours. ⊠ *5 Salmon Landing, Ketchikan* ☎ *907/225–8100, 877/686–8100* ⊕ *www. allenmarinetours.com.*

Sights

Longhouse

INDIGENOUS SIGHT | Constructed in 1972 to resemble a traditional Tsimshian longhouse, this cedar structure serves as a gathering place for community events. Two totem poles stand in the back of the building, and a Northwest Coast design featuring the four Tsimshian clans—Raven, Eagle, Killer Whale, and Wolf—covers the front. ✉ *Metlakatla* ☎ *907/886–4441* ⊕ *www.metlakatla.com.*

William Duncan Memorial Church

CHURCH | This clapboard church is one of tiny Metlakatla's nine churches. The original burned in 1948. The current version, topped with two steeples, was rebuilt several years later. Nearby, **Father Duncan's Cottage,** maintained to appear exactly as it would have in 1891, contains original furnishings, personal items, and a collection of turn-of-the-20th-century music boxes. ✉ *4th Ave. and Church St., Metlakatla* ☎ *907/886–4441* ⊕ *www. metlakatla.com.*

Yellow Hill

VIEWPOINT | A boardwalk 2 miles from town leads up the 540-foot Yellow Hill. Distinctive yellow sandstone rocks and panoramic vistas make this a worthwhile detour on clear days. ✉ *West of Airport Rd., 2 miles south of town, Metlakatla.*

Prince of Wales Island

43 miles northwest of Ketchikan.

Prince of Wales Island stretches more than 130 miles from north to south, making it the largest island in Southeast Alaska. Only two other American islands—Kodiak in Alaska and Hawaii in the Hawaiian chain—are larger. Prince of Wales (or "P.O.W." as locals call it) has a multitude of landforms, a plethora of wildlife, and exceptional sportfishing, especially for steelhead, salmon, and trout anglers, with the Karta and Thorne rivers among the favorite fishing areas.

In the past, the island was a major source of timber, both from Tongass National Forest lands and those owned by Native corporations, but things are changing. Environmental restrictions on the U.S. Forest Service's activities on public lands have greatly reduced logging activity and in 2021 the regional Native corporation, Sealaska, announced it was shutting down its logging operations on the island and elsewhere. The island's economy is now supported by small-scale logging operations, tourism, and commercial fishing.

About 5,800 people live full-time on Prince of Wales Island, scattered in small villages and towns, including Southeast's main Haida communities, Hydaburg and Kasaan. A network of 1,500 miles of roads—nearly all built to access clear-cuts—crisscrosses the island, providing connections to even the smallest settlements.

GETTING HERE AND AROUND

The Inter-Island Ferry Authority operates a daily vehicle and passenger ferry between Ketchikan and Prince of Wales Island. The ferry terminal is in the settlement of Hollis, 31 miles from Craig on a paved road. The relative abundance of roads, combined with ferry and air access from Ketchikan, makes it easy to explore the island.

FERRY INFORMATION Inter-Island Ferry Authority. ☎ *907/225–4848, 866/308–4848* ⊕ *www.interislandferry.com.*

ESSENTIALS

VISITOR INFORMATION Prince of Wales Chamber of Commerce. ✉ *6488 Klawock-Hollis Hwy., Klawock* ☎ *907/775–2626* ⊕ *www.princeofwale-scoc.org.*

◉ Sights

Craig

TOWN | The primary commercial center for Prince of Wales is Craig, on the island's western shore. This town of 1,200 retains a hard-edged aura fast disappearing in the many Inside Passage towns where tourism now holds sway. Although sightseeing attractions are slim, the town exudes a frontier spirit, and its small-boat harbors buzz with activity. ✉ *Craig* ⊕ *www.princeofwalescoc.org/visitors.*

El Capitan Cave

CAVE | The best known of the large natural caverns that pockmark northern Prince of Wales Island has one of the deepest pits in the United States. Paleontologists have found a wealth of black bear, brown bear, and other mammal fossils in the cave's 13,000 feet of passageways, including some that date back more than 12,000 years. The Forest Service leads free, two-hour tours of El Capitan Cave several times a week in summer. It takes some work to get to the cave's mouth, but if you're up for a 1,100-foot hike up a 367-step stairway, it's well worth the effort. The rangers pause along the way to give visitors time to catch their breath. Reservations are required at least two days ahead, and no children under age seven are permitted. Bring a flashlight and wear hiking or rubber boots. A light jacket is also helpful, as the cave gets quite cool. ✉ *Mile 51, N. Prince of Wales Rd., Prince of Wales Island* ☎ *907/828–3304 Ranger station* ⊕ *www.adfg.alaska.gov.*

Hydaburg

TOWN | While Alaskans of Haida ancestry live throughout Southeast, Hydaburg and Kasaan are the two main Haida communities in the state. The Alaskan Haida population can be traced back to a migration from Canada in the 1700s; the majority of tribal members continue to live in Canada, in Haida Gwaii (an area of British Columbia formerly called the Queen Charlotte Islands). The village of Hydaburg lies approximately 40 miles south of Klawock (via chip-sealed road), along scenic Sukkwan Strait. A small collection of totem poles occupies the center of town, and a nearby carving shed allows visitors to view artists at work. Contact the Hydaburg Cooperative Association *(www.hcatribe.org)* for details. ✉ *Hydaburg* ⊕ *www.princeofwalescoc.org/visitors.*

Klawock

TOWN | A half-dozen miles from Craig is the Tlingit village of Klawock, with a sawmill, cannery, hatchery, and the island's only airport. The town is best known for its striking totem poles in Totem Park. Several of these colorful poles were moved here in the 1930s; others are more recent carvings. You can watch carvers restoring old totems at the carving shed, across the road from the grocery store. Along the bay you'll find the Catholic church St. John by the Sea, with stained-glass windows picturing Native Alaskans. ✉ *Klawock* ☎ *907/755–2261* ⊕ *www.princeofwalescoc.org/visitors.*

Klawock River Hatchery

OTHER ATTRACTION | Klawock is also home to the Klawock River Hatchery, one of the state's most effective hatcheries. Though the facility isn't open to the public, visitors can watch the coho and sockeye salmon in the river (but keep an eye out for bears). ✉ *Mile 9 Klawock-Hollis Hwy., Klawock* ☎ *907/755–2231* ⊕ *www.ssraa. org/klawock-river-hatchery.*

♨ Restaurants

Zat's Pizza

$ | PIZZA | With its bright red tables and tall wooden booths, this informal pizza spot serves beer on tap and is a fun place to come with a group. As is typical in this part of the world, your experience will be vastly improved if you're not in a hurry—Zat's is known for its friendly service, but not necessarily its speed. **Known for:** lively local crowd;

build-your-own pizza; meatball subs. [$] *Average main: $10* ✉ *420 Port Bagial Blvd., Craig* ☎ *907/826–2345* ⏲ *Closed Sun. and Mon.*

Hotels

Dreamcatcher Bed & Breakfast
$$ | **B&B/INN** | Within walking distance of downtown Craig, the Dreamcatcher has three rooms with outside entrances and private baths. **Pros:** rooms have patios; beautiful water views; close to shops and restaurants. **Cons:** bathrooms can be small; often booked up; basic breakfast. [$] *Rooms from: $139* ✉ *1405 E. Hamilton Dr., Craig* ☎ *907/826–2238* 🌐 *www.dreamcatcherbandb.com* 🛏 *3 rooms* 🍴 *Free Breakfast.*

Shelter Cove Lodge
$$$$ | **ALL-INCLUSIVE** | Tall windows front the water at this modern lodge along Craig's South Boat Harbor that offers all-inclusive fishing packages starting at $2,850 per person for four nights at the lodge, with three full days out fishing (six person minimum). **Pros:** good wildlife viewing opportunities; all-inclusive amenities; harbor-view rooms. **Cons:** no elevator; expensive; food can be heavy. [$] *Rooms from: $1424* ✉ *703 Hamilton Dr., Craig* ☎ *907/826–2939, 888/826–3474* 🌐 *www.sheltercovefishinglodge.com* ⏲ *Restaurant closed Sept.–May* 🍴 *All-Inclusive* 🛏 *10 rooms.*

★ **Waterfall Resort**
$$$$ | **RESORT** | Guests at this upscale fishing lodge a 45-minute floatplane ride from Ketchikan can choose from several accommodation styles, eat bountiful meals with all the trimmings, and fish from custom-built 25-foot cabin cruisers under the care of expert fishing guides. **Pros:** opportunity to spot wildlife; plenty of saltwater fishing; good views. **Cons:** remote location; most kitchens in the condos aren't used, since meals are provided by the resort; uninteresting room decor. [$] *Rooms from: $1895* ✉ *West coast of Prince of Wales* ☎ *907/225–9461, 800/544–5125* 🌐 *www.waterfallresort.com* ⏲ *Closed Sept.–late May* 🍴 *All-Inclusive* 🛏 *44 rooms.*

Wrangell

87 miles north of Ketchikan.

An unassuming timber and fishing community, Wrangell sits on the northern tip of Wrangell Island, near the mouth of the fast-flowing Stikine River—North America's largest undammed river. The Stikine plays a large role in the lives of many Wrangell residents, including those who grew up homesteading on the islands that pepper the area. Trips on the river with local guides are highly recommended for the insight they provide into the Stikine and a very Alaskan way of life. Like much of Southeast, Wrangell has suffered in recent years from a declining resource-based economy. But locals are working to build tourism. Bearfest celebrates Wrangell's proximity to the Anan Wildlife Observatory, where you can get a close-up view of brown and black bears.

Part of the ancestral homelands of the Stikine Tlingit, Wrangell has also flown three national flags in its time. Russia established Redoubt St. Dionysius here in 1834. Five years later Great Britain's Hudson's Bay Company leased the southern Alaska coastline, renaming the settlement Ft. Stikine. It was rechristened Wrangell when the Americans took over in 1867; the name came from Baron Ferdinand Petrovich von Wrangel, director of the Russian-American Company and the first governor of the Russian settlements.

Rough-around-the-edges Wrangell is off the track of the larger cruise ships, so it doesn't get the same seasonal traffic that Ketchikan and Juneau do. Its downtown is nearly devoid of the souvenir shops that dominate so many of its counterparts elsewhere, and the gift shops and art galleries that are here sell locally created work. Wrangell is very welcoming to visitors; independent travelers would do well to add a stop here during their Southeast wanderings.

GETTING HERE AND AROUND

Alaska Marine Highway System ferries connect Wrangell and other Southeast ports, and some small cruise ships stop here. Alaska Airlines operates daily flights from Seattle and Juneau. The town is fairly compact, and most sights are within walking distance of the city dock or ferry terminal.

FERRY CONTACT Alaska Marine Highway System. ⊠ *Wrangell* ☎ *907/465–3941, 800/642–0066* ⊕ *www.dot.state.ak.us/amhs.*

ESSENTIALS

VISITOR INFORMATION Tongass National Forest Wrangell Ranger District. ⊠ *525 Bennett St., Wrangell* ☎ *907/874–2323* ⊕ *www.fs.usda.gov/tongass.* **Wrangell Visitor Center.** ⊠ *296 Campbell Dr., in Nolan Center, Wrangell* ☎ *907/874–2829, 800/367–9745* ⊕ *www.travelwrangell. com.*

Sights

★ Anan Wildlife Observatory

NATURE PRESERVE | A prime spot to view brown and black bears, Anan lies within the Tongass National Forest. Each summer as many as 30 or 40 bears gather at Anan Creek to feed on huge runs of pink salmon. On an average visit of about three hours you might spot bears while strolling the half-mile viewing boardwalk. Once on the platform, you will likely see many. For 30-minute intervals, five people at a time can slip into a photo blind, accessible from the platform, that provides opportunities to shoot close-up, stream-level images of bears catching salmon. Anan is accessible only by boat or floatplane. Passes are required from July 5 to August 25 for the limited number of visits the Forest Service permits

each day. Unless you have experience navigating the Stikine by boat and walking through bear country, it's best to visit Anan with a local guide. Most guide companies provide passes. ⊠ *Wrangell* ⊹ *About 30 miles southeast of Wrangell* ☎ *907/874–2323 Wrangell Ranger District* ⊕ *www.travelwrangell.com/anan-bears.*

Chief Shakes Island and Tribal House

INDIGENOUS SIGHT | A footbridge from the bottom of Shakes Street provides access to this small island in the center of Wrangell's protected harbor. The Tribal House, constructed in 1940 as a replica of the original 19th-century structure, was completely restored by local carvers in 2012 and 2013, as were the surrounding totem poles. The interior of the building can be viewed for a fee; arrangements should be made through the Wrangell Cooperative Association *(www. wca-t.com).* ⊠ *Off Shakes St., Wrangell* ☎ *907/874–4304* ⊕ *www.travelwrangell. com/chief-shakes-tribal-house* ⊠ *$4.*

Chief Shakes's Grave Site

INDIGENOUS SIGHT | Buried here is Shakes V, who led the local Tlingit during the first half of the 19th century. A white picket fence surrounds the grave, and two killer-whale totem poles mark his resting spot, which overlooks the harbor. ⊠ *Case Ave, Wrangell.*

Irene Ingle Public Library

LIBRARY | The library, behind the post office, has two ancient petroglyphs out front and is home to a large collection of Alaskan books and computers with free Internet access. ⊠ *124 2nd St., Wrangell* ☎ *907/874–3535* ⊕ *www. wrangell.com/library.*

Kiks.ádi Totem Park

INDIGENOUS SIGHT | The Kiks.ádi Totem, one of several in the park, bears crests owned by the clan and other animal figures, including a frog, a beaver, and a raven. The totem is a replica carved in 1987. ⊠ *Front St., Wrangell* ⊕ *www. travelwrangell.com/totem-park.*

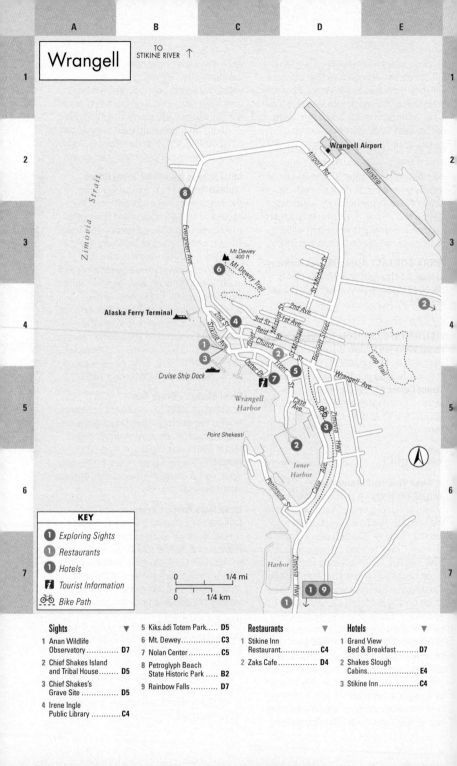

Wrangell

TO
STIKINE RIVER ↑

Zimovia Strait

Wrangell Airport

Airport Rd.

Airstrip

Evergreen Ave.

Mt Dewey
400 ft

Mt Dewey Trail

Alaska Ferry Terminal

2nd St.

Stikine Ave.

3rd St.

St. Michael St.

2nd Ave.

1st Ave.

3rd St.

Reid St.

Church St.

Bennett Street

Front St.

Outer Dr.

Cruise Ship Dock

Wrangell Ave.

Wrangell
Harbor

Case Ave.

Point Shekesti

Zimovia Hwy.

Inner
Harbor

Peninsula St.

Case Ave.

Zimovia Hwy.

Harbor

Loop Trail

KEY

① Exploring Sights

① Restaurants

① Hotels

🛈 Tourist Information

🚲 Bike Path

0 ——— 1/4 mi
0 ——— 1/4 km

Sights ▼

1 Anan Wildlife
Observatory **D7**

2 Chief Shakes Island
and Tribal House **D5**

3 Chief Shakes's
Grave Site **D5**

4 Irene Ingle
Public Library **C4**

5 Kiks.ádi Totem Park..... **D5**

6 Mt. Dewey **C3**

7 Nolan Center **C5**

8 Petroglyph Beach
State Historic Park **B2**

9 Rainbow Falls **D7**

Restaurants ▼

1 Stikine Inn
Restaurant **C4**

2 Zaks Cafe **D4**

Hotels ▼

1 Grand View
Bed & Breakfast **D7**

2 Shakes Slough
Cabins **E4**

3 Stikine Inn **C4**

Walking Around Wrangell

Start on Campbell Drive at the **Nolan Center**, where the informative and entertaining exhibits at the town museum will help you bone up on local history and biology. Head away from the water on Outer Drive and turn right on Front Street to check out **Kiks.ádi Totem Park**. Continue on Front Street to Shakes Street, following it to the footbridge that leads to the town's prize attraction, **Chief Shakes Island** and its **Tribal House**. Soak in the harbor view from here and examine the totem poles. For a more elevated harbor view, reverse course and turn right on Case Avenue, which leads up a hill to **Chief Shakes's Grave Site**. From the grave site, head up Church Street to the **Irene Ingle Public Library**, where you'll find ancient petroglyphs out front. About a half mile north of the ferry terminal along Evergreen Avenue lies **Petroglyph Beach**. Most of the beach's noteworthy ancient etchings are scattered along the rocky shore.

Petroglyph Beach and Chief Shakes Island are about a mile and a half apart. Plan on taking three hours to complete this walk and sightsee a little.

If you're game for more walking, climb **Mt. Dewey**, the woodsy hill right behind town. Five miles south of town lies **Rainbow Falls**, another fun hike.

Mt. Dewey

VIEWPOINT | Despite the name, this landmark is more a hill than a peak. Still, it's a steep 15-minute climb up the John Muir Trail from town to the top. The observation platform there provides views of waterways and islands whose names—among them Zarembo, Vank, and Woronkofski—recall the area's Russian history. The trail is named for naturalist John Muir, who, in 1879, made his way up the trail and built a campfire. Locals didn't realize there was anybody up on Mt. Dewey and the light from the fire caused a commotion below. Access the trail, which passes through a second-growth forest, on 3rd Street behind the high school. ⊠ *Wrangell* ⊕ *www. travelwrangell.com/mt-dewey*.

Nolan Center

HISTORY MUSEUM | The nexus of cultural life in Wrangell, the center houses the town's museum and visitor center as well as convention and performance facilities and a gift shop. Exhibits at the Wrangell Museum chronicle the region's rich history. On display here are the oldest known Tlingit house posts (dating from the late 18th century), decorative posts from Chief Shakes's clan house, petroglyphs, century-old spruce-root and cedar-bark baskets, masks, gold-rush memorabilia, and fascinating photographs. If you're spending any time in town, don't pass this up. The Wrangell Visitor Center, staffed when the museum is open, has information about local touring options. ⊠ *296 Campbell Dr., Wrangell* ☎ *907/874–3770* ⊕ *www. nolancenter.org*.

Petroglyph Beach State Historic Park

STATE/PROVINCIAL PARK | Scattered among other rocks at this public beach are three dozen or more large stones bearing designs and pictures chiseled by unknown ancient artists. No one knows why the rocks at this curious site were etched the way they were, or even exactly how old the etchings are. You can access the beach via a boardwalk, where you'll find signs describing the site, along with carved replicas of the petroglyphs. Most of the petroglyphs are to the right between the viewing deck and a large outcropping of rock in the tidal beach area. Because the original petroglyphs can be damaged by physical contact, only photographs are permitted. But you are welcome to use the replicas to make a rubbing with rice paper and charcoal or crayons (available in local stores). ✉ ½ mile north of ferry terminal, off Evergreen Ave., Wrangell ⊕ dnr.alaska.gov/parks/aspunits/southeast/wrangpetroshs.htm.

Rainbow Falls

WATERFALL | The trail to this scenic waterfall starts across the road from Shoemaker Bay, 5 miles south of Wrangell. A ¾-mile trail climbs uphill through the rain forest, with long stretches of boardwalk steps, ending at an overlook just below the falls. Hikers with more stamina can continue another 3 miles and 1,500 vertical feet to Shoemaker Bay Overlook. ✉ Wrangell ⊕ www.wrangell.com/recreation/rainbow-falls-trail.

Activities

AIR CHARTERS

Sunrise Aviation

AIR EXCURSIONS | This charter-only air carrier flies to the Anan Wildlife Observatory, LeConte Glacier, and Forest Service cabins. ✉ Wrangell Airport, Airport Rd., Wrangell ☎ 907/874–2319, 800/874–2311 ⊕ www.wrangell.com/organization/sunrise-aviation.

BICYCLING

A waterfront trail connects Wrangell with Shoemaker Bay Recreation Area, 4½ miles south of town. The trail is mainly flat; more adventurous souls can brave the dozens of miles of logging roads that crisscross the island.

BOATING

★ Breakaway Adventures

BOATING | This well-established outfitter, in business for nearly three decades, leads a variety of jet-boat trips, including a tour to Chief Shakes Glacier and the nearby hot springs. Tours can be

arranged for groups of up to 50 people. You can catch one of their water taxis to Petersburg or Prince of Wales Island, as well as to one of the area's U.S. Forest Service cabins. ✉ City dock, Wrangell ☎ 907/874–2488, 888/385–2488 ⊕ www.breakawayadventures.com ⛴ From $160.

FISHING

Wrangell Visitor Center

FISHING | Numerous companies schedule salmon- and trout-fishing excursions ranging in length from an afternoon to a week. Contact the visitor center for information on guide services and locations. ✉ Nolan Center, 296 Campbell Dr., Wrangell ☎ 800/367–9745 ⊕ www.travelwrangell.com.

WILDLIFE VIEWING

The following Wrangell-based guide companies are authorized to run trips to Anan.

Alaska Charters and Adventures

ADVENTURE TOURS | This outfit leads small group tours (six guests or fewer) to Anan for day trips of seven or eight hours. Most of the time is spent above Anan Creek on an observation deck reached via a half-mile trail. Reservations are recommended well in advance. The same company also offers whale-watching tours, kayak adventures, and fishing trips. ✉ 1003 Case Ave., Wrangell ☎ 888/993–2750 ⊕ www.alaskaupclose.com ⛴ From $368.

Alaska Vistas

ADVENTURE TOURS | Watch bears feeding on salmon at a small waterfall from an observatory deck with this reliable outfitter. Like other Anan tours, this one includes an hour-long boat ride from Wrangell. Alaska Vistas also leads rafting trips down the Stikine River and sea-kayaking adventures. ✉ City Dock, Wrangell ☎ 907/874–3006, 888/874–3006 ⊕ www.alaskavistas.com ⛴ From $270.

Alaska Waters

ADVENTURE TOURS | This family-owned business leads six-hour tours from late June to August. Cofounder Wilma Stokes-Leslie, who is of Tlingit and Haida descent, was born and raised in Wrangell, as were many of the other members of her team. ✉ *7 Stikine Ave., Wrangell* ☎ *907/305-0495* 🌐 *www.alaskawaters.com* 🎟 *From $290.*

Restaurants

Stikine Inn Restaurant

$$$ | **AMERICAN** | With views overlooking the water, the Stikine Inn's restaurant (often called the Stik) is easily the prettiest place to dine in Wrangell. Given the town's scarcity of options, the place could just assemble a get-by menu, but the salads, pizzas, burgers, and hearty soups here are seriously tasty. **Known for:** awesome views; delicous burgers; oversized desserts. [$] *Average main: $25* ✉ *107 Stikine Ave., Wrangell* ☎ *907/874-3388* 🌐 *www.stikineinn.com/dining* ⏲ *Closed Nov.–Mar.*

Zak's Cafe

$$ | **AMERICAN** | The café has a no-frills look, but it serves good food at reasonable prices. Check out the dinner specials, or try the steaks, seafood, and salads. **Known for:** good steak; low-key, local atmosphere; excellent seafood chowder. [$] *Average main: $16* ✉ *316 Front St., Wrangell* ☎ *907/874-3355* ⏲ *No dinner Sun.*

Hotels

Grand View Bed & Breakfast

$$ | **B&B/INN** | An unassuming beachfront home 2 miles from town, the Grand View offers spectacular vistas across Zimovia Strait. **Pros:** free Wi-Fi; amazing location and views; visitors get the inside scoop from a true local. **Cons:** transaction fees for credit cards; outside of town; options for evening activities limited. [$] *Rooms from: $165* ✉ *Mile 2, Zimovia Hwy., Wrangell* ☎ *907/874-3225* 🌐 *www.grandviewbnb.com* 🍴 *Free Breakfast* 🛏 *3 rooms.*

Shakes Slough Cabins

$ | **HOUSE** | In addition to offering stunning views of Popof Glacier and Mt. Basargin, these remote and very rustic Forest Service cabins are a 4-mile boat ride from Shakes Slough Hot Springs, where you can soak in open-air and enclosed hot tubs. **Pros:** wildlife viewing; open-air hot tub; stunning, remote location. **Cons:** hard to get to except with a local boat guide; cabins have no electricity or water; tend to book up fast. [$] *Rooms from: $40* ✉ *Wrangell Ranger District, 525 Bennett St., Wrangell* ☎ *907/874-2323, 877/444-6777 National Recreation Reservation Service* 🌐 *www.recreation.gov* 🍴 *No Meals* 🛏 *2 cabins.*

Stikine Inn

$$$ | **B&B/INN** | Half the rooms at Wrangell's largest inn have excellent ocean views, and others look out on Mt. Dewey and downtown. **Pros:** good restaurant; nice views; scenic water-front location. **Cons:** nighttime activities limited; no elevator; uninspired decor. [$] *Rooms from: $240* ✉ *107 Stikine Ave., Wrangell* ☎ *907/874-3388, 888/874-3388* 🌐 *www.stikineinn.com* 🛏 *34 rooms* 🍴 *No Meals.*

Shopping

Angerman's Sporting Goods

SOUVENIRS | This is primarily a place for locals to stock up on practical outdoor clothing and fishing gear, but Angerman's also sells souvenir T-shirts, jewelry, gifts, and other tourist items. ✉ *2 Front St., Wrangell* ☎ *907/874-3640.*

Petersburg

22 miles north of Wrangell.

Getting to Petersburg is an experience, whether you take the "high road" by air or the "low road" by sea. Alaska Airlines claims one of the shortest jet flights in the world, from takeoff at Wrangell to landing at Petersburg. The schedule calls for 20 minutes of flying, but it's usually more like 15. At sea level only ferries and smaller cruisers can squeak through the Wrangell Narrows with the aid of more than 50 buoys and range markers along the 22-mile waterway, which takes almost four hours to negotiate. But the inaccessibility of Petersburg is also part of its charm: you'll never be overwhelmed here by hordes of cruise passengers. The town's Scandinavian heritage is most evident during the Little Norway Festival, held annually on the weekend closest to May 17th, while its Tlingit roots are highlighted through the work of the Petersburg Indian Association; one recent high-profile project involved the creation of a mural of Petersburg-born Tlingit civil rights activist Elizabeth Peratrovich in the center of town.

One of the most pleasant things to do in Petersburg is to roam among the fishing vessels tied up dockside in the harbor. This is one of Alaska's busiest, most prosperous fishing communities, with an enormous variety of seacraft. You'll see small trollers, big halibut vessels, and sleek pleasure craft. By watching shrimp, salmon, or halibut catches being brought ashore (though be prepared for the pungent aroma), you can get a real appreciation for this industry.

On clear days Petersburg's scenery is second to none. Across Frederick Sound the sawlike peaks of the Stikine Ice Cap scrape clouds from the sky, looking every bit as malevolent as their monikers suggest. (Some of the most wickedly named summits include Devil's Thumb, Kate's Needle, and Witches' Tits.)

Although Petersburg is nice to explore, commercial fishing is more important than tourism—in other words, you'll find more hardware stores than jewel merchants. But that authenticity lends it its allure. The main attractions are the town's Norwegian and Tlingit heritage, its vibrant community, and its magnificent mountain-backed setting. The country around Petersburg provides an array of outdoor fun, from whale watching and glacier gazing to hiking and fishing.

GETTING HERE AND AROUND

Once you arrive in Petersburg by ferry on the Alaska Marine Highway or by airplane, a host of activities await. For help finding tours of the area, contact travel agency Viking Travel or the Petersburg Visitor Information Center.

FERRY CONTACTS Alaska Marine Highway System. ✉ *Petersburg* ☎ *907/465–3941, 800/642–0066* ⊕ *www.dot.state.ak.us/amhs.*

ESSENTIALS

TOUR INFORMATION Viking Travel. ✉ *Petersburg* ☎ *907/772–3818, 800/327–2571* ⊕ *www.alaskaferry.com.*

VISITOR INFORMATION Petersburg Visitor Information Center. ✉ *1st and Fram Sts., Petersburg* ☎ *907/772–4636, 866/484–4700* ⊕ *www.petersburg.org.*

Sights

Blind Slough Recreation Area

NATURE SIGHT | This recreation area includes a number of sites scattered along the Mitkof Highway from 15 to 20 miles south of Petersburg. Blind River Rapids Trail is a wheelchair-accessible 1-mile boardwalk that leads to a three-sided shelter overlooking the river—one of Southeast's most popular fishing spots—before looping back through the muskeg. Not far away is a bird-viewing area where several dozen trumpeter swans spend the winter. In summer you're likely to see many ducks and other waterfowl. At Mile 18 the state-run hatchery releases thousands of king and coho salmon each year. The kings return in June and July, the coho in August and September. Nearby is a popular picnic area. Four miles south of the hatchery is a Forest Service campground. ⊠ *Petersburg* ☎ *907/772–3871 USFS Petersburg Ranger District* ⊕ *www.fs.us-da.gov/detail/r10/specialplaces.*

Clausen Memorial Museum

OTHER MUSEUM | The exhibits here explore commercial fishing and the cannery industry, the era of fish traps, the social life of Petersburg, and Tlingit culture. Don't miss the 126½-pound king salmon—the largest ever caught commercially—as well as the Tlingit dugout canoe; the Cape Decision lighthouse station lens; and *Earth, Sea and Sky,* a 3-D wall mural outside. ⊠ *203 Fram St., Petersburg* ☎ *907/772–3598* ⊕ *www.clausenmuseum.com* ☉ *Closed Sun.*

Eagle's Roost Park

CITY PARK | Just north of the Petersburg Fisheries cannery, this small roadside park is a great place to spot eagles, especially at low tide. On a clear day you will also discover dramatic views of the sharp-edged Coast Range, including the 9,077-foot summit of Devil's Thumb. ⊠ *617 N. Nordic Dr, Petersburg.*

Hammer Slough

BODY OF WATER | Houses on high stilts and the historic Sons of Norway Hall border this creek that floods with each high tide, creating a photogenic reflecting pool. ⊠ *Hammer Slough Trail, Petersburg.*

★ LeConte Glacier

NATURE SIGHT | Petersburg's biggest draw lies at the foot of the Stikine Ice Cap. Accessible only by air or water, LeConte Glacier is the continent's southernmost tidewater glacier and one of its most active, often calving off so many icebergs that the tidewater bay at its face is

carpeted shore to shore with them. ⊠ *25 miles northeast of Petersburg, Petersburg* ☎ *907/772–4636 Petersburg visitor information* ⊕ *www.petersburgak.org.*

Sons of Norway Hall

OTHER ATTRACTION | Built in 1912, this large, white, barnlike structure just south of the Hammer Slough is the headquarters of an organization devoted to keeping alive the traditions and culture of Norway. Petersburg's Norwegian roots date back to 1897, when Peter Buschmann arrived and founded the Icy Strait Packing Company cannery. As his business and family flourished, others arrived to join them, many of Norwegian descent. By 1920, they and the area's Tlingit residents had established a year-round community of 600 residents. The hall, its red shutters decorated with colorful Norwegian rosemaling designs, is listed on the National Register of Historic Places. Outside sits a replica of a Viking ship that is a featured attraction in the annual Little Norway Festival each May. On the building's south side is a bronze tribute to deceased local fishermen. ⊠ *23 S. Sing Lee Alley, Petersburg* ☎ *907/772–4575* ⊕ *www.petersburgsons.org.*

Activities

BOATING

Jensen's Boat Rentals

BOATING | This outfit's fleet of skiffs range from 18 to 22 feet and include safety items, coolers, and fish dip nets and crab pots. Other fishing equipment is available for rental. ⊠ *Petersburg* ☎ *907/772–4635* ⊕ *www.jensensboatrentals.com* ⌂ *From $160/day.*

Whale Song Cruises

BOAT TOURS | A great way to experience the Petersburg area from the water, these cruises take place aboard a custom-built, 29-foot aluminum boat suitable for 14 passengers. Choose from a half-day sightseeing trip to LeConte Bay to view the southernmost tidewater

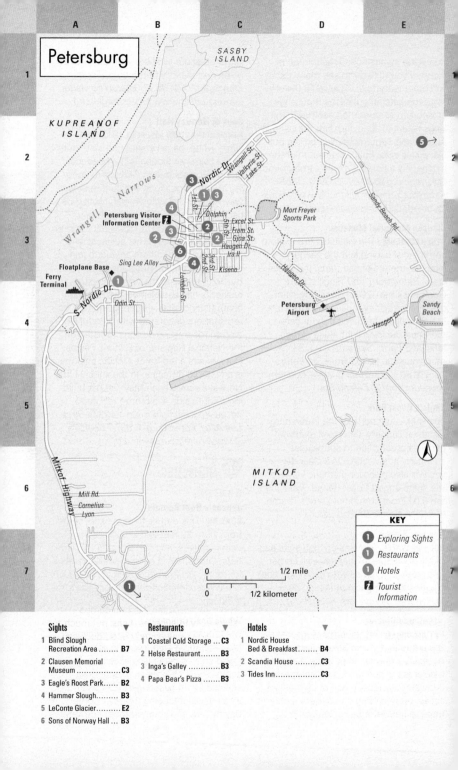

Petersburg

KUPREANOF ISLAND

SASBY ISLAND

Nordic Dr.

Wrangell Narrows

Wrangell St.
Valkyrie St.
Lake St.

1st St.

Dolphin

Petersburg Visitor
Information Center

Excel St.
Fram St.
Gjoa St.
Haugen Dr.
Ira II

Mort Freyer
Sports Park

Sandy Beach Rd.

Sing Lee Alley

3rd St.
2nd St.

Kiseno

Haugen Dr.

Floatplane Base

Ferry
Terminal

S. Nordic Dr.

Odin St.

Lumber St.

Petersburg
Airport

Sandy
Beach

Haugen Dr.

MITKOF ISLAND

Mitkof Highway

Mill Rd.

Cornelius
Lyon

0   1/2 mile
0   1/2 kilometer

KEY

- **1** *Exploring Sights*
- **1** *Restaurants*
- **1** *Hotels*
- **7** *Tourist Information*

Sights ▼

1 Blind Slough
   Recreation Area **B7**
2 Clausen Memorial
   Museum **C3**
3 Eagle's Roost Park **B2**
4 Hammer Slough **B3**
5 LeConte Glacier **E2**
6 Sons of Norway Hall ... **B3**

Restaurants ▼

1 Coastal Cold Storage ... **C3**
2 Helse Restaurant **B3**
3 Inga's Galley **B3**
4 Papa Bear's Pizza **B3**

Hotels ▼

1 Nordic House
   Bed & Breakfast **B4**
2 Scandia House **C3**
3 Tides Inn **C3**

glacier in North America or a full-day whale-watching trip into Frederick Sound. Hot beverages and snacks are included. The captain, longtime local Ron Loesch, also runs the *Petersburg Pilot*, the town's weekly newspaper. ✉ *207 N. Nordic Dr., Petersburg* ☎ *907/772–9393* 🌐 *www.whalesongcruises.com* 🎟 *Call for pricing.*

HIKING

Raven's Roost Cabin Hike

HIKING & WALKING | A 4.2-mile trail begins at the southern edge of the Petersburg airport's runway and winds 1,800 feet in elevation to Raven's Roost Cabin. Along the way you take in a panorama that reaches from the ice-bound Coast Range to the protected waters and forested islands of the Inside Passage far below. Get details on these and other hikes from the Petersburg Visitor Information Center or the Petersburg Ranger District. The two-story Forest Service cabin is available for rent ($40 per night). ✉ *Petersburg Ranger District, 12 N. Nordic Dr., Petersburg* ☎ *907/772–3871* 🌐 *www.fs.usda.gov/recarea/tongass/recarea/?recid=79036.*

🍴 Restaurants

Coastal Cold Storage

$ | **SEAFOOD** | This busy little seafood deli in the heart of Petersburg is a great place for a quick bite en route to your next adventure. Live or cooked crab is available for takeout, and the shop can process your sport-caught fish. **Known for:** full-service fish processing; beer-battered halibut bits; outdoor seating. [$] *Average main: $10* ✉ *306 N. Nordic Dr., Petersburg* ☎ *907/772–4177.*

Helse Restaurant

$ | **AMERICAN** | Locals flock to this cheery spot for lunch; it's the closest thing to home cooking Petersburg has to offer, and most days it's open from 8:30 to 4, even in winter. Helse also doubles as an ice cream and espresso stand. **Known for:** mom-and-pop atmosphere; perfect halibut chowder; tasty ice cream. [$] *Average main: $12* ✉ *13 Sing Lee Alley, Petersburg* ☎ *907/772–3444* 🕒 *Closed Sun.*

Inga's Galley

$ | **PACIFIC NORTHWEST** | Locally sourced ingredients—including Southeast seafood and organic produce—are at the heart of casual Inga's menu. The dishes at this local favorite, a glorified food cart with picnic tables, change "with season, availability, and mood," and most go superbly well with the Baranof Island Brewery beers poured here (there's also wine). **Known for:** vegetarian options; smoked salmon chowder; outdoor, picnic-style dining. [$] *Average main: $12* ✉ *104 N. Nordic Dr., Petersburg* ☎ *907/772–2090* 🌐 *www.facebook.com/IngasGalley* 🕒 *Closed mid-Sept.–mid-Apr.*

Papa Bear's Pizza

$ | **PIZZA** | This oft-crowded restaurant specializes in pizza, Italian sandwiches, tortilla wraps, and ice cream. Traditional pizzas are on the menu but also ones with fanciful add-ons, such as barbecued chicken. **Known for:** local following; chubby chicken pizza; thin crust pizzas. [$] *Average main: $12* ✉ *219 S. Nordic Dr., Petersburg* ☎ *907/772–3727* 🌐 *www.papabearspizza.com* 🕒 *Closed Sun.*

🛏 Hotels

Nordic House Bed & Breakfast

$$ | **B&B/INN** | Just three blocks from the ferry terminal and within easy walking distance of town, Nordic House is a great home base from which to explore Petersburg. **Pros:** great views; central waterfront location; kitchen comes stocked with supplies. **Cons:** not much to do at night; uninspired decor; deck can be noisy. [$] *Rooms from: $180* ✉ *806 S. Nordic Dr., Petersburg* ☎ *907/772–3620* 🌐 *www.nordichouse.net* 🍽 *Free Breakfast* 🛏 *4 rooms.*

Scandia House

$$ | **HOTEL** | On Petersburg's main drag, Scandia House offers some rooms with kitchenettes and king-size beds, and others with in-room hot tubs and harbor views. **Pros:** central location; some pets allowed; airport and ferry shuttle. **Cons:** small rooms; fourth-floor rooms (including the three suites) are not accessible by elevator; dated decor. *§ Rooms from: $130 ⊠ 110 Nordic Dr., Petersburg ☎ 907/772–4281, 800/722–5006 ⤴ 33 rooms ⦿ No Meals.*

Tides Inn

$$ | **HOTEL** | Petersburg's largest hotel is a block uphill from the town's main thoroughfare, and its rooms, some with kitchenettes, have comfortable but timeworn furnishings. **Pros:** friendly staff; central location; harbor views from the newer rooms. **Cons:** no frills; rooms in the old wing are dark and dated; limited breakfast options. *§ Rooms from: $154 ⊠ 307 N. 1st St., Petersburg ☎ 907/772–4288, 800/665–8433 ⊕ www.tidesinnalaska.net ⤴ 45 rooms ⦿ Free Breakfast.*

Nightlife

Harbor Bar

BARS | With ships' wheels, nautical pictures, and a mounted red snapper, the Harbor Bar's decor stays true to Petersburg's seafaring spirit. The bar's liquor store has a separate entrance. *⊠ 310 N. Nordic Dr., Petersburg ☎ 907/772–4526.*

Shopping

FireLight Gallery

ART GALLERIES | This gallery sells jewelry, gifts, and art, including paintings, prints, and handmade pottery, by local and Alaskan artists. *⊠ 211 N. Nordic Dr., Petersburg ☎ 907/772–2161 ⊕ firelight-gallery.com.*

Northern Lights Smokeries

FOOD | Owner Thomas Cumps has made a name for himself with his hot-smoked white king, red king, and sockeye salmon, along with a local favorite, cold-smoked black cod. It's best to call ahead to make sure Cumps will be around before you stop by. You can take your fish with you or have it shipped. *⊠ 501 Noseeum St., Petersburg ☎ 907/518–1616 ⊕ www.nlsmokeries.com.*

Sing Lee Alley Books

BOOKS | Off an alley in a big, beautiful white house that served as a boardinghouse for fishermen and schoolteachers, this shop stocks books on Alaska, best sellers, cards, and gifts. *⊠ 11 Sing Lee Alley, Petersburg ☎ 907/772–4440.*

Tonka Seafoods

FOOD | Sample smoked or canned halibut and salmon at Tonka Seafoods, located in the old Mitkof Cannery building. Be sure to taste the white king salmon—an especially flavorful type of chinook that the locals swear by. Tonka will also ship. *⊠ 1200 S. Nordic Dr., Petersburg ☎ 888/560–3662 ⊕ www.tonkaseafoods.com.*

Sitka

110 miles west of Petersburg.

It's hard not to like Sitka, with its eclectic blend of Alaska Native, Russian, and American history and its dramatic and beautiful open-ocean setting. This is one of the best Inside Passage towns to explore on foot, with St. Michael's Cathedral, the Sheldon Jackson Museum, Castle Hill, Sitka National Historical Park, and the Alaska Raptor Center topping the must-see list.

Sitka was home to the Kiks.ádi clan of the Tlingit people for centuries prior to the 18th-century arrival of the Russians under the direction of territorial governor Alexander Baranof, who believed the region was ideal for the fur trade. The governor also coveted the Sitka site for its beauty, mild climate, and economic potential; in the island's massive timber forests he saw raw materials for shipbuilding. Its location offered trading routes as far west as Asia and as far south as California and Hawaii. In 1799 Baranof built St. Michael Archangel—a wooden fort and trading post 6 miles north of the present town.

Strong disagreements arose shortly after the settlement. The Tlingits attacked the settlers and burned their buildings in 1802. Baranof, however, was away in Kodiak at the time. He returned in 1804 with a formidable force—including shipboard cannons—and attacked the Tlingits at their fort near Indian River, site of the present-day 105-acre Sitka National Historical Park, forcing many of them north to Chichagof Island.

By 1821 the Tlingits had reached an accord with the Russians, who were happy to benefit from the tribe's hunting skills. Under Baranof and succeeding managers, the Russian-American Company and the town prospered, becoming known as the Paris of the Pacific. The community built a major shipbuilding and repair facility, sawmills, and forges, and even initiated an ice industry, shipping blocks of ice from nearby Swan Lake to the booming San Francisco market. The settlement that was the site of the 1802 conflict is now called Old Sitka. It is a state park and listed as a National Historic Landmark.

The town declined after its 1867 transfer from Russia to the United States, but it became prosperous again during World War II, when it served as a base for the U.S. effort to drive the Japanese from the Aleutian Islands. Today its most important industries are fishing, government, and tourism.

GETTING HERE AND AROUND

Sitka is a common stop on cruise routes for smaller ships and a regular stop along the Alaska Marine Highway System. Alaska Airlines also operates flights from Seattle and other Alaskan cities to Sitka. The best way to see the town's sights is on foot.

AIRLINE CONTACTS Alaska Airlines.
☒ *Sitka* ☎ *800/252–7522* ⊕ *www.alaskaair.com.***Alaska Seaplanes.** ☒ *Juneau* ☎ *907/789–3331* ⊕ *www.flyalaskaseaplanes.com.*

FERRY CONTACTS Alaska Marine Highway System. ☒ *Petersburg* ☎ *907/465–3941, 800/642–0066* ⊕ *www.dot.state.ak.us/amhs.***Sitka Ferry Terminal.** ☒ *5307 Halibut Point Rd., Sitka* ☎ *907/747–8737.*

ESSENTIALS

VISITOR INFORMATION Sitka Convention and Visitors Bureau. ☒ *104 Lake St., Sitka* ☎ *907/747–8604* ⊕ *www.sitka.org.*

 Sights

Alaska Raptor Center

NATURE PRESERVE | FAMILY | Above Indian Creek, a 20-minute walk from downtown, Alaska's only full-service avian hospital rehabilitates from 100 to 200 birds each year. Well-versed guides provide an introduction to the center (there's also a short video), and guests can visit with one of these majestic birds. The primary attraction is an enclosed 20,000-square-foot flight-training center, built to replicate the rain forest, where injured eagles relearn survival skills, including flying and catching salmon. Visitors watch through one-way glass windows. A large deck out back faces an open-air enclosure for eagles and other raptors whose injuries prevent them from returning to the wild. Additional mews with hawks, owls, and other birds lie along a rain forest path. The gift shop sells all sorts of eagle

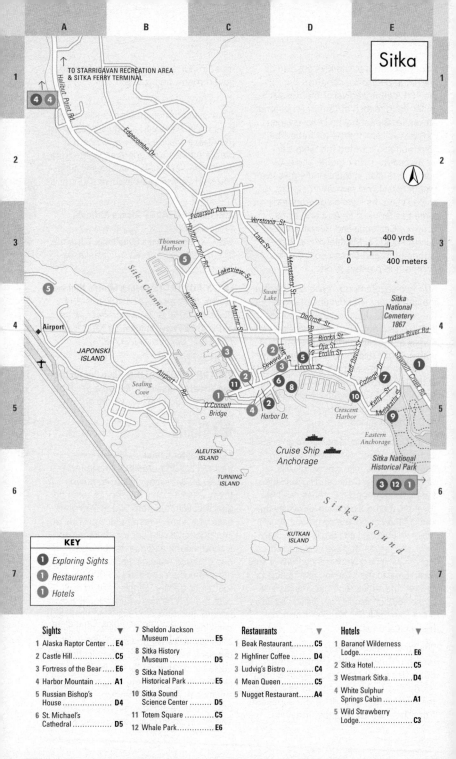

Sitka

TO STARRIGAVAN RECREATION AREA
& SITKA FERRY TERMINAL

Halibut Point Rd.

Edgecombe Dr.

Peterson Ave.

Thomsen Harbor

Halibut Point Rd.

Sitka Channel

Lakeview St.

Verstovia St.

Lake St.

Monastery St.

Swan Lake

DeGroff St.

Sitka National Cemetery 1867

Indian River Rd.

Airport

JAPONSKI ISLAND

Nathan St.

Marine St.

Seward St.

Lake St.

Baranof St.

Biorka St.
Oja St.
Etolin St.

Jeff Davis St.

Sawmill Creek Rd.

College Dr.

Kelly St.

Metlakatla St.

Airport Rd.

Sealing Cove

O'Connell Bridge

Harbor Dr.

Lincoln St.

Crescent Harbor

Eastern Anchorage

Sitka National Historical Park

ALEUTSKI ISLAND

Cruise Ship Anchorage

TURNING ISLAND

KUTKAN ISLAND

Sitka Sound

KEY

- **1** Exploring Sights
- **1** Restaurants
- **1** Hotels

Sights ▼

1. Alaska Raptor Center ... **E4**
2. Castle Hill **C5**
3. Fortress of the Bear **E6**
4. Harbor Mountain **A1**
5. Russian Bishop's
   House **D4**
6. St. Michael's
   Cathedral **D5**
7. Sheldon Jackson
   Museum **E5**
8. Sitka History
   Museum **D5**
9. Sitka National
   Historical Park **E5**
10. Sitka Sound
    Science Center **D5**
11. Totem Square **C5**
12. Whale Park **E6**

Restaurants ▼

1. Beak Restaurant......... **C5**
2. Highliner Coffee **D4**
3. Ludvig's Bistro **C4**
4. Mean Queen **C5**
5. Nugget Restaurant...... **A4**

Hotels ▼

1. Baranof Wilderness
   Lodge.................... **E6**
2. Sitka Hotel.............. **C5**
3. Westmark Sitka.......... **D4**
4. White Sulphur
   Springs Cabin **A1**
5. Wild Strawberry
   Lodge.................... **C3**

0   400 yards
0   400 meters

Walking Around Sitka

Many visitors begin tours of Sitka under the distinctive onion dome of **St. Michael's Cathedral**, right in the town center. A block behind the cathedral along Harbor Drive is **Harrigan Centennial Hall**, a low-slung convention hall that houses the smallish **Sitka Historical Society and Museum** and an information desk that opens when cruise ships are in port. A block east, along Lincoln Street, you'll find the **Russian Bishop's House**, one of the symbols of Russian rule. Continue out on Lincoln Street along the bustling boat harbor to Sheldon Jackson College, where the worthwhile **Sheldon Jackson Museum** is packed with Native cultural artifacts. Close by is the **Sitka Sound Science Center**, which has an aquarium touch tank, a killer-whale skeleton, and other marine-related items of interest. Another half mile out along gently curving Metlakatla Street is the **Sitka National Historical Park**, where you can chat with Native artisans as they craft carvings and silver jewelry. Behind the main building a network of well-signed paths takes you through the rain forest past more than a dozen totem poles and to the site of a Tlingit fort from the battle of 1804. A signed trail crosses the Indian River (watch for spawning salmon in late summer) and heads across busy Sawmill Creek Road to the **Alaska Raptor Center**, for an up-close look at bald eagles.

Return to town along Sawmill Creek Road. On your right, you'll see the white headstones of the small Sitka National Cemetery. Back downtown, you can browse the many shops or walk along Harbor Drive and take the path to the summit of **Castle Hill**, where Russia transferred Alaska to American hands—these are the best views in town. If you follow the path down the other side of the hill, check out the impressive **Sitka Pioneer Home**, with the statue of pioneer "Skagway Bill" Fonda. Across the street is **Totem Square**, with its tall totem pole and three ancient anchors. Adjacent to the Pioneer Home is the **Sheet'ka Kwaan Naa Kahídi** community house.

Sitka has many attractions, and you can easily spend a full day exploring this culturally rich area. You can accomplish the walk in two to three hours if you do not spend much time at each stop.

paraphernalia, the proceeds from which fund the center's programs. ✉ *1000 Raptor Way, off Sawmill Creek Rd., Sitka* ☎ *907/747–8662* ⊕ *www.alaskaraptor.org* ✇ *$15* ⊗ *No tours Oct.–Apr.*

Castle Hill

MONUMENT | On this hill, Alaska was formally handed over to the United States on October 18, 1867, and the first 49-star U.S. flag was flown on January 3, 1959, signifying Alaska's statehood. To reach the hill, take the first right off Harbor Drive just before O'Connell Bridge; then enter the paved path switchbacks to the top, where you can read the interpretive signs on the area's Tlingit and Russian history and take in the views of Crescent Harbor and downtown Sitka. On a clear day, look for the volcanic flanks of Mt. Edgecumbe on the horizon. ✉ *Harbor Rd., Sitka* ☎ *907/747–6249 DNR Sitka Ranger Station* ⊕ *dnr.alaska.gov/parks/aspunits/southeast/baranofcastle.htm.*

Fortress of the Bear

NATURE PRESERVE | FAMILY | An independently operated animal rescue center, Fortress of the Bear offers the chance to see bears up close without worry for safety. The center, 5 miles east of Sitka, shelters a handful of brown and black bears, both adults and cubs, in large enclosures that allow them to interact and play. In addition to creating a hospitable environment for bears that might otherwise be euthanized, the center educates visitors about proper human–animal interaction. ⊠ *4639 Sawmill Creek Rd., Sitka* ☎ *907/747–3032* ⊕ *www.fortressofthebear.org* ⊠ *$15.*

Harbor Mountain

VIEWPOINT | During World War II the U.S. Army constructed a road to the 2,000-foot level of Harbor Mountain, a perfect spot from which to watch for invading Japanese subs or ships (none were seen). This road has been improved over the years, and it is possible to drive 5 miles to a spectacular summit viewpoint across Sitka Sound. A trail climbs uphill from the parking lot, then follows the ridge 2½ miles to a Forest Service shelter. From there, ambitious hikers can continue downhill another 3½ miles to Sitka via the **Gavan Hill Trail.** ⊠ *Harbor Mountain Rd, Sitka.*

Russian Bishop's House

HISTORIC HOME | The Russian–American Company built this registered historic landmark for Bishop Innocent Veniaminov. Completed in 1843 and one of Alaska's few remaining Russian-built log structures, the house, which faces the harbor, contains exhibits on the history of Russian America. In several places, portions of the structure are peeled away to expose Russian building techniques. The ground level is a free museum. The National Park Service operates the house and rangers lead guided tours of the second floor, which holds the residential quarters and a chapel. ⊠ *501 Lincoln St., Sitka* ☎ *907/747–0110* ⊕ *www.nps.gov/sitk.*

Sheldon Jackson Museum

HISTORY MUSEUM | This octagonal museum that dates from 1895 contains priceless Alaska Native items collected by Dr. Sheldon Jackson (1834–1909), who traveled the remote regions of Alaska as an educator and missionary. The collection represents every Alaska Native culture. On display are carved masks, Chilkat blankets, dogsleds, kayaks, and even the impressive helmet worn by the famous Tlingit warrior Katlian during an 1804 battle against the Russians. The museum's small but well-stocked gift shop carries books, paper goods, and handicrafts created by Alaska Native artists. ⊠ *104 College Dr., Sitka* ☎ *907/747–8981* ⊕ *www.museums.state.ak.us* ⊠ *$9 May–Sept., $7 Apr.–Oct.*

Sitka Historical Society and Museum

OTHER MUSEUM | A Tlingit war canoe sits beside this brick building officially named Harrigan Centennial Hall. Check out the museum's collection of Tlingit, Victorian-era, and Alaska-purchase historical artifacts, including spruce-root basketry, nautical instruments, and mining tools. ⊠ *330 Harbor Dr., Sitka* ☎ *907/738–3766 museum* ⊕ *www.sitkahistory.com* ⊠ *Free.*

★ Sitka National Historical Park

HISTORY MUSEUM | The main building at this 113-acre park houses a small museum with fascinating historical exhibits and photos of Tlingit Native culture. Highlights include a brass peace hat given to the Sitka Kiks.ádi by Russian traders in the early 1800s and Chilkat robes. Head to the theater to watch a 12-minute video about Russian–Tlingit conflict in the 19th century. Ask a ranger to point you toward the Centennial Totem Pole, installed in 2011 to honor the park's 100th anniversary. Also here is where Native artisans demonstrate silversmithing, weaving, wood carving, and basketry. Make an effort to strike up a conversation with the artists; they're on-site to showcase and discuss their work and Tlingit cultural traditions. At the far end of the building are seven totems (some more than a century old) that have been brought indoors to protect them from decay. Behind the center a wide, 2-mile path winds through the forest and along the shore of Sitka Sound. Scattered along the way are some of the most skillfully carved Native totem poles in Alaska. Keep going on the trail to see spawning salmon from the footbridge over Indian River. In summer, Park Service rangers lead themed walks that focus on the Russian–Tlingit conflict, the area's natural history, and the park's totem poles. ⊠ 106 Metlakatla St., Sitka ☎ 907/747–0110 visitor center ⊕ www. nps.gov/sitk ⊠ Free.

Sitka Sound Science Center
SCIENCE MUSEUM | FAMILY | The exhibits and activities at this waterfront facility highlight Sitka's role as a regional hub for whale biologists, fisheries-management experts, and other specialists. Attractions include a touch tank, five wall-mounted aquariums, a killer-whale skeleton, and a fish hatchery. Well-placed signs throughout this working science center describe what's going on, providing a great introduction for kids to hands-on environmental science. ⊠ 834 Lincoln St., Sitka ☎ 907/747–8878 ⊕ www. sitkascience.org ⊠ $7.

St. Michael's Cathedral
CHURCH | One of Southeast's best-known landmarks, the onion-dome cathedral is so treasured by locals that in 1966, as a fire engulfed the building, townspeople risked their lives and rushed inside to rescue precious Russian icons, religious objects, and vestments. An almost exact replica of St. Michael's was completed in 1976. Today you can view what may well be the largest collection of Russian icons in the United States, among them Our Lady of Sitka (also known as the Sitka Madonna) and the Christ Pantocrator (Christ the World Judge), displayed on the altar screen. ⊠ 240 Lincoln St., Sitka ☎ 907/747–8120 ⊕ stmichaelcathedral.org.

Totem Square
PLAZA/SQUARE | On this grassy square across the street from the Sitka Pioneer Home are three anchors discovered in local waters and believed to be of 19th-century British origin. Look for the double-headed eagle of czarist Russia carved into the cedar of the park's totem pole. ⊠ 200 Katlian St., Sitka.

Whale Park
CITY PARK | FAMILY | This small waterside park sits in the trees 4 miles east of Sitka right off Sawmill Creek Road. Boardwalk paths lead to five viewing platforms and steps lead down to the rocky shoreline. A gazebo next to the parking area contains signs describing the whales that visit Silver Bay, and you can listen to their sounds from recordings and an offshore hydrophone. ⊠ Sawmill Creek Rd, Sitka.

 Activities

BICYCLING
Yellow Jersey Cycle Shop
BIKING | If it isn't raining, rent a high-quality mountain bike from Yellow Jersey Cycle Shop and head out on the nearby dirt roads and trails. Staffers know Sitka's many mountain- and road-bike routes well. ⊠ 329 Harbor Dr., Sitka ☎ 907/747–6317 ⊕ www.yellowjerseycycles.com ⊠ From $20.

BOAT AND KAYAK TOURS
Alaska Travel Adventures
BOATING | Alaska Travel Adventures leads a three-hour kayaking tour in protected waters south of Sitka. The tour includes friendly guides, basic kayak instruction, and snacks at a remote cabin on the water. ⊠ Sitka ☎ 800/323–5757 ⊕ www. bestofalaskatravel.com ⊠ $154.

Allen Marine Tours
BOATING | One of Southeast's largest and best-known tour operators leads several boat-based Sitka Sound tours throughout the summer. The Wildlife Quest tours provide a fine opportunity to view humpback whales, sea otters, puffins,

eagles, and brown bears in a spectacular setting; it also includes a stop at Fin Island Lodge, located on a private island. Other stops on the company's Sitka tours include the Fortress of the Bear and Alaska Raptor Center. Private catamaran tours for up to six guests can also be arranged. ⊠ *1512 Sawmill Creek Rd., Sitka* ☎ *907/747–8100, 888/747–8101* ⊕ *www.allenmarinetours.com* ☎ *Call for rates.*

Sitka Sound Ocean Adventures

KAYAKING | The guide company's waterfront operation is easy to find: just look for the big blue bus at Crescent Harbor next to the Sitka Historical Society. Sitka Sound runs various guided kayak trips through the mysterious and beautiful outer islands off the coast of Sitka. Guides help new-to-the-area paddlers understand Sitka Sound's wonders, and for day trips the company packs a great picnic. Experienced paddlers who want to go it alone can rent gear. ⊠ *Harbor Dr., at Centennial Hall, Sitka* ☎ *907/752–0660* ⊕ *www.kayaksitka.com* ☎ *From $79.*

BUS TOURS AND HISTORICAL WALKS

Sitka Tours

GUIDED TOURS | Longtime local business Sitka Tours meets ferries and cruise ships and leads both bus tours and historical walks. ⊠ *1004 Halibut Point Rd,, Sitka* ☎ *907/747–5800* ⊕ *www.sitkatoursalaska.com.*

Tribal Tours

CULTURAL TOURS | This company conducts bus and walking tours that emphasize Sitka's rich Tlingit culture and include Naa Kahídi dance performances at the tribal community house. Cruise passengers can book through their cruise agent and independent travelers through Viking Travel. ⊠ *Sitka* ☎ *907/747–7137* ⊕ *www.sitkatours.com.*

FISHING

Sitka is home to a fleet of charter boats. The Chamber of Commerce Visit Sitka website (*visitsitka.org*) has descriptions of and links to several dozen sportfishing operators.

The Boat Company

FISHING | This outfitter offers multiday wildlife-watching and fishing trips departing from Sitka and Juneau. ⊠ *Sitka* ☎ *360/697–4242, 877/647–8268* ⊕ *www.theboatcompany.org.*

HIKING AND WILDLIFE VIEWING

Sitka Trail Works

HIKING & WALKING | You can pick up a good map of local trails from this nonprofit organization that helps maintain them and also leads group hikes on Saturdays in the summer; check the website for details. ⊠ *801 Halibut Point Rd., Sitka* ☎ *907/747–7244* ⊕ *www.sitkatrailworks.org.*

Starrigavan Recreation Area

BIRD WATCHING | This recreation area 7 miles north of Sitka is a peaceful place to explore the rain forest. The state ferry terminal is less than a mile from Starrigavan, and a popular Forest Service campground is also here. Several easy trails pass through the area. ⊠ *Halibut Point Rd., Sitka* ☎ *907/747–6671.*

🍴 Restaurants

Beak Restaurant

$$ | SEAFOOD | On a clear day, the deck at this popular eatery is likely to be overflowing with a lively local crowd devoted to chef Renée Trafton's creative dishes and sustainable practices—that includes a living wage for staff and no tipping (if you do leave a tip, it will be donated to local charities). It's located near the bridge in a historic building that also houses the local radio station, KCAW. **Known for:** fresh, local ingredients; cedar-plank salmon; homemade donuts.

Continued on page 133

AMAZING WHALES
OF ALASKA

It's unforgettable: a massive, barnacle-encrusted humpback breaches skyward from the placid waters of an Alaskan inlet, shattering the silence with a thundering display of grace, power, and beauty. Welcome to Alaska's coastline.

Alaska's cold, nutrient-rich waters offer a bounty of marine life that's matched by few regions on earth. Eight species of whales frequent the state's near-shore waters, some migrating thousands of miles each year to partake of Alaska's marine buffet. The state's most famous cetaceans (the scientific classification of marine mammals that includes whales, dolphins, and porpoises) are the humpback whale, the gray whale, and the orca (a.k.a. the killer whale).

130

BEST REGIONS TO VIEW WHALES

Whales can be viewed throughout the world; after all, they are migratory animals. But thanks to its pristine environment, diversity of cetacean species, and jaw-dropping beauty, Alaska is perhaps the planet's best whale-watching locale.

From April through October, humpbacks visit many of Alaska's coastal regions, including the Bering Sea, the Aleutian Islands, and Prince William Sound. The **Inside Passage,** though, is the best place to see them: it's home to a migratory population of up to 600 humpbacks. Good bets for whale-viewing include taking a trip on the **Alaska Marine Highway,** spending time in **Glacier Bay National Park,** or taking a day cruise out of any of Southeast's main towns. While most humpbacks return to Hawaiian waters in

A gray whale greets whale-watchers

the winter, some spend the whole year in Southeast Alaska.

Gray whales favor the coastal waters of the Pacific, which terminate in the Bering Sea. Their healthy population—some studies estimate that 30,000 gray whales populate the west coast of North America—make them relatively

THE HUMPBACK: Musical, Breaching Giant

Humpbacks' flukes allow them to breach so effectively that they can propel two-thirds of their massive bodies out of the water.

Known for their spectacular breaching and unique whale songs, humpbacks are captivating. Most spend their winters in the balmy waters off the Hawaiian Islands, where females, or sows, give birth. Come springtime, humpbacks set off on a 3,000-mile swim to their Alaskan feeding grounds.

Southeast Alaska is home to one of the world's only groups of bubble-net feeding humpbacks. Bubble-netting is a cooperative hunting technique in which one humpback circles below a school of baitfish while exhaling a "net" of bubbles, causing the fish to gather. Other humpbacks then feed at will from the deliciously dense group of fish.

The Song of the Humpback

All whale species communicate sonically, but the humpback is the most musical. During mating season, males emit haunting, songlike calls that can last for up to 30 minutes at a time. Most scientists attribute the songs to flirtatious, territorial, or competitive behaviors.

QUICK FACTS:

Scientific name: *Megaptera novaeangliae*

Length: Up to 50 ft.

Weight: Up to 90,000 pounds (45 tons)

Coloring: Dark blue to black, with barnacles and knobby, lighter-colored flippers

Life span: 30 to 40 years

Reproduction: One calf every 2 to 3 years; calves are generally 12 feet long at birth, weighing up to 2,000 pounds (1 ton)

easy to spot in the spring and early summer months, especially around **Sitka** and **Kodiak Island** and south of the **Kenai Peninsula,** where numerous whale-watching cruises depart from Seward into **Resurrection Bay**.

Orcas populate nearly all of Alaska's coastal regions. They're most commonly viewed in the **Inside Passage** and **Prince William Sound,** where they reside year-round. A jaunt on the Alaska Marine Highway is one option, but so is a kayaking or day-cruising trip out of **Whittier** to Prince William Sound.

When embarking on a whale-watching excursion, don't forget rain gear, a camera, and binoculars!

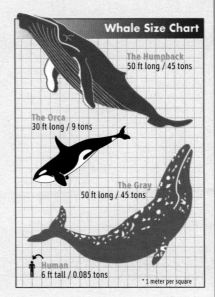

Whale Size Chart

The Humpback
50 ft long / 45 tons

The Orca
30 ft long / 9 tons

The Gray
50 ft long / 45 tons

Human
6 ft tall / 0.085 tons

* 1 meter per square

THE GRAY WHALE: Migrating Leviathan

Though the average lifespan of a gray whale is 50 years, one individual was reported to reach 77 years of age—a real old-timer.

While frequenting Alaska during the long days of summer, gray whales tend to stay close to the coastline. They endure the longest migration of any mammal on earth—some travel 14,000 miles each way between Alaska's Bering Sea and their mating grounds in sunny Baja California.

Gray whales are bottom-feeders that stir up sediment on the sea floor, then use their baleen—a comblike collection of long, stiff hairs inside their mouths—to filter out sediment and trap small crustaceans and tube worms.

Their predilection for near-shore regions, coupled with their easygoing demeanor—some "friendly" gray whales have even been known to approach small tour boats—cements their spot on the short list of Alaska's favorite cetacean celebrities. (Gray whales aren't always in such amicable spirits: whalers dubbed mother gray whales "devilfish" for the fierce manner in which they protected their young.)

QUICK FACTS:

Scientific name: *Eschrichtius robustus*

Length: Up to 50 ft.

Weight: Up to 90,000 pounds (45 tons)

Coloring: Gray and white, usually splotched with lighter growths and barnacles

Life span: 50 years

Reproduction: One calf every 2 years; calves are generally 15 feet long at birth, weighing up to 1,500 pounds (3/4 ton)

AN AGE-OLD CONNECTION

Nearly every major Native group in Alaska has relied on whales for some portion of its diet. The Inupiaq and Yup'ik counted on whales for blubber, oil, meat, and intestines to survive. Aleuts used whale bones to build their semisubterranean homes. Even the Tlingit, for whom food was perennially abundant, considered a beached whale a bounty.

Subsistence whaling lives on in Alaska: although gray-whale hunting was banned in 1996, the Eskimo Whaling Commission permits the state's Native populations to harvest 50 bowhead whales every year.

Other Alaskan whale species:
Bowhead, northern right, minke, fin, and beluga whales also inhabit Alaskan waters.

barnacles

BARNACLES These ragged squatters of the sea live on several species of whales, including humpbacks and gray whales. They're conspicuously absent from smaller marine mammals, such as orcas, dolphins, and porpoises. The reason? Speed. Scientists theorize that barnacles are only able to colonize the slowest-swimming cetacean species, leaving the faster swimmers free from their unwanted drag.

THE ORCA: Conspicuous, Curious Cetacean

Why the name killer whale? Perhaps for this animal's skilled and fearsome hunting techniques, which are sometimes used on other, often larger, cetaceans.

Perhaps the most recognizable of all the region's marine mammals, orcas (also called killer whales) are playful, inquisitive, and intelligent whales that reside in Alaskan waters year-round. Orcas travel in multigenerational family groups known as pods, which practice cooperative hunting techniques.

Orcas are smaller than grays and humpbacks, and their 17-month gestation period is the longest of any cetacean. They are identified by their white-and-black markings, as well as by the knifelike shape of their dorsal fins, which, in the case of mature males, can reach 6 feet in height.

Pods generally adhere to one of three common classifications: residents, which occupy inshore waters and feed primarily on fish; transients, which occupy larger ranges and hunt sea lions, squid, sharks, fish, and whales; and offshores, about which little is known.

QUICK FACTS:

Scientific name:
Orcinus orca

Length: Up to 30 ft.

Weight: Up to 18,000 pounds (9 tons)

Coloring: Smooth, shiny black skin with white eye patches and chin and white belly markings

Life span: 30 to 50 years

Reproduction: One calf every 3 to 5 years; calves are generally 6 feet long at birth, weighing up to 400 pounds (0.2 ton)

[$] *Average main: $16* ✉ *2 Lincoln St., Sitka* ☎ *907/966–2326* 🌐 *www.beakrestaurant.com* ⏲ *Closed Mon.*

Highliner Coffee
$ | **AMERICAN** | Sitkans' favorite spot for coffee, Highliner also serves great bagels for breakfast and sandwiches at lunch. **Known for:** breakfast burritos; house brews; free Wi-Fi. [$] *Average main: $8* ✉ *327 Seward St., Sitka* ☎ *907/747–4924* 🌐 *stores.highlinercoffee.com.*

★ **Ludvig's Bistro**
$$$ | **MEDITERRANEAN** | Food lovers pack into Ludvig's to sample chef-owner Colette Nelson's remarkably creative cuisine, which means there's often a wait, but rest assured that your meal will be worth it. Seafood (particularly king salmon and scallops) is the specialty, and organic ingredients are used whenever possible. **Known for:** excellent wine list; king salmon and scallops; great reputation throughout the region. [$] *Average main: $28* ✉ *256 Katlian St., Sitka* ☎ *907/966–3663* 🌐 *www.ludvigsbistro.com* ⏲ *Closed Sun. mid-Sept.–Apr.*

Mean Queen
$$ | **PIZZA** | Carefully crafted pizza and generously sized salads are the draw at the Mean Queen, a casual, friendly pub near the bridge. The views of Sitka Harbor make it a great spot to linger. **Known for:** $3 beer on tap; nice views; creative pizzas. [$] *Average main: $20* ✉ *205 Harbor Dr., Sitka* ☎ *907/747–0616* 🌐 *www.meanqueensitka.com.*

Nugget Restaurant
$$ | **AMERICAN** | Travelers flying out of Sitka's airport retreat to the Nugget while waiting for their plane to arrive. The Nugget serves American classics for breakfast, lunch, and dinner, but the homemade pies are the real attraction. **Known for:** Friday night prime rib; homemade pie; better-than-usual airport dining. [$] *Average main: $24* ✉ *Sitka Airport Terminal, 600 Airport Dr., Sitka* ☎ *907/966–2480* 🌐 *www.nuggetrestaurant.com.*

Hotels

Baranof Wilderness Lodge
$$$$ | **B&B/INN** | A quick floatplane ride from Sitka, this cozy fishing lodge is on Baranof Island, a remote and magnificent location from which to explore the surrounding landscape and view wildlife that includes bears, whales, and eagles. **Pros:** rate is all-inclusive from Sitka; spacious rooms; beautiful surroundings. **Cons:** five-day stays only; might be too remote for some; expensive. [$] *Rooms from: $2340* ✉ *Warm Springs Bay, Sitka* ☎ *907/738–3597, 800/613–6551* 🌐 *www.flyfishalaska.com* ⏲ *Closed Oct.–May* 🛏 *8 rooms* 🍴 *All-Inclusive.*

Sitka Hotel
$$ | **HOTEL** | An affordable option in downtown Sitka, the renovated Sitka Hotel offers clean, spacious rooms, friendly staff, and a central base from which to explore Sitka's many treasures. **Pros:** good-size rooms; central location; free airport shuttle. **Cons:** street noise; very basic; lackluster breakfast options. [$] *Rooms from: $185* ✉ *118 Lincoln St., Sitka* ☎ *907/747–3288* 🌐 *www.sitkahotel.com* 🍴 *No Meals* 🛏 *50 rooms.*

Westmark Sitka
$$$ | **HOTEL** | The Westmark has large rooms, many overlooking Crescent Harbor; the best are the corner suites (but all could use an update). **Pros:** good restaurant on-site; nice views; big rooms. **Cons:** rooms a bit outdated; lacks charm; high rates. [$] *Rooms from: $250* ✉ *330 Seward St., Sitka* ☎ *907/747–6241, 800/544–0970 in U.S.* 🌐 *www.westmarkhotels.com/sitka.php* 🛏 *105 rooms* 🍴 *No Meals.*

White Sulphur Springs Cabin
$ | **HOUSE** | With incredible views and proximity to a hot-springs bathhouse, this isolated retreat 65 miles northwest of Sitka is one of Southeast's most prized public-use cabins. **Pros:** completely private; close to hot springs; Pacific Ocean views. **Cons:** requires boat ride to

location; guests must bring own bedding and cooking utensils; no good drinking water source nearby. $ *Rooms from: $60* ✉ *West Chichagof–Yakobi Wilderness Area, Sitka* ☎ *907/747–6671 information, 877/444–6777 reservations* ⊕ *www.recreation.gov* ⇨ *1 cabin* ⦿ *No Meals.*

★ Wild Strawberry Lodge

$$$$ | **B&B/INN** | At this fishing lodge with waterfront cabins, you'll gather for home-cooked meals after a long day of fishing to socialize and scheme for the next day's adventure; all-inclusive packages start at $2,075 per person. **Pros:** friendly hosts; great food; lots of accommodation options. **Cons:** arrival-night dinner not included; expensive; can be noisy. $ *Rooms from: $2075* ✉ *724 Siginaka Way, Sitka* ☎ *800/770–2628* ⊕ *www.wildstrawberrylodge.com* ⇨ *13 rooms* ⦿ *All-Inclusive.*

Nightlife

Baranof Island Brewing Company

BARS | Beer lovers will want to check out the brewery's taproom, open daily from 2 to 8 pm. Under state law, patrons can only consume up to 36 ounces in one visit (that's for breweries only). ✉ *1209 A Sawmill Creek Rd., Sitka* ☎ *907/747–2739* ⊕ *www.baranofislandbrewing.com.*

Bayview Pub

BARS | In addition to its selection of Alaska and Pacific Northwest craft beers, "The Pub" is known for handcrafted classic cocktails made with freshly squeezed juices. If you're tired of seafood, this is a solid choice; dinner options include racks of lamb, top sirloins, and French dip sandwiches. The pub has a stage for live music; nonmusical diversions include two pool tables, a dart area, and plenty of wide-screen TVs. ✉ *407 Lincoln St., Sitka* ☎ *907/747–5300* ⊕ *www.sitkabayviewpub.com.*

Pioneer Bar

BARS | As far as the locals are concerned, the few green-and-white-vinyl booths at this bar across from the harbor make a fine destination. The Pioneer is vintage Alaska, with pool tables, rough-hewn locals clad in Carhartts and XtraTuf boots, hundreds of pictures of local fishing boats, and occasional live music. ✉ *212 Katlian St., Sitka* ☎ *907/747–3456.*

 Performing Arts

New Archangel Dancers of Sitka

FOLK/TRADITIONAL DANCE | Dedicated to preserving Alaska's Russian history, this all-female troupe has performed in Sitka since 1969. The 30-minute performances showcase authentic dances from the surrounding regions and Russia. ✉ *208 Smith St., Sitka* ☎ *907/747–5516* ⊕ *www.newarchangeldancers.com.*

Sheet'ka Kwaan Naa Kahidi Dancers

FOLK/TRADITIONAL DANCE | Tlingit dancers in full regalia perform at the Sheet'ka Kwaan Naa Kahidi community house on Katlian Street. Tickets are sold through cruise lines or, for independent travelers, as part of package tours offered through Viking Travel. ✉ *204 Katlian St., Sitka* ☎ *907/747–7137* ⊕ *www.sitkatours.com/pages/Dancers.html.*

Shopping

ART GALLERIES

Artist Cove Gallery

ART GALLERIES | In this tiny yet inviting gallery, you'll find a selection of interesting jewelry, ceramics, artwork, and carvings hand-picked by the owner, a Czech-born artist. ✉ *241 Lincoln St., Sitka* ☎ *907/747–6990* ⊕ *www.artistcovegallery.com.*

Island Artists Gallery

ART GALLERIES | A co-op of local artists, this storefront gallery sells their jewelry, pottery, fine-art prints, and other works. ✉ *205 Lincoln St., Sitka* ☎ *907/747–6536* ⊕ *www.islandartistsgallery.com.*

Sitka Rose Gallery

ART GALLERIES | In an 1895 Victorian next to the Bishop's House, the gallery, Sitka's most charming shop, sells Alaskan paintings, sculptures, Native art, and jewelry. ⊠ *419 Lincoln St., Sitka* ☏ *907/747–3030* ⊕ *www.sitkarosegallery.com.*

BOOKSTORES

Old Harbor Books

BOOKS | The knowledgeable staff and impressive collection of Alaska titles make a visit to Old Harbor a pleasure. **The Backdoor Café** (*sitkabackdoor.com*), a cozy politically progressive hangout behind the bookstore, serves excellent espresso and fresh-baked pastries. ⊠ *201 Lincoln St., Sitka* ☏ *907/747–8808* ⊕ *www.oldharborbooks.net.*

GIFTS

WinterSong Soap Company

SOUVENIRS | The colorful and scented soaps sold at this shop near St. Michael's Cathedral are handcrafted on the premises. ⊠ *202 Lincoln St., Sitka* ☏ *907/747–8949, 888/819–8949* ⊕ *www.wintersongsoap.com.*

Juneau

100 miles northeast of Sitka.

Juneau, Alaska's capital and third-largest city, is on the North American mainland but can't be reached by road. Bounded by steep mountains and water, the city's geographic isolation and compact size make it much more akin to an island community like Sitka than to other Alaskan urban centers, such as Fairbanks or Anchorage. Juneau is full of contrasts. Its dramatic hillside location and historic downtown buildings provide a frontier feeling, but the city's cosmopolitan nature comes through in fine museums, noteworthy restaurants, and a both literate and outdoorsy populace. You can visit cultural institutions like the Alaska State Museum or the Walter Soboleff Building, which offers visitors a chance to learn about the Indigenous cultures of Southeast Alaska—Tlingit, Haida, and Tsimshian. Other Juneau highlights include the Mt. Roberts Tramway, plenty of densely forested wilderness areas, quiet bays for sea kayaking, and even a famous drive-up glacier, Mendenhall Glacier. For goings-on, pick up the *Juneau Empire*, which keeps tabs on state politics, business, sports, and local news.

GETTING HERE AND AROUND

Juneau is an obligatory stop on the Inside Passage cruise and ferry circuit. Hence, the town has an overabundance of visitors in midsummer. Alaska Airlines also flies here, and Delta Airlines offers seasonal service from Memorial Day through September. Downtown Juneau is compact enough that most of its main attractions are within walking distance of one another. Note, however, that the city is very hilly, so your legs will get a real workout. Keep an eye out for the abundant wayfinding signs, installed in 2020, that feature a Northwest Coast formline design of red salmon.

ESSENTIALS

VISITOR INFORMATION Alaska Department of Fish & Game. ⊠ *1255 W. 8th St., Juneau* ☏ *907/465–4180 sportfishing seasons and regulations, 907/465–2376 license information* ⊕ *www.adfg.alaska.gov.* **Alaska Division of Parks.** ⊠ *400 Willoughby Ave., Juneau* ☏ *907/465–4563* ⊕ *dnr.alaska.gov/parks.* **Juneau Convention & Visitors Bureau.** ⊠ *800 Glacier Ave., Suite 201, Juneau* ☏ *907/586–2201, 888/581–2201* ⊕ *www.traveljuneau.com.*

Sights

Alaska State Capitol

GOVERNMENT BUILDING | Completed in 1931, this unassuming building houses the governor's office and hosts state legislature meetings in winter, placing it at the epicenter of Alaska's animated political discourse. Historical photos line the upstairs walls. You can pick

Did You Know?

On the Trail of Time, see the physical signs of Mendenhall Glacier's history. Dark (old) and light (new) green vegetation meet at the highest point reached by the glacier's ice.

Juneau's History

Tlingit residents of the area originally made their home in nearby Auke Bay, where the rain is less oppressive and the vistas are more open, but in summers they frequently moved down the channel to what is now the Aak'w Village District of Juneau. Miners began arriving in the 1880s, including two colorful sourdoughs, Joe Juneau and Richard Harris. Led by a Tlingit chief named Kowee, Juneau and Harris discovered rich reserves of gold at Snow Slide Gulch, the drainage of Gold Creek around which the town was eventually built. Shortly thereafter a modest stampede resulted in the formation of a mining camp, which quickly grew to become the Alaska district government capital in 1906. The city may well have continued under its original appellation—Harrisburg, after Richard Harris—were it not for Joe Juneau's political jockeying at a miner's meeting in 1881.

For some 60 years after Juneau's founding, gold was the mainstay of the economy. In its heyday the AJ (for Alaska Juneau) Gold Mine was the biggest low-grade ore mine in the world. It was not until World War II, when the government decided it needed Juneau's manpower for the war effort, that the AJ and other mines in the area ceased operations. After the war, mining failed to start up again and government became the city's principal employer (mining does continue in some areas, such as the Greens Creek mine on Admiralty Island). The city's largest private-sector employer is tourism.

up a self-guided tour brochure as you enter. ✉ *Seward and 4th Sts., Juneau* ☎ *907/465–4648* ⊕ *www.akleg.gov* 🎟 *Free.*

★ Alaska State Libraries, Archives, and Museums

HISTORY MUSEUM | FAMILY | The Father Andrew P. Kashevaroff Building, which houses the State Libraries, Archives, and Museums (LAM), opened in 2016 on the site of the old state museum and is among the most impressive cultural attractions in Alaska. In the permanent gallery, visitors weave through interconnected spaces that present Alaska's unique stories through carefully selected objects and culturally diverse narratives. Three temporary galleries host an ever-changing selection of solo shows and exhibits, offering in-depth views of notable contemporary Alaskan artists and art forms. Kids will love the pirate ship (built for them to climb on) and the eagle tree in the lobby, viewable from multiple levels. The new state-of-the-art building also houses Alaska's most important books, photographs, and documents, offering increased opportunities for researchers as well as more casual visitors. ✉ *395 Whittier St., Juneau* ☎ *907/465–2901* ⊕ *lam.alaska.gov/home* 🎟 *$14 summer, $9 winter.*

DIPAC Macaulay Salmon Hatchery

OTHER ATTRACTION | FAMILY | Salmon are integral to life in Southeast Alaska, and Alaskans are proud of their healthy fisheries. A visit to the hatchery is a great introduction to the complex considerations involved in maintaining the continued vitality of this crucial resource. Watch through an underwater window as salmon fight their way up a fish ladder from mid-June to mid-October. Inside the busy hatchery, which produces almost 125 million young salmon annually, you will learn about the environmental considerations of commercial fishermen and the lives of salmon. A retail shop sells gifts and salmon products. The salmon hatchery is part of a larger nonprofit, Douglas Island Pink and Chum, Inc., and is usually referred to locally by its acronym, DIPAC. ✉ *2697 Channel Dr., Juneau ✛ 3 miles northwest of downtown Juneau* ☎ *907/463–4180* ⊕ *www.dipac.net* ✉ *$4, including short tour* ⊘ *Closed Oct.–Apr.*

Glacier Gardens Rainforest Adventure

FOREST | One of the upsides to living in a rain forest is the lush proliferation of plants and trees. At Glacier Gardens, they've turned local flora into an art form. Spread over 50 acres of rain forest, the family-owned Glacier Gardens has ponds, waterfalls, hiking paths, a large atrium, and gardens. The roots of fallen trees, turned upside down and buried in the ground, act as bowls to hold planters that overflow with begonias, fuchsias, and petunias. Guided tours in covered golf carts lead you along the 4 miles of paved paths, and a 580-foot-high overlook provides dramatic views of the Mendenhall wetlands wildlife refuge, the Chilkat Range, and downtown Juneau. A café and gift shop are here, and the conservatory is a popular wedding spot. Admission includes a guided tour. The Juneau city bus, which departs from multiple locations downtown, stops in front of Glacier Gardens (but be prepared for a meandering journey). ✉ *7600 Glacier Hwy., Juneau ✛ 6½ miles northwest of downtown Juneau* ☎ *907/790-3377* ⊕ *www.glaciergardens.com* ✉ *$29* ⊘ *Closed Oct.–Apr.*

Governor's Mansion

HISTORIC HOME | This stately Colonial-style home completed in 1912 overlooks downtown Juneau. With 14,400 square feet, 6 bedrooms, and 10 bathrooms, it's no miner's cabin. Out front is a totem pole that tells three tales: the history of man, the cause of ocean tides, and the origin of Alaska's ubiquitous mosquitoes. Unfortunately, tours of the residence are not permitted. ✉ *716 Calhoun Ave, Juneau.*

Juneau-Douglas City Museum

HISTORY MUSEUM | **FAMILY** | Exhibits at this city-run museum interpret pioneer, mining, and Tlingit history. A diorama of a fire assay lab shows how the Bureau of Mines measured the gold content of rock samples, and there's a reconstructed Tlingit fish trap. Pioneer artifacts include a century-old store and kitchen. Digital story kiosks shed light on Alaska's quest for statehood, how government works here, civil rights in Alaska, and the cultures of Juneau. In the hands-on room, youngsters can try on clothes similar to ones worn by the miners and look at gold-rush stereoscopes. Engaging historic walking tours of downtown ($30) take place from May through September. ✉ *114 4th St., Juneau* ☎ *907/586-3572* ⊕ *www.juneau.org/library/museum/index. php* ✉ *$6 May–Sept., free Oct.–Apr.; $30 walking tour (includes museum admission)* ⊘ *Closed Mon.–Wed. Oct.–Apr.*

Last Chance Mining Museum

OTHER MUSEUM | A 1½-mile hike or taxi ride behind town, this small museum is housed in the former compressor building of Juneau's historic AJ Gold Mine. The collection includes old mining tools, railcars, minerals, and a 3-D map of the ore body. If you have time, and didn't arrive on foot, meander down back toward town. Unlike most of Juneau, Basin Road is flat and relatively quiet. The surrounding country is steep and wooded, with trails leading in all directions, including one to the summit of Mt. Juneau. At the base of the Perseverance Trail, not far from the museum, you can see the boarded-up opening to an old mining tunnel; even from a safe distance you can feel a chilly breeze wafting through the cracks. ✉ *1001 Basin Rd., Juneau* ☎ *907/586-5338* ✉ *$5.*

★ Mendenhall Glacier

NATURE SIGHT | **FAMILY** | Glaciers are abundant in Southeast Alaska, but only a very few are as accessible as Mendenhall Glacier. Alaska's most-visited drive-up glacier spans 12 miles and is fed by the massive Juneau

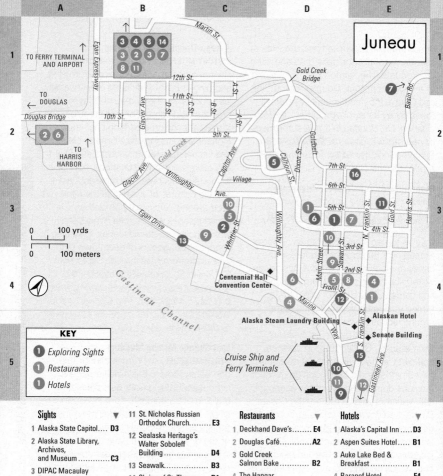

Juneau

TO FERRY TERMINAL AND AIRPORT

TO DOUGLAS

Douglas Bridge

TO HARRIS HARBOR

Gastineau Channel

0   100 yrds
0   100 meters

Martin St.

12th St.

11th St.

10th St.

9th St.

Gold Creek Bridge

Gold Creek

Willoughby Ave.

Egan Drive

Glacier Ave.

Egan Expressway

Village

Centennial Hall Convention Center

Calhoun St.

Golbelt

Dixon St.

Main Street

Seward St.

Front St.

Marine

Way

Alaska Steam Laundry Building

Alaskan Hotel

Senate Building

7th St.

6th St.

5th St.

4th St.

3rd St.

2nd St.

N. Franklin St.

Gold St.

Harris St.

Basin Rd.

S. Franklin St.

Gastineau Ave.

Cruise Ship and Ferry Terminals

KEY

1 *Exploring Sights*

1 *Restaurants*

1 *Hotels*

Sights ▼

1 Alaska State Capitol.... **D3**
2 Alaska State Library, Archives, and Museum **C3**
3 DIPAC Macaulay Salmon Hatchery **B1**
4 Glacier Gardens Rainforest Adventure **B1**
5 Governor's Mansion.... **D2**
6 Juneau-Douglas City Museum **D3**
7 Last Chance Mining Museum **E1**
8 Mendenhall Glacier **B1**
9 Mt. Roberts Tramway .. **D5**
10 Red Dog Saloon.........**D5**

11 St. Nicholas Russian Orthodox Church.........**E3**
12 Sealaska Heritage's Walter Soboleff Building **D4**
13 Seawalk.................**B3**
14 Shrine of St. Therese... **B1**
15 South Franklin St.........**E5**
16 Wickersham State Historic Site **E3**

Restaurants ▼

1 Deckhand Dave's........ **E4**
2 Douglas Café............**A2**
3 Gold Creek Salmon Bake **B2**
4 The Hangar on the Wharf **D4**
5 Heritage Coffee Company.................**D4**
6 Island Pub **A2**
7 Rainbow Foods...........**E3**
8 The Rookery Café........ **E4**
9 Salt **D4**
10 The Sandpiper Café **C3**
11 Tracy's King Crab Shack........ **D5**
12 Twisted Fish Company.................**E5**

Hotels ▼

1 Alaska's Capital Inn **D3**
2 Aspen Suites Hotel **B1**
3 Auke Lake Bed & Breakfast **B1**
4 Baranof Hotel **E4**
5 Driftwood Lodge **C3**
6 Four Points by Sheraton Juneau.... **D4**
7 Grandma's Feather Bed **B1**
8 Pearson's Pond Luxury Inn and Adventure Spa **B1**
9 Ramada by Wndham....**C3**
10 Silverbow Inn **D3**
11 U.S. Forest Service Cabins...................**B1**

Walking Around Juneau

The most common starting spot is **Marine Park**, right along the cruise-ship dock. From there, head up to Front Street to the **Walter Soboleff Building,** an Alaska Native arts and cultural center, one of the few modern buildings in this part of town. From there, walk up Main Street to the **State Office Building,** where you'll find an observation deck with vistas across Gastineau Channel. The snug but cheery **Juneau–Douglas City Museum,** a local treasure, sits a short distance away at 4th and Main Streets. The looming, banklike building across Main Street is the **Alaska State Capitol.** For a far more attractive example of governmental architecture, continue southwest on 4th Street until it becomes Calhoun Street and then head north to the **Governor's Mansion.** On your way back toward town, head down the public stairs on Calhoun and follow the signs to the new **Alaska State Library, Archives, and Museum.**

After viewing the museum, head back downtown to peruse the historic buildings and busy shops before dipping inside the always crowded **Red Dog Saloon** at the intersection of South Franklin Street and Admiralty Way. Try a microbrew, and then continue down the street to the **Mt. Roberts Tramway,** a popular way to reach alpine country for a hike overlooking Juneau and Gastineau Channel. Next door is the colorful new Juneau Visitor Center. From here you can stroll down the **Seawalk,** which parallels South Franklin.

To cover downtown Juneau's many interesting sights, you should allow at least three or four hours for exploring. Add at least another hour if you're a museum fan or if you plan to ride the **Mt. Roberts Tramway.** Don't miss drive-up **Mendenhall Glacier;** it's a few miles out of town, so you'll need to take a car, taxi, or bus to get there.

Icefield. Like many other Alaska glaciers, it is retreating, losing more than 100 feet a year as huge chunks of ice calve into the small lake separating the glacier from the Mendenhall Visitor Center. The center has interactive and traditional exhibits, a theater and bookstore, and panoramic views. Nature trails lead along Mendenhall Lake, to Nugget Falls, and into the mountains overlooking Mendenhall Glacier; the trails are marked by posts and paint stripes delineating the historic location of the glacier, providing a sharp reminder of Mendenhall's hasty retreat. An elevated viewing platform allows visitors to look for spawning sockeye and coho salmon—and the bears that eat them—at Steep Creek, a half mile south of the visitor center along the Moraine Ecology Trail.

Several companies lead bus tours to the glacier; ask at the visitor information center. You can also get within a mile and a half of the glacier on the city bus, which is $2 one-way. For a different perspective, you can travel by helicopter to the surface of the glacier, or hire a guide to take you to one of the amazing, electric blue ice caves. Note that because the caves are inherently unstable, the Forest Service doesn't recommend self-guided tours. ⊠ *End of Glacier Spur Rd. off Mendenhall Loop Rd., Juneau* ✛ *13 miles north of downtown Juneau* ☎ *907/789–0097* ⊕ *www.fs.usda.gov/detail/tongass/about-forest/offices* ⌫ *Visitor center $5 May–Sept., free Oct.–Apr.* ☉ *Closed Mon.–Thurs. Oct.–Apr.*

★ Mt. Roberts Tramway

VIEWPOINT | FAMILY | One of Southeast's most popular tourist attractions whisks you from the cruise-ship docks 1,800 feet up the side of Mt. Roberts. After the six-minute ride, you can take in a film on the history and culture of the Tlingits, visit the nature center, go for an alpine walk on hiking trails (including the 5-mile round-trip hike to Mt. Roberts's 3,819-foot summit), purchase Native art and peruse the on-site gallery, or enjoy a meal while savoring mountain views. You can also get an up-close view of an "education" eagle in her mew. A local company leads guided wilderness hikes from the summit, and the bar serves locally brewed beers. Plan to spend one to two hours at the top. For a workout, hike up the mountain from town or hike to Father Brown's Cross from the top; each takes about an hour. ⊠ *490 S. Franklin St., Juneau* ☎ *907/463–3412, 888/461–8726* ⊕ *www.mountrobertstramway.com* ⌑ *$45* ⊙ *Closed Oct.–Apr.*

Red Dog Saloon

RESTAURANT | The frontierish quarters of the Red Dog have housed an infamous Juneau watering hole since 1890. Nearly every conceivable surface in this two-story bar is cluttered with graffiti, business cards, and memorabilia, including a pistol that reputedly belonged to Wyatt Earp, who failed to reclaim the piece after checking it in at the U.S. Marshall's office on June 27, 1900. The saloon's food menu includes halibut, reindeer sausage, potato skins, burgers, and locally brewed beers. A little atmospheric sawdust covers the floor, and musicians pump out ragtime piano tunes when cruise ships are docked. ⊠ *278 S. Franklin St., Juneau* ☎ *907/463–3658* ⊕ *www.reddogsaloon.com.*

St. Nicholas Russian Orthodox Church

CHURCH | Newly baptized Orthodox Natives and Siberian gold miners built what's now Southeast's oldest Russian church in 1894. Refurbished in the late 1970s, the onion-dome white-and-blue structure is a national historic landmark. Services sung in Slavonic, English, and Tlingit take place on weekends. A small visitor center and gift shop are located next door in the rectory. ⊠ *326 5th St., Juneau* ☎ *907/586–1023* ⊕ *www.stnicholasjuneau.org.*

★ Sealaska Heritage's Walter Soboleff Building

INDIGENOUS SIGHT | This center devoted to Alaska Native art, culture, and language is operated by Sealaska Heritage Institute and named for a local Tlingit elder who died at age 102 in 2011. It includes an exhibits gallery, a traditional clan house, research areas, and a shop selling work by Northwest Coast artists. The building's three major public art pieces—exterior red metal panels, a carved cedar house front in the lobby, and a modern glass screen in the clan house—were created by three of the top Northwest Coast artists in the world (Robert Davidson, David A. Boxley, and Preston Singletary), and represent the three Indigenous tribes of Southeast Alaska—Haida, Tsimshian, and Tlingit, respectively. The art pieces also highlight the center's dual role in honoring tradition while remaining forward-facing and contemporary. Among the goals of this facility are promoting Juneau's role as a hub of Northwest Coast art and fostering cross-cultural understanding. Across the street from the building, an arts campus devoted to both goals is set to open in early 2022. ⊠ *105 Seward St., Juneau* ☎ *907/463–4844* ⊕ *www.sealaskaheritage.org* ⌑ *$5* ⊙ *Store closed Sun. and Mon. Oct.–Apr.*

Seawalk

MARINA/PIER | Constructed as part of a long-range waterfront improvement plan, Juneau's Seawalk currently exists in two unconnected segments: the southern portion runs from the end of South Franklin Street to Marine Park, and the northern section extends along Egan Drive to the whale sculpture below the Juneau–Douglas Bridge. The southern

Seawalk provides a calmer pedestrian alternative to the narrow, crowded sidewalks of South Franklin Street and includes the Juneau Visitor Center, the Mt. Roberts Tram building, and a statue of a beloved local dog named Patsy Ann. One section passes between the Taku Smokeries fish-processing plant and an offloading dock for fishermen, allowing an occasional glimpse of an industry that remains an important part of Alaskan life. The northern section of the Seawalk offers beautiful views of Gastineau Channel and Douglas Island; signage provides information on local history, flora, and fauna. At the end in Overstreet Park, Juneau's iconic whale sculpture rises above a fountain, providing the perfect backdrop for photos and an opportunity to rest up for the walk back. ⊠ *S. Franklin St, Juneau.*

Shrine of St. Thérèse

CHURCH | If the crowds become overwhelming, and you have access to a vehicle, consider a visit to the Shrine of St. Thérèse, "out the road"—it's a peaceful site that's perfect for quiet contemplation. Built in the 1930s, this beautiful stone church and its 15 stations of the cross are the only structures on a serene tiny island accessible via a 400-foot-long pedestrian causeway. Visitors enjoy the Merciful Love Labyrinth, the black-granite Columbarium, and the floral gardens along the Good Shepherd Rosary Trail. Sunday services are held at 1:30 pm from June through August. For those wishing to explore the area for more than a few hours, the shrine offers a lodge and four rental cabins that run the gamut from rustic to resplendent. A round-trip taxi ride may cost $60 or more. ⊠ *Mile 23 Glacier Hwy., Juneau* ✛ *23 miles northwest of downtown* ☎ *907/586–2227* ⊕ *www.shrineofsainttherese.org.*

South Franklin Street

STREET | The buildings on South Franklin Street and neighboring Front Street house curio and crafts shops, snack shops, and a salmon shop. Though some have fallen into disrepair, many reflect the architecture of the 1920s and 1930s; the older structures are located closer to the center of town. When the small Alaskan Hotel opened in 1913, Juneau was home to 30 saloons; the Alaskan gives today's visitors the most authentic glimpse of the town's whiskey-rich history—and, true to that history, is still a bit rough around the edges. Topped by a wood-shingled turret, the 1901 Alaska Steam Laundry Building now houses a toy store and other shops. The Senate Building, another of South Franklin's landmarks, is across the street. ⊠ *S. Franklin St, Juneau.*

Wickersham State Historic Site

HISTORIC HOME | At the top of the hill behind the capitol, on a rise sometimes known as "Chicken Ridge," stands the former residence of James Wickersham, pioneer judge, delegate to Congress, prolific author, and gutsy outdoorsman. The white New England–style home, constructed in 1898, contains memorabilia from the judge's travels throughout Alaska—from rare Native basketry and ivory carvings to historic photos and a Chickering grand piano that came "'round the Horn" to Alaska in the 1870s. The tour provides a glimpse into the life of this dynamic man. ⊠ *213 7th St., Juneau* ☎ *907/586–9001* ⊕ *dnr.alaska.gov/parks/units/wickrshm. htm* 🖃 *Free* ⊗ *Closed Oct.–Apr.*

🏃 Activities

BIKING

Cycle Alaska

BIKING | Rentals from Cycle Alaska include everything from a helmet and minipump to a bottle of water and a granola bar. You can reserve a bike online at their website. Be sure to check out Juneau's new free bike map on the Juneau Rides website (*juneaurides.org/ juneau-bike-map/*). ⊠ *1107 W. 8th St., Juneau* ☎ *907/780–2253* ⊕ *www.cycleak. com* 🖃 *From $38.*

BOATING, CANOEING, AND KAYAKING

Above & Beyond Alaska

BOATING | Juneau-based Above & Beyond conducts day and overnight camping trips, ice-climbing adventures, and Mendenhall Glacier and sea-kayaking trips. They are located in Auke Bay. ⊠ *Auke Bay Harbor, 11521 Glacier Hwy., Auke Bay* ☎ *907/364–2333* ⊕ *www.beyondak.com* ⌕ *Tours from $240.*

★ Adventure Bound Alaska

BOATING | All-day trips to Sawyer Glacier within Tracy Arm in summer are available from Adventure Bound Alaska. ⊠ *76 Egan Dr., Juneau* ☎ *907/463–2509, 800/228–3875* ⊕ *www.adventureboundalaska.com* ⌕ *$165.*

Alaska Discovery

BOATING | Operated by Mountain Travel Sobek, Alaska Discovery leads 13-day trips down the Alsek River and 7-day kayaking trips in Glacier Bay, among other adventures. ⊠ *Juneau* ☎ *888/974–0300* ⊕ *www.mtsobek.com/trips/alaska-north-america/alaska* ⌕ *From $4495.*

Alaska Travel Adventures

BOATING | Mendenhall River floats, lake kayaking, and lake canoeing are among the Juneau-area tours this outfit offers; lunch at a creek-side salmon bake is a popular add-on. ⊠ *9085 Glacier Hwy., Juneau* ☎ *800/323–5757, 907/789–0052* ⊕ *www.alaskatraveladventures.com* ⌕ *From $119.*

Allen Marine Tours

BOATING | Family-owned Allen Marine Tours conducts catamaran trips to Tracy Arm fjord, whale-watching adventures out of Auke Bay, and several land-and-water combination tours. Book through your cruise line, or call for prices. ⊠ *13391 Glacier Hwy,, Juneau* ☎ *907/789–0081, 888/289–0081* ⊕ *www.allenmarinetours. com.*

FISHING

Juneau Convention & Visitors Bureau

FISHING | The website and office for the Juneau Convention & Visitors Bureau has a complete list of people and companies that lead sportfishing trips from Juneau. ⊠ *800 Glacier Hwy.* ☎ *907/586–2201, 888/581–2201* ⊕ *www.traveljuneau.com.*

FLIGHTSEEING

Several local companies operate helicopter flightseeing trips to the spectacular glaciers flowing from Juneau Icefield. Most have booths along the downtown cruise-ship dock. All include a touchdown on a glacier, providing the opportunity to romp on these rivers of ice. Some also lead trips that include a dogsled ride on the glacier. Note that although we recommend the best companies, even some of the most experienced pilots have had accidents; always ask a carrier about its recent safety record before booking a trip.

★ Alaska Seaplanes

AIR EXCURSIONS | Besides daily scheduled air service to 14 Southeast communities, Alaska Seaplanes also offers flightseeing tours and charters to other Southeast destinations. ⊠ *Juneau International Airport, 1873 Shell Simmons Dr.,* ☎ *907/789–3331* ⊕ *www.flyalaskaseaplanes.com.*

Coastal Helicopters

AIR EXCURSIONS | These helicopters land on several glaciers within the Juneau Icefield during a 2½-hour tour; 1½-hour dogsled adventures are another popular option. ⊠ *8995 Yandukin Dr., Juneau* ☎ *907/789–5610, 800/789–5610* ⊕ *www. coastalhelicopters.com* ⌕ *$315 for ice field tour.*

NorthStar Trekking

AIR EXCURSIONS | No experience is necessary at NorthStar, which has three levels of excellent glacier hikes. The lowest level includes a one-hour interpretive walk, while the highest consists of a three-hour hike that includes the chance to practice basic climbing and rope techniques. Dogsled adventures are also available. Book through your cruise line, or call for prices. ✉ *1910 Renshaw Way, Juneau* ☎ *907/790–4530* ⊕ *www.north-startrekking.com* 🖘 *From $404.*

Temsco Helicopters

AIR EXCURSIONS | The self-proclaimed pioneers of Alaska glacier helicopter touring, Temsco Helicopters offers glacier tours, dogsled adventures, and year-round flightseeing. Book through your cruise line or contact the company for pricing. ✉ *1650 Maplesden Way, Juneau* ☎ *907/789–9501, 877/789–9501* ⊕ *www.temscoair.com* 🖘 *From $329.*

Ward Air

AIR EXCURSIONS | Take flightseeing trips to Glacier Bay, the Juneau Icefield, Elfin Cove, Tracy Arm, and Pack Creek with Ward Air, or charter a floatplane to access remote U.S. Forest Service cabins. Charter flights to Gustavus and Bartlett Cove are also available on request. ✉ *8991 Yandukin Dr., Juneau* ☎ *907/789–9150* ⊕ *www.wardair.com.*

★ Wings Airways and Taku Glacier Lodge

AIR EXCURSIONS | This Juneau-based company specializes in glacier sightseeing followed by a salmon feast at a remote, historic Alaskan lodge, complete with glacier views in their Taku Lodge Feast & 5 Glacier Discovery Tour—one of the best day trips out of the state capital. The 5 Glacier Discovery Tour is also available as a stand-alone flightseeing trip. ✉ *2 Marine Way, Suite 175, Juneau* ☎ *907/586–6275* ⊕ *www.wingsairways.com* 🖘 *$230 for glacier tour, $330 for tour/lodge combo.*

GOLD-PANNING

AJ Mine Gastineau Mill Tour

SPECIAL-INTEREST TOURS | Former miners lead two-hour tours of the historic AJ Gold Mine south of Juneau. The tours, which depart from downtown by bus, include a gold-panning demonstration and time in the old tunnels that lace the mountains. ✉ *Sheep Creek Mine Rd.,*

Juneau ☎ *907/463–5017* ⊕ *www.ajgastineauminetour.com* 🖘 *Call for prices.*

Alaska Travel Adventures

SPECIAL-INTEREST TOURS | **FAMILY** | Gold panning is fun, especially for children, and Juneau is one of Southeast's best-known gold-panning towns. Sometimes you actually discover a few flecks of the precious metal in the bottom of your pan. You can buy a pan at almost any Alaska hardware or sporting-goods store. Alaska Travel Adventures has gold-panning tours near the famous Alaska-Juneau Mine. ✉ *Juneau* ☎ *800/323–5757, 907/789–0052* ⊕ *www.alaskatraveladventures.com* 🖘 *From $71.*

HIKING

★ Gastineau Guiding

HIKING & WALKING | This company leads a variety of hikes in the Juneau area. Especially popular are the Mt. Roberts Extended Trek tours, which include a tram ride up Mt. Roberts followed by a strenuous 4- to 6-mile hike farther up the mountain through alpine meadows. ✉ *1330 Eastaugh Way, Suite 2, Juneau* ☎ *907/586–8231* ⊕ *www.stepintoalaska.com* 🖘 *Call for pricing.*

U.S. Forest Service

HIKING & WALKING | Hikers can contact the U.S. Forest Service for trail books and maps; some are available online for easy downloading. ✉ *Juneau Ranger District office, 8510 Mendenhall Loop Rd., Juneau* ☎ *907/586–8800* ⊕ *www.fs.usda.gov/detail/tongass/maps-pubs.*

SIGHTSEEING AND GLACIERS

Juneau Convention & Visitors Bureau

ADVENTURE TOURS | The bureau maintains a list of companies that conduct tours of Mendenhall Glacier and others that provide boat trips to Tracy Arm's Sawyer Glacier, about 50 miles southeast of Juneau. The recently opened Juneau Visitor Center, next to the Mt. Roberts Tramway building on South Franklin Street, is the bureau's most convenient location for summertime visitors, and a fun example of local architecture. ✉ *800 Glacier Ave., Suite 201, Juneau* ☎ *907/586–2201, 888/581–2201* 🌐 *www.traveljuneau.com.*

SKIING

Eaglecrest

SKIING & SNOWBOARDING | Southeast's only downhill ski area is on Douglas Island, 30 minutes from downtown Juneau. The resort typically offers skiing and snowboarding from late-November to mid-April on 620 acres of well-groomed and off-piste terrain. Amenities include four double chairlifts, cross-country trails, a beginner's slope, a ski school, a ski-rental shop, a cafeteria, and a tri-level day lodge. In the summer, hikers and bikers can explore the mountain via the service road that runs from the bottom of Eaglecrest to the top of the chairlift, a 2-mile trek with a heart-pumping 1,400-foot elevation gain. The road is usually snow-free by June. ✉ *Eaglecrest Ski Area, 3000 Fish Creek Rd., Juneau* ☎ *907/790–2000* 🌐 *skijuneau.com.*

Foggy Mountain Shop

SKIING & SNOWBOARDING | Find groomed cross-country ski trails near the Eaglecrest Ski Area and at Mendenhall Campground in the winter. You can rent skis and get advice about touring the trails and ridges around town from Foggy Mountain Shop. The shop also outfits hikers and climbers in summer. ✉ *134 N. Franklin St., Juneau* ☎ *907/586–6780* 🌐 *www.foggymountainshop.com.*

WHALE-WATCHING

Alaska Galore Tours

WILDLIFE-WATCHING | This company offers small-group whale-watching excursions of up to 20 guests aboard a luxury yacht with an onboard naturalist, as well as a combination whale-watching-and-flightseeing tour over the Juneau Icefield. ✉ *Juneau* ☎ *877/794–2537* 🌐 *www.alaska-galore-juneau-whale-watching.com* 🎫 *From $149.*

Harv & Marv's Outback Alaska

WILDLIFE-WATCHING | Experienced local captains lead these whale-watching excursions for groups of up to 6 or up to 18 passengers. Private tours can also be arranged. ✉ *Juneau* ☎ *866/909–7288, 907/209–7288* 🌐 *www.harvandmarvs-alaska-whale-watching.com* 🎫 *From $165.*

★ Weather Permitting Alaska

WILDLIFE-WATCHING | The small-boat luxury whale-watching trips of Weather Permitting last four hours, including van travel. Visitors get plenty of time to view whales, bears, sea lions, eagles, porpoises, and other animals, all the while enjoying dramatic scenery. With only 10 customers on a trip (excepting single groups of up to 12), this is among the most intimate and comprehensive whale watches anywhere. For a truly unique experience, schedule a customized trip with an "Alaskan celebrity," such as the famous whale photographer and marine biologist Flip Nicklin (if he's available). ✉ *Juneau* ☎ *907/789–5843* 🌐 *www.weatherpermittingalaska.com* 🎫 *From $189.*

🍴 Restaurants

★ Deckhand Dave's

$ | **SEAFOOD** | A former park in the middle of downtown Juneau has been transformed into a vibrant outdoor food court thanks to Deckhand Dave, a commercial fisherman who has acquired a loyal local following for his foodtruck-prepared rockfish and halibut tacos. The backyard patio atmosphere includes tents, heat lamps, firepits, and a ship-shaped bar. **Known for:** local hot spot; outdoor seating; fresh fish tacos. [$] *Average main: $12* ✉ *139 South Franklin St., Juneau* 🌐 *www.deckhanddaves.com.*

Douglas Café

$$ | **AMERICAN** | In the heart of quiet Douglas, across the bridge and a couple of miles from downtown Juneau, this family diner has Formica tables and a menu that includes omelets, sandwiches, kids' favorites, and burgers that are often cited as the best in the city. This is a good

choice for those seeking an alternative to downtown Juneau's midsummer crowds. **Known for:** local crowd; burgers and fries; hearty breakfasts. $ *Average main: $16* ⊠ *916 3rd St., Douglas* ☎ *907/364–3307* ⊘ *Closed Mon.*

Gold Creek Salmon Bake

$$$$ | **SEAFOOD** | Trees, mountains, and the rushing water of Salmon Creek surround the comfortable, canopy-covered benches and tables at this authentic, all-you-can-eat salmon bake operated through Alaska Travel Adventures. After dinner you can pan for gold in the stream, wander up a hill to explore the remains of a gold mine, or roast marshmallows over a fire. **Known for:** picnic-style eating; fresh-caught salmon cooked over fire; forest experience. $ *Average main: $56* ⊠ *1061 Salmon Lane Rd., Juneau* ☎ *907/789–0052, 800/323–5757* ⊕ *www. bestofalaskatravel.com/alaska_day_tours/ pages/j_gold_creek_salmon.htm* ⊘ *Closed Oct.–Apr.*

The Hangar on the Wharf

$$ | **ECLECTIC** | Crowded with locals and travelers, the Hangar occupies the building where Alaska Airlines started business, and though flight-theme puns (e.g., "Pre-flight Snacks" and the "Plane Caesar") dominate the menu, the comfortably worn wood and the vintage airplane photos create a casual experience that trumps the kitsch. Every seat has views of Gastineau Channel and Douglas Island, and on warm days you can sit outdoors. **Known for:** wide selection of beers on tap, including local options; prime rib; gorgeous views. $ *Average main: $18* ⊠ *Merchants Wharf Mall, 2 Marine Way, Juneau* ☎ *907/586–5018* ⊕ *www. hangaronthewharf.com.*

Heritage Coffee Company

$ | **CAFÉ** | Established in 1974, Heritage Coffee serves locally roasted coffees, along with gelato, fresh pastries, and a variety of sandwiches. The flagship store sits on the corner of Front and Seward Streets, while other locations include

smaller cafés at 230 South Franklin and 124 South Franklin (inside the Baranof Hotel), a branch inside Foodland IGA market, the Glacier Cafe in the Mendenhall Valley, and a kiosk at the University of Alaska Southeast. **Known for:** delicious baked goods; good espresso; lively atmosphere. $ *Average main: $9* ⊠ *130 Front St., Juneau* ☎ *907/586–1088* ⊕ *www.heritagecoffee.com.*

Island Pub

$ | **PIZZA** | Fast service, a full bar, views of Gastineau Channel, and occasional live music have turned this Douglas pub into an area hot spot, but the real draw is pizza: thin, 13-inch focaccia crusts prepared fresh daily, topped with creative ingredients, and baked in a copper wood-fired oven. If you don't get too full, try a dessert pizza—bizarre, but surprisingly good. **Known for:** local gathering spot; inventive topping combinations; thin focaccia crusts. $ *Average main: $13* ⊠ *1102 2nd St., Douglas* ☎ *907/364–1595* ⊕ *www.theislandpub.com.*

Rainbow Foods

$ | **VEGETARIAN** | This crunchy natural foods market with a weekday buffet offers an ever-changing selection of hot entrées, salads, soups, and pizza, along with self-serve coffee and freshly baked breads. Check their website for a daily menu, and arrive at 11 am for the best choices; a few tables are available inside. **Known for:** vegetarian options; organic, healthy snacks; lunch buffet. $ *Average main: $8* ⊠ *224 4th St., Juneau* ☎ *907/586–6476* ⊕ *www.rainbow-foods.org.*

The Rookery Café

$$ | **ECLECTIC** | This lively café fills up quickly at noon with locals on lunch break, making it a great place for people-watching while munching on a salad. You can also grab a great breakfast here, including fresh-baked *pain au chocolat*, buttermilk corn cakes, and Stumptown coffee. **Known for:** popularity with locals; baked goods; creative lunch options. $ *Average main: $14* ⊠ *111 Seward St.,*

Juneau ☎ 907/463–3013 ⊕ www.therook-erycafe.com.

Salt

$$$ | **MEDITERRANEAN** | Upscale American and Mediterranean fare is served at Salt, one of Juneau's nicest dining options, and though it's a bit pricey, the ambience and service make it worth the extra expense. It's also a good spot to stop for a cocktail if you can snag a spot at the tiny bar in the back. **Known for:** filet mignon; upscale dining; craft cocktails. Ⓢ Average main: $28 ⊠ 200 Seward St., Juneau ☎ 907/780–2221 ⊕ www.saltalaska.com ⊗ Closed Sun.

The Sandpiper Café

$ | **AMERICAN** | This busy and bright café in the Aak'w Village District, about a five-minute walk from the center of town, is a popular destination for brunch on weekends. It's also a good choice for lunch if you're visiting the state museum, as it's less than a block away. **Known for:** weekend brunch; French toast; Reuben sandwiches. Ⓢ Average main: $12 ⊠ 429 W. Willoughby Ave. ☎ 907/586–3150 ⊕ www.sandpiper.cafe ⊗ No dinner.

★ Tracy's King Crab Shack

$$ | **SEAFOOD** | Alaskan king crab—a not-to-be-missed Alaskan delicacy—is the specialty of popular Tracy's. There's often a line to place your order, but the wait is entirely worth it. **Known for:** casual, fun vibe; perhaps Alaska's best crab bisque; Bristol Bay king crab legs with butter. Ⓢ Average main: $15 ⊠ 432 S. Franklin St., Juneau ☎ 907/790–2722 ⊕ www.kingcrabshack.com ⊗ Closed Oct.–Apr.

Twisted Fish Company

$$$ | **SEAFOOD** | Downtown Juneau's liveliest eatery, housed in a log-frame waterfront building adjacent to the base of the Mt. Roberts Tramway, serves fish as fresh as you'll find. Grab a seat on the deck and enjoy prime-time Gastineau Channel gazing over a glass of wine or locally brewed beer. **Known for:** fresh halibut; Captain Ron's chowder; waterfront dining. Ⓢ Average main: $24 ⊠ 550 S. Franklin St., Juneau ☎ 907/463–5033 ⊕ www.twistedfishcompany.com ⊗ Closed Oct.–Apr.

 Hotels

★ Alaska's Capital Inn

$$$ | **B&B/INN** | Gold-rush pioneer John Olds built this American foursquare home in 1906, and a major restoration transformed it into downtown Juneau's most elegant B&B. **Pros:** gourmet breakfasts; antique decor; beautiful restoration of 1906 mansion. **Cons:** room rates are a little high; the inn sits atop a steep incline from the main section of downtown; less privacy than some other properties. Ⓢ Rooms from: $254 ⊠ 113 W. 5th St., Juneau ☎ 907/586–6507, 888/588–6507 ⊕ www.alaskacapitalinn.com ➪ 7 rooms ⦿ Free Breakfast.

Aspen Suites Hotel

$$ | **HOTEL** | A standard all-suites hotel near the airport, the Aspen is well suited for business travelers and travelers with children. **Pros:** close to the airport; walking distance to Mendenhall Wetlands Trail; complimentary Wi-Fi. **Cons:** housekeeping is weekly, not daily; not near downtown attractions; basic hotel decor. Ⓢ Rooms from: $189 ⊠ 8400 Airport Blvd., Juneau ☎ 907/500–7700 ⊕ www.aspenhotelsak.com/juneau ➪ 78 rooms ⦿ No Meals.

Auke Lake Bed & Breakfast

$$ | **B&B/INN** | A stay at this lakeside B&B about 4½ miles northwest of Juneau's airport provides a glimpse into local living—you can explore small, quiet Auke Lake by paddleboat, canoe, or kayak; enjoy it from the shoreside hot tub; or walk the 3-mile trail that circles it. **Pros:** walking distance to bus stop; secluded residential area; lakefront location. **Cons:** few restaurant options nearby; outside town; no laundry facilities. Ⓢ Rooms from: $175 ⊠ 11595 Mendenhall Loop Rd., Juneau ☎ 907907/957–9263 ⊕ www.aukelakebb.com ⦿ Free Breakfast ➪ 5 rooms.

Baranof Hotel

$$ | **HOTEL** | Once Juneau's most prestigious hotel, the Baranof Hotel has begun to show its age, although it does retain some of its old glamour. **Pros:** 1930s ambience; elegant public areas; central location. **Cons:** some rooms are small; lower floors are noisy; dated room decor. $ *Rooms from: $169* ✉ *127 N. Franklin St., Juneau* ☎ *907/586–2660, 800/780–7234* ⊕ *www.bestwestern.com* ⤳ *200 rooms* ❍ *No Meals.*

Driftwood Lodge

$$ | **HOTEL** | This workaday downtown motel is a good option for guests on a budget who are interested in preparing their own meals and exploring downtown Juneau on foot. **Pros:** ferry and airport shuttle service; well-equipped kitchenettes in many rooms; easy walking distance to downtown sights. **Cons:** spare and dated decor; not very accessible for those with disabilities; parking lot out front. $ *Rooms from: $159* ✉ *435 W. Willoughby Ave., Juneau* ☎ *907/586–2280, 800/544–2239* ⊕ *www.dhalaska.com* ❍ *No Meals* ⤳ *62 rooms.*

Four Points by Sheraton Juneau

$$$ | **HOTEL** | A high-rise by Juneau standards, the seven-story Four Points by Sheraton (formerly the Goldbelt) is one of the city's better lodgings, with decent, if somewhat overpriced, rooms. **Pros:** great views from many rooms; walking distance to downtown sights; restaurant on-site. **Cons:** a little pricey; street-side rooms are noisy; no room service. $ *Rooms from: $288* ✉ *51 W. Egan Dr., Juneau* ☎ *907/586–6900* ⊕ *www.fourpointsjuneau.com* ⤳ *106 rooms* ❍ *No Meals.*

Grandma's Feather Bed

$$$ | **B&B/INN** | This charming Victorian-style hotel—the smallest property in the Best Western chain—is less than a mile from the airport in the Mendenhall Valley and has spacious and homey rooms. **Pros:** beds topped with feather comforters; delicious breakfast; deluxe suites with in-room whirlpool baths. **Cons:** books up quickly; outside downtown; not set up for children. $ *Rooms from: $215* ✉ *2358 Mendenhall Loop Rd., Juneau* ☎ *907/789–5566, 800/780–7234* ⊕ *www.grandmasfeatherbed.com* ❍ *Free Breakfast* ⤳ *14 rooms.*

★ Pearson's Pond Luxury Inn and Adventure Spa

$$$$ | **B&B/INN** | On a small pond near Mendenhall Glacier, this large, jaw-droppingly landscaped home may be Alaska's finest B&B. **Pros:** kayaks and bicycles for guest use; close to the glacier and hiking trails; private balconies with excellent views. **Cons:** not very accessible for those with disabilities; limited public transportation; two-night minimum during summer. $ *Rooms from: $399* ✉ *4541 Sawa Circle, Juneau* ☎ *907/789–3772* ⊕ *www.pearsonspond.com* ❍ *Free Breakfast* ⤳ *5 rooms.*

Ramada by Wyndham

$$ | **HOTEL** | A short walk west of downtown, this nicely appointed but visually unremarkable hotel (formerly known as the Prospector) is a favorite with business travelers year-round and lawmakers during the winter legislative session. **Pros:** restaurant on-site; convenient location; most pets accepted. **Cons:** rooms could use updating; lackluster exterior and lobby; street noise on the water side. $ *Rooms from: $189* ✉ *375 Whittier St., Juneau* ☎ *907/586–3737* ⊕ *www.wyndhamhotels.com/ramada/juneau-alaska/ramada-juneau/overview* ⤳ *56 rooms* ❍ *No Meals.*

Silverbow Inn

$$$ | **B&B/INN** | Conveniently located in Juneau's historic downtown, the Silverbow has contemporary, charming hotel rooms on two upper levels. **Pros:** rooftop hot tub; central location; easy walk to the sights. **Cons:** limited parking; no laundry facilities; small rooms. $ *Rooms from: $239* ✉ *120 2nd St., Juneau* ☎ *907/206–5693, 800/586–4146* ⊕ *www.silverbow-inn.com* ⤳ *11 rooms* ❍ *Free Breakfast.*

★ U.S. Forest Service Cabins

$ | HOUSE | Scattered throughout the Tongass National Forest, these rustic cabins—most of which are reached by floatplane or boat—offer a cheap and charming escape. **Pros:** amazing views; a unique experience; affordable rates. **Cons:** no electricity or water; remote; outdoor bathroom. ⓢ *Rooms from: $45* ✉ *Juneau Ranger District, 8510 Mendenhall Loop Rd., Juneau* ☎ *907/586–8800, 877/444–6777 reservations* ⊕ *www.recreation.gov* ⍐| *No Meals* ⤳ *150 cabins.*

ⓨ Nightlife

Alaskan Brewing Company

BARS | The company's tasty, award-winning beers—including Alaskan Amber, Icy Bay IPA, White, and Freeride Pale Ale—are brewed and bottled in Juneau. This is no designer brewery—it's in Juneau's industrial area, and there is no upscale café-bar attached—but the gift shop sells T-shirts and beer paraphernalia. You can also visit the brewery's Downtown Depot, on Franklin Street; though you can't sample the beer there, you can find out more about the brewing process and purchase Alaskan Brewing Company gear. From the Depot you can also take a shuttle to the brewery; $25 includes round-trip shuttle, brewery tour, and six beer samples. Shuttles run hourly in the summer. ✉ *5364 Commercial Blvd., Juneau* ☎ *907/780–5866* ⊕ *www. alaskanbeer.com.*

Alaskan Hotel Bar

BARS | A sign frequently placed outside this historic bar reads: "Have an Alaskan with an Alaskan at the Alaskan," referring to the locally made beer, the clientele, and the bar itself. And it's true that this triple convergence can be found here any night of the week—the bar always has at least one type of Alaskan Brewing Company beer on tap, and the crowd is primarily local, even in summer. On the ground floor of the Alaskan Hotel, this is Juneau's most historically authentic watering hole, with flocked-velvet walls, antique chandeliers, and vintage frontier-brothel decor. Just keep in mind that in recent years the vintage charm has begun to look decidedly worn out, but it's still worth visiting just the same. ✉ *167 S. Franklin St., Juneau* ☎ *907/586–1000* ⊕ *www.thealaskanhotel.com.*

Amalga Distillery

BARS | In the tasting room at the Amalga Distillery, you can sample Amalga's small-batch gin (up to two drinks per visit) while seated next to the brass and copper still in which the gin was made. The well-designed space also includes high ceilings and huge windows perfect for people-watching. ✉ *134 N. Franklin St., Juneau* ☎ *907/209–2015* ⊕ *www. amalgadistillery.com.*

Imperial Saloon

BARS | A remodeled former dive where locals like to drink, shoot pool, and meet singles, the Imperial retains mounted moose and bison heads and other vestiges of its divey decor. Other noteworthy features include the original pressed-tin ceiling and what is reputed to be the longest bar in Alaska. The Imperial Grill, located within the bar, serves food until 1 am on weekends. ✉ *241 Front St., Juneau* ☎ *907/586–1960.*

The Narrows

BARS | An upscale alternative to Juneau's somewhat rowdy bar scene, The Narrows is the best place in the city to enjoy a classy, carefully prepared cocktail. The bar gets its name from the shape of the space—long and skinny—and its exposed brick walls, fireplace, and leather couches in back add to the intimate vibe. ✉ *148 S. Franklin St., Juneau* ☎ *415/205–3704* ⊕ *the-narrows.business.site.*

Performing Arts

Juneau Symphony

MUSIC | A high-caliber volunteer organization, the symphony performs classical works from October through June in high school auditoriums and local churches. ✉ 522 W. 10th St., Juneau ☎ 907/586–4676 ⊕ www.juneausymphony.org.

Perseverance Theatre

THEATER | Alaska's only professional theater company performs classics and new productions from September through May. The company also stages plays in Anchorage each season, and some shows have toured more extensively, among them the all-Tlingit version of Shakespeare's *Macbeth,* which traveled to the Smithsonian's National Museum of the American Indian in Washington, D.C. Perseverance is Juneau's most high-profile troupe, but also worth checking out are **Theatre in the Rough,** a fantastic all-volunteer theater troupe that's been staging Shakespearian works and other classics twice a year since 1991, and two opera companies, **Juneau Lyric Opera** and **The Orpheus Project.** ✉ 914 3rd St., Douglas ☎ 907/364–2421 ⊕ www.ptalaska.org.

Shopping

ART GALLERIES

Annie Kaill's Gallery

ART GALLERIES | This gallery displays a mix of playful and whimsical original prints, pottery, jewelry, and other art and crafts from Alaska artists. If you're in town on the first Friday of any month, ask the staff for a map of the First Friday Art Walk; more than a dozen downtown galleries participate in this monthly event by hosting evening exhibit openings, most of which feature the works of local artists. ✉ 244 Front St., Juneau ☎ 907/586–2880 ⊕ www.anniekaills.com.

Caribou Crossings

ART GALLERIES | Locally owned and operated, this gallery sells artworks, craft items, and other creations—from sculptures to fossilized ivory bracelets to children's books—created by Alaskans. ✉ 497 S. Franklin St., Juneau ☎ 877/586–5008, 907/586–5008 ⊕ www.cariboucrossings.com.

Juneau Artists Gallery

ART GALLERIES | The cooperatively run gallery, on the first floor of the old Senate Building, sells a mix of watercolors, jewelry, oil and acrylic paintings, etchings, photographs, art glass, ceramics, fiber art, and pottery from more than 20 local artists. ✉ 175 S. Franklin St., Juneau ☎ 907/586–9891 ⊕ www.juneauartistsgallery.org.

Kindred Post

ART GALLERIES | Kindred Post is more than the downtown area's sole post office. The local owner, a poet and artist, has transformed the space into an elegant gallery that features locally made jewelry, ceramics, prints, and other works of art. ✉ 145 S. Franklin St., Juneau ☎ 907/523–5053 ⊕ www.kindredpost.com.

Mt. Juneau Trading Post

ART GALLERIES | A Tlingit family owns this crowded shop that specializes in traditional Northwest Coast artworks, from carved silver bracelets to high-end masks. They also have a second location across the street. ✉ 151 S. Franklin St., Juneau ☎ 907/586–3426 ⊕ mtjuneautradingpost.com.

Rie Muñoz Gallery

ART GALLERIES | Rie Muñoz, one of Alaska's best-known artists, was the creator of a stylized, simple, and colorful design technique that is much copied but rarely equaled. This gallery run by her son is located in the Mendenhall Valley, a 10-minute walk from the airport. ✉ 2101 N. Jordan Ave., ☎ 907/789–7411, 800/247–3151 ⊕ www.riemunoz.com.

Sealaska Heritage Store

ART GALLERIES | On the Front Street side of the Walter Soboleff Building, Juneau's regional Alaska Native arts and cultural center, this shop and gallery sells work by Northwest Coast and Alaska Native artists from Seattle to Yakutat and farther north. Here you'll find a wide range of items, from moderately priced earrings and T-shirts to high-end, one-of-a-kind art pieces. ✉ *105 Front St., Juneau* ☎ *907/463–4844* 🌐 *www.sealaskaheritage.org.*

GIFTS

Wm. Spear Design

OTHER ACCESSORIES | Lawyer-turned-artist Bill Spear produces fun and colorful enameled pins and zipper pulls. His quirky shop has something for everyone. ✉ *230 Seward St., Juneau* ☎ *907/586–2209* 🌐 *www.wmspear.com.*

SEAFOOD

Taku Store

FOOD | At the south end of town near the cruise-ship docks and Mt. Roberts Tramway, Taku Store processes nearly 6 million pounds of fish a year, mostly salmon. The smoked sockeye fillets make excellent gifts. You can view the smoking procedure through large windows, and then purchase the packaged fish in the deli-style gift shop or have some shipped back home. ✉ *550 S. Franklin St., Juneau* ☎ *907/463–3474, 800/582–5122* 🌐 *www.takustore.com.*

Juneau's Nearby Villages

Though Juneau has a vibrant and active Native community, a visit to one of the surrounding villages can be a great way to increase your understanding of Southeast's Indigenous cultures. Life is slower here than in Juneau, people are generally friendlier, and there's less competition for visitors' attention. From Juneau, you can fly or take one of the Alaska Marine Highway's ferries to **Kake, Angoon, Klukwan,** or **Hoonah.** All four are predominantly Tlingit. Kake's attractions include one of the world's tallest totem poles (132 feet), a historic salmon cannery, and the beautiful beaches of Kupreanof Island (*www.visitkake.com*). Angoon, on Admiralty Island, is a popular departure point for kayaking and sportfishing trips. Klukwan (*chilkatindianvillage.org*), located 22 miles outside Haines, is home to the Jilkaat Kwaan Cultural Heritage Center and Bald Eagle Preserve Visitor Center. Hoonah's cannery building has been beautifully restored and serves as part of Huna Totem Corporation's **Icy Strait Point** (*www.icystraitpoint.com*) cruise port. Highlights at Icy Strait Point include one of the world's longest zip lines, Tlingit dance performances, and whale-watching trips to nearby Point Adolphus. Icy Strait Point is only open when cruise ships are in port, so book well in advance whether you're coming via cruise or not.

Independent travelers won't find much organized touring in Kake or Angoon, but you will find hotels (reservations strongly suggested), and guided fishing and natural-history trips can be arranged by asking around.

Hotels

★ **Favorite Bay Lodge**

$$$$ | **B&B/INN** | This high-end sportfishing lodge—often cited among the top three luxury lodges in Alaska—offers guests an opportunity to fish in both the saltwater and freshwater areas of Admiralty Island with local guides. **Pros:** rate includes transportation, meals, activities, and fish processing; pristine wilderness setting; local fishing expertise. **Cons:** pricey; remote location; three-day minimum stay. [$] *Rooms from: $5335* ✉ *917 Killisnoo Rd., Angoon* ☎ *866/788–3344, 907/788–3344* 🌐 *www.favoritebay.com* 🛏 *12 rooms* 🍴 *All-Inclusive.*

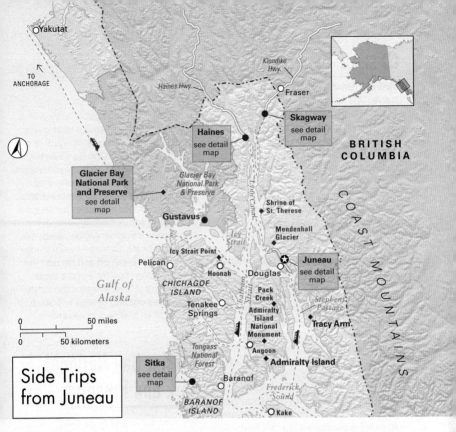

Icy Strait Lodge

$$ | B&B/INN | One of Hoonah's few lodging options, the Icy Strait Lodge is a great base from which to explore this small, friendly Tlingit community. **Pros:** beautiful views; on-site restaurant; boat and car rentals available. **Cons:** can be noisy at night; rooms a bit dated; nighttime activities limited. *$ Rooms from: $140 ⊠ 435 Airport Rd., Hoonah ☎ 907/945–3636 ⊕ www.icystraitlodge.com ⏐⭘⏐ No Meals ⤳ 14 rooms.*

Keex' Kwaan Lodge

$$ | B&B/INN | In Kake, the Keex' Kwaan Lodge offers a serene setting, views of the water, and helpful hosts who can give you inside tips on their community. **Pros:** near the beach and local store; waterfront views; free Wi-Fi and breakfast. **Cons:** basic decor; limited breakfast options; no restaurant on-site. *$ Rooms from: $149 ⊠ 538 Keku Rd., Kake ☎ 907/723–8386 ⊕ www.kakealaska.com ⤳ 12 rooms ⏐⭘⏐ Free Breakfast.*

Admiralty Island

40 miles south of Juneau.

There's only one year-round community—Angoon—on this huge island; the rest is wilderness, home to healthy populations of bears, eagles, deer, birds, salmon, and whales. A visit to Admiralty offers an unparalleled introduction to the nonhuman inhabitants of this area and their unspoiled habitat.

Sights

Admiralty Island

ISLAND | The island is famous for its lush old-growth rain forest and abundant wildlife, including one of the largest concentrations of brown bears anywhere on the planet. The Tlingit name for the island is Kootznoowoo (Xootsnoowú), meaning "Fortress of the Bears." Ninety miles long, with 678 miles of coastline, Admiralty—the second-largest island in Southeast Alaska—is home to an estimated 1,600 bears, almost one per square mile. ⊠ *Admiralty Island, Juneau* ⊕ *www.nps.gov/glba/learn/nature/admiralty-island-province.htm.*

Admiralty Island National Monument

NATURE PRESERVE | The Forest Service's Admiralty Island National Monument has a canoe route that crosses the island via a chain of lakes and trails, and some of the region's best sea kayaking and sportfishing happens here. The area is said to have the world's highest density of nesting bald eagles, and there are large concentrations of humpback whales. Fourteen public-use cabins are available for overnight stays. ⊠ *Admiralty Island, Juneau* ⊕ *www.fs.usda.gov/recmain/tongass/recreation.*

★ Pack Creek

BODY OF WATER | More than 90% of Admiralty Island is preserved within the Kootznoowoo Wilderness. Its chief attraction is Pack Creek, where you can watch brown bears feeding on salmon. One of Alaska's premier bear-viewing sites, Pack Creek is comanaged by the U.S. Forest Service and the Alaska Department of Fish and Game. Permits are required during the main viewing season, from June 1 through September 10. If you're headed to Pack Creek without a guide or an experienced visitor, be sure to cover the basics of bear safety before your trip. Permits for Pack Creek can be processed through *www.recreation.gov.* ⊠ *Admiralty Island, Juneau* ☎ 907/586–8800 ⊕ *www.fs.usda.gov/recarea/tongass/recreation* 🖼 *From $20.*

Tracy Arm

45 miles south of Juneau.

One of the most popular and rewarding day trips out of Juneau is a boat trip to Tracy Arm. The narrow fjord south of the city offers access to two-part Sawyer Glacier. En route the boats pass through twisting passageways between nearly vertical rock walls, dodging vibrant blue icebergs and stopping to let passengers catch glimpses of passing wildlife, including whales, dolphins, eagles, seals, sea lions, and bears. Calving—when pieces of the glacier break off and fall into the water—is common here and a breathtaking thing to see, even for the locals. Companies offering service to Tracy Arm include Allen Marine and Adventure Bound Alaska.

Glacier Bay National Park and Preserve

60 miles northwest of Juneau.

Glacier Bay is a wild, magical place that rewards nature lovers of all persuasions, particularly those who get out on the water—aboard a cruise ship, on a day-boat tour, or in a sea kayak.

Humpback whales breach, spout, and slap their tails against the water. Coastal brown bears feed on sedge, salmon, and berries. Bald eagles soar overhead. The mountains of the Fairweather Range come into and out of view. And then there are the formations that give the bay its name. Indeed, coming here is like stepping back into the Little Ice Age.

Though many of the park's estimated 1,000 glaciers are remote terrestrial or lakewater formations, it's one of the few places in the world where you can approach massive tidewater glaciers. Bergs the size of 10-story office buildings crash from the "snouts" of these glaciers, reverberating like cannon fire, sending water and spray skyward, and propelling mini–tidal waves outward from the point of impact. Johns Hopkins Glacier calves so often and with such volume that large cruise ships can seldom come within 2 miles of its face. Although most of the bay's glaciers are retreating, some—such as Johns Hopkins, despite its calving, and Marjorie—receive enough snow to maintain their size or even grow.

Glacier Bay and the surrounding area is the homeland of the Huna Tlingit. Before the mini–ice age of the 18th century, an outwash plain existed where the bay now resides. The advancing glaciers displaced the Huna Tlingit, and they founded the village of Hoonah on the south side of the Icy Strait. After the glacier's retreat, they remained in Hoonah but continued to hunt and fish in the area. It wasn't until October 1879 that naturalist and writer John Muir, accompanied by several Huna Tlingit paddlers, explored the bay. His eloquent prose helped make it a hot spot for adventurers and sightseers.

Glacier Bay was designated a national monument in 1925 at the urging of scientist William Cooper. He recognized the area's unique opportunities for the study of plant succession after glaciation in real time, and his work continues today. Over time, the size of the protected area increased, and, in 1980, Glacier Bay was made a national park.

Because of all its glacial activity, the bay itself is a still-forming body of water that supports a variety of wildlife and ecosystems, including lush spruce-and-hemlock rain forest. Be on the lookout for the region's rare glacier bears (aka blue bears), a variation of the black bear, which is also found here along with the brown bear. In late spring and early summer, watch for mountain goats. Humpback whales are most abundant from June through early August. In addition, more than 200 species of birds have been spotted in the park, and it's all but guaranteed that you'll see a bald eagle.

GETTING HERE AND AROUND

Although Glacier Bay and the nearby community of Gustavus are technically on the mainland, there is no road connecting them to Juneau. The only way to get to the area is by plane or the ferry system, which does offer car transport.

Flights from Juneau to Gustavus are 30 minutes. Alaska Airlines has daily service in the summer, as do other smaller, light-aircraft companies like Alaska Seaplanes.

As Glacier Bay is best experienced from the water, it's fitting to arrive in the park by sea. Although its schedule can vary and winter service can be sporadic, the Alaska Marine Highway ferry generally sails from Juneau to Gustavus once or twice a week in summer. From there, it's a 10-mile shuttle/car ride to the park.

Although two cruise ships per day are permitted in the park during the summer months, there is no port of call for them either in Glacier Bay or Gustavus. Nor do they anchor in area waters. They simply sail through the region—with passengers enjoying the scenery from the deck—as part of a greater Alaska itinerary that might also pass along the park's outer coast.

For most visitors who aren't traveling aboard a cruise ship, the best way to see the park's shoreline woodlands, its marine life, and its key tidewater glaciers is aboard the day boat. It departs early each morning in the summer season from the Glacier Bay Lodge dock, travels up the bay's West Arm—to Margerie Glacier and, on occasion, John Hopkins—and returns late in the afternoon.

It's a 20-minute drive from the ferry dock or airport in Gustavus—a tiny community at the intersection of the region's two main roads—to Bartlett Cove, home to Glacier Bay Lodge and the park's visitor center and visitor information station.

Glacier Bay Lodge offers its guests free shuttle service, which is generally correlated with the departures and arrivals of flights, ferries, and fishing and whale-watching tours. If there's space, most shuttle drivers will let you ride to and from Gustavus to explore the town or pick up supplies. Many Gustavus B&Bs and other lodges also provide free pickup and drop-off service at the ferry dock and airport.

There are a couple of locally owned taxi services in Gustavus, and drivers are happy to share their knowledge of the area. A run between Bartlett Cove and Gustavus costs around $20 each way.

PARK FEES AND PERMITS
There is no fee to enter Glacier Bay National Park. The Bartlett Cove Campground and backcountry permits are also free.

PARK HOURS
The park is open year round, though most amenities are open only seasonally. The visitor information station (VIS) is open from early May through late September. The tour boats and Glacier Bay Lodge, which is home to the park visitor center, start to ramp up on Memorial Day and cease operations around Labor Day.

TOURS
Gustavus Water Taxi
Local kayak operators often use this company, which specializes in kayak drop-offs and pickups. It also offers private tours, including whale-watching excursions, and custom sightseeing packages, with forays to the outer coast and nearby Inian Islands. No more than six passengers are allowed on the company's vessel, the *Taurus*, and prices start at $300; after that, costs depend on the time and distance involved. ⊠ *1508 Glacier Ave., Juneau* ☎ *907/209–9833* ⊕ *gustavuswatertaxi.com.*

Fairweather Folly

In 1778, Captain Cook gave the name Mt. Fairweather to the magnificent snow-clad mountain towering over the head of the bay, known to the Tlingit as Tsalxhaan. As the story goes, Cook's naming took place on one of Southeast's most beautiful blue days—and the mountain was not seen again during the following century. Overcast, rainy weather is the norm here.

⊙ Sights

Glacier Bay National Park Visitor Center
VISITOR CENTER | FAMILY | Located on the second floor of the lodge, the visitor center has a small theater where the 30-minute film *Beneath the Reflections* showcases park highlights. A few basic and somewhat dated exhibits outside the theater provide details on some of the bay's flora, fauna, and glaciers. A small kiosk sells books on the area, including a couple by local authors. ⊠ *Glacier Bay Lodge, 179 Bartlett Cove Rd., Gustavus* ☎ *907/697–2627* ⊕ *www.nps.gov/glba.*

John Hopkins Glacier
NATURE SIGHT | The inlet to John Hopkins cuts deep into the Fairweather Range, making it another of the lucky few glaciers that have remained stable in recent years. Although it is tidewater, it isn't visited as often as Margerie Glacier because it takes longer to travel down the inlet to it. Further, this inlet is closed to motorized traffic for the first half of the summer as it's a critical habitat for pupping harbor seals. ⊠ *Glacier Bay National Park, Gustavus* ⊹ *Johns Hopkins Inlet, West Arm of upper Glacier Bay, 63 nautical miles northwest of Bartlett Cove.*

Geology In Glacier Bay

Glacier Bay's impressive landscape—much of it the result of plate tectonics—is a geologist's dream come true. The upper bay is still mostly exposed bedrock since the vegetation hasn't had time to grow back since the glacier's retreat. Indeed, several types of bedrock intersect within the park, which also sits directly above a chaotic intersection of fault lines, making it a hot spot for earthquakes.

On September 10, 1899, the area was rocked by a temblor registering 8.4 on the Richter scale. The quake, which had its epicenter in Yakutat Bay, rattled Glacier Bay so much that the entire bay was choked with icebergs. On July 9, 1958, another earthquake—7.9 on the Richter scale—triggered an epic landslide in nearby Lituya Bay: 40 million cubic yards of rock tumbled into the bay, creating a tidal wave that reached 1,720 feet.

Of course, no discussion of Glacier Bay would be complete without touching on isostatic rebound, which sounds more complicated than it is. Imagine pressing your hand down on a sponge and watching it slowly rise when you take your hand off. The same concept applies in Glacier Bay and its environs, with the rate of rebound correlated with how long the land has been out from under the glaciers. In some areas, the land is rising as fast as a human's fingernails grow.

Margerie Glacier

NATURE SIGHT | The final destination for most tour vessels and cruise ships, charismatic Margerie frequently calves large chunks of ice off its 350-foot face. Unlike most of the world's glaciers, Margerie has maintained a relatively stable position over the past several years thanks to high precipitation levels in the Fairweather Mountains where it originates. ⊠ *Glacier Bay National Park, Gustavus* ⊹ *West Arm of upper Glacier Bay, 55 nautical miles northwest of Bartlett Cove.*

Xunaa Shuká Hít (*Huna Tribal House*)

INDIGENOUS SIGHT | **FAMILY** | This 2,500-square-foot, recreated, cedar post-and-plank clan house, dedicated in 2016, is a space for the Huna Tlingit clans—whose ancestral homeland is Glacier Bay—to gather for meetings and ceremonies. It's also a place where visitors can learn about traditional food, art, crafts, dance, and other aspects of Tlingit culture. Xunaa Shuká Hít (*roughly translated as "Huna Ancestor's House"*) was a collaborative project between the National Park Service and the Hoonah Indian Association. ⊠ *Glacier Bay National Park, Gustavus* ⊹ *Just south of Glacier Bay Lodge* ☎ *907/697–2230* ⊕ *www.nps. gov/glba.*

🏃 Activities

National Park Service naturalists come aboard cruise ships to explain the great glaciers and to help spot bears, mountain goats, whales, porpoises, and birds. Several experienced operators can also guide you or set you up to explore on your own.

BOATING AND LOCAL INTEREST

Glacier Bay Day Boat

BOATING | Each day in the summer season, a high-speed, 150-passenger catamaran leaves at 7:30 am (boarding is at 7) from the dock at Bartlett Cove for sails up the West Arm of Glacier Bay to Margerie Glacier. Operated by Glacier Bay Lodge and Tours, the eight-hour excursion is narrated by a park ranger and includes a light lunch. Campers and sea kayakers heading up the bay ride the same boat. ☒ *179 Bartlett Cove Rd., Gustavus* ☎ *888/229–8687* ⊕ *www. visitglacierbay.com.*

CAMPING

The one maintained campground in Glacier Bay National Park has many amenities and is free. Although the National Park Service has considered expanding the Bartlett Cove amenities to include an RV park, at this time there is no dedicated RV parking anywhere in Bartlett Cove or Gustavus.

Backcountry camping requires a permit (free), which you can organize at the dockside Visitor Information Station (VIS). You'll be asked to provide basic information (e.g., the number of people in your party, a description of your tents and other gear) as well as a trip itinerary. The day boat makes two designated backcountry stops to pick up and drop off campers on its daily tour of the bay. Bear in mind that Glacier Bay is a "paddler's park" with no backpacking trails; the best way to experience these wild areas really is by kayak rather than on foot.

Bartlett Cove Campground. Sites are just inside the tree line at this free, well-maintained, tents-only campground, which is about a half mile from the VIS. Securing a tent-site is rarely an issue, so reservations aren't required. Before your first night, you must, however, attend an hour-long orientation at the VIS. Afterward, you can use one of the available wheelbarrows to haul your gear to the campground along a groomed path. Amenities include a firepit and firewood near the shore, a warming hut for drying clothes, and multiple bear-proof food caches. (Wildlife is common in this area, so take proper bear-safety precautions at all times.) For a fee, you can take a hot shower or use the laundry facilities at Glacier Bay Lodge, a 10-minute walk away. *907/697–4000, www.nps.gov/ glba/planyourvisit/campground.htm.*

HIKING
Bartlett Lake Trail

TRAIL | The longest of the Bartlett Cove trails is an offshoot of the Bartlett River Trail. Look for the trailhead about a mile down the river trail on your right. After climbing a moraine, you weave through the woods for approximately 4 miles before reaching the lake. The serenity and the views make the total 12-mile journey—a seven- to eight-hour, out-and-back endeavor—worth the effort. *Moderate–difficult.* ☒ *Glacier Bay National Park, Gustavus* ⊕ *Trailhead: Off Bartlett River Trail* ⊕ *www.nps.gov/glba.*

Bartlett River Trail

TRAIL | This 5-mile, round-trip route borders an intertidal lagoon, runs alongside an old glacial moraine, zigzags through the woods, and spits you out in a designated wilderness area at the Bartlett River estuary. From the trailhead, located a short walk from Glacier Bay Lodge, it's about 2 miles to the river, and although this portion can be muddy and slippery, the park service does maintain it. The stretch that continues along the riverbank for a couple more miles isn't maintained, and segments of it can be difficult to navigate, depending on the tide or recent rainfall. Bear sightings are common here, especially when the salmon are running. *Moderate–difficult.* ☒ *Glacier Bay National Park, Gustavus* ⊕ *Trailhead: East of Glacier Bay Lodge in Bartlett Cove* ⊕ *www.nps.gov/glba.*

Forest Loop Trail

TRAIL | **FAMILY** | Of the handful of trails in the Bartlett Cove area, this is the shortest and easiest. It's a 1-mile round-trip route that starts just across the road from Glacier Bay Lodge and travels through the rain forest and along the beach. Boardwalks make up the first half of the trail, allowing those using wheelchairs to access the two viewing platforms that overlook a pond where moose can sometimes be spotted. *Easy.* ☒ *Glacier Bay National Park, Gustavus* ⊕ *Trailhead:*

Across from Glacier Bay Lodge in Bartlett Cove 🌐 *www.nps.gov/glba.*

SEA KAYAKING

The most adventurous way to explore Glacier Bay is by paddling your own kayak through the bay's icy waters and inlets. But unless you're an expert, you're better off joining a guided tour.

Alaska Mountain Guides

KAYAKING | Take day kayaking trips for whale watching at Point Adolphus, a premier humpback gathering spot, as well as multiday sea-kayaking expeditions next to tidewater glaciers in Glacier Bay National Park with Alaska Mountain Guides. ✉ *Gustavus* ☎ *907/313–4422, 800/766–3396* 🌐 *www.alaskamountainguides.com* 🎫 *Day trips from $460.*

★ Glacier Bay Sea Kayaks

KAYAKING | Kayak rentals and single- and multiday trips with knowledgeable guides can be arranged in Bartlett Cove with this official park concessionaire. You will be given instructions on handling the craft plus camping and routing suggestions for unescorted trips. ✉ *Gustavus* ☎ *907/697–2257* 🌐 *www.glacierbayseakayaks.com* 🎫 *Guided day trips from $95.*

★ Spirit Walker Expeditions

KAYAKING | Spirit Walker's single- and multiday kayak trips (from $399) travel through the Icy Strait region and focus on the marine mammal hotbed at Point Adolphus. Trips to Glacier Bay and other remote areas of Southeastern Alaska, including Fords Terror and West Chichagof, are also offered on a limited basis. ✉ *Gustavus* ☎ *800/529–2537* 🌐 *www.seakayakalaska.com.*

WHALE-WATCHING

The TAZ Whale Watching Tours

WILDLIFE-WATCHING | Step aboard the M/V *TAZ* and check out the Icy Strait and Point Adolphus, near the entrance to Glacier Bay, for awesome views of humpback whales and many other marine mammals. All tours out of Gustavus include binoculars, snacks, and hot beverages. Half-day tours and custom charters accommodating up to 28 passengers are offered, as well as "Weddings with the Whales," where you can get married while surrounded by humpbacks. ✉ *Gustavus* ☎ *907/321–2302, 888/698–2726* 🌐 *www.tazwhalewatching.com* 🎫 *From $123.*

🍴 Restaurants

Fairweather Dining Room

$$ | **AMERICAN** | **FAMILY** | The menu at the restaurant in Glacier Bay Lodge, which serves three meals a day and is open to both nonguests and guests, has a decent selection of sandwiches, salads, burgers, and other American fare as well as pasta, steak, and seafood entrees. Sometimes, the indoor dining room requires reservations, but there's almost always room on the sheltered outdoor deck, which has better views of Bartlett Cove and the Fairweather Mountains. **Known for:** both buffet and à la carte breakfasts; the only restaurant in the park; fresh Alaskan seafood. [$] *Average main: $24* ✉ *Glacier Bay National Park, 179 Bartlett Cove Rd., Glacier Bay Lodge, Gustavus* ☎ *907/697–4000* 🌐 *www.visitglacierbay.com* 🕓 *Closed post–Labor Day weekend until Memorial Day weekend.*

🛏 Hotels

Glacier Bay Lodge

$$$ | **HOTEL** | Built of massive timbers and blending well with the surrounding rain forest, the only accommodation in the national park has rustic rooms (accessible by a boardwalk); a large porch overlooking Glacier Bay; and a roster of activities that includes whale-watching excursions, kayaking trips, guided hikes, and boat tours of the bay. **Pros:** packages include meals, transfers, and boat tour of Glacier Bay; ample hiking trails nearby; good local seafood at restaurant. **Cons:** location is somewhat remote; dining options within the park are all on the property;

Kayaking through Glacier Bay is one of the best and most popular ways to get up-close and personal with the region's glaciers.

dated decor. $ Rooms from: $250
✉ Glacier Bay National Park, 179 Bartlett Cove Rd., Gustavus ☎ 888/229–8687 reservations, 907/697–4000 ⊕ www.visit-glacierbay.com ⏱ Closed post–Labor Day weekend until Memorial Day weekend ⦿ No Meals ⇄ 49 rooms.

Gustavus

50 miles west of Juneau, 75 miles south of Skagway.

For airborne visitors, Gustavus is the gateway to Glacier Bay National Park and Preserve. The long, paved jet airport, built as a refueling strip during World War II, is all the more impressive because of the limited facilities at the field. Gustavus itself is less of a town than a scattering of homes, farmsteads, a craft studio, fishing and guiding charter companies, an art gallery, and other tiny enterprises run by hospitable individualists. Visitors enjoy the unstructured outdoor activities in the area, including beach and trail hiking in the Nature Conservancy's Forelands Preserve.

GETTING HERE AND AROUND
Alaska Airlines serves Gustavus daily in the summer from Juneau. Smaller, light-aircraft companies also serve the community out of Juneau. The Alaska Marine Highway System stops in Gustavus twice a week. Glacier Bay is best experienced from the water, whether from the deck of a cruise ship, on a tour boat, or from the level of a sea kayak.

 Activities

HIKING
The entire Gustavus beachfront was set aside by the Nature Conservancy, enabling visitors to hike the shoreline for miles. The beachfront is part of the Alaska Coastal Wildlife Viewing Trail. The spring and fall bird migrations are exceptional on Gustavus estuaries, including the Dude Creek Critical Habitat Area, which provides a stopover before crossing the ice fields for sandhill cranes. Maps and wildlife-viewing

information are available from the Alaska Division of Wildlife Conservation (*wildlife. alaska.gov*).

Restaurants

Fireweed Gallery Coffee and Tea House

$ | **AMERICAN** | Inside a gallery that features work by local and regional artists, this café at Four Corners offers light fare such as crepes, pastries, and cookies, as well as milkshakes and specialty espresso drinks and teas. The café's drive-up window is groundbreaking for Gustavus (but if you're a visitor, you'll want to go in to see the art and crafts). **Known for:** drive-through option; espresso and sweet treats; local art. $ *Average main: $8* ⊠ *1250 Gustavus Rd., Gustavus* ☎ *907/697–3013* ⊕ *www.fireweedcoffee. com.*

Hotels

Annie Mae Lodge

$$ | **B&B/INN** | This quiet two-story lodge, one of the few Gustavus places open year-round, faces the Good River, has beautiful grounds, and is a five-minute walk from the beach. **Pros:** amazing food with meal plan; good views; some rooms open to wraparound veranda. **Cons:** two of the rooms share a bathroom; property is not on the beach; spotty Internet reception. $ *Rooms from: $200* ⊠ *2 Grandpas Farm Rd.,* ☎ *907/697–2346, 800/478–2346* ⊕ *www.anniemae.com* ☞ *11 rooms* ⦙⦚ *Free Breakfast.*

Bear Track Inn

$$$$ | **B&B/INN** | Built of spruce logs on a 97-acre property facing the Icy Strait, this inn's strengths include an inviting lobby with a central fireplace and moose antler chandeliers and spacious and luxuriously furnished guest rooms. **Pros:** great restaurant; views; rate includes meals and air from Juneau. **Cons:** no room TVs; high room rate; spotty Internet reception. $ *Rooms from: $435* ⊠ *255 Rink Creek Rd., Gustavus* ☎ *907/697–3017* ⊕ *www.*

beartrackinn.com ⊘ *Closed Oct.–Apr.* ⦙⦚ *All-Inclusive* ☞ *14 rooms.*

Glacier Bay Country Inn

$$$ | **ALL-INCLUSIVE** | Choose your own adventure at the Glacier Bay Country Inn, from basic rates (one-night stay plus meals) to extensive (four nights, all meals, a two-day fishing excursion, and a one-day Glacier Bay cruise). **Pros:** gorgeous location; flexible itineraries; highly rated restaurant. **Cons:** not on the water; spotty Wi-Fi; limited on-site activities. $ *Rooms from: $249* ⊠ *35 Tong Rd., Gustavus* ☎ *480/725–3446* ⊕ *www. glacierbayalaska.com* ⊘ *Closed Oct.–Apr.* ⦙⦚ *All-Inclusive* ☞ *5 rooms, 5 cabins.*

Haines

75 miles north of Gustavus, 80 miles northwest of Juneau.

Haines encompasses an area that has been occupied by Tlingit peoples for thousands of years on the collar of the Chilkat Peninsula, a narrow strip of land that divides Chilkat and Chilkoot Inlets. It's hard to imagine a more beautiful setting—a heavily wooded peninsula with magnificent views of Portage Cove and the snowy Coast Range. Unlike most other towns in Southeast Alaska, Haines can be reached by car on the 152-mile Haines Highway, which connects at Haines Junction with the Alaska Highway. It's also accessible by the state ferry and by planes on scheduled service from Juneau. The Haines ferry terminal is 4½ miles northwest of downtown, and the airport is 4 miles west.

Haines is an interesting community, its history the product of equal parts Tlingit homeland, enterprising gold-rush boomtown, and regimented military outpost. A cultural center in Klukwan, a small Tlingit village 20 miles up the road, is a good place to learn about the area's Native roots and ongoing traditions. The region's gold-rush history is evidenced by Jack

Dalton, who in the 1890s maintained a toll route from the settlement of Haines into the Yukon, charging $1 for foot passengers and $2.50 per horse. His Dalton Trail later provided access for miners during the 1897 gold rush to the Klondike.

The town's military roots are visible at Ft. William Henry Seward, at Portage Cove just south of town. For 17 years (1923–39) prior to World War II, the post, renamed Chilkoot Barracks in commemoration of the gold-rush route, was the only military base in the territory. The fort's buildings and grounds are now part of a National Historic Landmark.

Today the Haines community is recognized for its abundance of artists and writers and for the superb fishing, camping, and outdoor recreation to be found at Chilkoot Lake, Portage Cove, Mosquito Lake, and Chilkat State Park on the shores of Chilkat Inlet. Northwest of the city is the Alaska Chilkat Bald Eagle Preserve. Thousands of eagles come here each winter to feed on a late run of chum salmon, making it one of Alaska's premier bird-watching sites.

The downtown area is small, and the town exudes a down-home friendliness. Perhaps this is because Haines sees fewer cruise ships, or maybe it's the grand landscape and ease of access to the mountains and sea. Whatever the cause, visitors should be prepared for a relative lack of souvenir and T-shirt shops compared to other ports. Local weather is drier than in much of Southeast Alaska.

Smoking is banned in all businesses, including bars, restaurants, and shops. Accommodations are allowed to have smoking rooms; be sure to reserve one if needed.

GETTING HERE AND AROUND
Haines is connected to other towns in Southeast Alaska by the Alaska Marine Highway, and from here you can connect with smaller vessels serving Bush communities. The Haines–Skagway Fast Ferry, a catamaran, connects its two namesake cities in 45 minutes, with several trips weekly in summer. Special rates are available for guests who also book a ride on Skagway's White Pass Summit Train. Alaska Fjordlines offers express service to Juneau.

Haines is among Southeast Alaska's few towns accessible by road; be aware that the weather and wildlife in this area present hazards on the highway. Take the Alaska Highway to Haines Junction and then drive southwest on the Haines Highway to the Alaska Panhandle. The town is a delightful place to explore on foot. Alaska Seaplanes serves Haines from Juneau and Skagway.

AIRLINE CONTACTS Alaska Seaplanes.
✉ *Juneau* ☎ *907/789–3331* ⊕ *www. flyalaskaseaplanes.com.*

FERRY CONTACTS Alaska Fjordlines. ✉ *Skagway* ☎ *907/766–3395, 800/320–0146* ⊕ *www.alaskafjordlines.com.***Haines– Skagway Fast Ferry.** ✉ *39 Beach Rd., Haines* ☎ *907/766–2100, 888/766–2103* ⊕ *www.hainesskagwayfastferry.com.*

ESSENTIALS
VISITOR INFORMATION Haines Alaska Convention & Visitors Bureau. ✉ *122 2nd Ave. S, Haines* ☎ *907/766–6418* ⊕ *www. visithaines.com.*

Sights

Alaska Chilkat Bald Eagle Preserve
NATURE PRESERVE | In winter, the section of the preserve between Mile 19 and Mile 21 of the Haines Highway harbors the largest concentration of bald eagles in the world. In November and December, more eagles gather outside Haines than live in the continental United States. Thousands come to feast on the late run of salmon in the clear, ice-free waters of the Chilkat River, which is heated by underground warm springs. ✉ *Haines Hwy., Haines* ☎ *907/766–2292* ⊕ *dnr.alaska.gov/parks/ aspunits/southeast/chilkatbep.htm.*

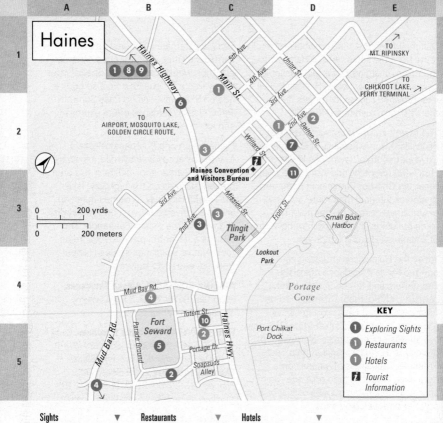

Haines

A **B** **C** **D** **E**

TO MT. RIPINSKY

TO CHILKOOT LAKE, FERRY TERMINAL

Haines Highway

5th Ave.

4th Ave.

Union St.

Main St.

3rd Ave.

2nd Ave.

Detten St.

TO AIRPORT, MOSQUITO LAKE, GOLDEN CIRCLE ROUTE,

Willard St.

Haines Convention and Visitors Bureau

3rd Ave.

2nd Ave.

Mission St.

Front St.

Tlingit Park

Small Boat Harbor

Lookout Park

Portage Cove

Mud Bay Rd.

Mud Bay Rd.

Parade Ground

Fort Seward

Totem St.

Haines Hwy.

Portage Dr.

Soapsuds Alley

Port Chilkat Dock

Port Chilkat Dock

0   200 yrds
0   200 meters

KEY

1 Exploring Sights
1 Restaurants
1 Hotels
🛈 Tourist Information

Sights ▼

1 Alaska Chilkat Bald Eagle Preserve.......... **B1**
2 Alaska Indian Arts...... **B5**
3 American Bald Eagle Foundation................ **C3**
4 Chilkat State Park....... **A5**
5 Ft. William H. Seward National Historic Landmark................ **B5**
6 Haines Highway **B2**
7 Hammer Museum **D2**
8 Jilkaat Kwaan Heritage Center......... **B1**
9 Kroschel Wildlife Center.................... **B1**
10 Port Chilkoot Distillery...**C5**
11 Sheldon Museum and Cultural Center.......... **D3**

Restaurants ▼

1 Bamboo Room **D2**
2 Fireweed Restaurant.... **C5**
3 Mountain Market........ **C2**

Hotels ▼

1 Aspen Suites Hotel Haines **C1**
2 Captain's Choice Motelight **D2**
3 The Cliffhanger **C3**
4 Hotel Halsingland........ **B4**

Walking Around Haines

A stroll through downtown Haines is best started at the **Haines Alaska Convention and Visitors Bureau**, at 2nd and Willard Streets, where you can pick up a walking-tour brochure. To learn a bit about the area's natural and cultural history, head to the **Sheldon Museum and Cultural Center**, on Main Street. From here, you can see the busy docks of Portage Cove, filled with commercial fishing boats and pleasure craft. Head down the hill (turning right on Front Street) to follow the shoreline a quarter mile to Lookout Park, a fine place to take in the view on a sunny day—which, in Haines, occurs more often than you might guess. Just up the hill from here is a small cemetery with graves dating from the 1880s. From the cemetery, steps emerge on Mission Street; follow it to 2nd Avenue, where a left turn will bring you to the **American Bald Eagle Foundation**, a museum and research center for these majestic birds. Another nearly third of a mile out 2nd Avenue is perhaps the most interesting sight in Haines: **Ft. William H. Seward National Historic Landmark**. Nearby is **Alaska Indian Arts**, inside the old fort hospital.

Alaska Indian Arts

INDIGENOUS SIGHT | FAMILY | Dedicated to the preservation and continuation of Alaska Native art, this nonprofit organization occupies what was Ft. Seward's hospital. You can watch artisans doing everything from carving totem poles to creating delicate silver jewelry. ✉ *Ft. Seward, south side of parade ground, Haines* 🕾 *907/766–2160* ⊕ *www.alaskaindianarts.com* 🕮 *Free.*

American Bald Eagle Foundation

OTHER MUSEUM | FAMILY | The main focuses at this natural history museum are bald eagles and associated fauna of the Chilkat Preserve. Lectures, displays, videos, and a taxidermy-heavy diorama help tell their stories, and there's a raptor center that has live presentations and an aviary displaying live eagles. ✉ *113 Haines Hwy., Box 49,* 🕾 *907/766–3094* ⊕ *www.baldeagles.org* 🕮 *$15* 🕙 *Closed weekends.*

Chilkat State Park

STATE/PROVINCIAL PARK | This park on Chilkat Inlet has beautiful and accessible viewing of both the Davidson and Rainbow glaciers. The Seduction Point Trail, about 7 miles one way, takes hikers to the very tip of the peninsula upon which Haines sits. ✉ *Mile 7, Mud Bay Rd., Haines* 🕾 *907/766–2292 Haines Ranger Station, 800/458–3579* ⊕ *dnr.alaska.gov/parks/aspunits/southeast/chilkatsp.htm.*

Ft. William H. Seward National Historic Landmark

MILITARY SIGHT | Stately clapboard homes stand against a mountain backdrop on the sloping parade grounds of Alaska's first U.S. Army post. As you enter you'll soon see the gallant, white-columned former commanding officer's quarters, now part of the Hotel Hälsingland. Circle the parade ground if you like, passing the other homes along Officers Row. On the parade ground's south side at Alaska Indian Arts, you can watch artists at work. The Haines Alaska Convention & Visitors Bureau has a walking-tour brochure of the fort. ✉ *Ft. Seward Dr., Haines* ⊕ *www.nps.gov/places/fort-william-h-seward.htm.*

★ Haines Highway

SCENIC DRIVE | The breathtaking Haines Highway, a National Scenic Byway, starts at Mile 0 in Haines and continues 152 miles to Haines Junction. You don't have to drive the entire length to experience its beauty, as worthwhile stops are all along the route. At about Mile 6 a delightful picnic spot is near the Chilkat River. At Mile 9.5 the view of Cathedral Peaks, part of the Chilkat Range, is magnificent. At Mile 9 begins the Alaska Chilkat Bald Eagle Preserve. In winter the stretch between Mile 19 and Mile 21 harbors the largest concentration of bald eagles in the world. At Mile 33 is a roadside restaurant called, aptly, 33-Mile Roadhouse (*www.33mileroadhouse.com*), where you can fill your tank and coffee mug. Grab a burger and, most important, a piece of pie—do not leave without trying the pie. The United States–Canada border lies at Mile 42; stop at Canadian customs and set your clock ahead one hour. ⊠ *Haines Hwy., Haines* ☎ *907/766–2234 HCVB* ⊕ *www.visithaines.com.*

Haines Sheldon Museum

HISTORY MUSEUM | In the 1880s, Steve Sheldon began assembling Native artifacts, items from historic Ft. Seward, and gold-rush memorabilia, such as Jack Dalton's sawed-off shotgun, and started an exhibit of his finds in 1925. Today his collection is the core of this museum's impressive array of artifacts, including Chilkat blankets, a model of a Tlingit tribal house, and the original lens from the Eldred Rock lighthouse just south of Haines on Lynn Canal. Repatriated Bear Clan items such as an 18th-century carved ceremonial Murrelet hat are also on display. ⊠ *11 Main St., Haines* ☎ *907/766–2366* ⊕ *www.sheldonmuseum.org* ⊠ *$10* ⊗ *Closed Sun.*

Hammer Museum

OTHER MUSEUM | The owner started his impressive collection of 1,800 hammers decades ago and founded the museum—the world's first—in 2001.

Noteworthy specimens include a Roman battle hammer and 6-foot-long posting hammers used to secure advertisements to exterior walls. ⊠ *108 Main St., Haines* ☎ *907/766–2374* ⊕ *www.hammermuseum.org* ⊠ *$5* ⊗ *Closed Sun.*

Jilkaat Kwaan Heritage Center

INDIGENOUS SIGHT | Built near Klukwan, a Native village 23 miles up the road from Haines, this site offers visitors the chance to learn more about Tlingit culture, language, and traditions. Visit the site's Clan House, built using traditional methods; find out about traditional Native art forms, including wood carving and the distinctive Chilkat weavings; see the process for smoking salmon; and much more. ⊠ *32 Chilkat Ave., Klukwan* ☎ *907/767–5485* ⊕ *jilkaatkwaanheritagecenter.org* ⊠ *$15* ⊗ *Closed mid-Sept.–mid-May; Sun.*

Kroschel Wildlife Center

ZOO | A must for animal lovers, this privately run operation 28 miles north of Haines provides an up-close look at Alaskan wildlife, including bears, caribou, moose, wolverines, porcupines, foxes, and wolves. More sanctuary than zoo, the center hosts small group tours, usually booked through cruise lines or other tourist outlets, but with notice may be able to arrange a visit for independent travelers. ⊠ *Mile 1.8 Mosquito Lake Rd., Haines* ☎ *907/766–2050* ⊕ *www.kroschelfilms.com* ⊠ *Rates vary depending on tour; expect to pay about $50.*

Port Chilkoot Distillery

DISTILLERY | Located in Ft. Seward in a renovated old bakery, the Port Chilkoot Distillery offers craft cocktails and samples of its locally made spirits, such as vodka, gin, and bourbon. As in other distilleries around the state, patrons are limited to two drinks on the premises. ⊠ *34 Blacksmith St., Haines* ☎ *907/917–2102* ⊕ *www.portchilkootdistillery.com* ⊗ *Closed Sun. year-round and Tues. Nov.–Apr.*

⚡ Activities

AIR TOURS

Fly Drake

AIR EXCURSIONS | The company offers Glacier Bay flightseeing tours from Haines and Skagway—including a single-passenger tour aboard a Super Cub—and operates an awe-inspiring custom tour of the Outer Coast that takes in mountain and sea. ☎ 907/314–0675 ⊕ www.flydrake. com ✉ From $220.

Mountain Flying Service

AIR EXCURSIONS | A few doors up the street from the visitor center, this company leads flightseeing trips to nearby Glacier Bay National Park in a 1956 rebuilt propeller plane, a DeHavilland Beaver, that seats up to seven passengers. Its Grand Flight package also includes a spin by a few mountains before heading out to the Gulf of Alaska. In late spring and early summer, glacier landings and snowfield takeoffs are offered for an additional $75. ✉ 132 2nd Ave., Haines ☎ 907/766–3007 ⊕ www.mountainflyingservice.com ✉ From $200.

BICYCLING

Sockeye Cycle Company

BIKING | Guided mountain- and road-bike tours along the roads and trails of Haines, including the breathtaking 360-mile Golden Circle route that connects Haines and Skagway via the Yukon Territory, are Sockeye's specialty. The outfit also rents, services, and sells bikes. ✉ 24 Portage St., Haines ☎ 907/766–2869, 877/292–4154 ⊕ www.cyclealaska.com ✉ Rentals from $12.

BOATING AND FISHING

Haines Convention and Visitors Bureau

BOATING | For information on numerous sportfishing charter boats in town, contact the Haines Convention and Visitors Bureau. ✉ 122 2nd Ave. S, Haines ☎ 907/766–6418, 800/458–3579 ⊕ www. visithaines.com/activities.

HIKING

Alaska Mountain Guides

HIKING & WALKING | The very experienced hands at this guide service and rock-climbing school lead hiking and mountaineering excursions from Haines, from half-day trips to 24-day expeditionary courses for hiking, sea kayaking, fly-fishing, ice climbing, rock climbing, skiing, and mountaineering. Sea-kayak rentals are also available. ✉ 170 Sawmill Rd., Haines ☎ 907/313–4422, 800/766–3396 ⊕ www.alaskamountainguides.com ✉ From $86.

Battery Point Trail

HIKING & WALKING | A fairly level path that hugs the shoreline for 1.2 miles, Battery Point provides fine views across Lynn Canal. The trail begins a mile east of town, and a campsite can be found at Kelgaya Point near the end. For other hikes, pick up a copy of "Haines Is for Hikers" at the Haines Alaska Convention & Visitors Bureau. ✉ Beach Rd., east end, Haines ⊕ www.seatrails.org/com_haines/trl-battery.htm.

NATURE AND WILDLIFE VIEWING

Alaska Fjordlines

WILDLIFE-WATCHING | The company operates a high-speed catamaran from Skagway and Haines to Juneau and back throughout the summer, stopping along the way to watch sea lions, humpbacks, and other marine mammals. One-way service is also available. ✉ Skagway small-boat harbor, Skagway ☎ 907/766–3395, 800/320–0146 ⊕ www. alaskafjordlines.com ✉ $179 round-trip, $135 one-way.

Alaska Nature Tours

WILDLIFE-WATCHING | This company conducts bird-watching and natural-history tours through the Alaska Chilkat Bald Eagle Preserve, operates brown bear–watching excursions in July and August, and leads hiking treks in summer. ✉ 109 2nd Ave., Haines ☎ 907/766–2876 ⊕ www.alaskanaturetours.net ✉ From $65.

Chilkat River Adventures
WILDLIFE-WATCHING | The flat-bottom jet-boat tours offered by Chilkat River Adventures are a great way to experience the bald eagle preserve in the majestic Chilkat River Valley. ✉ *Haines* ☎ *800/478–9827, 907/766–2050* 🌐 *www.jetboatalaska.com* 🎫 *From $155.*

🍴 Restaurants

Bamboo Room
$ | **AMERICAN** | Pop culture meets greasy spoon in this unassuming coffee shop with red-vinyl booths that has been in the same family for more than 50 years. The menu doesn't cater to light appetites—it includes sandwiches, burgers, fried chicken, chili, and halibut fish-and-chips—but the place really is at its best for an all-American breakfast (available until 2 pm). **Known for:** retro, relaxed atmosphere; diner-style breakfast; great burgers. [$] *Average main: $12* ✉ *11 2nd Ave., near Main St., Haines* ☎ *907/766–2800* 🌐 *www.bamboopioneer.net.*

Fireweed Restaurant
$$ | **AMERICAN** | A local favorite, the Fireweed serves unusual pizza, pasta, and fish dishes you can wash down with beer on tap from the Haines Brewing Company. The casual restaurant is so popular that you may have to wait a bit for your food—a perfect opportunity to try the Spruce Tip Ale and gaze out at the water. **Known for:** local beer on tap; historic Ft. Seward building; seafood specials. [$] *Average main: $18* ✉ *Bldg. No. 37, Blacksmith Rd., Haines* ☎ *907/766–3838* 🌐 *www.fireweed-restaurant.com* 💳 *No credit cards* 🕒 *Closed Sun. and Mon. Oct.–Mar.*

Mountain Market
$ | **AMERICAN** | Meet the locals over espresso, brewed from fresh-roasted beans, and a fresh-baked pastry at this busy corner natural-foods store, deli, café, wine-and-spirits shop, de facto meeting hall, and hitching post. Mountain Market is great for lunchtime sandwiches, wraps, soups, pizza, and salads. **Known for:** one-stop shop; coffee roasted on the premises; pizza beloved by locals. [$] *Average main: $8* ✉ *151 3rd Ave., Haines* ☎ *907/766–3340* 🌐 *www.mountain-market.com.*

🛏 Hotels

Aspen Suites Hotel Haines
$$$ | **HOTEL** | This mid-range, all-suites hotel, which is among the town's more modern properties, offers spacious, comfortable rooms with kitchenettes. **Pros:** kitchenettes in all rooms; large rooms; centrally located. **Cons:** can be noisy; very basic; lacks charm. [$] *Rooms from: $239* ✉ *409 Main St., Haines* ☎ *907/766–2211* 🌐 *www.aspenhotelsak.com/haines* 🍽 *No Meals.*

Captain's Choice Motel
$$ | **HOTEL** | In the summer, overflowing flower boxes surround this Haines motel, where the accommodations are plain and somewhat dated, but most rooms have great views. **Pros:** pet-friendly; beautiful grounds; easy walk to town. **Cons:** amenities are limited; some rooms are dark; dated decor. [$] *Rooms from: $157* ✉ *108 2nd Ave. N, Box 392, Haines* ☎ *907/766–3111, 800/478–2345* 🌐 *www.capchoice.com* 🍽 *Free Breakfast* 🔑 *40 rooms.*

The Cliffhanger
$$$ | **B&B/INN** | On the outskirts of Haines, straddling Mt. Ripinski, the Cliffhanger makes the most of its spectacular surroundings, providing unrestricted views of the Chilkat Range and Lynn Canal from the wraparound deck and from the giant windows of the two suites. **Pros:** dog-friendly; mountainside views; private setting. **Cons:** somewhat difficult to access; remote location; not good for travelers with young children. [$] *Rooms from: $229* ✉ *Mile 2, Haines Hwy., Haines* ☎ *907/314–0099* 🌐 *www.cliffhangerbnb.com* 🔑 *2 rooms* 🍽 *Free Breakfast.*

Hotel Hälsingland

$$ | HOTEL | On the National Register of Historic Places, this gracious yet somewhat tired hotel housed in former officers' quarters has original claw-foot bathtubs, nonworking fireplaces decorated with Belgian tiles, and charming and nicely maintained rooms. **Pros:** unique and quirky; historic property; rental cars on-site. **Cons:** small rooms; small showers; some rooms share a bath. $ *Rooms from: $129 ⊠ 13 Ft. Seward Dr., Haines* ☎ *907/766–2000, 800/542–6363* ⊕ *www.hotelhalsingland.com* ⊘ *Closed mid-Nov.–Mar.* ❐ *No Meals* ⤳ *35 rooms.*

▼ Nightlife

Fogcutter Bar

BARS | A friendly spot to grab a beer and a snack while checking email—or visiting with the locals—the Fogcutter epitomizes the laid-back, unpretentious vibe for which Alaskans are known. ⊠ *122 Main St., Haines* ☎ *907/766–2555.*

Haines Brewing Company

BARS | This downtown microbrewery sells beer by the sample glass or pint glass and in liter growlers to go. Captain Cook's Spruce Tip Ale is a good choice, best enjoyed on the back deck if the weather complies. Just note that the brewery is cash only. In recent years Haines has become known as a hub for the craft beer movement; in May, the town hosts the Great Alaska Craft Beer & Home Brew Festival, a wildly popular event. ⊠ *4th and Main Sts., Haines* ☎ *907/766–3823* ⊕ *www.hainesbrewing.com.*

▣ Shopping

Wild Iris Gallery

ART GALLERIES | Haines's most charming gallery displays attractive jewelry, prints, and fashion wear created by owner Fred Shields and his daughter Melina. Other local artists are also represented. The gallery is just up from the cruise-ship

dock, and its summer gardens alone are worth the visit. ⊠ *22 Tower Rd., Haines* ☎ *907/766–2300.*

Skagway

14 miles northeast of Haines.

Located at the northern terminus of the Inside Passage, Skagway is a one-hour ferry ride from Haines. By road, however, the distance is 359 miles, as you have to take the Haines Highway up to Haines Junction, Yukon, then take the Alaska Highway 100 miles south to Whitehorse, and then drive a final 100 miles south on the Klondike Highway to Skagway. North-country folk call this sightseeing route the Golden Horseshoe or Golden Circle tour, because it passes a lot of gold-rush country in addition to spectacular lake, forest, and mountain scenery.

On the surface, the town is an amazingly preserved artifact from North America's biggest, most-storied gold rush. Most of the downtown district forms part of the Klondike Gold Rush National Historical Park, a unit of the National Park System dedicated to commemorating and interpreting the frenzied stampede of 1897 that extended to Dawson City in Canada's Yukon.

For locals, however, the town is better known for its community spirit, outdoor opportunities, and abundance of artists and writers. The North Words Writers Symposium, an annual event since 2010, has attracted keynote speakers such as Mary Roach and Susan Orlean. Like other communities in northern Southeast, Skagway is also part of the Tlingit homeland; its name comes from a Tlingit word "Shgagwei," often translated as "rugged or wrinkled up water."

Nearly all the interesting sights are within a few blocks of the cruise-ship and ferry dock, allowing visitors to meander through the town's attractions

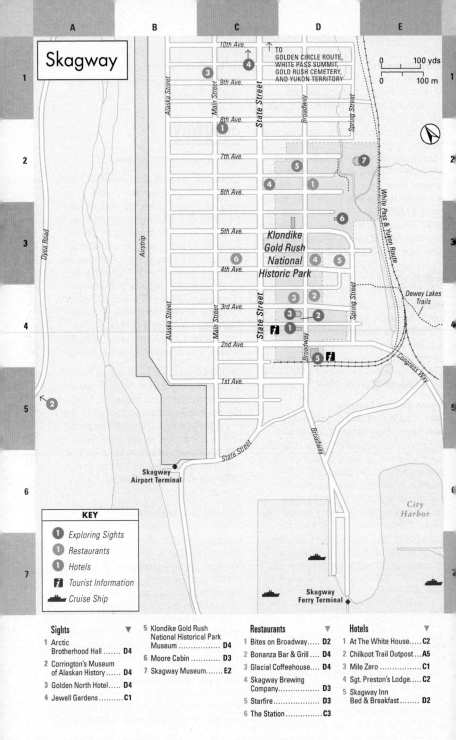

Skagway

10th Ave.

9th Ave.

8th Ave.

7th Ave.

6th Ave.

5th Ave.

4th Ave.

3rd Ave.

2nd Ave.

1st Ave.

Alaska Street

Main Street

State Street

Broadway

Spring Street

TO
GOLDEN CIRCLE ROUTE,
WHITE PASS SUMMIT,
GOLD RUSH CEMETERY,
AND YUKON TERRITORY

White Pass & Yukon Route

Dewey Lakes
Trails

Congress Way

Klondike
Gold Rush
National
Historic Park

Dyea Road

Airstrip

Alaska Street

Main Street

State Street

Broadway

Skagway
Airport Terminal

City
Harbor

Skagway
Ferry Terminal

0   100 yds
0   100 m

KEY

1 *Exploring Sights*

1 *Restaurants*

1 *Hotels*

7 *Tourist Information*

Cruise Ship

Sights ▼

1 Arctic
Brotherhood Hall **D4**

2 Corrington's Museum
of Alaskan History **D4**

3 Golden North Hotel..... **D4**

4 Jewell Gardens **C1**

5 Klondike Gold Rush
National Historical Park
Museum **D4**

6 Moore Cabin **D3**

7 Skagway Museum....... **E2**

Restaurants ▼

1 Bites on Broadway..... **D2**

2 Bonanza Bar & Grill **D4**

3 Glacial Coffeehouse.... **D4**

4 Skagway Brewing
Company................. **D3**

5 Starfire.................. **D3**

6 The Station **C3**

Hotels ▼

1 At The White House..... **C2**

2 Chilkoot Trail Outpost ... **A5**

3 Mile Zero **C1**

4 Sgt. Preston's Lodge..... **C2**

5 Skagway Inn
Bed & Breakfast **D2**

at whatever pace they choose. Unless you're visiting in winter or hiking into the backcountry on the Chilkoot Trail, you aren't likely to find a quiet Alaska experience around Skagway.

GETTING HERE AND AROUND

Skagway offers one of the few opportunities in the region to arrive by car. Take the Alaska Highway to the Canadian Yukon's Whitehorse and then drive on Klondike Highway to the Alaska Panhandle. Southeast Alaska's only railroad, the **White Pass & Yukon Route,** operates several different tours departing from Skagway; Fraser, British Columbia; and on some days, Carcross, Yukon. The tracks follow the historic path over the White Pass summit—a mountain-climbing, cliff-hanging route of as far as 67½ miles each way. Bus connections are available at Fraser to Whitehorse, Yukon. While the route is primarily for visitors, some locals use the service for transportation between Skagway and Whitehorse. The Haines–Skagway Fast Ferry, a passenger catamaran, makes several runs weekly (45 minutes each way) in summer between Skagway and Haines. Special rates are available for guests who book a ride on the White Pass Summit Train. A catamaran to Juneau is operated seasonally by Alaska Fjordlines (3 hours, with a stop in Haines), and the Alaska Marine Highway serves Skagway five days a week in the summer, three in winter. Another alternative is to book an Alaska Seaplanes flight from Juneau (45 minutes); the airport is within walking distance of town.

AIRLINE CONTACTS Alaska Seaplanes. ✉ *Juneau* ☎ *907/789–3331* ⊕ *www. flyalaskaseaplanes.com.*

FERRY CONTACTS Alaska Fjordlines. ✉ *Skagway* ☎ *907/766–3395, 800/320–0146* ⊕ *www.alaskafjordlines.com.***Haines– Skagway Fast Ferry.** ✉ *39 Beach Rd., Haines* ☎ *907/766–2100, 888/766–2103* ⊕ *www.hainesskagwayfastferry.com.*

VISITOR AND TOUR INFORMATION

Klondike Gold Rush National Historical Park. ✉ *Visitor center, 291 Broadway, at 2nd Ave., Skagway* ☎ *907/983–9200* ⊕ *www. nps.gov/klgo.***Skagway Convention & Visitors Bureau.** ✉ *205 Broadway, Skagway* ☎ *907/983–2854, 888/762–1898* ⊕ *www. skagway.com.***White Pass & Yukon Route.** ✉ *201 Second Ave., Skagway* ☎ *907/983– 2217, 800/343–7373* ⊕ *www.wpyr.com.*

 # Sights

Arctic Brotherhood Hall

NOTABLE BUILDING | The local members of the Arctic Brotherhood, a fraternal organization of Alaska and Yukon pioneers, built their hall's (now renovated) false front out of 8,833 pieces of driftwood and flotsam from local beaches. The result: one of the most unusual buildings in all of Alaska. The AB Hall now houses the **Skagway Convention & Visitors Bureau,** along with public restrooms. ✉ *Broadway between 2nd and 3rd Aves., Skagway* ☎ *907/983–2854, 888/762–1898 message only* ⊕ *www.skagway.com.*

Corrington's Museum of Alaskan History

HISTORY MUSEUM | Located in the Golden North Hotel building, this impressive (and free) scrimshaw museum highlights more than 40 exquisitely carved walrus tusks and other exhibits that detail Alaska's history. The museum was founded by Dennis Corrington, a onetime Iditarod Race runner, who passed away in July 2021. ✉ *298 Broadway, Skagway* ☎ *907/983–3939* ⊕ *www.alaskabest-shopping.com* 🖘 *Free.*

Golden North Hotel

HOTEL | Built during the 1898 gold rush, the Golden North Hotel was—until closing in 2002—Alaska's oldest hotel. Despite the closure, the building has been lovingly maintained and still retains its gold rush–era appearance; a golden dome tops the corner cupola. Today the downstairs houses shops. ✉ *3rd Ave. and*

*Broadway, Skagway ⊕ www.nps.gov/
articles/klgo-golden-north.htm.*

Jewell Gardens

GARDEN | This unusual attraction incorporates two of Southeast Alaska's strengths: art and nature. Visitors can take a guided walk through the lush gardens while admiring the glass sculptures on display, and then watch glassblowing in action in the art studio—or even try it themselves under the watchful eye of local artisans. Tea or lunch can also be arranged. ⊠ *Klondike Hwy., just northwest of Alaska St., Skagway* ☎ *907/983–2111* ⊕ *www.jewellgardens.com.*

Klondike Gold Rush National Historical Park Museum

HISTORY MUSEUM | Housed in the former White Pass & Yukon Route Depot, this wonderful museum contains exhibits, photos, and artifacts from the White Pass and Chilkoot Trails. It's a must-see for anyone planning on taking a White Pass train ride, driving the nearby Klondike Highway, or hiking the Chilkoot Trail. Films, ranger talks, and walking tours are offered. ⊠ *2nd Ave., south of Broadway, Skagway* ☎ *907/983–2921, 907/983–9224* ⊕ *www.nps.gov/klgo* ☑ *Free.*

Moore Cabin

NOTABLE BUILDING | Built in 1887 by Captain William Moore and his son Ben Moore, the tiny cabin was the first structure erected in Skagway. An early homesteader, Captain Moore prospered from the flood of miners, constructing a dock, warehouse, and sawmill to supply them, and selling land for other ventures. Next door, the larger **Moore House** (1897–98) contains interesting exhibits on the Moore family. Both structures are maintained by the Park Service, and the main house is open daily in summer. ⊠ *5th Ave. between Broadway and Spring St., Skagway* ☎ *907/983–2921* ⊕ *www.nps.gov/klgo.*

Skagway Museum

HISTORY MUSEUM | This nicely designed museum—also known as the Trail of '98 Museum—occupies the ground floor of the beautiful building that also houses Skagway City Hall. Inside, you'll find a 19th-century Tlingit canoe (one of only two like it on the West Coast), historic photos, a red-and-black sleigh, and other gold rush–era artifacts, along with a healthy collection of contemporary local art and post–gold-rush history exhibits. ⊠ *7th Ave. and Spring St., Skagway* ☎ *907/983–2420* ☑ *$5.*

 Activities

BIKING

Sockeye Cycle Company

BIKING | Based in Haines, Sockeye also does business in Skagway during summer. The company specializes in guided bike tours, including a train–bike ride combo, and from May through September rents bikes. ⊠ *381 5th Ave., Skagway* ☎ *907/983–2851* ⊕ *www.cyclealaska.com* ☑ *From $12.*

BOATING

Alaska Fjordlines

BOATING | Passengers board a high-speed catamaran at 8 am and stop along the way to watch sea lions, humpbacks, and other marine mammals on this popular day tour from Skagway and Haines to Juneau and back. The boat gets to Juneau at 11 am, where a bus transports visitors into town and to Mendenhall Glacier, returning to the boat at 4:30 pm for the ride back to Skagway, where the boat docks back at 8 pm. Call or check their website for the schedule—up to six trips a week in the summer is common. ⊠ *Skagway* ☎ *907/766–3395, 800/320–0146* ⊕ *www.alaskafjordlines.com* ☑ *$179 round-trip; $135 one-way.*

Continued on page 178

THE KLONDIKE GOLD RUSH

At the end of the 19th Century, scoundrels and starry-eyed gold seekers alike made their way from Alaska's Inside Passage to Canada's Yukon Territory, with high hopes for heavy returns.

"There are strange things done in the midnight sun
By the men who moil for gold. . . ."
—Robert Service, "The Cremation of Sam McGee"

Miners have moiled for gold in the Yukon for many centuries, but the Klondike Gold Rush was a particularly strange and intense period of history. Within a decade, the towns of Skagway, Dyea, and Dawson City appeared out of nowhere, mushroomed to accommodate tens of thousands of people, and just about disappeared again. At the peak of the rush, Dawson City was the largest metropolis north of San Francisco. Although only a few people found enough gold even to pay for their trip, the rush left an indelible mark on the nation's imagination.

A 1898 engraving shows a typical gold miner camp in the Klondike

A GREAT STAMPEDE

Historians squabble over who first saw the glint of Yukon gold. All agree that it was a member of a family including "Skookum" Jim Mason (of the Tagish tribe), Kate and George Carmack, and Dawson Charlie, who were prospecting off the Klondike River in 1896. Over the following months, word spread and claims were quickly staked. When the first boatload of gold reached Seattle in July 1897, gold fever ignited with the *Seattle Post-Intelligencer's* headline: "GOLD! GOLD! GOLD! Sixty-Eight Rich Men On the Steamer Portland." Within six months, 100,000 people had arrived in Southeast Alaska, intent upon making their way to the untold riches.

Skagway had only a single cabin standing when the gold rush began. Three months after the first boat landed, 20,000 people swarmed its raucous hotels, saloons, gambling houses, and dance halls. By spring 1898, the town was labeled "little better than a hell on earth." When gold was discovered in Nome the next year and in Fairbanks in the early 1900s, Skagway's population dwindled to 700 souls.

(above) Buildings in Skagway today still reflect what life was like during the Gold Rush

A GRITTY REALITY

To reach the mining hub of Dawson City, prospectors had to choose between two risky routes from the Inside Passage. From Dyea, the Chilkoot Trail was steep and bitterly cold. The longer, bandit-ridden White Pass Trail from Skagway killed so many pack animals that it earned the nickname Dead Horse Trail. After the mountains, there were still over 500 miles to travel. For those who arrived, dreams were quickly washed away, as most promising claims had already been staked by the Klondike Kings. Many ended up working as laborers. The disappointment was unbearable.

KLONDIKE KATE

The gold rush was profitable for clever entrepreneurs. Stragglers, outfitters, and outlaws took advantage of every opportunity to make a buck. Klondike Kate, a brothel keeper and dance-hall gal, had an elaborate song-and-dance routine that involved 200 yards of bright red chiffon.

TWO ENEMIES DIE IN A SKAGWAY SHOWDOWN

CON ARTIST "SOAPY" SMITH

Claim to Fame: Skagway's best-known gold-rush criminal, Soapy was the de facto leader of the town's loosely organized network of criminals and spies.

Cold-Hearted Snake: Euphemistically referred to as "colorful," he ruthlessly capitalized on the naïveté of prospectors.

Famous Scheme: Soapy charged homesick miners $5 to wire a message home in his counterfeit Telegraph Office (the wires ended in a tangled pile behind a shed).

Shot Through the Heart: In 1898, just days after he served as grand marshal of Skagway's 4th of July parade, Soapy barged in on a meeting set up by his rival, Frank Reid. There was a scuffle, and they shot each other.

Famous Last Words: When he saw Reid draw his gun, Soapy shouted, "My God, don't shoot!"

R.I.P.: Soapy's tombstone was continually stolen by vandals and souvenir seekers; today's grave marker is a simple wooden plank in Skagway's Gold Rush Cemetery.

GOOD GUY FRANK REID

Claim to Fame: Skagway surveyor and all-around good fellow, Frank Reid was known for defending the town against bad guys.

The Grid Man: A civil engineer, Reid helped to make Skagway's streets wide and gridlike.

Thorn in My Side: Reid set up a secret vigilante meeting to discuss one very thorny topic: Soapy Smith.

In Skagway's Honor: Reid killed Soapy during the shootout on the city docks, breaking up Soapy's gang and freeing the town from its grip.

Dyin' Tryin': Reid's heroics cost him his life—he died some days later from the injuries he sustained.

R.I.P.: The town built a substantial monument in Reid's memory in the Gold Rush Cemetery, which you can visit to this day; the inscription reads: "He gave his life for the honor of Skagway."

(above) Soapy Smith (front), so named for his first con, which involved selling "lucky soap," stands with five friends at his infamous saloon.

FOLLOWING THE GOLD TRAIL TODAY

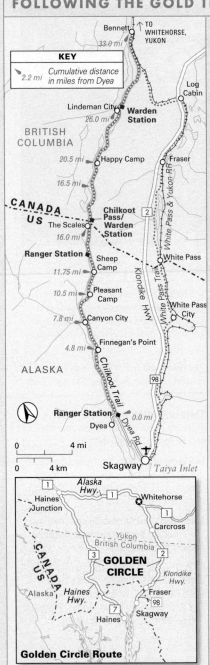

KEY

2.2 mi — Cumulative distance in miles from Dyea

THE HISTORIC CHILKOOT TRAIL

If you're an experienced backpacker, consider hiking the highly scenic Chilkoot Trail, the 33-mile route of the 1897–98 prospectors from Skagway into Canada. Most hikers will need four to five days. The trail is generally in good condition, with primitive campsites strategically located along the way. Expect steep slopes and wet weather, along with exhilarating vistas at the summit. Deep snow often covers the pass until late summer. The trail stretches from Dyea (just outside of Skagway) to Lake Bennett. The National Park Service maintains the American side of the pass as part of **Klondike Gold Rush National Historical Park;** the Canadian side is part of the **Chilkoot Trail National Historic Site**. A backcountry permit is required.

■**TIP**→ **To return to Skagway, hikers usually catch the White Pass & Yukon Route train from Lake Bennett. The fare is $97. For more information, visit www.wpyr.com/chilkoottrail.html.**

For more details, including backcountry permits (C$61.30), contact the summer-only **Chilkoot Trail Center** ☎ 907/983–9234 ⊕ www.nps.gov/klgo. Or you can call Parks Canada ☎ 800/661–0486 ⊕ www.pc.gc.ca/chilkoot.

GOLDEN DRIVES

The Golden Circle Route starts in Skagway on the Klondike Highway, then travels to Whitehorse. The route continues to Haines Junction, and then south to Haines. On the much longer Klondike Loop, you'll take Klondike Highway past Whitehorse, all the way to Dawson City, where the Klondike Highway meets the Alaska Highway. From start to finish, this segment covers 435 miles. From there, you can continue west and then south on the Alaska Highway, past Kluane National Park, and back down to Haines, a total distance of 890 miles. If you're

(top left) Trekking the Chilkoot Trail (right) White Pass & Yukon Route (bottom left) A bridge on Chilkoot Trail

taking the Klondike Highway north from Skagway, you must stop at Canadian customs, Mile 22. If you're traveling south to Skagway, check in at U.S. Customs, Mile 6.

WHITE PASS & YUKON ROUTE

You can travel the gold-rush route aboard the historic White Pass & Yukon Route (WP & YR) narrow-gauge railroad. The diesel locomotives tow vintage-style viewing cars up steep inclines, hugging the walls of precipitous cliffs with views of craggy peaks, forests, and plummeting waterfalls. It's open mid-May to late September only, and reservations are highly recommended.

■ TIP→ Most of the commentary is during the first half of the trip and relates to sights out of the left side of the train, so sit on this side. A "seat exchange" at the summit allows all guests a canyonside view.

Several options are available, including a fully narrated 3-hour round-trip excursion to White Pass summit (fare: $125). Sights along the way include Bridal Veil Falls, Inspiration Point, and Dead Horse Gulch. Through service to Whitehorse, Yukon (4 hours), is offered daily as well—in the form of a train trip to Fraser, where bus connections are possible on to Whitehorse (entire one-way fare to Whitehorse: $129). Also offered are the Chilkoot Trail hikers' service and a 4-hour roundtrip to Fraser Meadows on Thursday and Monday (fare: $159).

Call ahead or check online for details and schedules. ☎ 907/983–2217 or 800/343–7373 ⊕ www.wpyr.com.

Walking Around Skagway

Skagway's rowdy history is memorialized at the corner of 1st Avenue and Main Street, where a marker notes the infamous 1898 gun battle between Soapy Smith and Frank Reid. From the marker, head two blocks east along 1st Avenue and turn left on Broadway into the heart of the town. Inside the old White Pass & Yukon Railroad Depot at 2nd Avenue and Broadway, you'll find the **Klondike Gold Rush National Historical Park Museum**, one of Southeast's best museums.

The next block north on Broadway—the heart of historical Skagway—contains several of the town's best-known buildings. The two-centuries-old **Red Onion Saloon** remains a favorite place to imbibe under the watchful eyes of "working girl" mannequins. Next door is the **Arctic Brotherhood Hall**, the facade of which is constructed entirely of driftwood. Inside, you'll find the helpful **Skagway Convention & Visitors Bureau**, which is full of friendly faces and useful local information. The golden dome of the **Golden North Hotel**, built in 1898, sits across the street from the old Mascot Saloon.

Inside the Golden North Building, you'll find **Corrington's Museum of Alaskan History**, with its large collection of scrimshaw (carved ivory) art. Continue up Broadway and make a right turn on 5th Avenue to find the Park Service's **Moore Cabin**, Skagway's oldest structure. The beautifully restored Skagway City Hall is housed in the same granite-front building as the **Skagway Museum.** Return to Broadway and follow it to 6th Avenue, where you can see *The Days of '98 with Soapy Smith* show inside historic Eagles Hall.

If you are up for a longer walk, continue 2 miles out of town along Alaska Street to the Gold Rush Cemetery, where you'll find the graves of combatants Soapy Smith and Frank Reid. The cemetery is also the trailhead for the short walk to Lower Reid Falls, an enjoyable jaunt through the valley's lush forest. (A city bus takes you most of the way to the cemetery for $2 each direction.) No tour of Skagway is complete without a train ride on the famed **White Pass & Yukon Route.** Trains depart from the corner of 2nd Street and Broadway several times a day in summer.

The six blocks that compose the heart of downtown Skagway can be explored in a half hour, but budget two hours to see the Park Service's historic buildings and the Skagway Museum. (If you include the 4-mile round-trip walk to the Gold Rush Cemetery, plan on three to four hours.) Leave some time to explore Skagway's many shops and restaurants.

BUS TOURS

Skagway Street Car Company

BUS TOURS | Revisit the gold-rush days in modern restorations of the bright yellow 1920s sightseeing buses with Skagway Street Car Company. Costumed conductors lead these popular 90-minute tours, but advance reservations are recommended for independent travelers, since most seats are sold aboard cruise ships. Call a week ahead in peak season to reserve a space. ⊠ *270 2nd Ave., Skagway* ☎ *907/983–2908* ⊕ *skagway-streetcar.com.*

Dyea

Seven and a half miles outside Skagway, the town of Dyea was once a busy hub for miners-to-be preparing to head up the Chilkoot Trail. Prior to that, it was the staging area for a major Tlingit trade route (the name Dyea comes from the Tlingit word "*dayéi," meaning "to pack*"). Today, it's the starting place for hikers braving the 33-mile Chilkoot Trail. A few people still live in the area, but for the most part, Dyea functions as both a fascinating historic site and a stunning place of beauty. Dyea is part of Klondike Gold Rush National Historical Park, and the National Park Service offers tours of the area. Or, for those who really want to experience Dyea's quiet, consider camping here.

OUTDOOR ADVENTURES

★ Alaska Excursions

ADVENTURE TOURS | Booking independently with Alaska Excursions, which leads wheeled (no snow) sled-dog tours, horseback-riding tours, and zip-line adventures, can be difficult, as cruise-ship groups reserve the bulk of available slots. Plan well ahead to join these tours. ✉ *5th Ave., Skagway* ☎ *907/983–4444* 🌐 *www.alaskaexcursions.com* 🎟 *From $169.*

★ Beyond Skagway Tours

ADVENTURE TOURS | This family-operated tour company's customizable private tours include trips to Dyea, gold panning in Emerald Lake, a visit to a dog-mushing camp, and train rides over White Pass. Passports are required for some tours. ✉ *703 Alaska St., Skagway* ☎ *907/612–0499* 🌐 *www.beyondskagwaytours.com.*

Packer Expeditions

HIKING & WALKING | This company offers guided hikes on wilderness trails not accessible by road. One trip includes a helicopter flight, a 2-mile hike toward Laughton Glacier, and a one-hour ride back to town on the White Pass Railroad. A longer hike on the same trail uses the train for access in both directions and includes time hiking on the glacier. They also guide kayaking trips on Lake Bernard, part of the waterways utilized by the gold stampeders in the 1890s. ✉ *4th Ave. and State St., Skagway* ☎ *907/983–3005* 🌐 *www.packerexpeditions.com* 🎟 *From $205.*

Temsco Helicopters

ADVENTURE TOURS | This company flies passengers to Denver Glacier for an hour of learning about mushing and riding on a dogsled. Guided tours of other area glaciers are also conducted. ✉ *901 Terminal Way, Skagway* ☎ *907/983–2900, 866/683–2900* 🌐 *www.temscoair.com* 🎟 *From $339.*

🍴 Restaurants

Bites on Broadway

$ | **BAKERY** | A 10-minute walk from the cruise-ship docks, this friendly eatery is a good stop for a cheese biscuit and coffee in the morning or soup and a sandwich in the afternoon. You'll also find sweet treats such as muffins, tortes, and cakes. **Known for:** good espresso; breakfast sandwiches; cheese biscuits. [$] *Average main: $7* ✉ *648 Broadway Ave., Skagway* ☎ *907/983–2166* 🌐 *www.bitesonbroadway.com.*

Bonanza Bar & Grill

$$ | **AMERICAN** | Expect a lively crowd at the Bonanza, and possibly live music or bingo if you're here in the evening. The pub serves well-prepared American food with no surprises; if you're a sports fan, this is a good place to watch a game. **Known for:** upbeat atmosphere; seafood chowder; halibut and chips. [$] *Average main: $15* ✉ *320 W. Broadway, Skagway* ☎ *907/983–6214.*

Glacial Coffeehouse

$ | **CAFÉ** | A local hang-out, this coffeehouse offers a wide range of breakfast options to accompany your morning joe, and nearly everything on the menu is made on-site. Customers can cool down with a Mango Madness or Blueberry Blues smoothie year round and with soft-serve ice cream in summer. **Known for:** soup and sandwich combo; fresh fruit smoothies; locally sourced ingredients. [$] *Average main: $9* ✉ *336 3rd Ave., Skagway* ☎ *907/983–3223* 🌐 *www.glacialcoffeehouse.com* ⏲ *No dinner.*

Skagway Brewing Company

$$ | **AMERICAN** | Though beer is the primary business of Skagway Brewing, this local pub has a diverse dinner menu that includes burgers, halibut and chips, pasta dishes, hearty salads, and vegetarian options such as falafel. Whatever you order, sampling the locally made ale is a must; Skagway's five staples are Prospector Pale, Chilkoot Trail IPA, Boom Town Brown, Blue Top Porter, and Spruce Tip Blonde Ale. **Known for:** crowded with locals; beer samplers; burger night. [$] *Average main: $17* ✉ *250 4th Ave., Skagway* ☎ *907/983–2739* 🌐 *www.skagwaybrewing.com.*

★ Starfire

$$ | **THAI** | A popular spot with the locals, and known to attract repeat customers from as far away as Juneau, this Thai restaurant fills up very quickly in the summer around dinner hour; it's best to call ahead. One reason for the crowds is the authenticity of the traditional Thai cuisine; Starfire's American chef learned his recipes during visits to Thailand, where he watched local friends and their grandmothers at work in their kitchens. **Known for:** outdoor dining; gang dang red curry; fresh herbs grown on-site. [$] *Average main: $17* ✉ *4th Ave. and Spring St., Skagway* ☎ *907/983–3663* 🌐 *www.starfirealaska.com* ⏲ *Closed winter.*

The Station

$ | **AMERICAN** | Housed in a former gas station, this year-round restaurant is known for its comfort-food specials. The huge calzones are stuffed and served piping hot with sides of house marinara and ranch dressing—build your own or choose one of the chef's creations. **Known for:** friendly local staff; build-your-own calzones; cheesy bread. [$] *Average main: $10* ✉ *444 4th St., Skagway* ☎ *907/983–2200* 🌐 *www.facebook.com/thestationskagway.*

🛏 Hotels

At the White House

$$ | **B&B/INN** | Built in 1902 by Lee Guthrie, a gambler and owner of one of the town's most profitable gold-rush saloons, the white-clapboard two-story inn—about two blocks from downtown Skagway—is furnished with original Skagway antiques and handcrafted quilts. **Pros:** antique furnishings; one room is wheelchair accessible; conveniently located. **Cons:** no breakfast; no shuttle service; most rooms require climbing stairs. [$] *Rooms from: $169* ✉ *475 8th Ave., Skagway* ☎ *907/983–9000* 🌐 *www.atthewhitehouse.com* 🛏 *10 rooms* 🍴 *No Meals.*

Chilkoot Trail Outpost

$$ | **B&B/INN** | A great choice for visitors planning to make the famous 33-mile Chilkoot Trail hike, this lodging is a half mile from the trailhead and offers special packages for hikers that include pre- and posttrail lodging, train transportation from the trail's end at Lake Bennett, and several meals. **Pros:** friendly hosts; quiet setting; flexible cabin layouts. **Cons:** few amenities; 7 miles from town; unreliable Internet. [$] *Rooms from: $165* ✉ *Dyea Rd., 7 miles northwest of Skagway, Skagway* ☎ *907/983–3799* 🌐 *www.chilkoottrailoutpost.com* 🛏 *8 cabins* 🍴 *Free Breakfast.*

Mile Zero

$$ | **B&B/INN** | In a quiet residential area a few blocks from downtown, this comfortable inn has spacious and well-insulated guest rooms, all with private entrances, phones, and baths. **Pros:** close to town; large rooms; communal areas are comfortable and clean. **Cons:** not much of a view; limited room amenities; no kitchen access. [$] *Rooms from: $169* ✉ *901 Main St., Skagway* ☎ *907/983–3045* 🌐 *www.mile-zero.com* 🛏 *7 rooms* 🍴 *No Meals.*

Sgt. Preston's Lodge

$$ | **HOTEL** | A good choice for budget-conscious travelers and hikers, this motel-like lodge occupies a former army barracks where the rooms range from economy doubles to spacious family suites. **Pros:** pets allowed for a small fee; convenient downtown location; accessible room for those with disabilities. **Cons:** some rooms are small; some rooms shaped oddly; basic decor. [$] *Rooms from: $129* ✉ *370 6th Ave., Skagway* ☎ *907/612–0296, 866/983–2521* 🌐 *www.sgtprestonskagway.com* 🍴 *No Meals* 🛏 *20 rooms.*

Skagway Inn Bed & Breakfast

$$ | **B&B/INN** | Each room in this family-friendly downtown Victorian inn (once a not-so-family-friendly bordello) is named after a different gold-rush gal. **Pros:** antique furnishings; large breakfast served; historic atmosphere. **Cons:** walls are thin; floors are creaky; some rooms without private bathrooms. [$] *Rooms from: $226* ✉ *655 Broadway, Skagway* ☎ *907/983–2289, 888/752–4929* 🌐 *www.skagwayinn.com* 🕒 *Closed Oct.–Apr.* 🛏 *10 rooms* 🍴 *Free Breakfast.*

Nightlife

Red Onion Saloon

BARS | Skagway was once host to dozens upon dozens of watering holes in its gold-rush days, but the Red Onion is pretty much the sole survivor. The upstairs was Skagway's first bordello, and you'll find a convivial crowd of Skagway locals and visitors among the scantily clad mannequins who represent the building's former illustrious tenants. A ragtime pianist tickles the keys in the afternoons, and local musicians strut their stuff on Thursday night. Pizza and nachos are available in the bar. The saloon closes up shop for winter. ✉ *201 Broadway, Skagway* ☎ *907/983–2414* 🌐 *www.redonion1898.com.*

Performing Arts

The Days of '98 with Soapy Smith

THEATER | Since 1927 locals and visiting actors have performed a show at Eagles Hall called *The Days of '98 with Soapy Smith.* You'll see cancan dancers (including Molly Fewclothes, Belle Davenport, and Squirrel Tooth Alice), learn a little local history, and watch desperado Soapy Smith being sent to his reward. At the evening show you can enjoy a few warm-up rounds of mock gambling with Soapy's money. Performances of Robert Service poetry start a half hour before showtime. Shows take place from one to four times daily, from mid-May through mid-September. ✉ *590 Broadway, Skagway* ☎ *907/983–2545 mid-May–mid-Sept.* 🌐 *www.thedaysof98show.com.*

🛍 Shopping

Skaguay News Depot & Books

BOOKS | This small but quaint bookstore carries Alaska titles, children's books, magazines, maps, and gifts. Its moniker is a throwback to the town name's former spelling. The owner, Jeff Brady, ran the local newspaper, the *Skagway News,* for more than 30 years. ✉ *208 Broadway, Skagway* ☎ *907/983–3354* ⊕ *www.skagwaybooks.com.*

Taiya River Arts

CRAFTS | A tiny gallery tucked next to the bookstore, Taiya River is operated by a multigenerational family of artists who create one-of-a-kind carvings and jewelry in wood, silver, and other materials. The black-and-white "Made in Skagway" sign in the window here and elsewhere makes it easy to support local artists and businesses. ✉ *252 Broadway, Skagway* ☎ *907/612–0664* ⊕ *www.taiyariverarts.com.*

THE KENAI PENINSULA AND SOUTHCENTRAL ALASKA

Updated by
Teeka Ballas

⊙ Sights	🍴 Restaurants	🛏 Hotels	🛍 Shopping	🍸 Nightlife
★★★★★	★★☆☆☆	★★★☆☆	★★★☆☆	★★☆☆☆

WELCOME TO THE KENAI PENINSULA AND SOUTHCENTRAL ALASKA

TOP REASONS TO GO

★ **Fishing:** In summer, salmon fill the rivers and you can fish on the bank or from your own boat with a guide. Fishing for halibut and rockfish is also possible from charter boats out of most seaside towns.

★ **Animal life :** Urban moose, black and brown bears, sea lions, Dall sheep, gray whales, and bald eagles are all common in the region.

★ **Scenery:** Boasting views of volcanoes and mountains that fall right into the water, the Kenai Peninsula is a buffet for the eyes.

★ **Glaciers:** There are loads of opportunities here to get up close and personal with a glacier: you can ski, dogsled, or hike a glacier's surface, or even paddle out to one.

1 Chugach State Park. One of the largest state parks in the United States.

2 Portage Glacier. A shrinking glacier located at the entrance to the Whittier Tunnel that was once the most visited site in Alaska.

3 Whittier. A former Army base, now a major cruise port.

4 Chugach National Forest. A national forest filled with diverse geography.

5 Valdez. Prince William Sound's largest port.

6 Cordova. The gateway to the Copper River delta.

7 Hope. A gold-mining community with small town charm.

8 Seward. A railroad town and fishing hub in the middle of incredible scenery.

9 Kenai Fjords National Park. A rare opportunity to see glaciers up-close.

10 Cooper Landing. One of Alaska's most popular fishing locations.

11 Kenai National Wildlife Refuge. The best moose habitat in the region.

12 Kenai, Sterling, and Soldotna. Three towns offering fishing and moose sightings.

13 Homer. A unique town that blends art, fishing, dining, and tourism.

14 Kachemak Bay State Park and State Wilderness Park. Alaska's first state park.

15 Seldovia. A small town with a strong Russian heritage.

16 Kodiak. One of the busiest fishing ports in the country.

17 Kodiak National Wildlife Refuge. The bear-viewing capital of Alaska.

18 Lake Clark National Park and Preserve. Home to two volcanoes and a salmon-filled lake.

19 Palmer. The state's major agricultural hub.

20 Wasilla. The heart of Alaska's agriculture industry.

21 Talkeetna. A quirky town that serves as the base for climbing Denali.

22 Denali State Park. The national park's quieter and less crowded sibling.

23 Glennallen. A good base for visiting Wrangell-St. Elias.

24 Wrangell–St. Elias National Park and Preserve. A national park encompassing one of the tallest peaks in North America and plenty of outdoor adventures.

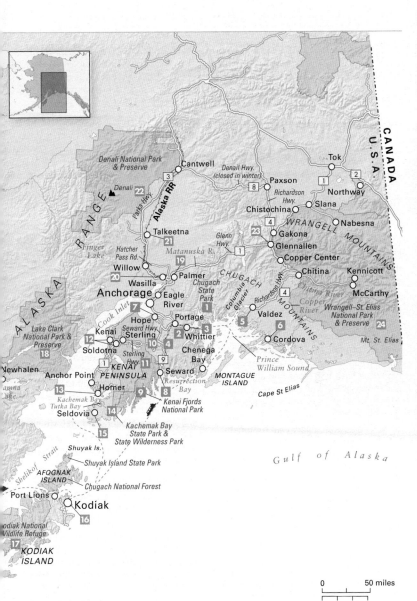

Few places in the United States offer as diverse an array of natural beauty as Southcentral Alaska. From grizzly bears to migrating whales, and moose to spawning salmon, from icy peaks to calving glaciers, and ocean bays to rain forests, there is something to satiate every nature-lover.

The wonders of this area are traversable or viewable by car. Unlike other regions in Alaska, roads connect most towns, villages, and cities here. Most visitors to the Kenai Peninsula and Southcentral tend to begin and end their journey in Anchorage, the region's transportation hub. During summer, planes, trains, buses, and automobiles depart from there on a daily basis. RV rentals are also popular in Anchorage, and recreational vehicles can be seen in droves on the Seward Highway along Cook Inlet. Most highways have two lanes and are paved, but summertime traffic can be frustrating. Be wary of impatient drivers trying to get around slow-moving RVs. Stay aware of wildlife as well. Every year motorists kill hundreds of moose, and in turn there are many driver fatalities.

Southcentral Alaska is bordered on the south and the west by ocean waters: the Gulf of Alaska, Prince William Sound, and Cook Inlet. This region is lined with a smattering of quaint port towns. From the city of Kodiak—a commercial fishing port on Kodiak Island—to Homer, a funky artists' colony, each town has its own personality. Inland, the remnants of mining towns continue to grow and prosper in different ways. Talkeetna, a small village on the region's northern edge

at the base of Denali, is a starting point for many mountaineers. In the center of Southcentral is Alaska's farmland, the Matanuska-Susitna Valley, generally referred to as the "Mat-Su Valley," the "Matsu," or just "the Valley." The region boasts 75-pound cabbages and gigantic award-winning rhubarb.

All of Southcentral is wrapped in the embrace of several mountain ranges. In a crescent shape south and east of Anchorage lies the 300-mile-long Chugach Mountain Range, which bends all the way around the gulf to Valdez, where it meets Wrangell–St. Elias National Park. The Chugach, St. Elias, and Wrangell mountain ranges are so immense that they are often referred to, collectively, as the "mountain kingdom of North America."

The mountain peaks don't end there, however. Across Cook Inlet, easily viewed from Anchorage, is the Alaska Range, which, on clear days, offers impressive views of a distant but looming Denali. The Alaska Range's southwest tip meets the 600-mile Aleutian Range, which spreads out across the Gulf of Alaska atop the Aleutian Islands. These islands are riddled with both dormant and active volcanoes and are part of the Pacific Ocean's great Ring of Fire.

Whether you're hoping to explore mountains or ocean, tundra, taiga, or forest—from the coastal rain forests around Seward and Kodiak to the rough Arctic chill of glaciers flowing off the Harding Icefield—each climate zone and ecosystem is available in this region.

MAJOR REGIONS

Prince William Sound. Tucked into the east side of the Kenai Peninsula, the sound is a peaceful escape from the throngs of people congesting the towns and highways. Enhanced with steep fjords, green enshrouded waterfalls, and calving tidewater glaciers, Prince William Sound is a stunning arena. It has a convoluted coastline, in that it is riddled with islands, which makes it hard to discern just how vast the area is. The sound covers almost 15,000 square miles—more than 12 times the size of Rhode Island—and is home to more than 150 glaciers. The sound is vibrantly alive with all manner of marine life, including salmon, halibut, humpback whales, orcas, sea otters, sea lions, and porpoises. Bald eagles are easily seen soaring above, and often brown and black bears, Sitka black-tailed deer, and gray wolves can be spotted on the shore. On the west side of the sound, Chugach State Park is just outside Anchorage, with access to the once impressive Portage Glacier, while Whittier serves as a major port for the Sound. Chugach National Forest is found east of the sound, along with Valdez and Cordova.

Kenai Peninsula. The Kenai Peninsula, thrusting into the Gulf of Alaska south of Anchorage, is Southcentral's playground, offering salmon and halibut fishing, spectacular scenery, and wildlife viewing. Commercial fishing is important to the area's economy; five species of Pacific salmon run up the aqua-color Kenai River every summer. Campgrounds and trailheads for backwoods hiking are strung along the roads. Along the way you can explore three major federal holdings on the peninsula—the western end of the sprawling Chugach National Forest, Kenai National Wildlife Refuge, and Kenai Fjords National Park. Towns like Hope, Seward, Cooper Landing, Kenai, Sterling, and Soldotna make good bases for your stay.

Homer. Literally the end of the road, Homer is an alluring blend of commercial fishermen, artists, bohemians, and tourists. With bluffs sloping down to Kachemak Bay, it's hard to find a spot in town without a view of the ocean or mountains. Be sure to try the excellent restaurants and sip a locally brewed beer. Nearby Kachemak Bay State Park and State Wilderness Park and the settlement of Seldovia make for good side trips from Homer.

Kodiak Island. The second-largest island in the United States, Kodiak Island is part of a 177-mile-long archipelago. Kodiak City, in the northeastern part of the island, is the way station for supplies to the six neighboring island villages and those visiting the 1.6-million-acre Kodiak National Wildlife Refuge, where tourists hope to spot the enormous Kodiak brown bears. Russian explorers discovered Kodiak Island in 1763, and the city of Kodiak served as the original headquarters of the Russian-American Company, which was managed by Alexander Baranov with the intent of colonization for exploitation of resources. Because it was the original headquarters of the company, Kodiak is often referred to as the "first capital of Russian America." Situated as it is in the northwestern Gulf of Alaska, Kodiak has been subjected to several natural disasters. In 1912 a volcanic eruption on the nearby Alaska Peninsula covered the town site in knee-deep drifts of ash and pumice. The 1964 earthquake and resulting tsunami destroyed the island's large fishing fleet and smashed Kodiak's low-lying downtown area

Mat-Su Valley and Beyond. Giant home-grown vegetables and the headquarters of the best-known dogsled race in the world are among the most prominent attractions of the Matanuska-Susitna (Mat-Su) Valley. The Valley, an hour north of Anchorage by road, draws its name from its two largest rivers, the Matanuska and the Susitna, and is bisected by the Parks and Glenn Highways. Southwest of Anchorage, Lake Clark National Park and Preserve is only accessible via small plane, but is one of the hidden gems of the area. The region has two small but prominent cities, Wasilla (on the Parks Highway) and Palmer (on the Glenn Highway). To the east, the Glenn Highway connects to the Richardson Highway by way of several high mountain passes sandwiched between the Chugach Mountains to the south and the Talkeetnas to the north. The town of Talkeetna serves as the gateway to Denali State Park, while Glennallen is a good base for those visiting Wrangell–St. Elias National Park and Preserve.

Planning

When to Go

Summer is the peak season all over the state. In the Kenai Peninsula and Southcentral this means it is rarely too hot or too cold, particularly along the coast, although rainfall occurs often and without warning. Long daylight hours make it possible to enjoy the beauty and the bounty of Alaska around the clock. If you're hoping to catch more hours of darkness, however, there are always the shoulder seasons. Unfortunately, the weather in spring and fall tends to be more unpredictable than in summer, with random appearances of snow and dramatic drops in temperature. Autumn starts early, with the deciduous trees beginning to show color in mid-August. Visitor services generally close by the end of September.

FESTIVALS

Alaska State Fair

Giant vegetables are big attractions at Palmer's Alaska State Fair. Shop for Alaskan-made gifts and crafts, and whoop it up with midway rides, livestock and 4-H shows, bake-offs, home-preserved produce contests, food, and live music. The fair runs for 12 to 14 days, starting in late August and ending on Labor Day. ⊠ *Mile 40.2, Glenn Hwy., Palmer* ☎ *907/745–4827* ⊕ *www.alaskastatefair.org* 🖃 *$13.*

Copper River Delta Shorebird Festival

The arrival of as many as 5 million birds in the Copper River Delta each May is cause for three to five days of festivities during the first week of the month that include workshops and guided field trips. The birds, mostly western sandpipers and dunlins, feed and rest here on their long migration to their northern nesting grounds. Alaska Airlines often offers discounted fares to festivalgoers—check the chamber website for details. ⊠ *Cordova* ☎ *907/424–7260* ⊕ *www.cordovachamber.com.*

Copper River Salmon Jam!

In mid-July, this small-town festival draws an impressive number of artists, musicians, and athletes for the celebration of salmon (of course!) and the Salmon Runs Marathon. It's a terrific event for the entire family. ⊠ *Cordova* ☎ *907/424–7260* ⊕ *www.salmonjam.org* 🖃 *$30.*

Ice Worm Festival

To shake off the winter blues, the residents of tiny Cordova gather for a weeklong celebration in early February. The festivities include a parade and numerous entertaining activities, including the Ice Worm Variety Show and the Miss Ice Worm Coronation. ⊠ *Cordova* ☎ *907/424–7260* ⊕ *www.icewormfestival.com.*

Kachemak Bay Shorebird Festival

Early-summer visitors to Homer join thousands of migrating shorebirds for the Kachemak Bay Shorebird Festival on the second weekend in May. Experts offer bird-watching trips and photography demonstrations, and the simultaneous Wooden Boat Festival provides a chance to meet some of Alaska's finest boat-builders. Various kids' events add to the fun. ⊠ *Homer* ⊕ *www.kachemakshore-bird.org.*

Mt. Marathon Race

An event held every July 4 since 1915, this race attracts runners and spectators from near and far while the entire town of Seward celebrates. The whole affair takes less than an hour, but the route is arduous: straight up the mountain (3,022 feet) and back down to the center of town. Racers are chosen on a lottery basis; enter before April for a chance, and be sure to book a hotel room well in advance. ⊠ *Seward* ⊕ *mountmarathon.com.*

Salmonfest

Every August, thousands of people from all over the state and country converge on the tiny town of Ninilchik, on the Kenai Peninsula 37 miles outside of Homer, to celebrate music, food, and fish. Over the course of a three-day weekend, countless vendors of art and crafts set up shop while approximately 50 musical acts take to the four stages, drawing awareness and bolstering support for the protection of Bristol Bay waters and fishing habitat. ⊠ *Kenai Peninsula* ☎ *907/435–0525* ⊕ *www.salmonfestalaska.org* 🍽 *$175 for 3-day pass.*

Seward Halibut Tournament

For the whole month of June, locals and visitors set out to catch the largest halibut of the season. There are daily winners and end-of-tournament winners. The current record holder is a 337-pound catch. ⊠ *Seward* ☎ *907/224–8051* ⊕ *halibut.seward.com* 🍽 *$10.*

Seward Music and Arts Festival

The Seward Arts Council hosts this family-friendly indoor festival between the end of September and the first weekend of October. The three-day festival draws some of Alaska's finest musicians. Many art activities take place, and artists and craftspeople sell their works in booths. ⊠ *913 Port Ave., Seward* ⊕ *www.seward-festival.com.*

Seward Silver Salmon Derby

For more than 60 years, anglers from near and far have been gathering every mid-August for the state's oldest and most popular fishing derby. Vying for the largest tagged coho (silver salmon), they can win up to $50,000. ⊠ *Seward* ☎ *907/224–8051* ⊕ *www.seward.com* 🍽 *$10.*

Talkeetna Winterfest

The monthlong celebration known as Winterfest encourages visitors to visit Talkeetna during the very snowy and very cold month of December, offering plenty of activities, events, and live music. Part of this is the tongue-in-cheek Wilderness Woman Contest, where women compete in a variety of events like fishing, sawing wood, and yes, sandwich prep (that's the tongue-in-cheek part, don't worry). Afterward, women are invited to the annual Bachelor Auction & Ball, where they can purchase a dance from any of Talkeetna's eligible bachelors. Proceeds from both events go to funding local domestic violence programs. ⊠ *Talkeetna* ⊕ *www.alaska.org/detail/talkeetna-winterfest.*

Getting Here and Around

BOAT AND FERRY

With its glaciers, mountains, fjords, and sea mammals, the coast is great to experience by ferry. The ferries between Valdez and Whittier run by way of Columbia Glacier in summer, where it is not unusual to witness giant fragments of ice calving from the face of the glacier into Prince William Sound.

The Alaska Marine Highway, the state-run ferry operator, has scheduled service to Valdez, Cordova, Whittier, Homer, and Seldovia on the mainland; to Kodiak and Port Lions on Kodiak Island; and to the port of Dutch Harbor in the Aleutian Islands. These connect to the ferries that operate in Southeast Alaska, but the two systems connect only on once-a-month sailings. Ferries operate on two schedules; summer (May through September) sailings are considerably more frequent than winter (October through April) service. Check your schedules carefully: ferries do not stop at all ports every day. Reservations are required on all routes and should be made as far in advance as possible.

Many major cruise lines also use Whittier as a port of embarkation/disembarkation for cruises through Alaska's Southeastern Peninsula.

CONTACTS Alaska Marine Highway.
☎ 800/642–0066 from outside Alaska, 907/465–3941 ⊕ www.dot.state.ak.us/amhs.

BUS

For bus service in the region, contact Interior Alaska Bus Line, Park Connection Motor Coach, or Seward Bus Line.

CONTACTS Interior Alaska Bus Line. ⊠ Tok ☎ 800/770–6652 ⊕ www.interioralaskabusline.com.**Park Connection Motor Coach.** ⊠ Anchorage ☎ 800/266–8625 ⊕ alaskacoach.com.**Seward Bus Line.** ⊠ Anchorage ☎ 888/420–7788 ⊕ www.sewardbuslines.net.

CAR

Car is definitely the way to go when exploring the Kenai Peninsula and South-central Alaska; the road system is more developed than in other regions, and is mostly paved. It also has some great driving routes that involve putting your car on a ferry. If you're renting, know that not all rental companies will let you do this, so aim to get your ducks in a row about two or three months in advance before the ferry-friendly rental agencies are all booked for your dates.

TRAIN

Anchorage is the region's hub, connected by rail and road to major ports in Southcentral. To the east, you can reach McCarthy and Valdez by an indirect but scenic drive on the Glenn and Richardson Highways. The Seward and Sterling Highways connect to nearly every town on the Kenai Peninsula. The Alaska Railroad Corporation operates the Alaska Railroad, which runs 470 miles between Seward and Fairbanks via Anchorage. There's daily service between Anchorage and Fairbanks in summer, and in winter there's one round-trip per week. Service to Seward from Anchorage runs every weekend from mid-May to September.

CONTACTS Alaska Railroad. ⊠ 327 W Ship Creek Ave., Anchorage ☎ 800/544–0552 ⊕ www.alaskarailroad.com.

Health and Safety

In Southcentral, it's important to stick to basic principles of Alaska safety: hiring a guide for anything outside your comfort zone might just prove to be the most important investment you've ever made. Always follow bear safety rules, and know that moose can be the more common and more dangerous encounter, so use extreme respect and caution.

Money Matters

Nothing is too surprising on the financial front here: try to bring cash if you're traveling to a small town, and even if you've prepaid for a guide's services, remember to bring a little something to tip with at the end of the day or trip. Food, lodging, and sundries are going to be significantly higher in Alaska than the rest of the country, especially the more remote you go—remember, almost everything gets to Alaska via barge or approximately 2,000 miles of highway.

Restaurants

The best way to describe the hospitality industry in Alaska is "informal," and this applies all over the state—even in Anchorage. Don't worry if you still have your hiking clothes on when you go out to eat. Every kind of food is available, especially in larger towns, but options decline considerably from mid-September through April.

Hotels

Accommodations in Alaska, particularly in the sparsely populated areas, can be quite rugged. You will find a lot of establishments have only shared bathrooms, and amenities, such as a coffeepot, television, and Internet access, are scant, although the latter is beginning to find its way even into remote villages. In the most rural of places it is not entirely unheard of to find no bathrooms in the establishment, but rather an outhouse or "honey bucket" out back or in a closet. If such things are important to you, it's wise to inquire in advance.

Restaurant and hotel reviews have been shortened. For full information, visit Fodors.com. Restaurant prices are the average cost of a main course at dinner or, if dinner is not served, at lunch. Hotel prices are the lowest cost of a standard double room in high season.

What It Costs			
$	$$	$$$	$$$$
RESTAURANTS			
under $14	$14–$22	$23–$30	over $30
HOTELS			
under $100	$100–$200	$201–$300	over $300

Chugach State Park

Bordering Anchorage to the east.

One of the largest state parks in the United States, Chugach State Park covers approximately 495,000 acres. Located entirely in Southcentral, it lies mostly within the Municipality of Anchorage—just 7 miles from Downtown.

GETTING HERE AND AROUND

Chugach forms the backdrop of Anchorage, and trailheads are accessible at the top of O'Malley, Huffman, and DeArmoun Roads; south of Anchorage at Potter Valley, McHugh Creek, and Bird Ridge on the Seward Highway; and to the north of town at Arctic Valley Road (6 miles out) and Eagle River Road (13 miles out).

ESSENTIALS

VISITOR INFORMATION Chugach State Park Headquarters. ⊠ *18620 Seward Hwy.,* ☎ *907/345–5014* ⊕ *dnr.alaska.gov/parks/aspunits/chugach/chugachindex.htm.*

Sights

Chugach State Park
STATE/PROVINCIAL PARK | Comprising nearly a half million acres, Chugach State Park is the third-largest state park in the United States. On the edge of Anchorage, the park is Alaska's most accessible wilderness, with nearly 30 trails for hikers of all abilities. Totaling more than 150 miles, the hiking trails range in length from 2 miles to 30 miles. Although Chugach,

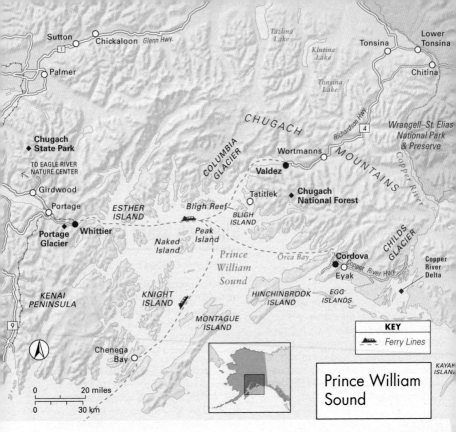

Prince William Sound

KEY
Ferry Lines

connected as it is to Alaska's largest city, is technically an urban park, this is far from being a typical urban setting. Hardly tame, this is real wilderness, home to Dall sheep, mountain goats, brown and black bears, moose, and several packs of wolves. Miners who sought the easiest means of traversing the mountain peaks and passes initially blazed most of the park's trails. Today they are restored every spring and maintained by park rangers and various volunteer groups. Hiking in the park is free whether you're here for an afternoon or a week, though a $5 daily parking fee is charged at several popular trailheads. The park serves up some truly intoxicating views, and, depending on what perch you're looking down from, you can see across the bay to the looming white mountains of the Alaska Range, the great tides of Cook Inlet, and, on clear days, Denali in

all its glory. One of the best and most easily accessible places to seek out such a view is from Flattop Mountain, on the park's western edge. The peak is the most popular destination within Chugach Park. A 1-mile hike leads to the top, and hikers of all abilities make the trek, but be aware it is strenuous, particularly toward the top. ⊕ dnr.alaska.gov/parks/aspunits/chugach/chugachindex.htm ☑ Free; $5 parking fee at some trailheads.

Eagle River Nature Center

VISITOR CENTER | Eagle River Road leads 12 miles into the mountains from the bedroom community of Eagle River. The nature center, at the end of the road, has wildlife displays, telescopes for wildlife spotting, and 9 miles of hiking trails. Volunteers are on hand to answer questions, lead hikes, and host naturalist programs. A cabin that sleeps eight and

a pair of yurts (round insulated tents) that sleep four and six are available to rent ($65 per night). A 1½-mile hike in is required. Amenities include wood stoves, firewood, and outdoor latrines. The center is also the trail end for the Crow Pass Trail, a 26-mile section of the Iditarod National Historic Trail that starts in Girdwood. ⊠ *32750 Eagle River Rd., Eagle River* ☎ *907/694–2108* ⊕ *www. ernc.org* ☒ *Parking $5.*

♿ Activities

The **Little Rodak Trail** is less than 1 mile long and has a viewing platform that overlooks Eagle River Valley. The **Albert Loop Trail** behind the nature center has markers that coordinate with a self-guided hike along its 3-mile route; pick up a brochure at the Eagle River Nature Center.

HIKING

Several trailheads along the edge of Anchorage lead into the park and its 3,000- to 5,000-foot-tall peaks. The park's most popular day climb is **Flattop Mountain,** which towers 3,500 feet above sea level. It's reached via the Glen Alps Trailhead off Upper Huffman Road on Anchorage's Hillside. A 1-mile trail climbs 1,300 feet from the Glen Alps parking area to the top. On a bright summer day you'll encounter plenty of company. Bring along a daypack with plenty of water and energy bars, a rainproof jacket, good hiking boots, and trekking poles.

Every summer solstice, locals climb to the top of Flattop Mountain to celebrate the longest day of the year. If you're in town for this event, it's great fun; there's even an impromptu concert by musicians who lug their instruments to the top of the mountain. Parking spots are at a premium, so arrive early.

MOUNTAIN BIKING

Mountain biking has become very popular in the park, and most, but not all, trails are open to bikes; check the signs and symbols at the trailheads if in doubt. The Powerline Pass trail from the Glen Alps parking lot is wide and well maintained for bikes and offers a great view from the pass, as well as opportunities to spot moose, Dall sheep, bears, and maybe even wolves. Be sure to share the trails when they are multiuse.

Pablo's Bicycle Rentals

BIKING | You can rent mountain and road bikes from Pablo's. ⊠ *415 L St., Anchorage* ☎ *907/272–1600* ⊕ *www.pablobicyclerentals.com.*

Portage Glacier

54 miles southeast of Anchorage.

Until recently Portage Glacier was the most visited site in Alaska. The glacier has receded dramatically in the past decade, and these days it is easier to see where it used to be. The road to the glacier follows Portage Lake, where icebergs calved from the glacier still lazily float, impressing visitors with their aqua blue colors.

GETTING HERE AND AROUND

Accessible by car from Anchorage, Portage Glacier lies within the Chugach National Forest just west of the tunnel to Whittier. In summer, Gray Line of Alaska leads boat tours along the face of Portage Glacier aboard the 200-passenger *Ptarmigan.*

ESSENTIALS

VISITOR AND TOUR INFORMATION
Begich-Boggs Visitor Center. ⊠ *Portage Lake Loop, Girdwood* ☎ *907/783–2326 summer, 907/783–3242 winter* ⊕ *www. fs.usda.gov/detail/chugach.*

Sights

Alaska Wildlife Conservation Center

NATURE PRESERVE | FAMILY | The center is a 144-acre, 2-mile drive-through loop with places where you can see up close the many animals the park has adopted and rescued. For more than a decade the center has been raising wood bison, which had been extinct in Alaska since the 1800s and were endangered in Canada. In 2015, the center reintroduced 100 wood bison to the wild, 340 miles west of Anchorage; a small herd remains at the center. Visitors can see moose, elk, eagles, musk ox, porcupines, and the elusive lynx. An elevated walkway at the center also allows visitors the thrilling experience of seeing bears at eye level. ⊠ *Mile 79, 43640 Seward Hwy., Anchorage* ☎ *907/783–2025* ⊕ *www.alaskawildlife.org* ⧨ *$15*.

Byron Glacier

NATURE SIGHT | The mountains surrounding Portage Glacier are covered with smaller glaciers. A 1-mile hike off Byron Glacier Road—the trail begins about a mile south of Begich-Boggs Visitor Center—leads to the Byron Glacier overlook. The glacier is notable for its accessibility—this is one of the few places where you can hike onto a glacier from the road system. In summer, naturalists lead free weekly treks in search of microscopic ice worms. ⊠ *Byron Glacier Rd., off Portage Glacier Rd.* ⊕ *www.alaska.org/detail/byron-glacier-trail*.

Indian Valley Meats

STORE/MALL | A popular place where for almost 40 years Alaskans have had their game processed, Indian Valley Meats has a shop that sells smoked salmon and reindeer, along with buffalo sausage made on the premises. The folks here will smoke, can, and package any fish you've caught, and they'll arrange for shipping. ⊠ *200 Huot Circle, off Seward Hwy. at Mile 104 (follow Indian Rd. northeast to Poppy La.), Indian* ☎ *907/653–7511* ⊕ *www.indianvalleymeats.com*.

Portage

RUINS | The 1964 earthquake destroyed the town of Portage. The ghost forest of dead spruce in the area was created when the land subsided by 6 to 10 feet after the quake and saltwater penetrated inland from Turnagain Arm, killing the trees. ⊕ *www.alaska.org/guide/portage-valley*.

Portage Glacier

NATURE SIGHT | The glacier is one of Alaska's most frequently visited tourist destinations. A 6-mile side road off the Seward Highway leads to Begich-Boggs Visitor Center on the shore of Portage Lake, named after two U.S. congressmen who disappeared on a small-plane journey out of Anchorage in 1972. The center is staffed by Forest Service personnel, who can help plan your trip and explain the natural history of the area. A film on glaciers is shown hourly, and icebergs sometimes drift down to the center from Portage Glacier. Due to global climate change, Portage, like most of the glaciers in Alaska, has receded from view in recent years. ⊠ *Portage Lake Loop, Girdwood* ⊕ *www.fs.fed.us/r10/chugach*.

Turnagain Arm

BODY OF WATER | Several hiking trails are accessible from the Seward Highway, including the steep paths up Falls Creek and Bird Ridge. Both offer spectacular views of Turnagain Arm, where explorer Captain Cook searched for the Northwest Passage. The arm has impressive tides, and notably, the second-largest bore tide in North America. These bore tides can reach up to 40 feet, and move at an impressive 30 miles per hour (an average tide flows at 10 to 15 miles per hour). An increasingly popular, yet somewhat dangerous, sport is windsurfing the tidal bore. To view the bore tide, station yourself at one of the turnoffs along the arm about 2½ hours after low tide in Anchorage.

During the summer, beluga whales are frequent visitors to the arm as they patrol the muddy waters in search of salmon and hooligan, a variety of smelt. During high tide from July to August, when the surface of the water is calm, belugas are often spotted from the highway, frequently causing traffic jams as tourists and residents pull off the road for a chance to take in this increasingly rare sight. For reasons that are still unclear to scientists, Southcentral's beluga population has declined from 1,300 in 1980 to fewer than 290 today; they are currently listed as critically endangered, making a sighting of them even more exciting.

 ## Activities

COMBINATION TRIPS
★ NOVA
ADVENTURE TOURS | In business since 1975, this company conducts river rafting, glacier hiking, and backcountry combo trips from its office near Matanuska Glacier. ⊠ *38100 Glenn Hwy., Glacier View* ☎ *800/746–5753* ⊕ *www.novalaska. com* ⊠ *From $100.*

PORTAGE GLACIER TOURS
Portage Glacier Cruises
BOATING | The only boat still operating on the lake, the Portage Glacier Cruise takes you just 300 yards from Portage Glacier. Watch for fractures of ice breaking off the glacier and crashing into the water below. ⊠ *1500 Byron Glacier Rd., Girdwood* ☎ *800/544–2206* ⊕ *www. portageglaciercruises.com* ⊠ *$45.*

ROCK AND ICE CLIMBING
Alaska Rock Gym
ROCK CLIMBING | For information about rock- and ice-climbing activities, stop by Alaska Rock Gym. There's a great indoor gym here, and staffers can point you to the routes local climbers have set along the Seward Highway just south of town. ⊠ *665 E. 33rd Ave., Anchorage* ☎ *907/562–7265* ⊕ *www.alaskarockgym. com.*

Whittier

60 miles southeast of Anchorage.

The entryway to Whittier is unlike any other: a 2½-mile drive atop railroad tracks through the Anton Anderson Memorial Tunnel, cut through the Chugach Mountain Range. Once on the other side of the tunnel, you enter the mysterious world of Whittier, the remnants of a military town developed during World War II. The only way to get to Whittier was by boat or train until the tunnel opened to traffic in 2000.

This quaint hamlet, nestled at the base of snow-covered peaks at the head of Passage Canal on the Kenai Peninsula, has an intriguing history. In the 1940s the U.S. Army constructed a port in Whittier and built the Hodge and Buckner Buildings to house soldiers. These enormous monoliths are eerily reminiscent of Soviet-era communal apartment buildings. The Hodge Building (now called Begich Towers) houses almost all of Whittier's 215 year-round residents. The town averages 30 feet of snow in the winter, and in summer gets a considerable amount of rainfall. Whittier's draw is primarily fishing, but there are a number of activities to be had on Prince William Sound, including kayaking and glacier tours with some of the best glacier viewing in Southcentral Alaska.

Whittier is very small, and there is not much to look at in town, but the location is unbeatable. Surrounding peaks cradle alpine glaciers, and when the summer weather melts the huge winter snow load, you can catch glimpses of the brilliant blue ice underneath. Sheer cliffs drop into Passage Canal and provide nesting places for flocks of black-legged kittiwakes, while sea otters and harbor seals cavort in the small-boat harbor and salmon return to spawn in nearby streams. A short boat ride out into the sound reveals tidewater glaciers, and an alert wildlife watcher can catch sight of mountain goats clinging to the rocks and black bears patrolling the beaches and hillsides in their constant search for food.

Many companies' phones in Whittier are disconnected from October through April. If you can't get through to a number with prefix 472, check the company's website for an alternate number.

GETTING HERE AND AROUND

Unless you come in on a cruise ship, ferry, or other boat, your only way in and out of Whittier is through the tunnel. Its access, however, is limited by the railroad schedule, so it's not always possible to breeze in and out of town. For up-to-date tunnel information and schedules, check the tunnel's website.

Tolls are $13 for passenger vehicles and $22 to $38 for RVs and trailers; waits of up to an hour are possible, and summer hours are from 5:30 am until 11 pm. You can also arrive via the Alaska Railroad, with tickets starting at $90.

ESSENTIALS

TUNNEL INFORMATION Anton Anderson Memorial Tunnel. ⊠ *Portage Glacier Rd., Whittier* ☎ *877/611–2586* ⊕ *dot.alaska. gov/creg/whittiertunnel.*

Sights

Portage Pass

TRAIL | Historically a route used by the Chugach Alaska Natives, Russian fur traders, and early settlers, this 1-mile hike (one-way) now offers tremendous views of Portage Glacier. To access the hike, drive through the Anton Anderson Memorial Tunnel to Whittier and take the first right after the railroad tracks, onto a gravel road marked "Forest Access." The trail will be just a short way up from there on the right. There's a 750-foot elevation gain, so bring your hiking poles. ⊠ *Whittier.*

Activities

BOATING AND WILDLIFE VIEWING

Alaska Sea Kayakers

KAYAKING | This outfit supplies sea kayaks and gear for exploring Prince William Sound and conducts guided day trips, multiday tours, instruction, and boat-assisted and boat live-aboard kayaking trips. The company practices a leave-no-trace camping ethos and is very conscientious about avoiding bear problems. All guides are experienced Alaska paddlers, and group sizes are kept small. ⊠ *Whittier* ☎ *907/472–2534* ⊕ *www.alaskaseakayakers.com* ⊠ *Day trips from $89.*

Lazy Otter Charters

BOATING | With three boats and two landing craft, Lazy Otter runs sightseeing trips, operates a water taxi to Forest Service cabins, drops off sea kayakers at scenic points, and has ride-along and share-a-ride programs, a way to see Prince William Sound on a smaller budget. Customized sightseeing trips last from four to nine hours. Day trips include lunch from the Lazy Otter Café. ⊠ *Whittier* ☎ *800/587–6887, 907/694–6887* ⊕ *www.lazyotter.com* ⊠ *Custom sightseeing trips from $255 per person (minimum of four).*

Major Marine Tours

BOATING | Major Marine Tours runs a five-hour cruise from Whittier that visits two tidewater glaciers. The waters of Prince William Sound are well protected and relatively calm, making this a good option if you tend to get seasick. Seabirds, waterfowl, and bald eagles are always present, and the chance to get close to the enormous walls of glacier ice is not to be missed. A number of different cruises are available from mid-March to mid-September, ranging from $95 to $240 per person. ⊠ *Whittier* ☎ *907/224–8030* ⊕ *www.majormarine.com* ⊠ *From $95 per person.*

On many tours in Prince William Sound, you'll spot sea lions sunning themselves on rocks.

★ **26 Glacier Cruise**

BOATING | Phillips Cruises & Tours has been running the 26 Glacier Cruise through Prince William Sound for many years. The high-speed catamaran covers 135 miles of territory in 4½ hours, leaving Whittier and visiting Port Wells, Barry Arm, and College and Harriman Fjords. The boat is a very stable platform, and even visitors prone to seasickness take this cruise with no ill effects. The heated cabin has large windows, upholstered booths, and wide aisles, and a snack bar and a saloon are onboard. Potential wildlife sightings include humpback and orca whales, sea otters, harbor seals, sea lions, bears, mountain goats, and eagles. You can drive to Whittier and catch the boat at the dock, or you can arrange with the company to travel from Anchorage by rail or bus. The tour rate includes a hot lunch of smoked salmon chowder or vegetable chili. ✉ *Cliffside Marina, 100 W. Camp Rd., Whittier* ☎ *907/276–8023* 🌐 *www.phillipscruises.com* 🎟 *$159.*

🍴 Restaurants

China Sea

$$ | CHINESE | This classic Chinese restaurant features local seafood and amazingly fresh vegetables. The grilled halibut is fantastic, and for nonfish lovers, the Mongolian beef and kung pao chicken are excellent choices. **Known for:** fresh fish and vegetables (a rarity in these parts); location right near the ferry terminal; one of the best Chinese restaurants in Southcentral Alaska. [$] *Average main: $15* ✉ *6 Harbor Rd., Whittier* ☎ *907/472–3663* 🕐 *Closed mid-Sept.–late May.*

Lazy Otter Café & Gifts

$$ | CAFÉ | Amid the summer shops and docks, this little café offers warm drinks and soups, sandwiches, and fresh-baked pastries, along with an Alaskan favorite, soft-serve ice cream. The busy shop has only a couple of indoor seats, but there's outdoor seating overlooking the harbor, which is quite pleasant on sunny days. **Known for:** only good coffee in town; excellent seafood chowder and salmon spread; outdoor seating with views of harbor. $ *Average main: $16* ✉ *Lot 2, Whittier Harbor, Whittier* ☎ *907/694–6887* 🌐 *www.lazyottercharters.com/boxed-lunches* 🕒 *Closed late Sept.–early May.*

Varly's Ice Cream & Pizza Parlor
$ | PIZZA | On a hot summer day and even on not-so-hot days, locals yearn for some Varly's ice cream, or if the weather's cold and rainy, for some decent pizza. The owners (who also manage Varly's Swiftwater Seafood Café) take great pride in what they do, and it shows: the homemade pizza here is certainly something to write home about. **Known for:** authentic frontier feel; homemade pizza dough and breads; outdoor seating. $ *Average main: $10* ✉ *Lot 1A Triangle Lease Area, Whittier Harbor, Whittier* ☎ *907/472–2547* 🕒 *Closed Oct.–Apr. and Wed.*

Varly's Swiftwater Seafood Café
$$ | SEAFOOD | The epicurean heart of Whittier for more than two decades, Varly's offers delightful surprises like its famed calamari burger—squid tenderized and fried in a secret batter. Other menu items include burgers, homemade chowders, rockfish, halibut, and salmon. **Known for:** true fishermen's wharf atmosphere; best fried fish in the state; fresh seafood straight out of the water. $ *Average main: $20* ✉ *Harbor Loop, Whittier* ☎ *907/472–2550* 🌐 *varlys-seafood-cafe.edan.io* 🕒 *Closed mid-Sept.–May.*

Hotels

Inn at Whittier
$$ | HOTEL | With its lighthouse-tower design and its weathered-looking gray slats, this hotel set among shanties and harbor boats blends in well with its surroundings. **Pros:** nice restaurant and bar; comfortable beds; great views. **Cons:** some downstairs rooms have only parking lot views; no kitchen amenities; some rooms don't have working televisions. $ *Rooms from: $199* ✉ *5a Harbor Rd., Whittier* ☎ *907/472–1007, 907/472–3200* 🌐 *www.innatwhittier.com* 🕒 *Closed Oct.–Mar.* 🍴 *No Meals* 🛏 *25 rooms.*

Chugach National Forest

40 miles east of Anchorage.

The 6,908,540 acres of national forest—a little larger than New Hampshire—stretch across the Kenai Peninsula and Southcentral region, from southeast of Cordova to northwest of Seward. The diverse geography here includes the shorelines, glaciers, forests, and rivers of the Copper River delta, the Eastern Kenai Peninsula, and Prince William Sound.

GETTING HERE AND AROUND

Your best bet for getting around the area is by rental car. The Seward Highway between Anchorage and Seward has a number of trail access points. (Check the highway for mile markers, with the distance measured from Seward.) At Mile 64, just south of Turnagain Pass, is the turnoff to the Johnson Pass Trail, a relatively flat trail to walk. Seven miles farther south, take the Hope Highway 18 miles to its end and find the Porcupine Campground. From there the Gull Rock Trail follows the shore of Turnagain Arm for 5 miles, offering scenic views across the arm and the chance to spot beluga whales foraging for salmon. Farther south on the Seward Highway, at Mile 23, the Ptarmigan Creek Trail starts at the campground and climbs 3½ miles into the mountains, ending next to a lake surrounded by snowy peaks. Bears are common in these areas, so always be aware of your surroundings.

ESSENTIALS

VISITOR INFORMATION Forest Headquarters. ✉ *161 E. 1st Ave., Anchorage* ☎ *907/743–9500 Anchorage* 🌐 *www.fs.usda.gov/chugach.*

Sights

Chugach National Forest

FOREST | Sprawling east of Chugach State Park, the Chugach National Forest encompasses nearly 6 million acres. The forest covers most of the Kenai Peninsula and parts of Prince William Sound and is the second-largest national forest in the United States, exceeded in size only by the Tongass in Southeast Alaska. The forest has abundant recreational opportunities: hiking, camping, backpacking, fishing, boating, mountain biking, horseback riding, hunting, and flightseeing. Southcentral Alaska is not the best terrain for rock climbing (aside from Denali), as the rock is predominantly composed of hardened ocean sediments that are weak and crumbly. There are, however, some places for great bouldering, and in the wintertime ice climbing is quite popular, as are snowshoeing, skiing, snowmachining, and dog mushing. Hiking trails offer easy access into the heart of the forest. You can spend a day hiking or looking for wildlife, or you can embark on a multi-day backpacking excursion. At all but the most popular trailheads, a five-minute stroll down a wooded trail can introduce you to the sights, smells, and tranquility of backcountry Alaska.

Be prepared to be self-sufficient when entering the Chugach Forest. Trailheads typically offer nothing more than a place to park and perhaps an outhouse. Running water, trail maps, and other amenities are not available. Also, be "bear aware" whenever you travel in bear country—and all of Alaska is bear country. ☎ *907/743–9500* ⊕ *www.fs.usda.gov/chugach.*

Activities

Crow Pass Trail

HIKING & WALKING | This 26-mile backpacking trail begins outside Girdwood and ends at the Eagle River Nature Center. Part of the Iditarod National Historic Trail, Crow Pass is a truly great hike. The first 3 miles are the most strenuous—after that the worst things hikers have to contend with are snow above the tree line and icy-cold river crossings. During summer in Alaska it's wise to cross through rivers only in the morning to avoid the rising waters throughout the day as snow and glaciers melt under the many hours of sunshine. In addition to offering splendid views, the Crow Pass Trail winds around the front of the amazing Raven Glacier terminus. The glacier is a half mile wide and more than 2 miles long, with many deep crevasses. You can camp anywhere along the trail, though it's important to know that camping near the glacier, even at the peak of summer, is a chilly endeavor. The one cabin along the trail sits above the tree line at 3,500 feet, just across from rich crystalline-blue Crystal Lake. The cabin is almost always booked at least six months in advance. ☎ *907/743–9500 cabin reservations* ⊕ *www.fs.usda.gov/chugach.*

Resurrection Pass Trail

HIKING & WALKING | Its colorful summer wildflowers are the big draw of this 39-mile backpacking trail through the Chugach National Forest. There's also a chance to spot wildlife: moose, caribou, Dall sheep, mountain goats, black and brown bears, wolves, coyotes, and lynx all traverse the forest. The trail's northern leg starts south of the town of Hope, following an old mining trail through the Kenai Mountains to its end near Cooper Landing. The trail branches off at one point to the Devil's Pass trailhead along the Seward Highway. Besides cabins, the U.S. Forest Service has provided several "official" campsites along the trail, where you'll find a cleared patch of ground and a fire ring. You are free, however, to pitch your tent wherever you'd like to. ☒ *Resurrection Creek Rd ⊹ At Mile 15 Hope Highway in Hope, turn south onto Resurrection Creek Road, then drive 4 miles to trailhead parking* ☎ *907/743–9500* ⊕ *www.fs.usda.gov/chugach* ⛨ *Free.*

Hotels

U.S. Forest Service Cabins
$ | **HOUSE** | Along trails, near wilderness alpine lakes, in coastal forests, and on saltwater beaches, these rustic cabins offer retreats for solo hikers or groups. **Pros:** beautiful surroundings; remote locations; cheap prices. **Cons:** often booked months in advance for summer; extremely basic; mice often inhabit them. [$] *Rooms from: $65* ☎ *877/444–6777 reservations* 🌐 *www.recreation.gov* 🛏 *41 cabins* 🍴 *No Meals.*

Valdez

6 hours northeast of Whittier by water, 304 miles east of Anchorage.

Valdez (pronounced val- *deez*) is the largest of the Prince William Sound communities. This year-round ice-free port was the entry point for people and goods going to the Interior during the gold rush. Today that flow has been reversed, as Valdez Harbor is the southern terminus of the Trans-Alaska Pipeline, which carries crude oil from Prudhoe Bay and surrounding oil fields nearly 800 miles to the north. This region, with its dependence on commercial fishing, is still feeling the aftereffects of the 1989 massive oil spill that released 11 million gallons of oil into Prince William Sound. Much of Valdez looks modern because the business area was relocated and rebuilt after its destruction by the 1964 Good Friday earthquake. Even though the town is younger than the rest of developed Alaska, it's quickly acquiring a lived-in look, especially due to its extreme annual snowfall.

Many Alaskan communities have summer fishing derbies, but Valdez may hold the record for the number of such contests, stretching from late May into September for halibut and various runs of salmon. If you go fishing, by all means enter the appropriate derby. Every summer the newspapers run sob stories about tourists who landed possible prizewinners but couldn't share in the glory (or sizable cash rewards) because they hadn't forked over the five bucks to officially enter the contest. The **Valdez Silver Salmon Derby** is held the entire month of August, and fishing charters abound in this area of Prince William Sound .

GETTING HERE AND AROUND

Valdez is road-accessible, and the 304-mile drive from Anchorage is stunning if a bit long to do in one day. The Richardson Highway portion of the drive takes you through Thompson Pass, high alpine country with 360-degree views. As you approach the town, the road descends into a steep canyon with rushing waterfalls—a popular ice-climbing destination in winter. Valdez's port is a stop on the Alaska Marine Highway, from which you can also sail to Cordova and Whittier. There's also a commercial airport.

The downtown is above the harbor, and two main avenues—Hazelet and Meals—run north–south, with smaller streets branching off.

RENTAL CARS Valdez U-Drive. ✉ *300 Airport Rd., Valdez* ☎ *907/835–4402.*

ESSENTIALS

VISITOR AND TOUR INFORMATION
Valdez Convention & Visitor's Bureau. ✉ *309 Fairbanks Dr., Valdez* ☎ *907/835–2984* 🌐 *www.valdezalaska.org.*

Sights

Columbia Glacier
NATURE SIGHT | A visit to Columbia Glacier, which flows from the surrounding Chugach Mountains, should definitely be on your Valdez agenda. Its deep aquamarine face is 5 miles across, and it calves icebergs with resounding cannonades. This glacier is one of the largest and most readily accessible of Alaska's coastal glaciers. The state ferry travels past its

face, and scheduled tours of the glaciers and the rest of the sound are available by boat and aircraft from Valdez, Cordova, and Whittier. ⊠ *Valdez* ⊕ *www.alaska.org/ detail/columbia-glacier.*

Maxine & Jesse Whitney Museum

OTHER MUSEUM | This museum contains one of the largest collections of Alaska Native artifacts. Over the course of several decades, Maxine Whitney, a gift-shop owner, amassed the ivory and baleen pieces, masks, dolls, fur garments, and other objects. Whitney donated her collection to Prince William Sound Community College in 1998; the museum is adjacent to the college. ⊠ *Prince William Community College, 303 Lowe St., Valdez* ☎ *907/834–1690* ⊕ *www.mjwhitneymuseum.org* ⊠ *Free* ⊗ *Closed Oct.–Apr.*

Valdez Museum & Historical Archive

HISTORY MUSEUM | FAMILY | The museum has two sections, the Egan and the Hazelet, named after their respective streets. The highlights of the museum at 436 S. Hazelet include a 35- by 40-foot model of what Old Town looked like before the 1964 earthquake and artifacts of the historic event that registered 9.5 on the Richter scale. An award-winning film that screens often describes the quake. Two blocks away, the 217 Egan site explores the lives, livelihoods, and events significant to Valdez and surrounding regions. On display are a restored 1880s Gleason & Bailey hand-pump fire engine, a 1907 Ahrens steam fire engine, and a 19th-century saloon, and there are exhibits about local Alaska Native culture, early explorers, bush pilots, and the 1989 oil spill. Every summer the museum hosts an exhibit of quilts and fiber arts made by local and regional artisans, and other exhibits are presented seasonally. ⊠ *217 Egan Dr., Valdez* ☎ *907/835–2764 Egan Dr., 907/835–5407 S. Hazelet Ave.* ⊕ *www.valdezmuseum.org* ⊠ *$7* ⊗ *Egan location closed Mon.*

🏃 Activities

ADVENTURE EXCURSIONS

Anadyr Adventures

KAYAKING | For more than a quarter century this company has led sea-kayak trips into Alaska's most spectacular wilderness, Prince William Sound. Guides will escort you on day trips, multiday camping trips, "mother ship" adventures based in a remote anchorage, or lodge-based trips for the ultimate combination of adventure by day and comfort by night. If you're already an experienced kayaker, Anadyr will outfit you and you can travel on your own. Also available are guided hiking and glacier trips, ice caving at Valdez Glacier, soft-adventure charter-boat trips in the sound, and water-taxi service to or from anywhere on the eastern side of the sound. ⊠ *225 N. Harbor Dr., Valdez* ☎ *907/835–2814, 800/865–2925* ⊕ *www. anadyradventures.com* ⊠ *Day trips from $79.*

Pangaea Adventures

KAYAKING | Since 1996, Pangaea has been navigating the aquatic world surrounding Valdez with guided trips via kayak, raft, sailboat, and water taxi. They also offer multiday hiking and camping adventure trips. ⊠ *Valdez* ☎ *800/660–9637, 907/835–8442* ⊕ *www.alaskasummer. com* ⊠ *From $79.*

Vertical Solutions Helicopter Flightseeing

AIR EXCURSIONS | These copters deliver a bird's-eye view of Prince William Sound, Valdez, and Columbia Glacier. They also provide heli-taxi services and glacier landings—an exciting way to experience this amazing place. All the helicopters have big bubble windows, maximizing the viewing pleasure. ⊠ *290 Airport Rd., Valdez* ☎ *907/831–0643* ⊕ *www.vshelicopters.com* ⊠ *From $295.*

BOATING AND WILDLIFE VIEWING

Lu-Lu Belle Glacier Wildlife Tours

BOATING | The "Limousine of the Prince William Sound," Valdez-based *Lu-Lu Belle* sets sail on small-group whale-watching and wildlife-viewing cruises that also go up close to massive Columbia Glacier. Cruises last about seven hours. There's a snack bar onboard, but it's good to pack a lunch, too. Private and large group tours are available. ⊠ *Valdez* ☎ *800/411–0090* ⊕ *www.lulubelletours.com* 🛥 *$150.*

Sound Eco Adventures

BOAT TOURS | Woman-owned and-operated, Sound Eco can guide you through Prince William Sound almost any way possible. From helicopter to kayak, whale watching to hiking adventures, the company employs a team of expert navigators well versed in the history, flora, and fauna of the region. The boat is fitted with an eco-friendly outboard engine, and trips are limited to six to minimize the environmental impact. ⊠ *Valdez* ☎ *907/835–8687* ⊕ *www.soundecoadventures.com* 🛥 *From $75.*

Stan Stephens Glacier & Wildlife Cruises

BOATING | This outfit conducts two different Prince William Sound glacier and wildlife-viewing tours. The nine-hour Meares Glacier Excursion takes in the glacier but also detours to spots where orcas, harbor seals, and other sea creatures are often sighted. Lunch and late-afternoon soup are provided. A light snack is served on the seven-hour Columbia Glacier Cruise, which also makes wildlife-viewing stops. Both tours include commentary about local commercial-fishing operations, the Alyeska Pipeline terminal, the 1964 earthquake, and defunct gold mines. ⊠ *Valdez* ☎ *866/867–1297* ⊕ *www.stanstephenscruises.com* 🛥 *$170 Meares tour, $140 Columbia tour.*

🍴 Restaurants

Fat Mermaid

$$ | SEAFOOD | This funky waterfront eatery delivers tasty breakfast, lunch, and dinner dining year-round indoors as well as outside on a smoke-free patio on warm summer days. The menu includes gourmet pizzas, Alaskan seafood, burgers, and plenty of vegetarian and healthy options. **Known for:** outside harbor-view seating; 15 craft beers on tap; great specialty cocktails. 🖇 *Average main: $20* ⊠ *143 N. Harbor Dr., Valdez* ☎ *907/835–3000* ⊕ *www.thefatmermaid.com.*

MacMurray's Alaska Halibut House

$$ | SEAFOOD | At this very casual family-owned establishment you order at the counter, sit at the Formica-covered tables, and check out the photos of local fishing boats. The battered halibut is excellent—light and not greasy. **Known for:** amazing fried halibut; old-school fish-and-chips; relaxed atmosphere. 🖇 *Average main: $15* ⊠ *208 Meals Ave., Valdez* ☎ *907/835–2788* 🕙 *Closed Sun. and Mon. No dinner.*

Roadside Potatohead Valdez

$ | AMERICAN | This cozy little converted house overlooks the harbor and is the go-to place for locals in the summer. Whether it's for breakfast, lunch, or dinner, they're all about the potato—be sure to try the potatohead burrito or the spuds with gravy. **Known for:** all things potatoes; excellent breakfast burritos; tastiest fries for hundreds of miles. 🖇 *Average main: $10* ⊠ *225 North Harbor Dr., Valdez* ☎ *907/835–3058* ⊕ *www.theroadsidepotatohead.com* 🕙 *Closed Oct.–Apr.*

A Rogue's Garden

$ | CAFÉ | For a quarter century, this downtown natural foods store has been serving Valdez and its visitors espresso and organic coffees, delicious fresh-baked goods, and fruit smoothies. There's also a sandwich bar for paninis and soups made from scratch. **Known for:** great selection of natural foods and kitchen items; fresh rustic bread; best lunch destination in town. $ *Average main: $10* ✉ *354 Fairbanks St., Valdez* ☎ *907/835–5880* ⊕ *www.roguesgarden. com* ✆ *Closed Sun.*

 Hotels

If you roll into town without reservations, especially if it's after hours, stop at the Valdez Convention & Visitor's Bureau on the corner of Fairbanks. It posts vacancies in bed-and-breakfasts on the window when it closes for the day.

Best Western Valdez Harbor Inn
$$$ | HOTEL | Near the harbor, this hotel comes complete with views of mountains, sea otters, seals, and waterfowl. **Pros:** very clean; lovely location on an inlet; great views. **Cons:** some rooms are cramped; standard-issue decor; hot water is inconsistent. $ *Rooms from: $235* ✉ *100 Harbor Dr., Valdez* ☎ *907/835–3434, 888/222–3440* ⊕ *www. valdezharborinn.com* ⇌ *88 rooms* ❄ *Free Breakfast.*

Totem Hotel & Suites
$$$ | HOTEL | This hotel is one of the newer lodgings in Valdez and looks the part, with its sleek corrugated metal siding and slick rectangular lines. **Pros:** delicious Continental breakfast; great location; modern, updated rooms. **Cons:** a little pricey; not all rooms have mountain views; walls are a bit thin. $ *Rooms from: $297* ✉ *144 East Egan Dr., Valdez* ☎ *888/808–4431* ⊕ *www.totemhotelandsuites.com* ⇌ *91 rooms* ❄ *Free Breakfast.*

Cordova

6 hours southeast of Valdez by water, 150 miles east of Anchorage by air.

A small town with the spectacular backdrop of snowy Mt. Eccles, Cordova is the gateway to the Copper River delta—one of the great birding areas of North America. Originally named Puerto Cordova by Spanish explorer Salvador Fidalgo in 1790, this peaceful fishing town of approximately 2,300 inhabitants is perched at the head of Orca Inlet in eastern Prince William Sound. Early in the 20th century, Cordova became the port city for the Copper River and Northwestern Railway, which was built to serve the Kennicott Copper mines 191 miles away in the Wrangell Mountains. Since the mines and the railroad shut down in 1938, Cordova's economy has depended heavily on fishing. Attempts to develop a road along the abandoned railroad line connecting to the state highway system were dashed by the 1964 earthquake, so Cordova remains isolated, accessible only by plane or ferry.

GETTING HERE AND AROUND
Take the scenic ferry or a water taxi from either Whittier or Valdez along the Alaska Marine Highway; you can also catch a commercial flight from Anchorage or Juneau via Yakutat. If taking the ferry from Valdez, be sure your operator points out Bligh Reef—it's where the Exxon Valdez oil spill occurred, along with numerous other shipwrecks.

Once in Cordova, the center of town is walkable, but you'll want some wheels for heading down the Copper River Highway, a scenic drive to the Copper River delta, the largest contiguous wetlands along the Pacific Coast in North America, and a temporary refueling station for 5 million migrating shorebirds every May.

FERRY INFORMATION Alaska Marine Highway. ☎ *800/642–0066 from outside Alaska, 907/465–3941* ⊕ *www.dot.state. ak.us/amhs.*

RENTAL CARS Chinook Auto Rentals. ⊠ *Mudhole Smith Airport, Mile 13, Copper River Hwy., Cordova* ☎ *907/424–2277* ⊕ *www.chinookautorentals.com.*

ESSENTIALS

VISITOR INFORMATION Cordova Chamber of Commerce. ⊠ *404 1st St., Cordova* ☎ *907/424–7260* ⊕ *www.cordovachamber.com.*

Sights

Copper River Delta

BODY OF WATER | This 35-mile-wide wetlands complex east of Cordova, a crucial habitat for millions of migratory birds on the Pacific Flyway, is one of North America's most spectacular vistas. The delta's nearly 700,000 acres are thick with marshes, forests, streams, lakes, and ponds. Numerous terrestrial mammals, including moose, wolves, lynx, mink, and beavers, live here, and the Copper River salmon runs are world-famous. When the red and king salmon hit the river in spring, there's a frantic rush to net the tasty fish and rush them off to markets and restaurants all over the country. The delta is connected by the Million Dollar Bridge, an impressive feat of engineering notable for its latticework.

The Forest Service had built an imposing viewing pavilion across the Copper River from Childs Glacier—famous for the spectacle of its calving icebergs and tidal waves—but in 2011, a natural change in the river's flow compromised Bridge 339 at Mile 36, and then several years later it washed out at Mile 44. With every new administration, there are talks of reconstructing the bridge and road, but due to continued budgetary constraints and the hefty price tag of repair, it is unlikely road access will be recreated any time in the near future. The only way to see the

glacier now is to book a private helicopter or plane tour or float the 140 miles or so from Chitina. The rules for these float trips are continually changing, but while you're in town, it's worth investigating if there are any motorboat outfitters currently permitted to give rides upriver to the glacier. This difficulty of getting to Childs Glacier has only slightly deterred visitors, as travelers from all over the world still come just to see the awe-inspiring glacier; though in recent years, it has ceased to calve with much frequency due to the receding of the ice and the lowering of river waters. ⊠ *Copper River Hwy, Cordova* ⊕ *www.fs.usda.gov/ recarea/chugach/recarea/?recid=6654.*

Cordova Historical Museum

HISTORY MUSEUM | Located in the Cordova Center, the Cordova Historical Museum documents early explorers to the area, Alaska Native culture, the Kennicott Mine and Copper River and Northwestern Railway era, and the growth of the commercial fishing industry. Additionally, the museum often features touring exhibits by Alaskan and (occasionally) non-Alaskan artists. The gift shop sells local postcards, Cordova and Alaska gifts, and regional history books. ⊠ *The Cordova Center, 601 1st St., Cordova* ☎ *907/424–6665* ⊕ *www.cordovamuseum.org* 🎫 *Donations encouraged* ⊗ *Closed Sun. and Mon.*

Activities

Alaganik Slough

BIRD WATCHING | A dedicated bird-watcher can spend hours at Alaganik Slough peering into the vegetation, seeking out interesting avian species. A 5-mile road off the Copper River Highway leads to a wheelchair-accessible boardwalk as well as covered viewing shelters, vaulted toilets, and four picnic areas. ⊠ *Turnoff at Mile 17, Copper River Hwy., Cordova* ⊕ *www.fs.usda.gov/recarea/chugach/ recarea/?recid=6935.*

Alaskan Wilderness Outfitting Company

FISHING | This outfit operates an air-taxi service out of Cordova and arranges fresh- and saltwater fly-out fishing experiences. Services range from drop-offs to guided tours with lodge accommodations. Alaskan Wilderness also provides access to floating cabins in Prince William Sound, a private fly-in cabin in Wrangell–St. Elias, and a full-service lodge for silver salmon fishing on the Tsiu River. ✉ *Cordova* ☎ *907/424–5552* 🌐 *www.alaskawilderness.com* 🎫 *Call for prices.*

Copper River Delta

BIRD WATCHING | Spring migration to the Copper River delta provides some of the finest avian spectacles in the world as millions of birds descend upon the region. Species include the western sandpiper, American dipper, orange-crowned warbler, and short-billed dowitcher. Trumpeter swans and dusky Canada geese can also be viewed. ✉ *Cordova* 🌐 *www.adfg.alaska.gov/index.cfm?adfg=copperriverdelta.main.*

🍴 Restaurants

Baja Taco & Espresso Bar

$ | **MEXICAN** | A funky bus turned food stand with an attached dining room, Baja Taco serves creative Tex-Mex dishes. Some come with a little added Alaska pizzazz, like the halibut-cheek tacos or the fish of the day. **Known for:** location right next to the water; super groovy school-bus kitchen; best salsas and tacos in the region. [$] *Average main: $12* ✉ *1 Harbor Loop Rd., Cordova* ☎ *907/424–5599* 🌐 *www.bajatacoak.com* 🕓 *Closed Oct.–May.*

OK Restaurant

$$ | **CHINESE** | This Asian food dining destination specializing in Chinese and Korean cuisine is a favorite with locals who want a little diversity in their palate. OK is particularly known for its outstanding Mongolian beef and fresh sushi in summer. **Known for:** delicious homemade kimchi; only Asian eatery that doesn't require a boat ride; fantastic interiors. [$] *Average main: $19* ✉ *616 1st St., Cordova* ☎ *907/424–3433* 🕓 *Closed Sun.*

Powder House Bar and Grill

$$$ | **SEAFOOD** | On clear summer evenings, you can relax on this roadside bar's deck overlooking Eyak Lake and enjoy whatever the cook's in the mood to make. Located inside a former storage shed for railroad explosives, this place serves homemade soups, burgers, and sushi (on Friday); seasonal seafood, including shrimp, scallops, razor clams, and whatever else is fresh, is also available every night. **Known for:** scenic mountain views from the back porch; fantastic burger specials; rustic charm. [$] *Average main: $25* ✉ *Mile 2.1, Copper River Hwy., Cordova* ☎ *907/424–3529* 🌐 *www.facebook.com/igotblasted.*

Reluctant Fisherman Restaurant

$$$ | **SEAFOOD** | This restaurant is about the closest thing to fine dining in Cordova, and it's generally packed with tourists, fishermen, and locals who appreciate both the food and the drinks. Each summer, the chef blows the menu up with something new and fabulous, but you're guaranteed to find a number of excellent fish dishes always fresh and right off the fishing boats. **Known for:** ceviche and grilled salmon; great outdoor seating; location next to the boat docks. [$] *Average main: $25* ✉ *407 Railroad Ave., Cordova* ☎ *907/424–3272* 🌐 *www.reluctantfisherman.com.*

🛏 Hotels

Northern Nights Inn

$ | **B&B/INN** | Commanding a dramatic view of Orca Inlet a few blocks from downtown Cordova, this turn-of-the-20th-century inn has three roomy suites and one "sleeping room" furnished with antiques. **Pros:** suites have full kitchens; great location; big bright rooms. **Cons:**

three rooms accessible only by stairs; views aren't great; no air-conditioning. $ Rooms from: $95 ✉ 500 3rd St., Cordova ☎ 907/424–5356 ⤴ 4 rooms ❙◯❙ Free Breakfast.

★ Orca Adventure Lodge

$$ | **B&B/INN** | This converted cannery at the end of the road offers a peek into what life in the region must have been like in the 1880s. **Pros:** excellent food; full slate of amenities, including outdoor activities; views include sea otters congregating outside. **Cons:** no television; 3 miles outside of town; dim lighting in rooms. $ Rooms from: $175 ✉ 301 Orca Rd., Cordova ☎ 907/424–7249, 866/424–6722 ⊕ www.orcaadventurelodge.com ☉ Restaurant closed Oct.–May ⤴ 38 rooms ❙◯❙ No Meals.

Reluctant Fisherman Inn

$$ | **HOTEL** | At this waterfront fisherman's hotel you can watch the commercial-fishing fleet and other maritime traffic sail by. **Pros:** clean and comfortable rooms; perfect location in the heart of Cordova; great view of the marina or the mountains. **Cons:** no kitchen amenities; rooms on north side can be noisy with nightlife activity; only harbor-view rooms have balconies. $ Rooms from: $174 ✉ 407 Railroad Ave., Cordova ☎ 907/424–3272 ⊕ www.reluctantfisherman.com ⤴ 45 rooms ❙◯❙ No Meals.

U.S. Forest Service Cabins

$ | **HOUSE** | The Cordova Ranger District of the Chugach National Forest maintains a series of simple backcountry cabins for rent. **Pros:** perfect for experiencing true wilderness; beautiful and remote; affordable. **Cons:** zero amenities (including running water); you must be self-sufficient and comfortable in the wilderness; must be booked six months in advance. $ Rooms from: $75 ✉ Cordova ☎ 877/444–6777 ⊕ www.recreation.gov ⤴ 17 cabins ❙◯❙ No Meals.

🛍 Shopping

Copper River Fleece

MIXED CLOTHING | All over Southcentral you'll find locals sporting American-made fleece hoodies, jackets, vests, and hats with decorative trim featuring Tglingit and Haida designs. Cordova resident Jennifer Park designed the clothing and commissioned Alaska Native artist Michael Webber to create the trim. Found in many souvenir shops around the state, they can also be purchased online—but the only outlet store for these nifty articles of clothing is in Cordova. ✉ 504 1st St., Cordova ☎ 800/882–1707 ⊕ www.copperriverfleece.com.

Hope

88 miles south of Anchorage, 74 miles north of Seward.

The little gold-mining community of Hope is located across the Turnagain Arm from Anchorage. To visit, however, you must drive the 88 miles all the way around the arm. Your reward is a quiet little community that is accessible to but not overrun by tourists. Miners founded Hope in 1896, and the old log cabins and weathered frame buildings in the town center are favorite photography subjects. At its peak, Hope had a population of 3,000. Now, according to the 2010 census, there are just 192 residents. You'll find gold-panning, fishing, and hiking opportunities here, and the northern trailhead for the 39-mile-long Resurrection Pass Trail is nearby. Contact the U.S. Forest Service for information on campgrounds, cabin rentals, and hikes in the area.

GETTING HERE AND AROUND

The only way to get to Hope is by car. Head south on the Seward Highway out of Anchorage. About 40 miles past the Girdwood turnoff look for the Hope exit. From there a two-lane road meanders

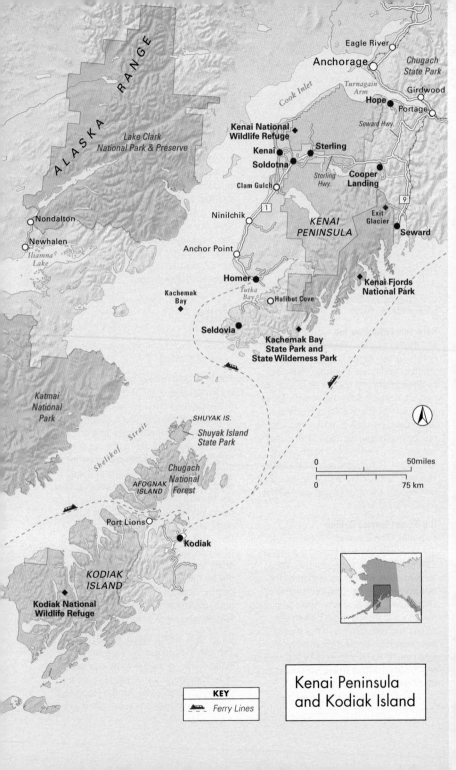

Kenai Peninsula
and Kodiak Island

through the forest for 16 miles before ending in the town center.

Activities

MOUNTAIN BIKING

The Kenai Peninsula offers outstanding opportunities for mountain bikers seeking thigh-busting challenges amid extraordinary scenery. **Crescent Creek Trail** (at Mile 44.9 of Sterling Highway; drive 3 miles to the trailhead at end of gravel road); **Devil's Pass** (at Mile 39½ of Seward Highway); **Johnson Pass** (at Miles 32.6 and 63.7 of Seward Highway); and the **Resurrection Pass trail systems** offer miles of riding for a wide range of expertise. Cyclists here are subject to highly fickle mountain weather patterns. But remember that you're never really alone in wild Alaska: be sure to bring along bear spray and bug dope (repellent). For maps and descriptions of trails, visit the website of the state's Department of Natural Resources (*dnr.alaska.gov/parks/aktrails/ explore/trailmapguide.htm*).

KAYAKING

Turnagain Kayak

KAYAKING | This outfitter rents gear, including kayaks, paddleboards, wet suits, and camping equipment, and also offers instruction and guided packrafting and white-water kayaking trips. ✉ *19796 Hope Hwy., Hope* ☎ *907/715–9365* ⊕ *www.turnagainkayak.com* ⚑ *From $30.*

 Restaurants

Creekbend Cafe & the Acres

$$ | **AMERICAN** | This roadhouse diner is a great place to grab a bite and a libation and soak up the sun (when it makes an appearance) on the outside deck; you might even catch a show at the Acres, the adjacent outdoor music and events venue. The café offers an array of dishes, but they're particularly known for their spicy crispy chicken sandwich and their excellent variety of burgers. **Known for:**

fantastic outdoor concert venue; great burgers and sandwiches; roadside stop perfect for weekend breakfast. $ *Average main: $16* ✉ *Mile 16½, 19842 Hope Hwy., Hope* ☎ *907/782–3274* ⊕ *www. creekbendco.com* ☉ *Closed Mon.–Wed.*

Dirty Skillet

$$ | **AMERICAN** | This restaurant and acoustic music venue (adjacent to Bear Creek Lodge) prides itself on epic meals with a twist, like two-layer crab cakes and deep-fried cheesy rice and Alaska sausage. The food is delicious, but the interior, with its one wall that opens up to let the delightful summer outdoors in, really makes this a terrific place to dine, drink, and enjoy great music. **Known for:** rustic diner atmosphere; palate-pleasing menu with something for everyone; live music. $ *Average main: $20* ✉ *19702 Hope Hwy., Hope* ☎ *907/349–7777* ⊕ *www. dirtyskillet.com* ☉ *Closed Mon. No lunch.*

Seaview Cafe & Bar

$$ | **AMERICAN** | With its rusty roof set against a breathtaking inlet and mountain backdrop, the Seaview is one of the original buildings in Hope at nearly 120 years old. It serves terrific seafood chowder and halibut-and-chips as well as one of the best Reuben sandwiches in Alaska. **Known for:** live music on weekends and Thursday; excellent seafood chowder; outdoor seating. $ *Average main: $16* ✉ *18416 B St., Hope* ☎ *907/782–3800* ⊕ *www.seaviewcafealaska.com* ☉ *Closed Tues. and Wed.*

Turnagain Kayak Coffeehouse

$ | **CAFÉ** | This is the only combination kayak rental shop and coffeehouse in Hope—maybe anywhere. They offer up great coffee, fresh fruit smoothies, and house-made pastries. **Known for:** nearby kayaking excursions; terrific coffee; excellent smoothies and baked goods. $ *Average main: $10* ✉ *19796 Hope Hwy., Hope* ☎ *907/715–9365* ⊕ *www.turnagainkayak.com/coffee-house* ☉ *Closed Thurs. and Fri.*

Hotels

Bear Creek Lodge
$$ | B&B/INN | This lodge is comprised of eight cabins either situated creekside or around a pond. **Pros:** very peaceful; excellent food at restaurant; nightly campfire around the pond. **Cons:** 16 miles off the main highway; some cabins have shared bathhouse; no cable or television. [$] *Rooms from: $150* ✉ *Mile 15.9, Hope Hwy., Hope* ☎ *907/349–7777* 🌐 *www.bearcreeklodgeak.com* 🛏 *8 cabins* 🍴 *No Meals.*

Coldwater Lodge & Market
$$ | HOUSE | Comprised of two cabins and four guest rooms right above the town's market and liquor store, plus a few yurts, this is a charming and affordable place to spend your time in Hope. **Pros:** close to good dining options; great location; quiet atmosphere. **Cons:** basic amenities; no Wi-Fi; decor very no-frills. [$] *Rooms from: $100* ✉ *19742 Hope Hwy., Hope* ☎ *907/782–3223* 🌐 *www.creekbendco.com/coldwater* 🍴 *No Meals* 🛏 *4 rooms, 2 cabins, 3 yurts.*

Shopping

Coldwater Lodge & Market
CONVENIENCE STORE | Located just as you enter town, this is Hope's only option for basic and essential groceries, liquor, propane, and firewood. There's also a small laundromat and an information desk for guided Kenai River trips. ✉ *19742 Hope Hwy., Hope* ☎ *907/782–3223* 🌐 *www.creekbendco.com/coldwater.*

Seward

74 miles south of Hope, 127 miles south of Anchorage.

It is hard to believe that a place as beautiful as Seward exists. Surrounded on all sides by Kenai Fjords National Park, the Chugach National Forest, and Resurrection Bay, Seward offers all the quaint realities of a small railroad town with the bonus of jaw-dropping scenery. This hamlet of about 2,750 citizens was founded in 1903, when survey crews arrived at the ice-free port and began planning a railroad to the Interior. Since its inception, Seward has relied heavily on tourism and commercial fishing. It is also the launching point for excursions into Kenai Fjords National Park, where it is quite common to see marine life and calving glaciers.

GETTING HERE AND AROUND

As a cruise-ship port, Seward has several routes in and out. Arrive by boat via the Alaska Marine Highway, or from Anchorage take a luxury Ultradome railcar, or drive the 127 miles from Anchorage. Although there's a small airport, only private planes use it. It's possible to walk around town or from the harbor to downtown, or hop onto the free shuttle that runs during summer.

ESSENTIALS

VISITOR AND TOUR INFORMATION
Seward Chamber of Commerce. ✉ *2001 Seward Hwy., Seward* ☎ *907/224–8051* 🌐 *www.seward.com.*

Sights

★ **Alaska SeaLife Center**
WILDLIFE REFUGE | FAMILY | A research center as well as visitor center, Alaska SeaLife rehabilitates injured marine wildlife and provides educational experiences for the general public. The facility includes massive cold-water tanks and outdoor viewing decks as well as interactive displays of cold-water fish, seabirds, and marine mammals, including harbor seals and a 2,000-pound sea lion. The center was partially funded with reparations money from the *Exxon Valdez* oil spill. Films, hands-on activities, a gift shop, and private small group tours where you can interact with different animals complete the offerings. ✉ *301*

Railway Ave., Seward ☎ *888/378–2525* ⊕ *www.alaskasealife.org* 🔊 *$29.95* 🕐 *Closed Mon.*

Iditarod National Historical Trail

TRAIL | The first mile of the historic original trail—at first called the Seward-to-Nome Mail Trail—runs along the beach and makes for a nice, easy stroll. ✉ *Mile 2.1 Seward Hwy., Seward* ⊕ *www.alaska. org/detail/iditarod-national-historic-trail.*

Lowell Point

FOREST | If you drive south from the Alaska SeaLife Center, after about 10 minutes you'll reach Lowell Point, a wooded stretch of land along the bay with access to beach walking, hiking, and kayaking. This is a great day-trip destination, and camping is also an option. ✉ *Lowell Point Rd., Seward* ⊕ *dnr.alaska.gov/parks/aspunits/kenai/lowellptsrs.htm.*

Nash Road

VIEWPOINT | For a different view of the town along a less-traveled road, drive out Nash Road, around Resurrection Bay, and look down at Seward, nestled at the base of the surrounding mountains like a young bird in its nest. ✉ *Nash Rd., Seward* ⊕ *www.alaska.org/detail/ nash-road.*

Seward Community Library & Museum

HISTORY MUSEUM | Seward's museum, community center, and library is a one-stop attraction, with the museum just downstairs from the library. The museum displays art by prominent Alaskan artists as well as relics that weave together the stories of the gold rush, Russian settlements, Alaska Native history, and the upheaval created by the 1964 earthquake. A movie illustrating the disaster and one about the Iditarod Trail are played back-to-back daily. ✉ *239 6th Ave., Seward* ☎ *907/224–3902* ⊕ *www. cityofseward.us/libmus* 🔊 *Museum $5; movie $5 suggested donation* 🕐 *Closed Mon.*

Activities

ADVENTURE AND WILDLIFE VIEWING

Exit Glacier Guides

ADVENTURE TOURS | This highly regarded outfit conducts tours of Exit Glacier, and not just to the moraine, where most tourists stop; the guides also lead travelers right onto the glacier. The company also offers guided hikes on the Harding Icefield, remote camping trips, and, for experienced climbers, backcountry heli- and fly-ins to remote peaks. ✉ *1013 3rd Ave., Seward* ☎ *907/224–5569* ⊕ *www. exitglacierguides.com* 🔊 *From $40.*

BOATING

Major Marine Tours

BOATING | This family-run operation has been offering aquatic tours of the fjords for more than 25 years. Onboard, a National Park Service ranger narrates the half- and full-day cruises of Resurrection Bay and Kenai Fjords National Park. Some trips include a deli-style lunch. Whether whale watching or glacier gazing, you're sure to have extraordinary wildlife sightings and awe-inspiring views. Major Marine can arrange transportation between Anchorage and Seward. ✉ *1412 4th Ave., Seward* ☎ *800/764–7300* ⊕ *www.majormarine.com* 🔊 *From $94.*

FISHING

Crackerjack Sportfishing

FISHING | With a fleet of five custom-made sportfishing boats, Crackerjack runs half-day salmon and full-day halibut fishing charters as well as two- to five-day fishing expeditions in Kenai Fjords National Park and beyond. The local captains have been guiding in Seward for years and offer trips year-round. ✉ *1302 4th Ave., Seward* ☎ *907/224–2606* ⊕ *www.crackerjackcharters.com* 🔊 *From $235.*

The Fish House

FISHING | This booking agency has a fleet of more than 40 Resurrection Bay and Kenai Peninsula fishing charters specializing in silver salmon and halibut fishing. You can book a half- or full-day charter (full-day only for halibut). The Fish House is also a supplier of tackle, gear, and clothing. ✉ *1303 4th Ave., Seward* ☎ *907/224–3674, 800/257–7760* 🌐 *www.thefishhouse.net* 🎟 *From $299.*

HIKING

For a comprehensive listing of all the trails, cabins, and campgrounds in the Seward Ranger District of Chugach National Forest, check the website of the U.S. Forest Service (*www.fs.fed.us*).

Caines Head Trail

HIKING & WALKING | This 4½-mile trail that starts at Lowell Point allows easy, flat hiking south along the coast, but with a hitch. Much of the hike is over tidal mudflats, so care must be taken to time it correctly: with tides here running in the 10- to 20-foot range, bad planning isn't just a case of getting your feet wet. It's officially advised that the trail be hiked only during very low tide in the summer. Two cabins can be rented at Derby Cove and Callisto Canyon (*www.dnr.alaska.gov*). ✉ *Seward* ☎ *907/269–8700* 🌐 *dnr.alaska.gov/parks/aspunits/kenai/caineshеadsra.htm.*

Lost Lake/Primrose Trail

HIKING & WALKING | A 15-mile end-to-end hike, this moderate to difficult trail winds through spruce forests and up into the high alpine area. The Lost Lake trailhead is near Mile 5 of the Seward Highway, and the other end is at the Primrose campground, at Mile 17 along the same highway. The trails are steep and usually snow-covered through late June, but the views along the Lost Lake valley are worth the climb. Above the tree line you're in mountain-goat country—look for white, blocky figures perched precariously on the cliffs. The lake is a prime spot for rainbow trout fishing. As usual, be bear-aware. The Dale Clemens cabin, at Mile 4½ from the Lost Lake trailhead, has propane heat and a captivating view of Resurrection Bay. Cabins must be booked in advance. ✉ *Seward* ☎ *907/288–3178* 🌐 *www.fs.usda.gov/recarea/chugach/recarea/?recid=16811&actid=50.*

KAYAKING

Kayak Adventures Worldwide

KAYAKING | Take a guided trip in sea kayaks from Kayak Adventures Worldwide, an outfit comprising a staff passionate about kayaking and the aquatic world. They offer half-day and full-day trips to Resurrection Bay and Aialik Bay. This Seward-based outfitter also runs multiday trips in Kenai Fjords, offers customized booking dates, teaches sea kayaking and safety skills, and is a great resource for weather updates and travel insurance. ✉ *328 3rd Ave., Seward* ☎ *907/224–3960* 🌐 *www.kayakak.com* 🎟 *From $89.*

★ Sunny Cove Sea Kayaking

KAYAKING | Whether in the bay, around the islands, or on a glacial lake, this woman-owned-and-operated outfitter has been touring the fjords for more than 26 years. They offer exemplary kayaking, hiking, and glacier cruise opportunities, with a strong "leave no trace" ethic. Both multiday ($450) and single-day ($95) excursions are available, but be sure to book well in advance. ✉ *1304 4th Ave., Seward* ☎ *907/224–4426* 🌐 *www.sunnycove.com* 🎟 *From $95.*

🍴 Restaurants

★ Chinooks Bar

$$$ | **SEAFOOD** | Just about everything at this restaurant in the small-boat harbor is made on-site, from the salad dressings to the infused liquors in the inventive libations. The award-winning chef prepares only sustainable Alaskan seafood, and information is provided about where it comes from and when it's in season. **Known for:** upstairs seating with views of the harbor and mountains; fantastic cocktail menu; inventive fresh seafood dishes. [$] *Average main: $25* ✉ *1404 4th Ave., Seward* ☎ *907/224–2207* 🌐 *www.chinooksak.com* 🕒 *Closed Mon., Tues., Jan., and Feb.*

The Cookery & Oyster Bar

$$$ | AMERICAN | Featuring local oysters harvested daily along with locally sourced meats and vegetables, this eating and drinking establishment is a favorite. In addition to freshly shucked and broiled oysters, the Cookery is also known for its melding of flavors to make scrumptious and wildly popular dishes like the wild and tame mushroom toast. **Known for:** exceptional food for a small fishing town; freshest oysters in town; beautiful food presentation. $ Average main: $30 ✉ 209 5th Ave., Seward ☎ 907/422–7459 ⊕ www.cookeryseward.com ⊗ Closed Mon., Tues., and Sept.–May.

★ Le Barn Appétit

$$ | FRENCH FUSION | This little restaurant and inn serves some of the finest crepes in Alaska with options that range from savory, like creamed beef and spinach, to sweet, like strawberries, Nutella, and whipped cream. The delightful proprietor is known to throw together fantastic French dinners for parties that call ahead, and if you're lucky, you'll also taste his quiche lorraine or chicken cordon bleu. **Known for:** best French crepes in Alaska; good for groups; great hospitality. $ Average main: $18 ✉ 11786 Old Exit Glacier Rd., Seward ☎ 907/224–8706 ⊕ www. lebarnappetit.com ⊗ No dinner (except by special advance reservation).

Ms. Gene's Place

$$$ | AMERICAN | A warm and inviting wood-paneled restaurant and Victorian lounge inside Hotel Seward, Ms. Gene's is one of the town's only fine dining establishments, serving breakfast and dinner year-round. The dinner menu changes often, but dishes such as seared ahi tuna, filet mignon, and halibut cheeks appear with frequency and are revered. **Known for:** fantastic halibut cheeks dishes; romantic dining; limited seating, so reservations a must. $ Average main: $30 ✉ 221 5th Ave., Seward ☎ 907/224–6447 ⊕ www.hotelsewardalaska.com ⊗ No lunch. No dinner Mon.

Railway Cantina

$$ | MEXICAN | This harbor-area hole-in-the-wall is locally renowned for its flavorful burritos, quesadillas, and great halibut and rockfish tacos. Various hot sauces, some contributed by customers who brought them from their travels, and beer complement the fare. **Known for:** excellent hot sauce collection; fantastic blackened halibut burrito; grab-and-go hot food. $ Average main: $14 ✉ 1401 4th Ave., Seward ☎ 907/224–8226 ⊕ www. railwaycantina.com.

Resurrection Roadhouse

$$$ | AMERICAN | Part of Seward Windsong Lodge, the Roadhouse offers locally sourced food and a deck that overlooks the Resurrection River and the surrounding mountains. Standard Alaska seafood fare fills the menu, along with multiple Alaska-brewed beers on tap. **Known for:** Alaskan microbrews; quiet and away from town; outdoor seating with views of the mountains and the Resurrection River. $ Average main: $25 ✉ 31772 Herman Leirer Rd., Mile ½, Exit Glacier Rd., Seward ☎ 800/808–8068 ⊕ www.sewardwindsong.com ⊗ Closed mid-Sept.–mid-May.

The Sea Bean Cafe

$ | CAFÉ | This splendid café offers a good selection of teas and organic coffee, as well as soups, wraps, pastries, and smoothies. **Known for:** great place to eat and read or work on your computer; grab-and-go options for those heading off on tours; vegetarian, vegan, and gluten-free options. $ Average main: $10 ✉ 225 4th Ave., Seward ☎ 907/224–6623 ⊕ www. seabeancafe.com.

Seward Brewing Company

$$ | AMERICAN | This two-story microbrewery serves up diverse and wildly unusual pub grub prepared with locally sourced ingredients. The restaurant's interior and exterior design blends rustic-chic, modern deco, and industrial elements, with two highlights being the high ceilings and enormous copper fish welded by a

local artist. **Known for:** salted watermelon salad; mostly locally sourced ingredients; only locally brewed craft beer in town. $ *Average main: $16* ✉ *139 4th Ave., Seward* ☎ *907/422–0337* ⊕ *www. sewardbrewery.com* ⊙ *Closed Tues. and Wed.*

Hotels

Breeze Inn
$$ | **HOTEL** | Across the street from the small-boat harbor, this modern 100-room hotel is very convenient if you're planning an early-morning fishing trip. **Pros:** free shuttle to nearby attractions and shopping; walking distance to downtown; Wi-Fi available. **Cons:** one section of the inn is older and a little more dated; rooms are bland and chain motel–like; can be busy. $ *Rooms from: $189* ✉ *1306 Seward Hwy., Seward* ☎ *888/224–5237* ⊕ *www.breezeinn.com* ⇌ *100 rooms* ⧘ *No Meals.*

Hotel Edgewater
$$$$ | **HOTEL** | The rooms at this hotel overlook Resurrection Bay, and on clear days the panorama of mountains, glaciers, and the bay is breathtaking. **Pros:** comfortable rooms; convenient to attractions, restaurants, and shops; breakfast included. **Cons:** lacks local flare; more expensive than other waterfront lodgings in town; not all rooms have balconies or views. $ *Rooms from: $364* ✉ *202 5th Ave., Seward* ☎ *907/224–2700, 800/780–7234* ⊕ *www.bestwestern.com* ⊙ *Closed Oct.–Apr.* ⇌ *76 rooms* ⧘ *Free Breakfast.*

Hotel Seward
$$ | **HOTEL** | Originally built in the 1940s as the best and most beautiful hotel in town, Hotel Seward is conveniently located downtown near a number of eateries, shopping, and the Alaska SeaLife Center. **Pros:** free access to gym next door; cool historic building; fine dining restaurant on-site. **Cons:** some rooms in the historic wing have shared bathrooms; no elevator for the historic wing; no free breakfast.

$ *Rooms from: $179* ✉ *221 5th Ave., Seward* ☎ *907/224–8001, 800/440–2444* ⊕ *www.hotelsewardalaska.com* ⧘ *No Meals* ⇌ *62 rooms.*

Kenai Fjords Wilderness Lodge
$$$$ | **HOTEL** | On a private parcel of land on Resurrection Bay's Fox Island, this beautiful retreat is only a 45-minute boat ride from Seward. **Pros:** tranquil setting; very comfortable beds; tremendous views. **Cons:** not the best food; no urban amenities; limited adventuring to be found on the island. $ *Rooms from: $695* ✉ *Fox Island, Seward* ☎ *800/808–8068* ⊕ *www.kenaifjordslodge.com* ⊙ *Closed Sept.–May* ⇌ *8 cabins* ⧘ *All-Inclusive.*

Seward Windsong Lodge
$$ | **HOTEL** | In a thickly forested setting near the bank of the Resurrection River, this lodging 2 miles north of Seward has the feel of a mountain time-share cabin. **Pros:** away from the bustle of cruise ship pedestrians; incredible river valley views; on-site Resurrection Roadhouse is convenient for dining. **Cons:** has an overall corporate feel; outside of town, so guests must rent a car or rely on the lodge's shuttle; many of the staff are uninformed about in-town destinations. $ *Rooms from: $179* ✉ *31772 Herman Leirer Rd., Mile ½, Exit Glacier Rd., Seward* ☎ *800/808–8068* ⊕ *www. sewardwindsong.com* ⧘ *No Meals* ⇌ *196 rooms.*

Stoney Creek Inn
$$ | **B&B/INN** | Sandwiched between two streams—one glacial, the other salmon-on-spawning—this B&B about 6 miles outside Seward offers respite from the summer buzz. **Pros:** has sauna and Jacuzzi; quiet location; not too far from town. **Cons:** far from urban conveniences; car might be necessary to get here; decor a bit dated. $ *Rooms from: $175* ✉ *33422 Stoney Creek Ave., Seward* ☎ *907/224–3940* ⊕ *www.stoneycreekinn.net* ⇌ *5 rooms, 1 guesthouse* ⧘ *Free Breakfast.*

★ **Teddy's Inn the Woods**
$$ | HOUSE | A sole, beautifully decorated cabin nestled in the woods across from Kenai Lake, Teddy's is surrounded by mountains and hiking trails. **Pros:** very clean and comfortable; fantastic setting; charming and hospitable owners. **Cons:** lacks some urban amenities; nearest restaurant and grocery store are a bit of a drive away; so quiet at night it might be difficult for urban dwellers to sleep. [$] *Rooms from: $200* ✉ *Mile 23, 29792 Seward Hwy., Seward* ☎ *907/288–3126* 🌐 *www.seward.net/teddys* 🛏 *1 cabin* 🍴 *No Meals.*

Van Gilder Hotel
$$$ | HOTEL | Built in 1916 and listed on the National Register of Historic Places, the Van Gilder is steeped in local history. **Pros:** entertaining decor; historic site; central location. **Cons:** some rooms have shared bathrooms; no kitchen; a little on the rustic side. [$] *Rooms from: $249* ✉ *308 Adams St., Seward* ☎ *907/224–3079* 🌐 *www.vangilderseward.com* 🛏 *20 rooms* 🍴 *No Meals.*

Shopping

Ranting Raven
SOUVENIRS | FAMILY | The shelves at this gallery and art shop are packed with local artwork, Alaska Native crafts and jewelry, and ravens—lots of them, including a couple of murals that adorn the side exterior. ✉ *238 4th Ave., Seward* ☎ *907/224–2228.*

Resurrect Art Coffeehouse
SOUVENIRS | A gorgeous coffeehouse and gallery–gift shop, Resurrect is located inside a 1932 church—the ambience and the views from the old choir loft are reason enough to stop by. This is a good place to get great coffee, enjoy fresh pastries, and find Alaskan gifts—many of them made by local artists and craftspeople, so they aren't mass-produced. ✉ *320 3rd Ave., Seward* ☎ *907/224–7161* 🌐 *www.resurrectart.com.*

Kenai Fjords National Park

125 miles south of Anchorage.

Kenai Fjords National Park is a vast, jagged masterpiece of mountains, nunataks (peaks that poke out from beneath ice), glacial moraines and valleys, temperate coastal rain forest, islands, narrow jetties, and abundant wildlife. It's an ever-changing landscape—one that's continuously shaped by the dynamics of water and the rivers of ice known as glaciers.

The park's 38 glaciers all flow off the 700-square-mile Harding Icefield (the country's largest), whose elevation has been decreasing by 10 to 12 feet every year, causing the fjord waters to rise. The impact of this on the park and its glaciers has been, and continues to be, significant. It's important to stay abreast of conditions and heed warnings, particularly involving ice chunks released into Resurrection Bay and Bear Lagoon and on land along the toe of Exit Glacier.

Archaeological findings indicate that indigenous peoples have been in the region for thousands of years, many living in permanent settlements, including one village that appears to have been maintained for almost 900 years. As the rising waters have reclaimed land, though, most evidence of early coastal sites has been erased.

In the mid-1700s, the first Europeans to arrive in the region—primarily Russian fur trappers—encountered the Unegkurmiut, an Alutiiq (Sugpiaq)–speaking people whose communities were spread across most of the outer southeastern coast of the Kenai Peninsula.

Most English, Russian, and Spanish interests avoided the outer Kenai Peninsula coast, as the tidewater glaciers and narrow jetties made the region less attractive for the development of permanent settlements. Trappers and traders, however, were attracted to the region's vast resources, and in the late 1700s, Resurrection Bay became the site of a Russian trading post and shipyard. Subsequent battles and transgressions between Russian and European armies and interests ensued. Missionaries descended on the peninsula, and Russian companies forced or paid the Unegkurmiut and other Sugpiat communities to consolidate. Largely due to the influx of foreign diseases (particularly smallpox, which decimated an enormous portion of the Alaska Native population all over the territory during the mid- to late 1800s) and because they were either persuaded or forced to leave their homes, the Unegkurmiut population declined to the point of no longer existing anywhere along the outer coast of the peninsula by the time the City of Seward was incorporated as an American town. Ancestors of the Unegkurmiut now live in the communities of Port Graham and Nanwalek, which are located on the (inner) southwest end of the Kenai Peninsula.

The United States purchased the Alaska Territory from Russia in 1867, and about 10 years later the first American-identified inhabitants arrived in the Kenai Fjords region. Frank Lowell and his wife Mary (who was Russian and Alaska Native) and their nine children set up a trade station at the head of Resurrection Bay. When fur-trading began to steeply decline, Frank was transferred to a station hundreds of miles away, but Mary and six of her children stayed on for more than 15 years without him. In 1903 they were witness to the steamships that arrived with hordes of American settlers looking for work building the railroad. Mary sold her holdings to the founders of the City of Seward, which was officially incorporated in 1912, just before she died in 1906. Although fur trading in the area was no longer viable, as the sea otter had become practically extinct from over-harvesting, the fjords became a dominant destination for the fishing industry.

President Jimmy Carter, in 1978, established the Kenai Fjords as a national monument under the Antiquities Act, and following the passage of the Alaska National Interest Lands Conservation Act (ANILCA) in 1980, he declared it a national park with the hopes of preserving and maintaining the wildlife and natural wonders of the region. Today, the harbor town of Seward (population 3,000), on the north end of Resurrection Bay, is the gateway to Alaska's fifth-most-popular national park, which has approximately 350,000 visitors per year. In addition to being the location for the park's headquarters, it's a beautiful town nestled into the crook of Resurrection Bay, loaded with excellent eateries, lodgings, and camping options.

GETTING HERE AND AROUND
Ted Stevens Anchorage International Airport (ANC) is the nearest major airport to Kenai Fjords National Park, 126 miles away. Travelers can catch a 40-minute flight with Rust's Flying Service, or grab a shuttle to Lake Hood, just a mile away from the international airport, and take a flight on a floatplane with Seward Air Tours. Seward has a small airport that accommodates air taxis and flightseeing outfits, the latter of which is the only way to visually grasp how massive the Harding Icefield is, and the only way to see all of the region's glaciers.

The only part of the park you can drive to is Exit Glacier, which is accessible off the Seward Highway, eight miles north of Seward, 126 miles south of Anchorage. There are a number of car rental companies located directly at the airport, but it's important to book a car in advance as many of them are booked solid during the summer months.

A four-and-a-half-hour scenic railroad trip from Anchorage to Seward with Alaska Railroad is an excellent way to begin your park visit. It's a fair jaunt from the depot to the boat harbor, but there are free shuttles if you're slated to do a boat or kayaking trip.

ESSENTIALS
PARK FEES AND PERMITS
There are no entrance fees or camping fees within the park, however, public use cabins must be reserved in advance and are $75 a night.

PARK HOURS
Access to the park is open year-round, but the Kenai Fjords National Park Visitor's Center and the Exit Glacier Nature Center are only open June through September.

VISITOR INFORMATION Kenai Fjords National Park. ☎ *907/422–0500* ⊕ *www. nps.gov/kefj.*

TOURS
Adventure 60 North
This year-round kayaking outfitter offers a number of excellent adventures that can only be had in the Kenai Fjords. Chill out while quietly gliding through the iceberg monoliths of Bear Glacier Lake, or kayak back and forth between the massive calving Aialik and Holgate Glaciers in Aialik Bay. Spend a day, or spend a few; get heli-dropped or take a 2-hour water-taxi ride chock-full of wildlife viewing to get to your paddle-dipping destination. ☒ *31872 Herman Leirer Rd., Seward* ☎ *907/224–2600* ⊕ *www.adventure60. com* ☒ *Day trips start at $499; multi-day trips start at $799.*

Exit Glacier Guides
With single and multiday hikes and climbs available, fly-in or paddle-to, Exit Glacier Guides offers small group or private guided adventures throughout the park and surrounding areas. ☒ *1013 3rd Ave., Seward* ☎ *907/224–5569* ⊕ *www. exitglacierguides.com.*

Kenai Fjords Tours
This company offers multiple day trips through Resurrection Bay and into the park for glacier viewing, whale watching, and evening stops for dinner at Fox Island. ☎ *800/808–8068* ⊕ *www. alaskacollection.com/day-tours/ kenai-fjords-tours.*

 ## Sights

Exit Glacier
NATURE SIGHT | One of the few accessible valley glaciers in the state, Exit is the only destination in the park accessible by car. Named for being a mountaineering expedition's exit from the first recorded successful crossing of the Harding Icefield in 1968, this glacier is the park's most popular destination. ☎ *907/422– 0500* ⊕ *www.nps.gov/kefj.*

Exit Glacier Nature Center
VISITOR CENTER | Open daily from Memorial Day to Labor Day, the center includes a bookstore, exhibits of topographical maps, stories of explorers and adventurers, and geological and glaciological artifacts. The center is ADA compatible and has rangers on staff to answer questions and guide short tours of the immediate area. ☒ *24620 Herman Leirer Rd., Seward* ☎ *907/422–0500* ⊕ *www. nps.gov/kefj.*

Harding Icefield
NATURE SIGHT | This is the largest ice field located entirely in the United States. It began forming during the Pleistocene Epoch, about 23,000 years ago, and is now comprised of a number of interconnected glaciers. As it's not possible to see through the ice, it's hard to gauge the depth of it, but radio wave studies have indicated that it's at least 1,500 feet deep in a ridge above Exit Glacier. The surface area is relatively easy to study, however, and research shows that over the past 10 years, the ice field's melt has increased, dropping it 10–12 feet in elevation every year. ☎ *907/422–0500* ⊕ *www. nps.gov/kefj.*

Kenai Fjords
NATURE SIGHT | The Kenai Fjords explode with glaciers, rain forests, and wildlife sights. The marine mammals you'll likely see are the Dall's porpoises, sea lions, otters, seals, dolphins, and whales (orca, humpback, gray, minke, sei, and fin). In the air, on the water, and populating the

many islands and outcroppings along the way are almost 200 species of birds that call this region home, including falcons, eagles, and puffins. ☎ *907/422–0500* ⊕ *www.nps.gov/kefj.*

Kenai Fjords National Park Visitor Center

VISITOR CENTER | Located in Seward's small-boat harbor, the main visitor center is open daily from June to mid-September. The small center has a few things for sale, issues marine tour tickets, and offers free viewings of a short 2-minute film narrated from the perspective of a wilderness kayaker, a marine ecologist, and a Sugpiaq family whose ancestors hailed from the region. Park rangers are on staff to answer questions about the area. ⊠ *1212 4th Ave., Seward* ☎ *907/422–0500* ⊕ *www.nps.gov/kefj* ☾ *Closed mid-Sept.–May.*

Resurrection Bay

BODY OF WATER | Serving as the port for the city of Seward, this 18-mile long fjord is the epic destination for kayakers from all over the world, as well as the entry point to Kenai Fjords National Park. Framed by snow-tip peaks, this scenic body of water is an exciting place for viewing birds and marine life in the summer months. ☎ *907/422–0500* ⊕ *www. nps.gov/kefj.*

 Activities

BOATING

Phillips Cruises Alaska

BOAT TOURS | This locally owned and operated tour company got its start in 1958 in Whittier and now offers a 5-hour, 115-mile catamaran cruise of Kenai Fjords National Park. It's a terrific way to see the abundant marine and avian life of the region. The trip includes a complimentary hot meal and even guarantees you won't get seasick. ⊠ *Seward* ☎ *800/544–0529* ⊕ *www.kenaifjordscruise.com* ⏛ *$159.*

CAMPING

Because the majority of Kenai Fjords is only ice and water, there is just one campground in the entire park. There are only a couple of places along remote shorelines in the parklands where primitive camping is advisable and just two summer public-use cabins—all of which can only be accessed by floatplane or motorized boat. Kayaking to these destinations is strongly discouraged as the water can be quite treacherous. It is also important to note that some of the coastline within the parklands is owned by the Alaska Native–owned Port Graham Village Corporation. A permit must be obtained in order to camp on those lands. Though a camping experience is difficult to come by within the park, there are several privately owned campgrounds in Seward as well as camping options in the nearby Chugach National Forest.

Exit Glacier Campground. There is a 12-site, walk-in, tent-only campground located along the road to the glacier. Two sites are ADA accessible. Sites are first come, first served, with a 14-day maximum stay, and there is no fee. Drinking water and pit toilets are available, but pets are not allowed. Bear bins are provided. *Mile 8, Herman Leirer Rd. www.nps.gov/kefj/ planyourvisit/campgrounds.htm.*

HIKING

Hiking opportunities in Kenai Fjords National Park are limited to the small portion of the park that is on dry land. The only designated and maintained hiking trails are found at Exit Glacier; there are a few short, easy hikes that all begin at the Nature Center, but the most noteworthy is the Harding Icefield Trail—an epic 8.2-mile strenuous route that offers stunning views and breathtaking vantage points. The rest of the parklands is considered trailless—if you do find a trail, it's most likely a bear trail and should be avoided. Off-trail hiking in the park is not recommended as the terrain is steep, rugged, and unreliable.

Glacier View Loop

TRAIL | A 1-mile, wheelchair-accessible trail that offers excellent viewing angles of Exit Glacier. *Easy.* ✣ *Trailhead: The Nature Center.*

KAYAKING

Kayaking is the primary athletic sport in the region. People come from all over the world to experience putting their paddle into Resurrection Bay, which is surrounded by snowcapped peaks and abundant marine life. Traveling with a guide is strongly recommended in these waters. The fjords are exposed to the excessive rain and winds that blow in from the Gulf of Alaska, making for treacherous waters and rough surf.

🛏 Hotels

Kenai Fjords Glacier Lodge

$$$$ | **ALL-INCLUSIVE** | Located in Aialik Bay, this is the only wilderness lodge within the 700,000 acres of Kenai Fjords National Park. **Pros:** excellent food; stunning views; all-inclusive rates. **Cons:** very remote; a bit pricey; no tech amenities. [$] *Rooms from: $915* ✉ *Kenai Fjords National Park, Seward* ☎ *800/334–8730* 🌐 *www.alaskawildland.com/lodges/kenai-fjords-glacier-lodge* 🍴 *All-Inclusive* 🛏 *16 cabins.*

Cooper Landing

100 miles south of Anchorage.

Centrally located on the Kenai Peninsula, Cooper Landing is within striking distance of some of Alaska's most popular fishing locations. Here the Russian River flows into the Kenai River, and fishing opportunities abound. Solid lines of traffic head south from Anchorage every summer weekend, and the confluence of the two rivers gets so crowded with enthusiastic anglers that the pursuit of salmon is often referred to as "combat fishing." However, a short walk upstream will separate you from the crowds and afford a chance to enjoy these gorgeous blue rivers.

The Russian River supports two runs of red (sockeye) salmon every summer, and it's the most popular fishery in the state. The Kenai River is famous for its runs of king (chinook), red, pink, and silver (coho) salmon, as well as large rainbow trout and Dolly Varden char. A number of nearby freshwater lakes, accessible only by hiking trail, also provide excellent fishing for rainbow trout and Dolly Varden.

Don't let the presence of dozens if not hundreds of fellow anglers lull you into a sense of complacency: in recent years the amount of brown bear activity at the Russian River has increased noticeably. This needn't deter you from enjoying yourself, though. Be aware of the posted signs warning of recent bear sightings, observe the local "rules of the road" about fishing and disposing of carcasses, and keep your senses tuned.

Cooper Landing serves as a trailhead for the 39-mile-long Resurrection Pass Trail, which connects to the village of Hope and the Russian Lakes/Resurrection River trails, which run south to Exit Glacier near Seward. The town's central location also affords easy access to saltwater recreation in Seward and Homer.

GETTING HERE AND AROUND

Follow the line of traffic flowing south out of Anchorage on the Seward Highway; take a right at the "Y" onto the Sterling Highway and soon you'll be there—just don't blink or you'll miss it. Look for the lodges and tackle shops that spring up from the wilderness, dotting either side of the highway. Cooper Landing does not have a commercial airport.

Continued on page 224

ALASKA'S GLACIERS
NOTORIOUS LANDSCAPE ARCHITECTS

(opposite and above) Facing the Taku Glacier challenge outside Juneau.

Glaciers—those massive, blue-hued tongues of ice that issue forth from Alaska's mountain ranges—perfectly embody the harsh climate, unforgiving terrain, and haunting beauty that make this state one of the world's wildest places. Alaska is home to roughly 100,000 glaciers, which cover almost 5% of the state's land.

FROZEN GIANTS

A glacier occurs where annual snowfall exceeds annual snowmelt. Snow accumulates over thousands of years, forming massive sheets of compacted ice. (Southeast Alaska's **Taku Glacier**, popular with flightseeing devotees, is one of Earth's meatiest: some sections measure over 4,500 feet thick.) Under the pressure of its own weight, the glacier succumbs to gravity and begins to flow downhill. This movement results in sprawling masses of rippled ice (Alaska's **Bering Glacier**, at 127 miles, is North America's longest). When glaciers reach the tidewaters of the coast, icebergs calve, or break off from the glacier's face, plunging dramatically into the sea.

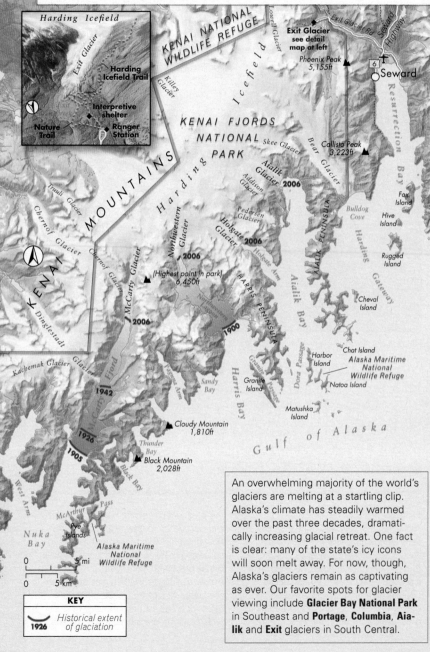

THE RAPIDLY RETREATING GLACIERS IN KENAI FJORDS NATIONAL PARK

Harding Icefield

Exit Glacier

Harding Icefield Trail

◆ **Interpretive shelter**

Nature Trail

◆ **Ranger Station**

KENAI NATIONAL WILDLIFE REFUGE

Exit Glacier see detail map at left

Lowell Glacier

Phoenix Peak 5,155ft ▲

6

○ **Seward**

Exit Glacier Rd

Seward Highway

Killey Glacier

Icefield

KENAI FJORDS NATIONAL PARK

Skee Glacier

Atalik Glacier **2006**

Addison Glacier

Bear Glacier

Callisto Peak 3,223ft ▲

Resurrection Bay

Fox Island

Harding

Mountains

Truuli Glacier

Chernof Glacier

Chernof Glacier

Northwestern Glacier

2006

Pedersen Glacier

Holgate Glacier **2006**

Harding

Bulldog Cove

Harding Gateway

Hive Island

Rugged Island

KENAI MOUNTAINS

McCarty Glacier

(Highest point in park) 6,450ft

2006

Holgate Arm

Harris Peninsula

1900

Aialik Peninsula

Aialik Bay

Cheval Island

Dinglestadt Glacier

Dinglestadt Glacier

Northwestern

Northwestern Fjord

Harbor Island

Chat Island
Alaska Maritime National Wildlife Refuge

Dora Passage

Kachemak Glacier

Glacier

1942

Pederson Arm

Sandy Bay

Harris Bay

Granite Island

Granite Passage

Natoa Island

Matushka Island

1926

▲ Cloudy Mountain 1,810ft

Gulf of Alaska

1905

Thunder Bay

▲ Black Mountain 2,028ft

Black Bay

West Arm

McArthur Pass

Pye Islands

Nuka Bay

Alaska Maritime National Wildlife Refuge

0 ___ 5 mi
0 ___ 5 km

KEY

1926 ⌣ *Historical extent of glaciation*

An overwhelming majority of the world's glaciers are melting at a startling clip. Alaska's climate has steadily warmed over the past three decades, dramatically increasing glacial retreat. One fact is clear: many of the state's icy icons will soon melt away. For now, though, Alaska's glaciers remain as captivating as ever. Our favorite spots for glacier viewing include **Glacier Bay National Park** in Southeast and **Portage**, **Columbia**, **Aialik** and **Exit** glaciers in South Central.

ICY BLUE HIKES & THUNDEROUS BOATING EXCURSIONS

Glaciers enchant us with their size and astonishing power to shape the landscape. But let's face it: nothing rivals the sheer excitement of watching a bus-size block of ice burst from a glacier's face, creating an unholy thunderclap that resounds across an isolated Alaskan bay.

Most frequently undertaken with a seasoned guide, **glacier trekking** is becoming increasingly popular. Many guides transport visitors to and from glaciers (in some cases by helicopter or small plane), and provide ski excursions, dogsled tours, or guided hikes on the glacier's surface. Striding through the surreal landscape of a glacier, ice crunching underfoot, can be an otherworldly experience. Whether you're whooping it up on a dogsled tour, learning the fundamentals of glacier travel, or simply poking about on a massive field of ice, you're sure to gain an acute appreciation for the massive scale of the state's natural environment.

You can also experience glaciers via boat, such as the Alaska Marine Highway, a cruise ship, a small chartered boat, or even your own bobbing kayak. Our favorite out of Seward is the ride with Kenai Fjords Tours. Don't be discouraged by rainy weather. Glaciers often appear even bluer on overcast days. When piloting your own vessel, be sure to keep your distance from the glacier's face.

DID YOU KNOW?

What do glaciers and cows have in common? They both *calve*. While bovine calving refers to actual calf-birth, the word is also used to describe a tidewater glacier's stunning habit of rupturing icebergs from its terminus. When glacier ice meets the sea, steady tidal movement and warmer temperatures cause these frequent, booming deposits.

GLACIER-VIEWING TIPS

■ The most important rule of thumb is never to venture onto a glacier without proper training or the help of a guide.

■ Not surprisingly, glaciers have a cooling effect on their surroundings, so wear layers and bring gloves and rain gear.

■ Glaciers can powerfully reflect sunlight, even on cloudy days. Sunscreen, sunglasses, and a brimmed hat are essential.

■ Warm, thick-soled waterproof footwear is a must. Crampons are highly recommended.

■ Don't forget to bring a camera and binoculars (preferably waterproof).

Taking in the sights at Mendenhall Glacier

Activities

FISHING

Most lodges in Cooper Landing cater to the fishing crowd; ask when you make your reservation.

Alaska River Adventures

FISHING | These Cooper Landing–based guides take small groups fishing throughout the region, with self-professed "well-seasoned old pros." Alaska River Adventures is only one of two operators permitted to offer trips on the Goodnews River. Horseback riding, river rafting, hiking, gold panning, and lodging are also available. Book early for the Goodnews River: only six trips are allowed each year. ✉ *35269 King Salmon Dr., Cooper Landing* ☎ *907/595–2000* 🌐 *www.alaskariveradventures.com* 🎟 *From $175.*

Alaska Troutfitters

FISHING | Guided trout and salmon fly-fishing on the Kenai River is the specialty of this outfit that also offers classes that cover everything from casting technique to fishing entomology. Alaska Troutfitters conducts hike-in, drift-boat, and fly-in trips. Package deals include instruction, fishing, transportation, and lodgings that resemble camp cabins. ✉ *Cooper Landing* ☎ *907/595–1212* 🌐 *www.aktroutfitters.com* 🎟 *From $195.*

Alaska Wildland Adventures

FISHING | From the lodge in Cooper Landing, south of Anchorage, these folks provide fishing adventures on the upper and lower Kenai River, some of which may include a stay at either their Riverside, Glacier, or Backcountry Lodge. They also offer a number of other adventures that don't all include fishing. ✉ *Cooper Landing* ☎ *800/334–8730* 🌐 *www.alaskawildland.com* 🎟 *From $315.*

HORSEBACK RIDING

Alaska Horsemen Trail Adventures

HORSEBACK RIDING | This Cooper Landing–based company offers single- and multiday horseback trips into the Kenai Mountains via Crescent Lake, Resurrection, and other area trail systems. ✉ *Cooper Landing* ☎ *907/595–1806* 🌐 *www.alaskahorsemen.com* 🎟 *From $109.*

Restaurants

Kingfisher Roadhouse

$$ | AMERICAN | With a back side that faces Kenai Lake and offers splendid views, and food equally worth your attention, this unassuming roadhouse is *the* place to stop in Cooper Landing. The halibut crab cakes with an excellent homemade tartar sauce come highly recommended, and there are always great fish options at the peak of the season. **Known for:** great seafood options; extraordinary views of Kenai Lake; live music venue in the evenings. [$] *Average main: $20* ✉ *Mile 47.3, 19503 Sterling Hwy., Cooper Landing* ☎ *907/595–2861* 🌐 *www.letseat.at/kingfisherak* 🕒 *Closed Mon. and Tues. Sept.–mid-Jun. No dinner Sept.–mid-Jun. No lunch Mon. and Tues. mid-Jun.–Sept.*

Sunrise Inn

$$ | AMERICAN | FAMILY | The owners of this cheerful little restaurant on the shore of Kenai Lake call it a "backwoods bistro." The very reasonably priced menu includes excellent breakfast foods, homemade soups and chowders, wraps and vegetarian items, and hand-grated french fries. Dinners often feature fresh Alaska fish, and they also have a late-night menu for the pub. **Known for:** live music in summer; amazing interior woodwork and a fish stream floor; late-night food stop. [$] *Average main: $15* ✉ *Mile 45, Sterling Hwy., Cooper Landing* ☎ *907/595–1222* 🌐 *www.sunriseinncooperlandingalaska.com.*

Hotels

Eagle Landing Resort
$$$$ | **B&B/INN** | Cabins here come in three variations—regular, deluxe, and riverfront, all with private bath, heat, and kitchen. **Pros:** fantastic kitchens; accommodations that fit any budget; great views. **Cons:** certain upstairs rooms are only semi-private; some staircases are steep; lacks many urban amenities. [$] *Rooms from: $350* ✉ *Mile 48.1, Sterling Hwy., Box 748, Cooper Landing* ☎ *907/595–1213, 866/595–1213* 🌐 *www.eaglelandingresort.net* 🍴 *No Meals* 🛏 *12 cabins.*

Grizzly Ridge Lodge
$$ | **HOTEL** | This lodge is conveniently located along the Sterling Highway, with quick and easy access to trailheads and fishing holes. **Pros:** perfect for fishing excursions; full kitchens in all rooms; convenient location. **Cons:** not the most comfortable beds; some rooms only have stair access; few amenities. [$] *Rooms from: $200* ✉ *18280 Sterling Hwy., Cooper Landing* ☎ *907/595–1260* 🌐 *www.grizzlyridgeak.com* 🛏 *6 rooms* 🍴 *No Meals.*

Gwin's Lodge
$$ | **B&B/INN** | One of Alaska's oldest roadhouses, Gwin's is the epicenter of much activity on the peninsula and a one-stop shop providing food, lodging, and fishing tackle. **Pros:** very quaint and historic; everything you need in one place; pretty decent food. **Cons:** can sometimes have rowdy patrons in the evenings; lofts have very low ceilings; restaurant closed in off-season. [$] *Rooms from: $100* ✉ *Mile 52, 14865 Sterling Hwy., Cooper Landing* ☎ *907/595–1266* 🌐 *www.gwinslodge.com* 🛏 *17 cabins* 🍴 *No Meals.*

Kenai Princess Wilderness Lodge
$$$ | **HOTEL** | "Elegantly rustic" might best describe this sprawling complex approximately 45 miles from Seward. **Pros:** quiet atmosphere; cozy rooms have fireplaces; beautiful location. **Cons:** caters mainly to cruise passengers and those on tours; rooms don't have views of the river; food is cruise-ship quality. [$] *Rooms from: $229* ✉ *Mile 47.7, Sterling Hwy., Cooper Landing* ☎ *907/595–1425, 800/426–0500* 🌐 *www.princesslodges.com/princess-alaska-lodges/kenai-lodge* ⏲ *Closed mid-Sept.–May* 🛏 *86 rooms* 🍴 *No Meals.*

Kenai Riverside Lodge
$$$$ | **RESORT** | Run by Alaska Wildland Adventures, this collection of cabins on the bank of the Kenai River offers a "roughing it in authentic comfort" all-inclusive, two-night package, with cabins that have private baths. **Pros:** relaxing sauna; beautiful wooded location; great adventure and expedition packages. **Cons:** two-night minimum stays, which can get pricey; cabins are a bit small; fishing excursions not included. [$] *Rooms from: $1175* ✉ *Mile 50.1, 16520 Sterling Hwy., Cooper Landing* ☎ *800/334–8730* 🌐 *www.kenairiversidelodge.com* ⏲ *Closed Oct.–mid-May* 🍴 *All-Inclusive* 🛏 *16 cabins.*

Kenai National Wildlife Refuge

95 miles northwest of Kenai Fjords National Park, 150 miles southwest of Anchorage.

The refuge, which encompasses nearly 2 million acres, was originally established to protect the Kenai moose, and it remains the finest moose habitat in the region. Wildlife viewing is popular, of course, and the canoeing and kayaking opportunities attract many visitors each summer.

Moose are the most commonly seen large animals in the refuge—it was originally named the Kenai National Moose Range.

GETTING HERE AND AROUND

There are several roads in the refuge, and the Sterling Highway bisects it, but the best access is by canoe.

■ TIP→ **Road access to the canoe trailheads is off the Swanson River Road at Mile 83.4 of the Sterling Highway.**

Other than canoeing, the only way to get into the far reaches of the refuge is by airplane. Floatplane services in Soldotna, where the refuge is headquartered, can fly you into the backcountry. The refuge office maintains lists of transporters, air taxis, canoe rentals, and big-game guides that are permitted to operate on refuge lands. To reach the main visitor center–refuge office on Ski Hill Road, turn south on Funny River Road in Soldotna just west of the Kenai River Bridge, and follow the signs.

ESSENTIALS

VISITOR INFORMATION Kenai National Wildlife Refuge Visitor Center. ⊠ *1 Ski Hill Rd., Soldotna* ☎ *907/260–2820 recreational info, 907/262–7021 permits* ⊕ *kenai.fws.gov.*

 Sights

Kenai National Wildlife Refuge

NATURE PRESERVE | The refuge's nearly 2 million acres include a portion of the Harding Icefield as well as two large and scenic lakes, Skilak and Tustumena. This is the area's premier moose habitat, and the waterways are great for canoeing and kayaking. The refuge maintains two visitor centers. The main center, in Soldotna, has wildlife dioramas, free films and information, and a bookstore and gift shop. There's also a seasonal "contact" center at Mile 58 of the Sterling Highway, open from mid-June to mid-August. Wildlife is plentiful even by Alaskan standards. Although caribou seldom appear near the road, Dall sheep and mountain goats live on the peaks near Cooper Landing, and

black and brown bears, wolves, coyotes, lynx, beavers, and lots of birds reside here, along with many moose.

The refuge's canoe trail system runs through the Swan Lake and Swanson River areas. Covering more than 140 miles on 100 lakes and the Swanson River, this route escapes the notice of most visitors and residents. It's a shame because this series of lakes linked by overland portages offers fantastic access to the remote backcountry, well away from what passes for civilization in the subarctic. The fishing improves exponentially with distance from the road system. ⊕ *www.fws.gov/refuge/Kenai.*

 Activities

CANOEING

The best way to experience the refuge's backcountry is by canoe. The **Swan Lake Canoe System** and the **Swanson River Canoe System** are accessed from the road system at the turnoff at Mile 83.4 of the Sterling Highway. Several loop trips enable visitors to fish, hike, and camp away from the road system and motorized boat traffic. Fishing for trout, salmon, and Dolly Varden is excellent, and the lakes and portages offer access to more than 100 miles of waterways. The Kenai National Wildlife Refuge Visitor Center has a thorough list of canoeing outfitters.

Alaska Canoe & Campground

CANOEING & ROWING | Whether you're looking for a canoe, kayak, raft, or drift boat—or tackle or camping gear—this company comes highly recommended by locals and travelers alike. They'll properly outfit you and send you on your Refuge adventure, on your own or with a guide. They also have cabin rentals and an RV park. ⊠ *25292 Sterling Hwy., Sterling* ☎ *907/262–2331* ⊕ *www.alaskacanoetrips.com* ⊠ *From $45 for half-day.*

HIKING

Hiking trails branch off from the Sterling Highway and the Skilak Lake Loop. The degree of difficulty ranges from easy ½-mile walks to strenuous climbs up to mountain lakes. Bring topographic maps, water, food, insect repellent, and bear awareness. You won't find toilets, water fountains, or signposts. Remember: brown and black bears are numerous on the Kenai Peninsula.

Hotels

Kenai Backcountry Lodge

$$$$ | **ALL-INCLUSIVE** | Getting off the road and the beaten track is the most authentic way to experience Alaska, and Kenai Backcountry Lodge is about as true as it gets, with access only by boat across Skilak Lake. **Pros:** experienced and knowledgeable guides; backcountry experience without roughing it too much; gorgeous remote location. **Cons:** no major amenities; no Wi-Fi; can be pricey. [$] *Rooms from: $2000* ✉ *Kenai Peninsula* ☎ *800/334–8730* 🌐 *www.alaskawildland.com/kenaibackcountrylodge.htm* 🕓 *Closed Sept.–May* 🍴 *All-Inclusive* 🛏 *8 cabins.*

USFWS Cabins

$ | **HOUSE** | These cabins are in remote areas of the Kenai National Wildlife Refuge accessible only by air or boat. **Pros:** peace and quiet; the true experience of being off the grid; beautiful surroundings. **Cons:** no amenities; making an online reservation is not easy; comfort depends on what you bring with you. [$] *Rooms from: $75* ✉ *Soldotna* ☎ *877/444–6777* 🌐 *www.fws.gov/refuge/Kenai/cabin.html* 🛏 *16 cabins* 🍴 *No Meals.*

Kenai, Sterling, and Soldotna

116 miles northwest of Seward, 148 miles southwest of Anchorage.

Because of their proximity to each other, the towns of Kenai, Sterling, and Soldotna are often mentioned together, and all three are within the Kenai Peninsula Borough. Soldotna and Sterling, with their strategic location on the peninsula's northwest coast, serve as the Kenai Peninsula's commercial and sportfishing hub. Along with Kenai, whose onion-dome Holy Assumption Russian Orthodox Church is a highlight of its Old Town, they are home to Cook Inlet oil-field workers and their families. Sterling and Soldotna's commercial center stretches along the Sterling Highway, making this a good stopping point for those traveling up and down the peninsula. The town of Kenai lies near the end of a road that branches off the Sterling Highway in Soldotna. Near Kenai is Captain Cook State Recreation Area, one of the least-visited state parks on the road system. This portion of the peninsula is level and forested, with numerous lakes and streams pocking and crisscrossing the area. Trumpeter swans return here in spring, and sightings of moose are common.

GETTING HERE AND AROUND

As you're driving either north or south on the Sterling Highway from Cooper Landing or Homer, you'll know you've hit Soldotna when you're suddenly stuck in traffic in between strip malls. From the north the slowdown is gradual, but from Homer, it's quite sudden. Kenai is 11 miles up the Kenai Spur Highway, which originates in central Soldotna. Commercial flights are available to Kenai from Anchorage.

ESSENTIALS

VISITOR INFORMATION Kenai Visitor and Convention Bureau. ⊠ *11471 Kenai Spur Hwy., Kenai* ☎ *907/283–1991* ⊕ *kenai-chamber.org.*

 Sights

Clam Gulch

NATURE SIGHT | FAMILY | In addition to fishing, clam digging is popular at Clam Gulch, 24 miles south of Soldotna on the Sterling Highway. This is a favorite of local children, who love any excuse to dig in the muddy, sloppy goo. Ask locals on the beach how to find the giant razor clams (recognized by their dimples in the sand). Ask also for advice on how to clean the clams—cleaning is pretty labor-intensive, and it's easy to get into a clam-digging frenzy when the conditions are favorable, only to regret your efforts when cleaning time arrives. The clam digging is best when tides are minus 4 or 5 feet. A sportfishing license, available at grocery stores, sporting-goods shops, and drugstores, is required for clam diggers 16 years old and older. ⊠ *Soldotna* ⊕ *dnr.alaska.gov/parks/aspunits/kenai/clamgulchsra.htm.*

 Activities

FISHING

Anglers from around the world come for the salmon-choked streams and rivers, most notably the Kenai River and its companion, the Russian River. Knowledgeable fishery professionals figure it's only a matter of time before someone with sportfishing gear catches a 100-pounder (the record is currently a 97-pound, 5-ounce fish caught in 1987). There are two runs of kings up the Kenai every summer. The first run starts in mid-May and tapers off in early July, and the second run is from early July until the season ends on July 31. Generally speaking, the first run has more fish, but they tend to be smaller than second-run fish.

"Smaller," of course, has a whole different meaning when it comes to these fish. Fifty- and 60-pounders are unremarkable here, and 40-pound fish are routinely tossed back as being "too small." The limit is one king kept per day, five per season, no more than two of which can be from the Kenai—unless an emergency order states otherwise. In addition to a fishing license, you must obtain a special Alaska king salmon license stamp and a harvest record. These can be purchased on the Alaska Department of Fish and Game website, or check with your guide, as most guides sell them. The river also supports two runs of red (sockeye) salmon every year, as well as runs of silver (coho) and pink (humpback) salmon. Rainbow trout of near-mythic proportions inhabit the river, as do Dolly Varden char. Limits vary from place to place, so be sure to check your fishing booklet.

Farther up the river, between Kenai Lake in Cooper Landing and Skilak Lake, motorboats are banned, so a more idyllic experience can be had. Scores of guide services ply the river, and if you're inexperienced at the game, consider hiring a guide for a half-day or full-day trip. Deep-sea fishing for salmon and halibut out of Deep Creek is challenging Homer's position as the preeminent fishing destination on the southern Kenai Peninsula. This fishery is unusual in that tractors launch boats off the beach and into the Cook Inlet surf. The local campground and RV lot is packed on summer weekends.

Some 300 fishing charters and guides operate here, and all of them stay busy during the summer fishing season.

Alaska Wildland Adventures

FISHING | Head down the Kenai River and learn about the area and its wildlife on an eight-hour fishing trip. Trips include lunch and all your gear, and they will filet your fish for free. Fish processing and vacuum packing are available for $1.75 per pound.

✉ *Soldotna* ☎ *800/334–8730* ⊕ *www. alaskarivertrips.com* 💲 *$315 full-day trips.*

MULTISPORT OUTFITTERS

Alaska Canoe & Campground

CANOEING & ROWING | This company operates fishing, rafting, paddleboarding, kayaking, canoeing, and glacier-viewing trips. It also has cabins, offers instruction, and operates shuttles to put-in and take-out points. ✉ *35292 Sterling Hwy., Soldotna* ☎ *907/262–2331* ⊕ *www. alaskacanoetrips.com* 💲 *From $250 for guided kayaking.*

 Restaurants

Burger Bus

$ | **BURGER** | A great spot to hit after a day of fishing, the Burger Bus is just as it sounds: an old school bus converted into a kitchen, with a shack built around it, and delicious burgers on offer. The portions are big and the flavors are great. **Known for:** unique school-bus kitchen setup; excellent halibut burger; great grub-on-the-go stop before or after a fishing excursion. 💲 *Average main: $11* ✉ *409 Overland Ave., Kenai* ☎ *907/283–9611* ☉ *Closed Sun. and Mon.*

The Duck Inn Cafe

$$ | **AMERICAN** | With pizzas, burgers, chicken, steaks, and seafood on the Duck Inn's menu, there's something for everyone. Portions are generous, and the prices are reasonable. **Known for:** duck-themed artwork; unique and varied halibut dishes; greatly accommodating menu for diverse eaters. 💲 *Average main: $20* ✉ *Mile 19½, 43187 Kalifornsky Beach Rd., Soldotna* ☎ *907/262–2656* ⊕ *www.duckinnalaska.net.*

Louie's Steak and Seafood

$$$ | **AMERICAN** | As its name suggests, Louie's specializes in steak and Alaska seafood, but they have a number of other alternatives on the menu as well. The clam chowder gets quite the rave

reviews, and the clam and mussel appetizer is outstanding. **Known for:** excellent prime rib; family-friendly menu; eccentric decor. 💲 *Average main: $30* ✉ *47 Spur View Dr., Kenai* ☎ *907/283–3660* ⊕ *www. louiessteakandseafood.com.*

St. Elias Brewing Company

$$ | **AMERICAN** | Everything at St. Elias is homemade: the beer, the Neapolitan-style stone-fired rustic pizza, the sandwiches, and even the desserts. The calzones are to die for, and the Mt. Redoubt chocolate cake with a molten center is simply divine. **Known for:** locally brewed beer; fantastic rustic pizzas; great live music concerts in the summer. 💲 *Average main: $17* ✉ *434 Sharkathmi Ave., Sterling* ☎ *907/260–7837* ⊕ *www. steliasbrewingco.com.*

 Hotels

Aspen Hotel Soldotna

$$ | **HOTEL** | This Soldotna hotel sits on a bluff overlooking the Kenai River, and if you get a river-view room you'll have a front-row seat for the fishing action during salmon runs. **Pros:** riverfront location; hot tub for all guests; great swimming pool. **Cons:** urban setting, despite being along the river; bland corporate feel; no air-conditioning for the rare hot days. 💲 *Rooms from: $189* ✉ *326 Binkley Cir., Soldotna* ☎ *907/260–7736* ⊕ *www. aspenhotelsak.com* 🛏 *63 rooms* ☉| *No Meals.*

Best Western King Salmon Motel

$$ | **HOTEL** | Large rooms, including some with kitchenettes, make this motel a great option for families. **Pros:** meticulously cleaned; food voucher for the café next door; coffee and food in walking distance. **Cons:** pillows are lumpy; surrounded by strip malls; beds are hard. 💲 *Rooms from: $159* ✉ *35546–A Kenai Spur Hwy., Soldotna* ☎ *907/262–5857* ⊕ *bestwesternalaska.com/hotels* 🛏 *49 rooms* ☉| *Free Breakfast.*

Salmon Catcher Lodge

$$$ | HOTEL | For a break from hotel mayhem or to immerse yourself in the world of angling, this upscale lodge delivers both tranquil beauty and a flurry of fishing activity. **Pros:** rates include unlimited processing of your fishing catch; plenty of tranquility; great angling opportunities. **Cons:** very fishing focused; setting may be too remote for some; no TV. [$] *Rooms from: $210* ✉ *37911 Ralph La., Kenai* ☎ *907/335–2001* 🌐 *www.salmoncatcherlodge.com* 🛏 *46 rooms* 🍴 *No Meals.*

Homer

77 miles south of Soldotna, 226 miles southwest of Anchorage.

At the southern end of the Sterling Highway lies the city of Homer, at the base of a narrow spit that juts 4 miles into beautiful Kachemak Bay. Glaciers and snowcapped mountains form a dramatic backdrop across the water.

Founded in the late 1800s as a gold-prospecting camp, this community was later used as coal-mining headquarters. Chunks of coal are still common along local beaches; they wash into the bay from nearby slopes where the coal seams are exposed. Today the town of Homer is an eclectic community with most of the tacky tourist paraphernalia relegated to the Spit (though the Spit has plenty else to recommend it, not the least of which is the 360-degree view of the surrounding mountains); the rest of the town is full of local merchants and artisans. The community is an interesting mix of fishermen, actors, artists, and writers. Much of the commercial fishing centers on halibut, and the popular Homer Jackpot Halibut Derby is often won by fish weighing more than 300 pounds. The local architecture includes everything from dwellings that are little more than assemblages of driftwood to steel commercial buildings and magnificent homes on the hillside overlooking the surrounding bay, mountains, forests, and glaciers.

GETTING HERE AND AROUND

The Sterling Highway ends in Homer, and the drive in is beautiful. Once there, you'll see signs on your left for Pioneer Avenue, Homer's commercial district. On the right is the historic town center, and if you keep to the road you'll hit the Spit. Homer also has a commercial airport, with flights daily to and from Anchorage, Seldovia, and elsewhere. If you're traveling on the Marine Highway system, ferries to Kodiak and beyond dock several times a week in summer.

ESSENTIALS

VISITOR INFORMATION Visit Homer.
✉ *201 Sterling Hwy., Homer* ☎ *907/235–7740* 🌐 *www.homeralaska.org.*

👁 Sights

★ Homer Spit

PROMENADE | FAMILY | Protruding into Kachemak Bay, the Homer Spit provides a sandy focal point for visitors and locals. A 4½-mile paved road runs the length of the Spit, making it the world's longest road into the ocean. A commercial-fishing-boat harbor at the end of the path has restaurants, hotels, charter-fishing businesses, sea-kayaking outfitters, art galleries, and on-the-beach camping spots. Fly a kite, walk the beaches, drop a line in the Fishing Hole, or just wander through the shops looking for something interesting; this is one of Alaska's favorite summertime destinations. ✉ *Homer.*

★ Islands and Ocean Visitors Center

VISITOR CENTER | FAMILY | This center provides a wonderful introduction to the Alaska Maritime National Wildlife Refuge. The refuge covers some 3½ million acres spread across some 2,500 Alaskan islands, from Prince of Wales Island in the south to Barrow in the north. The 37,000-square-foot eco-friendly facility with towering windows facing Kachemak Bay is a must for anyone interested in the abundant aquatic, avian, and land mammal life of the region. A film takes visitors along on a voyage of the Fish and Wildlife Service's research ship, the MV *Tiglax*. Interactive exhibits detail the birds and marine mammals of the refuge (the largest seabird refuge in America), and one room even re-creates the noisy sounds and pungent smells of a bird rookery. In summer, guided bird-watching treks and beach walks are offered, and you can take a stroll on your own on the walkways in Beluga Slough, where Alaskan poet Wendy Erd's commissioned work lines the way. ✉ *95 Sterling Hwy., Homer* ☎ *907/235–6961* ⊕ *www.islandsandocean.org* 💲 *Free.*

Kachemak Bay

BODY OF WATER | The bay abounds with wildlife, including a large population of puffins and eagles. Tour operators take visitors past bird rookeries or across the bay to gravel beaches for clam digging. Most fishing charters include an opportunity to view whales, seals, porpoises, and birds close-up. At the end of the day, walk along the docks on one of the largest coastal parks in America. ✉ *Homer.*

Pratt Museum

OTHER MUSEUM | FAMILY | The Pratt is an art gallery and a cultural and natural-history museum rolled into one. In addition to monthly exhibits showcasing some of Alaska's finest artists, the museum has an exhibit on the 1989 *Exxon Valdez* oil spill; botanical gardens; nature trails; a gift shop; and pioneer, Russian, and Alaska Native displays. You can spy on wildlife with robotic video cameras set up on a seabird rookery and at the McNeil River Bear Sanctuary. A refurbished homestead cabin and outdoor summer exhibits are along the trail out back. ✉ *3779 Bartlett St., Homer* ☎ *907/235–8635* ⊕ *www. prattmuseum.org* 💲 *$15* 🕐 *Closed Mon., Tues., and Jan.*

 ## Activities

BEAR WATCHING
Emerald Air Service

WILDLIFE-WATCHING | Homer is a favorite departure point for viewing Alaska's famous brown bears in Katmai National Park. Emerald Air is one of several companies offering one-hour flightseeing trips, as well as day-long and custom photography trips. ✉ *1344 Lake Shore Dr., Homer* ☎ *907/235–4160, 877/235–9600* ⊕ *www.emeraldairservice.com* 💲 *From $350.*

Smokey Bay Air

WILDLIFE-WATCHING | This outfitter supplies the surrounding area with air-taxi services but also provides excellent bear-viewing trips at Katmai and Lake Clark National Parks. On the way, you'll have a chance to view volcanoes and glaciers, then land and peruse the terrain while carefully spying on bears. ✉ *2100 Kachemak Bay Dr., Homer* ☎ *888/482–1511, 907/235–1511* ⊕ *www.smokeybayair.com* 💲 *From $100.*

BOATING AND FISHING

Homer is a major commercial fishing port (especially for halibut) and a popular destination for sport anglers in search of giant halibut or feisty king and silver salmon. Quite a few companies offer charter fishing in summer, from about $250 to $350 per person per day, including bait and tackle. The pricing is usually based on how many different types of fish you're going after.

Annual Homer Halibut Tournament

FISHING | With live music, food trucks, random drawings, and activities, this two-day fishing tournament is loads of fun for everyone. The tournament entry fee lets you fish both days to try for the grand slam as well as a number of side challenges. ✉ *Homer* ☎ *907/235–7740* ⊕ *www.homerhalibuttournament.com* 💲 *$100.*

Central Charters & Tours

BOATING | This hyper-local, small but mighty charter can arrange fishing trips in outer Kachemak Bay and Lower Cook Inlet—areas known for excellent halibut fishing. Boat sizes vary considerably; some have a six-person limit, whereas others can take up to 16 passengers. The company also conducts non-fishing boat tours and bear-viewing trips. ✉ *4241 Homer Spit Rd., Homer* ☎ *907/235–7847* 🌐 *www.centralcharter.com* 🎫 *Boat tours from $69, fishing trips from $120, bear viewing from $595.*

Fishing Hole

BOATING | Near the end of the Spit, Homer's famous Fishing Hole, aka the Nick Dudiak Fishing Lagoon, is a small bight stocked with king and silver salmon smolt (baby fish) by the Alaska Department of Fish and Game. The salmon then head out to sea, returning several years later to the Fishing Hole, where they are easy targets for wall-to-wall bankside anglers throughout summer. The Fishing Hole isn't anything like casting for salmon along a remote stream, but your chances are good and you don't need to drop $800 for a flight into the wilderness. Fishing licenses and rental poles are available from fishing-supply stores on the Spit. ✉ *Homer.*

Homer Ocean Charters

FISHING | Locally owned and operated, Homer Ocean Charters has been in business since 1979, setting up half-day to multiday fishing excursions, as well as sea-kayaking and hiking adventures. They also offer water-taxi services and bare-bones cabin rentals on Otter Cove. ✉ *4287 Homer Spit Rd., Homer* ☎ *907/235–6212* 🌐 *www.homerocean.com* 🎫 *From $195.*

Inlet Charters

FISHING | This family-owned-and-run charter has been operating in Homer since 1991. They provide salmon, halibut, and rockfish charters as half- and full-day excursions. They also provide water-taxi services, lodging, sea kayaking, and wildlife cruises. ✉ *4287 Homer Spit Rd., Homer* ☎ *800/770–6126* 🌐 *www.halibutcharters.com* 🎫 *From $265.*

SEA KAYAKING

True North Kayak Adventures

KAYAKING | Several local companies offer guided sea-kayaking trips to protected coves within Kachemak Bay State Park and nearby islands. True North has a range of such adventures, including a three-day trip and a boat and kayak day trip to Yukon Island (both trips include round-trip water taxi to the island base camp, guide, all kayak equipment, and meals). ✉ *4308 Homer Spit Rd., Homer* ☎ *907/235–0708* 🌐 *www.truenorthkayak.com* 🎫 *Day trips from $125; overnight from $425.*

🍴 Restaurants

Fat Olives Restaurant

$$ | **MEDITERRANEAN** | Pumpkin-color walls, light streaming through tall front windows, and a playful collection of Italian posters add to the appeal of this fine Tuscany-inspired bistro. The menu encompasses enticing appetizers, salads, sandwiches, calzones, and pizzas throughout the day, along with oven-roasted chicken, fresh seafood, pork loin, and other fare in the evening. **Known for:** classic Italian cuisine; excellent pizza options; good wine selection. [$] *Average main: $15* ✉ *276 Ohlson La., Homer* ☎ *907/235–8488* 🌐 *www.fatoliveshomer.com.*

Fritz Creek General Store

$ | **ECLECTIC** | Be sure to check out this old-fashioned country store, gas station, liquor store, post office, video-rental shop, and deli. The latter is the primary reason for stopping at Fritz's: the food is amazingly good—brisket smoked right out back, homemade bread, pastries, and pizza by the slice. **Known for:** off-the-beaten-path vibe; best sandwiches in town; great place to mingle with locals. [$] *Average main: $10* ✉ *Mile 8.2, 55770 E. End Rd., Homer* ☎ *907/235–6753.*

★ La Baleine

$ | AMERICAN | Open at 7 am, this place is a perfect stop before a day of fishing, but lunch is an equally fulfilling experience. La Baleine serves fantastic breakfast sandwiches on fresh ciabatta rolls—complimentary cup of locally roasted coffee included. **Known for:** locally sourced ingredients; fantastic homemade ramen bowls; best breakfast sandwiches in town. $ *Average main: $12 ✉ 4450 Homer Spit Rd., Homer ☎ 907/299–6672 ⊕ www.labaleinecafe.com ☻ Closed Mon. and Tues. No dinner.*

★ Little Mermaid

$$$ | AMERICAN | This hot spot draws crowds from all over the world, despite the fact it's too small to fit them all (reservations are essential). The emphasis here is on local ingredients, each bite making Homer feel a little more like home. **Known for:** famed Hot Stone Bowl with local fish and veggies; best seafood destination in town; cozy ambience. $ *Average main: $25 ✉ Harborview Boardwalk, 4246 Homer Spit Rd., Homer ☎ 907/399–9900 ⊕ www.littlemermaid-homer.com ☻ Closed Sun. and Mon.*

Two Sisters Bakery

$ | CAFÉ | This very popular café is a short walk from Bishops Beach, Beluga Slough, and the Islands and Ocean Visitors Center. In addition to fresh breads and pastries, Two Sisters specializes in deliciously healthy lunches, such as vegetarian focaccia sandwiches, homemade soups, quiche, and salads. **Known for:** wraparound porch perfect for summer; fantastic fresh bread; best place to drink coffee and read the morning paper. $ *Average main: $10 ✉ 233 E. Bunnell Ave., Homer ☎ 907/235–2280 ⊕ www. twosistersbakery.net ☻ Closed Sat.– Mon. No dinner.*

Wild Honey Bistro

$ | BISTRO | Located in Old Town next to the Bunnell Street Arts Center, Wild Honey features sweet and savory crepes along with housemade soups and salads, most of which showcase ingredients the owners have harvested themselves. Everything else is bought from local farmers. **Known for:** cozy ambience; great outdoor seating; Drunken Monkey (strawberry and banana) mimosas. $ *Average main: $14 ✉ 106 W Bunnell Ave., Homer ☎ 907/435–7635 ⊕ www.wildhoneybistro.com ☻ Closed Mon.–Wed. No dinner.*

Hotels

Alaskan Suites

$$$ | HOTEL | The five modern cabins here each offer a million-dollar view from a hilltop on the west side of Homer. **Pros:** quaint but classy; crow's-nest views; highway location with no highway noise. **Cons:** views so beautiful you may never want to go home; not within walking distance of anything; not as remote as it could be. $ *Rooms from: $270 ✉ 3255 Sterling Hwy., Homer ☎ 907/299–7450 ⊕ www.alaskansuites.com ⟲ 5 cabins ⦿ No Meals.*

Driftwood Inn

$$ | B&B/INN | With an RV park, four deluxe lodges, two cottages, and a historic inn, the Driftwood accommodates a range of travelers. **Pros:** close to Bishop's Beach; accommodations for every budget; relaxed, cozy atmosphere. **Cons:** some rooms are only accessible by stairs; some of the inn's rooms are small; decor a little old-fashioned. $ *Rooms from: $124 ✉ 135 W. Bunnell Ave., Homer ☎ 907/235–8019 ⊕ www.thedriftwoodinn.com ⟲ 42 rooms ⦿ No Meals.*

Homer Inn & Spa

$$$ | B&B/INN | Along with a fabulous view of the ocean, this waterfront boutique inn offers six guest rooms, all decorated with local art and character. **Pros:** great spa services on-site; all rooms are ocean-facing; incredible views of the bay, glaciers, and volcanoes. **Cons:** no beach access; no restaurant on-site; Old Town and main commerce area are not in close walking distance. $ *Rooms from: $250 ✉ 895*

Ocean Dr. Loop, Homer ☎ *907/235–1000* 🌐 *www.homerinnandspa.com* 🛏 *6 suites* 🍴 *No Meals.*

Land's End Resort and Lodges

$$ | HOTEL | Spread across the best real estate on the Spit, Land's End offers splendid bay views from variously styled rooms and suites. **Pros:** great dining on-site; the Spit-end location puts you well into the bay; great views of the bay and mountains. **Cons:** large, corporate feel; you might be disappointed if you get a room without a view; location makes it a bit of a drive to Old Town. [$] *Rooms from: $189* ✉ *4786 Homer Spit Rd., Homer* ☎ *907/235–0400, 800/478–0400* 🌐 *www.lands-end-resort.com* 🛏 *145 rooms* 🍴 *No Meals.*

Old Town Bed & Breakfast

$$ | B&B/INN | In the oldest commercial building in Homer, this bright and cozy B&B offers peace, convenience, and sweeping views of the bay and mountains. **Pros:** great views; warm and inviting; good location. **Cons:** have to climb a set of stairs; some rooms have shared baths; the stairs are at an angle so it feels as though you're inebriated. [$] *Rooms from: $120* ✉ *106 W. Bunnell Ave., in Old Inlet Trading Post, Homer* ☎ *907/235–7558* 🌐 *www.oldtownbedandbreakfast.com* 🍴 *Free Breakfast* 🛏 *3 rooms.*

Nightlife

Alice's Champagne Palace

LIVE MUSIC | Dance to lively bands on weekends at Alice's, which attracts nationally known singer-songwriters. When you're all danced out, be sure to fill up on their great bar grub or grab a "bag of burgers" to eat back at your hotel room (a deal that consists of 6 cheeseburgers and fries for $40). ✉ *195 E. Pioneer Ave., Homer* ☎ *907/235–6909.*

Salty Dawg Saloon

BARS | The Spit's infamous Salty Dawg is a tumbledown lighthouse of sorts, sure to be frequented by a carousing fisherman or 20, along with half the tourists in town. ✉ *4380 Homer Spit Rd., Homer* ☎ *907/235–6718* 🌐 *www.saltydawgsaloon.com.*

Performing Arts

Pier One Theater

THEATER | For more than four decades, this community theater has presented locally written and outside plays. Recent seasons have seen a Molière comedy and narratives of people in the fishing industry. The theater is in an old barnlike building on the Homer Spit. ✉ *3858 Homer Spit Rd., Homer* ☎ *907/235–7333* 🌐 *www.pieronetheatre.org.*

Shopping

ART AND GIFTS

A variety of art by the town's residents can be found in the galleries on and around Pioneer Avenue.

Bunnell Street Arts Center

ART GALLERIES | The gallery, which occupies the first floor of a historic trading post, showcases and sells innovative Alaskan-made contemporary art. It also hosts workshops, lectures, musical performances, and other community events. ✉ *106 W. Bunnell Ave., at Main St., Homer* ☎ *907/235–2662* 🌐 *www.bunnellarts.org.*

Ptarmigan Arts

ART GALLERIES | A cooperative gallery, Ptarmigan shows photographs, paintings, pottery, jewelry, woodworking, and other pieces by local fine and craft artists. ✉ *471 E. Pioneer Ave., Homer* ☎ *907/235–5345* 🌐 *www.ptarmiganarts.com.*

CLOTHING

The Fringe

SECOND-HAND | Located in the belly of Bunnell, Fringe is a used and new clothing boutique. Its biggest draw are the locally made wearable art pieces that range from groovy hats to clever, funky dresses and linens. ⊠ *106 W. Bunnell St., Homer* ☎ *907/235–4999.*

Homer's Jeans

MIXED CLOTHING | This shop offers name-brand outdoor wear in addition to more utilitarian gear. Buy your cute shoes and your hiking boots here. ⊠ *564 E. Pioneer Ave., Suite 1, Homer* ☎ *907/235–6234* ⊕ *www.homersjeans.com.*

Nomar

MIXED CLOTHING | The company manufactures equipment and clothing for commercial fishermen. Its Homer shop sells PolarFleece garments and other rugged outerwear, plus duffels, rain gear, and children's clothing. ⊠ *104 E. Pioneer Ave., Homer* ☎ *800/478–8364* ⊕ *www. nomaralaska.com.*

FOOD

Coal Point Seafood Company

FOOD | Homer is famous for its halibut, salmon, and Kachemak Bay oysters. For fresh fish, head to Coal Point Seafood Company, which can also package and ship fish that you catch. ⊠ *4306 Homer Spit Rd., Homer* ☎ *907/235–3877, 800/325–3877* ⊕ *www.welovefish.com.*

Salmon Sisters

FOOD | Created by two sisters who grew up harvesting seafood on Alaska commercial fishing boats, Salmon Sisters is an all-woman-run shop where you can stock up on your filleted, smoked, jarred, or frozen wild Alaska salmon and halibut. They also sell fishing gear and Alaska-made cards, books, and clothing. ⊠ *1554 Homer Spit Rd., Homer* ☎ *907/299–5615* ⊕ *www.aksalmonsisters.com.*

Kachemak Bay State Park and State Wilderness Park

10 miles southeast of Homer.

Kachemak Bay is Alaska's first state park and only wilderness park. It protects roughly 400,000 acres of coast, mountains, glaciers, forests, and wildlife on the lower Kenai Peninsula. The park encompasses a line of snowcapped mountains and several large glaciers. The prominent one visible from the Homer Spit is Grewingk Glacier. One of the most popular trails in the park is a 3-mile hike that ends at the lake in front of the glacier.

GETTING HERE AND AROUND

There are more than 80 hiking trails and a number of lodges and campsites in Kachemak Bay State Park and State Wilderness Park. They are only accessible by boat, except for a few that are also accessible by floatplane. Mako's Water Taxi and Danny J Ferry provide boat service to the park.

WATER TAXI CONTACTS Danny J Ferry. ⊠ ☎ *907/399–2683* ⊕ *www.thesaltry.com/danny-j-ferry.* **Mako's Water Taxi.** ⊠ *Homer Spit Rd., Homer* ☎ *907/235–9055* ⊕ *www.makoswatertaxi.com.*

 ## Sights

Halibut Cove

TOWN | A small artists' community directly across from the tip of the Homer Spit, Halibut Cove is a fine place to spend time meandering along the boardwalk and visiting galleries. The cove is lovely, especially during salmon runs, when fish leap and splash in the clear water. The *Danny J* ferries people across from the Spit, with a tour of the rookery at Gull Island ($66) and three hours to walk around Halibut Cove. The *Danny J* also provides a daily dinner cruise to The Saltry Restaurant

($41). Central Charters and The Saltry Restaurant handle all bookings. Several lodges are on this side of the bay, on pristine coves away from summer crowds. Mako's Taxi also provides service to most of the lodging destinations in the area. ✉ *Homer* ☎ *907/399–2683* ⊕ *www. halibutcove.com* ⊘ *Closed Oct.–Apr.*

Kachemak Bay State Park and State Wilderness Park

STATE/PROVINCIAL PARK | Recreational opportunities in this beautiful park, which encompasses about 400,000 acres, include boating, sea kayaking, fishing, hiking, and beachcombing. Among the attractions here are Grewingk Glacier, Poot Peak, China Poot Bay, Halibut Cove Lagoon, Tutka Bay, Humpy Creek, and China Poot (Leisure) Lake—trails accessible from Kachemak Bay lead to all of them. Facilities are minimal but include 20 primitive campsites and five public-use cabins. Most Homer water-taxi operators can drop you off and pick you up at specific points and can provide advice about hiking, camping, and kayaking trips. ✉ *Homer* ☎ *907/235–7024* ⊕ *dnr.alaska.gov/parks/aspunits/kenai/ kachemakbaysp.htm.*

 **Restaurants**

Halibut Cove Live

$$$$ | **SEAFOOD** | Set on a superb floating stage on Halibut Cove, HCL hosts dinner several times a summer, each featuring a renowned guest chef from somewhere in the state, locally grown produce, and fresh seafood. There's also live jazz music. **Known for:** very romantic ambience; unique (and expensive) dining and music experience; fantastic fresh seafood dishes. $ *Average main: $250* ☎ *907/235–0541* ⊕ *www.halibutcovelive. com* ⊘ *Closed Sept.–May.*

★ The Saltry Restaurant

$$$ | **SEAFOOD** | At the top of the dock overlooking Halibut Cove, this is one of Southcentral's most beautiful places to

Camping on Kachemak Bay

Twenty primitive, free campsites with pit toilets and fire rings are scattered along the shores of Kachemak Bay across from Homer and are accessible by boat (water taxis operate here daily in summer). The sites are available on a first-come, first-served basis, and camping is allowed nearly everywhere in the park (not restricted to developed sites). Large groups can reserve sites, which are listed on the park's website. 907/235–7024or 907/262–5581.

sit and soak up the pleasures of a summer afternoon. Locally caught seafood, the restaurant's specialty, is prepared with finesse, and the dish for vegetarians is always a mouthwatering delight. **Known for:** location on art-filled boardwalk; romantic dining; one of the best Alaskan culinary experiences. $ *Average main: $28* ✉ *9 W. Ismilof Rd., Halibut Cove* ☎ *907/399–2683* ⊕ *www.thesaltry.com* ⊘ *Closed Sun., Mon., and late Sept.–early May.*

 Hotels

Alaska State Parks Cabins

$ | **HOUSE** | Three public-use cabins are within Kachemak Bay's Halibut Cove lagoon area, another is near Tutka Bay lagoon, and a fifth is at China Poot Lake. **Pros:** true wilderness; total solitude; great views. **Cons:** all cabins except one accessible only by boat; remote locations with no amenities; no running water or electricity. $ *Rooms from: $75* ✉ *Homer* ☎ *907/262–5581* ⊕ *dnr.alaska.gov/parks/ aspcabins* ⇥ *5 cabins* ⊘ *No Meals.*

Kachemak Bay Wilderness Lodge

$$$$ | **RESORT** | Across Kachemak Bay from Homer, this lodge provides wildlife-viewing opportunities and panoramic mountain and bay vistas in an intimate setting for up to 12 guests. **Pros:** stunning location; extraordinary facility; sauna and outdoor hot tub. **Cons:** might be too remote for some; pricey; few standard hotel amenities. [$] *Rooms from: $3700* ✉ *Homer* ☎ *907/235–8910* 🌐 *www.alaskawildernesslodge.com* 🕒 *Closed Oct.–Apr.* 🛏 *5 cabins* 🍴 *All-Inclusive.*

★ **Tutka Bay Lodge**

$$$$ | **RESORT** | In a small cove 9 nautical miles from Homer Spit (boat ride included in the room rates), this resort offers luxury and relaxation. **Pros:** incredible food; experienced guide on all trips; amazing location. **Cons:** cell phone service may be dodgy; a bit pricey; three-night minimum stay. [$] *Rooms from: $6250* ✉ *Homer* ☎ *907/274–2710* 🌐 *withinthewild.com/lodges/tutka-bay* 🛏 *5 cabins* 🍴 *All-Inclusive.*

Seldovia

16 miles south of Homer.

The town of Seldovia is an off-the-road-system settlement on the south side of Kachemak Bay that retains the charm of an earlier Alaska. The town's Russian bloodline shows in its onion-dome church and its name, which means "herring bay." For many years this was the primary fishing town on the bay, but today the focus is on tourism. The town was heavily damaged in the 1964 earthquake, but a few stretches of old boardwalk survive and houses stand on stilts along Seldovia Slough. Seldovia has several restaurants and lodging places, plus a small museum and the hilltop Russian Orthodox church. The area abounds with hiking, mountain-biking, and sea-kayaking options, and is a favorite performance destination for many Alaskan musicians during the summer months.

GETTING HERE AND AROUND

Seldovia's not an island, but it is only accessible by the Alaska Marine Highway ferry, by water taxi, or by air from Homer.

🍴 Restaurants

Linwood Bar & Grill

$$ | **AMERICAN** | With a great outdoor deck and a heap of local company, the Linwood emphasizes its "bar" side at night and serves up hearty grilled burgers, pizzas, and seafood by day and into the early evening. Musicians from all over the state take the boat over to perform for Seldovians here. **Known for:** great pub food; live music from around the state; excellent outdoor deck. [$] *Average main: $15* ✉ *257 Main St., Seldovia* ☎ *907/234–7674* 🌐 *www.linwoodbar.com.*

🛏 Hotels

Sea Parrot Inn

$$ | **B&B/INN** | In view of the harbor and just a short walk away, the Sea Parrot Inn is hard to miss. **Pros:** robust breakfast included in rate; convenient harbor location; welcoming hosts. **Cons:** boat ride required to get there; setting may be too cozy for some guests; can get loud on live music nights. [$] *Rooms from: $135* ✉ *226 Main St., Seldovia* ☎ *844/377–7829, 907/234–7829* 🌐 *www.seaparrotinn.com* 🕒 *Closed Memorial Day–Labor Day* 🛏 *4 rooms* 🍴 *Free Breakfast.*

Seldovia Boardwalk Hotel

$$ | **HOTEL** | With fabulous views of the harbor and tastefully decorated rooms, the Boardwalk has many of the simple amenities found in an urban hotel, but with a cozy B&B feel. **Pros:** beautiful sundeck overlooking the water; in-town location; great waterfront views. **Cons:** takes a boat to get here; some rooms primarily have street views; small rooms. [$] *Rooms from: $165* ✉ *239 Main St.,*

Seldovia ☎ *907/234–7816* ⊕ *www.seldo-viahotel.com* ⮌ *11 rooms* ⦿ *No Meals.*

Kodiak

248 miles southwest of Anchorage by air.

For over 7,000 years, the Alutiiq people inhabited the region now known as Kodiak (Sun'aq). In the 18th century, Russian explorers arrived, and today, commercial fishing is king in Kodiak. Despite its small population—about 5,583 people scattered among the several islands in the Kodiak Borough—the city is among the busiest fishing ports in the United States. The harbor is also an important supply point for small communities on the Aleutian Islands and the Alaska Peninsula.

Visitors to the island tend to follow one of two agendas: either immediately fly out to a remote lodge for fishing, kayaking, or bear viewing; or stay in town and access whatever pursuits they can reach from the limited road system. If the former is too pricey an option, consider combining the two: drive the road system to see what can be seen inexpensively, then add a fly-out or charter-boat excursion to a remote lodge or wilderness access point.

Floatplane and boat charters are available from Kodiak to many remote attractions, chief among them Kodiak National Wildlife Refuge, which includes most of the terrain of four islands in the Kodiak Archipelago: Kodiak, Afognak, Ban, and Uganik.

GETTING HERE AND AROUND
Access to the island is via the Alaska Marine Highway ferry (which makes several stops a week) or by plane. A few roads stretch out of town, perfect for a day of sightseeing. The action, however, is in town. Your first exploring stop should be the Kodiak Island Convention & Visitors Bureau. Here you can pick up brochures, pamphlets, and lists of all

the visitor services on Kodiak and the surrounding islands, and get help with planning your adventures. If you want to strike out and hike the local trails, there's an informative *Hiking and Birding Guide* published by the Kodiak Audubon Society.

ESSENTIALS
VISITOR INFORMATION Kodiak Island Convention & Visitors Bureau. ⊠ *100 E. Marine Way, Suite 200, Kodiak* ☎ *907/486–4782* ⊕ *kodiak.org.*

Sights

Alutiiq Museum and Archaeological Repository
HISTORY MUSEUM | Home to one of the largest collections of Alaska Native materials in the world, the Alutiiq Museum contains archaeological and ethnographic items dating back 7,500 years. The more than 150,000 artifacts include harpoons, masks, dolls, stone tools, seal-gut parkas, grass baskets, and pottery fragments. The museum store sells Alaska Native art and educational materials. ⊠ *215 Mission Rd., Suite 101, Kodiak* ☎ *844/425–8844* ⊕ *www.alutiiqmuseum.org* ⮌ *$7* ⊙ *Closed Sun. and Mon.*

Fort Abercrombie State Historical Park
MILITARY SIGHT | **FAMILY** | As part of America's North Pacific defense during World War II, Kodiak was the site of an important naval station, now occupied by the Coast Guard fleet that patrols the surrounding fishing grounds. Part of the old military installation has been incorporated into this park north of town. Self-guided tours take you past concrete bunkers and gun emplacements, and trails wind through moss-draped spruce forest. There's a highly scenic overlook, great for bird and whale watching, and inside a bunker a volunteer group runs the **Kodiak Military History Museum.** ⊠ *1400 Abercrombie Dr., Kodiak* ☎ *907/486–6339* ⊕ *dnr.alaska.gov/parks/aspunits/kodiak/fortabercrombieshp.htm* ⮌ *$5.*

Holy Resurrection Russian Orthodox Church
CHURCH | The ornate Russian Orthodox church is a visual feast, both inside and out. The cross-shaped building is topped by two onion-shaped blue domes, and the interior contains brass candelabra, distinctive chandeliers, and numerous icons representing Orthodox saints. Three different churches have stood on this site since 1794. The present structure, built in 1945, is on the National Register of Historic Places. ✉ *385 Kashevaroff Ave., Kodiak* ☎ *907/486–5532 parish priest* 🌐 *www.oca.org/parishes/oca-ak-kodhrc* 🎟 *Free.*

Kodiak History Museum
HISTORY MUSEUM | Formerly the Baranov Museum, this spot has been designed to collect, educate about, and inform on the many diverse perspectives and stories of Kodiak's rich past—from the 7,500 years of Alutiiq history to the role of the region in World War II. The museum's permanent and temporary exhibits are housed in an old building first commissioned in the 1800s by Alexander Baranov, the chief manager for the fur-trading Russian-American Company. This building is considered the oldest building in the state that is not an Alaska Native structure. ✉ *101 Marine Way, Kodiak* ☎ *907/486–5920* 🌐 *www.kodiakhistorymuseum.org* 🎟 *$10* 🕒 *Closed Sun.–Tues.*

Kodiak National Wildlife Refuge Visitor Center
VISITOR CENTER | **FAMILY** | Indispensable for those exploring the wildlife refuge, this center a block from the downtown ferry dock is an interesting stop on its own. Wander through exhibits about the refuge's flora and fauna, attend an interpretive talk, and marvel at the complete 36-foot hanging skeleton of a male gray whale on the second floor. ✉ *402 Center Ave., Kodiak* ☎ *907/487–2626* 🌐 *www.fws.gov/refuge/kodiak.*

Activities

Adventure Kodiak
WILDLIFE-WATCHING | This high-end company offers seven-day yacht cruises that explore a number of the area's bays. You might choose from activities like photography lessons, bear viewing, wildlife viewing, birding, beachcombing, and tidal pool exploration. ✉ *Kodiak* ☎ *907/337–6532* 🌐 *www.adventurekodiak.com* 🎟 *From $1500.*

Kodiak Outdoor Guide
FOUR-WHEELING | This outfitter will hook you up with an ATV or UTV sightseeing tour or a boat for fishing adventures, getting you to places you couldn't access otherwise. ✉ *1713 E Rezanof Dr.,* ☎ *907/654–7357, 907/654–7356* 🌐 *www.kodiakoutdoorguide.com* 🎟 *From $350.*

Restaurants

Henry's Great Alaskan Restaurant
$$$ | **AMERICAN** | A big, boisterous, friendly place near the small-boat harbor, Henry's has a menu that's equally big. There's fresh local seafood, of course, but also everything from barbecue and rack of lamb to gourmet salads, pastas, and even some Cajun dishes. **Known for:** very relaxed environment; great post-fishing dining destination; flavorful seafood bowls. [$] *Average main: $30* ✉ *512 W. Marine Way, Kodiak* ☎ *907/486–8844* 🌐 *www.henrysgreatalaskan.com.*

Java Flats
$ | **CAFÉ** | This great coffee shop represents the true essence of Kodiak life. Fantastic breakfast burritos, vegetarian sandwiches, and excellent coffee make this the perfect place to stock up on provisions before embarking on exciting bear-watching and salmon-fishing adventures. **Known for:** best coffee in town; tasty vegetarian sandwiches; grab-and-go options. [$] *Average main: $12* ✉ *11206 W. Rezanof Dr., Kodiak* ☎ *907/487–2622* 🌐 *www.javaflats.com* 🕒 *Closed Mon. and Tues.*

Kodiak Hana Restaurant

$$ | **SEAFOOD** | This converted powerhouse facility allows a close-up view of Near Island and the channel connecting the boat harbors with the Gulf of Alaska. Enjoy fine steaks and classic seafood dishes or fresh sushi and sashimi while watching the procession of fishing boats gliding past on their way to catch or bring back your next meal. **Known for:** diverse fresh fish dishes; excellent sushi; great views of marine wildlife. $ *Average main: $20* ✉ *516 E. Marine Way, Kodiak* ☎ *907/481–1088* ⊕ *www.kodiakhana. com* ⊙ *No lunch Sun.*

Rendezvous Bar & Grill

$$ | **AMERICAN** | A shanty roadhouse of sorts, Rendezvous serves drinks all night and caters to locals with great grub and live music from artists that hail from all over the country. And every afternoon (except Monday), the locals and tourists show up in droves to fill their bellies with the tastiest eats on the island. **Known for:** no food (just drinks) after 7:30 pm; amazing fish tacos; laid-back ambiance. $ *Average main: $15* ✉ *11652 Rezanof Dr. W, Kodiak* ☎ *907/487–2233* ⊕ *www. facebook.com/rendezvous.kodiak* ⊙ *No lunch or dinner Mon.*

Hotels

Best Western Kodiak Inn

$$$ | **HOTEL** | Rooms here have soothing floral decor, and some overlook the harbor. **Pros:** free Wi-Fi; downtown location; local seafood at restaurant. **Cons:** quiet rooms don't have great views; harbor-view rooms are on the street; despite location, it's still a corporate chain. $ *Rooms from: $207* ✉ *236 W. Rezanof Dr., Kodiak* ☎ *907/486–5712* ⊕ *www.bestwestern.com* ⇱ *82 rooms* ⋈ *Free Breakfast.*

A Channel View Bed & Breakfast

$$ | **B&B/INN** | Owned and operated by a fifth-generation Kodiak Alaskan, this emerald-isle favorite has sea views and is conveniently located less than 1 mile from downtown Kodiak. **Pros:** nicely furnished; channel views; very hospitable owners. **Cons:** must take stairs to get to some rooms; slightly inconvenient if you don't have a car and aren't keen on a 20-minute walk into town; two-night minimum. $ *Rooms from: $199* ✉ *1010 Stellar Way, Kodiak* ☎ *907/486–2470* ⊕ *www.kodiakchannelview.com* ⋈ *Free Breakfast* ⇱ *4 rooms.*

Cliff House B&B

$$ | **B&B/INN** | Perched on Kodiak's rocky coastline, this house contains a suite of three rooms with a common sitting area, private entrance, shared bath, and kitchen facilities, complete with a bottomless jar of homemade granola. **Pros:** cliffside deck; excellent views; cozy library for rainy-day relaxation. **Cons:** decor a bit dated; some rooms share a bathroom; activities cost extra. $ *Rooms from: $190* ✉ *1223 W. Kouskov St., Kodiak* ☎ *907/486–5079* ⊕ *www.galleygourmet. biz* ⇱ *4 rooms* ⋈ *Free Breakfast.*

Quality Inn Kodiak

$$ | **HOTEL** | This chain property is a five-minute walk from the main terminal at the airport, about 4½ miles from downtown (free airport transportation is provided). **Pros:** friendly staff; can fish for salmon in the river out back; comfortable and clean rooms. **Cons:** no air-conditioning for the hot days; a bit out of town, so you might need a vehicle; not very attractive from the outside. $ *Rooms from: $180* ✉ *1395 Airport Way, Kodiak* ☎ *907/487– 2700* ⊕ *www.choicehotels.com/alaska/ kodiak/quality-inn-hotels* ⇱ *50 rooms* ⋈ *Free Breakfast.*

Nightlife

Kodiak Island Brewing Co.

BARS | Freshly brewed, unfiltered beer is the specialty here, sold in liters, growlers, pigs, and kegs, so you can stock up for your wilderness expedition and avoid beer withdrawal. Drop on by for a couple

Kodiak brown bears are often spotted near rivers and streams, fishing for salmon.

of pints in the tasting room. ⊠ *117 Lower Mill Bay Rd., Kodiak* ☎ *907/486–2537* ⊕ *www.kodiakbrewery.com.*

Kodiak National Wildlife Refuge

50 miles south of Katmai National Park, 300 miles southwest of Anchorage.

Many visitors to Kodiak National Wildlife Refuge come here to view Kodiak bears. Seeing these beautiful animals, which weigh a pound at birth but up to 1,500 pounds when fully grown, is worth the trip to this rugged country. The bears are spotted easily in July and August, feeding along salmon-spawning streams. Chartered flightseeing trips go to the area, and exaggerated tales of encounters with these impressive beasts are frequently heard.

GETTING HERE AND AROUND

The refuge is accessible only by boat or plane. The Alaska Marine Highway ferry stops at the town of Kodiak several times a week in summer. The visitor bureau there has lists of the numerous guides, outfitters, and air taxis that service the refuge.

 Sights

★ **Kodiak National Wildlife Refuge**
WILDLIFE REFUGE | The opportunity to view Kodiak brown bears alone is worth the trip here. Approximately 3,000 Kodiak brown bears, the biggest brown bears anywhere—sometimes topping out at more than 1,500 pounds—share the refuge with a few other land mammals: red foxes, river otters, short-tailed weasels, and tundra voles. Additionally, a number of mammals have been introduced to the archipelago: Sitka black-tailed deer, snowshoe hare, beavers, muskrat, Roosevelt elk, and mountain goats. The 1.9-million-acre refuge lies mostly on Kodiak Island and neighboring Afognak

and Uganik Islands, in the Gulf of Alaska. All are part of the Kodiak Archipelago, separated from Alaska's mainland by stormy Shelikof Strait.

Within the refuge are rugged mountains, tundra meadows and lowlands, and thickly forested hills, plus lakes, marshes, and hundreds of miles of pristine coastland. No place in the refuge is more than 15 miles from the ocean. The weather here is generally wet and cool, and storms born in the North Pacific often bring heavy rains. Dozens of species of birds flock to the refuge each spring and summer, including Aleutian terns, horned puffins, black oystercatchers, ravens, ptarmigan, and chickadees. At least 600 pairs of bald eagles live on the islands, building the world's largest bird nests on shoreline cliffs and in tall trees. Six species of Pacific salmon—chums, kings, pinks, silvers, sockeyes, and steelhead—return to Kodiak's waters from May to October. Other resident species include rainbow trout, Dolly Varden (an anadromous trout waiting for promotion to salmon), and arctic char. The abundance of fish and bears makes Kodiak National Wildlife Refuge popular with anglers, hunters, and wildlife watchers. ⊠ *Kodiak* ⊕ *www.fws.gov/refuge/kodiak.*

Activities

Kodiak Brown Bear Center

WILDLIFE-WATCHING | Part of the Kodiak Regional Native Corporation, this outfit has exclusive access to 112,000 acres that are free of motorized distractions. KBBC limits its tours to groups of six, ensuring an extraordinary bear-viewing experience. Lodging is within a series of modern cabins with porches facing Karluk Lake. Gourmet meals are prepared every day, and a traditional Alutiiq steam bath is on the premises. ⊠ *Kodiak* ☎ *877/335–2327* ⊕ *www.kodiakbearcenter.com* ☜ *Packages from $5425.*

Hotels

Kodiak Refuge Public-Use Cabins

$ | **HOUSE** | One of Kodiak National Wildlife Refuge's lesser-known wonders is its collection of eight fantastic cabins scattered throughout the refuge. **Pros:** affordable; true Alaska wilderness; plenty of solitude. **Cons:** roughing it is not for everyone; zero amenities; the chance of getting weathered in for a couple of days requires a loose schedule. $ *Rooms from: $45* ⊠ *1390 Buskin River Rd., Kodiak* ☎ *907/487–2600* ⊕ *www.recreation. gov* ⦿ *No Meals* ☜ *8 cabins.*

Lake Clark National Park and Preserve

100 miles southwest of Anchorage by air.

Lake Clark might have fewer visitors than other national parks, but it's hardly short on reasons to visit. Among them are abundant wildlife, salmon-filled rivers, enormous glaciers, and endless acres of solitude.

The park and preserve's 4 million acres were first declared a national monument under the Antiquities Act by President Jimmy Carter in 1978 to protect both the nature and the ruins and artifacts of the region's early inhabitants. In 1980, the region was established as a national park and preserve by the Alaska National Interest Lands Conservation Act (ANILCA). It now protects coastal rain forest; 900 square miles of glaciers; tributaries to the world's largest salmon run; Mt. Iliamna and Mt. Redoubt, two active volcanoes that sit on the Ring of Fire; large populations of brown bear, moose, caribou, Dall sheep, and eagles; and years of human history.

Evidence of the first human settlers in the region dates back nearly 10,000 years, at the end of the last great ice age. The region was a rich source of food, with abundant animal and plant life. Additionally, the coast provided opportunities for large sea-mammal hunting, as evidenced by the 2,000-year-old rock paintings—the only known rock paintings in the Alaska National Park system—in Tuxedni and Chinitna Bays.

For nearly 1,000 years, along the shores of Lake Clark (originally called Qizhjeh Vena, which translates to "Place Where People Gather Lake"), Qizhjeh village sprawled across 25 acres. It was inhabited by the Dena'ina Athabaskan, and people came from villages across the region to trade. In the late 1800s, European-American settlers arrived, and in 1902, a flu–measles epidemic struck the village. By 1909, it was abandoned as the survivors fled to nearby Nondalton, and Qizhjeh is now a National Historical Landmark maintained by the park service. The area holds more than a dozen archeological sites, and hikers still walk the Telaquana Route, which once connected Qizhjeh to what is now the northern part of the park at Telequana Lake. This is truly an outdoor explorer's backcountry trail that taps into all the scout badges you earned growing up.

Lake Clark National Park and Preserve offers endless opportunities for adventure. There are no roads, there are no shops, and there are no restaurants—it's just 4 million acres of nature and a smattering of remote lodges. The most reliable means of getting here, one that doesn't risk the rough seas or require climbing mountain ranges, is by plane. Most air-taxi services that travel from Anchorage to the parklands also offer flightseeing tours and wilderness adventure drops, just as most lodges offer guided fishing, wildlife-viewing, and adventure trips.

GETTING HERE AND AROUND
Although the eastern shore of the Lake Clark parklands is accessible by boat, it requires a two- to four-hour crossing of rough open waters and navigating the

extreme tides of Tikahtnu Inlet. Thus, flying into the park via wheeled craft or floatplane is the standard form of entry. The nearest international airport is the Ted Stevens International in Anchorage. Several air taxis depart from there, but most—especially floatplanes—depart from Lake Hood, just 2 miles down the road from the international airport.

ESSENTIALS
PARK FEES AND PERMITS
There are no entrance fees or permits needed for any park recreational activities, including backpacking, camping, river running, bear viewing, or visiting Dick Proenneke's cabin. There are fees for the two public-use cabins in the parklands, and online reservations are required (⊕ *www.nps.gov/lacl/public-use-cabins. htm*). Additionally, licenses and fees are needed for fishing; many outfitters provide the licensing.

PARK HOURS
Lake Clark National Park and Preserve is open 24 hours a day all year long. The Port Alsworth visitor center is only open form late May through September.

VISITOR INFORMATION Lake Clark National Park and Preserve. ✉ *Port Alsworth* ☎ *907/781–2218* ⊕ *www.nps.gov/lacl.*

◉ Sights

Lake Clark
BODY OF WATER | Centrally located, the park's namesake lake is 50 miles long and filled with nooks, crannies, coves, and islands. Port Alsworth, which is on the lake's south-central shore, is the jumping off point for hundreds of possible adventures: kayaking to a remote campsite, hiking to a public-use cabin, catching a floatplane to a hidden lakeside lodge. Although the lake is an access point for lodges and campsites, it offers sublime solitude and awe-inspiring nature. ✉ *Lake Clark National Park and Preserve.*

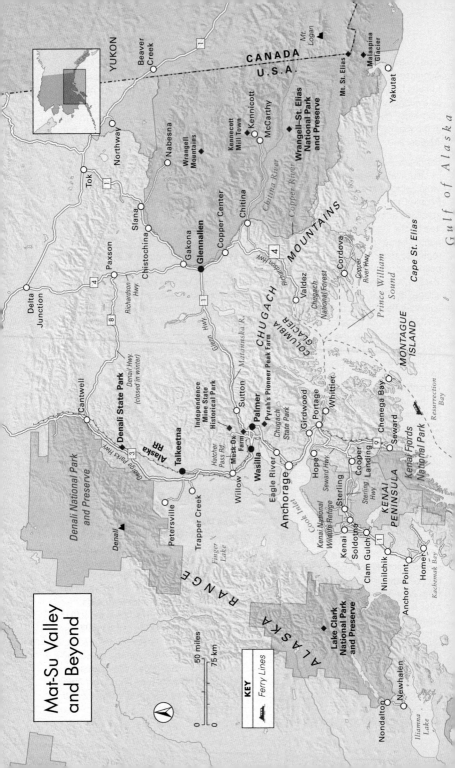

Mt. Iliamna

VOLCANO | The peak of this 10,016-foot stratovolcano, which is in the southeast corner of the park, is home to 10 glaciers. Although not active, it is expected to erupt at some time in the future. It's noted as being the 25th most prominent peak in North America. ☒ *Lake Clark National Park and Preserve.*

Mt. Redoubt

VOLCANO | This active volcano, located north of Tuxedni Bay on the eastern side of the park, can be seen from many different vantage points in Southcentral Alaska, but from within Lake Clark National Park, it is a truly impressive sight. Its sister, Mt. Iliamna, has blown plumes of ash and smoke but has had no recorded erruptions, unlike Redoubt, which has errupted 30 times in the past 10,000 years, including four times just in the last century. ☒ *Lake Clark National Park and Preserve.*

Port Alsworth Visitor Center

VISITOR CENTER | Only open in the summer months (late May through mid-September), the visitor center is a place to register for outings, learn about the area, pick up a couple of gifts, and start off on your exploration. ☒ *Lake Clark National Park and Preserve, Port Alsworth* ☎ *907/781–2117* ⊕ *www.nps.gov/lacl.*

Tuxedni Glacier

NATURE SIGHT | Most of the park's glaciers are found in the Chigmit Mountains. The longest is 19-mile Tuxedni Glacier, which is one of 10 that radiates from the Mt. Iliamna volcano. ☒ *Lake Clark National Park and Preserve.*

 Activities

★ Alaska Alpine Adventures

ADVENTURE TOURS | Whether you want to raft, paddle, hike, or climb, this outfitter can hook you up on 4- to 10-day (or longer) guided excursions. Renowned for their expertise and experience, the guides have a thorough, safe, and extensive track record. ☒ *300 E. 76th Ave., Unit B, Anchorage* ☎ *877/525–2577* ⊕ *www.alaskaalpineadventures.com* ☒ *From $3,350 per person.*

 Hotels

Alaska Backcountry Fishing Lodge

$$$$ | ALL-INCLUSIVE | Located on the beach of Lake Clark, this lodge organizes day trips and fishing or rafting adventures, whether you want a guide or prefer to head out on your own. **Pros:** very friendly; close to the national park visitor center; terrific views. **Cons:** fishing license not included; there could be a bear outside your door; must make your own travel arrangements. Ⓢ *Rooms from: $1400* ☒ *Port Alsworth* ☎ *907/310–1165* ⊕ *www.alaskabackcountryfishing.com* ⓘ⃝ *All-Inclusive* ⇆ *4 rooms.*

Chulitna Lodge and Wilderness Retreat

$$$$ | ALL-INCLUSIVE | Though large enough to accommodate a small wedding party, this remote lodge tends to keep things intimate with just five to eight guests at a time, a rugged but comfortable style, and warm hospitality. **Pros:** excellent guides and hospitality; remote, pristine, natural experience; fantastic food. **Cons:** no internet; no cell service; no alcohol allowed in cabins. Ⓢ *Rooms from: $415* ⊕ *Lake Clark, across from Port Alsworth* ☎ *907/781–3144* ⊕ *chulitnalodge.com* ⇆ *7 cabins* ⓘ⃝ *All-Inclusive.*

Redoubt Mountain Lodge

$$$$ | ALL-INCLUSIVE | The only privately owned property and lodge on 9-mile Crescent Lake offers excellent meals, plenty of comfort, memorable adventures, and a fantastic view of Mt. Redoubt—the park's volcano—8 miles away. **Pros:** Internet and phone available in common areas; arranges outdoor activities; sauna and hot tub. **Cons:** a little pricey; super remote; no televisions or Internet in rooms. Ⓢ *Rooms from: $3300* ⊕ *Crescent Lake* ☎ *866/733–3034* ⊕ *redoubtlodge.com* ⓘ⃝ *All-Inclusive* ⇆ *6 cabins.*

Palmer

40 miles northeast of Anchorage.

With mountain-ringed farms, Palmer is charming and photogenic. This is the place to search for 100-pound cabbages and fresh farm cheese. Historic buildings are scattered throughout the Mat-Su Valley; in 1935 the federal government relocated about 200 farm families here from the Depression-ridden Midwest. Now it has developed into the state's major agricultural region. Good growing conditions of rich soil and long hours of summer sunlight result in some huge vegetables.

GETTING HERE AND AROUND

The Glenn Highway heads north out of Anchorage and right through Palmer. The Chugach Range lines both sides of Palmer's valley, and if you continue past the town you'll find yourself smack in the middle of the mountains.

ESSENTIALS

VISITOR INFORMATION Mat-Su Convention & Visitors Bureau. ⊠ *610 S. Bailey Street, Suite 201, Palmer* ☎ *907/746–5000* ⊕ *www.alaskavisit.com.* **Palmer Chamber of Commerce.** ⊠ *550 S. Alaska St., Palmer* ☎ *907/745–2880* ⊕ *www. palmerchamber.org.*

Sights

Independence Mine State Historical Park

HISTORIC SIGHT | Gold mining was an early mainstay of the Mat-Su Valley's economy. You can tour the long-dormant Independence Mine on the Hatcher Pass Road, a loop that in summer connects the Parks Highway just north of Willow to the Glenn Highway near Palmer. The stunningly scenic drive travels past forested streams and alpine meadows and winds high above the tree line. The road to Independence Mine from the Palmer side is paved; the section between the mine and Willow is gravel. In the 1940s the

mine employed as many as 200 workers. Today it is a 271-acre state park that has good cross-country skiing in winter. Only the wooden buildings remain; one of them, the red-roof manager's house, is now used as a visitor center. ⊠ *Hatcher Pass Rd., 19 miles northwest of Glenn Hwy., Palmer* ☎ *907/745–3975* ⊕ *www. dnr.alaska.gov/parks/units/indmine.htm* 🅿 *$5 day-use parking.*

Musk Ox Farm

FARM/RANCH | FAMILY | Fifty or so animals roam at the Musk Ox Farm, which conducts 30-minute guided tours. There's a hands-on museum and a gift shop featuring hand-knitted items made from the cashmere-like underfur (qiviut) combed from the musk ox. The scarves, caps, and more are made by Oomingmak, an Alaska Native collective. ⊠ *Mile 50.1, Glenn Hwy., Palmer* ☎ *907/745–4151* ⊕ *www. muskoxfarm.org* 🅿 *$11.*

Pyrah's Pioneer Peak Farm

FARM/RANCH | FAMILY | On a sunny day the town of Palmer looks like a Swiss calendar photo, with its old barns and log houses silhouetted against craggy Pioneer Peak. On nearby farms on the Bodenburg Loop off the Old Palmer Highway, you can pay to pick your own raspberries and other fruits and vegetables. The peak picking time at Pyrah's Pioneer Peak Farm, which cultivates 35 kinds of fruits and vegetables, occurs around mid-July. ⊠ *Mile 2.6, 4350 Bodenburg Loop Rd., Palmer* ☎ *907/745–4511* ⊕ *www.pppfarm.net* ⊗ *Closed Sept.–June.*

Restaurants

Palmer City Alehouse

$$ | AMERICAN | A hot meeting place in the old train depot, Palmer City echoes with the sound of local chatter. Though it doesn't provide much of a romantic dining experience, it has a great ambience, and the standard pub fare—salads, pizzas made in a firebrick oven, and handmade burgers—are better than average. **Known for:** good pub food; historic location; wide beer selection. $ *Average main: $15* ⊠ *320 E. Dahlia Ave., Palmer* ☎ *907/746–2537* ⊕ *www.alaskaalehouse.com.*

Vagabond Blues

$ | **CAFÉ** | The folks at this aroma-filled spot serve up fresh and tasty pastries, quiches, wraps, salads, panini and other sandwiches, and espresso drinks. A convivial setting for meetings, board games, and pleasant conversation by day, Vagabond is a popular venue for touring musical acts several times a month. **Known for:** healthy food options; grab-and-go meals; best coffee in town. $ *Average main: $12* ⊠ *642 S. Alaska St., Palmer* ☎ *907/745–2233.*

Hotels

Alaska's Harvest B&B

$$ | **B&B/INN** | Two miles outside Palmer on 15 acres of wooded land, the Hand family's peaceful inn has tremendous views of snowcapped mountains from across a sheep pasture. **Pros:** kitchens stocked with breakfast food; beautiful views; hospitable hosts. **Cons:** alcohol not allowed; only three rooms have private bathrooms; could use some updating. $ *Rooms from: $149* ⊠ *2252 N. Love Dr., Palmer* ☎ *907/745–4263* ⊕ *www.alaskasharvest.com* ⊃ *6 rooms, 1 cabin* �ⓞ *Free Breakfast.*

Colony Inn

$$ | **B&B/INN** | All guest rooms in this lovingly restored historic building are tastefully decorated with antiques and quilts. **Pros:** centrally located; quiet; charming. **Cons:** rooms are small; front desk a five-minute walk away at Valley Hotel; no air-conditioning for any abnormally warm days. $ *Rooms from: $100* ⊠ *325 E. Elmwood Ave., Palmer* ☎ *907/745–3330* ⊕ *www.akcolonyinn.com* ⓞ *No Meals* ⊃ *12 rooms.*

Hatcher Pass Lodge

$$ | **B&B/INN** | This lodge has spectacular views and can serve as a base camp for hiking, berry picking, and—in fall and winter—skiing. **Pros:** comfortable beds; views and nature right outside your door; food is quite tasty. **Cons:** not all rooms have private baths; no kitchens and a bit far from town, so dining options are limited; decor a bit dated. $ *Rooms from: $150* ⊠ *Mile 17, Hatcher Pass Rd., Box 763, Palmer* ☎ *907/745–5897, 907/745–1200* ⊕ *www.hatcherpasslodge.com* ⊃ *3 rooms, 9 cabins* ⓞ *No Meals.*

Nightlife

Arkose Brewery

BARS | This microbrewery has a flavor portfolio inspired by both Germany and the Pacific Northwest. Expect to find seven fresh-brewed staples as well as one seasonal beer. Have a pint at the bar or fill a growler and head off on an adventure. Due to strict Alaska brewery laws, food can be purchased to accompany your beverage at a food truck parked outside—always sure to be a delicious treat. ⊠ *650 E. Steel Loop, Palmer* ☎ *907/746–2337* ⊕ *www.arkosebrewery.com.*

Wasilla

42 miles north of Anchorage, 10 miles west of Palmer.

Wasilla made national news in 2008 when Sarah Palin, the former governor of the state and former mayor of the town, was picked to be the Republican vice-presidential candidate. Wasilla is one of the valley's original pioneer communities, and over time has served as a supply center for farmers, gold miners, and mushers. Today fast-food restaurants and strip malls line the Parks Highway. Rolling hills and more scenic vistas can be found by wandering the area's back roads.

■ TIP→ Wasilla is the best place for stocking up if you're heading north to Talkeetna or Denali.

GETTING HERE AND AROUND

Wasilla is accessible by car. Going north along the Glenn Highway, turn off just before Palmer and head west. You'll soon be in Wasilla. With its abundant strip malls, the town is not known for glamour or beauty, but take a side road or cruise past one of the many lakes in the region and you're sure to grab some great pictures.

ESSENTIALS

VISITOR INFORMATION Wasilla Chamber of Commerce. ✉ *415 E. Railroad Ave., Wasilla* ☎ *907/376–1299* 🌐 *www.wasilla-chamber.org.*

Sights

Iditarod Trail Headquarters

OTHER ATTRACTION | FAMILY | The famous competition's headquarters displays dogsleds, mushers' clothing, and trail gear, and you can watch video highlights of past races. The gift shop sells Iditarod items. Dogsled rides take place year-round; in summer rides on wheels are available for $10. ✉ *2100 S. Knik–Goose Bay Rd., Wasilla* ☎ *907/376–5155* 🌐 *www.iditarod.com* 🎟 *Free.*

Museum of Alaska Transportation and Industry

OTHER MUSEUM | FAMILY | On a 20-acre site the museum exhibits some of the machines that helped develop Alaska, from dogsleds to jet aircraft and everything in between. The Don Sheldon Building houses aviation artifacts as well as antique autos, trains, and photographic displays. There is also a snowmachine (Alaskan for snowmobile) exhibit. ✉ *3800 W. Museum Dr., off Mile 47 Parks Hwy., Wasilla* ☎ *907/376–1211* 🌐 *www.museumofalaska.org* 🎟 *$8* 🕑 *Closed Tues.–Thurs.*

Restaurants

Cadillac Cafe

$$ | CAFÉ | Hearty fare fills the menu at this diner-style café, including homemade pies, juicy burgers, burritos, pasta dishes, and pizzas turned out of a wood-fired oven. The owner describes the decor as "Alaska minimalist," but the booths are plush and comfortable, and hand-rubbed wood is evident. **Known for:** family dining destination; diverse menu; best pies in town. [$] *Average main: $15* ✉ *Pittman Rd. and Parks Hwy., at Mile 49, Wasilla* ☎ *907/357–5533.*

The Grape Tap

$$$ | AMERICAN | With a menu that ebbs and flows with the seasons yet consistently delivers fantastic dishes, try The Grape Tap. This 60-seat restaurant and European wine cellar is set in a 1930s pioneer home that's been renovated with contemporary colors and style. **Known for:** romantic ambience; excellent fine dining; fantastic wine selection. [$] *Average main: $30* ✉ *322 N. Boundary St., Wasilla* ☎ *907/376–8466* 🌐 *www.thegrapetap.com* 🕑 *Closed Sun.–Tues. No lunch.*

Hotels

Best Western Lake Lucille Inn

$$ | HOTEL | This well-maintained resort on Lake Lucille provides easy access to several recreational activities, including boating in summer and ice-skating and snowmachining in winter. **Pros:** beautiful lakefront property; comfortable rooms; very clean. **Cons:** rooms do not have microwaves; not all rooms have a lake view; sound of nearby powerboats can get annoying. [$] *Rooms from: $169* ✉ *1300 W. Lake Lucille Dr., Mile 43½, Parks Hwy., Wasilla* ☎ *907/373–1776, 800/528–1234* 🌐 *www.bestwestern.com* 🍴 *Free Breakfast* 🛏 *54 rooms.*

⭐ **Pioneer Ridge Bed and Breakfast Inn**
$$ | B&B/INN | Each of the spacious, log-partitioned rooms in the converted old Fairview Dairy barn and award-winning inn is decorated according to a theme. **Pros:** excellent breakfast; cozy and warm; gorgeous views. **Cons:** walls are thin; not very accessible for those with disabilities; not every room has a private bath. Ⓢ *Rooms from: $139* ✉ *2221 Yukon Circle, HC31, Box 5083K, Wasilla* ☎ *907/376–7472, 800/478–7472* ⊕ *www.pioneerridge.com* ⦿ *Free Breakfast* ⤳ *6 rooms, 1 cabin.*

Talkeetna

56 miles north of Wasilla, 112 miles north of Anchorage.

Located at the end of a spur road off Mile 99 of the Parks Highway, the town of Talkeetna has an artsy, groovy vibe mixed with a mountain-climber verve and practicality. There's a small, unpaved downtown area surrounding a central green area. When it's clear enough, Denali looms in the distance; but keep in mind, the big mountain makes its own weather and is often not seen for weeks.

Mountaineers congregate here to begin their journey to Denali in Denali National Park; those just off the mountain are recognizable by their tanned faces with white "raccoon eyes" where their sunglasses protected their skin from the sun. The Denali mountain rangers have their climbing headquarters here, as do most glacier pilots who fly climbing parties to the mountain. A carved pole at the town cemetery honors deceased mountaineers.

If driving between Anchorage and Denali or Fairbanks, Talkeetna makes for a great stop. Its locals are a true cast of characters, and the pebbly shore of the Susitna River reveals fantastic views. While here, you're likely to hear tales of the former mayor of Talkeetna, Stubbs, an affable orange cat who served as the town's leader for 19 years before he died in 2017.

Sights

Talkeetna Historical Society Museum
HISTORY MUSEUM | Exhibits at this downtown museum explore the history of mountain climbing in Denali as well as the town's eclectic history. Residents founded the organization in 1972 to protect the original Talkeetna schoolhouse. The group publishes a walking-tour map and operates a gift area, too. ✉ *Mile 14½, Talkeetna Spur and D St., Talkeetna* ☎ *907/733–2487* ⊕ *www.talkeetna-historicalsociety.org* 🎟 *$5* ⊘ *Closed Mon., Tues., and all winter except by appointment.*

Activities

BOATING, FLOATING, AND FISHING
Mahay's Riverboat Service
BOATING | FAMILY | With the immense peaks of Denali as its backdrop, Mahay's operates jet-boat sightseeing and adventure tours on the Susitna and Talkeetna Rivers. The company also conducts a Devil's Canyon Tour, a 130-mile round-trip river excursion through Denali State Park and into Devil's Gorge. They also do private tours. ✉ *22333 Talkeetna Spur Rd., Talkeetna* ☎ *907/733–2223* ⊕ *www.mahaysriverboat.com* 🎟 *From $75.*

Phantom Tri-River Charters
FISHING | Phantom operates fishing trips out of Talkeetna and on the nearby Deshka River using covered, heated boats. They provide all the necessary tackle and gear as well as drop-offs for guests looking to catch grayling, rainbows, and Alaska king salmon. ✉ *22228 Talkeetna Spur Rd, Talkeetna* ☎ *907/733–2400* ⊕ *phantomsalmoncharters.com* 🎟 *From $190.*

The First Known to Summit Denali

Between 1903 and 1912 eight expeditions walked the slopes of 20,310-foot Denali. But none had reached the absolute top of North America's highest peak. Thus the stage was set for Hudson Stuck, a self-described American amateur mountaineer.

Missionary Man

Stuck came to Alaska in 1904, drawn not by mountains but by a missionary calling. As the Episcopal Church's archdeacon for the Yukon River region, he visited Alaska Native villages year-round. His passion for climbing was unexpectedly rekindled in 1906, when he saw from afar the "glorious, broad, massive uplift" of Denali, the "father of mountains."

The Team

Five years after that wondrous view, Stuck pledged to reach Denali's summit—or at least try. For his climbing party he picked three Alaskans experienced in snow and ice travel, though not in mountaineering: Harry Karstens, a well-known explorer and backcountry guide who would later become the first superintendent of Mt. McKinley National Park; Robert Tatum, Stuck's missionary assistant; and Walter Harper, of Koyukun Athabascan and Irish descent, who served as Stuck's interpreter and later became the lead climber during their summit attempt.

The Climb

Assisted by two sled-dog teams (and two Gwich'in teenagers), the group began its expedition on St. Patrick's Day, 1913, at Nenana, a village 90 miles northeast of Denali. A month later they began their actual ascent of the great peak's northern side, via Muldrow Glacier. The glacier's surface proved to be a maze of crevasses, some of them wide chasms with no apparent bottom. Carefully working their way up-glacier, the climbers established a camp at 11,500 feet. From there the team chopped a staircase up several miles—and 3,000 vertical feet—of rock, snow, and ice. Their progress was delayed several times by high winds, heavy snow, and near-zero visibility.

By May 30 the climbers had reached the top of the ridge and moved into a high glacial basin. Despite temperatures ranging from subzero to 21°F, they kept warm at night by sleeping on sheep and caribou skins and covering themselves with down quilts, camel-hair blankets, and a wolf robe.

The Summit

On June 6 the team established its high camp at 18,000 feet. The following morning was bright, cloudless, and windy. Three of the climbers suffered headaches and stomach pains, but given the clear weather everyone agreed to make an attempt. They left camp at 5 am and by 1:30 pm stood within a few yards of Denali's summit. Harper, who had been leading all day, was the first to reach the top, soon followed by the others. After catching their breath, the teammates shook hands, said a prayer of thanks, made some scientific measurements, and reveled in their magnificent surroundings.

FLIGHTSEEING

★ K2 Aviation

AIR EXCURSIONS | With a long, storied history in Alaska mountain-flying circles, this company offers flightseeing tours that give guests a bird's-eye view of Denali's famous peaks. They offer routes that range from an hour to two hours, with options to land on glaciers. A sister company provides standard air-taxi services. ✉ *14052 E. 2nd St., Talkeetna* ☎ *907/733–2291, 800/764–2291* 🌐 *www.flyk2.com* 🎟 *From $230.*

Talkeetna Air Taxi

AIR EXCURSIONS | Check out Denali from the air, then swoop down to a glacier to test your boots. Talkeetna Air gives you the option to land on glaciers or to take longer flights that soar farther, sometimes above Denali itself. They also offer support for mountain-climbers and backcountry adventurers, helicopter flightseeing and heli-hiking tours, and even a 10-day Iditarod package that trails the mushers in the air throughout the entire race. ✉ *14212 E. Second St., Talkeetna* ☎ *907/733–2218, 800/533–2219* 🌐 *www.talkeetnaair.com* 🎟 *From $220.*

HIKING

Alaska Mountaineering School

MOUNTAIN CLIMBING | This outfitter will take you on Denali, Foraker, and Hunter mountain expeditions and also offers workshops, custom climbing trips, and training intensives. The AMS is famous for making climbers out of novices by teaching important mountain skills, such as glacier travel, backpacking, ski mountaineering, and skillsets specific to Denali and mountain rescue. ✉ *13765 Third St., Talkeetna* ☎ *907/733–1016* 🌐 *www.climbalaska.org* 🎟 *From $250.*

🍴 Restaurants

Denali Brewing Company BrewPub

$$ | **AMERICAN** | Like every good brewery, Denali Brewing Company has a large outdoor porch for sunny days, and a menu of savory items to soak up the beer. Burgers, fish-and-chips, and a host of appetizers pack their menu. **Known for:** locally produced cider, mead, and spirits also available; award-winning microbrews; great outdoor seating. [$] *Average main: $20* ✉ *13605 N. Main St., Talkeetna* ☎ *907/733–2537* 🌐 *www.denalibrewing-company.com.*

Mountain High Pizza Pie

$$ | **PIZZA** | Flatbreads, pizzas, calzones, and an excellent array of salads and garlic-filled dishes are the reasons locals congregate at this laid-back downtown eatery all year long. The calzones are true works of art. **Known for:** favorite hangout for locals; great pizzas and calzones; family-friendly atmosphere. [$] *Average main: $15* ✉ *22165 S. C St., Talkeetna* ☎ *907/733–1234* 🌐 *www.pizzapietalkeetna.com.*

Talkeetna Spinach Bread

$ | **ECLECTIC** | **FAMILY** | This iconic food truck is known for its highly popular cheesy spinach bread and also serves breakfast and rotating daily specials, like Thai curry, Ethiopian beans and rice, and a Hawaiian poke bowl. Just look for the shiny metal trailer with a long line of people waiting for their favorite meal. It's worth the wait, and don't forget to grab some Brazilian limeade to wash it all down. **Known for:** long lines that are worth the wait; heavenly spinach bread; tasty breakfasts. [$] *Average main: $12* ✉ *13487 E. Main St., Talkeetna* ☎ *907/671–3287* 🌐 *talkeetna-spinach-bread.business.site* 🕒 *Closed Tues. and in winter.*

Hotels

★ Susitna River Lodging

$$ | B&B/INN | On the bank of the Susitna River and an easy half-mile walk from downtown Talkeetna, this year-round lodge is idyllic. **Pros:** great gathering space outside with firepits; comfortable beds and pillows; gorgeous river and mountain views. **Cons:** a short walk to town; no breakfast served; no televisions in the cabins. [$] *Rooms from: $199* ✉ *23094 S. Talkeetna Spur, Talkeetna* ☎ *907/733–0505* 🌐 *www.susitnariverlodge.com* 🍴 *No Meals* 🛏 *4 suites, 4 cabins.*

Swiss Alaska Inn

$$ | B&B/INN | Family-run since 1976, this rustic-style property is well-known among those who come to fish in the Talkeetna, Susitna, and Chulitna Rivers. **Pros:** very quiet; friendly staff; hearty breakfast. **Cons:** no air-conditioning for rare hot days; a little off-the-beaten-path; about a half mile from town. [$] *Rooms from: $130* ✉ *East Talkeetna, by boat launch, 22056 S. F St.,* ☎ *907/733–2424* 🌐 *www.swissalaska.com* 🍴 *Free Breakfast* 🛏 *20 rooms.*

Talkeetna Alaskan Lodge

$$$ | HOTEL | This lodge sits on a choice spot with great hiking trails and splendid views of Denali. **Pros:** dining on-site; tremendous views of Denali on clear days and of forests on rainy ones; comfortable rooms. **Cons:** none of Talkeetna's charm; 2 miles from Talkeetna's town center; no air-conditioning. [$] *Rooms from: $209* ✉ *Mile 12½, 23601 Talkeetna Spur Rd., Talkeetna* ☎ *800/808–8068, 907/733–9500* 🌐 *www.talkeetnalodge.com* 🍴 *No Meals* 🛏 *212 rooms.*

Talkeetna Roadhouse

$ | B&B/INN | This circa-1917 log roadhouse has a common sitting area and rooms of varying sizes. **Pros:** delicious food; perfectly situated location; down-home Alaska at its best. **Cons:** rooms are very basic; walls are thin; shared bathrooms. [$] *Rooms from: $55* ✉ *13550 E. Main St., Talkeetna* ☎ *907/733–1351* 🌐 *www.talkeetnaroadhouse.com* 🛏 *7 rooms, 1 cabin, 1 apartment* 🍴 *No Meals.*

Shopping

Dancing Leaf Gallery

CRAFTS | Featuring contemporary art and crafts made by Alaskans, this is the go-to stop for gifts, a touch of Alaska, and an education. The high-ceiling, spacious gallery was constructed out of repurposed historic railroad timber. Be sure to give yourself enough time to browse as there is a lot to see. ✉ *13618 Main St., Talkeetna* ☎ *907/733–5323* 🌐 *www.thedancingleafgallery.com.*

★ Nagley's General Store

GENERAL STORE | Opened around 1900, this is the only grocery store in town, and it's where most locals go to get caught up on the gossip. Nagley's is also where you can go to get a great cup of hot coffee, a scoop of ice cream, adult libations, and other standard trading post items. In addition, this is the former home of Stubbs the Cat, the town's mayor until his death, and workers are happy to tell you about the many store cats who came before and after him. ✉ *13650 Main St., Talkeetna* ☎ *907/733–3663* 🌐 *www.nagleysstore.com.*

Denali State Park

34 miles north of Talkeetna, 132 miles north of Anchorage.

A 2½ to 3-hour drive from Anchorage, this state park is nearly split in half by the Parks Highway, the major road link between Anchorage and Fairbanks. With the Talkeetna Mountains to the east and the Alaska Range to the west, the park offers a vast area for people to fish, hike, paddle, and just plain explore. The terrain varies from lowland streams to alpine tundra, with the

Kesugi Ridge a popular multiday hiking area at the eastern half of the park.

GETTING HERE AND AROUND

The Parks Highway bisects Denali State Park and offers not only a majestic view of year-round snow-covered mountaintops, but also a mad array of easy and not so easy opportunities to see wildlife. The highway is paved, but after the breakup of winter ice it tends to be riddled with potholes. It's always wise when driving in Alaska to have at least one good spare tire.

ESSENTIALS

VISITOR INFORMATION Alaska State Parks, Mat-Su Area Office. ✉ *7278 East Bogard Rd., Wasilla* ☎ *907/745–3975* 🌐 *dnr.alaska.gov/parks/units/denali1.htm.*

Sights

Denali State Park

STATE/PROVINCIAL PARK | Overshadowed by the larger and more charismatic Denali National Park and Preserve, the 325,240-acre "Little Denali," or Denali State Park, offers excellent road access, beautiful views of Denali, scenic campgrounds, and prime wilderness hiking and backpacking opportunities within a few miles of the road system. The terrain here varies from the verdant, low-lying banks of the Tokositna River to alpine tundra. Moose, wolves, and grizzly and black bears inhabit the park, along with lynx, red foxes, land otters, beavers, porcupines, and myriad other species.

Activities

Kesugi Ridge

HIKING & WALKING | Denali State Park offers remarkable views of Denali and the Alaska Range on a clear day and also gives folks one of the best and most accessible multiday hikes to do in the state. Hiking Kesugi Ridge can cover around 30 miles depending on where you start and finish. Many begin at the Little Coal Creek trailhead (mile 163.9) and hike to the Byers Lake Campground trail (mile 147) to minimize elevation gain. Some do a longer trek by continuing to the Troublesome Creek trailheads. The strenuous but very doable climb to the ridge can reveal spectacular vistas, weather allowing, while the rest of the hike offers mostly gentle up-and-down terrain with a few common hazards like weather, mosquitoes, and bears, especially around Troublesome Creek in late summer when the salmon runs are in full force. Plan for three days of hiking. 🌐 *dnr.alaska.gov/parks/units/denali1.htm.*

Peters Hills

HIKING & WALKING | Backcountry travelers can also reach the western part of the park via Peters Hills, an area accessible from Petersville Road out of Trapper Creek. This old mining road on the southern side of Denali National Park covers about 34 miles, mostly unpaved. Denali State Park borders the hills, where primitive trails and campgrounds are used year-round. It's especially popular with snowmachiners in winter and mountain bikers in summer. ✉ *Peterson Highway, Trapper Creek* 🌐 *dnr.alaska.gov/parks/units/denali1.htm.*

Hotels

Alaska State Parks Cabins

$ | **HOUSE** | Three public-use cabins are in Denali State Park, along the shores of Byers Lake. **Pros:** great way to experience Alaska; more accessible than most wilderness cabins; stunning surroundings. **Cons:** no running water or electricity; can get booked up quickly; no indoor bathrooms. [$] *Rooms from: $80* ✉ *Byers Lake, Anchorage* ☎ *907/269–8700* 🌐 *dnr.alaska.gov/parks/aspcabins/index.htm* 🛏 *3 cabins* 🍴 *No Meals.*

Mt. McKinley Princess Wilderness Lodge

$$ | HOTEL | When the sky is clear and Denali is visible, this lodge has excellent views of North America's highest peak, especially from the lobby, which has two-story windows. **Pros:** delicious food; has everything you might need; great location. **Cons:** somewhat bland decor; too huge for some; many large tour groups. $ *Rooms from: $189* ✉ *Mile 133, Parks Hwy., Trapper Creek* ☎ *907/733–2900, 800/426–0500* ⊕ *www.princesslodges.com/princess-alaska-lodges/mckinley-lodge* ⊘ *Closed mid-Sept.–mid-May* 🛏 *464 rooms* ⦿ *No Meals*.

Glennallen

187 miles northeast of Anchorage.

This community of about 500 residents is a good spot to gas up and grab some food before continuing toward Wrangell–St. Elias National Park and Preserve 124 miles away. Glennallen is also the service center for the Copper River basin and a fly-in base for several outfitters that take visitors flightseeing, fishing, rafting, and wildlife viewing. The town of Glennallen was established in the mid-1940s as a highway construction camp for the Glenn Highway, and it now sits along the highway, close to where it intersects with the Richardson Highway. There are several recreation areas near the town with trails, fishing, and camping. The 17-mile road to Lake Louise State Recreation Area is west of Glennallen on the Glenn Highway while the small Dry Creek State Recreation Site is 4 miles north of town on the Richardson Highway.

GETTING HERE AND AROUND

The Glenn Highway from Anchorage to Glennallen is relatively well maintained all year round, but it's still important to pack what you might need in all conditions whenever traveling by car.

ESSENTIALS

VISITOR INFORMATION Bureau of Land Management. ✉ *Glennallen Field Office, Glennallen* ☎ *907/271–5960, 907/822–3217* ⊕ *www.blm.gov/office/glennallen-field-office*.

Restaurants

Ernesto's Mobile Grill

$$ | MEXICAN | Located at the Copper River Valley Visitor Information Center, Ernesto's serves an array of mostly Mexican food, including street tacos, burritos, tamales, and chili rellenos, along with burgers and breakfast. The food usually comes out fast and hot. **Known for:** convenient and hearty food; Mexican breakfasts; street tacos. $ *Average main: $16* ✉ *The HUB, 189 Glenn Hwy., Glennallen* ☎ *907/822–4500* ⊕ *www.ernestosmobilegrill.com*.

Tok Thai

$$ | THAI | Originally a large purple bus parked next to the gas station in the town's crossroads, this window-service eatery is by far the best place in town. It serves surprisingly fresh vegetables and delightfully spicy dishes. **Known for:** various spicy dishes; unique window-service setting; great pad Thai. $ *Average main: $15* ✉ *189 Glenn Hwy., Glennallen* ☎ *907/259–3311*.

Hotels

Caribou Hotel

$$ | HOTEL | This super-convenient, easy to find, and modern hotel offers rooms and a few suites with Alaska decor and amenities like Wi-Fi, big-screen TVs, and queen beds in every room. **Pros:** decent amenities; restaurant next door; comfortable rooms. **Cons:** nothing glamorous; located along the highway; no views. $ *Rooms from: $159* ✉ *Mile 187, Glenn Hwy., Glennallen* ☎ *907/822–3302* ⊕ *www.caribouhotel.com* 🛏 *61 rooms* ⦿ *No Meals*.

Glennallen's Rustic Resort

$$ | **B&B/INN** | This charming resort offers seven rooms and one cabin along with a shared kitchen and beautiful outdoor areas. **Pros:** modern Alaska ambience; very quiet but still close to downtown Glennallen; breakfast included. **Cons:** not all rooms have private baths; rooms can book up quickly; amenities on the basic side. $ *Rooms from: $189* ⊠ *Mile 187.5 Glenn Hwy., Glennallen* ☎ *907/259–2002* ⊕ *www.glennallenresort.com* ⦿ *Free Breakfast* ⇆ *7 rooms, 1 cabin.*

Wrangell–St. Elias National Park and Preserve

77 miles southeast of Glennallen, 264 miles east of Anchorage.

Encompassing 13.2 million acres (it's nearly the size of West Virginia), this park stretches from one of the tallest peaks in North America, Mt. St. Elias (elevation 18,009 feet), to the ocean.

Alaska is chock full of spectacularly beautiful mountains, but those in Wrangell–St. Elias Park and Preserve are possibly the finest of them all. The extraordinarily compact cluster of immense peaks here belongs to four different mountain ranges, which attract climbers from all over the world and which rise through many eco-zones.

The park's interior has been inhabited by the Ahtna Athabascan people for thousands of years. They once used the raw copper found throughout the region to create pots, tools, arrowheads, spear tips, and elaborate shields that were largely symbolic of personal wealth. Surveyors and explorers were introduced to the copper veins, and, in the early 1900s, the McCarthy/Kennecott region became a destination for mineral extraction.

From 1911 to 1934, the Kennecott Mine—located at the terminus of Kennicott Glacier (the spelling discrepancy is thought to be due to a "clerical error" that occurred in 1899)—processed more than $200 million of copper. At the peak of its operation, between 200 and 300 people worked in the mine camp, and 300 resided in the mill town, which consisted of a general store, school, skating rink, tennis court, recreation hall, hospital, and cow dairy.

Now the mine site is a National Historic Landmark and includes Kennicott Glacier Lodge. Just a couple of miles down the road is the town of McCarthy, accessible by road from the west only as far as the river. From there, you must enter on foot. Much of the character from the early 1900s is still present today. There are a couple of eateries, two places to board, and one bar. During the summer months, musicians amble into town, and several guide operations set up shop.

You don't have to be a backcountry camper to experience this park—it's possible to stay in comfortable lodgings in Kennecott or McCarthy, hike to massive glaciers, go on a flightseeing tour, or book a guided rafting trip—for a day or a week.

GETTING HERE AND AROUND

The nearest major airports are Fairbanks International and Ted Stevens Anchorage International. Reeve Air (*907/646–0538, reeveairalaska.com*) has direct flights from Anchorage to Glennallen, connecting to McCarthy, year-round; it also flies direct to McCarthy from May through September. Copper Valley Air Service (*907/822–4200, www.coppervalleyairservice.com*) flies direct from Anchorage to McCarthy. Alaska Airlines offers flights direct from Anchorage to Yakutat along the park's southern edge. Floatplanes to many of the region's remote lodges usually depart from either Anchorage or Glennallen. If you want to spend time in the town of McCarthy without driving the unpaved road to it, consider flying in from Chitina Airport with the flightseeing operator Wrangell Air. The flight takes about 30 minutes, and you'll see glaciers along the way.

From Fairbanks, 260 miles northwest of the park, take AK–2 east to AK–1 (Glenn Highway) and follow it south to the Tok Cutoff and the village of Slana (which has no services), gateway for the scenic Nabesna Road. Alternatively, follow AK–4 (Richardson Highway) south for 258 miles from Fairbanks to the community of Copper Center, home to the park's main visitor center. From Anchorage, AK–1 travels 196 miles northeast to Copper Center. From here, Chitina, gateway to the scenic McCarthy Road, is 52 miles south via AK–4 and AK–10 (Edgerton Highway). Because the scenic roads are quite narrow in places, they're best suited to small RVs and high-clearance 4WD vehicles.

Note that some car rental companies will not allow you to drive into Wrangell–St. Elias on either scenic road due to the wear and tear it puts on a vehicle.

Potholes and old railroad ties or spikes along Nabesna and McCarthy Roads may cause tire damage; to avoid being stranded, make sure your vehicle has a working jack and a properly inflated, full-size spare before heading out.

ESSENTIALS
PARK FEES AND PERMITS
There is no fee to enter or camp in Wrangell–St. Elias National Park and Preserve; however, private-land campgrounds along McCarthy Road do charge fees. If you're fishing with an outfitter, be sure to inquire about any necessary licenses or permits.

PARK HOURS
The park is open 24/7 year-round, but many of its services are seasonal, and, even during peak season, you should call ahead to confirm hours. In general, the main Copper Center Visitor Center and Slana and Chitina ranger stations are open daily 9–5 from mid-May through mid-September. The Kennecott Visitor Center is open from Memorial Day through Labor Day; daily operating hours and services vary. Note, too, that the Nabesna and McCarthy Roads into the park are often impassable in winter.

VISITOR INFORMATION Wrangell–St. Elias National Park. ☎ *907/822–5234* ⊕ *www. nps.gov/wrst.*

 Sights

Copper Center Complex Visitor Center
VISITOR CENTER | FAMILY | Situated in the community of Copper Center near the town of Glennallen and 87 miles south of Slana (gateway for the Nabesna Road) and 52 miles north of Chitina (gateway for the McCarthy Road), the main visitor center is an excellent place to learn about the park's geography and natural and cultural history. The complex includes an exhibit hall, a theater and amphitheater, and the Ahtna Cultural Center, with displays on the region's Native peoples. It also has a bookstore that sells crafts as well as a good selection of titles by local authors, restrooms, a picnic shelter, and tables. It's open daily from 9 to 5 between May and September (exact opening and closing dates vary). ⊠ *Wrangell–St. Elias National Park, Mile 106.8, Richardson Hwy., Copper Center* ☎ *907/822–7250* ⊕ *www.nps.gov/wrst.*

Kennecott Mill Town
HISTORIC SIGHT | The Ahtnu and Upper Tanana Athabascan peoples who inhabited the Copper River Region for thousands of years used and traded copper found in the region. These ore deposits were noted by European surveyors in the late 1800s, and, by the early 1900s, prospectors began staking claims in the mountains above Kennicott Glacier. The Kennecott Copper Corporation soon built a mine, a railway (now the McCarthy Road), and a company town and camp for about 300 workers.

By 1935, however, the copper ore was depleted, and the company ceased operations, leaving behind equipment, facilities, and debris. Today, the abandoned mine is one of Wrangell–St. Elias National Park and Preserve's main attractions, and restoration works have been an ongoing effort for more than a decade. The best way to see the mine is on a tour with one of the area operators, though only St. Elias Alpine Guides is authorized to take you into some of the restored buildings.

While exploring the area, it's hard not to notice the different spellings of the mine and the glacier, which was named after Robert Kennicott, a geologist who surveyed the area in 1899. Believed to have been caused by a clerical error, the discrepancy can be confusing, unless you look at it as a way to differentiate the man-made landmarks from the natural ones. ⊠ Wrangell-St. Elias National Park.

Kennecott Visitor Center

VISITOR CENTER | **FAMILY** | Set in the historic Blackburn Schoolhouse at the center of the Kennecott Mill Town historic site, this is a great place to pick up trail maps and brochures, book a trip, or take a history or nature tour with a park ranger. It's open from Memorial Day through Labor Day, but hours and offerings vary, so check before heading out. ⊠ Kennecott Mill Town, Wrangell-St. Elias National Park ☎ 907/205–7106 ⊕ www.nps.gov/wrst.

Malaspina Glacier

NATURE SIGHT | Wrangell–St. Elias's coastal mountains are frequently wreathed in snow-filled clouds, their massive height making a giant wall that contains the great storms brewed in the Gulf of Alaska. As a consequence, they bear some of the continent's largest ice fields, with more than 100 glaciers radiating from them. One of these, Malaspina Glacier, includes 1,500 square miles—larger than the state of Rhode Island. This tidewater glacier has an incredible pattern of black-and-white stripes made by the other glaciers that coalesced to form it. If you fly between Juneau and Anchorage, look for Malaspina Glacier on the coast north of Yakutat. ⊠ Wrangell-St. Elias National Park.

McCarthy Road

SCENIC DRIVE | The better-known of the two scenic routes into the park travels for 60 bumpy miles (fill the tank and the cooler ahead of time) along an old railroad bed from Chitina to the Kennicott River, a drive of at least 2½ hours. Just past Chitina, as you cross over the Copper River, keep an eye out for floating metal and wood contraptions that look like steampunk rafts. These are salmon fishwheels, which can only be used by Alaska residents. All along this road you will come across numerous relics of the region's mining past and countless opportunities to have your breath stolen away by glorious park vistas. At the end of the road, you must park and walk across the bridge—only residents of McCarthy are allowed to drive across it—to reach the town and the Kennecott site beyond. It's about a 15-minute walk into town; most outfitters and lodgings offer shuttles. ⊠ Wrangell-St. Elias National Park.

Mt. St. Elias

MOUNTAIN | The white-iced spire of Mt. St. Elias, in the range of the same name, reaches more than 18,000 feet. It's the second-highest peak on the North American continent and the crown of the planet's highest coastal range. It also has the world's longest ski descent. ⊠ Wrangell-St. Elias National Park.

Wrangell Mountains

MOUNTAIN | Covering a 100-by-70-mile area, the Wrangells tower over the 2,500-foot-high Copper River Plateau, with the peaks of mounts Jarvis, Drum, Blackburn, Sanford, and Wrangell rising from 15,000 feet to 16,000 feet above sea level. ⊠ Wrangell-St. Elias National Park.

Activities

★ St. Elias Alpine Guides

ADVENTURE TOURS | FAMILY | With more than three decades of experience, this is the go-to company not only for tours of historic Kennecott (St. Elias Alpine Guides is the only park concessionaire allowed to take visitors *into* historic mine buildings) but also for half-or full-day hikes and longer, more adventurous outings on land or water. Reservations are essential for the two-hour Kennecott Mill Town Tours ($28 per person; three tours daily in summer) to see a mining community and mine operations that were abandoned in 1938. Along the way, guides share the tales of the men and women who lived, loved, toiled, and died in the quest for copper here.

Don't miss the chance to explore Root Glacier on guided 5- to 6-mile half-day or 8- to 10-mile full-day hikes ($95 or $130 per person). Other short or long hikes, mountaineering lessons, ice climbs, multiday backpacking expeditions, and custom trips are also available. If you'd rather raft than hike, the company's Copper Oar (*www.copperoar.com*) sister operation has single- and multiday river trips into the heart of the wilderness. ✉ *Wrangell–St. Elias National Park, Motherlode Powerhouse, McCarthy* ☎ *888/933–5427 toll free, 907/554–4445 local, 907/231–6395 cell* ⊕ *www.stelias-guides.com* 🖃 *From $95.*

CAMPING

Most campgrounds within Wrangell–St. Elias National Park and Preserve are privately owned and charge fees, particularly in the McCarthy area. Along the Nabesna Road, you'll find the park's free Kendesnii Campground and five primitive camping spots at rest areas. As with camping anywhere in Alaska, it is imperative that you be bear-aware and bear-wise. Store food, stove fuel, and personal items like body wash and toothpaste in bear barrels.

Base Camp Kennicott. You can pitch a tent ($25 per day) at this privately operated campsite at the end of the McCarthy Road. That said, the rocky region is a better place to park a car ($5–$10 per day) or set up an RV (small rigs only as the road here is rough; no hookups or dump stations; $40 per night) before heading over the river to McCarthy. *Mile 59. 2 McCarthy Rd. www.basecampkennicott.com.*

Glacier View Campground. This private campground is a social, inviting place to lay out your spread and get your bearings before traveling off into the unfamiliar. You can park your vehicle here for the day (free, though overnight parking is $15) before crossing the Kennicott River en route to McCarthy, or you can park a small RV or your car, pitch a tent, and stay for the night ($20 per night including vehicle and one tent; $10 for each additional tent). There's also a small camp store and cabins for rent (from $95 per night). *McCarthy Rd. glacierviewcampground.com.*

Kendesnii Campground. The only park-service-maintained camping area in Wrangell–St. Elias has 10 sites with picnic tables, fire rings, trails, and restrooms. This is a great place to fish and view wildlife. A ½-mile hike will take you to Jack Lake and more beautiful views of the Wrangell Mountains. Sites are free and don't require reservations. As the road here is best suited to passenger vehicles, this campground is geared to tents rather than RVs. *Mile 27.8, Nabesna Rd. www.recreation.gov.*

HIKING

Exploring the great outdoors on foot is the best way to access and experience the abundant nature of this region. There are only a few short trails along the McCarthy Road, though Kotsina Trail traverses a couple of miles before reaching a network of impressive backcountry trails. Along the Nabesna Road, five primary trails range from easy day hikes to strenuous overnighters.

It's important to note that there are no maintained trails within the parklands, and Alaska's outdoors can be deadly. Before heading out on any hike, it's imperative that you prepare for extreme inclement weather, rough trail conditions, water crossings, and dangerous wildlife. You must also be equipped with maps, bear spray, bear barrels, and proper food and clothing. Be sure to check in with the Slana Ranger Station (*www.nps.gov/wrst/planyourvisit/slana-ranger-station.htm*) before trekking along the Nabesna Road.

🍴 Restaurants

Meatza Wagon

$$ | AMERICAN | This food truck is like no other: not only is everything made from scratch, but because it's situated so far from the main road system, the chef has no choice but to rely heavily on locally sourced ingredients. Be sure to try the Copper River salmon cakes and the slow-cooked Kenny Lake pork tacos. **Known for:** grab-and-go meals; fantastic pork tacos; vegetarian and gluten-free options. [$] *Average main: $15* ✉ *McCarthy* 🌐 *www.meatzawagon.com.*

The Potato

$ | AMERICAN | What started as a food truck with an indoor-order bar is now a full-blown restaurant. This is where locals come for tasty comfort food, live music, and a super laid-back vibe. **Known for:** live-music venue; fries, fries, and more fries; fun and relaxed ambience. [$] *Average main: $10* ✉ *McCarthy* ☎ *907/554–4405* 🌐 *www.theroadsidepotatohead.com* 🕒 *Closed Oct.–Apr.*

★ **The Salmon and Bear Restaurant**

$$$$ | AMERICAN | A remote town with only 50 year-round residents seems an unlikely place to find a five-star meal, but that's exactly what the chefs here deliver, creatively assembling dishes using ingredients grown, caught, and raised in the region. The changing menu might include local yak, red angus, Kenny Lake pork, or Copper River salmon—all paired with fantastic wines. **Known for:** romantic ambience; fine dining where you'd least expect it; seared local duck. [$] *Average main: $40* ✉ *Ma Johnson's Historical Hotel, 101 Kennicott Ave., McCarthy* ☎ *907/554–4402* 🌐 *majohnsonshotel.com* 🕒 *Closed Oct.–Apr. No lunch.*

🛏 Hotels

Aspen Meadows of McCarthy B&B

$$ | B&B/INN | Three miles before the Kennicott River footbridge to McCarthy, this bed-and-breakfast offers rustic-but-comfortable cabins with cozy beds and an Alaskan-wilderness feel. **Pros:** peaceful; breakfast includes freshly baked rolls; welcoming hosts. **Cons:** only two cabins have running water and bathrooms; bare-bones amenities; driving directions are a little complicated. [$] *Rooms from: $150* ✉ *McCarthy No. 42, Wrangell-St. Elias National Park* ☎ *907/554–4454, 866/487–7657* 🌐 *wsen.net* 🕒 *Closed Sept.–May* 🛏 *4 cabins* 🍴 *Free Breakfast.*

Copper River Princess Wilderness Lodge

$$ | HOTEL | A wall of windows two stories high provides dramatic views of the Wrangell–St. Elias Range and the Copper and Klutina Rivers at this lodge near the national park's main visitor center. **Pros:** plenty of activities offered; comfortable lodge in the wilderness; dramatic views. **Cons:** frequently occupied by tour groups; little else nearby in the way of amenities; no Wi-Fi in rooms. [$] *Rooms from: $150* ✉ *1 Brenwick Craig Rd., Mile 102, Richardson Hwy., Copper Center* ☎ *800/426–0500 reservations* 🌐 *www.princesslodges.com* 🕒 *Closed mid-Sept.–mid-May* 🍴 *No Meals* 🛏 *85 rooms.*

Kennicott Glacier Lodge

$$$ | **HOTEL** | At the top of the 10-mile gravel road from McCarthy is an astounding site: a red-and-white lodge with manicured lawns set amid the aged and worn Kennecott Mine and a receding glacier—all with a backdrop of snow-crested peaks. **Pros:** outdoor activities can be arranged for a fee; lots of character and delicious food; shuttle service to/from McCarthy. **Cons:** no air-conditioning; some rooms have shared bath; family-style dinner not for everyone. [$] *Rooms from: $210* ✉ *15 Kennicott Millsite, Kennicott* ✣ *5 miles north of McCarthy* ☎ *800/582–5128* 🌐 *www.kennicottlodge.com* 🍴 *All-Inclusive* ⏲ *Closed mid-Sept.–mid-May* 🛏 *35 rooms.*

Ma Johnson's Historical Hotel

$$$ | **B&B/INN** | A restored boarding house from McCarthy's early-1900s mining heyday is now a characterful B&B decorated with antiques and artifacts. **Pros:** pickup and drop-off at the airport or foot bridge included; fantastic restaurant; cute, historical property. **Cons:** very small rooms; no electrical outlets in rooms (charge devices in the lobby); shared bathrooms. [$] *Rooms from: $249* ✉ *McCarthy* ☎ *907/554–4402* 🌐 *majohnsonshotel.com* ⏲ *Closed Oct.–Apr.* 🍴 *Free Breakfast* 🛏 *20 rooms.*

Ultima Thule Outfitters

$$$$ | **RESORT** | This remote fly-in-only lodge on the Chitina River in Wrangell–St. Elias National Park and Preserve offers four-night "air-safari adventures" packages (starting at $8,550 per person) that include flightseeing, rafting, climbing, hiking, fishing, mushing, and skiing excursions. **Pros:** stunning views; adventure with creature comforts; fantastic food. **Cons:** very remote; ultra-expensive; cost only covers five days. [$] *Rooms from: $8550* ✉ *Chitina* ☎ *907/854–4500* 🌐 *www.ultimathulelodge.com* 🍴 *All-Inclusive* 🛏 *6 cabins.*

🍸 Nightlife

Golden Saloon

BARS | Hang out with locals and seasonal guides at the only bar in town, right on the main drag. Thursday is open mic night featuring old-favorite sing-along songs and tall-tale spoken-word performances. On weekend nights, there's sure to be live music outside on the grass. ✉ *McCarthy* ☎ *907/554–4402* 🌐 *wp.mccarthylodge.com.*

Chapter 6

DENALI NATIONAL PARK AND PRESERVE

Updated by
David Cannamore

🏕 Camping 🛏 Hotels 🏃 Activities 👁 Scenery 👥 Crowds
★★★★★   ★★★☆☆   ★★★★★   ★★★★★   ★★★★☆

WELCOME TO DENALI NATIONAL PARK AND PRESERVE

TOP REASONS TO GO

★ **Backcountry hiking:** Getting off the road system and into the park's managed units allows for a true wilderness experience, limited only by time and the strength of your legs. For on-trail hiking, try the Savage River Loop or Mt. Healy Overlook Trail.

★ **Denali flightseeing:** Soar over river valleys and up glaciers to the slopes of Denali to see the continent's wildest scenery. Some tours also offer landings on Ruth Glacier.

★ **Sled-dog demonstrations:** Watch half-hour demonstrations at the nation's oldest working dogsled kennel. Since the 1920s, sled dogs have been hauling rangers and workers to Denali's interior.

★ **Rafting:** Experience Denali on its wild rapids or serene flat water.

★ **Wonder Lake:** It takes all day to get to Wonder Lake via bus, but your chances of spotting wildlife are excellent. And from Wonder Lake the view of the massive slopes of Denali is something you'll never forget.

1 **The Entrance.** Just outside the park you'll find a strip of hotels, restaurants, and shops; just inside the park are the official visitor center, the least scenic campsites in Denali, and a level of chaos—at least in high season—that does not reflect the park's amazing beauty. Just put all this at your back as soon as you can.

2 **Eielson Visitor Center.** Deep in the heart of the park, near a favored caribou trail, Eielson offers great mountain views and sweeping vistas of the glaciated landscape. If you can't make it all the way to Wonder Lake, at least make it here.

3 **The Mountain.** Call it Denali or just "the Mountain." It's the highest spot on the continent, a double-edged peak that draws more than 1,000 climbers a year. Fewer than half make it to the top, but that's okay: it's easy enough to enjoy the view from below.

4 **Wonder Lake.** The end of the road for most vehicles, the lake is a full day's ride on one of the park buses. For your time, when the weather allows, you get the best view of the mountain anywhere in the park.

SNOHOMISH HILLS

DENALI NATIONAL PRESERVE

Castle Rocks 2079ft ▲

COTTONWOOD HILLS

SLOW FORK HILLS

Heart Mtn 6500ft ▲

A L A S K A

Mt Russell 11670ft ▲

Yentna

Mount Dall 8756ft ▲

DENALI NATIONAL PRESERVE

0   10 miles
0   10 kilometers

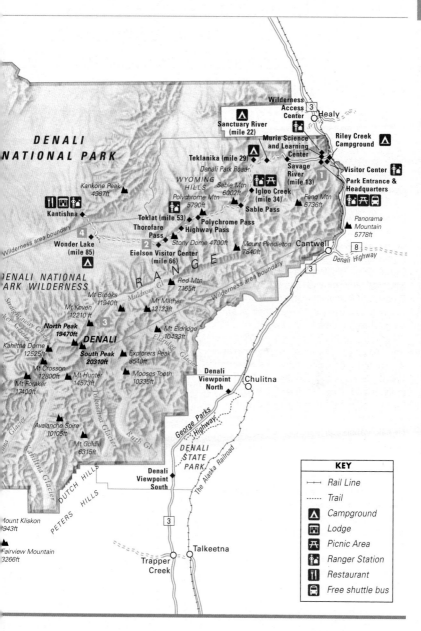

DENALI NATIONAL PARK

Wilderness Access Center

Healy

Sanctuary River (mile 22)

Murie Science and Learning Center

Riley Creek Campground

Teklanika (mile 29)

Denali Park Road

Savage River (mile 13)

Visitor Center

Park Entrance & Headquarters

WYOMING HILLS

Sable Mtn 6002ft

Igloo Creek (mile 34)

Fang Mtn 6736ft

Kankone Peak 4987ft

Polychrome Mtn 5790ft

Sable Pass

Panorama Mountain 5778ft

Kantishna

Toklat (mile 53)

Polychrome Pass

Thorofare Pass

Highway Pass

Stony Dome 4700ft

Wonder Lake (mile 85)

Eielson Visitor Center (mile 66)

Mount Pendleton 7840ft

Cantwell

Denali Highway

8

3

DENALI NATIONAL PARK WILDERNESS

RANGE

Red Mtn 7165ft

Wilderness area boundary

Mt Brooks 11940ft

Muldrow Gl

Mt Mather 12123ft

Mt Keven 12210 ft

North Peak 19470ft

DENALI

Mt Eldridge 10433ft

Kahiltna Dome 12525ft

South Peak 20310ft

Explorers Peak 8540ft

Mt Crosson 12800ft

Mt Hunter 14573ft

Mooses Tooth 10335ft

Denali Viewpoint North

Chulitna

Mt Foraker 17400ft

Avalanche Spire 10105ft

Mt Goldie 6315ft

George Parks Highway

DENALI STATE PARK

The Alaska Railroad

DUTCH HILLS

Denali Viewpoint South

PETERS HILLS

Mount Kliskon 3943ft

3

Fairview Mountain 3266ft

Trapper Creek

Talkeetna

KEY	
⊢—⊣	Rail Line
······	Trail
⛺	Campground
🏠	Lodge
⛩	Picnic Area
👫	Ranger Station
🍴	Restaurant
🚌	Free shuttle bus

Denali National Park and Preserve is Alaska's most visited attraction for many reasons. The most accessible of Alaska's national parks and one of only three connected to the state's highway system, the 6-million-acre wilderness offers spectacular mountain views, a variety of wildlife, striking vegetation, and unforgettable landscapes.

Denali National Park lies 120 miles south of Fairbanks and 240 miles north of Anchorage on the George Parks Highway. The keystone of the park is Mt. Denali itself. The mountain was named Mt. McKinley from 1917 to 2015, but President Obama changed the name of this peak back to Denali, an Athabascan name meaning "the High One." It is often referred to by Alaskans simply as "the Mountain." The peak measures in at 20,310 feet, the highest point on the continent. Denali is also the tallest mountain in the world—yes, Mt. Everest is higher, but it sits on the Tibetan plateau, as if it was standing on a chair to rise above Denali, which starts barely above sea level.

Denali is part of the Alaska Range, a harsh, rigid 600-mile backbone of snow, ice, and rock that cuts sharply through the center of the park. The 92-mile park road runs parallel to the north side of the range, winding along its foothills. Mt. Hunter (14,573 feet) and Mt. Foraker (17,400 feet) stand sentinel to the south of Denali, with glaciers flowing across the entire range.

Another, smaller group of mountains— the Outer Range, north of Denali's park road—is a mix of volcanics and heavily metamorphosed sediments. Though not as breathtaking as the Alaska Range, the Outer Range is popular with hikers and backpackers because its summits and ridges are not as technically difficult to reach.

But despite its dizzying height, Denali is not always easy to see. Like most great mountains, it has a tendency to create its own weather, which for a majority of the time involves a large amount of clouds. The mountain is only visible from the park about a third of the time in summer. The deeper you travel into the park and the longer you linger in her shadow, the better the odds are that the cloudy veil will be lifted.

While you wait to catch a glimpse of Denali, there's plenty more to look for. Dozens of mammal species populate the park, including the "Big Five" of Alaskan animals: the moose, grizzly bear, wolf, Dall sheep, and caribou. Snowshoe hare and arctic ground squirrels watch with suspicious eyes from the roadside, and the sky is filled with the calls of

Denali National Park in One Day

You can do a bus tour of the park in a single day. Allow for all day, and try to go at least as far as Eielson Visitor Center. If you can, set out to Wonder Lake. A few buses go a few miles farther to Kantishna, but the views from Wonder Lake are better; there's no reason to ride those last miles unless you're staying at one of the inholding lodges.

If you have more than a single day, the best thing to do is camp in the park.

The longer you stay, the better chance you'll have of seeing Denali, which, on average, is only visible one day out of three. Again, Wonder Lake is the spot of choice.

It's also easy to fill a day around the park entrance, taking rafting trips on the Nenana River or going on some of the short hikes near the main visitor center.

willow ptarmigan and eagles. Tundra and spruce-laden Taiga forests lead to the rocky foothills of the Alaska Range, populated by lichens and small grasses favored by caribou. There are also the harsh glaciers and sharp peaks of the mountains themselves, but be aware that mountaineering in this region is not a casual endeavor. Only about half of those who attempt to summit North America's highest peak succeed and careful planning is required months in advance.

But for those who would prefer not to risk the thin air of Denali's summit, there are still several ways to experience the park, from half-day excursions to weeklong adventures. Hiking trails dot the area near the visitor center while the more bold might try a multiday backpacking trip through the tundra. Tour buses cover the length of the park road, with six campgrounds available along it. The buses feature informative and keen-eyed drivers, who are constantly looking to spot wildlife. Flightseeing tours are offered from the nearby community of Healy, which, barring bad weather, will get you up close to the mountains (Denali included), and many even include a glacier walk.

Several of Denali's most spectacular landforms are found deep in the park but are still visible from the park road. The multicolor volcanic rocks at Cathedral Mountain and Polychrome Pass reflect the vivid hues of the American Southwest. The braided channels of glacially fed streams, such as the Teklanika, Toklat, and McKinley Rivers, serve as highway routes for both animals and hikers. The debris- and tundra-covered ice of Muldrow Glacier, one of the largest glaciers to flow out of Denali National Park's high mountains, is visible from Eielson Visitor Center, at Mile 66 of the park road. Wonder Lake, a narrow kettle pond that's a remnant of Alaska's ice ages, lies at Mile 85, just a few miles from the former gold-boom camp of Kantishna.

Planning

When to Go

Denali's main season runs mid-May through early September. About 90% of travelers come in these months, and with good reason: warmish weather, long days, and all the facilities are open. Shoulder seasons (early May and late

AVERAGE HIGH/LOW TEMPERATURES					
Jan.	Feb.	Mar.	Apr.	May	June
11/-5	17/-2	26/1	39/16	54/31	65/41
July	Aug.	Sept.	Oct.	Nov.	Dec.
67/45	61/40	50/31	32/14	17/1	15/-1

September) can be incredibly beautiful in the park, with few people around; plus, you can often drive your own car a fair way down the park road since the buses don't run. Exact opening and closing dates for seasonal properties tend to vary year to year, and when traveling close to a shoulder season, it's best to inquire directly before your visit to ensure a place is open. In winter the only way into the park is on skis or snowshoes or by dog-sled. You'll have the place almost entirely to yourself—most of the businesses at the park entrance are closed—and if you're comfortable in deep snow and freezing weather, there is no better time to see Denali.

No matter how much time you have, plan ahead. Bus and campsite reservations are available for the summer season beginning December 1.

■ TIP→ **Reserve tickets for buses ahead of time; call the numbers provided in this chapter or log on to www.reservedenali. com.**

Although you can often just walk up and get on something, it may not be the experience you're after. Advance planning makes for the best trips.

Getting Here and Around

AIR

Fairbanks International Airport (FAI), the closest international airport to Fairbanks, is 120 miles to the north. Bush planes fly into the community of Healy just north of the park entrance or Talkeetna 150 miles to the south. These two smaller strips are

where the majority of the flight seeing tours for Denali depart from.

CAR

The park is 120 miles south of Fairbanks, or 240 miles north of Anchorage, on the George Parks Highway, which is the most common access route.

There is a second, seldom-used road to the park: the Denali Highway leads from Paxon, which is accessible from the Rich-ardson Highway (it connects Fairbanks and Valdez) to Cantwell, coming out just south of the park entrance. This 134-mile road is mostly unpaved, with few ser-vices. Only people with high-clearance cars should try it. The Denali Highway is closed in winter.

Unless you are staying at the Teklanika Campground at Mile 29 (a three-day min-imum stay is required), personal vehicles are only allowed along the first 15 miles of the Denali road. There is a road lottery for a day in September (the exact date varies every year) where you can drive your personal vehicle into the park, but these days are often crowded and traf-fic-filled even if you come sans-vehicle.

SHUTTLE

Only one road penetrates Denali's expansive wilderness: the 92-mile Denali Park Road, which winds from the park entrance to Wonder Lake (as far as the regular buses go) and on the inholding of Kantishna, the historic mining district in the heart of the park, where there are a couple of private lodges. The first 15 miles of the road are paved and open to all vehicles. During the summer months, the road beyond the checkpoint at Savage River is limited to tour buses, special permit holders, and the community members of Kantishna. To get around the park, you need to get on one of the buses or start hiking.

TRAIN

For those who don't want to drive, Denali National Park is a regular stop on the Alaska Railroad's Anchorage–Fairbanks route. The railway sells packages that combine train travel with hotels and trips into the park. There are great views along the way, especially when crossing the Hurricane Gulch Bridge, and the train is a lovely, comfortable way to travel. The final approach to the park is much prettier by train than via car.

Inspiration

A story that has captured the imagination of some and the frustration of others, Jon Krakauer's book *Into the Wild* (and subsequent 2007 movie directed by Sean Penn) follows the mysterious journey of Chris McCandless from the east coast to the wilds of Alaska. The iconic bus along the Stampede Trail where his body was discovered has been the site of much frustration for search and rescue crew ever since as backpackers and sightseers attempt to reach it. The bus has since been removed although you can still see the model used in the film at the nearby 49th State Brewing Company in Healy.

One of the most recognized and important naturalists of the 20th century, Adolph Murie will be forever remembered for his work within Denali National Park. Well researched but condensed and easy to read, you don't need to be a PhD carrying scientist to appreciate the wealth of knowledge and history of the area in *A Naturalist in Alaska.*

It isn't necessary to stand on the highest peak in North America to appreciate Art Davidson's vivid descriptions in *Minus 148.* The book details the first winter ascent of the mountain and is best enjoyed next to a roaring fire with a hot beverage of your choice.

Denali National Park, Alaska Guide to Hiking, Photography, and Camping is an intensive look at the park's geography and a must for backpackers. Ike Waits keeps updating this guidebook, the most recent one highlights more than 40 hikes and backpacking trips through the park's tundra.

Park Essentials

ACCESSIBILITY

While many of the wilderness areas are impossible to reach for those with disabilities, the park has done a good job of configuring several areas to make them accessible for the majority of visitors. All campground talks and theater programs take place in wheelchair accessible areas. When possible, ASL translations of ranger programs can be made available. Since Denali is such a remote setting, the earlier you can make this request, the more likely the park will be able to provide this service.

Most trails in the park have a base of native vegetation punctuated by rocks and roots, but several trails around the park entrance like the Bike Loop and Horseshoe Lake Trails are made of compacted gravel and are the easiest for a wheelchair to navigate.

All campgrounds that admit vehicles have some level of accessibility, the best of which is Riley Creek campground. Here you'll find specific campsites that have been surfaced with compact gravel and are located close to the mercantile.

Some of the tour buses have a wheelchair lift. Like the ASL translation option, the sooner that you can request one of these specific buses for your tour the better. The same service is available to reach the sled dog kennels 1.5 miles from the entrance. The kennel

6

Denali National Park and Preserve PLANNING

amphitheater has limited seating, so it's best to show up early to ensure a spot.

Two wheelchairs are available at the Denali Visitor Center, which are available on a first come, first served basis.

PARK FEES AND PERMITS
Admission to Denali is $15 per person for a seven-day entrance permit.

PARK HOURS
The park never closes. There may not be anybody around to accept the admission fee in deep winter, but the gates are always open.

CELL PHONE RECEPTION
Don't count on cell-phone reception past the first mile or two beyond the visitor center.

Restaurants

There's a small grill-style restaurant near the park's visitor center, but otherwise there are no traditional restaurants or grocery stores inside the park so you'll need to carry in your food. Just outside the park entrance, in the area known as Glitter Gulch, you'll find dozens of restaurants open during the summer only. Year-round grocery stores are found ten miles north of the entrance in the town of Healy.

Restaurant and hotel reviews have been shortened. For full information, visit Fodors.com. Restaurant prices are the average cost of a main course at dinner or, if dinner is not served, at lunch. Hotel prices are the lowest cost of a standard double room in high season

What It Costs

	$	$$	$$$	$$$$
RESTAURANTS				
	under $14	$14–$22	$23–$32	over $32
HOTELS				
	under $100	$100–$175	$176–$250	over $250

Hotels

There are plenty of options right outside the park entrance, but don't expect to find anything open in winter. Year round lodgings can be found in Healy.

Tours

Don't be alarmed by the crowded park entrance; that gets left behind very quickly. After the chaos of private businesses that line the George Parks Highway and the throngs at the visitor center, there's pretty much nothing else in the park but wilderness. From the bus you'll have the opportunity to see Denali's wildlife in natural settings, as the animals are habituated to the road and vehicles, and go about their daily routine with little bother. In fact, the animals really like the road: it's easier for them to walk along it than to work through the tundra and tussocks.

Bus trips take time. The maximum speed limit is 35 mph, and the buses don't hit that very often. Add in rest stops, wildlife sightings, and slowdowns for passing, and it's an 8- to 11-hour day to reach the heart of the park and the best Denali views from Miles 62–85. Buses run from May 20 to September 13, although if you're running up close against one of those dates, call to make sure.

■ TIP → **If you decide to tour the park by bus, you have two choices: a sightseeing bus tour or a ride on the shuttle bus. The differences between the two are significant.**

BUSES AND SHUTTLES
Camper Buses

These buses serve permitted backpackers and those staying in campgrounds along the road. Seats in the back of the bus are removed for gear storage and there is room for two bikes (the bike spaces must be reserved ahead of time). While there is no formal narration, bus drivers aren't likely to let you miss anything important. The $60 pass includes transportation anywhere down the road as far as Wonder Lake for the length of the backpacker's stay; kids under 15 are free. Tell the driver ahead of time where you'd like to get out. ⊠ *Denali National Park* ☎ *800/622–7275* ⊕ *www.reservedenali.com* ⊠ *$60* ☉ *Closed mid-Sept.–mid-May.*

Shuttle Buses

The park's shuttle and transit buses are a more informal, cheaper, and independent way to experience Denali. These buses are green-painted, converted school buses while the formally narrated tour buses are tan. While these trips are not formally narrated, the majority of bus drivers enjoy sharing information with riders, and the buses are equipped with speakers. Transit buses offer the freedom to disembark virtually anywhere along the road system and explore the park for yourself. Catching a ride back is as simple as returning to the road and waiting for the next transit bus to come by. Note that full buses will not stop, so it's possible to wait for an hour or more for your ride back. Like the narrated tours, transit buses are operated by Doyon/Aramark and bookings are made through the concessionaire. Reservations are not required, and about a quarter of the seats are saved for walk-ons. But if you're visiting during peak season, it's best to make reservations ahead of time to ensure availability. Schedules can be found on the National Park Service's Denali website; departure times are relatively reliable although they can fluctuate during the summer. ⊠ *Denali National Park* ☎ *800/622–7275* ⊕ *www.reservedenali.com* ⊠ *Free–$60* ☉ *Closed mid-Sept.–mid-May.*

Tour Buses

Guided bus tours offer the most informative introduction to the park. Each trip is led by a trained naturalist who drives the bus and gives a full narration. All tours include rest stops approximately every 90 minutes. Unlike the transit buses, you are not allowed to wander off on your own. The shortest is the five-hour Natural History Tour that travels to Teklanika at Mile 27. Besides moose and the occasional caribou, chances of seeing the park's large mammals are limited on this route, and glimpses of Denali are possible but not probable. The next longest option is the seven to eight-hour Tundra Wilderness Tour that reaches Stony Brook at Mile 62; this is the best choice for wildlife and photography enthusiasts. The longest narrated tour is the Kantishna Experience, a 12-hour extravaganza that runs the full 92 miles of park road to the old mining town of Kantishna. Advance reservations are required for all bus tours, and they can be made starting on December 1, with exact departure times fluctuating depending on demand and time of year. It's best to consult Doyon/Aramark for an exact schedule as departure times are often not set until a few days before. ⊠ *Denali National Park* ☎ *800/622–7275* ⊕ *www.reserve-denali.com* ⊠ *From $101.75* ☉ *Closed mid-Sept.–mid-May.*

Visitor Information

CONTACTS Denali National Park Headquarters. ⊠ *Denali National Park* ☎ *907/683–2294 information* ⊕ *www.nps.gov/dena.*

Bus	Experience	Route	Frequency	Round-Trip Duration	Approximate Cost
Riley Creek Loop	Like taking a bus downtown.	Among buildings at park entrance	Approximately every 30 minutes	30 minutes	Free
Savage River Shuttle	An easy way to see the wooded areas near the park entrance; good chance of moose sightings.	First 14 miles of park road	Hourly in summer	2 hours	Free
Natural History Tour	Focuses on the park's history; includes an hour of interpretive stops. Fully narrated.	First 27 miles of park road	Twice a day, morning and evening	5 hours	$101.75 adults; $43.50 15 and under
Tundra Wilderness Tour	From the park entrance to the Toklat River; emphasis on park history and wildlife. Fully narrated.	To the Stony Overlook at Mile 62	Twice a day, morning and evening	7–8 hours	$162.50 adults; $73.75 15 and under
Kantishna Experience	The grand tour of Denali: from forest to tundra beyond Wonder Lake. Fully narrated.	To the end of the park road	Two morning departures daily	13 hours	$240.75 adults; $113 15 and under
Transit Bus	The park's own bus: get on and off wherever you want. No formal narration. Most flexible option.	To the end of the park road	Depends on how far out the particular bus goes; schedule and departure times vary throughout the summer	6–7 hours Toklat, 8 hours Eielson, 11 hours Wonder Lake, 12 hours Kantishna	Round-trip: $50 to Toklat; $60 to Eielson, free 15 and under; $60 to Wonder Lake and Kantishna
Camper Bus	Transport to all park campgrounds. No formal narration. Reserved for those with camping permits.	To Wonder Lake, with stops at all campgrounds along the way	Several times a day, varies throughout the summer	Times vary	$60; free 15 and under

In the Park

With a landmass larger than Massachusetts, Denali National Park and Preserve has too much area for even the most dedicated vacationer to explore in one go. When planning your trip, consider whether you want to strike out on your own as a backcountry traveler or to stay at a lodge nearby and enjoy Denali as a day hiker with the help of a tour or shuttle bus. Both options require some advance planning, for bus tickets or backcountry permits. But both options also offer a magnificent experience.

Sights

GEOLOGICAL FORMATIONS

★ Denali

MOUNTAIN | In the heart of mainland Alaska, within 6-million-acre Denali National Park and Preserve, the continent's most majestic peak rises into the heavens. Formerly known as Mt. McKinley, this 20,310-foot massif of ice, snow, and rock has been renamed to honor its Alaska Native name, Denali, or "the High One." Some simply call it "the Mountain." One thing is certain: it's a giant among giants, and the most dominant feature in a land of extremes and superlatives. Those who have walked Denali's slopes know it to be a wild, desolate place. As the highest peak in North America, Denali is a target of mountaineers who aspire to ascend the "seven summits"—the tallest mountains of each of the seven continents. A foreboding and mysterious place, it was terra incognita—unclimbed and unknown to most people—as recently as the late 1890s. Among Athabascan tribes, however, the mountain was a revered landmark; many generations regarded it as a holy place and a point of reference. The mountain's vertical rise is the highest in the world. This means that at 18,000 feet over the lowlands (which are some 2,000 feet above sea level), Denali's vertical rise is even greater than that of Mt. Everest at 29,035-feet (which sits 12,000 feet above the Tibetan plateau, some 17,000 feet above sea level). Denali's awesome height and its subarctic location make it one of the coldest mountains on Earth, if not *the* coldest. Primarily made of granite, Denali undergoes continual shifting and uplift thanks to plate tectonics (the Pacific Plate pushing against the North American Plate); it grows about 1 millimeter per year. ✉ *Denali National Park*.

PICNIC AREAS

There are a handful of dedicated picnic spots within Denali.

Riley Creek Picnic Area

OTHER ATTRACTION | A covered pavilion is located near Riley Creek just inside the park entrance. It's accessible year round and there are a couple of bathrooms nearby. ✉ *Denali National Park* ⊕ *www. nps.gov/places/dena-riley-picnic-area. htm*.

Denali's Dinosaurs

On June 27, 2005, a geologist discovered the track of a theropod, or a three-toed carnivorous dinosaur, in 65- to 70-million-year-old Cretaceous sedimentary rock, just 35 miles west of the park entrance. This is the first hard evidence of dinosaurs in the Interior of Alaska. While the initial discoveries were made by geologists, subsequent finds were uncovered by participants in a teacher workshop with the Murie Science and Learning Center.

Mountain Vista

OTHER ATTRACTION | Near the end of the road system open to private vehicles is the Mountain Vista Picnic area. In addition to multiple picnic tables, bathroom facilities are available along with the chance to glimpse the mountain on a clear day. For day trips, the Savage River Alpine Trail is located next to the picnic area. The spot can be windy so plan accordingly. ⊠ *Denali National Park* ✛ *13½ miles inside the park along the Denali Highway* ⊕ *www.nps.gov/places/dena-mountain-vista.htm.*

Savage River

OTHER ATTRACTION | Located another couple of miles down the road, the Savage River picnic area is as far as private vehicles can go. There's a couple of uncovered picnic tables along with seasonally available bathroom facilities, both of which are right along the river. Two trailheads start at the picnic area. One of these, the Savage Alpine Trail connects with the Mountain Vista picnic spot while another, the Savage Canyon Trail, runs along the river. Like the picnic area at Mountain Vista, it can be windy so be prepared. ⊠ *Denali National Park* ✛ *15 miles inside the park along the Denali Highway* ⊕ *www.nps.gov/dena/planyourvisit/savagecanyon.htm.*

SCENIC DRIVES

If you're camping nearby and have your own vehicle, a drive to Savage River at first light or sunset is a good way to avoid the crowds. Wildlife tends to be more active during these quiet hours, especially if the forecast has been hot and dry.

Denali Park Road

OTHER ATTRACTION | No matter whether you visit on foot, bike, or bus, you'll want to utilize the Denali road system as much as possible. Personal vehicles are only allowed the first 15 miles of the 92-mile long road, and most of the best potential views and wildlife are beyond

this 15-mile marker. The view from the Eielson Visitor Center and Wonder Lake are the park's most iconic and these are located at miles 66 and 85 respectively. But amazing views of the rolling tundra, foothills, and grizzly bears can be had almost anywhere. Take your time and if possible, spend multiple days either taking bus tours, hiking, or biking through the park to give yourself the best chance of an unforgettable view or wildlife encounter.

While the park is never technically closed, much of the road is snowed in during the winter months. Depending on the snowfall, travel along the park road can be hampered in spring and fall as well. The road is generally open up to Mountain Vista (mile 13) by mid-February. ⊠ *Denali National Park* ⊕ *www.nps.gov/dena/planyourvisit/visiting-denali.htm* ⊙ *Weather dependent in spring, fall, and winter. Generally open to mile 13 by mid-Feb.*

SCENIC STOPS

Private vehicles are unable to access Stony Hill, Polychrome, or any of the other iconic stops in the park like Eielson Visitor Center and Wonder Lake. However, most bus tours make stops at most of them.

TRAILS

The park offers plenty of options for those who prefer to stay on marked and groomed pathways. The entrance area has more than a half-dozen forest and tundra trails such as the Taiga Loop and Triple Lakes. These range from easy to challenging, so there's something suitable for all ages and hiking abilities. All of the maintained trails within Denali can be hiked in one day and none of the trails have campgrounds or any other amenities along the way.

Some, like the **Taiga Loop Trail** and **McKinley Station Loop Trail**, are less than 1½ miles; others, like the **Rock Creek Trail**

Continued on page 277

DENALI

In the heart of mainland Alaska, within 6-million-acre Denali National Park & Preserve, the continent's most majestic peak rises into the heavens. Formerly known as Mount McKinley, this 20,310-foot massif of ice, snow, and rock has been renamed to honor its Alaska Native name Denali, or "the High One." Some simply call it "The Mountain." One thing is certain: It's a giant among giants, and the most dominant feature in a land of extremes and superlatives.

Those who have walked Denali's slopes know it to be a wild, desolate place. As the highest peak in North America, Denali is a target of mountaineers who aspire to ascend the "seven summits"—the tallest mountains on each continent. A foreboding and mysterious place, it was terra incognita—unclimbed and unknown to most people—as recently as the late 1890s. Among Athabascan tribes, however, the mountain was a revered landmark; many generations regarded it as a holy place and a point of reference.

NAMING TERRA INCOGNITA

Linguists have identified at least eight native Alaskan names for the mountain, including Deenaalee, Doleyka, Traleika, and Dghelay Ka'a. The essence of all the names is "the High One" or "Big Mountain." The first recorded sighting of Denali by a foreign explorer was in 1794, when Captain George Vancouver spotted it in the distance. More than a century later, after a summer of gold-seeking, Ivy Leaguer William Dickey reported his experiences in the *New York Sun*. His most significant news was of a massive peak, which he dubbed "Mt. McKinley," after Republican William McKinley of Ohio. Mountaineer Hudson Stuck, who led the first mountaineering team to "McKinley's" summit, was just one in a long line of Alaskans to protest this name. In Stuck's view, the moniker was an affront to both the mountain and Alaska's native people. For these very reasons, a vast majority of Alaskans called the continent's highest peak by its original name, Denali. On August 28, 2015 President Obama changed the name of the mountain back to Denali.

Denali Facts & Figures

■ The mountain's vertical rise is the highest in the world. This means that at 18,000 feet over the lowlands (which are some 2,000 feet above sea level), McKinley's vertical rise is even greater than Mt. Everest, at 29,035-feet (which rises 12,000 feet above the Tibetan plateau, some 17,000 feet above sea level).

Halfway to the summit, Denali's weather is equivalent to that of the North Pole in severity. In summer, night temperatures may reach -40° F.

11,000' Camp

Route proceeds behind ridge

Kahiltna Pass 10,320'

West Buttress Route

Climbers begin expeditions by flying to the Kahiltna Glacier Base Camp at 7,200 ft.

Kahiltna Glacier

■ The safest route to the summit is the West Buttress. Eighty to 90% of climbers attempting to ascend the peak take this route, with only about half reaching the top.

■ More than 30 people—including some world-class mountaineers—have been killed on the West Buttress.

■ From base camp to high camp, climbers must trek some 16 miles and 10,000 vertical feet—a trip that takes two to three weeks.

■ The most technically challenging stretch is the ascent to 18,200-foot Denali Pass; climbers must cross a steep snow-covered slope

■ In addition to coping with severe weather, climbers face avalanches, open crevasses, hypothermia, frostbite, and high-altitude illnesses. More than 120 people have died on the mountain and hundreds more have been seriously injured.

■ Denali's awesome height and its subarctic location make it one of the coldest mountains on Earth, if not the coldest.

■ Primarily made of granite, Denali undergoes continual shifting and uplift thanks to plate tectonics (the Pacific plate pushing against the North American Plate); it grows about 1 mm per year.

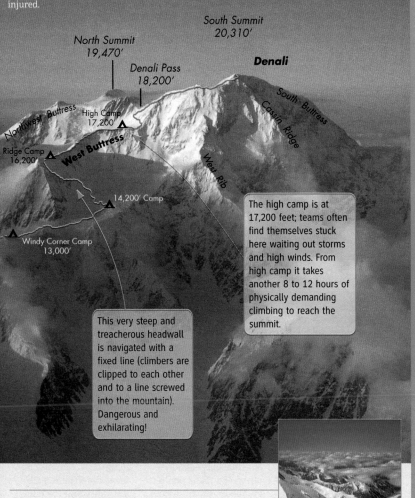

South Summit
20,310'

North Summit
19,470'

Denali Pass
18,200'

Denali

Northwest Buttress

South Buttress

High Camp
17,200'

Cassin Ridge

West Buttress

Ridge Camp
16,200'

West Rib

14,200' Camp

Windy Corner Camp
13,000'

The high camp is at 17,200 feet; teams often find themselves stuck here waiting out storms and high winds. From high camp it takes another 8 to 12 hours of physically demanding climbing to reach the summit.

This very steep and treacherous headwall is navigated with a fixed line (climbers are clipped to each other and to a line screwed into the mountain). Dangerous and exhilarating!

then a shallow bowl called the Football Field.

■ Then, still roped together, climbers ascend an 800-foot snow-and-ice wall to reach the "top of the continent" itself.

Fearless climbers facing the icy challenge at 16,400 feet on the West Buttress Route.

EARLY MILESTONES

Climbing Mt. McKinley in the early 1900s

■ In 1903, two different expeditions made the first attempts to climb Denali. The highest point reached? 11,000 feet. Over the next decade, other expeditions would try, and fail, to reach the top.

■ Finally, in 1913, a team led by Hudson Stuck reached the summit. The first person to the top was Walter Harper, a native Alaskan.

■ After the Stuck party's success in 1913, no attempts were made to climb the mountain until 1932. That year, for the first time, a pilot landed a small plane on one of the mountain's massive glaciers. Another first: a party climbed both the 20,320-foot South Peak and 19,470-foot North Peak. More tragically, the first deaths occurred on the mountain.

■ Alaskans Dave Johnston, Art Davidson, and Ray Genet completed the first winter ascent of Denali in February 1967. Japanese climber Naomi Uemura completed the first solo ascent in 1970.

A FLIGHT TO REMEMBER

Talkeetna is the home of the popular Denali Flyers. Pilots take you on a variety of air tours into the Alaska Range in small, ski-equipped planes. Flights usually include a passage through the Ruth Glacier's Great Gorge, which is bordered by breathtaking granite spires. Leaving the gorge, you'll enter immense glacial basins of the Don Sheldon Amphitheater (named in honor of the first Denali Flyer). Most trips also include flights past Denali's southern flanks and show glimpses of its climbing routes. Longer tours circle the mountain, passing among the perennially ice-capped upper slopes, saw-toothed ridges, and vertical rock faces. Flights generally range from 30 minutes to 3 hours and cost $200 to $400 per person.

FLOWER QUEST

Though most visitors to Denali have things quite large on their minds (grizzlies, moose, the mountain itself), it's often the little things that people remember long after their visits are over. Dozens and dozens of varieties of wildflowers bloom throughout the summer (though early July is the best time). In 2012, one of the park's rangers, Jake Frank, set out to photograph at least 120 species in the park. His final tally? 185. Over ten weeks, Frank photographed everything from the Alaska state flower, Alpine forget-me-nots to bright magenta Chukchi primroses, delicate arctic poppies, and much more. Along with counting flowers on a multi-mile hike, either just off the road or deep in Denali backcountry, consider going micro, too. Hike up above the treeline, grab a seat, and count the number of tiny alpine flowers (and fruit plants, including lowbush blueberries and cranberries) crowded into just a few inches of the tundra.

and **Triple Lakes Trail,** are several miles round-trip, with an altitude gain of hundreds of feet. Along these paths you may see beavers working on their lodges in Horseshoe Lake, red squirrels chattering in trees, red foxes hunting for rodents, sheep grazing on tundra, golden eagles gliding over alpine ridges, and moose feeding on willow.

The **Savage River Trail,** farthest from the park entrance and as far as private vehicles are allowed, offers a 1¾-mile round-trip hike along a raging river and under rocky cliffs. Be on the lookout for caribou, Dall sheep, foxes, and marmots.

Some argue that the park's best hiking isn't along a trail system but out in the tundra. The park's wilderness areas are broken into sectors, ensuring that backpackers and hikers have the solitude that's so highly valued in Denali. Consult with park staff for day or overnight hikes in these memorable locations. Make sure that all permits are in order, and you are comfortable hiking in bear country.

McKinley Station Trail

TRAIL | The Station trail begins at the Visitor Center and follows a winding path down toward the Riley and Hines Creeks. While the trail drops more than 100-feet during its 1½ mile long path, the grade is never very steep and the trail is made of compacted gravel for easy walking. *Easy. ⊠ Denali National Park ⊹ Trailhead: A one way trail with access points at the Denali Visitor Center and Riley Creek Campground ⊕ www.nps.gov/dena/planyourvisit/dayhiking.htm.*

Mt. Healy Overlook Trail

TRAIL | An offshoot from some of the tamer trails near the park entrance, this rugged trail is made of mostly native plant life, rocks, and roots so footing can be challenging on the steep portions and the switchbacks. It gains 1,700 feet in 2½ miles and takes about four hours round-trip, with outstanding views of the Nenana River below and the Alaska Range,

including the upper slopes of Denali. You are permitted to continue hiking along the ridge but it is not maintained and can be dangerous. From the top hikers can take in the view of the park entrance and area to the south. It's often cold and windy at the summit so wear appropriate clothing. *Difficult. ⊠ Denali National Park ⊹ Trailhead: Denali Visitor Center as an offshoot of the Taiga Trail ⊕ www.nps.gov/dena/planyourvisit/dayhiking.htm.*

Rock Creek Trail

TRAIL | After following the Taiga Trail for a short time, the Rock Creek Trail splits to the west and offers a steeper, challenging, and quieter journey through the woods. Further from the road than many of the trails near the park entrance, this 30" wide trail can have a steep grade at times of up to 15%. All together the trail runs about 2.5 miles one way, ending at the Sled Dog Kennels. *Moderate ⊠ Denali National Park ⊹ Trailhead: One way trail with access from the Denali Visitor Center and Sled Dog Kennels ⊕ www.nps.gov/dena/planyourvisit/dayhiking.htm.*

Taiga Loop Trail

TRAIL | A simple forested trail that winds around the Denali Visitor Center and other buildings and connects with the bus and train depot. The trail is made of gravel with minimal grade, most explorers should be able to complete the loop in less than an hour. ■TIP→ **Access may be limited by snowfall in winter.** *Easy. ⊠ Denali National Park ⊹ Trailhead: Looped trail with access from the Visitor Center and Bus Depot ⊕ www.nps.gov/dena/planyourvisit/dayhiking.htm.*

Triple Lakes Trail

TRAIL | At 9½ miles one-way, the Triple Lakes Trail has the distinction of being the longest trail in the park. It starts at the Denali Visitor Center and runs south, crossing a pair of creeks and offering vistas of a trio of lakes. The trail is a mixed of gravel, roots, dirt, and rocks and can feature a relatively steep 20%

grade at times. Plan on it taking about five-miles one way before you reach the other trailhead near Highway 3, about 7 miles south of the park entrance. *Diffi-cult. ☒ Denali National Park ⚓ Trailhead: Denali Visitor Center and on the west side of Highway 3 about 7 miles south of the park entrance ⊕ www.nps.gov/dena/planyourvisit/dayhiking.htm.*

Savage Alpine Trail

TRAIL | Running about four miles, this trail system connects the Savage River pull-out and campground areas. You can use the Savage River Shuttle to access the trailhead or your personal vehicle. Note that if you're using your own vehicle, the trail spits you out about two miles down the road system. ■TIP➔ **The trail isn't accessible for most of the winter.** *Moderate. ☒ Denali National Park ⚓ Trailhead: Located at the Savage River and Mountain Vista Picnic Areas.*

Savage River Loop

TRAIL | True to its name, the River Loop follows the Savage River up the valley carved between Mount Margaret and Healy Ridge for about a mile. The trail crosses a bridge before traveling down the valley and re-connecting with the Savage River Picnic Area. ■TIP➔ **The trail is inaccessible during winter months.** *Moderate. ☒ Denali National Park ⚓ Trailhead: Savage River Picnic Area ⊕ www.nps.gov/dena/planyourvisit/savagecanyon.htm.*

VISITOR CENTERS
Denali Education Center

COLLEGE | FAMILY | Situated on 10 acres of forest across from Denali National Park, this nonprofit offers intensive learning experiences that range from a variety of all-inclusive weeklong Road Scholar programs to weeklong youth programs, including hands-on research in conjunction with the National Park Service or backpacking trips for high schoolers. Public events as well as day and evening dinner programs are offered at intervals throughout the summer months. On the first weekend of August the center sponsors the Fundraising Auction, which draws in hundreds of people and thousands of articles for sale, all for a fantastic cause. *☒ Parks Hwy., Box 212, Denali National Park ⚓ Mile 231 ☎ 907/683–2597 ⊕ www.denali.org ⊗ Closed mid-Sept.–mid-May.*

Denali Visitor Center

VISITOR CENTER | Open from mid-May through mid-September, the center is a mile-and-a half beyond the park's entrance, and includes two floors' worth of displays detailing the park's natural and cultural history along with several life-size representations of the park's largest animals. A theater on the main floor plays the 20-minute film *The Heart-beats of Denali* twice an hour. The center is the starting point for most interpretive ranger hikes and several other trails you can explore independently. This is also the place to go for your backcountry camping permits (permits aren't necessary for day hikes). Nearby facilities include the railroad and bus depots, the Morino Grill, and the Alaska Geographic bookstore. *☒ Denali National Park Rd., Denali National Park ☎ 907/683–9532 ⊕ www.nps.gov/dena ⊗ Closed mid-Sept.–mid-May.*

Eielson Visitor Center

VISITOR CENTER | Famous for its views of Denali, the Eielson Visitor Center is found at Mile 66 of the park road. Park rangers are present throughout the day either leading presentations or hikes such as the leisurely Eielson Stroll. While there is a small gallery of Denali-inspired art here, this visitor center is all about the view, dominated, with a little luck, by the mountain itself. The center opens on June 1 and closes on the second Thursday after Labor Day; it's open daily 9–5:30. It's accessible by any of the shuttle buses that pass Mile 66, excluding the Kantishna Experience tour. For backpackers, the bathrooms remain unlocked 24-hours a day during the summer. *☒ Park Rd., Denali National Park ⚓ Mile*

66 🌐 www.nps.gov/dena/planyourvisit/the-eielson-visitor-center.htm 🕒 Closed early Sept.–May.

Murie Science and Learning Center
COLLEGE | Next to the Denali Visitor Center, Murie Science and Learning Center is the foundation of the park's science-based education programs, and also serves as the winter visitor center when the Denali Visitor Center is closed. Hours during the summer vary, and the center usually opens only for special presentations. During off-season camping at the Riley Campground, it's the go-to spot for ranger information and, yes, bathrooms with running water. *✉ Park Rd., Denali National Park ✣ Mile 1.5 ☎ 907/683–6432 🌐 www.nps.gov/rlc/murie.*

Wilderness Access Center
VISITOR CENTER | Also known as the Bus Depot, this center just inside the park entrance is where you can reserve campgrounds and bus trips into the park. For those that arrive after 7 pm, campground reservations can be made at the Riley Creek Mercantile until 11 pm. There's also a coffee stand—your last chance for a cup of joe unless you bring the makings for campsite coffee with you. *✉ Park Rd., Denali National Park ✣ Mile 0.5 ☎ 907/683–9532 🌐 www.nps.gov/dena/planyourvisit/wildernessaccesscenter.htm 🕒 Closed mid-Sept.–mid-May.*

🍴 Restaurants

The Denali Doghouse
$ | **AMERICAN** | It's all about the dog at this casual, dog-decorated and hot dog–theme joint whose menu includes hot dogs topped with gourmet bacon, cheese, kraut, slaw, or chili. The owners are locals and rely on made-in-Alaska products so all quarter-pound burger patties are hand-pressed while fries and onion rings are fresh. **Known for:** one of the cheaper (and most filling) options in Glitter Gulch; quick lunch and dinners; reindeer hot dogs. *[$] Average main: $9 ✉ Parks Hwy., Denali National Park ✣ Mile 238.6 ☎ 907/683–3647 🌐 www.denalidoghouse.com 🕒 Closed mid-Sept.–mid-May.*

Denali Park Salmon Bake
$$ | **SEAFOOD** | Affectionately known as "The Bake," this upbeat and lively spot does everything it can to make every night a party: from frequent live music events, to karaoke, to cramming every holiday into the summer season, there's always something happening. While salmon and other Alaska seafood is on the menu, there is no traditional all-you-can-eat salmon buffet. **Known for:** Alaska beers on tap; live music (by local musicians) and dancing; Alaska-sourced elk burger. *[$] Average main: $18 ✉ Parks Hwy., Denali National Park ✣ Mile 238.5 ☎ 907/683–2733 🌐 www.denaliparksalmonbake.com 🕒 Closed late Sept.–early May.*

Moose-AKa's
$$ | **EASTERN EUROPEAN** | Just as unique as its name, Moose-AKa's brings something different to the table for those in Glitter Gulch. Specializing in authentic European items, they offer crepes, stuffed peppers, and, of course, moussaka. **Known for:** cozy atmosphere; fantastic European-inspired menu where you'd least expect it; Serbian-inspired tempura fried crepes. *[$] Average main: $19 ✉ George Parks Hwy., Denali National Park ✣ Mile 238.9 ☎ 907/687–0003 🌐 www.moose-akas.com 🕒 Closed mid-Sept.–mid-May.*

★ Prospector's Historic Pizzeria and Ale House
$$ | **AMERICAN** | **FAMILY** | Built to have an old-time-saloon feel, this restaurant serves a seemingly endless selection of handcrafted pizzas, as well as salad, soup, pastas, and brick-oven sandwiches. Farm-to-table ingredients are used whenever possible and include locally grown greens, Alaska raised meat, and seafood. **Known for:** wide-ranging menu that includes gluten-free, vegetarian, and vegan options; Deadliest Catch pizza that comes with a pound of king crab legs;

Plants and Wildlife in Denali

Mammals

Thirty-seven species of mammals reside in the park, from wolves and bears to little brown bats and pygmy shrews that weigh a fraction of an ounce. The most sought-after species among visitors are the large mammals: grizzlies, wolves, Dall sheep, moose, and caribou. All inhabit the forest or tundra landscape that surrounds Denali Park Road. You can expect to see Dall sheep finding their way across high meadows and peppering distant mountaintops (look for the tiny white dots), grizzlies and caribou frequenting stream bottoms and tundra, moose in the forested areas both near the park entrance and deep in the park, and the occasional wolf or fox that may dart across the road.

Birds

The park also has a surprisingly large avian population in summer, with 167 identified species. Most of the birds migrate in fall, leaving only two-dozen year-round resident species, including ravens, boreal chickadees, and hawk owls. Some of the summer birds travel thousands of miles to nest and breed in subarctic valleys, hills, and ponds. The northern wheatear migrates from southern Asia, warblers arrive from Central and South America, and the arctic tern annually travels 24,000 miles while commuting between the Arctic and Antarctica.

Taiga

Vegetation in the park consists largely of taiga and tundra. Taiga is coniferous forest in moist areas below a tree line of 2,700 feet and consists mainly of white and black spruce trees. Due to the layer of permafrost that lies just under the surface of the land, the trees have shallow root systems. This means they are very susceptible to wind and weather conditions, and it's not at all unusual to see entire sections of forest, usually black spruce, leaning to one side, or leaning every which way like a bunch of jackstraws. Called a "drunken forest," the lean comes from trees trying to make their home in permafrost that thaws, freezes, and thaws again, shifting the soil right under the roots. Ground cover in the taiga forest includes dwarf birch, blueberry, and willow shrubs.

Tundra

The rest of the landmass not covered by ice and snow is carpeted by tundra, consisting of a variety of delicate plants such as lichens, berries, bright wildflowers, and woody plants. This complex carpet of low-lying vegetation generates brilliant color, especially in August, when the fall weather begins. Take a really close look at tundra: it's like being a giant and looking down on a forest, it's all so perfect and detailed and tiny. A single square foot of tundra can hold 40 or 50 different species. The park as a whole contains more than 650 species of flowering plants, plus who knows how many mosses, fungi, and lichen. While you're busy watching for moose and bears, don't forget to check out the plants.

In the fall, the mountains of Denali National Park are surrounded by brilliant orange and red foliage.

largest and most diverse beer selection around. $ *Average main: $20* ✉ *Parks Hwy., Denali National Park* ✛ *Mile 238.9* ☎ *907/683–7437* ⊕ *www.prospectorspizza.com* ⊗ *Closed late Sept.–early May.*

 Hotels

If you can afford it, stay at a wilderness lodge within Denali, like Camp Denali and North Face Lodge or the Kantishna Roadhouse.

★ Camp Denali and North Face Lodge
$$$$ | RESORT | The legendary, family-owned and-operated Camp Denali and North Face Lodge both offer stunning views of Denali and active learning experiences deep within Denali National Park, at Mile 89 on the park road. **Pros:** only in-park lodge with a view of Denali; knowledgeable and attentive staff; strong emphasis on learning. **Cons:** alcohol is BYO; steep rates and three-night minimum stay; credit cards not accepted. $ *Rooms from: $1310* ✉ *Denali Park Rd., Denali National Park* ✛ *Mile 89* ☎ *907/683–2290* ⊕ *www.campdenali.com* ▭ *No credit cards* ⊗ *Closed mid-Sept.–late May* ⤴ *18 cabins (Camp Denali), 15 rooms (North Face Lodge)* ¶◯¶ *All-inclusive.*

Kantishna Roadhouse
$$$$ | RESORT | Run by the Athabascan Doyon Tourism, this establishment at Mile 95 on the park road offers an enriching wilderness getaway. **Pros:** transport from the train station is provided; guided hikes with naturalists; home to the only saloon in the Denali backcountry. **Cons:** two-night minimum stay; lacks a direct view of Denali; no connection to the outside world besides a phone booth. $ *Rooms from: $1135* ✉ *Denali Park Rd., Denali National Park* ✛ *Mile 92* ☎ *800/942–7420, 907/374–3041* ⊕ *www.kantishnaroadhouse.com* ⊗ *Closed mid-Sept.–early June* ⤴ *32 rooms.*

⚒ Activities

BIKING

Mountain biking is allowed along the entire park road, and no permit is required for day trips. Bikes can be transported for free on the park's shuttle buses, though space is limited and available on a first come, first served basis. Before heading out, you should check with the park rangers at the visitor center; if there has been a wolf kill or a lot of bear sightings by the road, bike access might be limited. Bring proper gear including a bike repair kit.

The road is unpaved after the first 15 miles. Beyond the Savage River checkpoint the road is dirt and gravel, and during the day the road is busy with the park buses, which can leave bikers choking on dust. The road can get really sloppy in the rain, too. The best time to bike is late evening, when the midnight sun is shining and buses have stopped shuttling passengers for the day. When biking on the road, you need to be aware of your surroundings and observe park rules. Do not try to outride bears, moose, or wolves as it's a race you won't win. Off-road riding is forbidden, and some sensitive wildlife areas are closed to hiking and biking. The Sable Pass area is always closed to off-road excursions on foot or bike because of the high bear population, and other sites are closed due to denning activity or recent signs of carcass scavenging.

Bike Denali rents mountain bikes and all the necessary gear you'll need for biking the park road whether you plan on being out of the afternoon or days at a time.

Bike Denali

BIKING | Locally owned and situated in Glitter Gulch just outside the park entrance, Bike Denali specializes in rentals instead of tours. You get more than just a bike with your rental though, as the basic packages include everything you need for a day on Denali's roadsystem including a lock, tire repair kit, high visibility day pannier (special bags that attach to the bike frame), and bear spray with a holster. Even cargo and child trailers are available. Longer rentals extending more than a week are also possible for those that want to experience the park in this unique style. Additional gear is available to help make bike camping possible. 24-hour bike rentals start at $75. ⊠ *Parks Highway, Denali National Park* ⬦ *Mile 238.5* ☏ *907/378–2107* ⊕ *bikedenali.com.*

BOATING AND RAFTING

Several privately owned raft and tour companies operate along the Parks Highway near the entrance to Denali, and they schedule daily rafting, both in the fairly placid areas on the Nenana and through the 10-mile-long Nenana River canyon, which has stretches of Class IV–V rapids—enough to make you think you're on a very wet roller coaster. The Nenana is Alaska's most accessible white water, and if you don't mind getting a little chilly, a river trip is not just a lot of fun, it's also a fantastic way to see a different side of the landscape. Most outfitters lend out dry suits for river trips; it takes a few minutes to get used to wearing one (they feel tight around the neck) but they're essential gear to keep you safe if you fall into the water.

Denali Raft Adventures

WHITE-WATER RAFTING | This outfitter launches its rafts several times daily on two- and four-hour scenic and white-water trips on the Nenana River. GORE-TEX dry suits are provided. Guests under the age of 18 must have a release waiver signed by a parent or guardian. Contact the company for copies before the trip. Courtesy pickup at hotels and the train depot is available within a 7-mile radius of their location. Two-hour, half-day, and full-day tours are available, starting at $102 per person. ⊠ *Mile 238.6, Parks Hwy., Denali National Park* ☏ *907/683–2234, 888/683–2234* ⊕ *www.denaliraft.com* ⊙ *June–mid-Sept.*

CAMPING

If you want to camp in the park, either in a tent or an RV, there are six campgrounds, with varying levels of access and facilities. Two of the campgrounds—Riley Creek (near the park entrance, essentially no scenery at all) and Savage River (Mile 13; on a very clear day, you might be able to see the mountain from here, but not much of it)—have spaces that accommodate tents, RVs, and campers. Visitors with private vehicles can also drive to the Teklanika campsite (Mile 29; a three-night minimum stay helps keep the traffic down), but they must first obtain park-road travel permits. Sanctuary River (Mile 22, the smallest campground in the park, ideal if you want to be alone but can't backpack), Igloo Creek (Mile 43, comparable to Sanctuary River), and Wonder Lake (Mile 85, the cream of the crop in Denali camping—best views of the mountain and great easy hikes) have tent spaces only. The camper buses offer the only access to these sites. Riley Creek is the only campground open year-round, but does not have potable water during the winter and other amenities may not be available. Visit ⊕ *www. reservedenali.com* for details.

Visitors to the Sanctuary and Igloo Creek campsites should come prepared: both campgrounds lack treated drinking water. All campgrounds have vault toilets and food lockers. Individual sites are beyond sight of the park road, though within easy walking distance.

Fees for individual sites range from $15 to $30 per night (higher rates are for the RV sites); Wonder Lake has an additional one-time reservation fee of $6.50. Campsites can be reserved in advance online, through the Denali National Park website (⊕ *www.reservedenali.com*). Reservations can also be made in person at the park. It's best to visit Denali's website before making reservations, both to see the reservation form and to learn whether any changes in the reservation system have been made.

Riley Creek. A wooded campground with plenty of amenities, Riley Creek serves as a staging area for deeper forays into the park and is the only campground open year round. There is still cell phone reception here, and while there aren't any electrical hookups, all the conveniences of Glitter Gulch are a short drive away. There's a small camp store near the campground with ice and firewood available for purchase. ⊠ *1/4 mile inside park* ⊕ *www.nps.gov/dena/planyourvisit/ campgrounds.htm.*

Savage River. Nestled within a spruce forest, many of the campsites are a short walk from the Savage River, a beautiful braided stream where glimpses of Denali can be had on clear days. This is the first campground where you lose cell phone service. Potable water and staff are available on site and there are spots for both tents and RVs. ⊠ *14 miles inside park* ⊕ *www.nps.gov/dena/planyourvisit/ campgrounds.htm.*

Sanctuary River. While a lot of the area around the campground is brushy, if you're willing to push through the foliage you'll have access to the nearby mountains and the memorable hiking that can be found close to Sanctuary River's seven campsites. It's a tent-only sight (no RVs), and there are no reservations, so it's first come, first served; there also isn't potable water or staff. Open fires are not permitted so bring a cookstove for your meals. ⊠ *22 miles inside park* ⊕ *www.nps.gov/dena/planyourvisit/ campgrounds.htm.*

Teklanika River. The only way to drive your personal vehicle more than 15 miles into the park is by reserving a three-night stay at Teklanika. Once you've arrived, your vehicle must remain in the campground for the duration of your stay, though it's easy to catch rides on the camper or tour buses that pass by daily. Potable water and park rangers are both on site. ⊠ *29 miles inside park* ⊕ *www.nps.gov/dena/ planyourvisit/campgrounds.htm.*

Moose and Bear Safety

Moose

Commonly underestimated by visitors and locals alike, moose can pose a threat despite their lack of claws and sharp teeth. They may look gangly, but are fast moving and will charge when threatened. Per park guidelines, moose should be enjoyed from a respectable distance of at least 25 yards. If the animal's behavior changes, you're too close. Give mother moose and their calves extra distance as they can be especially unpredictable. If a moose charges, seek shelter in a thick stand of trees or behind any large object that it can't get through. Remember: moose can kick with either their front *or* back hooves.

Bears

Most visitors seek the Goldilocks bear encounter: not too far, not too close, but just right. But bears are capable of reaching speeds of 35 miles per hour, which can turn "just right" into "oh no!" in a heartbeat. The best method is to prevent bad bear encounters before they happen. This means giving bears lots of space, making plenty of noise while hiking, and keeping a clean camp with food stored properly in bear cans away from your tent. Park-issued, bear-proof containers come in two sizes that weigh three and seven pounds, respectively. Small containers

hold 3–5 days worth of food for one person. Bigger ones can hold enough food for 7–10 days. Some personal bear containers are also accepted; check the park website for other approved containers. If you do come across a bear at close range, do not run as a bear perceives anything that runs as food. Speak calmly to the bear. Make yourself appear as big as possible (i.e., open up your jacket, spread your legs, or if in a group, stand together to form a "super creature") and back away slowly in the direction from which you came. Scan the surrounding area for cubs or a moose kill, both of which a bear will defend passionately.

Bears that choose to approach or stand on their hind legs are not necessarily aggressive. Most are simply curious and want a better look at you. A bear standing sideways to show its full profile, huffing, or jaw-popping are signs of potential aggression. Should a bear charge, stand your ground and deploy bear spray at a close distance. Most charges are simply bluffs. Play dead as a last resort by falling to the ground, curling in a ball, and wrapping your hands around your neck to protect it. Signs are peppered across the park with additional bear safety tips and park rangers are well-versed in bear safety.

Igloo Creek. Another small, tent-only campground, Igloo Creek has seven sites that are first come, first served. There's no potable water or staff on site, and open fires aren't permitted so bring a cook stove for your meals. ⊠ *35 miles inside park* ⊕ *www.nps.gov/dena/plan-yourvisit/campgrounds.htm.*

Wonder Lake. The furthest campsite in the park, Wonder Lake has 28 tent-only spots. The area is favored for its incredible views of the Mountain when weather allows. Amenities are rudimentary but flush toilets are available seasonally as is an amphitheater. Be prepared with bug nets and spray, the mosquitoes can be brutal at times. ⊠ *85 miles inside park* ⊕ *www.nps.gov/dena/planyourvisit/campgrounds.htm.*

HIKING

There are few places in the world wilder and more beautiful to hike than Denali's wilderness regions. It's easy to get lost in the beauty and the desire to climb just one more ridge, but know your limits and consult park staff before you head out. Also be sure to follow "Leave No Trace" etiquette, be prepared for bear encounters, and bring all necessary equipment.

With the exception of the trails near the entrance and at the Savage River checkpoint, the park is essentially trailless. Distances may look attainable from a distance, with foothills off the side of the road appearing no more than an hour away. Be wary of such predictions. Distances in the tundra are farther than they appear and while it may look smooth, bogs, willows, alder, and other obstacles can quickly hinder the best-laid plans. Be conservative with your goals, take your time, and leave a hike plan with someone that includes your intended destination and when to expect to hear from you. Once you finalize this plan, do not deviate from it.

A big draw for more experienced hikers and backpackers are the foothills and ridges accessible from the park road. As long as you don't go deep into the Alaska Range, it's possible to reach some summits and high ridges without technical climbing expertise. Stamina and physical fitness are required however. Once up high, hikers find easy walking and sweeping views of braided rivers, tundra benches and foothills, and ice-capped mountains.

GUIDED HIKES

In addition to exploring the park on your own, you can take free ranger-guided discovery hikes and learn more about the park's natural and human history. Rangers lead daily hikes throughout summer. Inquire at the visitor center. You can also tour with privately operated outfitters.

The Stampede Trail

One of Healy's greatest attractions is the **Stampede Trail**, perhaps most famous to today's traveler for being where Christopher McCandless of *Into the Wild* fame met his end. On the Stampede Trail you can enter Denali by snowmobile, dogsled, cross-country skis, or mountain bike. This wide, well-traveled path leads all the way to Kantishna, 90 miles inside the park. To get here, take the George Parks Highway 2 miles north of Healy to Mile 251.1, where Stampede Road intersects the highway.

Rangers will talk about the area's plants, animals, and geological features. Before heading into the wilderness, even on a short hike, check in at the Backcountry Information Center located in the visitor center. Rangers will update you on conditions and make route suggestions. Because this is bear country, the Park Service provides backpackers with bearproof food containers. These containers are mandatory if you're staying overnight in the backcountry.

MOUNTAIN CLIMBING

Alaska Mountaineering School

MOUNTAIN CLIMBING | This outfitter leads backpacking trips in wilderness areas near Talkeetna and elsewhere in the state, including the Brooks Range, and glacier treks that can include overnighting on the ice. It also conducts mountaineering courses that run from 6 to 12 days, expeditions to Denali (figure on at least three weeks; prices from $11,000) and other peaks in the Alaska Range, and climbs for all levels of expertise. A weeklong novice course, which should be enough to get you comfortable in the mountains, runs about $2,900. Custom trips, backpacking, and workshops are also offered throughout the summer ranging from day courses to weeklong adventures. While you're in Talkeetna, check out the AMS mountain and gear shop on F Street. ⊠ *13765 3rd St., Talkeetna* ☎ *907/733–1016* ⊕ *www. climbalaska.org.*

SCENIC FLIGHTS

A flightseeing tour of the park is one of the best ways to get a sense of the Alaska Range's size and scope. Flight-seeing is also the best way to get close-up views of Denali and its neighboring giants, and maybe even stand on a glacier, all without the hassle of days of hiking and lugging food and gear.

Most Denali flightseeing is done out of Talkeetna, a small end-of-the-road town between Anchorage and Denali, and the operators will offer several tours, includ-ing a quick fly-by, a summit tour, a glacier landing—something for everybody. But there are a few outfitters nearer to the park that fly either from McKinley Park airstrip or the small airfield in Healy, 20 miles north. It's best to take the longest, most detailed tour you can afford, so you don't go back home wishing you'd had a chance to see more.

Fly Denali

AIR EXCURSIONS | This is the only flight-seeing company based in Healy with a permit to land on the glaciers of Denali. Prices are $599 for adults, and include more than 100 minutes of flight time and 20–30 minutes on the Ruth Glacier and its amphitheater. ⊠ *Healy Airport, Healy Rd., Healy* ⊹ *Turn right off George Parks Highway at Mile 238.7 and follow 2 miles* ☎ *907/683–2359, 877/770–2359* ⊕ *www. flydenali.com.*

WINTER SPORTS

Snowshoers and skiers generally arrive with their own gear and park or camp at the Riley Creek Campground at the park entrance. The Park Service does keep some loaner snowshoes on hand;

check at the Murie Science and Learning Center (which doubles as the winter visitor center). Dog mushing can also be done with your own team, or you can contact one of the park concessionaires that run single-day or multi-day trips.

Denali Dog Sled Expeditions

LOCAL SPORTS | Owned by the couple behind Earthsong Lodge, Denali Dog Sled Expeditions is the only dogsled-ding company that has the National Park Service okay to run trips in Denali National Park. And, midwinter, the park will feel as if it's all yours. The company specializes in multiday trips of 2 to 10 days (starting at $2,775 per person). Early in the season and between trips, they also offer day trips of one to four hours (from $140); call ahead to check availability. Denali Dog Sled Expeditions also offers cross-country skiers and mountaineers dogsled team support for multiday winter cabin and hut trips in the park. ⊠ *Mile 4, Stampede Rd., Healy* ⊹ *17 miles northwest of Denali National Park* ☎ *907/683–2863* ⊕ *www.earthsong-lodge.com* ⊡ *From $140.*

What's Nearby

There are two areas near the park entrance with a variety of amenities and accommodations within 15 miles of the park entrance. The nearest of these is "Glitter Gulch," which contains a long strip of hotels, guide shops, and restaurants. The Gulch is predominately seasonal, so don't expect to find any businesses open in winter. While there's no shortage of restaurants ranging from sit-down to grab-and-go selections, you won't find grocery stores or anything of that nature.

A little further north along the road system is the community of Healy. This town of almost 1,000 people provides some more substantial offerings as it also supports the nearby mining sites along with serving as a jumping off point for independent travelers. Here you'll find year round accommodations from cozy B&Bs like the Dome Home to more traditional inns like the Aurora Denali Lodge. The 49th State Brewery, one of the area's best restaurants, offers an excellent range of in-house beer as well as several locally grown dishes.

To the south is Denali State Park. A little ways north of Talkeetna, this protected wilderness encompasses almost 300,000 acres including foothills, mountains, streams, glaciers, and lakes. Camping, hiking, and canoeing are popular activities within the state park. Fishing is also possible with all five species of salmon spawning within the park along with numerous types of trout and dolly varden.

Glitter Gulch

Hotels, motels, RV parks, campgrounds, and some restaurants are clustered along the George Parks Highway near the park entrance in an area known as Glitter Gulch, which is at Mile 237.3. You can judge distance from the park by mileage markers; numbers increase northward and decrease southward.

🍴 Restaurants

McKinley Creekside Cafe

$$ | AMERICAN | This is the place for hearty, delicious food, including breakfast, lunch, dinner, and weekend brunch. While the menu does offer some very good salads, the real treats include the mooster burger (made of locally sourced beef, as wild game can't be sold in restaurants), grilled halibut tacos, and Alaskan salmon with a rotating cast of sides and marinades. **Known for:** generous boxed lunches; fantastic desserts baked in-house; weekend brunch menu with rotating specials. $ *Average main: $18* ⊠ *Parks Hwy., Denali National Park* ✛ *Mile 224*

☎ *907/683–2277* ⊕ *www.mckinleycabins. com* ⊗ *Closed mid-Sept.–mid-May.*

Panorama Pizza Pub

$$ | PIZZA | Situated in a cluster of restaurants and cabins along Carlo Creek, Panorama is one of the more lively and festive options. Hand-tossed pizzas include one with Alaskan microbrewed beer baked into the crust. **Known for:** wide array of pizzas and sandwiches; live music venue including open mike nights; deck with views of Carlo Creek. $ *Average main: $20* ⊠ *Parks Hwy., in front of Perch Cabins, Carlo Creek* ✛ *Mile 224* ☎ *907/683–2623* ⊗ *Closed Oct.–Apr. No lunch.*

The Perch Restaurant, Bar, and Cabins

$$$ | AMERICAN | Built on top of an old glacier moraine, the Perch offers dining in a more removed and relaxed setting than elsewhere in the area. Steak and seafood make up the menu—local ingredients are used when possible—although gluten-free and vegetarian options are also available. **Known for:** working closely with local organic farmers; impressive wine selection; bay windows overlooking the mountains. $ *Average main: $25* ⊠ *Parks Hwy., Carlo Creek* ✛ *Mile 224* ☎ *888/322–2523, 907/683–2523* ⊕ *www.denaliperchresort.com* ⊗ *Closed mid-Sept.–mid-Apr.*

★ 229 Parks Restaurant and Tavern

$$$ | AMERICAN | Led by a two-time James Beard Award–nominated chef, this hot spot is spoken of with reverential tones by locals. With its own veggie gardens and daily changing menu that's sourced from nearby farms, this is as local as you can get; dinner is the only seated meal offered, box lunches are available for tours through Denali. ■ TIP→ **If you're lucky enough to pass by on a Sunday in winter, be sure to check out their brunch menu. Known for:** rotating art shows throughout the summer; daily-changing menu with all items made in-house; wintertime-only brunches on Sundays and Mondays. $ *Average main: $28* ⊠ *Parks*

Hwy., Denali National Park ✣ Mile 229.7 ☎ 907/683–2567 🌐 www.229parks.com 🕓 Closed May–mid-June and Tues.–Thurs. in Oct.–Apr. No lunch except Sun. and Mon. in Oct.–Apr. No dinner Sun. and Mon. in Oct.–Apr.

🛏 Hotels

Denali Cabins
$$ | RESORT | Cedar cabins built within the taiga forest have all the basic amenities (including TV and phone), private baths, and shared hot tubs at this complex along the highway 8 miles south of the park entrance. **Pros:** relaxing sauna and hot tub; quiet location; offers National Park day trips. **Cons:** cabins tucked close together; few extra amenities offered; not on the river. [$] *Rooms from: $169* ✉ *Mile 229, Parks Hwy., Denali National Park* ☎ *800/808–8068, 907/683–2643* 🌐 *www.alaskacollection.com* 🕓 *Closed mid-Sept.–mid–May* 🛏 *46 cabins.*

Denali Crows Nest Log Cabins
$$$$ | HOTEL | Sitting above the restaurants and other accommodations of Glitter Gulch, the Crows Nest offers a more secluded atmosphere while still being close to the park entrance. **Pros:** within walking distance of Glitter Gulch restaurants; beautiful cabins; hot tub and sauna with tremendous views. **Cons:** rough-cut wood on cabin exteriors catches clothing and skin easily; not very accessible for those with mobility problems; standard cabins are on the small side. [$] *Rooms from: $330* ✉ *Mile 238.5, Parks Hwy., Denali National Park* ☎ *907/683–2723* 🌐 *www.denalicrowsnestcabins.com* 🕓 *Closed mid-Sept.–late May* 🛏 *38 cabins.*

Denali Hostel and Cabins
$ | HOUSE | For those who wish to spend a night along an Alaskan river without breaking the bank, Mountain Morning Hostel and Cabins is a good option. **Pros:** one of the cheaper options in the region that books some tours at a discount; coffee, tea, and coin operated laundry available; great riverside location. **Cons:** Wi-Fi spotty in some cabins and no cell service; some of the private cabins are small with steep stairs or ladders; shared bathrooms. [$] *Rooms from: $115* ✉ *Parks Hwy., Denali National Park* ✣ *Mile 224.1* ☎ *907/683–7503* 🌐 *www.denalihostel.com* 🕓 *Closed mid-Sept.–mid-May* 🛏 *14 cabins.*

Denali Park Village
$$$$ | RESORT | This sprawling 20-acre resortlike property operated by one of the National Park Service's largest concessionaires, Aramark, sits just 7 miles south of the park entrance next to the Nenana River. **Pros:** close to both park and nearby dining; shuttle service for all guests; transfers to railroad depot. **Cons:** resort-style complex lacks local flavor; draws lots of big tour groups; not the place for quiet or to meet many (or any) locals. [$] *Rooms from: $390* ✉ *Parks Hwy., Denali National Park* ✣ *Mile 231* ☎ *800/276–7234* 🌐 *www.denaliparkvillage.com* 🕓 *Closed mid-Sept.–mid-May* 🛏 *338 rooms, 50 cabins.*

Ruth Glacier

Even the shortest flightseeing trips usually include a passage through the Great Gorge of **Ruth Glacier,** one of the major glaciers flowing off Denali's south side. Bordered by gray granite walls and gigantic spires, this spectacular chasm is North America's deepest gorge. Leaving the area, flightseers enter the immense, mountain-encircled glacial basins of Ruth Glacier's Don Sheldon Amphitheater. Among the enclosing peaks are some of the range's most rugged and descriptively named peaks, including Moose's Tooth and Rooster Comb. Truly, it's one of the most beautiful places on the planet.

McKinley Creekside Cabins

$$$ | **HOTEL** | These accommodations sit on 10 acres and are bordered on the south side by Carlo Creek, with 14 cabins right along the Creek and 13 rooms in a hotel-style building. **Pros:** barbecue and covered pavillion next to the creek; great location by the water; nice mountain views. **Cons:** cabins close together with little privacy; right off the side of the highway; no TVs in cabins may be considered a negative. $ *Rooms from: $229* ✉ *Parks Hwy., Carlo Creek* ✛ *Mile 224* ☎ *907/683–2277* ⊕ *www.mckinleycabins. com* ⊙ *Closed mid-Sept.–mid-May* ⌿ *32 cabins, 13 rooms, 3 house rentals.*

★ Tonglen Lake Lodge

$$$$ | **B&B/INN** | **FAMILY** | Tucked away from the bustling highway, Tonglen Lake Lodge provides a unique, community-oriented environment for those who desire a deeper and more intimate Alaskan experience. **Pros:** weekly performances showcase everything from theater to live music; the hub for the surrounding community of 150 residents; large yard complete with badminton and other lawn games. **Cons:** narrow, bumpy dirt road to property; no Wi-Fi in cabins; personal transportation required. $ *Rooms from: $445* ✉ *Mile 230, Parks Hwy., Denali National Park* ✛ *Heading north, take first turn after Mile 230 and follow handmade signs 0.8 miles* ☎ *907/683–2570* ⊕ *www. tonglenlake.com* ⊙ *Closed mid-Sept.– mid-May except 4 "guide" rooms* ⌿ *11 cabins, 4 rooms.*

Healy

13 miles north of the Denali Visitor Center via AK-3.

Healy is a small town just a 10 minute drive north of the park entrance. There's simple lodging, B&Bs, a few restaurants, and a grocery store.

 ## Restaurants

Black Diamond Grill

$$$ | **AMERICAN** | For a casual and family-oriented atmosphere, dine with a view in this lodge-style, off-the-beaten-path locals hangout. The menu features hand-pressed burgers, New York steaks, crab cakes, penne pasta, salads with local and organic greens, and fresh-baked desserts. **Known for:** large main dining room good for large groups; mountain views; outdoor seating. $ *Average main: $25* ✉ *Mile 1, Otto Lake Rd., Healy* ✛ *Off Mile 247, Parks Hwy.* ☎ *907/683–4653* ⊕ *www.blackdiamondtourco.com* ⊙ *Closed mid-Sept.–mid-May.*

★ 49th State Brewing Company

$$ | **AMERICAN** | Top-notch craft beer and plenty of food options makes 49th State Brewing Company a must when passing through Healy. Committed to using local ingredients whenever possible, they offer plenty of Alaska-grown dishes, the keystone being the Alaskan-raised, all-you-can-eat pig roast on Friday nights. **Known for:** outdoor beer garden with beers brewed on-site; Yak burger raised on a farm in southeast Alaska; live music throughout the summer. $ *Average main: $20* ✉ *Parks Hwy., Healy* ✛ *Mile 248.4* ☎ *907/683–2739* ⊕ *www.49statebrewing. com* ⊙ *Closed early Oct.–early May.*

Rose's Café

$$ | **AMERICAN** | A local hangout with friendly service, good American cuisine, generous portions, and fair prices makes Rose's Café the quintessential roadside diner suitable for any meal. Located just far enough north from the park entrance to be overlooked by most visitors, you're bound to be surrounded by Healy locals here. **Known for:** to-go food options; appropriately named one-pound Grizzly Burger; staying open year-round. $ *Average main: $15* ✉ *249 George Parks Hwy., Healy* ☎ *907/683–7673* ⊕ *www.facebook. com/healyrosescafe.*

Hotels

Aurora Denali Lodge

$$$ | **HOTEL** | Formerly the Motel Nord Haven, this property has wood trim throughout, and rooms have one or two queen-size beds; it's also on five wooded acres which minimizes the presence of the nearby George Parks Highway. **Pros:** one of the least expensive options in the area; open year-round; reading area with comfy couches. **Cons:** not directly on the road but traffic is still audible; no stove tops in kitchenettes; no elevator to second floor. [$] *Rooms from: $190* ✉ *Parks Hwy., Healy* ✣ *Mile 249.5* ☎ *907/683–4500, 800/683–4500* 🌐 *www.auroradenalilodge.com* 🛏 *28 rooms.*

Denali Dome Home

$$$ | **B&B/INN** | A 7,200-square-foot modified geodesic dome houses this year-round B&B, decorated with Alaskan and local art. **Pros:** car-rental and tour-booking service; thoughtful and knowledgeable owners; unique architecture. **Cons:** close to main road; anyone squeamish about animal hides should be warned the house is decorated with a few prize trophies; anyone with dog allergies should beware of an enthusiastic Scottish terrier. [$] *Rooms from: $250* ✉ *137 Healy Spur Rd., Healy* ☎ *907/683–1239, 800/683–1239* 🌐 *www.denalidomehome.com* 🛏 *8 rooms.*

★ EarthSong Lodge

$$$ | **B&B/INN** | Above the tree line at the edge of Denali National Park, EarthSong has 14 cabins of five different sizes, all with views of open tundra backed by peaks of the Alaska Range, along with a team of sled dogs that run winter tours into Denali Park. **Pros:** off the beaten path vibe with great views; nightly slideshows on dogsledding or Denali; owners offer a wealth of knowledge. **Cons:** no pickup or transportation service so rental car or personal vehicle a must; individual cabins don't have kitchenettes, so must share one coffeemaker, fridge, and microwave; 17-mile drive from the park entrance. [$] *Rooms from: $190* ✉ *Stampede Rd., Healy* ✣ *Mile 4* ☎ *907/683–2863* 🌐 *www.earthsonglodge.com* 🕒 *Closed mid-Sept.–mid-May* 🛏 *13 cabins.*

Chapter 7

FAIRBANKS, THE YUKON, AND THE INTERIOR

Updated by
J. Besl

⊙ Sights	🍴 Restaurants	🛏 Hotels	🛍 Shopping	🍸 Nightlife
★★★☆☆	★★★★☆	★★★★☆	★★★☆☆	★★★☆☆

WELCOME TO FAIRBANKS, THE YUKON, AND THE INTERIOR

TOP REASONS TO GO

★ **Gold-rush heritage:** The frontier spirit of the richest gold rush in Alaska remains alive in Fairbanks. From exploring dredges to panning for gold, chances to relive the past abound.

★ **Stern-wheeler cruises:** The Riverboat *Discovery* is an authentic stern-wheeler that cruises the Chena and Tanana Rivers, which served as "highways" long before there were roads.

★ **The gateway to the Arctic:** Fairbanks is an essential point for connections to northern Alaska—a vast land of the midnight sun and the northern lights.

★ **Dog mushing:** The Interior is Alaska's prime mushing spot. Many enthusiasts live here just so they can spend every free winter moment running sled dogs.

★ **The University of Alaska:** Fairbanks is home to Alaska's main university campus. This means great museums, endless cultural events, and all the other perks of a college town, albeit one where winter temperatures can drop to –50°F.

1 **Fairbanks.** The main hub of northern Alaska.

2 **Nenana.** A good Fairbanks side trip.

3 **Chena Hot Springs.** Home to an impressive hot springs resort.

4 **Central and Circle.** Small communities filled with history and nature.

5 **Steese and White Mountains.** Easily accessible mountains with plenty of hiking.

6 **Yukon-Charley Rivers National Preserve.** A gorgeous landscape perfect for solitude.

7 **The Dalton Highway.** The road connecting Interior Alaska to the oil bays of the North.

8 **North Pole and Salcha.** Two small towns celebrating Christmas and handicrafts.

9 **Delta Junction.** The western terminus of the Alaska Highway.

10 **Tok.** A pit stop for those traveling the Alaska Highway.

11 **Chicken.** The heart of the Fortymile Mining District.

12 **Eagle.** The former center of government for Interior Alaska.

13 **Dawson City.** The perfect gold-rush town.

14 **Whitehorse.** The capital of the Yukon.

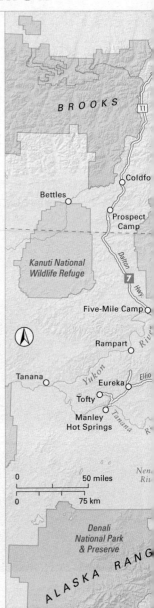

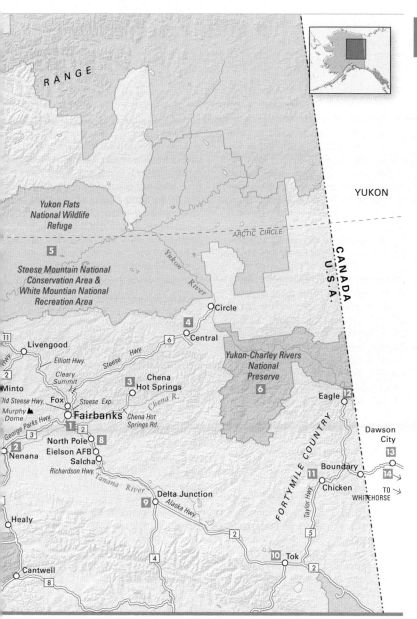

RANGE

YUKON

Yukon Flats
National Wildlife
Refuge

ARCTIC CIRCLE

C
A
N
A
D
A

U.
S.
A.

5

Steese Mountain National
Conservation Area &
White Mountian National
Recreation Area

Yukon River

Circle

4

11   Livengood

Elliott Hwy.

6   Central

Steese Hwy.

Cleary
Summit

3   Chena
Hot Springs

Yukon-Charley Rivers
National
Preserve

6

2

Minto

Old Steese Hwy.   Fox   Steese Exp.

Chena R.

Eagle   **12**

Murphy ▲
Dome

1   Fairbanks
2

Chena Hot
Springs Rd.

George Parks Hwy.

3

North Pole   **8**

2
Nenana

Eielson AFB
Salcha

Dawson
City

13

Richardson Hwy.

Tanana River

FORTYMILE COUNTRY

Boundary

14

11

Healy

Delta Junction

9   Alaska Hwy.

Taylor Hwy.

Chicken

TO
WHITEHORSE

2

Cantwell

8

4

2

10   Tok

5

2

Alaska's Interior remains the last frontier, even for the Last Frontier state. The northern lights sparkle above a vast, mostly uninhabited landscape that promises adventure for those who choose to traverse it.

Come here for wildlife-packed, pristine land and hardy locals, a rich and quirky history, gold panning, nonstop daylight in the summer, or ice-sculpting competitions under the northern lights in winter. Outdoor enthusiasts can enjoy outstanding hiking, rafting, fishing, skiing, and dogsledding. And don't forget to top off the experience with a soak in a hot spring. The geology of the Interior played a key role in history at the turn of the 20th century. The image of early 1900s Alaska, set to the harsh tunes of countless honky-tonk saloons and the clanging of pans, is rooted around the Interior's goldfields. Gold fever struck in Circle and Eagle in the 1890s, spread into Canada's Yukon Territory in the big Klondike gold rush of 1898, headed as far west as the beaches of Nome in 1900, then came back to Alaska's Interior when Fairbanks hit pay dirt in 1903. Through it all, the broad, swift Yukon River was the rush's main highway. Flowing almost 2,300 miles from Canada to the Bering Sea, just below the Arctic Circle, it carried prospectors across the north in search of instant fortune.

Although Fairbanks has grown into a bustling city with some serious attractions, many towns and communities in the Interior seem little changed from the gold-rush days. Visiting the galleries at the Morris Thompson Cultural and Visitors Center makes it clear how intertwined the Interior's past and present

lifestyles remain. When early missionaries set up schools in the Bush, the Alaska Native peoples were sent to racist regional centers for schooling and "salvation", a horrific practice that only ended in the 1970s. Today, Interior Alaska's Native villages have their own schools and a particularly Alaskan blend of modern life and tradition. Ft. Yukon, 145 miles northeast of Fairbanks on the Arctic Circle, is the largest Athabascan village in the state, with just over 500 residents.

Alaska's current gold rush—the pipeline carrying (a little less each year) "black gold" from the oil fields in Prudhoe Bay south to the port of Valdez—snakes its way through the Interior. The Richardson Highway, which started as a gold stampeders' trail, parallels the Trans-Alaska Pipeline on its route south of Fairbanks. And gold still glitters in the Interior: Fairbanks, the site of the largest gold operation in Alaska in pre–World War II days, is home to the Ft. Knox Gold Mine, which has approximately doubled Alaska's gold production. Throughout the region, with the price of gold still quite lofty, hundreds of tiny mines—from one-man operations to full-scale works—have geared up again, proving that what the poet Robert Service wrote more than 100 years ago still holds true: "There are strange things done in the midnight sun / By the men who moil for gold."

MAJOR REGIONS

Fairbanks. With a regional population of about 100,000, Fairbanks is Alaska's northern hub, home to the main campus of the University of Alaska and an important point along the Trans-Alaska oil pipeline. This rough-edged town has a symphony orchestra, Alaska's largest library, and a vibrant local art scene, including one of the best museums in the state.

North of Fairbanks. The Alaska wilderness is right at Fairbanks's door, with hundreds of miles of subarctic wilderness to explore. Follow the manageable **Chena Hot Springs Road** to its end and you'll find a natural hot spring that is a local favorite spot for aurora viewing. The **Steese Highway** connects to historic goldfields in Central and Circle, and the **Elliott Highway** leads northwest and, before shifting to the southwest, connects to the roughly north–south Dalton Highway (built to assist construction of the Trans-Alaska Pipeline System). All three roads provide access to countless starting points for hiking, skiing, camping, fishing, canoeing, and other outdoor-oriented adventures, including Yukon-Charley Rivers National Preserve and Manley Hot Springs. A few roads and isolated villages are the extent of civilization here.

Fortymile Country. A trip through Fortymile Country up the Taylor Highway will take you back in time more than a century—to when gold was the lure that drew travelers to Interior Alaska. It's one of the few places to see active mining without leaving the road system. In addition, remote wilderness experiences and float trips abound. If you're headed to Fortymile Country from Fairbanks, you'll drive along the historic Richardson Highway, once a pack-train trail (think mules with bags) and a dogsled route for mail carriers and gold miners in the Interior. As quirky places to turn off a highway go, North Pole, Salcha, Delta Junction, Tok, Chicken, and Eagle are up there with the best of them.

Yukon Territory, Canada. The happy, shining promise of gold is what called Canada's Yukon Territory to the world's attention with the Klondike gold rush of 1897–98. Maybe as many as 100,000 people set off for the confluence of the Yukon and Klondike Rivers, on the promise of nuggets the size of basketballs just waiting to be picked up. In the end, roughly only a dozen of them actually went home rich in gold, but all who returned did so rich in memories and stories that are still being told. Though the international border divides Alaska from the Yukon Territory, the Yukon River tends to unify the region. Early prospectors, miners, traders, and camp followers moved readily up and down the river with little regard to national boundaries. An earlier Alaska strike preceded the Klondike find by years, yet Circle was all but abandoned in the stampede to the creeks around Dawson City and Whitehorse. Later gold discoveries in Fortymile Country, Nome, and Fairbanks reversed that flow across the border into Alaska.

Planning

When to Go

June and July bring near-constant sun (there's nothing quite like walking out of a restaurant at 11 pm into broad daylight), sometimes punctuated by afternoon cloudbursts. In winter it gets so cold (−40°F or below) that boiling water flung out a window can land as ice particles.

Like most of Alaska, many of the Interior's main attractions are seasonal, open from mid-May to mid-September. A trip in May avoids the rush, but it can snow in Fairbanks in spring. Late August brings fall colors, ripe berries, active wildlife, and the start of northern lights season, with marvelous shows, if you hit the right night. Winter-sports fans should come in March, when the sun's back but there's still plenty of snow. Festivals are a big part of life in Fairbanks, with the months of February and March bringing the most revelry.

FESTIVALS

Fairbanks Summer Arts Festival

Alaska's premier cultural gathering takes place over two weeks in late July on the University of Alaska Fairbanks campus. The festivities, which began as a small jazz festival, now attract visitors worldwide for American roots and other music, dance, and literary, healing, visual, and culinary arts. Guests are encouraged to participate in one- or two-week classes and mini-workshops. ⊠ *Fairbanks* ☎ *907/474–8869* ⊕ *www.fsaf.org.*

Golden Days

A street fair and parade through the city cap several days of events at this July celebration of Fairbanks's gold-rush past. ⊠ *Fairbanks* ☎ *907/452–1105* ⊕ *www. fairbankschamber.org/golden-days.*

Tanana Valley State Fair

This weeklong event in early August is Interior Alaska's largest annual gathering. If you've ever wondered just what a 50-pound cabbage looks like, this fair might be your best chance to find out. You can also peruse the handiwork of local artisans. ⊠ *1800 College Rd., Aurora* ⊕ *www.tananavalleyfair.org* ☜ *$10.*

World Ice Art Championships

An ice-sculpting extravaganza, these competitive events that unfold from late February to late March draw ice artists from around the world. ⊠ *1800 College Rd., Fairbanks* ☎ *833/442–3278* ⊕ *www. icealaska.com* ☜ *From $16.*

Yukon Quest

The early February Yukon Quest calls itself the "toughest sled dog race in the world," passing through historic early-gold-rush territory. In odd-numbered years the 1,000-mile race starts in Whitehorse, in even-numbered ones in Fairbanks. Both the start and finish are festive events, with huge crowds

on hand even when the temperatures plunge. ⊠ *Fairbanks* ☎ *907/452–7954* ⊕ *www.yukonquest.com.*

Getting Here and Around

AIR

Fairbanks is the regional air hub. From Fairbanks you can catch a ride on regularly scheduled mail planes to small, predominantly Athabascan villages along the Yukon River or to Iñupiat settlements on the Arctic coast. All the smaller air services operate the mail runs on varying schedules. If you want to visit a particular village, or just have the desire to see a bit of Alaska Native village life, contact any one of the services. Do be aware that not all villages are interested in tourism; some are more prepared than others, and in a few, you're just going to be a nuisance. And what's happening where can change fast, with season, with hunting conditions, with weather. Ask advice from local air carriers before heading out.

With many scheduled flights to bush villages in northwestern Alaska and the Interior and on the North Slope of the Brooks Range, Ravn is a trusted bush-flight service. Warbelow's Air Ventures flies to 13 villages around Interior Alaska and offers charters and tours, including trips on mail runs to bush villages. From its Fairbanks base, Wright flies to Interior and Brooks Range villages.

AIRLINE CONTACTS Warbelow's Air Ventures. ☎ *907/474–0518,* ⊕ *www.warbelows.com.* **Wright Air Service.** ⊠ *3842 University Ave. S* ☎ *907/474–0502* ⊕ *www.wrightairservice.com.*

CAR

Interior Alaska is sandwiched between two monumental mountain ranges: the Brooks Range to the north and the Alaska Range to the south. In such a vast wilderness many of the region's residents define their area by a limited network of two-lane highways. You really need a car in the Interior, even if you're exploring primarily in and around Fairbanks.

The Steese Highway, the Dalton Highway, and the Taylor Highway (which is closed in winter) are well-maintained gravel roads. However, summer rain can make them slick and dangerous. Rental-car companies have varying policies about travel on gravel roads, so check in advance to see what's permitted.

The Parks Highway runs south to Denali National Park and Preserve and on to Anchorage, the state's largest city, 360 miles away on the coast. The Richardson Highway extends southeast to Delta Junction before turning south to Valdez, which is also 360 miles away.

Two major routes lead north. You can take the Elliott Highway to the Dalton Highway, following the Trans-Alaska Pipeline to its origins at Prudhoe Bay on Alaska's North Slope (you can't drive all the way to the end, but you can get close). Alternatively, explore the Steese Highway to its termination at the Yukon River and the town of Circle.

■ TIP → **Alaskans don't refer to highways by their route numbers; if you do, you'll most likely get blank stares.**

Tours

If you're interested in getting out into the wilderness or out to one of the villages, tours are the way to go. They are a far less stressful way to see this area, particularly if you have limited experience driving remote unpaved roads or traveling the backcountry of Alaska.

CUSTOM SIGHTSEEING
Airlink Shuttle & Tours
This outfitter offers small group shuttles and tours from Fairbanks to Denali and onward to Anchorage and Seward. ⊠ Fairbanks ☎ 907/452–3337, 855/454–8094 ⊕ www.airlinkalaska.com ⊠ From $45.

RIVER TRIPS
Riverboat Discovery
These popular three-hour tours in a traditional stern-wheeler include the opportunity to visit an Athabascan village and watch a bush-pilot flight demonstration. ⊠ 1975 Discovery Dr., Fairbanks ☎ 907/479–6673, 866/479–6673 ⊕ www.riverboatdiscovery.com ⊠ From $69.

SEA AND LAND TOURS
GoNorth Alaska Travel Center
Summer and winter tours include fishing, aurora viewing, dogsledding, and wildlife watching. ⊠ Fairbanks ☎ 907/479–7271, 855/236–7271 ⊕ www.gonorth-alaska.com ⊠ From $95.

Northern Alaska Tour Company
This Fairbanks-based tour company specializes in Arctic adventures, including half- and full-day excursions to the Arctic Circle, Utqiaġvik, and the Brooks Range. Aurora-watching trips take place in winter. ⊠ Fairbanks ☎ 907/474–8600, 800/474–1986 ⊕ www.northernalaska.com ⊠ From $179.

Restaurants

Most restaurants fly in fresh salmon and halibut from the coast. Meat-and-potatoes main courses, pastas, pizzas, and pub fare dominate most menus, but an increasing number of establishments serving healthier fare as well as ethnic restaurants (including more than a dozen Thai restaurants) have opened in and around Fairbanks in recent years. The food isn't the only thing full of local flavor: Alaskan pride runs strong, so expect to see snowshoes, bear hides, the state flag, and historic photos incorporated into restaurant decor. As for attire, even in the most elegant establishments Alaskans sometimes wear sweats or Carhartts.

Hotels

You won't find ultraluxury hotels in the Interior, but the region does have bed-and-breakfasts, rustic-chic lodges, and national chains, as well as homespun local spots. B&Bs are usually owned by locals eager to provide travel tips or an unforgettable story.

Restaurant and hotel reviews have been shortened. For full information, visit Fodors.com. Prices in the restaurant reviews are the average cost of a main course at dinner or, if dinner is not served, at lunch. Prices in the hotel reviews are the lowest cost of a standard double room in high season.

What It Costs			
$	$$	$$$	$$$$
RESTAURANTS			
under $14	$14–$22	$22–$30	over $30
HOTELS			
under $100	$100–$200	$200–$300	over $300

Health and Safety

The main health concerns for travelers to the Interior are high anxiety caused by mosquito attacks and, far more dangerous—and a year-round concern—hypothermia. To protect yourself mentally (and physically) when a cloud of mosquitoes descends, your best bet is to apply DEET, and lots of it.

Hypothermia, the lowering of the body's core temperature, is an ever-present threat in Alaska's wilderness. Wear layers of warm clothing when the weather is cool or wet; this includes a good wind- and waterproof parka or shell, warm hat and gloves, and waterproof or water-resistant boots. Heed the advice of locals who will tell you "cotton kills." It does nothing to move moisture away from your skin and can speed the onset of hypothermia. Any time you're in the wilderness, eat regularly to maintain energy, and stay hydrated.

Early symptoms of hypothermia are shivering, accelerated heartbeat, and goose bumps; these may be followed by clumsiness, slurred speech, disorientation, and unconsciousness. In the extreme, hypothermia can result in death. If you notice any of these symptoms in yourself or anyone in your group, stop, add layers of clothing, light a fire or camp stove, and warm up; a cup of tea or any hot fluid also helps. Avoid alcohol, which speeds hypothermia and impairs judgment. If your clothes are wet, change immediately. Be sure to put on a warm hat (most of the body's heat is lost through the head) and gloves. If there are only two of you, stay together: a person with hypothermia should never be left alone. Keep an eye on your traveling companions; frequently people won't recognize the symptoms in themselves until it's too late.

Money Matters

ATMs are widely available in all the cities and most of the towns; if you move out to the villages, though, take cash and don't expect to find much in the way of banking services.

Fairbanks

On a first drive around Fairbanks, the city appears to be a sprawling conglomeration of strip malls, chain stores, and other evidence of suburbia. But look beyond the obvious in the Interior's biggest town and you'll discover why thousands insist that this is the best place to live in Alaska—most citing the incredibly tight and supportive community.

The hardy Alaskans who refuse to leave during the cold and dark winters share a strong camaraderie. The fight to stave off cabin fever leads to creative festivals, from winter solstice celebrations to midnight baseball in summer. Quirky is celebrated in Fairbanks. But so is the ability to take care of business, no matter the obstacles (including seriously cold temperatures). It takes a special kind of confidence to live here, and that adds to the town's attractiveness.

Many old homes and commercial buildings trace their history to the city's early days, especially in the downtown area, with its narrow, winding streets following the contours of the Chena River. Even if each year brings more chain stores, the beautiful hillsides and river valleys remain. And the farmers' market here is a stunner. Of course, there is Fairbanks's fall, winter, and spring bonus: being able to see the aurora, or northern lights, an average of 243 nights a year.

These magic lights were a common sight to the Alaska Natives who lived and traveled through Interior Alaska for thousands of years. But outsiders started coming to Fairbanks for the view all because of one guy's bad day: in 1901 E. T. Barnette, a merchant traveling upstream, was forced to leave the boat with all his trading goods at a wooded spot in the middle of nowhere along the Chena River because the water was too shallow to pass. While awaiting passage farther east, Barnette's luck took a turn for the wonderful when an Italian prospector discovered gold 12 miles north of Barnette's settlement the next summer. The resulting gold rush created customers for his stockpile of goods and led to the birth of Fairbanks, which for a brief time became the largest and wealthiest settlement in Alaska.

The city is making some real efforts to preserve what's left of its gold-rush past, most notably in 44-acre Pioneer Park, where dozens of cabins and many other relics were moved out of the path of progress. Downtown Fairbanks began to deteriorate in the 1970s, before and after the boom associated with the building of the Trans-Alaska Pipeline. But the downward spiral has since ended, and most of downtown has been rebuilt.

One symbol of downtown's renaissance and a good first stop is the Morris Thompson Cultural and Visitors Center. The pride of downtown, the center represents a very successful collaboration between Explore Fairbanks (run by the city's convention and visitors bureau), the Alaska Public Lands Information Center, and Tanana Chiefs Conference, whose goals include preserving local languages, knowledge, and customs, and promoting pride among Alaska Native youth. In addition to an impressive museum that will introduce you to the region's wonders, you'll find everything you need to plan the rest of your touring. You should also check out the University of Alaska Museum of the North, whose building is full of soothing, swooping lines that evoke glaciers, mountains, and sea life. The museum's collection of material about Alaska is among the state's best.

GETTING HERE AND AROUND

AIR
Alaska Airlines and Delta offer nonstop service between Fairbanks and Seattle. Alaska Airlines flies the Anchorage–Fairbanks route. Hotel shuttles, rental cars, and taxis are available at the Fairbanks airport.

BUS
Alaska/Yukon Trails connects Fairbanks, Denali, Anchorage, Talkeetna, Whitehorse, and Dawson City. Hotels run shuttle buses to and from the airport, but once in town you'll find getting around by public transportation can be cumbersome.

BUS CONTACTS Alaska Park Connection.
☎ 907/245–0200, 800/266–8625 ⊕ www.alaskacoach.com. **Alaska/Yukon Trails.**
✉ Fairbanks ☎ 800/770–7275, 907/452–3337 ⊕ www.alaskashuttle.com.

CITY BUS Fairbanks MACS Bus System.
⊠ *Fairbanks* ☎ *907/459–1010* ⊕ *fnsb.us/ transportation.*

CAR

Fairbanks is at the junction of three major highways, the Parks, Steese, and Richardson. The town is too spread out for walking, and though you can get around by taxi, the cost of cabs will add up fast. Save yourself frustration and rent a car.

TRAIN

Between late May and early September, the Alaska Railroad's daily passenger service connects Fairbanks to Anchorage, with stops at Talkeetna, Wasilla, and Denali National Park and Preserve. The route runs weekly through the winter, stopping in Talkeetna and Wasilla on the way to Anchorage. Standard trains have dining, lounge, and dome cars, as well as an outdoor viewing platform. Holland America and Princess offer luxurious travel packages as well.

TRAIN CONTACTS Alaska Railroad. ⊠ *Anchorage* ☎ *907/265–2494, 800/544–0552* ⊕ *www.alaskarailroad.com.* **Gray Line Alaska.** ☎ *888/425–1737* ⊕ *www.graylinealaska.com.*

ESSENTIALS

VISITOR INFORMATION Alaska Department of Fish and Game. ⊠ *1300 College Rd., Fairbanks* ☎ *907/459–7207 for sportfishing information, 907/459–7206 for hunting and wildlife-related information* ⊕ *www.adfg.alaska.gov.* **Alaska Public Lands Information Center.** ⊠ *101 Dunkel St., Fairbanks* ☎ *907/459–3730* ⊕ *www.alaskacenters.gov/visitors-centers/fairbanks.* **Explore Fairbanks.** ⊠ *101 Dunkel St., Fairbanks* ☎ *907/456–5774* ⊕ *www.explorefairbanks.com.* **Morris Thompson Cultural and Visitors Center.** ⊠ *101 Dunkel St., Fairbanks* ☎ *907/459–3700* ⊕ *www.morristhompsoncenter.org.*

TOURS

Gray Line Alaska

The company conducts scenic and informative tours of the Fairbanks area.

An eight-hour sightseeing package includes a stern-wheeler cruise and a tour of a historic goldfield operation. Other tours include visits to Iditarod kennels and ATV treks through the forest under the midnight sun. ⊠ *Fairbanks* ☎ *888/425–1737* ⊕ *www.graylinealaska.com* 💰 *From $74.*

 Sights

Alaska Range Overlook

VIEWPOINT | Much of the north side of the Alaska Range is visible from this overlook, a favorite spot for time-lapse photography of the midwinter sun just peeking over the southern horizon on a low arc. The three major peaks, called the Three Sisters, are nearly always distinguishable on a clear day. From your left are Mt. Hayes, 13,832 feet; Mt. Hess, 11,940 feet; and Mt. Deborah, 12,339 feet. Much farther to the right, toward the southwest, hulks Denali, the highest peak in North America. On some seemingly clear days it's not visible at all. At other times the base is easy to see but the peak is lost in cloud cover. Look for the parking area just east of the university's Museum of the North. ⊠ *West Ridge, University of Alaska Fairbanks campus, Yukon Dr., Fairbanks.*

Creamer's Field Migratory Waterfowl Refuge

NATURE PRESERVE | FAMILY | Thousands of migrating ducks, geese, and sandhill cranes stop here in spring as they head north to nesting grounds, and in late summer as they head south before the cold hits. It's amazing to watch them gather in huge flocks, with constant takeoffs and landings. This is also a great place to view songbirds and moose. Five miles of nature trails, open year-round, lead through fields, forest, and wetlands. Now on the National Register of Historic Places, Creamer's Dairy was the northernmost dairy in North America from 1910 to 1966. ⊠ *1300 College Rd., Fairbanks* ☎ *907/459–7307 visitor center,*

907/459–7307 winter number ⊕ www. adfg.alaska.gov ⊗ Visitor center closed Sun.–Fri. in mid-Sept.–May.

Fairbanks Ice Museum

OTHER MUSEUM | Housed inside the historic Lacey Street Theatre, this museum screens hourly films about ice carving and the tools of the trade. The *Ice Showcase*, a walkthrough display of intricate sculptures, is kept a consistent 20°F and includes something to dazzle just about everyone, including an ice slide, ice bar, and occasional live demonstrations. ⊠ *500 2nd Ave., Fairbanks* ☎ *907/451–8222* ⊕ *www.icemuseum.com* ⊠ *$15.*

★ Fountainhead Antique Auto Museum

OTHER MUSEUM | Among the world's finest auto museums, Fountainhead provides a fascinating survey of history, design, culture, and, of course, cars (specifically ones from 1898 to 1938). Obscure makes—Buckmobiles, Packards, and Hudsons among them—compete for attention with more familiar specimens from Ford, Cadillac, and Chrysler. The museum's holdings include the first car ever made in Alaska, built in Skagway out of sheet metal and old boat parts. Alongside the cars, all but three of them in running condition, are equally remarkable historical photographs and exhibits of vintage clothing that illustrate the era's evolution of style, especially for women. ⊠ *Wedgewood Resort, 212 Wedgewood Dr., Fairbanks* ☎ *907/450–2100* ⊕ *www. fountainheadmuseum.com* ⊠ *$15* ⊗ *Closed Mon., Tues., and Thurs.–Sat. mid-Sept.–mid-May.*

Georgeson Botanical Garden

GARDEN | FAMILY | When most people think of Alaska's vegetation, they conjure up images of flat, treeless tundra, so the variety of native and cultivated flowers on exhibit here is often unexpected. The garden, 4 miles west of downtown, is part of the University of Alaska Fairbanks. A major focus of research is Interior Alaska's unique, short but intense midnight-sun growing season, and the

results are spectacular. The nonstop daylight brings out rich and vibrant colors and—to the delight of locals and visitors—amazing vegetable specimens that don't grow anywhere near as big in the Lower 48. An adjacent children's garden includes a treehouse and hedge maze to explore. ⊠ *University of Alaska Fairbanks, 117 W. Tanana Dr., Fairbanks* ☎ *907/474–6921* ⊕ *www.georgesonbotanicalgarden. org* ⊠ *$7 suggested donation* ⊗ *Closed early Sept.–late May.*

Golden Heart Plaza

CITY PARK | This riverside park is the hub of downtown celebrations, including free evening concerts. The plaza is dominated by the towering statue of the Unknown First Family, encircled by plaques containing the names of 4,500 local families who contributed to the building of the plaza. ⊠ *1st Ave., east of Cushman St, Fairbanks.*

Large Animal Research Station

COLLEGE | FAMILY | On the fringes of the University of Alaska campus is a 134-acre home to dozens of musk ox and domestic reindeer. Resident and visiting scientists study these large ungulates to better understand their physiologies and adaptations to Arctic conditions. The station also serves as a valuable outreach program. Once nearly eradicated from Alaska, the shaggy, prehistoric-looking beasts known as musk oxen are marvels of adaptive physiques and behaviors. Their qiviut, the delicate undercoat of soft hair, is combed out (without harming the animals) and made into yarn for scarves, hats, and gloves. The station has this unprocessed wool and yarn for sale to help fund the care of the animals. On tours you visit the pens for a close-up look at the animals and their young while learning about the biology and ecology of the animals from a naturalist. Call ahead to arrange tours from mid-September through mid-May; otherwise you can just stop by. ⊠ *2220 Yankovich Rd., off Ballaine Rd., Fairbanks* ☎ *907/474–5724* ⊕ *www.lars.uaf.edu* ⊠ *Grounds free, tours $11 ($13 in winter).*

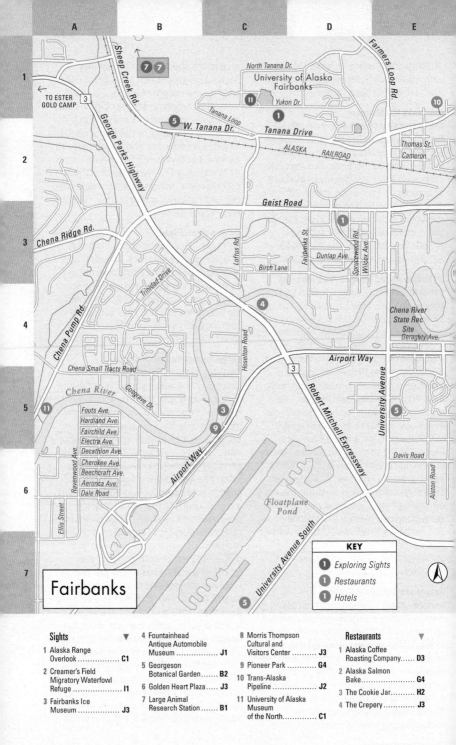

Fairbanks

KEY

- **1** Exploring Sights
- **1** Restaurants
- **1** Hotels

Map Labels

TO ESTER GOLD CAMP

7 **7**

North Tanana Dr.

University of Alaska Fairbanks

Yukon Dr.

11

1

W. Tanana Dr.

Tanana Loop

Tanana Drive

5

10

Thomas St.

Cameron

ALASKA RAILROAD

Geist Road

Sheep Creek Rd.

George Parks Highway

Farmers Loop Rd.

Chena Ridge Rd.

Fairbanks St.

Dunlap Ave.

Wilbox Ave.

Spruzeweld Rd.

Loftus Rd.

Birch Lane

1

Trinidad Drive

Chena Pump Rd.

Hoselton Road

4

Chena River State Rec. Site

Geraghty Ave.

Airport Way

Chena Small Tracts Road

Cosgrave Dr.

3

Chena River

Fouts Ave.

Hardland Ave.

Fairchild Ave.

Electra Ave.

Decathlon Ave.

Cherokee Ave.

Beechcraft Ave.

Aeronca Ave.

Dale Road

11

Ravenwood Ave.

9

Airport Way

Ellis Street

Floatplane Pond

Robert Mitchell Expressway

3

University Avenue

5

Davis Road

Alston Road

University Avenue South

5

Sights ▼

1 Alaska Range Overlook **C1**

2 Creamer's Field Migratory Waterfowl Refuge **I1**

3 Fairbanks Ice Museum **J3**

4 Fountainhead Antique Automobile Museum **J1**

5 Georgeson Botanical Garden...... **B2**

6 Golden Heart Plaza..... **J3**

7 Large Animal Research Station **B1**

8 Morris Thompson Cultural and Visitors Center **J3**

9 Pioneer Park **G4**

10 Trans-Alaska Pipeline **J2**

11 University of Alaska Museum of the North.............. **C1**

Restaurants ▼

1 Alaska Coffee Roasting Company...... **D3**

2 Alaska Salmon Bake...................... **G4**

3 The Cookie Jar.......... **H2**

4 The Crepery **J3**

F　　**G**　　**H**　　**I**　　**J**

TO CHENA HOT SPRINGS

College Road
Mack Blvd.
Totem Dr.
Capitol Ave.
Esquire Ave.
Carr Ave.
Central Ave.
Southern Ave.
College Rd.
Odonnot Rd.
Aspen St.
Bush St.
Aurora Drive
Dogwood St.
Evergreen St.
Wembley Ave.
Danby Street
Hanson Road
Illinois Street
College Rd.

Charles St.
Minnie St.
Well St.
Phillips Field Rd.

Phillips Field Road
Chena River
Growden
Memorial
Park
2nd Avenue
6th Ave.
7th Ave.
8th Ave.
Kellum St.
Cowles St.
2nd Ave.
4th Ave.
Barnette St.
Cushman St.
Noble Street
Coppet St.
Peger Rd.
Ivy Drive
Galena St.
Park Dr.
Coppet St.

Airport Way

Kiana
Park
Lillian St.
Peger Rd.
Wilbur Street
Gillam Way
Laurena St.
South Turner St.
17th Ave.
South Cushman St.
Richardson Highway

Hez Ray Sports
Complex
Lathrop Street
20th Ave.
21st Ave.
22nd Ave.
23rd Ave.
24th Ave.
25th Ave.
26th Ave.
27th Ave.
28th Ave.
East Cowles St.
Gillam Way
Rickert St.
Bernice
Allridge
Park
South Davis
Park
Hill Road
Davis Road

Robert Mitchell Expressway

Peger Rd.
30th Avenue
North Van Horn Rd.
Industrial Ave.
International St.
Lathrop St.
30th Ave.

0 ———— 0.5 mile
0 ———— 0.5 kilometer

★ Morris Thompson Cultural and Visitors Center

VISITOR CENTER | As with visitor centers elsewhere, you can get help with everything at this multifaceted facility, from taking in local attractions to negotiating a backcountry adventure. But the highlights here are the museum-quality displays about Interior Alaska. A walk-through exhibit re-creates a fish camp, and you can walk through a full-size public-use cabin similar to ones you can rent on your own. Alaska Native artists frequently sell jewelry and other wares at the center; in addition to making a unique purchase, you can chat with them about growing up in the villages or, in some cases, at fish camps such as the one the exhibit depicts. Named for a Tanana leader who dedicated his life to building bridges between Native and non-Native cultures, the center hosts summer programs showcasing Alaska Native art, music, storytelling, and dance; it's also home to the Explore Fairbanks Visitor Center and the Public Lands Information Center. On the edge of the center's parking lot is Antler Arch. Made from more than 100 moose and caribou antlers, it serves as a gateway to the bike and walking path along the Chena River. ⊠ *101 Dunkel St., Fairbanks* ☎ *907/459–3700* ⊕ *www.morristhompsoncenter.org* 🎫 *Free* ⊘ *Closed Sun. Jan.–May.*

Pioneer Park

CITY PARK | **FAMILY** | The 44-acre park is along the Chena River near downtown Fairbanks and has several museums, an art gallery, theater, civic center, children's playground, antique merry-go-round, minigolf course, and multiple restaurants. Owned and operated by the borough, the park also has a re-created gold-rush town with historic buildings saved from urban renewal, log-cabin gift shops, and a narrow-gauge train that circles the park. No-frills (dry) RV camping is available in the parking lot for $12 a night. No reservation is necessary. ⊠ *2300 Airport Way, at Peger Rd., Fairbanks* ☎ *907/459–1087* ⊕ *www.co.fairbanks.ak.us/pioneerpark* 🎫 *Park free; fees for some attractions* ⊘ *Some museums and shops closed early Sept.–late May.*

Trans-Alaska Pipeline

OTHER ATTRACTION | Just north of Fairbanks you can see and touch the famous Trans-Alaska Pipeline. This 48-inch-diameter pipe travels 800 miles from the oil fields on the North Slope of the Brooks Range over three mountain ranges and over more than 500 rivers and streams to the terminal in Valdez. There the crude oil is pumped onto tanker ships and transported to oil refineries in the Lower 48 states. Since the pipeline began operations in 1977, more than 18 billion barrels of North Slope crude have been pumped. Currently the pipe is carrying about 450,000 barrels per day (less than a quarter of its peak figures from 1988). ⊠ *Mile 8.4, Steese Hwy., Fairbanks* 🎫 *Free.*

★ University of Alaska Museum of the North

HISTORY MUSEUM | With sweeping exterior curves and graceful lines that evoke glaciers, mountains, and the northern lights, this don't-miss museum has some of Alaska's most distinctive architecture. Inside, two-story viewing windows look out on the Alaska Range, while the lobby features a 43-foot bowhead whale skeleton suspended from the ceiling. "Please touch" items include the molars of a mammoth and a mastodon, animal pelts, replica petroglyphs, and a massive quartz crystal found in Alaska's Brooks Range. The gallery also contains dioramas showing the state's animals and how they interact, and the fantastic collection of Alaska Native clothes, tools, and boats provides insights into the ways that different groups came to terms with climatic extremes. Another highlight is the Rose Berry Alaska Art Gallery, representing 2,000 years of Alaska's art, from ancient to modern times. ⊠ *University of Alaska Fairbanks, 1962 Yukon Dr., Fairbanks* ☎ *907/474–7505* ⊕ *www.uaf.edu/museum* 🎫 *$16.*

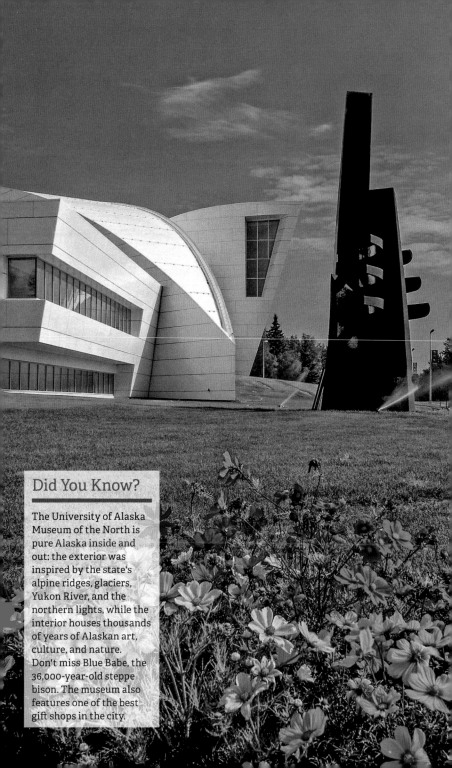

Did You Know?

The University of Alaska Museum of the North is pure Alaska inside and out: the exterior was inspired by the state's alpine ridges, glaciers, Yukon River, and the northern lights, while the interior houses thousands of years of Alaskan art, culture, and nature. Don't miss Blue Babe, the 36,000-year-old steppe bison. The museum also features one of the best gift shops in the city.

Winter in Fairbanks

The temperature gets down to −40°F every winter in Fairbanks, but school is almost never canceled, no matter how cold it gets. In recent years, in fact, the only times schools have closed were when rare winter warm spells created icy conditions on the roads that made it too hazardous for bus travel. Young Alaskans are so hardy that outdoor recess takes place down to −20°F.

The weather is a great unifying factor among Fairbanks residents. Winter conditions freeze the pipes of university presidents as well as laborers. After a night of 40 below, it's common to see cars bumping along as if the tires were flat; the bottoms of the tires freeze flat, and it takes a quarter mile or so before they warm up and return to round. Almost every car in Fairbanks has an electric plug hanging out front between the headlights. This is for a heater that prevents the car's engine block from getting so cold the engine won't start.

BASEBALL

Alaska Goldpanners

BASEBALL & SOFTBALL | Scores of baseball stars, including Tom Seaver and Dave Winfield, have passed through Fairbanks on their way to the major leagues. With a roster of college players on summer break, the Alaska Goldpanners play national teams at Growden Memorial Field from June through early August. The baseball park also hosts the W. G. & Eddie Stroecker Midnight Sun Game, a Fairbanks tradition for more than 115 years, in which the Goldpanners play late-night baseball on the summer solstice without the benefit of artificial lights. ⊠ *201 Wilbur St., Fairbanks* ☎ *907/451–0095* ⊕ *www.goldpanners. com* 🎫 *$7; $25 for Midnight Sun game.*

BICYCLING

Bicyclists in Fairbanks use the paved paths from the University of Alaska campus around Farmers Loop to the Steese Highway. Another path follows Geist and Chena Pump roads into downtown Fairbanks. A shorter, less strenuous route is the bike path between downtown and Pioneer Park along the south side of the Chena River. Mountain bikers can test their skills in summer on the ski trails of the University of Alaska Fairbanks and the Birch Hill Recreation Area or on many of the trails and dirt roads around Fairbanks.

CanoeAlaska

BIKING | In addition to canoes and paddleboards, this riverside shop near Pioneer Park also rents several styles of bikes, with rates starting at $20 for a half-day. Take advantage of the Bike and Boat package to paddle the Chena River one-way and pedal along the riverbank back. ⊠ *1101 Peger Rd., Pioneer Park* ☎ *907/457–2453* ⊕ *www.canoealaska. com.*

BOATING

For relaxing boating in or near Fairbanks, use Chena River access points at Nordale Road east of the city, at the Cushman and Wendell Street bridges near downtown, in Pioneer Park above the Peger River Bridge, at the state campground, and at the University Avenue Bridge.

The Tanana River, with a current that is fast and often shallow, is ideally suited for riverboats. On this river and others in the Yukon River drainage, Alaskans use long, wide, flat-bottom boats powered by one or two large outboard engines. The boats include a lift to raise the engine a few inches, allowing passage through the shallows; lately, it's more common just to get a jet boat, which doesn't have a propeller and so can go into much shallower waters. Arrangements for riverboat charters can be made in almost any river community. Ask at Explore Fairbanks, in the Morris Thompson Cultural and Visitors Center.

★ CanoeAlaska

CANOEING & ROWING | This outfit rents gear and arranges pickups and drop-offs for the Class I waters of the lower Chena River (the only real challenge for canoeists on the lower river is watching out for powerboats), as well as other local rivers. ⊠ *Pioneer Park Boat Dock, 1101 Peger Rd., along Chena River, Fairbanks* ☎ *907/457–2453* ⊕ *www.canoealaska. com* ✉ *From $55 for an 8-hr kayak or canoe.*

★ Riverboat Discovery

BOATING | Relive the city's riverboat history and the Interior's cultural heritage each summer aboard the Riverboat *Discovery*, a three-hour narrated trip by stern-wheeler down the Chena and Tanana Rivers to a rustic Alaska Native village on the Tanana. The cruise provides a glimpse of the lifestyle of the dog mushers, subsistence fishermen, traders, and Alaska Natives who populate the Yukon River drainage. Sights along the way include operating fish wheels, a bush airfield, floatplanes, a smokehouse and cache, log cabins, and dog kennels once tended by the late Susan Butcher, the first person to win the Iditarod four times. The Binkley family, with four generations of river pilots, has traveled the great rivers of the north for more than a century. ⊠ *1975 Discovery Dr., Fairbanks* ☎ *907/479–6673, 866/479–6673* ⊕ *www. riverboatdiscovery.com* ✉ *$70* ⊗ *Closed mid-Sept.–mid-May.*

CURLING

Hundreds of Fairbanksans participate each year in curling, a game in which people with brooms play a giant version of shuffleboard on ice. Curlers have an almost fanatical devotion to their sport, and they're eager to explain its finer points to the uninitiated.

Fairbanks Curling Club

LOCAL SPORTS | The club hosts an annual Yukon Title *bonspiel* (match) in early November and an international bonspiel on the first weekend of April. The club season runs from October to early April. Admission is free for those who want to watch a curling match or practice from the heated viewing area of the curling club arena. ⊠ *1962 2nd Ave., Fairbanks* ☎ *907/452–2875* ⊕ *www.curlfairbanks. org* ⊗ *Closed early Apr.–late Sept.*

DOG MUSHING

Throughout Alaska, sprint races, freight hauling, and long-distance endurance runs are held throughout the winter, with the majority running in late February and March, when longer days afford more enjoyment of the remaining winter snow. Men and women often compete in the same classes in the major races. For children, various racing classes are based on age, starting with the one-dog category for the youngest. The Interior sees a constant string of sled-dog races from November to March, culminating in the North American Open Sled-Dog Championship, which attracts international competitors.

Alaska Dog Mushers Association

LOCAL SPORTS | The association, one of the oldest organizations of its kind in Alaska, holds many races at its Jeff Studdert Sled Dog Race Grounds. ⊠ *925 Farmers Loop Rd., Mile 4, Fairbanks* ☎ *907/457–6874* ⊕ *www.alaskadogmushers.com.*

Paws for Adventure Sled Dog Tours

LOCAL SPORTS | Paws offers everything from a quick ride to mushing immersion courses. Experience the joys of mushing—and snap plenty of photos—on a one-hour ride, or learn how to drive a team at the three-hour mushing school. The multiday trips include mushing school plus overnight mushing, camping, and stays at Tolovana Roadhouse. ✉ *George Rd., at Herning Rd., on A Taste of Alaska Lodge property, Fairbanks* ☎ *907/699–3960* ⊕ *www.pawsforadventure.com* ☞ *From $80.*

Yukon Quest International Sled Dog Race

LOCAL SPORTS | **FAMILY** | This endurance race held in February covers more than 1,000 miles between Fairbanks and Whitehorse, Yukon Territory, via Dawson and the Yukon River. Considered much tougher and, among mushers, more prestigious than the more famous Iditarod, the Quest goes through more remote lands, with fewer checkpoints. The starting point alternates between the two cities each year (Fairbanks gets even-numbered years). ✉ *Fairbanks Yukon Quest office, 550 1st Ave., Fairbanks* ☎ *907/452–7954* ⊕ *www.yukonquest.com.*

FISHING

Although a few fish can be caught right in town from the Chena River, the best thing for an avid fishermen to do is hop on a plane or riverboat to get to the best areas for angling. Fishing trips include air charters to Lake Minchumina (an hour's flight from Fairbanks), known for good pike fishing and a rare view of the north sides of Denali and Mt. Foraker. Another charter trip by riverboat or floatplane will take you pike fishing in the Minto Flats, west of Fairbanks off the Tanana River, where the mouth of the Chatanika River spreads through miles of marsh and sloughs.

Salmon run up the Tanana River most of the summer, but they're not usually caught on hook-and-line gear. Residents take them from the river with gill nets and fish wheels, using special commercial and subsistence permits. The "Outdoors" section in the Friday *Fairbanks Daily News–Miner* often features fishing updates for the Interior.

You can purchase fishing licenses ($15 and up for nonresidents) good for one day or longer at many sporting goods stores and online at *www.admin.adfg. state.ak.us/license.*

Alaska Fishing and Rafting Adventures

FISHING | This outfit offers day trips for pike and grayling fishing across the region, as well as overnight float-and-fish trips on the Chena River in Fairbanks and Clearwater Creek in Delta Junction. Winter visitors can pair ice fishing with snowmobiles (called snowmachines by locals). ✉ *525 Halvorson Rd., Fairbanks* ☎ *800/819–0737* ⊕ *www.akrivertours. com* ☞ *From $189.*

GOLD PANNING

Gold Dredge 8

SPECIAL-INTEREST TOURS | From the comfort of a narrow-gauge railroad, Gold Dredge 8 offers a two-hour tour of a seasonal mining operation. Miners demonstrate classic and modern techniques, after which visitors get to try their luck panning for gold. Many historic elements from the old El Dorado Gold Mine have been transported here, so a tour provides a fairly complete look at how Fairbanks got rich. ✉ *1803 Old Steese Hwy. N, Fairbanks* ☎ *907/479–6673, 866/479–6673* ⊕ *www.golddredge8.com* ☞ *$43.*

GOLF

Chena Bend Golf Course

GOLF | Several holes meander alongside the Chena River at this well-maintained army course open to civilians. The 18-hole spread, at Ft. Wainwright, also has a restaurant and a pro shop. Civilians can book tee times three days in advance of play. The driving range is open 24 hours in summer. The course entrance is between the east end of the fort's airfield and the river. ✉ *Gaffney Rd., Bldg. 2092, Fairbanks* ☎ *907/353–6223* ⊕ *wainright.*

Aurora Borealis 101

The light show often begins simply, as a pale yellow-green luminous band that arches across Alaska's night sky. Sometimes the band will quickly fade and disappear. Other nights, however, it may begin to waver, flicker, and pulsate. Or the quiescent band may explode and fill the sky with curtains of celestial light that ripple wildly above the northern landscape. Growing more intense, these dancing lights take on other colors: pink, red, blue, or purple. At times they appear to be heavenly flames, leaping across the sky, or perhaps they're exploding fireworks, or cannon fire.

Where to See Them

The Fairbanks area is one of the best places in the world to see the aurora borealis—commonly called the northern lights. Here they may appear more than 200 nights per year; they're much less common in Anchorage, partly because of urban glare.

As you watch these dazzling lights swirling from horizon to horizon, it is easy to imagine why many Northern cultures, including Alaska's Native peoples, created myths to explain auroral displays. What start out as patches, arcs, or bands can be magically transformed into vaporous, humanlike figures. Some of Alaska's Native groups have traditionally believed the lights to be spirits of their ancestors. According to one belief, the spirits are celebrating with dance and drumming; another says they're playing games. Yet another tradition says the lights are torches, carried by spirits who lead the souls of recently deceased people to life in the afterworld.

Where Do They Come From?

During Alaska's gold-rush era some non-Native stampeders supposed the aurora to be reflections of ore deposits. Even renowned wilderness explorer John Muir allowed the northern lights to spark his imagination. In 1890, Muir once stayed up all night to watch a gigantic, glowing auroral bridge and bands of "restless electric auroral fairies" who danced to music "too fine for mortal ears."

Scientists have a more technical explanation for these heavenly apparitions. The aurora borealis is an atmospheric phenomenon that's tied to explosive events on the sun's surface, known as solar flares. Those flares produce a stream of charged particles, the "solar wind," which shoots off into space. When such a wind intersects with Earth's magnetic field, most of the particles are deflected; some, however, are sent into the upper atmosphere, where they collide with gas molecules such as nitrogen and oxygen. The resulting reactions produce glowing colors. The aurora is most commonly a pale green, but its borders are sometimes tinged with pink, purple, or blue. Especially rare is the all-red aurora, which appears when charged solar particles collide with oxygen molecules from 50 to 200 miles above Earth's surface.

Alaska's long hours of daylight hide the aurora in summer, so the best viewing is from September through March. Scientists at the University of Alaska Geophysical Institute give a daily forecast from late fall to spring of when the lights will be the most intense, at *auroraforecast.gi.alaska.edu.*

armymwr.com/programs/chena-bend-clubhouse-and-golf-course 🎫 *$48* ⛳ *18 holes, 6476 yards, par 72* 🕒 *Closed Oct.–Apr.*

Fairbanks Golf Course

GOLF | The 9-hole course here straddles Farmers Loop just north of the university and bills itself as the world's farthest north golf course. Watch for ravens stealing balls, though. ✉ *1735 Farmers Loop Rd., Fairbanks* ☎ *907/479–6555* 🌐 *www.fairbanksgolfcourse.com* 🎫 *$25 for 9 holes, $36 for 18 holes* ⛳ *9 holes, par 36.*

HIKING

Creamer's Field Migratory Waterfowl Refuge has three nature trails within its 1,800 acres on the edge of Fairbanks. The longest trail is 2 miles, and one is wheelchair-accessible.

SKIING

CROSS-COUNTRY

The Interior has some of the best weather and terrain in the nation for cross-country skiing, especially in late fall and early spring. Among the developed trails in the Fairbanks area, the ones at the **Birch Hill Recreation Area,** on the city's north side, and at the **University of Alaska Fairbanks** are lighted to extend their use into winter nights. Cross-country ski racing is a staple at several courses on winter weekends. The season stretches from October to late March or early April. Other developed trails can be found at **Chena Hot Springs Resort,** the **White Mountains National Recreation Area,** the **Chena Lake Recreation Area,** and the **Two Rivers Recreation Area.**

WILDLIFE-WATCHING

★ Running Reindeer Ranch

WILDLIFE-WATCHING | After just a few minutes communing with the ranch's herd of reindeer, it's hard not to get a little giggly. Before long it seems like second nature being surrounded by the herd, and by the time you've exhausted your camera snapping photos, that's when the fun begins. You just settle into listening to owner Jane Atkinson, whose love for the natural world, the animals she cares for, and indeed all of Alaska's wildlife, is infectious. If a reindeer walk seems too pedestrian, the ranch offers summer-only reindeer yoga as well. Reservations must be made in advance. ✉ *1470 Ivans Alley, Fairbanks* ☎ *907/455–4998* 🌐 *www.runningreindeer.com* 🎫 *$85 per guest.*

🍴 Restaurants

Alaska Coffee Roasting Company

$ | **CAFÉ** | With its tasty treats and eclectic artwork from around the world, this hangout is so popular that a line often curls out the door. It's a worthy stop either for a to-go lunch to bring on a hike or a well-made cup of joe and a cookie, a scone, or a muffin to savor inside. **Known for:** coffee roasted in-house; tasty cinnamon rolls and other pastries; wood-fired pizzas. [$] *Average main: $10* ✉ *4001 Geist Rd., Fairbanks* ☎ *907/457–5282* 🌐 *www.alaskacoffeeroasting.com.*

Alaska Salmon Bake

$$$$ | **SEAFOOD** | Salmon cooked over an open fire with a sauce of lemon and brown sugar is a favorite at this indoor-outdoor restaurant in Pioneer Park's Mining Valley. Guests select their main course—Bering Sea cod, prime rib, and snow crab are other popular options—and pick up sides, salads, and drinks at separate stations in this food-court-in-the-forest setting. **Known for:** cabin dedicated to just desserts; sunny outdoor seating; wood-grilled salmon. [$] *Average main: $31* ✉ *Airport Way and Peger Rd., Fairbanks* ☎ *907/452–7274* 🌐 *www.akvisit.com* 🕒 *Closed mid-Sept.–mid-May. No lunch.*

The Cookie Jar

$$ | **AMERICAN** | It's hard to believe the forever-in-motion staffers at the Cookie Jar can squeeze in the time to provide such friendly service, but they do. Don't miss the French toast made from sliced cinnamon rolls, but if you're not in a breakfast mood, don't worry: the menu includes everything from salads to coq au vin. **Known for:** massive waits on weekends; all-day breakfast options; homemade bread and biscuits. $ *Average main: $16* ✉ *1006 Cadillac Ct., Fairbanks* ☎ *907/479–8319* ⊕ *www.cookiejarfairbanks.com.*

The Crepery

$ | **BISTRO** | This crepes-all-day spot is the place to be on summer mornings, specifically if you can nab a seat on the expansive patio. Located in the center of downtown, the Crepery offers a lengthy menu of sweet and savory crepes stuffed with ingredients from brie and pear to salmon and crab. **Known for:** craft coffee and Bloody Marys; vegan options; downtown's most popular patio. $ *Average main: $10* ✉ *523 2nd Ave., Downtown* ☎ *907/450–9192* ⊕ *www.thecrepery.net* ☿ *Closed Mon.*

East Ramp Wood-Fired Pizza

$$ | **PIZZA** | **FAMILY** | Located just north of the control tower of Fairbanks International Airport, this place combines Alaska's love of airplanes with the universal love of pizza. Grab a paper menu from the waiting area, circle your preferred toppings from the extensive list, and a made-to-order pizza will be ready in minutes from the 700-degree wood-fired pizza oven. **Known for:** retro airplane seats in the lobby; spicy puttanesca sauce; large selection of toppings. $ *Average main: $14* ✉ *3788 S. University Ave., Fairbanks* ☎ *907/451–7492* ⊕ *www.eastramppizza.com.*

Geraldo's

$$$ | **ITALIAN** | No one in Fairbanks puts fresh chopped garlic to better use than Geraldo's, which has gourmet pizza, seafood, pasta, and veal dishes. A painting of Don Corleone hangs on the wall, and Frank Sinatra and Dean Martin provide background music for this cozy and often crowded spot near Wedgewood Resort. **Known for:** plenty of pizza; tasty baked lasagna; famous mozzarella bread. $ *Average main: $24* ✉ *701 College Rd., Fairbanks* ☎ *907/452–2299.*

Ivory Jack's

$$ | **AMERICAN** | Jack "Ivory" O'Brien used to deal ivory and whalebone out of this open and airy bar-restaurant tucked into the gold-rich hills of the Goldstream Valley on the outskirts of Fairbanks. These days, it's an Alaska-style sports bar, where you can choose from a dozen-and-a-half pub grub appetizers, followed by sandwiches, burgers, pizza, or entrées such as chicken Dijon and Alaska king crab. **Known for:** gluten-free options; crab-stuffed mushrooms; weekend ribs specials. $ *Average main: $22* ✉ *2581 Goldstream Rd., Fairbanks* ☎ *907/455–6665* ⊕ *www.ivoryjacksrestaurant.com.*

Lavelle's Bistro

$$$$ | **AMERICAN** | With offerings ranging from rack of lamb and lobster cakes to honey apple halibut and New York steaks, this impressive restaurant has won a loyal local following. Lavelle's also serves more than 30 wines by the glass and holds regular wine tastings and other events, lending the restaurant an air of sophistication far removed from the frontier image cultivated elsewhere in Fairbanks. **Known for:** entrée-worthy salads; late-night weekend menu; 3,000-bottle wine cellar. $ *Average main: $33* ✉ *SpringHill Suites, 575 1st Ave., Fairbanks* ☎ *907/450–0555* ⊕ *www.lavellesbistro.com* ☿ *No lunch.*

Pike's Landing

$$ | **AMERICAN** | The seats in the dining room of this extended log-cabin building are perfect for cooler weather, but the huge paddle-up deck dotted with firepits is the real draw here. The menu is mostly salads, sandwiches, and seafood, but the chance to enjoy the views over the Chena River and the landmark "Love Alaska" sign is what keeps diners coming. **Known for:** extensive waterfront deck; bacon burgers; crab-stuffed mushrooms. $ *Average main: $22* ✉ *4438 Airport Way, Fairbanks* ☎ *907/479–6500* ⊕ *www.pikes-landing.com.*

Pita Place

$ | **MIDDLE EASTERN** | Fairbanksans have been going mad for Nadav Weiss's falafel and hand-baked pitas ever since he started serving them at the Tanana Valley Farmers Market, and now they're available year round at this stand. In summer, enjoy the comfy outdoor seating, or pair lunch at the stand with a visit to the farmers market just a few blocks away at 2600 College Road. **Known for:** long lines that move quickly; great Middle Eastern classics; Turkish coffee. [$] *Average main: $8* ✉ *3300 College Rd., Fairbanks* ☎ *907/687–2456* 🌐 *www.pitasite.com* 🕒 *Closed Sun. and Mon. No dinner.*

Pump House Restaurant and Saloon

$$$ | **AMERICAN** | Alongside the Chena River, this upscale 1930s mining pump station–turned–restaurant claims to be the northernmost oyster bar in the world. Listed on the National Register of Historic Places, a grizzly bear in a glass case stands sentry here over a room full of Victorian-era antiques, and during the summer, be sure to enjoy the midnight sun on the deck out back by the river. **Known for:** good gluten-free options; wild game and seafood chowder; shareable small plates. [$] *Average main: $28* ✉ *796 Chena Pump Rd., Fairbanks* ☎ *907/479–8452* 🌐 *www.pumphouse.com* 🕒 *Closed Sun., Mon., and early Jan. No lunch.*

★ **Silver Gulch Brewing and Bottling Co.**

$$ | **AMERICAN** | Beer lovers should definitely make the 10-mile trip from town to North America's northernmost brewery. Several Silver Gulch brews can be found throughout the state, so be sure to check out the rotating specialty brews served only at the restaurant. **Known for:** summertime beer garden; reindeer sausage and beer cheese soup; inventive brick-oven pizzas. [$] *Average main: $22* ✉ *2195 Old Steese Hwy., Fairbanks* ☎ *907/452–2739* 🌐 *www.silvergulch.com* 🕒 *No lunch weekdays.*

★ **Thai House**

$$ | **THAI** | Fairbanks is famous for its number of Thai restaurants, and many locals consider downtown's Thai House the city's best. The food itself is complex, flavorful, and exceedingly fresh. **Known for:** variety of vegetarian options; Fairbanks's first and most popular Thai restaurant; staff dressed in elegant silks. [$] *Average main: $16* ✉ *412 5th Ave., Downtown* ☎ *907/452–6123* 🌐 *www.thaihousefairbanks.com* 🕒 *Closed Sun.*

Turtle Club

$$$$ | **AMERICAN** | Don't go to this wood-walled dining room expecting great variety, but you should go if you have a big appetite and are hungry for prime rib, lobster, prawns, or king crab. There's also a good salad bar, prompt service, and homemade bread that comes with every order. **Known for:** packed crowds on weekends; seafood dinners; dimly lit date nights. [$] *Average main: $33* ✉ *2098 Old Steese Hwy., Fox* ☎ *907/457–3883* 🌐 *www.turtleclubfairbanks.com* 🕒 *No lunch.*

Hotels

Bridgewater Hotel

$$ | **HOTEL** | In the heart of downtown Fairbanks, just above the Chena River, the Bridgewater welcomes guests with overflowing flower baskets and comfortable, modern rooms. **Pros:** the most character of any downtown Fairbanks hotel; great location; free airport and train shuttle. **Cons:** no refrigerators; small, modest rooms; some noise from the street. [$] *Rooms from: $169* ✉ *723 1st Ave., Downtown* ☎ *907/452–6661, 833/303–4760* 🌐 *www.bridgewaterhotel.net* 🛏 *93 rooms* 🍴 *No Meals.*

Pike's Waterfront Lodge

$$$ | **HOTEL** | Log columns and beams support the high ceiling in the lobby of this hotel and conference center designed to remind guests of the city's gold-rush past. **Pros:** close to the airport; location along the Chena River; Pike's

Landing next door is a hot spot. **Cons:** small gym; historic signs everywhere can become information overload; restaurant in a separate building. $ *Rooms from: $239* ✉ *1850 Hoselton Rd., Fairbanks* ☎ *907/456–4500, 877/774–2400* ⊕ *www. pikeslodge.com* ⦿ *No Meals* ⤴ *180 rooms, 28 cabins.*

River's Edge Resort

$$ | **HOTEL** | If you want the privacy of a cottage, a bit of elbow room, and the amenities of a luxury hotel, you'll find them all at this resort on the bank of the Chena River. **Pros:** shuttle service to both the airport and railroad terminal; prime Chena River location; private cabins. **Cons:** breakfast buffet is an added charge; no kitchenettes; half-mile to nearest shop or bar. $ *Rooms from: $179* ✉ *4200 Boat St., University West* ☎ *907/474– 0286, 800/770–3343* ⊕ *www.riversedge. net* ☾ *Closed mid-Sept.–mid-May* ⤴ *94 rooms* ⦿ *No Meals.*

Sophie Station Suites

$$$ | **HOTEL** | Its quiet location and very helpful staff make this spacious hotel near the airport one of Fairbanks's best. **Pros:** spacious suites; free shuttles to the airport and train station; full kitchens. **Cons:** fitness center is small; average interior decor; edge-of-town airport location. $ *Rooms from: $209* ✉ *1717 University Ave., Fairbanks* ☎ *907/479–3650, 800/528–4916* ⊕ *www.fountainheadho- tels.com/sophie-station* ⤴ *149 suites* ⦿ *No Meals.*

SpringHill Suites by Marriott

$$$ | **HOTEL** | At the center of the commercial district's former heart, the SpringHill Suites has 140 very comfortable suites, each with a microwave, a refrigerator, living-room furniture, and a well-lighted work area. **Pros:** location in the heart of downtown; on-site restaurant is a Fairbanks favorite; comfortable in-room work areas. **Cons:** moderate-sized gym; public traffic in lobby; small breakfast lounge. $ *Rooms from: $259* ✉ *575 1st Ave., Downtown* ☎ *907/451–6552,*

800/314–0858 ⊕ *www.marriott.com/faish* ⤴ *140 suites* ⦿ *Free Breakfast.*

A Taste of Alaska Lodge

$$ | **B&B/INN** | Though just a 20-minute drive from Fairbanks, A Taste of Alaska is far enough outside town to make you feel as though you're at a wilderness retreat; the 280-acre property, graced with fields and forested woodlands, has great views of the Alaska Range to the south, and in winter you can see the northern lights. **Pros:** interesting and unique history; eclectic decor; quiet, on-site trails. **Cons:** dated interior; 20 minutes to town; lodge rooms have private entrances, but some also open directly into dining area. $ *Rooms from: $195* ✉ *551 Eberhardt Rd., Fairbanks* ☎ *907/488–7855* ⊕ *www. atasteofalaska.com* ⤴ *11 rooms* ⦿ *Free Breakfast.*

★ Wedgewood Resort

$$$ | **RESORT** | Wild and cultivated flowers adorn the landscaped grounds of this 105-acre resort bordering the Creamer's Field Migratory Waterfowl Refuge. **Pros:** full-size kitchens; antique automobile museum on-site; trails through a wildlife sanctuary. **Cons:** apartment block appearance; one fitness center for seven buildings; away from other Fairbanks attractions. $ *Rooms from: $209* ✉ *212 Wedgewood Dr., Fairbanks* ☎ *907/452–1442, 800/528–4916* ⊕ *www. fountainheadhotels.com/wedgewood-re- sort* ⤴ *463 rooms* ⦿ *No Meals.*

Nightlife

Check the *Fairbanks Daily News-Miner* website (*www.newsminer.com*) for current nightspots, plays, concerts, and art shows.

Fairbanks Distilling Company

BARS | Housed in the former 1930s city hall, this family-staffed distillery is a labor of love for owner Patrick Levy. He provides tours by appointment; downstairs, the whiskey ages in a former Fairbanks Police Department holding cell. Visit any night and you'll likely find him behind the hand-built copper bar, radiating Fairbanks pride while pouring drinks made from local Fox Spring water and Nenana potatoes. ⊠ *410 Cushman St., Downtown* ☎ *907/452–5055* ⊕ *www.fairbanksdistilling.com.*

Goldie's

BARS | Operating out of a former firehouse, Goldie's swings open its double garage doors to host events like live music, open mic nights, and the occasional drag show. The bar—housed in a converted 1956 Airstream trailer—serves up beer, cocktails, and slushies, with rotating food trucks pulling up to the colorful patio. ⊠ *659 5th Ave., Downtown* ☎ *907/457–1064* ⊕ *www.goldiesak.com* Ⓜ *99701.*

★ HooDoo Brewing Company

BARS | The go-to spot for locals thirsting for well-crafted beer in Fairbanks is Hoo-Doo. The company sells growlers to go, but its beer is best enjoyed outdoors on a sunny afternoon around the brewery's spool tables—or if the weather gets bad, inside the airy taproom. The beer line is often long, but it moves quickly and it's a good place to meet new friends. The only issue is that it closes at 8 pm. Free brewery tours take place on Saturday at 4 pm. ⊠ *1951 Fox Ave., Fairbanks* ☎ *907/459–2337* ⊕ *www.hoodoobrew.com.*

Howling Dog Saloon

BARS | A local institution, the Howling Dog specializes in live blues and rock and roll. A party crowd of college students, airline pilots, tourists, miners, and bikers assembles for the cocktails, bar food, and music. Shows are played on a red-carpet stage acquired after Ronald Reagan and Pope John Paul II's visit to Fairbanks in 1984. ⊠ *2160 Old Steese Hwy. N, Mile 11.5, Fox* ☎ *907/456–4695* ⊕ *www.facebook.com/TheHowlingDogSaloon.*

Lavelle's Taphouse

BARS | This downtown bar boasts 36 taps that highlight a range of Alaska breweries, while the walls feature black-and-white images of Fairbanks history. The small space attracts a younger crowd and fills up quickly. ⊠ *414 2nd Ave., Downtown* ☎ *907/888–2220* ⊕ *www.lavellestaphouse.com.*

Senator's Saloon

BARS | On a warm summer evening, the saloon at the Pump House Restaurant is a fine place to listen to music alongside the Chena River. You can also peruse the wine list at the mahogany bar or shoot pool on the billiards table dating from 1898. ⊠ *796 Chena Pump Rd., Fairbanks* ☎ *907/479–8452* ⊕ *www.pumphouse.com.*

Performing Arts

Palace Theatre

THEATER | The theater hosts the *Golden Heart Revue,* a musical-comedy show about the founding and building of Fairbanks. ⊠ *Pioneer Park, Airport Way and Peger Rd., Fairbanks* ☎ *907/452–7274* ⊕ *www.akvisit.com/palace-theatre* 💲 *$24.*

Shopping

CRAFTS

Beads and Things

CRAFTS | This Alaska Native–owned shop sells handicrafts from around the state, along with a world's worth of beads for those who want to design their own pieces. ⊠ *537 2nd Ave., Downtown* ☎ *907/456–2323.*

Great Alaskan Bowl Company

CRAFTS | The big one-stop shop for Alaskan-made gifts and souvenirs, Great Alaskan specializes in lathe-turned bowls made out of Alaskan birch. ⊠ *4630 Old Airport Rd., Fairbanks* ☎ *907/474–9663* ⊕ *www.woodbowl.com.*

A Weaver's Yarn

CRAFTS | Artists Susan and Martin Miller own this shop that will delight knitters both new and experienced. It's the perfect place to buy a gift for that knitter back home or to pick up some qiviut, the pricey but exquisite undercoat wool of the musk ox that is some of the world's softest material. ✉ *1810 Alaska Way, College* ☎ *907/374–1995* 🌐 *www.aweaversyarn.com.*

JEWELRY

Judie Gumm Designs

JEWELRY & WATCHES | In her small shop, owner Judie Gumm fashions stunning and moderately priced silver and gold designs best described as sculptural interpretations of Northern images. Gumm, a longtime Ester resident, is a fun person to chat up about life in this small and quirky community tucked just off the highway west of Fairbanks; call ahead to make a appointment. ✉ *3600 Main St., Ester* ☎ *907/479–4568, 800/478–4568* 🌐 *www.judiegumm.com.*

Taylor's Gold-N-Stones

JEWELRY & WATCHES | Taylor's uses gemstones mined in Alaska and creates unique gold designs. ✉ *3578 Airport Way, University Avenue* ☎ *907/456–8369* 🌐 *www.taylorsgold.com.*

OUTERWEAR AND OUTDOOR GEAR

Apocalypse Design

SPORTING GOODS | In business since 1983, Apocalypse makes its own specialized cold-weather clothing for dog mushers and other winter adventurers. Travelers from colder areas of the Lower 48 will appreciate the double-layer fleece mittens, among other items. ✉ *201 Minnie St., Fairbanks* ☎ *907/451–7555, 877/521–7555* 🌐 *www.akgear.com.*

Beaver Sports

SPORTING GOODS | Stock up for all your adventures in the Interior at this store that sells the big names in backpacking, biking, paddling, and skiing gear. ✉ *3480 College Rd., College* ☎ *907/479–2494* 🌐 *www.beaversports.com.*

Nenana

56 miles southwest of Fairbanks, 75 miles north of Denali National Park.

For a break from the buzz of the George Parks Highway, take a detour in Nenana (rhymes with "banana"), a town of approximately 340 people, on the banks of the Tanana River and in the shadow of Toghotthele Hill or, in Athabascan, the "Hill on the River." The downtown avenue seems stuck in time, a relic of the early Alaska Railroad construction heyday from 1915 to 1923.

Nenana has several claims to fame: home to the world's second-largest single-span bridge, 700 feet long; the site where President Warren Harding drove the golden spike into Alaska's railroad to commemorate its completion (and possibly where he caught the case of pneumonia that contributed to his death a few weeks later); and the start of the 1925 serum run to Nome. It's also home to the Nenana Ice Classic, where Alaskans annually bet on the date and time of the river's spring breakup. Ongoing since 1917, the jackpot sometimes climbs to over $300,000.

🍴 Restaurants

Rough Woods Inn & Cafe

$$ | **DINER** | This spot could get away with a so-so menu in a town with few dining alternatives. Instead, the menu includes gems like the family-recipe herb bread, baked each morning and used in the restaurant's popular breakfast sandwiches that are served all day. **Known for:** Nenana's only year-round eatery; small-batch microbrews that can only be found on-site; homemade cinnamon rolls. [$] *Average main: $19* ✉ *2nd and A Sts., Nenana* ☎ *907/832–5299* 🕒 *Closed Tues.*

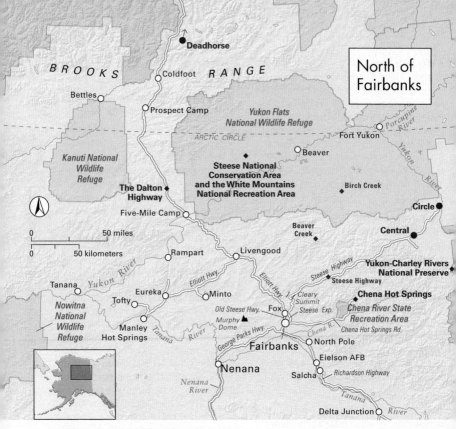

Chena Hot Springs

62 miles northeast of Fairbanks.

Nature is the star all along the road from Fairbanks that leads to **Chena Hot Springs Resort,** and even there it remains center stage thanks to the area's relaxing hot springs. The resort uses 165°F spring water to power three turbines, a feat that initially shocked geothermal experts who believed that water temperatures must be at least 220°F. This free source of power allows the resort to run greenhouses through the –40°F winters. The daily 2 pm and 4 pm free Renewable Energy tours end at these productive greenhouses, where row upon row of lettuce—up to 25 heads a day—and five varieties of tomatoes thrive off a hydroponic, or soil-free, system. Order a salad at the resort's restaurant and taste the special flavor of local, fresh-picked greens.

◉ Sights

Chena Hot Springs Road

SCENIC DRIVE | The 57-mile paved road, which starts 5 miles northeast of Fairbanks, leads to Chena Hot Springs Resort, a favorite playground of Fairbanks residents. From Mile 26 to Mile 51 the road passes through the Chena River State Recreation Area, a diverse nearly 400-square-mile wilderness. You can stop for a picnic, take a hike for an hour or an extended backpacking trip, fish for the beautiful yet gullible arctic grayling, or rent a rustic backcountry cabin to savor a truly wild Alaskan adventure. Grayling fishing in the Chena River is catch-and-release, single-hook, artificial-lure only. Several stocked lakes along the road allow catch-and-keep fishing for rainbow trout, well suited for the frying pan. Keep a sharp eye out for moose along the roadside. ✉ *Fairbanks.*

 Activities

HIKING
Granite Tors Trail
HIKING & WALKING | A 15-mile loop that can be done in a day, this trail provides an opportunity to see dramatic "tors"—fingers of rock protruding through grassy meadow—reminiscent of the *moai* monuments of Easter Island. The trail gains nearly 3,000 feet in elevation, but the views at the top make the climb worthwhile. Although the Interior landscapes lack the impressive mountain views of other parts of the state, the enormous expanse of rolling hills and seemingly endless tracts of forest are every bit as awe-inspiring. Come with adequate clothing, including rain gear, no matter how promising the skies look when you start. A shorter hike is the 3½-mile Angel Rocks Trail, near the area's eastern boundary. ✉ *Mile 39.5, Chena Hot Springs Rd.*

PADDLING
Alaska Wilderness Enterprises
BOATING | This company, in addition to multiday hunting expeditions, leads guided fishing tours and scenic float trips on the Chena River. Half-day and full-day options are available. When the temperatures drop, try your hand at ice fishing. ✉ *7445 Chena Hot Springs Rd., Fairbanks* ☎ *907/488–7517* ⊕ *www.wildernessenterprises.com* 🛶 *From $175.*

Chena River State Recreation Area
CANOEING & ROWING | The recreation area has numerous well-marked river-access points. The area's lower sections are placid, but the section above the third bridge, at Mile 44.1, can be hazardous for inexperienced boaters. The Chena Hot Springs Road parallels the Chena River, and canoeists use several put-in points along the way. ✉ *Fairbanks.*

 Hotels

Chena Hot Springs Resort
$$$ | RESORT | Soaking in the resort's hot springs has long been a popular experience for tourists and locals, especially in winter, when a soak is often paired with overhead aurora sightings. **Pros:** some of the state's best hot springs; 100% powered by geothermal energy; an activity for every interest. **Cons:** lots of public traffic on-site; fee for Wi-Fi; long access road gets icy in winter. $ *Rooms from: $209* ✉ *Mile 56.5, Chena Hot Springs Rd., Chena Hot Springs* ☎ *907/451–8104* ⊕ *www.chenahotsprings.com* 🛏 *86 rooms* ❌ *No Meals.*

Public-Use Cabins
$ | HOUSE | Usually reserved by locals and adventurers with extensive backcountry experience, these Alaska State Parks cabins have woodstoves, bunks, and tools for cutting wood; you have to supply everything else—food, bedding, water, cooking utensils, and, at some, firewood. **Pros:** a uniquely northern Alaska experience; four cabins are road-accessible; wilderness is at your doorstep. **Cons:** extremely popular and often booked; only amenities are the ones you bring along; farthest cabin is 13½ miles down the trail. $ *Rooms from: $45* ✉ *Chena River State Recreation Area, Miles 32 to 50, Chena Hot Springs Rd.* ☎ *907/451–2705* ⊕ *www.dnr.alaska.gov/parks/aspcabins* 🛏 *10 cabins* ❌ *No Meals.*

Thanks to the long hours of darkness this region sees every winter, Northern Lights viewing is particularly brilliant here.

Central and Circle

Central is 128 miles northeast of Fairbanks; Circle is 162 miles northeast of Fairbanks.

Though small, both of these communities on the Steese Highway loom large for those interested in history and nature. Central got its start in 1894 as a roadhouse called Central House. Mining remains a way of life here, with small private operations peppering the landscape. Claim jumpers definitely are not welcome. The Yukon River town of Circle is one of two entry points into the Yukon–Charley Rivers National Preserve.

Sights

Steese Highway

SCENIC DRIVE | The 161-mile Steese Highway follows the Chatanika River and several other creeks along the southern part of the White Mountains. The highway eventually climbs into weatherworn alpine mountains, peaking at Eagle Summit (3,624 feet), about 100 miles from Fairbanks, before dropping back down into forested creek beds en route to the town of Central. From Central you can drive the 30-plus miles on a winding gravel road to Circle, a small town on the Yukon River. The highway is paved to Mile 81 and is usually in good shape. A possible exception is in winter, when Eagle Summit is sometimes closed due to drifting snow.

Hotels

Chatanika Lodge

$ | **B&B/INN** | Rocket scientists from the nearby Poker Flat Research Range gather at this cedar lodge, as do mushers, snowmachiners, and local families (including the owners, who expanded the bar so much it consumed their cabin). **Pros:** friendly, longtime owners; a local favorite; decor is full of Alaskan character. **Cons:** shared bathrooms; long drive from Fairbanks; dated interiors. [$] *Rooms from: $80* ✉ *Mile 28.5, 5760*

*Steese Hwy., Chatanika ☎ 907/389–2164
⊕ www.chatanikalodge.com ⥅ 11 rooms
⧗⊙⧗ No Meals.*

Steese and White Mountains

30 miles north of Fairbanks via Elliott Hwy.

The Steese and White Mountains are readily accessible, just a quick jaunt up the Elliott Highway. Once you're here, you'll have a few hundred thousand acres pretty much to yourself, with opportunities for everything from a short hike to a monthlong expedition.

Sights

Beaver Creek
BODY OF WATER | Rising out of the White Mountains National Recreation Area, Beaver Creek makes its easy way north. If you have enough time, it's possible to run its entire length to the Yukon, totaling 360 river miles if done from road to road. If you make a shorter run, you will have to arrange a takeout via small plane. A lot of people make the trip in five or six days, starting from Nome Creek and taking out at Victoria Creek. Contact CanoeAlaska to schedule a shuttle. Don't try this on your own unless you're an expert in a canoe.

Birch Creek
BODY OF WATER | In the Steese National Conservation Area you can take a four- to five-day or 126-mile float trip on the lively, clear-water Birch Creek, a challenge with its several rapids; Mile 94 of the Steese Highway is the access point. Along the way you should see plenty of moose, caribou, and dozens of species of birds. This stream winds its way north through the historic mining country of the Circle District. The first takeout point is the Steese Highway Bridge, 25 miles from Circle. Most people exit here to avoid the

increasingly winding river and low water. From there Birch Creek meanders on to the Yukon River well below the town. Fairbanks outfitter CanoeAlaska can arrange shuttles for these trips.

Steese National Conservation Area and White Mountains National Recreation Area
NATURE PRESERVE | For those who want to immerse themselves in nature for several days at a time, the Steese National Conservation Area and the White Mountains National Recreation Area have opportunities for backcountry hiking and paddling. Both areas have road-accessible entry points, but you cannot drive into the Steese Conservation Area. The White Mountains Recreation Area has limited camping facilities from June to November; reservations are not accepted. Winter adventurers can snowmachine or snowshoe out to 12 public-use cabins and two shelters; none are accessible by car. ☎ *907/474–2200 Bureau of Land Management (BLM), 907/459–3730 Fairbanks Public Lands Information Center ⊕ www.blm.gov/visit/white-mountains.*

Activities

Tour companies are scarce in the area. Outdoor activities are generally do-it-yourself.

Chatanika River
CANOEING & ROWING | A choice spot for canoeists and kayakers, the Chatanika River is still fairly close to Fairbanks. The most northerly access point is at Cripple Creek campground, near Mile 60 on the Steese Highway. Other commonly used access points are at Long Creek (Mile 45, Steese Highway); at the state campground, where the Chatanika River crosses the Steese Highway at Mile 39; and at the state's Whitefish Campground, where the river crosses the Elliott Highway at Mile 11. The stream flows into the Minto Flats below this point, and river access is more difficult.

Water in the Chatanika River may or may not be clear, depending on mining activities along its upper tributaries. In times of very low water, the upper Chatanika River is shallow and difficult to navigate. Avoid the river in times of high water, especially after heavy rains, because of the danger of sweepers, floating debris, and hidden gravel bars. Contact the Alaska Public Lands Information Center for the status of river conditions before heading out on any of the area's waterways. ☎ *907/459–3730 river conditions information.*

Summit Trail
HIKING & WALKING | The Bureau of Land Management maintains the moderately difficult 20-mile Summit Trail, from the Elliott Highway, near Wickersham Dome, north into the White Mountains National Recreation Area. This nonmotorized trail can be explored as a day hike or in an overnight backpacking trip. It quickly rises into alpine country with 360-degree vistas that include abundant wildflowers and bird-watching in summer and blueberry picking in fall. This is not a loop trail, but ends at Beaver Creek—so you'll need to leave vehicles at both ends or arrange a ride back. Bring water, as sometimes the sources are scarce, and take advantage of the rest shelter at Mile 8. ✉ *Wickersham Dome Trailhead, Mile 28, Elliott Highway* ☎ *907/474–2200 Fairbanks BLM office* 🌐 *www.blm.gov/visit/summit-trail.*

Hotels

Public-Use Cabins
$ | **HOUSE** | The Bureau of Land Management runs 12 public-use cabins in the White Mountains National Recreation Area and one road-accessible cabin on the Elliot Highway, with 300 miles of interconnecting trails. **Pros:** a true Alaskan experience; remote locations allow for an intimate experience with the land; may be reserved up to 30 days in advance. **Cons:** most are inaccessible during summer; printed-out permits required; three-night maximum stay. [$] *Rooms from: $25* ✉ *Fairbanks District Office of BLM, 222 University Ave., Fairbanks* ☎ *907/474–2200* 🌐 *www.blm.gov/visit/white-mountains-national-recreation-area-alaska-cabins* 🛏 *12 cabins* 🍴 *No Meals.*

Yukon–Charley Rivers National Preserve

20 miles north of Eagle, 100 miles east of Fairbanks.

A dream landscape for adventurers who crave solitude, the preserve sits on the border of Canada and Alaska. The only ways in are by driving long gravel roads or taking a float trip or charter flight. Once here, miles of camping, hiking, canoeing, and fishing aplenty await—often with no one else in sight for days. Those who prefer their solitude dressed up with snow should schedule a winter mushing or snowmachining trip.

■ TIP→ Novices should refrain from exploring the preserve solo; consider hiring a guide familiar with the area or have an experienced outdoors person accompany you.

GETTING HERE AND AROUND

Byroads from the towns of Circle and Eagle lead into the preserve. You can also arrive by boat or floatplane.

Sights

Yukon–Charley Rivers National Preserve
NATURE PRESERVE | The stretch of the Yukon River between the former gold-rush towns of Eagle and Circle is protected in the 2.5-million-acre Yukon–Charley Rivers National Preserve. In the Charley River watershed, a crystalline white-water stream flows out of the Yukon-Tanana uplands, allowing for excellent river running for expert rafters. The field office

in Eagle and the NPS office in Fairbanks provide guidance to boaters.

In great contrast to the Charley, the Yukon River is a powerful waterway, dark with mud and glacial silt. The only bridge built across it in Alaska carries the Trans-Alaska Pipeline. The river surges deep, slow, and through this stretch, generally pretty flat, and to travel on it in a small boat is a humbling and magnificent experience. You can drive from Fairbanks to Eagle (via the Taylor Highway off the Alaska Highway) and to Circle (via the Steese Highway), and from either of these arrange for a ground-transportation shuttle back to your starting city at the end of your Yukon River trip. Weeklong float trips down the river from Eagle to Circle, 156 miles away, are also possible. There are several free first-come, first-served public cabins along the river, but no developed campgrounds or other visitor facilities within the preserve. Low-impact backcountry camping is permitted. ⊠ *Alaska Public Lands Information Center, 101 Dunkel St., Fairbanks* ☎ *907/459–3730, 907/547–2233 Eagle Visitor Center* ⊕ *www.nps.gov/ yuch* ⊘ *Eagle Visitor Center closed mid-Sept.–mid-May.*

 ## Activities

HIKING

Alaska Public Lands Information Center
HIKING & WALKING | The center has detailed information about federal lands in the Interior, including the trails in the Yukon–Charley Rivers National Preserve. ⊠ *101 Dunkel St., Fairbanks* ☎ *907/459–3730* ⊕ *www.alaskacenters. gov/visitors-centers/fairbanks.*

Circle-Fairbanks Historic Trail
HIKING & WALKING | The trail stretches 58 miles from the vicinity of Cleary Summit to Twelve-Mile Summit. This route, which is not for novices, follows the old summer trail used by gold miners; in winter they generally used the frozen Chatanika

River to make this journey. The trail has been cleared and roughly marked with mileposts and rock cairns, but there are no facilities and water is often scarce. Most of the trail is on state land, but it does cross valid mining claims that must be respected. It's easy to become disoriented; the State Department of Natural Resources strongly recommends that backpackers on this trail equip themselves with the following USGS topographical maps: Livengood A-1, Circle A-6, Circle A-5, and Circle B-4. ☎ *907/451–2705 DNR Public Information Center.*

Pinnell Mountain National Recreation Trail
HIKING & WALKING | The Bureau of Land Management maintains the Pinnell Mountain National Recreation Trail, connecting Twelve-Mile Summit and Eagle Summit on the Steese Highway. This 27-mile-long trail passes through alpine meadows and along mountain ridges, all above the tree line. It has two emergency shelters with water catchment systems, although no dependable water supply is available in the immediate vicinity. This is not a trip for novice hikers; most hikers spend three days making the traverse. ☎ *907/474–2200 Fairbanks BLM office* ⊕ *www.blm.gov/ak.*

RAFTING
Rafting trips on the Charley River are for experts only. With access via a small plane, you can put in a raft at the headwaters of the river and travel 88 miles down this exhilarating, bouncing waterway. Contact the National Park Service for more information. The river here is too rough for open canoes.

WINTER SPORTS
Once past Mile 20 of the Steese Highway you enter a countryside that seems to have changed little in 100 years, even though you're only an hour from downtown Fairbanks. Mountains loom in the distance, and in winter a solid snowpack of 4 to 5 feet makes the area great for snowshoeing, backcountry skiing, and snowmachine riding.

The Dalton Highway

Plenty of hardy, adventurous visitors "do the Dalton," a 414-mile gravel highway that connects Interior Alaska to the oil fields at Prudhoe Bay on the Beaufort Sea. Alaska's northernmost highway, the Dalton was built in the mid-1970s so that trucks could haul supplies to Prudhoe and Trans-Alaska Pipeline construction camps in Alaska's northern reaches. The Dalton is both an engineering marvel and a reminder of the state's economic dependence on oil production. It carries crude oil across three mountain ranges, 34 major rivers—including the Yukon—and hundreds of smaller creeks. It crosses permafrost regions and three major fault lines, too; half the pipeline runs aboveground and is held aloft by 78,000 vertical supports that proved their ability to withstand sudden, violent ground shifts in 2002, when a 7.9-magnitude earthquake hit along the Denali Fault.

GETTING HERE AND AROUND
Drive north out of Fairbanks and keep your compass needle pointed to the pole. That will get you to the Dalton, America's northernmost road.

◉ Sights

Coldfoot
TOWN | At Coldfoot, more than 250 miles north of Fairbanks, the summer-only Arctic Interagency Visitor Center provides information on road and backcountry conditions, along with recent wildlife spottings. The in-house bookstore is a good place to stock up on reading material about the area. A picnic area and a large, colorful sign mark the spot where the road crosses the Arctic Circle. ⊠ Coldfoot ☎ 907/678–5209 summer visitor center, 800/437–7021 winter BLM office ⊕ www.blm.gov/ak ⊙ Closed mid-Sept.–late May.

Dalton Highway
SCENIC DRIVE | The Trans-Alaska Pipeline is the main attraction for many who travel the Dalton. Thousands of 18-wheelers drive the formerly private highway each year, but since 1994 they've shared it with sightseers, anglers, and other travelers. That doesn't mean the Dalton is an easy drive, however. The road is narrow, often winding, and has several steep grades. Sections may be heavily potholed, and the road's coarse gravel is easily kicked up into headlights and windshields by fast-moving trucks. If you drive the Dalton in your own car, make sure you have windshield-replacement insurance because it's highly likely you'll need to make a repair when you return. There's mostly no cell service along the Dalton, few visitor facilities, and almost nowhere to get help if something goes wrong. With tow-truck charges of up to $5 per mile both coming and going, a vehicle breakdown can cost hundreds of dollars even before repairs. Before setting out, make sure everything in your car is working properly, and know how to change tires. Public access ends at **Deadhorse,** just shy of the Arctic coast. This town exists mainly to service the oil fields of Prudhoe Bay. The only lodging options are down-at-the-heels motels and camps that cater to truck drivers and other workers, or wilderness campgrounds. ⊕ www.blm.gov/visit/dalton-highway.

Activities

Although this is not a prime fishing area, fish, mostly grayling, populate the streams along the Dalton. You'll do better the farther you hike from the road, where less-motivated fishermen are weeded out. Lakes along the road contain grayling, and some have lake trout and arctic char. The Alaska Department of Fish and Game's pamphlet "Sport Fishing along the Dalton Highway" is available at the Alaska Public Lands Information Center.

Alaska Fly-In Fishing

FISHING | This company offers fly-ins to remote lakes for northern pike, rainbow trout, grayling, and silver salmon. Day trips and overnights are both available. ⊠ *1255 Shypoke Dr., Fairbanks* ☏ *907/388–9890* ⊕ *www.alaskaflyinfishing.com* ✈ *From $315.*

Coyote Air

AIR EXCURSIONS | The family-run Coyote Air bush-plane service specializes in scenic flights, backcountry trip support, and fall hunting trips in the Brooks Range. ⊠ *Mile 175, Dalton Hwy., Coldfoot* ☏ *907/678–5995, 907/687–3993 winter number* ⊕ *www.flycoyote.com.*

1st Alaska Outdoor School

DRIVING TOURS | This outfitter conducts year-round Dalton Highway tours in 15-passenger vans. Pickups are available from most Fairbanks hotels. Driving the Dalton yourself is difficult and will be hard on your car; if you're not feeling up to it, these tours are a great alternative. ⊠ *2240 Hanson Rd., Fairbanks* ⊕ *www.1stalaskatours.com.*

Northern Alaska Tour Company

GUIDED TOURS | The most established Dalton Highway tour company, Northern Alaska operates trips to the Arctic Circle and beyond, some with fly-drive options offered year-round. ⊠ *Fairbanks* ☏ *907/474–8600, 800/474–1986* ⊕ *www.northernalaska.com.*

 Hotels

Here are the most accessible options for the trip north.

Coldfoot Camp

$$$ | HOTEL | Fuel, tire repairs, and towing are available here, along with basic and clean rooms built from surplus pipeline-worker housing. **Pros:** café is staffed 24 hours a day; guided outdoor activities; boxed lunches available for on-the-go adventurers. **Cons:** truckers get a dinner menu, but summer guests get a buffet;

basic rooms; fee for Wi-Fi. **$** *Rooms from: $249* ⊠ *Mile 175, Dalton Hwy., Coldfoot* ☏ *866/474–3400, 907/474–3500* ⊕ *www.coldfootcamp.com* ⇆ *106 rooms* ⥢ *No Meals.*

Yukon River Camp

$$$ | HOTEL | The motel, built from surplus pipeline-worker housing, is basic and clean; there's a tire-repair shop, and you can buy gasoline, diesel, and propane here. **Pros:** a far better restaurant than you'd expect this far north; tire-repair shop handy for those driving; great hosts to answer questions. **Cons:** expensive for what you get; no private baths; extremely basic accommodations. **$** *Rooms from: $219* ⊠ *Mile 56, Dalton Hwy.* ☏ *907/474–3557* ⊕ *www.yukonrivercamp.com* ⇆ *42 rooms* ⥢ *No Meals.*

North Pole and Salcha

North Pole, 14 miles southeast of Fairbanks, may be a featureless suburb, but you'd have to be a Scrooge not to admit that this town's year-round acknowledgment of the December holiday season is at least a little bit of fun to take in. The Santa Claus House gift shop (on St. Nicholas Drive, of course) is a must-see stop. Sixteen miles farther along in Salcha, the Knotty Shop provides a new appreciation for twisted trees.

🛍 Shopping

The Knotty Shop

STORE/MALL | This shop has a large selection of Alaska handicrafts as well as a mounted wildlife display and a yard full of spruce-burl sculptures that photographers find hard to resist. Burls are actually caused by parasites in the living tree, and they create beautiful patterns in the wood. Don't forget to scoop up one of 50 ice cream flavors at the spruce-burl counter. ⊠ *Mile 332, 6565 Richardson Hwy., Salcha* ☏ *907/488–3014.*

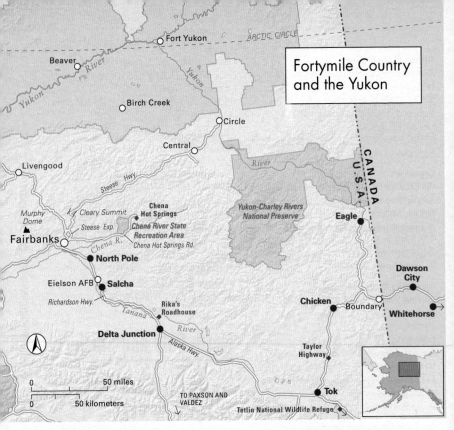

Santa Claus House

STORE/MALL | If you stop in North Pole, don't skip this shop. Look for the gigantic 42-foot Santa statue and the Christmas murals on the side of the building, as well as the year-round department-store-style display windows. Inside, you'll find toys, gifts, Alaska handicrafts, and, of course, Christmas cookies. Santa is on duty to talk to children in summer and during the holiday season. Also in summer, visit Antler Academy inside the red reindeer barn, where guests can interact with Santa's sleigh team. And yes, you can get your mail sent with a genuine North Pole postmark, a service offered since 1952. ⊠ *101 St. Nicholas Dr., North Pole* ☏ *907/488–2200, 800/588–4078* ⊕ *www.santaclaushouse.com.*

Delta Junction

100 miles southeast of Fairbanks, 108 miles northwest of Tok.

Delta is not only a handy stop on the Richardson Highway, it's the official western terminus of the Alaska Highway. In summer, this agricultural area becomes a bustling rest stop for road-weary travelers. The town is known for its access to good fishing and its proximity to the Delta Bison Range. Don't expect to see the elusive 500-strong bison herd, though, as the animals roam freely and generally avoid people.

GETTING HERE AND AROUND

Delta Junction is at the junction of the Alaska and Richardson Highways, a little less than a two-hour drive from Fairbanks and a five- to six-hour drive from Valdez.

Alaska Highway History

It's hard to overestimate the importance of the Alaska Highway in the state's history. Before World War II there was no road connection between Alaska's Interior and the rest of North America. The territory's population was centered in the coastal towns of Southeast's Panhandle region, and most of the state's commerce was conducted along its waterways. Access to the Interior was via riverboat until 1923, when the railroad connection from Seward through Anchorage and into Fairbanks was completed.

The onset of the Second World War changed everything. An overland route to the state was deemed a matter vital to national security in order to supply war material to the campaign in the Aleutians and to fend off a potential invasion by Japan. In a feat of amazing engineering and construction prowess (and hubris—the

United States started construction in Canada without bothering to ask the Canadian government if it was okay with them), the 1,500-mile-long route was carved out of the wilderness in eight months in 1942. Three regiments of Black soldiers—nearly a third of the highway's laborers—worked alongside white troops, and the Highway is credited for moving the military toward racial integration.

The original road was crude but effective (the first truck to travel it made a blazing average speed of 15 mph), and has been undergoing constant maintenance and upgrading ever since. Today the Alaska Highway is easily traversed by every form of highway vehicle imaginable, from bicycles and motorcycles to the biggest, most lumbering RVs, known not so affectionately by locals as "road barns."

◉ Sights

Delta Junction Visitor Center

VISITOR CENTER | In addition to finding out what's up in Delta Junction, you can purchase an "I Drove the Alaska Highway" certificate ($3) here—technically, the highway ends in Delta because there was already a road this far from Fairbanks. Across the street is the Sullivan Roadhouse Historical Museum (ask about hours at the visitor center, but it's generally open June through August). If you're in town on a Wednesday or Saturday between mid-May and early September, check out the wonderfully named Highway's End Farmers Market, open both days from 10 to 5. ⊠ 2855 Alaska Hwy., Delta Junction ⊙ Visitor center closed Sept.–May.

Rika's Roadhouse

HISTORIC SIGHT | The landmark Rika's Roadhouse, part of the 10-acre Big Delta State Historical Park, is a good detour for the free tours of the beautifully restored and meticulously maintained grounds, gardens, and historic buildings. In the past, roadhouses were erected at fairly regular intervals in the north, providing everything a traveler might need. Rika's, which operated from 1913 to 1947, is far and away the prettiest and best preserved of the survivors. It's a great place to get out, stretch, and buy homemade sandwiches and pies from the adjacent café. ⊠ Mile 274.5, Richardson Hwy., Delta Junction ☎ 623/696–5919 🖃 $5 ⊙ Closed mid-Sept.–mid-May.

Fairbanks, the Yukon, and the Interior   DELTA JUNCTION

7

🍴 Restaurants

Big Delta Brewing Company

$$ | **PIZZA** | The Delta area is one of Alaska's few agricultural hubs, and this brewery makes the most of its location. Sandwich meats and salad greens come from area farms, and the thin-crust pizzas are crafted from local barley. **Known for:** Alaska-grown ingredients from the Delta region; meat-heavy pizzas; local beers. [$] *Average main: $18* ✉ *1205 Richardson Hwy,, Delta Junction* ☎ *907/895–2222* 🌐 *www.bigdeltabrewingcompany.com* ⏲ *Closed Sun. and Mon.*

Buffalo Center Drive-In

$ | **AMERICAN** | **FAMILY** | This classic car hop sits right where the Richardson and Alaska Highways converge. It's all-American road-trip food—think burgers, fries, and ice cream—but the sunny patio next to Sullivan's Roadhouse provides a nice spot to unwind. **Known for:** summertime social hub; tasty buffalo burgers; generous milkshakes. [$] *Average main: $7* ✉ *265 Richardson Hwy., Delta Junction* ☎ *907/895–4055* 🌐 *www.facebook.com/BuffaloCenterDriveIn* ⏲ *Closed mid-Sept.–mid-May* 💳 *No credit cards.*

Tok

175 miles southwest of Dawson City, 200 miles southeast of Fairbanks.

Loggers, miners, old sourdoughs (Alaskan for "colorful local curmudgeons"), and hunting guides who live and work along Tok's streams or in the millions of acres of spruce forest nearby come here for supplies. The population of Tok is about 1,250 year-round, but its residents are joined each summer by thousands of travelers, among them adventurers journeying up the Alaska Highway from the Lower 48. Tok is more of a gateway to nearby attractions, such as the Tetlin National Wildlife Refuge, than a destination in itself, but its visitor center is worth a visit. The town also has markets, fueling stops, and some restaurants and hotels.

GETTING HERE AND AROUND

Tok sits at the junction of the Glenn and Alaska Highways. 40-Mile Air serves the town from Fairbanks with three flights per week and flies to the Tetlin National Wildlife Refuge and other wilderness locations. The refuge lies south of the Alaska Highway southeast of Tok.

A huge loop driving tour starting in Tok takes in many of Alaska's terrific landscapes. Head down the Tok Cutoff to the Richardson Highway and continue south to Valdez. From there, catch the ferry to Whittier, Cordova, or Seward. Explore the Kenai and Anchorage, then head north on the Seward Highway to the parks, to Denali, Fairbanks, and beyond. Loop back to Tok and you will have experienced most of what can be seen from the road system.

ESSENTIALS

AIRLINE CONTACT 40-Mile Air. ✉ *Mile 1313, Alaska Hwy., Tok* ☎ *907/883–5191* 🌐 *www.fortymileair.com.*

👁 Sights

Taylor Highway

SCENIC DRIVE | The 160-mile Taylor Highway runs north from the Alaska Highway at Tetlin Junction, 12 miles east of Tok. It's a narrow rough-gravel road that winds along mountain ridges and through valleys of the Fortymile River. The road passes the tiny community of Chicken and ends in Eagle at the Yukon River. This is one of only three places in Alaska where the Yukon River can be reached by road. The Top of the World Highway starts off the Taylor and leads to Dawson City in the Yukon Territory. The route is far more scenic, and shorter, than the alternative of taking the Alaska Highway

Continued on page 332

NATIVE ARTS AND CRAFTS

Intricate Aleut baskets, Athabascan birch-bark wonders, Inupiaq ivory carvings, and towering Tlingit totems are just some of the eye-opening crafts you'll encounter as you explore the 49th state. Alaska's native peoples—who live across 570,000 square miles of tundra, boreal forest, arctic plains, and coastal rain forest—are undeniably hardy, and their unique artistic traditions are just as resilient and enduring.

TIPS ON CHOOSING AN AUTHENTIC ITEM

1 The Federal Trade Commission has enacted strict regulations to combat the sale of falsely marketed goods; it's illegal for anything made by non-native Alaskans to be labeled as "Indian," "Native American," or "Alaska Native."

2 Some authentic goods are marked by a silver hand symbol or are labeled as an "Authentic Native Handicraft from Alaska."

3 The "Made in Alaska" label, often accompanied by an image of a polar bear with cub, denotes that the handicraft was made in the state.

4 Be sure to ask for written proof of authenticity with your purchase, as well as the artist's name. You can also request the artist's permit number, which may be available.

5 The Alaska State Council on the Arts, in Anchorage, is a great resource if you have additional questions or want to confirm a permit number. Call 907/269–6610 or 888/278–7424 in Alaska.

6 Materials must be legal. For example, only some feathers, such as ptarmigan and pheasant feathers, comply with the Migratory Bird Act. Only Native artisans are permitted to carve new walrus ivory. The seller should be able to answer your questions about material and technique.

THE NATIVE PEOPLE OF ALASKA

There are many opportunities to see the making of traditional crafts in native environments, including the Southeast Alaska Indian Cultural Center in Sitka and Anchorage's Alaska Native Heritage Center.

After chatting with the artisans, pop into the gift shops to peruse the handmade items. Also check out prominent galleries and museum shops.

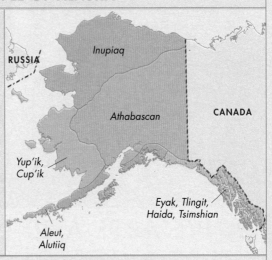

NORTHWEST COAST INDIANS: TLINGIT, HAIDA & TSIMSHIAN

Scattered throughout Southeast Alaska's rain forests, these highly social tribes traditionally benefited from the region's mild climate and abundant salmon, which afforded them a rare luxury: leisure time. They put this time to good use by cultivating highly detailed crafts, including ceremonial masks, elaborate woven robes, and, most famously, totem poles.

TOWERING TOTEM POLES

Throughout the Inside Passage's braided channels and forested islands, Native peoples use the wood of the abundant cedar trees to carve totem poles, which illustrate history, pay reverence, commemorate a potlatch, or cast shame on a misbehaving person.

Every totem pole tells a story with a series of animal and human figures arranged vertically. Traditionally the totem poles of this area feature ravens, eagles, killer whales, wolves, bears, frogs, the mythic thunderbird, and the likenesses of ancestors.

A Tlingit totem reaches for the skies in Ketchikan

K'alyaan Totem Pole

Carved in 1999, the K'alyaan totem pole is a tribute to the Tlingits who lost their lives in the 1804 Battle of Sitka between invading Russians and Tlingit warriors. Tommy Joseph, a venerated Tlingit artist from Sitka, and an apprentice spent three months carving the pole from a 35-ft western red cedar. It now stands at the very site of the skirmish, in Sitka National Historical Park.

Raven: Atop the pole sits the striking raven, the emblem of one of the two moieties (large multi-clan groups) of Tlingit culture.

Sockeye Salmon (above) and Dog/Chum Salmon (below): These two symbols signify the contributions of the Sockeye and Dog Salmon Clans to the 1804 battle. They also illustrate the symbolic connection to the tribe's traditional food sources.

Woodworm: The woodworm—a Tlingit clan symbol—is a wood-boring beetle that leaves a distinctive mark on timber.

Beaver: Sporting a fearsome pair of front teeth, this beaver symbol cradles a child in its arms, signifying the strength of Tlingit family bonds.

Frog: This animal represents the Kik.sádi Clan, which was very instrumental in organizing the Tlingit's revolt against the Russian trespassers. Here, the frog holds a raven helmet—a tribute to the Kik.sádi warrior who wore a similar headpiece into battle.

TOOLS AND MATERIALS
As do most modern carvers, Joseph used a steel adz to carve the cedar. Prior to European contact—and the accompanying introduction of metal tools—Tlingit artists carved with jade adzes. Totem poles are traditionally decorated with paint made from salmon-liver oil, charcoal, and iron and copper oxides.

ALEUT & ALUTIIQ

The Aleut inhabit the Alaska Peninsula and the windswept Aleutian Islands. Historically they lived and died by the sea, surviving on a diet of seals, sea lions, whales, and walruses, which they hunted in the tumultuous waters of the Gulf of Alaska and the Bering Sea. Hunters pursued their prey in *Sugpiaq*, kayaklike boats made of seal skin stretched over a driftwood frame.

WATERPROOF *KAMLEIKAS*

The Aleut prize seal intestine for its remarkable waterproof properties; they use it to create sturdy cloaks, shelter walls, and boat hulls. To make their famous cloaks, called *kamleikas*, intestine is washed, soaked in salt water, and arduously scraped clean. It is then stretched and dried before being stitched into hooded, waterproof pullovers.

FINE BASKETRY

Owing to the region's profusion of wild rye grass, Aleutian women are some of the planet's most skilled weavers, capable of creating baskets with more than 2,500 fibers per square inch. They also create hats, socks, mittens, and multipurpose mats. A long, sharpened thumbnail is their only tool.

ATHABASCANS

Inhabiting Alaska's rugged interior for 8,000 to 20,000 years, Athabascans followed a seasonally nomadic hunter-gatherer lifestyle, subsisting off of caribou, moose, bear, and snowshoe hare. They populate areas from the Brooks Range to Cook Inlet, a vast expanse that encompasses five significant rivers: the Tanana, the Kuskokwim the Copper, the Susitna, and the Yukon.

BIRCH BARK: WATERPROOF WONDER

Aside from annual salmon runs, the Athabascans had no access to marine mammals—or to the intestines that made for such effective boat hulls and garments. They turned to the region's birch, the bark of which was used to create canoes. Also common were birch-bark baskets and baby carriers.

FUNCTIONAL & ORNAMENTED PIECES

Much like that of the neighboring Iñupiat, Athabascan craftwork traditionally served functional purposes. But tools, weapons, and clothing were often highly decorated with colorful embroidery and shells. Athabascans are especially well known for ornamenting their caribou-skin clothing with porcupine quills and animal hair—both of which were later replaced by imported western beads.

IÑUPIAT, YUP'IK & CUP'IK

Residing in Alaska's remote northern and northwestern regions, these groups are often collectively known as the Iñupiat. They winter in coastal villages, relying on migrating marine mammals for sustenance, and spend summers at inland fish camps. Ongoing artistic traditions include ceremonial mask carving, ivory carving (not to be confused with scrimshaw), sewn skin garments, basket weaving, and soapstone carvings.

Thanks to the sheer volume of ivory art in Alaska's marketplace, you're bound to find a piece of ivory that fits your fancy—regardless of whether you prefer traditional ivory carvings, scrimshaw, or a piece that blends both artistic traditions.

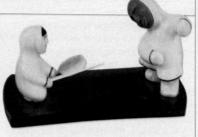

IVORY CARVING

While in Alaska, you'll likely see carved ivory pieces, scrimshaw, and some fake ivory carvings (generally plastic). Ivory carving has been a Native art form for thousands of years. After harvesting ivory from migrating walrus herds in the Bering Sea, artisans age tusks for up to one year before shaping it with adzes and bow drills.

KEEP IN MIND

The Marine Mammal Protection Act states that only native peoples are allowed to harvest fresh walrus ivory, which is legal to buy after it's been carved by a Native person. How can you tell if a piece is real and made by a native artisan? Real ivory is likely to be pricey; be suspect of anything too cheaply priced. It should also be hard (plastic will be softer) and cool to the touch. Keep an eye out for mastery of carving technique, and be sure to ask questions when you've found a piece you're interested in buying.

WHAT IS SCRIMSHAW?

The invention of scrimshaw is attributed to 18th-century American whalers who etched the surfaces of whale bone and scrap ivory. The etchings were filled with ink, bringing the designs into stark relief.

More recently the line between traditional Iñupiat ivory carving and scrimshaw has become somewhat blurred, with many native artisans incorporating both techniques.

TIPS

Ivory carving is a highly specialized native craft that is closely regulated. As it is a by-product of subsistence hunting, all meat and skin from a walrus hunt is used.

Ivory from extinct mammoths and mastodons (usually found buried underground or washed up on beaches) is also legal to buy in Alaska; many native groups keep large stores of it, as well as antique walrus tusk, for craft purposes. Many of the older pieces have a caramelized color.

to Whitehorse and then turning north, but it's another of those stretches for which it's good to make sure your insurance policy covers towing and windshield replacement. The highway is not plowed in winter, so it is snowed shut from fall to spring. If you're roughing it, know that the Bureau of Land Management also maintains three first-come, first-served campsites (as all BLM campsites are) on the Taylor Highway at Miles 49, 82, and 160; the last is located at the end of the road in Eagle. ⊘ *Closed winter.*

Tetlin National Wildlife Refuge

NATURE PRESERVE | This 700,000-acre refuge has most of the charismatic megafauna that visitors travel to Alaska to see, including black and grizzly bears, moose, Dall sheep, wolves, caribou, and tons of birds. Covering just south of the Alaska Highway east of the town of Tok all the way to the U.S.–Canada border, the refuge has a visitor center at Mile 1,229. A large deck here has spotting scopes, and inside are maps, books, and wildlife exhibits, as well as a board with information on current road conditions. At Mile 1,240 you can hike a 1-mile raised-plank boardwalk through lowland forest to scenic Hidden Lake. Basic lakefront campgrounds can be found at Miles 1,249 and 1,256 during the summer season. ✉ *Visitor Center, Mile 1,229, Alaska Hwy., Tok* ☎ *907/883–5312* ⊕ *www.fws.gov/refuge/tetlin* ⛁ *Free* ⊘ *Visitor center closed mid-Sept.–mid-May.*

Tok Main Street Visitor Center

VISITOR CENTER | To help with your planning, stop in at Tok's visitor center, which has travel information covering the entire state, as well as wildlife and natural-history exhibits. This is one of Alaska's largest info centers, and the staff is quite helpful. ✉ *Mile 1,314, Alaska Hwy., Tok* ☎ *907/883–5775* ⊕ *www.tokalaskainfo.com* ⛁ *Free* ⊘ *Closed Sept.–May.*

Border Crossing

Crossing into Interior Alaska from the Lower 48 or from the ferry terminals in Southeast requires border crossings into Canada and then into Alaska. Be very certain of all the requirements for crossing an international border before you travel, including restrictions on pets and firearms and the need for adequate personal identification for every member of the party. Citizens of Canada and the United States traveling between Alaska and Canada are required to have a passport—and they will be checked.

🍴 Restaurants

Fast Eddy's Restaurant

$$ | AMERICAN | Not the greasy fast-food joint its name might suggest, this relaxing place serves surprisingly interesting cuisine. Portions are sizable—that prime rib dinner will induce a nap—and the variety provides welcome relief from the roadhouse burgers served by most Alaska Highway restaurants (though there are plenty of burgers here, too). **Known for:** massive menu for a tiny town; deep-fried mushrooms; blueberry milkshakes. 💲 *Average main: $15* ✉ *Mile 1,313, Alaska Hwy., Tok* ☎ *907/883–4411* ⊕ *www.fasteddysrestaurant.com.*

🛏 Hotels

Burnt Paw and Cabins Outback

$$ | B&B/INN | One of Tok's nicer lodgings, Burnt Paw has seven comfortable, sod-roof cabins—each with two beds, a private bath, a microwave, a refrigerator, Wi-Fi, and satellite TV. **Pros:** best location in town; cozy cabins; homemade breakfast baskets. **Cons:** fee for pets;

no kitchenettes; road warriors from the Alaska Highway may arrive at any hour of the night. [$] *Rooms from: $159* ✉ *Mile 1,314.3, Alaska Hwy., Tok* ☎ *907/883–4121* 🌐 *www.burntpawcabins.com* 🛏 *7 cabins* 🍴 *Free Breakfast.*

Fox 'n Fireweed Cabins
$$ | **B&B/INN** | This family-run inn has picturesque private cabins and comfortable apartments. **Pros:** comfortable cabins; bikes available for guests; close to town. **Cons:** some cabins not accessible for those with disabilities; no kitchenettes in cabins; no guided activities. [$] *Rooms from: $120* ✉ *0.5 Sundog Trail, off Alaska Hwy. Mile 1,316.5, Tok* ☎ *907/505–0214* 🌐 *www.cleftoftherock.net* 🍴 *Free Breakfast* 🛏 *5 cabins, 2 apartments.*

Chicken

78 miles north of Tok, 109 miles west of Dawson City.

Chicken was, and still is, the heart of the southern Fortymile Mining District, and many of these works are visible along the highway. The second town in Alaska to be incorporated (Skagway was the first), the town got its name (or so the story goes) when its residents wanted to call it "Ptarmigan" but couldn't figure out how to spell that. Chicken has only a handful of permanent residents, mostly miners and trappers, creating an authentic frontier atmosphere.

Chicken is far from a prime shopping stop, but what it lacks in infrastructure, it makes up for in atmosphere. The town is small, so you don't have far to go to find everything you need. If you like bluegrass music, be sure to check out the Chickenstock Music Festival *(www.chickenstockmusicfest.com)* if you're passing through in mid-June.

On the Defensive

Ft. Greely, which is 5 miles south of Tok toward Valdez, contains a growing number of underground silos with missiles that are part of the Ballistic Missile Defense System. The missiles are connected to tracking stations elsewhere and would be launched to try to shoot down enemy missiles in space if the United States were ever so attacked.

GETTING HERE AND AROUND

Chicken sits off the Taylor Highway, a packed-gravel road that closes in winter. The town is accessible only by car or bush plane—or, during winter, dogsled or snowmachine. No major commercial flights come here. Most people fly to Fairbanks and drive the five hours or so to Chicken, or visit as part of a longer road trip.

Overland travel between Chicken and Dawson City winds along a gravel road. Some drivers love it, some white-knuckle it.

Sights

Chicken Creek RV Park & Cabins
VISITOR CENTER | Free gold panning and in-season tours of a historic schoolhouse are among the activities offered through this RV park's gift shop. The shop also has gas and diesel, an ATM, and free Wi-Fi. Not equipped with a full-size motorhome? Guests can also stay the night in suites, camping sites, and cabins. ✉ *Mile 66.8, at Chicken Creek Bridge, Chicken* ☎ *907/505–0231* 🌐 *www.townofchicken.com* ⏲ *Closed mid-Sept.–mid-May.*

Chicken Gold Camp & Outpost

HISTORIC SIGHT | Finders keepers is the name of the game at the Gold Camp, where you can pan for gold and tour a historic dredge. The Pedro Dredge scooped up 55,000 ounces of gold from Chicken Creek between 1959 and 1967, but apparently plenty was left behind in the creek and elsewhere. Guests can stay in the Gold Camp's cabins, campground, or RV park, and schedule a prospecting trip to the site's mining claims. Hungry gold seekers can fill up in the café on wood-fired pizzas, sandwiches, and baked goods, or fuel up with an espresso. Bluegrass lovers appreciate the family-friendly Chickenstock Music Festival, held the second weekend in June. ⊠ *Airport Rd. off Taylor Hwy., Chicken* ☏ *907/782–4427* ⊕ *www.chickengold. com* ⊗ *Closed mid-Sept.–mid-May.*

Downtown Chicken

TOWN | The longest-running business in town has classic wooden porches and provides multiple services. A fun place to explore, the complex includes the Chicken Creek Café, an eight-stool saloon, liquor store, and gift emporium. Free camping and overnight RV parking are available, with cabins and wall tents for rent. Gas and diesel are available from 7:30 am until the bar closes. The café serves baked wild Alaskan salmon for lunch and dinner, as well as chicken potpie and buffalo chili. ⊠ *Airport Rd. off Taylor Hwy., Chicken* ⊕ *www.chickenalaska.com* ⊗ *Most businesses closed mid-Sept.–mid-May.*

 ## Activities

Fortymile River

CANOEING & ROWING | The beautiful Fortymile River offers everything from a 38-mile run to a lengthy journey to the Yukon and then down to Eagle. Its waters range from easy Class I to serious Class IV (possibly Class V) stretches. Only experienced canoeists should attempt boating on this river, and rapids should be scouted beforehand. Several access points can be found off the Taylor Highway. ⊠ *Chicken* ⊕ *www.rivers.gov/ rivers/fortymile.php.*

Eagle

95 miles north of Chicken, 144 miles northwest of Dawson City (road closed in winter).

Eagle was once a seat of government and commerce for the Interior. An Army post, Ft. Egbert, operated here until 1911, and territorial judge and noted Alaska historian James Wickersham had his headquarters in Eagle until Fairbanks began to grow from its gold strike. The population peaked at 1,700 in 1898. Today there are fewer than 100 residents. Although the majority of the population is gone, the town still retains its frontier character and gold-rush architecture. John McPhee provides a fascinating account of life in Eagle during the 1970s in his renowned Alaska travelogue *Coming into the Country.* The local historical society has information about how the town was influenced by the Yukon River, which in the days before cars and trucks was also a vital mode of transportation.

GETTING HERE AND AROUND

Eagle is accessible by car, bush plane, or, during winter, dogsled or snowmachine. Commercial flights are available on Everts Air Alaska.

 ## Sights

Eagle Historical Society

HISTORY MUSEUM | The town's historical society has a two-hour walking tour that takes in historic buildings and includes tales of the famous people—among them Arctic explorer Roald Amundsen and aviation pioneer Billy Mitchell—who have passed through this historic Yukon River border town. The society also maintains an extensive archive, photo

Travel along the highway linking Chicken and Dawson City for some awe-inspiring scenery.

collection, and museum store stocked with regional history books and locally made items. Eagle is a sleepy town, so call ahead to schedule an appointment. If you can't reach the society, the Interagency Visitor Center can help coordinate a tour. ✉ *1st and Berry St., Eagle* 📠 *907/547–2325* ⊕ *www.eaglehistorical-society.com* ✉ *$7* ⊗ *Closed Labor Day–Memorial Day.*

Eagle Visitor Center

VISITOR CENTER | If you're even thinking of heading into the wilderness, the headquarters of the 2.5-million-acre Yukon–Charley Rivers National Preserve should be your first stop. Informal interpretive programs and talks take place here, and there are videos you can watch to prepare. You can also peruse maps and visit the reference library, and there are helpful books for sale. ✉ *100 Front St., off 1st Ave. by airstrip, Eagle* 📠 *907/547–2233 June–Sept., 907/459–3730 Oct.–May* ⊕ *www.nps.gov/yuch* ✉ *Free* ⊗ *Closed Oct.–May.*

Dawson City

109 miles east of Chicken.

Beautiful Dawson City is the prime specimen of a Yukon gold-rush town. Since the first swell of hopeful migrants more than 100 years ago, many of the original buildings have disappeared, victims of fire, flood, and weathering. But plenty remain, and it's easy to step back in time, by attending a performance at the Palace Theatre, erected in 1899, or stopping into a shop whose building originally served stampeders. In modern Dawson City, street paving is erratic, and the place maintains a serious frontier vibe. But it's also a center for the arts—the town's yearly summer music festival is one of Canada's biggest—and as the last touch of civilization before the deep wild, it's where hikers share tables with hard-core miners at quirky local restaurants.

In the years leading up to the turn of the 20th century, Dawson was transformed from a First Nations camp into the largest, most refined city north of Seattle and west of Winnipeg. It had grand buildings with running water, telephones, and electricity. In 1899 the city's population numbered almost 30,000—a jump of about 29,900 over the previous few years—which all but overwhelmed the Tr'ondëk Hwëch'in, the First Nations, Hän-speaking people who inhabited the area. Their chief, a man named Isaac, who is still revered as the savior of the culture, moved his people from the confluence, where they had hunted and fished for thousands of years, to the village of Moosehide a few miles downstream. The town they left behind grew into a place where a fresh egg could cost the equivalent of a day's salary down south, and where one of the most profitable jobs was panning gold dust out of the sawdust scattered on saloon floors.

Today Dawson City is home to about 1,300 people, 310 or so of whom are of First Nations descent. The city itself is now a National Historic Site of Canada. Besides being one of the hippest, funkiest towns in the north, Dawson also serves as a base from which to explore Tombstone Territorial Park, a natural wonderland with plants and animals found nowhere else, living in the spaces between high, steep mountain ranges.

GETTING HERE AND AROUND
Charter air service to Dawson flies from Fairbanks in summer. Air North, Yukon's Airline, offers direct service from Whitehorse to Dawson City in the summer.

Drivers traveling north- and southbound on the Alaska Highway can make a loop with the Taylor Highway route. This adds 100 miles to the trip but is worth it. Part with the Alaska Highway at Tetlin Junction and wind through Fortymile Country past the little communities of Chicken and Jack Wade Camp into Canada. The border is open from 8 am to 8 pm in summer. The Canadian section of the Taylor Highway is called Top of the

World Highway, and with most of it on a ridgeline between two huge valleys, the gravel road really does feel like the top of the world, opening broad views of range after range of tundra-covered mountains stretching in every direction. Join back with the Alaska Highway at Whitehorse.

Dawson City is small enough that you can walk end to end in about 20 minutes—even if you stop and spend five of those watching the river flow by. The Visitor Information Centre has an excellent walking map of the town, and following it is one of the best things you can do while here. Many old buildings have displays in the windows showing what they once were. A couple of older buildings have also been filled with historic photos and information. Walking tours—in English, French, and Dutch—leave regularly from the center.

AIRLINE INFORMATION Air North, Yukon's Airline. ✉ *Whitehorse* ☎ *800/661–0407* ⊕ *www.flyairnorth.com.*

ESSENTIALS
VISITOR AND TOUR INFORMATION
Klondike Visitors Association. ✉ *1102 Front St., Dawson City* ☎ *867/993–5575* ⊕ *www.dawsoncity.ca.* **Visitor Information Centre.** ✉ *Front and King Sts., Dawson City* ☎ *867/993–5566, 867/993–5575 Oct.–Apr.* ⊕ *www.dawsoncity.ca/ plan-your-trip.*

 ## Sights

Dänojà Zho Cultural Centre
INDIGENOUS SIGHT | Its inviting atmosphere makes the center a good stop to explore the heritage of Tr'ondëk Hwëch'in First Nations people. For countless generations Hän-speaking people lived in the Yukon River drainage of western Yukon and eastern Alaska. This specific language group settled around the mouth of the Klondike River. Through annually rotating displays, as well as tours, cultural activities, films, live radio broadcasts, and performances, you can learn about the

traditional and contemporary life of "the people of the river." Though somewhat sparse, the historical exhibits convey a sense of what the gold rush was like for the people who were here first. Special summer activities include music events and daily programs in beading, Indigenous medicine, and tea- and jelly-making. The gift shop sells fine First Nations art, clothing, and beaded footwear, and stocks music and books. Admission is valid for two days. ⊠ *1131 Front St., Dawson City* ☎ *867/993–7100 ext. 500* ⊕ *www.trondek.ca/danoja-zho-cultural-centre* ⌧ *C$10* ☺ *Closed mid-Sept.– late May and Sun.*

Dawson City Museum

HISTORY MUSEUM | The stories and experiences of the Yukon's First Nations peoples are one of the many topics explored throughout this museum on regional history. While touring the excellent displays of gold-rush materials, you may find it surprising just how luxurious Dawson was for the lucky few who could call themselves rich. Four restored locomotives and other railway cars and gear from the Klondike Mines Railway are housed in an adjacent building. The museum also has a library and archives, with staff on hand to help those seeking information about gold-rush ancestors. ⊠ *Old Territorial Administration Bldg., 595 5th Ave., Dawson City* ☎ *867/993–5291* ⊕ *www.dawsonmuseum.ca* ⌧ *C$9.*

Diamond Tooth Gerties Gambling Hall

CASINO | Adults-only Gerties presents live entertainment and high-energy performances, including a scintillating cancan three times nightly during the summer. This community nonprofit is the only authentic, legal gambling establishment operating in the entire North (it's also the oldest gambling hall in Canada), though the scene is mostly slots along with a few gaming tables. And there really was a Diamond Tooth Gertie—Gertie Lovejoy, a dance-hall queen who wore a diamond between her two front teeth.

⊠ *Queen St. and 4th Ave., Dawson City* ☎ *867/993–5575* ⊕ *www.diamondtoothgerties.ca* ⌧ *C$15* ☺ *Closed Nov., Dec., and Sun.–Thurs. late Sept.–mid-May.*

Gold Dredge No. 4

MINE | When this massive wooden-hull gold dredge was in operation (1913–59), it ate rivers whole, spitting out gravel and keeping the gold for itself—on one highly productive day it sucked up 800 ounces. These days the dredge—a Canadian National Historic Site—occupies a spot along Bonanza Creek about 10 miles southeast of Dawson. The dredge is still worth a look, even on your own, if only to ponder the geology and economics that made it viable to haul this enormous piece of equipment into the middle of nowhere at a time when gold only brought $20 an ounce. You can pan for gold yourself in Bonanza Creek, where the Klondike Visitors Association offers a free claim for visitors. Bring your own supplies (almost every gift shop in town sells pans). ⊠ *Mile 8, Bonanza Creek Rd.,* ⊕ *Exit Klondike Hwy. at Km marker 74* ☎ *867/993–2315* ⌧ *C$15* ☺ *Closed mid-Sept.–mid-May.*

Jack London Museum

OTHER MUSEUM | This reproduction of London's home from 1897 to 1898 is constructed with half the wood from his original wilderness home that was found south of Dawson in the 1930s. The other half was sent to Oakland, California, where a similar structure sits at Jack London Square. The small museum contains photos and documents from London's life and the gold-rush era. Half-hour talks are given twice daily during peak season. ⊠ *8th Ave. and Firth St., Dawson City* ☎ *867/993–5575* ⊕ *www.jacklondonmuseum.ca* ⌧ *C$5* ☺ *Closed Oct.–Apr.*

Robert Service Cabin

HISTORIC HOME | The poet Robert Service lived in this Dawson cabin from 1909 to 1912. From late May to early September, enjoy daily readings outside the cabin from Parks Canada. Stoke your inner poet and follow Service's footsteps on the nearby trail to Crocus Bluffs. ✉ *8th Ave. and Hanson St., Dawson City* ☎ *867/993–2315 in summer, 867/993–7200 in winter* 🎟 *C$7.*

Activities

Tombstone Territorial Park

HIKING & WALKING | Often described as "the Patagonia of the Northern Hemisphere," Tombstone has some of the best hiking and views of granite peaks in the Yukon. About 56 km (36 miles) northeast of Dawson City and bisected by the Dempster Highway, Tombstone occupies 2,200 square km (850 square miles) of wilderness supporting a vast array of wildlife and vegetation. Backcountry mountaineering and wildlife-viewing options abound, though for the most part the terrain is too difficult for hiking novices. The park maintains day-use trails at Km markers 58.5, 71.5 (two here), 74.4, and 78.2. At Km marker 71.5 is the Tombstone Interpretive Centre and Campground. The center has informative displays and great mountain views. Stop here to get a handle on everything the park has to offer, and to learn how animals make it through the winter. Flightseeing trips over the jagged Tombstone Range depart from Dawson City. ✉ *Dawson City* ☎ *867/993–7714 in Dawson City, 800/661–0408* 🌐 *www.env.gov.yk.ca/tombstone* 🎟 *Free* 🕒 *Interpretive Centre closed late Sept.–early May.*

Restaurants

Red Mammoth Bistro

$ | **BAKERY** | This coffee shop and its fresh-baked pastries provide a much-needed dose of warmth in Dawson's winter months. The chocolate-almond croissants are a local favorite. **Known for:** outdoor seating in summer; its namesake massive red coffee machine; from-scratch cakes and desserts. [$] *Average main: C$5* ✉ *932 2nd Ave.,* ☎ *867/993–3759* 🕒 *Closed weekends.*

Hotels

Bombay Peggy's

$$ | **B&B/INN** | Named and fashioned after one of the last of Dawson's legal madams, Peggy's is done in elaborate Victorian gold-rush style, with heavy, plush draperies, rich color schemes, and claw-foot tubs and pedestal sinks in the bathrooms. **Pros:** fun on-site pub; an engaging step back in time; nice touches such as fresh croissants and "Sherry Hour". **Cons:** small, social parlor can feel crowded; no elevator; three upstairs rooms, known as the Snugs, share a bathroom. [$] *Rooms from: C$185* ✉ *2nd Ave. and Princess St., Dawson City* ☎ *867/993–6969* 🌐 *www.bombaypeggys.com* 🍴 *No Meals* 🛏 *7 rooms.*

Eldorado Hotel

$$ | **HOTEL** | Though this hotel has a pioneer-style facade, its rooms are outfitted with modern amenities such as high-def TVs, and some suites even have Jacuzzis. **Pros:** good location; in-hotel bar and restaurant; kitchenettes in some rooms. **Cons:** free Wi-Fi has data limits; no elevator; no pets. [$] *Rooms from: C$179* ✉ *902 3rd Ave., Dawson City* ☎ *867/993–5451, 800/764–3536 from Alaska and the Yukon* 🌐 *www.eldoradohotel.ca* 🕒 *Closed mid-Dec.–mid-Jan.* 🍴 *No Meals* 🛏 *62 rooms.*

Triple J Hotel & Cabins

$$ | **HOTEL** | With a pretty white-and-blue annex of suites and standard rooms as well as a neighborhood of log cabins, Triple J offers choice for everyone from solo travelers to families. **Pros:** nice restaurant on-site; some cabins are pet-friendly; in-room kitchenettes in cabins and annex. **Cons:** kitchenettes lack ovens; smallish showers in cabins; some cabin porches face a gravel parking lot. [$] *Rooms from: C$179* ✉ *5th Ave. and Queen St., Dawson City* ☎ *867/993–5323, 800/764–3555* 🌐 *www.triplejhotel.com* 🛏 *58 rooms* 🍴 *No Meals.*

Whitehorse

337 miles southeast of Dawson City, 600 miles southeast of Fairbanks, 110 miles north of Skagway.

Near the White Horse Rapids of the Yukon River, Whitehorse began as an encampment in the late 1890s, a logical layover for gold rushers heading north along the Chilkoot Trail toward Dawson. The next great population boom came during World War II with the building of the Alcan—the Alaska-Canada Highway. Today this city of about 25,000 residents is Yukon's center of commerce, communication, and transportation, and the seat of the territorial government. It also has the only Tim Hortons café locations for hundreds of miles.

Besides being a great starting point for explorations of other areas of the Yukon, the town has plenty of diversions and recreational opportunities. You can spend a day exploring its museums and cultural displays—research the Yukon's mining and development history, look into the backgrounds of the town's founders, learn about its indigenous First Nations people, and gain an appreciation of the Yukon Territory from prehistoric times up to the present.

GETTING HERE AND AROUND

Air Canada flies to Whitehorse in summer from Anchorage through Vancouver. Air North, Yukon's Whitehorse-based airline, provides direct, seasonal air service from Whitehorse to several other Canadian cities, including Dawson City, Vancouver, and Calgary. Juneau-based Alaska Seaplanes also operates a service between Alaska's capital and Whitehorse.

To take in all the scenery along the way, you can drive yourself up the Alaska Highway. There are multiple rental-car companies, buses, and taxis in Whitehorse; Whitehorse Transit has a city bus circuit that will get you where you need to go. From Whitehorse you can also make your way to Skagway, at the northern end of the Inside Passage—the drive takes about three hours via the Klondike Highway.

AIRLINE CONTACTS Air North, Yukon's Airline. ☎ 800/661–0407 ⊕ *www.flyairnorth. com.*

CITY BUS Whitehorse Transit. ✉ *Whitehorse* ☎ 867/668–8396 ⊕ *www.whitehorse.ca/transit.*

TAXI CONTACTS Grizzly Bear Taxi. ✉ *Whitehorse* ☎ 867/667–4888.

ESSENTIALS
VISITOR AND TOUR INFORMATION
Whitehorse Visitor Information Centre. ✉ *100 Hanson St., Whitehorse* ☎ 867/667–3084, 800/661–0494 ⊕ *www. travelyukon.com.*

 ## Sights

Canyon City Historic Site
INDIGENOUS SIGHT | This archaeological dig site provides a glimpse into the past of the local First Nations people. Long before Western civilizations developed the Miles Canyon area, the First Nations people used it as a seasonal fish camp. From mid-June to late August, the Yukon Conservation Society sponsors two-hour, kid-friendly natural and historical hikes starting at the Miles Canyon bridge. Hikes provide the opportunity to experience the surrounding countryside with local naturalists and are occasionally led by topic experts like botanists, entomologists, and First Nations historians. A bookstore in the society's downtown office (302 Hawkins St.) specializes in the Yukon's history and wilderness and sells souvenirs, maps, and posters. ✉ *Miles Canyon Rd., Whitehorse* ☎ 867/668–5678 *Yukon Conservation Society* ▣ *Free.*

Kluane National Park and Reserve

NATIONAL PARK | About 170 km (100 miles) west of Whitehorse, the reserve has millions of acres for hiking. This is a completely roadless wilderness, with hundreds of glaciers and so many mountains over 14,000 feet high that most of them haven't been named yet (one exception: Mt. Logan, Canada's highest peak). Kluane, the neighboring Wrangell–St. Elias National Park in Alaska, and a few smaller parks, constitute the largest protected wilderness in all North America. The staff at the Haines Junction visitor center can provide hiking, flightseeing, and other information. ⊠ *Visitor center, 119 Logan St., Haines Junction* ☎ *867/634–7250* ⊕ *www.pc.gc.ca/kluane.*

MacBride Museum of Yukon History

HISTORY MUSEUM | The exhibits at the MacBride provide a comprehensive view of the colorful characters and groundbreaking events that shaped the Yukon. An old-fashioned confectionery and an 1898 miner's saloon are among the highlights of the Gold to Government Gallery illuminating gold-rush and Whitehorse history. The gold-related exhibits illustrate particularly well what people went through in quest of a little glint of color. Other displays investigate the Yukon's wildlife and geology, and there are fine collections of photography and First Nations beadwork. Outdoor artifacts include the cabin of Sam McGee, who was immortalized in Robert Service's famous poem "The Cremation of Sam McGee." ⊠ *1124 Front St., Whitehorse* ☎ *867/667–2709* ⊕ *www.macbridemuseum.com* ☜ *C$10* ☽ *Closed Sun. and Mon.*

Miles Canyon

NATURE SIGHT | Both scenic and historic, Miles Canyon is a short drive south of Whitehorse. Although the dam below the canyon makes its waters seem relatively tame, it was this perilous stretch of the Yukon River that determined the location of Whitehorse as the starting point for river travel north. The dam, built in 1958, created a lake that put an end to the infamous White Horse Rapids. Back in 1897, though, Jack London won the admiration—and cash—of fellow stampeders headed north to the Klondike goldfields because of his steady hand as pilot of hand-hewn wooden boats here. You can hike on trails along the canyon or rent a kayak and paddle on through. ⊠ *Miles Canyon Rd., Whitehorse.*

S.S. *Klondike*

HISTORIC SIGHT | You can't really understand the scale of the gold rush without touring a riverboat. The S.S. *Klondike*, a national historic site, is dry-docked on the bank of the Yukon River in central Whitehorse's Rotary Park, just a minute's drive from downtown. The 210-foot stern-wheeler was built in 1929, sank in 1936, and was rebuilt in 1937. In the days when the Yukon River was the transportation link between Whitehorse and Dawson City, the S.S. *Klondike* was the largest boat plying the river. Riverboats were as much a way of life here as on the Mississippi of Mark Twain, and the tour of the *Klondike* is a fascinating way to see how the boats were adapted to the north. In the old days they were among the few operations that provided Indigenous people paying jobs, so there's a rich First Nations and Alaska Native history as well. Entry fees include a self-guided tour brochure. Guided tours are available through Parks Canada for C$8. ⊠ *Robert Service Way at 4th Ave., on bank of Yukon River, Whitehorse* ☎ *867/667–4511 mid-May–mid-Sept., 867/667–3910* ⊕ *www.pc.gc.ca/ssklondike* ☜ *C$4* ☽ *Closed early Sept.–mid-May.*

Waterfront Walkway

PROMENADE | The walkway along the Yukon River passes by a few points of interest. Start along the river just east of the MacBride Museum entrance on Front Street. Traveling upstream (south), you'll see the old White Pass and Yukon Route Building on Main Street. The walk is a good way to get an overview of the old town site and just stretch your legs if you've been driving all day. ⊠ *Whitehorse.*

Whitehorse Fishway

DAM | **FAMILY** | Yukon Energy built the world's longest wooden fish ladder to facilitate the yearly chinook (king) salmon run around the Whitehorse Rapids hydroelectric dam. The salmon hold one of nature's great endurance records, the longest fish migration in the world—more than 2,000 miles from the Bering Sea to Whitehorse. There's a platform for viewing the ladder, and TV monitors display pictures from underwater cameras. Interesting interpretive exhibits, talks by local First Nations elders, and labeled tanks of freshwater fish enhance the experience. The best time to visit is August, when hundreds of salmon use the ladder to bypass the dam. ⊠ *Nisutlin Dr., Whitehorse* ☎ *867/633–5965* ☝ *C\$3 suggested donation.*

Yukon Beringia Interpretive Centre

HISTORY MUSEUM | The story of the Yukon during the last ice age comes alive at this center near the Whitehorse Airport. Beringia is the name given to the large subcontinental landmasses of eastern Siberia and Interior Alaska and the Yukon, which stayed ice-free and were linked by the Bering Land Bridge during the latest ice age. The area that is now Whitehorse wasn't actually part of this—it was glaciated—but lands farther north, among them what is present-day Dawson City, were in the thick of it, and miners are still turning up mammoth bones. Large dioramas depict the lives of animals in Ice Age Beringia, and there are skeleton replicas. A 26,000-year-old horsehide reveals that horses weren't as big back then as they are now. ⊠ *Mile 886, Alaska Hwy., Whitehorse* ☎ *867/667–8855* ⊕ *www.beringia.com* ☝ *C\$6* ⊗ *Closed weekdays mid-Sept.–early May.*

Yukon Permanent Art Collection

ART MUSEUM | The lobby of the Government of Yukon Main Administration Building displays selections from the Yukon Permanent Art Collection, featuring traditional and contemporary works by Yukon artists. The space also includes a 24-panel mural by artist David MacLagan depicting the historical evolution of the Yukon. In addition to the collection on the premises, the brochure *Art Adventures on Yukon Time,* available at visitor centers throughout the Yukon, guides you to artists' studios as well as galleries, festivals, and public art locations. ⊠ *2071 2nd Ave., Whitehorse* ☎ *867/667–5811* ☝ *Free* ⊗ *Closed weekends.*

Yukon Transportation Museum

OTHER MUSEUM | This museum takes a fascinating look at the planes, trains, trucks, and snowmachines that opened up the north. Even if big machines don't interest you, this is a cool place to learn about the innovations and adaptations that transport in the north has inspired. ⊠ *30 Electra Crescent, Whitehorse* ☎ *867/668–4792* ⊕ *www.goytm.ca* ☝ *C\$10* ⊗ *Closed Mon., Tues., and mid-Sept.–mid-May except by appointment.*

Yukon Wildlife Preserve

NATURE PRESERVE | The preserve provides a fail-safe way to photograph sometimes hard-to-spot animals in a natural setting. Animals roaming freely here include moose, elk, caribou, mountain goats, musk oxen, bison, mule deer, and Dall and Stone sheep. Bus tours take place throughout the day, and self-guided walking maps are available. ⊠ *Mile 5, Takhini Hot Springs Rd., Takhini Hot Springs* ☎ *867/456–7300* ⊕ *www.yukonwildlife.ca* ☝ *C\$16 self-guided tour, C\$24 bus tour.*

Activities

Yukon Quest International Sled Dog Race
LOCAL SPORTS | Because the terrain is rougher and there are fewer checkpoints, most dog mushers think this 1,000-mile race between Whitehorse and Fairbanks provides more intense competition than the higher-profile Iditarod. The Yukon Quest takes place in February; the starting line alternates yearly between the two cities. Twenty to 30 mushers participate, with most finishing in 9 to 14 days. ✉ *Whitehorse* ☎ *867/668–4711* 🌐 *www.yukonquest.com.*

Restaurants

The Chocolate Claim
$$ | **CAFÉ** | Choose from fresh-baked breads and pastries, homemade soups and sandwiches, and salads and quiches at this charming café and deli. Locals love the chocolate cake, a moist, rich delight. **Known for:** chocolate indulgences; outdoor seating; gluten-free options. [$] *Average main: C$15* ✉ *305 Strickland St., Whitehorse* ☎ *867/667–2202* 🌐 *www.theclaim.ca* 🕒 *Closed Sun.*

★ **Klondike Rib & Salmon**
$$$$ | **AMERICAN** | Wild-game dishes such as elk and bison are the Klondike's specialty, but it's also known for halibut, salmon, arctic char, and killer ribs. The restaurant meets vegetarians' needs with pasta and other meatless dishes. **Known for:** oldest operating building in Whitehorse; the best wild game in town; long waits. [$] *Average main: C$33* ✉ *2116 2nd Ave., Whitehorse* ☎ *867/667–7554* 🌐 *www.klondikerib.com* 🕒 *Closed mid-Sept.–mid-May.*

★ **Midnight Sun Coffee Roasters**
$ | **CAFÉ** | One of the hippest coffee shops you'll ever set foot in—but completely devoid of snobbery—shares space with a bicycle shop, cleverly named Icycle Sport. The service is superfriendly, and the coffee is, quite simply, stellar, as are the baked goods. **Known for:** fantastic flower boxes in summer; eclectic, family-run energy; small-batch coffee. [$] *Average main: C$6* ✉ *21 Waterfront Pl., Whitehorse* ☎ *888/633–4563, 867/633–4563* 🌐 *www.yukoncoffee.com* 🕒 *Closed weekends.*

Hotels

Coast High Country Inn
$$$ | **B&B/INN** | At this downtown hotel you'll find modern, comfortably appointed standard rooms and premium ones with Jacuzzis and kitchenettes. **Pros:** on-site dining at The Deck; free airport shuttle; central location. **Cons:** standard rooms are minimally decorated; some rooms lack air-conditioning; some rooms are very small. [$] *Rooms from: C$220* ✉ *4051 4th Ave., Whitehorse* ☎ *867/667–4471, 800/554–4471* 🌐 *www.coasthotels.com/coast-high-country-inn* 🛏 *82 rooms* 🍴 *No Meals.*

Edgewater Hotel
$$$ | **HOTEL** | Thanks to its small size, comfy bedding, sophisticated style, and emphasis on First Nations and Yukon art, the Edgewater has the ambience of a boutique hotel. **Pros:** free Wi-Fi; rich history; one block from the Yukon River. **Cons:** some noise from Main Street; no breakfast; adjacent parking is limited. [$] *Rooms from: C$225* ✉ *101 Main St., Whitehorse* ☎ *867/667–2572* 🌐 *www.edgewaterhotelwhitehorse.com* 🛏 *33 rooms* 🍴 *No Meals.*

Sternwheeler Hotel & Conference Centre
$$ | **HOTEL** | Rooms are standard issue but clean (suites have a little more personality) at this full-service downtown property, the largest hotel in the Yukon. **Pros:** pet-friendly; laundry facilities; great restaurant and lounge. **Cons:** breakfast available only at an extra charge; can get noisy; dated interiors. [$] *Rooms from: C$199* ✉ *201 Wood St., Whitehorse* ☎ *867/393–9700* 🌐 *www.sternwheelerhotel.ca* 🍴 *No Meals* 🛏 *181 rooms.*

Chapter 8

THE BUSH

8

Updated by
Dawnell Smith

⊙ Sights   🍴 Restaurants   🛏 Hotels   🛍 Shopping   🍸 Nightlife
★★★☆☆   ★★☆☆☆   ★★☆☆☆   ★☆☆☆☆   ★☆☆☆☆

WELCOME TO THE BUSH

TOP REASONS TO GO

★ **Alaska Native cultures:** Alaska's Indigenous communities continue to practice traditional ways of life while adapting to environmental and societal changes. In the Bush, you can meet and learn about Alaska Native people, traditions, and experiences.

★ **Bears:** The Alaska Peninsula has the world's largest concentrations of brown bears, which congregate in salmon streams every summer.

★ **Fishing:** You could see (and catch!) 50-pound salmon or 8-pound trout, and even try sheefish to learn why some folks prefer it to halibut.

★ **The land of the midnight sun:** In the summer, the sun stays above the horizon 24 hours a day north of the Arctic Circle; in Utqiaġvik, the sun doesn't set at all from mid-May to August.

★ **Nature adventures:** Need some space? Want to hike, climb, paddle, and fish? The Alaska Bush includes landscapes and parklands with little or no roads, trails, or facilities, but plenty to do, see, and experience.

1 **Bethel.**

2 **Yukon Delta National Wildlife Refuge.**

3 **Wood-Tikchik State Park.**

4 **Katmai National Park and Preserve.**

5 **Aniakchak National Monument and Preserve.**

6 **Becharof and Alaska Peninsula National Wildlife Refuges.**

7 **Aleutian Islands.**

8 **Unalaska/Dutch Harbor.**

9 **Pribilof Islands.**

10 **Nome.**

11 **Bering Land Bridge National Preserve.**

12 **Kotzebue.**

13 **Kobuk Valley National Park.**

14 **Noatak National Preserve.**

15 **Gates of the Arctic National Park and Preserve.**

16 **Utqiaġvik.**

17 **Prudhoe Bay.**

18 **Arctic National Wildlife Refuge.**

0		100 mi
0		100 km

St. Paul Island

PRIBILOF **9**
ISLANDS
Saint George Island

7 ISLANDS
ALEUTIAN
Unalaska/Dutch Harbor○ **8**

When Alaskans talk about going to the Bush, they usually mean anywhere off the grid, which pretty much includes most of Alaska. It also refers to those places beyond the state's major cities, towns, highways, and railroad corridors, stretching from the Kodiak Archipelago, Alaska Peninsula, and Aleutian Islands in the south to the Yukon-Kuskokwim Delta, the Seward Peninsula, and the Arctic to the north.

For the sake of this guide, the Bush refers to the remote areas that extend over two-thirds of Alaska, where caribou outnumber people and where the summer sun really does shine after midnight for months on end.

If you visit the Arctic in the summer, you'll see an array of bright wildflowers growing from a sponge of rich green tundra dotted with pools of melting snow. Willow trees barely an inch tall might be 100 years old, while spindly bushes grow massive (and delicious) berries. In the ice-and-snow-filled winter, a painter's-blue twilight rises at midday, and the nighttime moon can be bright enough to read by; on a clear night, you will sense the depth of sky and beyond. On the northern edge, the sun does not rise for months. In spring and fall, plants and animals prepare for growth or slumber, with trees, brush, and grasses greening up as snow melts or turning briefly brilliant with autumn colors before winter comes.

The Brooks Range, which stretches east–west across Alaska from the Chukchi Sea to the Canadian border, divides the Arctic from the rest of the state. This mountain superchain includes several mountain systems, from the pale, softly rounded limestone mountains in the east to the towering granite spires of the Arrigetch Peaks at its heart. Gates of the Arctic National Park and Noatak National Preserve include large portions of the middle and western Brooks Range while the Arctic National Wildlife Refuge contains its eastern reach.

North of the Brooks Range, a great apron of land called the North Slope tilts gently toward the Beaufort Sea and the Arctic Ocean. Here, frozen tundra brightens each summer with yellow Arctic poppies, bright red bearberry, and dozens of other wildflower species that pepper the landscape. Below the surface, the frozen ground known as permafrost has shifted and shaped this land for centuries, fragmenting it into giant polygons that make a fascinating pattern when viewed from the sky.

The thawing of this permafrost, caused by the climate crisis, is now impacting the people and animals in the region. Dozens of villages must try to find resources to move and safeguard entire communities in response to climate impacts like coastal erosion, rising sea levels, and severe storms. Thawing permafrost also disrupts animal migrations, alters animal habitats, and leads to a cascade of effects that threaten the Arctic and beyond. Worst yet, thawing permafrost releases gases previously held in the ground into the atmosphere, creating a destructive feedback loop.

These climate realities and continued fossil fuel extraction have in many ways defined Alaska's political and economic legacy for the past half century. In the Arctic, where land meets sea, the largest oil strike in the United States was found under Prudhoe Bay in 1968. At its peak, more than 2 million barrels a day of North Slope crude flowed from Prudhoe Bay and its neighboring basins to Valdez in Prince William Sound via the 800-mile Trans-Alaska Pipeline System. Today the flow has diminished and continues to decrease, the subject of political, social, and economic controversy. The pipeline was engineered to require a certain flow of oil to work properly, and maintaining that flow has become an argument for pushing for more fossil fuel extraction. Meanwhile, decades of policy decisions have driven economic dependency on oil, even in light of the climate issues that threaten Alaska communities, particularly in the Arctic.

The travel industry makes up another important sector in Bush Alaska's economy. Many village outfitters take travelers into remote places almost impossible to safely access without air taxis, water taxis, long miles on the ground or river systems, and experienced guides.

Living anywhere in Alaska means living where human and animal communities intermingle and navigating various waterways and landscapes. Many Alaskans who live in cities and larger towns spend a lot of time in the Bush, where they fish, hike, paddle, hunt, camp, and more. Others travel regularly to Bush Alaska as part of their work. Whether in a big city, a remote village, on a hunt, or at a fish camp, Alaska Native people have a deep relationship with the land that goes back thousands of years. Settlers who have made Bush Alaska their home, whether recently or generations ago, have a deep affection for the land, too. Though some talk about living independently or off-the-grid, remote living requires community, even a small or distant one. For many folks, a store-bought hamburger will never taste as good as fresh moose meat, and whatever they're missing by not having good Internet connectivity can't possibly be as interesting as the view out their window.

After experiencing the Bush, most people understand that the term "rural" really only applies to places in the Lower 48, where a nearby urban hub is easily accessible by car. If a village store in the Bush runs out of something, it might not be in stock again until the next delivery by boat or plane, and that can take anywhere from a week to a month, or maybe not even until the ice thaws. Those who live in Bush Alaska know transportation schedules like the backs of their hands, and they know that if they don't show up at the store within hours of the supply boat or plane's arrival, the odds of getting any fresh milk or vegetables can be zero.

Every region of Bush Alaska has its own climate, culture, communities, landscapes, and types of activities. Katmai National Park is a prime location for seeing brown bears, birds, and marine life. The Aleutian and Pribilof Islands are windswept regions teaming with bird and marine life. The Arctic promises landscapes without roads or trails, and plenty of paddling, hiking, and sightseeing that

8

The Bush

astounds with its vastness and life big and small. Wherever you go, you'll experience awe and wonder at the beauty and rawness of these places that have sustained animals and human communities for thousands and thousands of years.

MAJOR REGIONS

The Southwest. The Southwest region, below the Arctic Circle, encompasses some of Alaska's most remote, inaccessible, and rugged land and seascapes. Reaching from the Kodiak Archipelago to the Yukon-Kuskokwim Delta, this area nourishes a dense brown bear population and some of the world's greatest salmon runs. Given all this richness, it's no surprise to learn that Southwest Alaska has some of Alaska's premier park lands and refuges, from Katmai National Park and Wood-Tikchik State Park to Aniakchak National Monument and Preserve and Becharof and Alaska Peninsula National Wildlife Refuges. Here, too, are dozens of Alaska Native villages where people have lived in relationship with the land for millennia. Many visitors begin their trip to this region in Bethel, an important outpost of the Yukon-Kuskokwim Delta (YK Delta to locals), surrounded by the Yukon Delta National Wildlife Refuge.

Aleutian Islands and Pribilof Islands. Considered part of Southwest, the Aleutians are closer to Japan than to San Francisco. Unalaska, along with its famed Dutch Harbor, is the most populated destination in the Aleutian Islands, partially due to it being the setting of the Discovery Channel show *The Deadliest Catch*; it's also one of the busiest fishing ports in the world. The Pribilof Islands are the seasonal home of hundreds of thousands of seals and breeding birds, some seen nowhere else in North America.

The Northwest and the Arctic. This mostly roadless region, known for its dark, sunless winters and bright, midnight sun summers, is a place where Indigenous people have lived for thousands of years and where many continue to hunt, fish, and gather for most of their food. The region also sustains some of the world's largest caribou herds and populations of migrating birds. Other wildlife includes whales and polar bears, along with an array of other mammals, birds, fish, insects, and flora. The quest for gold and oil tells some of the story of the region's recent history in towns like Nome and Utqiaġvik. For most visitors, though, the source of awe remains in the area's remote communities and park lands, such as Bering Land Bridge National Preserve, Kobuk Valley National Park, Noatak National Preserve, Gates of the Arctic National Park, and the Arctic National Wildlife Refuge.

Planning

When to Go

Most people visit Bush Alaska in June, July, or August, when the weather is mildest (though it can be cool, wet, windy, and stormy) and daylight hours are longest. Because summer is so short, though, things happen fast, and seasonal activities may feel crammed into short time periods.

May and August are best for birding. The peak wildflower season is usually fleeting, particularly in the Arctic, when most flowers may not blossom until mid-June and then go to seed by late July.

Salmon runs vary from region to region, so it's best to do your homework before choosing dates. For the most part though, you're looking at July and sometimes August, when the tundra starts turning from its summer hues to autumnal colors. The best times for bear viewing coincide with salmon runs. Note that fishing, bear viewing, hunting, and other explorations often require licenses and permits that must be secured ahead of time, sometimes many months in advance. Few things about Alaska, especially during the summer season, can be arranged on the fly. Plan ahead for best results.

FESTIVALS

Remote communities often hold annual or special events all year, so it's smart to check city websites to see what's going on. Some annual festivals and events could well sway your decision about when to visit.

Cama-i Dance Festival

In the spring, the Bethel Council on the Arts hosts a regional celebration called the Cama-i Dance Festival (in Yup'ik, *cama-i* means "hello"). This three-day festival takes place in the local high school's gym in late March or the first half of April. Expect dancing, singing, art and crafts, and a community potluck for sharing food and stories. Cama-i brings people together from the Yukon-Kuskokwim Delta, along with dance groups and visitors from across Alaska and the world. ⊠ *Bethel High School, 1 Ron Edwards Memorial Dr., Bethel* ⊕ *www. camai.org.*

Heart of the Aleutians Festival

The city of Unalaska holds the Heart of the Aleutians Festival every August. A beloved local tradition, this free, two-day festival brings together residents of all ages to peruse art and crafts, listen to local music, eat specialty foods, participate in fun runs, and much more during a celebration of summer, friends, family, and community. ⊠ *Kelty Field, Unalaska* ☎ *907/581–1297* ⊕ *www. ci.unalaska.ak.us/parksrec/page/ heart-aleutians-festival.*

Iditarod Trail Sled Dog Race

Billed as "The Last Great Race," the Iditarod pulls in spectators and mushers from around the world to participate as racers, volunteers, and fans in this massive feat of endurance for mushers and their dogs. Many visitors watch the dog teams take off from the ceremonial start in Anchorage and then travel to the finish line in Nome to celebrate as teams come in. The race starts on the first weekend of March and covers about 1,049 snowy, icy, backcountry miles from its official start in Willow, 90 miles north of Anchorage, to Nome. ☎ *907/376–5155* ⊕ *www.iditarod.com.*

Kuskokwim 300 Sled Dog Race

Every January, the Kuskokwim 300 Sled Dog Race—"K300" to locals—brings mushers and fans to Bethel, where the 300-mile race both starts and ends. The best known of the middle-distance dog-sled races, the K300 course commemorates one of the earliest mail routes used in the Bush. The $150,000 or more purse comes as a welcome reward after negotiating the notoriously harsh and difficult weather and trail conditions. Smaller, shorter races happen later in the winter in Bethel as well. ⊠ *Downtown, Bethel* ☎ *907/545–3300* ⊕ *www.k300.org.*

Getting Here and Around

AIR

Alaska Airlines flies to most major communities in Alaska. Pen Air, Ravn Alaska, Wright Air Service, and Grant Aviation serve the smaller communities on the Alaskan Peninsula, the Aleutian and Pribilof Islands, and parts of the Arctic, Interior, and the Northwest.

Bush-based carriers such as Bering Air also offer flightseeing tours and, weather and politics permitting, specially arranged charter flights to the Provideniya Airport in Russia's Chukotka Region, on the Siberian coast across the Bering Strait. Currently, it is mandatory for Americans to obtain a visa, migration card, and permission to go to Russia in advance of travel—this can take time, as in months, so plan ahead. Applications for visas are available up to 90 days before travel. The visa fee starts at $160, not including a range of other administrative and processing fees. The Consulate General of the Russian Federation recommends working through a Russia-sponsored travel agent to secure a travel visa.

Information about certified air-taxi operations in Alaska is available from the Federal Aviation Administration. Individual parks and Alaska Public Lands Information Centers can also supply lists of reputable air-taxi services. Make your reservations in advance, and always plan for the unexpected; weather often delays a scheduled drop-off or pickup for days. If you are using adventure operators for part of your trip, you can ask for a list of air-taxi options they recommend.

AIR CONTACTS Alaska Airlines.
☎ 800/252–7522 reservations ⊕ www. alaskaair.com.**Bering Air.** ☎ 907/443–5464 Nome reservations, 800/478–5422 administration, 907/443–8988 Russian desk, 442–3943 Kotzebue reservations ⊕ www.beringair.com.**Federal Aviation Administration.** ☎ 907/271–5438 ⊕ www. faa.gov/airports/alaskan.**Grant Aviation.** ☎ 888/359–4726 general reservations, 907/543–2000 Bethel and Emmonak areas ⊕ www.flygrant.com.**Pen Air.** ☎ 907/771–2640, 800/448–4226, 907/771–2599 charter flight reservations ⊕ www.penair.com.**Ravn Alaska.** ☎ 907/266-8394 in Alaska, 800/866–8394 outside Alaska ⊕ www.flyravn.com. **Wright Air Service.** ☎ 907/474–0502 general reservations, 907/474–0542 charter flight reservations ⊕ www.wrightairservice.com.

BOAT
The Alaska Marine Highway, the state's amazing ferry system, makes one trip a month between Kodiak and Dutch Harbor/Unalaska in the Aleutians from April through October. It's not for the hurried traveler. Expect four to five days of travel each way and minimal on-boat luxuries. With many stops in far-flung towns, the ferry is a truly memorable way to get a full taste of Alaska's massive geography, unparalleled natural scenery, and medley of local cultures. Sailings can also take visitors all along Alaska's southern coast.

BOAT CONTACTS Alaska Marine Highway.
☎ 800/642–0066 from outside Alaska, 907/465–3941 ⊕ www.dot.state.ak.us/amhs.

CAR
The unpaved Dalton Highway connects with the state's paved highway system and traverses the Arctic, but it only leads to the oil fields of Prudhoe Bay. For those looking to tackle the journey north by road, prepare for flat tires, cracked windshields from flying debris, and a slow-going drive. Check with your rental-car company to confirm you are permitted to take the vehicle on the Dalton Highway. If so, consider investing in additional auto insurance as well as a basic roadside repair kit and a satellite phone. Pack extra food, gear, gas, and supplies in case of an accident or breakdown.

Health and Safety

When traveling in the Bush, you should never head out without a decent first-aid kit and navigation tools as you can be a very long way from help in case of an emergency. One health concern is hypothermia. Always carry more layers than you anticipate needing. Watch out for your travel mates, and pay attention to signs of dehydration and exhaustion. Seeing or finding yourself close to animals like moose, caribou, bears, and wolves is common, if not expected. Stay aware, keep your distance, and remember that these animals are not domesticated. They are often big, powerful, and unpredictable. However, a much more consistent nuisance than Alaska's mammals and birds are Alaska's insects—until you've experienced it, it's hard to understand just how thick the mosquitoes and other things that bite can get in summer. Bring plenty of DEET.

Money

Many small villages don't have bank offices, so visitors should bring cash. Most places within the larger Bush communities accept major credit cards, but don't take that for granted. Always be sure to confirm in advance what sort of payment tour companies, hotels, and restaurants accept. Hub communities that do have bank services are Nome, Bethel, Kotzebue, Barrow, and Unalaska.

Tours

Package tours are the most common way of traveling to Bush communities, where making your flight connections and having a room to sleep in at the end of the line are no small feats. During peak season (late May through Labor Day), planes, state ferries, hotels, and lodges are often crowded with travelers on organized tours. Creating a trip on your own can sometimes mean making reservations a year in advance for the really popular destinations. But the Bush is also large enough that there's always somewhere to go, and wherever you end up, it will amaze you.

The type of tour you choose will determine how you get there. In most cases this will be by air, since flying is the only way to access the vast majority of Bush communities. By flying to and from your destination, you can also enjoy an aerial perspective of the Arctic en route. Tours to Arctic towns and villages are usually short—one, two, or three days—so it's easy to combine them with visits to other regions. Road tours up the Dalton Highway are not common, but also not impossible. Northern Alaska Tour Company and Arctic Outfitters offer overland tours on the Dalton Highway, with the latter even renting road-ready vehicles for self-guided land tours. Driving the Dalton Highway has risks since the road is unpaved, mostly unmaintained, and

completely without modern roadside convenience stores and gas stations. Do research first and be prepared for a long, bumpy, and potentially hazardous ride (flat tires and cracked windshields are the norm). Before departing in a rented vehicle, check with your rental-car company about any provisions, exclusions, and extra insurance you might need to make the drive.

The Bush is home to many Alaska Native communities with people whose families have lived in these areas for thousands of years. Often, regional and local village Native corporations run tours, hotels, and attractions, and local people sell art and crafts made from materials such as bone, fur, hide, and baleen. Spending time with local guides and operators can be invaluable to understanding their way of life and the local people's connection to the surrounding lands and waters.

Northern Alaska Tour Company conducts highly regarded ecotours to the Arctic Circle, the Brooks Range, and Prudhoe Bay that emphasize natural and cultural history, wildlife, and geology. Groups are limited to 25 people on Arctic day tours and 10 people on Prudhoe Bay overnight trips. Some tours are completely ground-based; others include a mix of ground and air travel. Fairbanks-based Arctic Treks leads small groups on hiking, rafting, and backpacking adventures in places like the Arctic National Wildlife Refuge, Gates of the Arctic National Park, Noatak National Preserve, Kobuk Valley National Park, Cape Krusenstern National Monument, and the Bering Land Bridge National Preserve.

Arctic Outfitters
This company specializes in providing car rentals equipped for year-round use on the Dalton Highway. Based out of Fairbanks, Arctic Outfitters offers gravel road–ready automobiles, accommodation arrangements, and travel packages on and around the Dalton Highway.
✉ *3820 University Ave. S, Fairbanks*

Flying Through the Bush

Roads in the Bush are few and far between, so airplanes—from jetliners to helicopters to small bush planes—connect people to communities and the lands around them. Alaska has six times more pilots and 16 times more planes per capita than anywhere else in the country. Flying is truly a way of life here. Alaska's legendary pilots have earned something of a Wild West reputation for putting in thousands of flights miles through difficult terrain and predictably unpredictable and nasty weather. This comes with risk, of course. America's favorite humorist, Will Rogers, died in a crash with famed aviator Wiley Post in 1935. And a popular podcast, *Missing in Alaska*, centers on the disappearance of a small plane in 1972 with two congressmen on board, House Majority Leader Hale Boggs from Louisiana and House Member Nick Begich from Alaska.

☎ *907/474–3530* ⊕ *www.arctic-outfitters. com* ✈ *From $199 a day.*

Arctic Treks

Based in Fairbanks, this outfit offers hiking, boating, and base-camp trips of 7 to 12 days, including hiking in the Arrigetch Peaks, fall caribou-viewing in Gates of the Arctic, and hiking and camping trips that go to Gates of the Arctic and Kobuk Valley National Parks. The company offers other trips in the western Arctic and the Arctic National Wildlife Refuge, along with custom trips for groups of three to nine people. ⊠ *Fairbanks* ☎ *907/455–6502* ⊕ *www.arctictreksadventures.com* ✈ *From $4700.*

Explore Tours

This company helps visitors find tour packages from outfitters and vendors across the state. Options range from day trips to longer adventures and cover every region in Alaska, including the Bush. ☎ *800/523–7405* ⊕ *www.explore-tours.com* ✈ *From $99.*

Northern Alaska Tour Company

This company arranges shorter trips out of Fairbanks, including flightseeing excursions above the Arctic Circle and an evening flight tour that offers views of the Brooks Range before stopping at Anaktuvuk Pass, the only village in Gates of the Arctic National Park. From there, visitors can stage and begin longer backpacking or paddle trips. ⊠ *Fairbanks* ☎ *907/474–8600, 800/474–1986* ⊕ *www. northernalaska.com* ✈ *From $179.*

Tundra Tours

Operating out of the Top of the World Hotel in Utqiaġvik, Tundra Tours offers half-day excursions that give guests a chance to see wildlife, walk on the tundra, dip a toe in the Arctic Ocean, and learn about Utqiaġvik's cultural and historical sites. ⊠ *Top of the World Hotel, 3060 Eben Hopson St., Barrow* ☎ *907/852–3900* ⊕ *www.tundratoursinc. com* ✈ *From $162 per person.*

Wilderness Birding Adventures

This Homer-based outfitter takes small groups into the Alaska backcountry to watch birds and wildlife. These eco-adventures last from a few days to a few weeks and cover a wide range of Alaska from the Alaska National Wildlife Refuge and areas outside Utqiaġvik and Nome to the Pribilof Islands. They also do private trips that combine birding, hiking, and river-rafting. ⊠ *Homer* ☎ *907/299–3937* ⊕ *www.wildernessbirding.com* ✈ *From $1475.*

Restaurants

Dining options are few when traveling around Alaska's Bush. Smaller communities may have one or two eateries, if any at all. On the bright side, you won't need to worry about reservations. If they're open, they'll let you in, and you'll likely be surprised at the variety of foods available. In addition to Alaska seafood, game, and locally grown vegetables, Mexican and Asian fare are standard, even in the state's remotest corners. Most Bush restaurants feature two or three different cuisines, and many deliver. All food prices, including those at small grocery stores, reflect the high transportation costs, so be prepared to pay more than you would back home or even in Anchorage. Since many of these Bush restaurants will shut down for periods of time, particularly during the shoulder seasons, it never hurts to ask a local or call the eatery to confirm it's open before heading over.

Hotels

Lodging choices in the Bush are limited, but varied. Some communities have a single modern hotel, while the smallest may have none. Others have a mix of hotels, lodges, and bed-and-breakfasts. Some operators run lodges and camps remote from any villages, often offering all-inclusive pricing. As a rule, rooms have simple furnishings and are often not updated, though some offer full service food and bar service. Rooms go fast during the summer season, so book as far ahead as possible. And it never hurts to carry a tent as backup.

Restaurant and hotel reviews have been shortened. For full information, visit Fodors.com. Restaurant prices are the average cost of a main course at dinner, or if dinner is not served, at lunch. Hotel prices are the lowest cost of a standard double room in high season.

What It Costs			
$	$$	$$$	$$$$
RESTAURANTS			
under $14	$14–$22	$23–$30	over $30
HOTELS			
under $100	$100–$200	$201–$300	over $300

Visitor Information

CONTACTS Alaska Department of Fish and Game. ✉ *1255 W. 8th St., Juneau* ☎ *907/267–2257 hunting/wildlife information (statewide), 907/459–7346 sportfishing seasons/regulations (interior contact), 907/465–2376 licenses/permits (statewide)* ⊕ *www.adfg.alaska.gov.* **Alaska Public Lands Information Centers.** ✉ *605 W. 4th Ave., Suite 105, Anchorage* ☎ *907/644–3680 Anchorage office, 459–3730 Fairbanks office, 228–6220 Ketchikan office, 883–5667 Tok office* ⊕ *www.alaskacenters.gov.* **Alaska State Parks Information.** ✉ *550 W. 7th Ave., Suite 1260, Anchorage* ☎ *907/269–8400 Anchorage, 451–2705 Fairbanks* ⊕ *www. dnr.alaska.gov/parks.* **U.S. Fish and Wildlife Service Alaska Region.** ✉ *1011 E. Tudor Rd., Anchorage* ☎ *907/786–3309* ⊕ *www. fws.gov/alaska.*

Bethel

400 miles west of Anchorage.

About 6,000 people live in Bethel, the largest town in the region and a vital hub for the Yukon-Kuskokwim Delta. The town acts as a jumping-off point and trading center for over 50 villages in this western Alaska area that's roughly the size of Oregon.

The Yu'pik residents of a village that was later absorbed into Bethel were called the Mamterillermiut, meaning "Smokehouse People." The Yu'pik have lived in

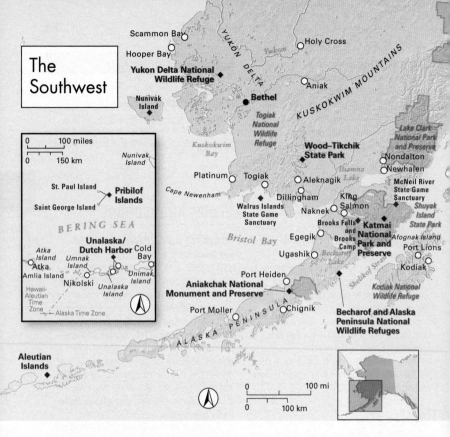

and moved through the area for thousands of years and make up the majority of Bethel's population today. In the late 19th century, the Alaska Commercial Company established a trading post in the town, and Moravian missionaries later moved it to the west side of the Kuskokwim River.

The surrounding lowland tundra shimmers in rich greens in summer and turns fiery shades of red, orange, and yellow in autumn, when plants burst with blueberries, cranberries, blackberries, and salmonberries. Salmon, arctic grayling, and Dolly Varden (a species of seagoing trout) fill the area's many lakes, ponds, and streams, providing excellent fishing. Pretty much everyone in Bethel smokes, dries, and freezes fish. The wetlands are also nourishing breeding grounds

for more than 60 species of birds, from shrikes to warblers.

Bethel serves as the northernmost freshwater port for oceangoing vessels. It supports a radio station, TV station, newspaper, theater, a range of businesses, and two colleges, including a tribal college.

Residents love where they live and all the nourishment it provides. A sense of community pervades this small tundra town, and many locals will talk your ear off about everything that makes their city great. Consider coming in late March to witness this enthusiasm during the Cama-i celebration, a dance festival that draws people from throughout the region and the world.

GETTING HERE AND AROUND

To get to Bethel, take a flight on Alaska Airlines. Once you're there, the town itself is quite walkable, or you can grab one of the many taxis (Bethel is known for its high cabs-to-people ratio).

 Sights

Nunivak Island

ISLAND | Due west of Bethel and separated from the Yukon-Kuskokwim Delta by the Etolin Strait, Nunivak Island is part of the Yukon Delta National Wildlife Refuge. The terrain includes interior craters and deep lakes from the island's volcanic origins, plus over 40 rivers and a tundra that gives way to shorelines and lagoons. The island sustains a large herd of reindeer managed by residents of the only permanent settlement on the island, the Cup'ik village of Mekoryuk. There's also a transplanted herd of musk ox, along with vast seabird colonies, migratory birds, and an array of sea mammals. For information on the island and travel options, contact the U.S. Fish and Wildlife Service in Bethel. ☎ *907/543–3151* ⊕ *www.fws. gov/refuge/yukon_delta.*

Pinky's Park

CITY PARK | **FAMILY** | Named after Thomas "Pinky" Sekanoff, who walked across the Bering Strait to escape the Russian Revolution in the early 1900s, the 22-acre Pinky's Park remembers his life in Bethel and constant goodwill toward the kids in the community. Take a stroll on the park's nearly 2 miles of wooden boardwalks, decks, and trails. These structures are engineered to hold up to the often harsh climate while not damaging the tundra underneath. There's also a nice community garden, along with a playground and multiuse sports field that acts as a hub for all of Bethel's July 4 festivities. ⊠ *301 Akiachak Ave., Bethel* ☎ *907/543–2047* ⊕ *www.cityofbethel.org.*

Yupiit Piciryarait Cultural Center

INDIGENOUS SIGHT | **FAMILY** | The cultural center hosts a range of community and art events, including classes, movie screenings, summer camps, concerts, and summer Saturday markets. The center also has a library and a museum, founded in 1965 as the Bethel Museum, with more than 2,500 artifacts, photographs, and art pieces from the Athabascan, Cup'ik, and Yup'ik cultures, including masks, statues, and intricate carvings in ivory, baleen, and whalebone. The Kuskokwim Art Guild also runs a gift shop on the site. ⊠ *420 Chief Eddie Hoffman Hwy., Bethel* ☎ *907/543–4504* ⊕ *www.uaf.edu/bethel/cultural-center* ⊙ *Library closed Sun.; gift shop closed Sun. and Mon.*

 Restaurants

Baba Pizza and Subs

$$ | **PIZZA** | In the local debate over who makes the best pizza, Baba regularly lands on top. In addition, it offers satisfying and filling American food like calzones, burgers, sandwiches, salads, and milkshakes. **Known for:** signature sauce that locals love; affordable burgers and pizza; late-night hours. $ *Average main: $20* ⊠ *1725 State Hwy., Bethel* ☎ *543–3500* ⊕ *www.babapizzasubs.com* ⊙ *Closed Sun.*

Fili's Pizza

$$ | **PIZZA** | **FAMILY** | This pizza, burger, and sandwich eatery has tables and bar space for dining in, or you can order for pickup using online ordering. You can choose from a nice selection of beer and wine along with an ample menu of calzones, pizzas, burgers, pastas, sandwiches, and jumbo wings. **Known for:** chicken wings for groups of all sizes; beer and wine when dining in; famed Fili's Mistake pie. $ *Average main: $21* ⊠ *110 Osage St., Bethel* ☎ *907/543–7010, 543–7011* ⊕ *filispizza.com* ⊙ *Closed Mon. No lunch.*

Hawaiian BBQ

$$ | HAWAIIAN | This newer restaurant offers barbeque and Korean dishes, with plenty of pork and other meat options on the menu. Choices include Hawaiian favorites, lunch bowls, fusion specials, and rolls from morning to night, with breakfast offered all day. **Known for:** Hawaiian favorites like loco moco; SPAM musubi sandwiches; all-day hours. $ *Average main: $18* ✉ *431 Ridgecrest Dr., Bethel* ☎ *543–5551* ⊘ *Closed Tues.*

Red Basket

$$ | ASIAN | Located next to the Long House Hotel, Red Basket offers an incredibly diverse menu. Options range from Mongolian beef, *yakisoba*, fettuccine Alfredo, and king crab to pancakes, omelets, and club sandwiches. **Known for:** traditional breakfast choices; early and late-night hours; varied, Asian-inspired menu with something for everyone. $ *Average main: $15* ✉ *751 3rd Ave., Bethel* ☎ *543–7001* ⊘ *Closed Mon.*

Snack Shack

$$ | CHINESE | FAMILY | This longtime Chinese and American restaurant is known for its rice and noodle dishes. Look for udon and egg foo yong, along with fried food baskets, sandwiches, and family dinner specials like the burger packs, which include four burgers with fries and soda. **Known for:** healthy portions; family-friendly burger packs; reliable Chinese dishes. $ *Average main: $19* ✉ *520 3rd Ave., Bethel* ☎ *543–2218.*

Tundra Restaurant

$$ | CHINESE | A longstanding Bethel eatery, Tundra focuses on Chinese, Korean, and American food. Choose from a range of rice and noodles dishes or mix it up with bento boxes and lunch or dinner combos. **Known for:** reasonable prices; bento boxes and lunch specials; popular Chinese dishes. $ *Average main: $17* ✉ *473 Ridgecrest Dr., Bethel* ☎ *543–5005* ⊘ *Closed Mon.*

Hotels

Bentley's B&B

$$$ | B&B/INN | FAMILY | Hospitality is never in short supply at this two-story, riverfront B&B in downtown Bethel. **Pros:** great breakfast by gourmet chef owner; river views; Wi-Fi available. **Cons:** not all rooms have baths; alcohol not allowed; some rooms need updating. $ *Rooms from: $210* ✉ *624 1st St., Bethel* ☎ *907/543–3552* ✉ *bentleybnbmartin@gmail.com* ⤴ *26 rooms* �‖ *Free Breakfast.*

Delta Cottages

$$$ | HOUSE | FAMILY | Enjoy single, double, and family-priced lodging with private bathrooms in these small cottages of various sizes, all of which come with a kitchen, phone, Wi-Fi, and television. **Pros:** comfortable rooms; good for families; quiet and clean. **Cons:** basic decor that's sometimes dated; no-frills amenities; not on or right near the river. $ *Rooms from: $235* ✉ *124 Gunderson Court, Bethel* ☎ *907/543–2387* ⊕ *delta-cottages-llc. business.site* �‖ *No Meals* ⤴ *19 rooms.*

Long House Bethel Hotel

$$$ | HOTEL | Within a three-story building about a half mile from the Bethel Airport, the Long House offers amenities that include Wi-Fi, refrigerators, microwaves, and filtered water in every room. **Pros:** Wi-Fi and cable television in every room; private bathrooms with filtered water; good restaurant on-site. **Cons:** no elevator; rooms can get hot in the summer; noise travels. $ *Rooms from: $239* ✉ *751 3rd Ave., Bethel* ☎ *907/543–4612* ⊕ *www.longhousebethel.com* �‖ *No Meals* ⤴ *39 rooms.*

Midtown Cottages

$$$ | HOUSE | These single-unit private cottages are conveniently located close to everything you need, come furnished with dining and sitting areas, and even provide extras like snacks and drinks. **Pros:** good location with easy walk to restaurants; extras like tea and candies;

private and comfortable rooms. **Cons:** limited Wi-Fi; on the small side; basic decor. $ *Rooms from: $210* ✉ *720 3rd Ave., Bethel* ☎ *907/545–6399* ⊕ *www.bethelmidtowncottages.com* ¶ *No Meals* ⌁ *12 units.*

Old Mission House–Alaskan Bed and Breakfast

$$ | **B&B/INN** | This B&B offers five cozy rooms in a large house with lots of windows and great views of the Kuskokwim River and surrounding areas. **Pros:** charming and cozy; wonderful views; free long-distance calls to the rest of the U.S.. **Cons:** limited space for group activities; shared bathrooms; not great if you're looking for alone time. $ *Rooms from: $190* ✉ *150 Torgerson St., Bethel* ☎ *907/543–2898* ⊕ *www.oldmissionhouse.net* ¶ *Free Breakfast* ⌁ *5 rooms.*

Suite 881

$$ | **HOTEL** | All 11 units at Suite 881 offer kitchen and work spaces, private bath, washer and dryer, and Internet access. **Pros:** cable and Wi-Fi; fully stocked kitchen; convenient long-term stays. **Cons:** some rooms lack great views; Bethel connectivity means no streaming; decor is generic. $ *Rooms from: $199* ✉ *81 3rd Ave., Bethel* ☎ *907/543–3883* ⊕ *www.suite881.net* ¶ *No Meals* ⌁ *10 rooms.*

Yukon Delta National Wildlife Refuge

The seemingly boundless lands and waters of the Yukon Delta National Wildlife Refuge support millions of animals. Ducks and geese breed here every year, and tens of thousands of caribou roam the hills during the fall and winter. Water mammals big and small are prevalent in the adjacent Bering Sea, and fish abound in the waters and wetlands created by the delta of the Yukon and Kuskokwim Rivers.

Alcohol in the Bush

Many Bush communities have elected to prohibit alcohol sales and possession. In these "dry" villages and towns, enforcement is strict, and bootlegging is a felony. A few towns are exceptions. Bethel got its first liquor store in 2016 after 40 years without one, while Nome supports many bars and restaurants that serve alcohol. Be sure to check local laws before bringing any alcohol into Bush communities.

GETTING HERE AND AROUND

There are no roads from Bethel to the wildlife refuge. To get there, first fly to Bethel and then catch a small plane or boat charter to one of the Delta villages or to a drop-off point for hiking, boating, camping, fishing, and other activities. You can visit the refuge visitor center while in Bethel by driving two miles down Chief Eddie Hoffman State Highway, the town's only paved road, to the end.

ESSENTIALS

VISITOR INFORMATION Visitor Center. ✉ *807 Chief Eddie Hoffman Rd., Bethel* ☎ *907/543–3151* ⊕ *www.fws.gov/refuge/yukon_delta.*

◉ Sights

Yukon Delta National Wildlife Refuge

WILDLIFE REFUGE | At 20 million acres, this is the nation's second-largest wildlife refuge, only a little smaller than the Alaska National Wildlife Refuge. Nearly one-third of the refuge is made up of water in the form of lakes, sloughs, bogs, creeks, and rivers, including both forks of the Andreafsky River, one of Alaska's specially designated Wild and Scenic Rivers. Rainbow trout, arctic char, and grayling flourish in upland rivers and creeks; pike,

Nesting Grounds

A true paradise for birders, Yukon Delta National Wildlife Refuge nourishes the largest grouping of water birds in the world. In terms of sheer density of birds and species diversity, the Delta is the most important shorebird nesting area in the country. Millions of shorebirds breed and feed in the refuge while over a million ducks and half a million geese breed there every year. Loons, grebes, swans, and cranes all return to the refuge every spring to nest.

Nearly a third of North America's northern pintails can be found in the refuge, along with cackling Canadian geese. More than half the continent's population of black brant (Pacific brant geese) are born here. Birds from throughout North America and from every continent that borders the Pacific Ocean also migrate to the refuge every year, including jaegers and the rare bristle-thighed curlew.

sheefish, and burbot thrive in the lowland streams. These abundant waters are also spawning grounds for five species of Pacific salmon. Other animal inhabitants include black and grizzly bears, moose, beavers, mink, and Arctic foxes. Occasionally, wolves venture into the delta's flats from neighboring uplands. Given the abundance of fish and wildlife, it's not surprising that the delta holds special importance to surrounding residents. The Yup'ik and Cup'ik people have lived here for thousands of years, and continue to hunt and gather food here. Athabaskan people have also inhabited these lands. Visitor facilities are minimal in the refuge, and access is only by boat or aircraft. Refuge staff can provide tips on recreational opportunities and recommend guides and outfitters who operate in the refuge. ☎ 907/543–3151 refuge headquarters, 907/543–1018 visitor center ⊕ www.fws. gov/refuge/yukon_delta.

🏃 Activities

Opportunities for seeing animals of all kinds abound in the Yukon Delta refuge. With so many lakes, ponds, streams, and wetlands, bird-watching is a given.

The refuge is also a great place for sportfishing, especially for rainbow trout, salmon, char, pike, grayling, and sheefish. Flat-water paddlers will never run out of water, although camping can be a bit marshy and DEET-dependent. Or try hiking and river floating in the uplands of the Andreafsky Wilderness area. As is the case with visiting all parklands in Alaska, you will be a long way from help when venturing here. Plan ahead, prepare for all conditions, and know what you're doing.

Float Alaska

FISHING | Travelers looking for the fishing journey of a lifetime can rent rafts and camping gear from this outfitter. You can count on Float to offer guidance on planning and preparing for trips on the remote rivers of the Yukon Delta National Wildlife Refuge, and to provide all the rental gear and logistical support you might need, from tents and tackle to arranging transportation. Actually catching the trout and salmon is up to you, though. ⊠ 198 H-Marker Rd., Bethel ☎ 208/602–1200 🚣 Raft, tent, and kitchen unit rental, from $150 per day.

★ Kuskokwim Wilderness Adventures

BOATING | This charter outfit operates four powerboats on the lower and upper Kuskokwim River and its tributaries. Traveling by boat can prove fast and affordable, with six people per boat and no luggage restrictions. All drivers are Coast Guard licensed and very knowledgeable of local waterways and conditions. ☒ *Bethel* ☎ *907/545–4092* ⊕ *www.kuskocharter. com* ☒ *From $175 per hour, 2 hour minimum.*

Papa Bear Adventures

ADVENTURE TOURS | This company can help gear you up for trips on the Yukon-Kuskokwim Delta and into the Togiak and Yukon Delta National Wildlife Refuges. They specialize in handling logistics and gear rentals for DIY fishing and rafting trips, and can customize adventures accordingly. They also run the Lakeside Lodge to cater to folks the nights before and after their trips. ☒ *198 H-Marker Lake Winter Rd., Bethel* ☎ *907/545–1155* ⊕ *www.pbadventures.com* ☒ *From $100 for an inflatable boat.*

Wood-Tikchik State Park

150 miles southeast of Bethel, 300 miles southwest of Anchorage.

The size of Delaware and Alaska's largest state park, 1.6-million-acre Wood-Tikchik State Park is an angler's dream come true. Five species of salmon as well as rainbow trout abound in the park's waters, and people come from around the world to fish here. South of Wood-Tikchik in the Bering Sea is the Walrus Islands State Game Sanctuary, a group of islands known for its—you guessed it—walruses. Make sure you get the appropriate access permits and fishing licenses before hopping in the plane or kayak.

GETTING HERE AND AROUND

The only way into Wood-Tikchik State Park is by air taxi or boat. The entire park is open to private aircraft landings. In the summer months it's not uncommon to see kayakers navigating their way through the river systems, their point of origin in the town of Dillingham or farther away via the waters of Bristol Bay. Kayaking the river system is suggested only for experienced kayakers who have very good navigational skills, as it is quite easy to get lost in the labyrinth of waterways. As always, prepare for mosquitoes.

ESSENTIALS

VISITOR INFORMATION Walrus Islands State Game Sanctuary. ☎ *907/267–2189* ⊕ *www.adfg.alaska.gov/index.cfm?adfg=walrusislands.main.***Wood-Tikchik State Park.** ☎ *907/842–2641 Dillingham Parks Office, Alekangik Ranger Station, 907/269–8700 Dept. of Natural Resources, Parks, & Outdoor Recreation* ⊕ *dnr. alaska.gov/parks/aspunits/woodtik/wtcindex.htm.*

Sights

Walrus Islands State Game Sanctuary

NATURE PRESERVE | Established in 1960 to protect one of the largest North American haul-out sites for the Pacific walrus, this sanctuary's 65 miles protects seven small islands and their adjacent waters in northern Bristol Bay, including Round Island, Summit Island, Crooked Island, High Island, Black Rock, and The Twins. The number of walruses fluctuates from year to year, but more than 14,000 have been counted on Round Island in a single day. These giant sea mammals come to the haul-out in such high numbers in the summer that you can barely see the rocks beneath the heaving red blubber. The islands also support an array of birds and mammals, including a large population of Steller sea lions and orca, humpback, and gray whales that feed in offshore waters. Transportation to the islands and permits for the sanctuary are limited, with access generally restricted to May through mid-August. Day-trip permits can be obtained on the island, but camping permits must be arranged in advance. Before planning a trip or applying for a permit, check the Alaska Department of Fish and Game website for an updated list of available transportation options from Togiak and Dillingham. ☎ *907/842–2334 Alaska Department Fish and Game, Dillingham* 🌐 *www.adfg.alaska.gov/index.cfm?adfg=walrusislands.main.*

Wood-Tikchik State Park

STATE/PROVINCIAL PARK | Located in the Bristol Bay region, this state park is the largest in the nation at 1.6 million acres. Two separate groups of interconnected lakes, some up to 45 miles long, dominate the park, making it a waterway-dense region despite being inland. Charismatic mammals like bears, caribou, porcupines, eagles, and loons abound in the park's forests and tundra, but Wood-Tikchik is best known for its fish. The park's lakes and streams are critical spawning habitat for five species of Pacific salmon. They also support healthy populations of rainbow trout, arctic char, arctic grayling, and northern pike. As a result, Wood-Tikchik draws anglers and boaters interested in fishing in a place without maintained trails (and with few visitor amenities). Most campsites here are primitive, and anyone planning to explore the park should be experienced in backcountry travel and camping. Besides the many large lakes and streams, the park's landscape includes rugged mountains, glaciers, and vast expanses of tundra. 🌐 *dnr.alaska.gov/parks/aspunits/woodtik/wtcindex.htm.*

Activities

Wood-Tikchik is most often explored by canoe, kayak, or raft. The most popular fly-in float trip is the 90-mile journey from Lake Kulik to Aleknagik, a Yup'ik village. Most people arrange for drop-off and pickup services with local charters or guides in Dillingham. The lakes are large enough to behave like small inland seas in stormy weather, so boaters need to show extreme caution in high winds and be prepared for bad weather. The fishing is often phenomenal for salmon and rainbow trout. Hiking is more difficult because of the dense brush, except for the uppermost part of the park, where the tundra makes walking easier.

Hotels

Fishing Bear Lodge

$$$$ | ALL-INCLUSIVE | This family-operated, all-inclusive lodge offers clean, comfortable cabins with twin beds and propane heating and lights, daily fishing and sightseeing by jet boat, and home-cooked meals, sometimes served along the water. **Pros:** intimate feel with only 8 guests per week; gorgeous location; daily fly-fishing excursions. **Cons:** very fishing focused, so not for everyone; stays are minimum six days; bathroom and shower facilities separate from cabins. [$] *Rooms from: $792* ☎ *800/552–2729* 🌐 *www.fishingbearlodge.com* ⏲ *Closed Oct.–May* 🍴 *All-Inclusive* 🛏 *4 cabins.*

★ **Tikchik Narrows Lodge**

$$$$ | B&B/INN | This remote, waterfront lodge in Wood-Tikchik State Park caters to anyone seeking great fishing accompanied by comfortable housing and delicious gourmet-style meals. **Pros:** provides some of the state's best sportfishing tours; knowledgeable owner who doubles as a guide; rates include delicious meals and all activities. **Cons:** mostly fishing focused; expensive; one-week minimum on all stays. [$] *Rooms from: $1314* ☎ *907/243–8450* 🌐 *www.tikchiklodge.com* 🍴 *All-Inclusive* 🛏 *7 cabins* ⏲ *Closed Oct.–May.*

Katmai National Park and Preserve

100 miles southeast of Wood-Tikchik, 290 miles southwest of Anchorage.

Remote Katmai receives very few annual visitors. Those who do make the effort, however, are richly rewarded with a dramatic, rugged landscape that offers truly unique experiences.

Katmai's once-in-a-lifetime opportunities include watching massive brown bears catch salmon; exploring a riveting assortment of volcanoes, glaciers, and waterways; and learning how people have thrived on these lands for thousands of years. Although the bears often steal the show, Katmai is also home to wolves, moose, lynx, and eagles. The salmon runs here are legendary, too.

The Sugpiat have lived in the Katmai area and throughout the coastal regions—from Prince William Sound to the Alaska Peninsula—for thousands of years. (The Sugpiat are also known as the Alutiiq people or the Aleut, a word introduced by Russian colonizers.) Before the 1912 Novarupta-Katmai eruption, one of the most powerful ever recorded, there were villages and many camps in what now falls within Katmai. Heavy ash from that eruption covered 46,000 miles and compelled many people to leave. The Sugpiat continue to live in relationship with the land of Katmai through their cultural and traditional practices, and they participate in park management through Alaska Native corporate and nonprofit organizations.

Katmai, which has 18 individual volcanoes, seven of which have been active since 1900, was designated as a monument in 1918 because of its volcanic activity—specifically, the Novarupta eruption, which formed the Valley of Ten Thousand Smokes, a 40-square-mile, 100-to-700-foot-deep pyroclastic flow.

There's a 6.6-mile (round-trip) trail into the valley that's accessible through a park tour and bus ride from Brooks Camp to the trailhead.

The park remained largely unvisited by travelers until the 1950s, when the area and surrounding lands were recognized by more people for their wide variety of wildlife, including an abundance of sockeye salmon and the brown bears that are drawn to them for food. After a series of boundary expansions, the present park and preserve were established in 1980 under the Alaska National Interest Lands Conservation Act.

Remote and expensive to reach, even by Alaska standards, the park offers limited visitor facilities beyond a single campground, a few wilderness lodges, and very few miles of designated and maintained trails. Most visitors rely on outfitters and lodges to help them arrange hiking, fishing, flightseeing, and other excursions. However, for those with the determination, the know-how, and the strength to carry their own gear, the park's remote areas offer plenty of space in which to hike and camp.

GETTING HERE AND AROUND

You can't drive to Katmai National Park. To get here, you can fly from Anchorage—enjoying amazing views of Cook Inlet and the lofty, snowy Alaska Range peaks—to King Salmon, near Bristol Bay. From there, you transfer to a floatplane for a 20-minute hop to Naknek Lake and Brooks Camp.

You can also travel from King Salmon to Brooks Camp by boat. On arrival, you must check in at the park ranger station, next to Brooks Lodge, for a mandatory bear-safety talk (for the safety of both you and the bears).

ESSENTIALS
PARK FEES AND PERMITS
There is no entrance fee for Katmai. The per-person camping fee at Brooks Camp is $12 a night. Although backcountry

camping is free and no permits are required, it's limited to 14 days in any one location.

PARK HOURS

Katmai is open 24 hours every day, though there are some backcountry camping closures at certain times of year. Check the park website for updates.

VISITOR INFORMATION

CONTACTS Katmai National Park and Preserve. ⊠ *1000 Silver St., Building 603, King Salmon* ☎ *907/246–4250 King Salmon Visitor's Center, 907/246–3305 park headquarters* ⊕ *www.nps.gov/katm.*

 Sights

Brooks Falls and Brooks Camp

WATERFALL | At Katmai's biggest draw, viewing platforms overlook Brooks Falls, a 6-foot cascade. Here, salmon leap upriver to their spawning grounds while brown bears stand on the edge of the falls to catch them, particularly in July and September. An access trail and boardwalk are separated from the river to avoid confrontations with bears. Note, too, that the daily tour to the Valley of Ten Thousand Smokes starts from nearby Brooks Lodge, and there's camping at Brooks Camp (just $12 a night, no permit required). ⊠ *Katmai National Park and Preserve* ☎ *907/246–4250 King Salmon Visitor Center, 907/246–3305 park headquarters* ⊕ *www.nps.gov/katm.*

Brooks River

BODY OF WATER | Just downstream from Brooks Falls, you can fish for salmon and rainbow trout in Brooks River. Note, though, that sometimes only fly-fishing is permitted, and there are seasonal closures to prevent contact with bears, so check locally for the latest information. ⊠ *Katmai National Park and Preserve* ☎ *907/246–3305* ⊕ *www.nps.gov/katm.*

★ McNeil River State Game Sanctuary and Refuge

STATE/PROVINCIAL PARK | At the northern end of the Alaska Peninsula, this sanctuary protects the world's largest gathering of brown bears. During the July to mid-August chum season, when salmon return to spawn, 50, 60, or even 70 brown bears congregate daily at the McNeil River falls to fish, eat, play, nap, and nurse cubs. The action happens within 15 to 20 feet of a viewing pad, so close that you can hear these magnificent creatures breathe and catch a whiff of their wet fur. Only 10 people a day can visit the viewing sites, and staffers (armed) are on hand to ensure that everyone behaves in nonthreatening, nonintrusive ways.

Because demand is so high, the Alaska Department of Fish and Game issues permits via a mid-March lottery. Applications and a nonrefundable $30 fee must be received by March 1, and Alaska residents get preferential treatment. Those who win pay an additional fee of just over $100 to $525, depending on the type of permit and the holder's residency. Air taxis to the sanctuary fly out of Homer on the Kenai Peninsula. Once in the sanctuary, all travel is by foot and guided by state biologists. Permit holders camp on gravel pads, in a protected area near a communal cook house, and must bring all their food. ⊠ *Anchorage* ☎ *907/267–2189 Alaska Dept. of Fish and Game, Wildlife Conservation* ⊕ *www.adfg.state.ak.us.*

Valley of Ten Thousand Smokes

NATURE SIGHT | This dramatically sculpted landscape demonstrates the power of volcanic eruptions and their effect on geology, flora, and fauna. The impact of the Novarupta eruption on the park's ecosystems can be both obvious and subtle, so it's helpful to have a guide. The park concessionaire offers a tour ($96, including lunch) that departs from Brooks Camp on a 46-mile (round-trip) bus ride to the valley, with an optional 3.4-mile hike

Alaskan Volcanoes

Earthquakes and Eruptions

First there were five days of violent earthquakes. Then, on June 6, 1912, the 2,700-foot Novarupta blew its top. For the next 60 hours, white-hot ash spiraled 100,000 feet into the atmosphere, coating the previously green valley and plunging Kodiak, over 100 miles away, into darkness during the season of the midnight sun. As Novarupta continued belching, the mountaintop peak of Mt. Katmai, 6 miles away, collapsed, creating a chasm almost 3 miles long and 2 miles wide and leaving a 2,000-foot deep caldera that now holds a lake.

During those cataclysmic 60 hours, more than 7 cubic miles of volcanic material was ejected, and people fled Katmai and Savonoski villages (miraculously no one was killed). Ash and pumice 300 feet deep covered more than 800 square miles of mountainous terrain around the volcano, and thousands of high-temperature fumaroles (holes in volcanic terrain that emit smoke) were created.

Volcanic Valley Is Born

By 1916, things had cooled off sufficiently to allow scientists to explore the area. A National Geographic Society expedition led by Dr. Robert F. Griggs reached the valley and found a moonlike landscape full of fumaroles and fountains emitting smoke and steam from springs and streams that had been smothered by ash. The report on what Griggs dubbed the Valley of Ten Thousand Smokes inspired Congress to declare the valley and the surrounding lands a national monument in 1918.

Although the steam has virtually stopped, an eerie sense of the Earth's forces remains, and several nearby volcanoes still smolder, threatening to blow every few years. Anchorage's airport will sometimes be shut down by smoke or ash from the peninsula's active volcanoes.

The Sugpiat who live in nearby communities continue using and maintaining a relationship with the land and animals of Katmai today. Scientists, naturalists, sightseers, anglers, hikers, climbers, boaters, and other visitors also come to Katmai to experience this dramatic and changing landscape.

8

The Bush KATMAI NATIONAL PARK AND PRESERVE

---

to the valley floor and back. This is also the bus to take for multiday backpacking trips up the valley to Mt. Katmai or the foot of Novarupta itself. ⊠ *Katmai National Park and Preserve* ⊕ *katmailand.com.*

🏃 Activities

The Katmai region offers an abundance of recreational opportunities, including bear viewing, fishing, hiking through the Valley of Ten Thousand Smokes, running the Alagnak River and other clear-water streams, flightseeing, exploring the outer coast, and backpacking through remote and seldom-visited backcountry wilderness.

CAMPING

Brooks Camp is the only developed camping area in Katmai.

Brooks Camp Campground. This National Park Service campground is a short walk from Brooks Lodge, where campers can pay to eat meals and shower. The camp includes designated cooking and eating shelters, latrines, well water, and a storage cache to protect food from the ever-present brown bears.

An electric-wire fence surrounds the camping area. Sites costs $12 per night per person, and reservations are required. *907/246–3305 for info, 877/444–6777 for reservations.*

FLIGHTSEEING
Katmai Air Services
AIR EXCURSIONS | Katmai Air offers flightseeing tours to the Valley of Ten Thousand Smokes and other areas of the park, along with one-day bear-viewing trips and charter flights from Anchorage and King Salmon to Brooks Camp. They also travel to multiple lodges and have scheduled flights from Anchorage to King Salmon. ⊠ *4125 Aircraft Dr., Anchorage* ☏ *800/544–0551 reservations, 907/243–5448 in Anchorage* ⊕ *www.katmailand. com* ✈ *From $225 for flightseeing, $950 roundtrip to Brooks Camp.*

Northwind Aviation
AIR EXCURSIONS | This Homer-based company offers flights to Katmai and the McNeil River, with one-day trips to Brooks Falls for bear viewing and Chinitna Bay and Hallo Bay for sightseeing and wildlife viewing. They also do flightseeing and charter trips. Their fleet includes a Cessna 206 and a de Havilland Otter. ⊠ *1184 Lakeshore Dr., Homer* ☏ *907/235–7482* ⊕ *www.northwindak. com* ✈ *From $825 for bear viewing trip to Brooks Falls.*

HIKING
In one sense, Katmai's hiking options expand as far as the eye can see. Where there's a way, there's a path for the will to follow. But hiking, backcountry camping, and climbing trips can include an array of hazards that require you to plan well and bring everything you might need for a range of weather and trail conditions, including windstorms, river crossings, and, of course, encounters with animals.

The park's few maintained trails start near Brooks River. The Brooks Falls trail is about 1.2 miles and wheelchair accessible; it basically goes from the lower Brooks River bear-viewing platform to the falls. The Dumpling Mountain trail climbs 800 feet through boreal forest, subalpine meadows, and alpine tundra to an overlook above Brooks Camp with expansive views. It's about 3 miles out and back, though you can continue another 2½ miles beyond the overlook to reach the summit of the mountain.

The Valley of Ten Thousand Smokes hike starts at Brooks Camp, too. You can either walk the 23-mile road to the Robert F. Griggs Visitor Center overlooking the valley or catch the bus tour that includes an optional 3.4-mile hike to the valley floor and back. Another trail offers a multiday backpacking adventure that includes creek crossings and walking on pumice-covered flats to the very volcanoes that erupted and gave the valley its name.

WILDLIFE VIEWING
Alaska Alpine Adventures–Katmai
ADVENTURE TOURS | **FAMILY** | This adventure outfitter based in Anchorage offers an array of 5- to 12-day hiking, backpacking, and multisport excursions into Katmai, with some trips designed for families. It also offers tours in the Alaska National Wildlife Refuge, Gates of the Arctic National Park, Aniakchak, and other public parklands. ⊠ *300 E. 76th Ave., Anchorage* ☏ *907/351–4193 Anchorage office* ⊕ *www.alaskaalpineadventures. com* ✈ *From $3,995 per person.*

Katmailand
GUIDED TOURS | This company offers trips geared toward fishing, sightseeing, and wildlife viewing within Katmai National Park, along with a day tour of the Valley of Ten Thousand Smokes. You can usually just pick up the day tour ($96 with lunch), which departs from Brooks Camp, on arrival, though it's best to book ahead during the busy month of July. ⊠ *6400 South Airpark Pl., Anchorage* ☏ *907/243–5448, 877/708–1391* ⊕ *www.katmailand. com* ✈ *Packages from $950.*

Ouzel Expeditions

ADVENTURE TOURS | This outfitter specializes in fishing and wildlife-viewing trips on American Creek in Katmai, starting at Hammersly Lake and ending at Lake Coville. The trip covers 40 miles in 8 days, with tons of chances to fish for rainbow trout. The company also leads adventure trips into the Arctic National Wildlife Refuge and the Brooks Range, on the Kongakut and Hula Hula Rivers, and to Kamchatka, Russia. ✉ *Girdwood* ☎ *907/783–2216 reservations* 🌐 *www.ouzel.com* 🎫 *From $5,500.*

Restaurants

Brooks Lodge

$$ | **AMERICAN** | **FAMILY** | Open to guests and nonguests, the dining room at Brooks Lodge serves both buffets and plated meals. It also offers beer, wine, and a small selection of cocktails. **Known for:** dairy- or gluten-free and vegetarian options; gift shop with basic food items; buffet-style meals. [$] *Average main: $19* ✉ *Brooks Lodge in Katmai National Park, King Salmon* ☎ *907/243–5448* 🌐 *www.katmailand.com/brooks-lodge* 🕓 *Closed Sept.–May.*

Hotels

The lodges listed here sit on privately owned lands inside protected areas within Katmai National Park. Most are along inland rivers; Katmai Wilderness Lodge is on the outer coast.

★ **Brooks Lodge**

$$$$ | **B&B/INN** | At the nexus of multiple lakes, rivers, and streams, this lodge makes a good base from which to fish—for rainbow or lake trout, arctic grayling, and, of course, salmon—and to visit the bear-viewing areas and the Valley of Ten Thousand Smokes. **Pros:** amazing access to fishing; private facilities; bear viewing at Brooks Falls. **Cons:** expensive; bunk beds only; requires flying or boating in. [$] *Rooms from: $1000* ☎ *907/243–5448* 🌐 *www.katmailand.com/brooks-lodge* 🕓 *Closed Sept.–May* 🛏 *16 cabins* 🍴 *No Meals.*

Grosvenor Lodge

$$$$ | **B&B/INN** | This intimate in-park lodge centers on fish, wildlife, and the lake system of the western Katmai. **Pros:** only four to six guests at a time; great access to fishing; accessible to two spawning streams. **Cons:** absolute seclusion not for everyone; bathhouse is outside the cabin; often booked far in advance. [$] *Rooms from: $2955* ☎ *907/243–5448 Anchorage office, 800/544–0551* 🌐 *grosvenorlodge.com* 🕓 *Closed Sept.–May* 🛏 *3 cabins* 🍴 *All-Inclusive.*

Katmai Wilderness Lodge

$$$$ | **B&B/INN** | This rustic but modern log-cabin lodge on Kukak Bay straddles the rugged outer coast of Katmai National Park, along the shores of the Alaska Peninsula. **Pros:** guide services; private rooms and bathrooms with hot showers; bear viewing guaranteed. **Cons:** you have to get to Kodiak first; pricey; minimum three-night stay. [$] *Rooms from: $4250* ☎ *800/488–8767, 907/486–8767 Anchorage office* 🌐 *www.katmai-wilderness.com* 🛏 *7 cabins* 🕓 *Closed Oct.–mid-May* 🍴 *All-Inclusive.*

Kulik Lodge

$$$$ | **B&B/INN** | Along the Kulik River between Nonvianuk and Kulik Lakes, this remote wilderness lodge sits in the northwest quadrant of the national park, near the boundary of the preserve. **Pros:** complimentary drinks when telling fish stories; great rainbow-trout fishing; modern facilities. **Cons:** fishing focused; need to bring your own tackle; minimum stay required. [$] *Rooms from: $4495* ☎ *907/243–5448, 877/708–1391* 🌐 *kuliklodge.com* 🕓 *Closed Sept.–May* 🍴 *All-Inclusive* 🛏 *12 cabins.*

Aniakchak National Monument and Preserve

100 miles southwest of Katmai National Park.

Need to check "Visit an active volcano" off your bucket list? A trip to remote Aniakchak will do the trick. The journey to this amazing landscape and its enormous caldera is not for the faint of heart or for those looking for some laid-back fun in the Alaska sun. The terrain is just as rugged (and bear-filled) as it was when the Aniakchak volcano first erupted 3,500 years ago. Travel options to this remote yet phenomenal national monument haven't changed much either.

GETTING HERE AND AROUND

Aniakchak National Monument and Preserve is expensive to reach, even by remote Alaska standards. The only easy access is by air, usually from the town of King Salmon. Few people visit this spectacular place—and those who do are likely to have the caldera all to themselves. Coming here will give you a unique and awe-inspiring Alaska vacation story, for sure.

ESSENTIALS

VISITOR INFORMATION Aniakchak National Monument and Preserve Headquarters.
⊠ *Aniakchak National Monument and Preserve, King Salmon* ☎ *907/246–3305 King Salmon office* ⊕ *www.nps.gov/ania.*

Sights

Aniakchak National Monument and Preserve

NATURE PRESERVE | This parkland of 586,000 acres contains an extraordinary living volcano that rises to the south of Katmai. Towering more than 4,400 feet above the landscape, the volcano also has one of the largest calderas in the world, with a diameter averaging 6 miles across and 2,500 feet deep. Although

Aniakchak last erupted in 1931, geologists place the first eruption after the last ice age because of the lack of glaciation. The Aniakchak climate brews mist, clouds, and serious wind much of the year. The caldera is so big that it can create its own weather patterns, and it really seems to like the bad stuff. Although the Aniakchak River (which drains Surprise Lake) is floatable, it has stretches of Class III and IV white water navigable only by expert river runners, and you must travel through open ocean waters to reach the nearest community, Chignik Bay (or get picked up by plane, along the coast). In other words, this is not a place for the unprepared or untested. An alternate way to enjoy Aniakchak is to wait for a clear day and fly to it in a small plane that will land you on the caldera floor or on Surprise Lake. There are no trails, campgrounds, ranger stations, or other visitor facilities here, though there are plenty of bears and mosquitoes. ☎ *907/246–3305* ⊕ *www.nps.gov/ania* ⊠ *Free.*

Activities

★ **Alaska Alpine Adventures–Aniakchak**
ADVENTURE TOURS | This year-round adventure outfitter offers a 12-day hiking and rafting excursion into Aniakchak Preserve during the summer. Alaska Alpine also operates adventure tours in the Alaska National Wildlife Refuge, Gates of the Arctic National Park, and Katmai National Park. ☎ *907/351–4193* ⊕ *www.alaskaalpineadventures.com* ⊠ *From $5195.*

Branch River Air Service
ADVENTURE TOURS | Branch River Air Service in King Salmon offers flightseeing, bear-viewing, and custom-charter trips around Bristol Bay and Katmai National Park, as well as charter flights to various remote locations on the Alaska Peninsula, including Aniakchak National Preserve. Rates are available upon request. ⊠ *King Salmon* ☎ *907/246–3437 June–Sept., 907/248–3539 Oct.–May* ⊕ *www.branchriverair.com.*

Ouzel Expeditions

ADVENTURE TOURS | This experienced outfitter guides weeklong fishing and float trips in Aniakchak National Monument and Preserve. The excursion starts at the caldera and ends in the Pacific Ocean. They also do other trips in Southwest Alaska, including to Katmai National Park, the Yukon Delta Wildlife Refuge, and Togiak Wildlife Refuge, as well as to Alaska's Arctic. ☎ 907/783–2216 ⊕ www.ouzel.com ⌨ From $3,500.

Becharof and Alaska Peninsula National Wildlife Refuges

Adjacent to Aniakchak National Monument and Preserve, 250 miles to 450 miles southwest of Anchorage.

The enormous Becharof and Alaska Peninsula National Wildlife Refuges are prime areas for volcano viewing. Couple these volcano-laden horizons with hundreds of species of birds, fish, and land mammals, and your Alaska experience will be hard to beat. Just be sure to dress appropriately and gear up for all conditions.

GETTING HERE AND AROUND

There are no visitor facilities here, and access is only by boat or plane. Most visitors begin their trips in King Salmon and use guides or outfitters.

ESSENTIALS

VISITOR INFORMATION Becharof National Wildlife Refuge Visitor Center. ⊠ 4 Bear Rd., King Salmon ☎ 907/246–3339 headquarters, 907/246–4250 visitor center ⊕ www.fws.gov/refuge/becharof.

 Sights

Becharof and Alaska Peninsula National Wildlife Refuges

WILDLIFE REFUGE | Stretching along the southern edge of the Alaska Peninsula, these two refuges encompass nearly 6 million acres of towering mountains, glacial lakes, broad tundra valleys, and coastal fjords. Volcanoes dominate the landscape—14 in all, nine of them active—and the waters are known for their salmon and grayling. The world-record grayling, nearly five pounds (most weigh a pound or less), was caught at Ugashik Narrows in 1981. Remote and rugged, with the peninsula's signature unpredictable weather, the Becharof and Alaska Peninsula Refuges draw mostly anglers and hunters. Backpackers, river runners, and mountain climbers also occasionally visit.

Some people hike the Kanatak Trail in Becharof, an ancient route between the Pacific Ocean and Bristol Bay via Becharof Lake. Early settlers continued using the trail and developed settlements, with oil exploration bringing people to the region in the 20th century. The last residents left in the 1950s. If you walk the trail now, you're likely to see plenty of animals and no other humans. It's not a long hike—about 5 miles—but the weather, terrain, and other elements can be challenging, so come prepared. ⊠ Becharof and Alaska Peninsula National Wildlife Refuges ☎ 907/246–3339 Becharof National Wildlife Refuge, 907/246–4250 King Salmon office ⊕ www.fws.gov/refuge/Becharof/about.html ⌨ Free.

Aleutian Islands

The Aleutians begin 540 miles southwest of Anchorage and stretch westward more than 1,200 miles.

The Aleutian Islands comprise a superchain of smaller island groups extending about 1,200 miles westward from the Alaska Peninsula toward the Kamchatka Peninsula in Russia, with the Bering Sea to the north and the Pacific Ocean to the south. The smaller island groups include the Andreanof, Delarof, Fox, Near, Rat, and Shumagin Islands and the Islands of Four Mountains. Together, they contain upward of 300 rocky, treeless islands of volcanic origin, with terrain alternating between towering (and frequently smoking) volcanic cones and high tablelands. The water on the Pacific side of the chain can be more than 25,000 feet deep, and the north side's Bering Canyon is twice as long as the Grand Canyon and twice as deep, bottoming out at 10,600 feet. The Aleutian Islands and surrounding coastal waters make up one of the most biologically rich areas in Alaska, with abundant seabirds, marine mammals, and lots and lots of fish (the Aleutians support one of the world's busiest fishing fleets).

The Indigenous people of the Aleutians call themselves Unangax̂. They have relied heavily on the ocean for thousands of years. The arrival of Russian fur traders in the mid-1700s brought a period of great violence, oppression, disease, and disruption, but the communities have continued to thrive. Today, Unangax̂ communities include **Nikolski,** on Umnak Island; **Atka,** on Atka Island; and **Cold Bay,** at the peninsula's tip. People in these communities forage, fish, hunt, and work in commercial fishing in canneries, as guides, and in other sectors. These communities are quite small, accommodations are scarce, and year-round travel is limited.

Visitors aren't allowed on Shemya Island, which has a remote U.S. Air Force base, without special permission. Because of downsizing, the military has closed its Adak operation, and the base provides the core infrastructure for what now is a small coastal community and commercial fishing port.

Unalaska/Dutch Harbor

Unalaska is a volcanic island in the Fox Islands group of the Aleutian chain.

The Alaska Marine Highway System

This much-loved form of Alaskan transport is best known for its routes along the Inside Passage. In summer these ferries also depart from Homer, in Southcentral, and pass by Kodiak on the three-plus-day trip to Unalaska/Dutch Harbor. Though slow-paced and far from luxurious, the ferry *(800/642–0066)* is an unforgettable way to see Southwest Alaska's dramatic landscapes.

The city of Unalaska actually lies on two islands—Unalaska Island and Amaknuk Island—which are connected by a bridge. Dutch Harbor is not a separate town, merely a harbor, albeit a very large one, on Amaknuk Island; it's usually referred to as simply "Dutch" (or, by people who spend winter here, "the Gulag").

Despite the often harsh weather—this region is known as the "Cradle of Storms" for good reason—the Indigenous people of the Aleutians (the Unangax̂) have occupied these islands and others for thousands of years. Today, Unalaska is the region's tourism center and the location for the annual Heart of the Aleutians Festival. The town's Parks, Culture, & Recreation department (PCR) manages eight public parks, an impressive community center (where visitors are welcome to use the indoor and outdoor sports facilities), and various arts and cultural amenities. They also publish an activity guide that includes local events. Dutch Harbor, best known from the Discovery Channel's hit show *Deadliest Catch,* is one of the busiest fishing ports in the world, processing a billion pounds of fish and crab each year. Scattered around both islands are reminders of recent history, specifically the Aleutian Campaign in World War II, which began when the Japanese bombed Dutch Harbor in June 1942 (unexploded ordnance may still be out there, so don't handle any odd metal objects you see while hiking). You can also still explore concrete bunkers built into mountainsides, gun batteries, and a partially sunken ship left over from the war.

GETTING HERE AND AROUND

Pen Air and Grant Aviation provide daily flights from Anchorage to Unalaska. Alaska Marine Highway ferries sail from Homer to Dutch Harbor once a month, May through September, with a journey time of 3½ days; Dutch Harbor welcomes several cruise ships in season.

ESSENTIALS

VISITOR INFORMATION Parks, Culture & Recreation department (PCR). ⊠ *37 S. 5th St., Unalaska* ☎ *907/581–1297* ⊕ *www. ci.unalaska.ak.us/parksrec.***Unalaska/Port of Dutch Harbor Convention and Visitors Bureau (CVB).** ⊠ *5 E. Broadway Ave., Unalaska* ☎ *907/581–2612, 877/581–2612* ⊕ *www.unalaska.org.*

Sights

It's worth the trip here on the ferry purely for the scenery along the way, but when travelers finally reach the islands they discover a surprisingly gentle landscape of tawny, rolling hills sheltering a town that is built for commercial fishing and other interests. The scenery is glorious on a sunny day, and the island's extensive trails provide dream routes for hikers and mountain-runners. Don't worry about opening hours: if the ferry (or a cruise ship) is in the harbor, the town's attractions are open.

Aleutian Islands World War II National Historic Area Visitor Center

MILITARY SIGHT | Through old newspapers, memorabilia, video footage, and exhibits about the Aleutian Campaign, this quaint

museum outside the Unalaska Airport preserves bits of history from Alaska's little-known role in the war. The Aleutian Islands saw heavy fighting through much of World War II; at the peak of the war, more than 60,000 servicemen were stationed here in the farthest and most brutal reaches of the United States. On June 3 and 4, 1942, the Japanese bombed Dutch Harbor and landed in the far reaches of the Aleutians a few days later. The Japanese military forces took entire villages and outposts captive in Kiska and Attu, with many of those captured transported to Japan as prisoners of war. The center is within easy walking distance of the ferry terminal.

The historic area also includes Ft. Schwatka, a U.S. Army base poised on a mountain and comprised of over 100 structures when fully built out. You can do a group or self-guided walking tour of the fort by getting an access permit from the Ounalashka Corporation at 400 Salmon Way or at the visitor center. ⊠ *2716 Airport Beach Rd., Unalaska* ☎ *907/581–9944* ⊕ *www. nps.gov/aleu/details.htm.*

Holy Ascension of Our Lord Cathedral

CHURCH | Undoubtedly the most dramatic human-made sight in Unalaska is the Holy Ascension Russian Orthodox church. The blue, onion-domed chapel right on the edge of Iliuluk Bay is arguably the most perfectly intact and authentic Russian church left in Alaska, and possibly the most scenic church anywhere. The extant buildings date to the 1890s, although there has been a church on the site since 1808. Now a National Historic Landmark, Holy Ascension is one of the oldest cruciform-style Russian churches in the nation, and it houses one of Alaska's richest collections of Russian artifacts, religious icons, and artwork. Next to the church is the Bishop's House. A walk in the graveyard between the two buildings captures some of the history of the area. Tours of the church can be arranged through the Unalaska/

Dutch Harbor Convention and Visitors Bureau. ✉ *W. Broadway Ave., between 1st and 2nd Sts., Unalaska* ☎ *907/581–5883 parish.*

Museum of the Aleutians

HISTORY MUSEUM | FAMILY | This remarkable museum highlights the cultural, military, and natural history of the Aleutian and Pribilof Islands. You'll find an array of objects representing some of the region's history, from gut parkas and repatriated religious artifacts to original drawings from Captain Cook's third voyage. The exhibits also give glimpses into the Unangax̂ way of life, as well as illustrating the impact of Russian contact and occupation, the gold rush, World War II, the fishing industry, and more. In the summer, the museum sponsors archaeological digs as well as periodic lectures by visiting scientists, historians, and researchers. ✉ *314 Salmon Way, Unalaska* ☎ *907/581–5150* 🌐 *www.aleutians.org* 🎫 *$7* ⏲ *Closed Sun. and Mon.*

World War II Military Installations

MILITARY SIGHT | The impact of World War II on Unalaska/Dutch Harbor is visible practically everywhere you look here: remnants of war bunkers, tunnels, Quonset huts, pillboxes, and other military relics are scattered throughout town. You can explore these pieces of history hands-on when at Bunker Hill, Memorial Park, Unalaska Lake, Mt. Ballyhoo, and other sites. ✉ *Unalaska, Unalaska.*

Activities

***Miss Alyssa* Bering Sea Excursions**

BOATING | The *Miss Alyssa* can take up to five passengers on epic backcountry skiing and climbing adventures, whale-watching and scuba-diving expeditions, and halibut fishing trips. The experienced crew welcomes other ideas for maritime adventures, too. Day and overnight charter packages include all meals, gear, and even drinks. ✉ *Dutch Harbor, Unalaska* ☎ *907/581–1386, 907/581–2386* 🌐 *www.missalyssa.com* 🎫 *From $2,000 a day.*

Ounalashka Corporation

HIKING & WALKING | Much of the land surrounding Unalaska and Dutch Harbor is owned by the Ounalashka Corporation. Before hiking, camping, or exploring off the main roads, purchase a land-use permit online or from the Alaska Native corporation office just around the corner from the Grand Aleutian. You can choose individual or family permits for a day, week, season, or year. ✉ *400 Salmon Way, Unalaska* ☎ *907/581–1276* 🌐 *ounalashka.com.*

★ **Wilderness Birding Adventures**

BIRD WATCHING | This Homer-based outfitter runs small group trips that cater to passionate birders. The Adak Island trip takes folks to the westernmost part of the United States to witness the area's spring migration birds. Other birding adventures include trips to Unalaska/Dutch Harbor and areas across Alaska, including the Pribilofs, the Gulf of Alaska, and the Arctic. Their guides can also do combined birding, hiking, and river-rafting trips. ✉ *40208 Alpenglow Circle, Homer* ☎ *907/299–3937* 🌐 *www.wildernessbirding.com* 🎫 *From $2,600.*

Restaurants

Amelia's Restaurant

$$ | INTERNATIONAL | This brightly colored all-day café next door to the Safeway has something for everyone, with enormous portions of breakfast fare, burgers, sandwiches, Asian options, house-made milkshakes, and Mexican dishes. Strands of beads hang from the ceiling, and various other kitschy items cover the walls. **Known for:** pretty decent Mexican dishes; big hearty breakfasts; view of the Bering Sea. [$] *Average main: $22* ✉ *2141 Airport Beach Rd., Unalaska* ☎ *907/581–2800.*

Cape Cheerful Lounge

$$$ | AMERICAN | This casual bar off the main lobby of the Grand Aleutian Hotel is the perfect spot to grab a bite to eat and a cold beer after a long day exploring. The menu features crab, steaks, burgers, salads, and sandwiches, and the bar has a surprisingly good selection of beers. **Known for:** Taco Tuesdays all year; standard pub fare; Friday night barbeques. $ *Average main: $30* ⊠ *Grand Aleutian Hotel, 498 Salmon Way, Dutch Harbor* ☎ *907/581–7130* ⊕ *www.grandaleutian.com* ☉ *No lunch Mon.–Sat.*

Chart Room

$$$$ | **AMERICAN** | By far the fanciest restaurant in Unalaska, the Chart Room serves food that very nearly parallels its spectacular views of the surrounding mountains and Margaret Bay. On most nights it's not difficult to grab a table, but consider planning ahead and making a reservation for the famous Wednesday-night seafood buffet or the Sunday brunch buffet. **Known for:** king crab entrées; Wednesday seafood buffets; incredible views when the weather's clear. $ *Average main: $35* ⊠ *Grand Aleutian Hotel, 498 Salmon Way, 2nd fl., Dutch Harbor* ☎ *907/581–7120* ⊕ *www.grandaleutian.com* ☉ *No lunch weekdays.*

Harbor Sushi

$$ | **SUSHI** | This sushi spot features wild-caught Alaska salmon and the usual selection of rolls and sashimi, with vegetarian choices and the usual sides. They also offer pork, beef, and chicken bowls and salads with or without ahi tuna or sockeye salmon. **Known for:** fresh seafood; tasty salmon rolls; scenic, harborside ambience. $ *Average main: $15* ⊠ *Grand Aleutian Hotel, 498 Salmon Way, Unalaska* ☎ *907/581–7191* ⊕ *www. grandaleutian.com* ☉ *No lunch.*

Pyramid Coffee

$$ | **CAFÉ** | You can get coffee here, of course, but you'll also find Dutch huevos rancheros, pancakes, chicken-fried steak, and an array of breakfast and lunch fare from 7 am to 6 pm every day. They also offer smoothies and milkshakes, and some quick bites and drinks. **Known for:** quick coffee service; delicious breakfast

sandwiches; surprisingly good beer menu. $ *Average main: $15* ⊠ *Grand Aleutian Hotel, 498 Salmon Way, Unalaska* ☎ *907/581–7117* ⊕ *www.grandaleutian.com* ☉ *No dinner.*

Hotels

Grand Aleutian Hotel

$$ | **HOTEL** | The airy, three-story atrium lobby with a large stone fireplace lends a European chalet sensibility to this hotel with brightly lit rooms and Alaska-themed artwork. **Pros:** bay-view rooms; several eateries on-site; helpful and enthusiastic staff. **Cons:** feels like a hotel that could be anywhere; generic interiors; less likely to connect with locals. $ *Rooms from: $199* ⊠ *498 Salmon Way, Box 921169, Dutch Harbor* ☎ *866/581–3844, 907/581–3844* ⊕ *www.grandaleutian.com* ❍ *No Meals* ⊐ *116 rooms.*

Nightlife

Harbor View Bar & Grill

BARS | Views, drinks, pizza, and pub food make this a perfect late-night hangout spot. Like with most sports bars, you'll get big screens, pool tables, darts, and live music on weekends. ⊠ *76–94 Gilman Way, Dutch Harbor* ☎ *907/581–7246* ⊕ *www.grandaleutian.com.*

Pribilof Islands

200 miles north of the Aleutian Islands, 800 miles southwest of Anchorage.

What the Bristol Bay region is to fly-fishing, the Pribilof Islands are to birding. Unfortunately, "the Pribs" are quite remote and visiting requires a bit of planning as well as patience and flexibility since even the best-laid plans fall victim to Mother Nature's whims. Fortunately, once there, you'll likely encounter a medley of people on the hunt for the exact same thing as you: a glimpse of some of the rarest birds on the planet.

GETTING HERE AND AROUND

For most travelers it is much easier and more efficient to sign up for package tours that arrange air travel from Anchorage, lodging, ground transportation on the islands, and guided activities. It can be nearly, if not completely, impossible to arrange such things after you arrive. Guest accommodations in the Pribilofs are very limited, with lodgings only on St. George and St. Paul. The best way to hop between islands is by air on Ravn Air, but both islands are notorious fog magnets; you should never plan on getting out quite as scheduled.

ESSENTIALS

AIRLINE CONTACT Ravn Air. ☎ 907/266–8394 ⊕ www.ravnalaska.com.

 Sights

Pribilof Islands

ISLAND | Rising out of the surging waters of the Bering Sea, the Pribilof Islands are a misty, fog-bound breeding ground of seabirds and northern fur seals that consist of five islets, all tiny, green, and treeless, with rippling belts of lush grass contrasting with volcanic rocks. In early summer, seals come home from far Pacific waters to mate, and the larger islands, St. Paul and St. George, are overwhelmed with frenzied activity. Although St. Paul and St. George are less than 50 miles apart, the island group itself is a 1,600-mile round-trip from Anchorage, over the massive snowy peaks of the Alaska Peninsula and north of the rocky islands of the Aleutian chain.

Few visitors go to the Pribilofs, save commercial fishermen and the most dedicated wildlife watchers. Yet together, St. Paul and St. George Islands are seasonal homes to hundreds of thousands of fur seals (about 80% of them on St. Paul) and nearly 250 species of birds. Some birds migrate from as far away as Argentina, while others are year-round residents.

Most spectacular of all is the islands' seabird population: each summer more than 2 million seabirds gather at traditional Pribilof nesting grounds; about 90% of them breed on St. George. ⊠ *Pribilof Islands, St. Paul Island* ⊕ *www.apiai.org.*

St. George Island

ISLAND | Though home to nearly 2 million nesting seabirds, St. George Island is rarely visited because no organized tours visit here, and accommodations are limited. People who live on St. Paul try to avoid going to St. George because of the weather. Avid bird- and wildlife watchers will find plenty to feast the eye on, however.

★ St. Paul Island

ISLAND | The largest of the Pribilof Islands at 40 square miles, St. Paul Island is home to the greatest concentration of northern fur seals in the world—500,000 of them—and more than 180 varieties of birds. Certainly it's hard to reach, but it's also a guaranteed treat for adventuresome naturalists. Russian fur traders claimed and named St. George, St. Paul, and St. Peter Islands, and they also enslaved the people of the Aleutian communities in Atka, Siberia, and Unalaska, relocating them to the islands to hunt for fur seals. About 500 descendants of Indigenous Aleutian-Russians live in St. Paul year-round, and the community has many elements of Aleutian cultures, as well as the Russian Orthodox Sts. Peter and Paul Church, built in 1907. The local museum provides details on how the U.S. government once controlled seal hunting on the island. ⊕ *www.stpaulak.com.*

Activities

The Pribilofs are considered a birders' paradise for good reason: species that are seldom, if ever, seen elsewhere in North America frequently show up here, including an array of "Asian vagrants" blown here by westerly winds. Birders can expect to find all manner of shorebirds, waterfowl, and seabirds, including puffins, murres, red- and black-legged kittiwakes, plovers—the list goes on and on. Tour guides are usually hired for their birding skills, but will also show visitors the best places to view seals (well, the seals are kind of hard to miss, since a lot of the adolescent males hang out near the roads) and maybe the occasional whale.

St. Paul Island Tours

BIRD WATCHING | Owned by the Tanad-gusix Native Corporation, this tour company takes visitors to St. Paul Island from May to October, with 3- to 8-day options that can include round-trip airfare from Anchorage, ground transportation on St. Paul, lodging at the King Eider Hotel, and tours led by experienced naturalists. ⊠ *St. Paul Island* ☎ *907/546–4158* ⊕ *www.stpaulislandtour.com* 🖅 *From $2,795.*

Wilderness Birding Adventures

BIRD WATCHING | This Homer-based operator takes small groups to the Pribilof Islands to see birds during their fall and spring migrations. Pricing includes flights to and from Anchorage, lodging, meals, and guides. The operator also takes travelers to remote locations across Alaska to sight birds and other wildlife. ⊠ *40208 Alpenglow Cir., Homer* ☎ *907/299–3937* ⊕ *www.wildernessbirding.com* 🖅 *From $4550.*

 Hotels

Aikow Inn

$$$ | **B&B/INN** | Bird and wildlife watchers can get a singular experience at St. George's only hotel, a small, rustic building with a dark-wood interior and a mix of modern and vintage furniture. **Pros:** European inn flavor in remote Alaska setting; bird-watcher's paradise; close to seals and other wildlife. **Cons:** seals might keep light sleepers awake; come ready for every weather condition

possible, all at once; must bring your own food. $ *Rooms from: $220* ⊠ *St. George Island* ☎ *907/272–9886 Anchorage office, 907/859–2255 St. George office* ⊕ *www.tanaq.com* 🖅 *10 rooms* ⦿ *No Meals.*

King Eider Hotel

$$$ | **HOTEL** | Close to birding spots and a mile from a seal rookery, the King Eider offers 40 rooms with basic amenities and meals, lodge-style common areas, and a simple gift shop with limited hours. **Pros:** comfortable common areas; close to airport; proximity to wildlife. **Cons:** unreliable Wi-Fi and cell service; small rooms; thin walls between rooms. $ *Rooms from: $250* ⊠ *St. Paul Island* ☎ *907/546–2477* ⊕ *www.stpaulislandtour.com/lodging-and-meals* 🖅 *40 rooms* ⦿ *No Meals.*

Nome

540 miles northwest of Anchorage.

More than a century has passed since a great stampede for gold put this speck of coastal land on Norton Sound on the Alaska map, but gold mining and noisy saloons are still mainstays in Nome. This community on the icy Bering Sea once boasted 20,000 people during the gold stampede in the 1890s, and now has about 3,800 year-round residents. At first glance the town may come off as a collection of ramshackle houses and low-slung commercial buildings—like a vintage gold-mining camp or, because of the spooky, abandoned, monolithic microwave towers from World War II that sit atop Anvil Mountain, the set for an Arctic horror movie—but only a couple of streets back you'll find tidy, modern homes and charming, hospitable shopkeepers. In fact, Nome is one of Alaska's storied places, very much itself, and the kind of town where the grocery store sells ATVs next to the meat counter. "There's no place like Nome" is the city's slogan for good reason.

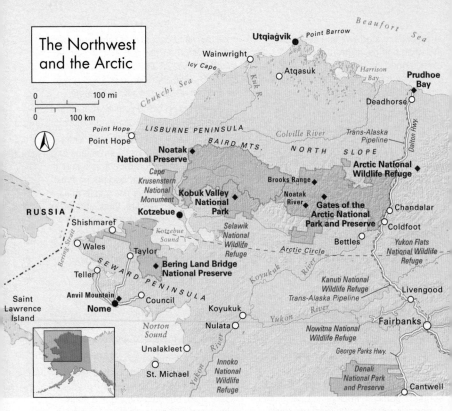

Beaufort Sea

Utqiaġvik   Point Barrow

Wainwright

Icy Cape

Atqasuk

Harrison Bay

Prudhoe Bay

Deadhorse

Chukchi Sea

Point Hope
Point Hope

LISBURNE PENINSULA

Colville River

Trans-Alaska Pipeline

Dalton Hwy.

BAIRD MTS.

NORTH   SLOPE

Kuk R.

Noatak National Preserve

Cape Krusenstern National Monument

Brooks Range

Arctic National Wildlife Refuge

Kobuk Valley National Park

Noatak River

Gates of the Arctic National Park and Preserve

Chandalar

Coldfoot

RUSSIA

Shishmaref

Kotzebue

Kotzebue Sound

Selawik National Wildlife Refuge

Arctic Circle

Bettles

Yukon Flats National Wildlife Refuge

Wales

Taylor

Bering Land Bridge National Preserve

Koyukuk River

Kanuti National Wildlife Refuge

Trans-Alaska Pipeline

Livengood

Teller

Bering Strait

SEWARD PENINSULA

Anvil Mountain

Nome

Council

Koyukuk

Nulata

Yukon River

Fairbanks

Saint Lawrence Island

Norton Sound

Unalakleet

Innoko National Wildlife Refuge

Nowitna National Wildlife Refuge

George Parks Hwy.

St. Michael

Yukon River

Denali National Park and Preserve

Cantwell

For centuries before Nome gained fame as a gold-rush town, the Iñupiat inhabited the area in hunting and fishing camps; an archaeological site south of town has the remains of some round pit houses.

For many, Nome is best known for the Iditarod Trail. Even though parts of the historic trail from Nome to Anchorage were long used as routes by Indigenous communities, the full trail gained fame in 1925 when Nome was hit with an outbreak of diphtheria. With no remedy in town, the serum was ferried by the Alaska Railroad to Nenana, 250 miles from Anchorage, and then a 20-dog sled team ran it the remaining 674 miles in –50°F temperatures over five days and seven hours; Nome was saved. In 1973, in honor of the original Iditarod (a word derived from the Athabascan word "haiditarod ," meaning "a far, distant place"), an annual

race for dog mushers was started. The now world-famous race begins in Anchorage and traverses snow and tundra for 1,049 miles, the odd 49 miles being added to commemorate Alaska's being the 49th state (the actual distance is give or take a few miles, of course; dogsleds don't come with odometers). Thousands of people converge in Nome each and every year (for some Lower-48ers, it's an annual tradition) to watch the dogs and mushers come over the finish line in March. Still more visitors come to Nome in the summer months to take advantage of the beautiful effulgent colors of wildflowers and green grass, its wildlife viewing and birding, and its marvelous end-of-the-world vibe. There is also still a steady flow of those looking to strike it rich panning for gold.

There are many relics of the past in and around the area. There are 44 abandoned gold dredges, enormous constructions of steel that are scattered from the outskirts of town to the surrounding miles of tundra beyond. Just east of town on the road out to Council, a quiet fishing village inhabited by many locals during the summer, you'll stumble across not only fantastic marshlands for birding but also the Last Train to Nowhere—a railway built to haul gold that was never finished—quietly rusting away. In the opposite direction, northeast of Nome on the road to Taylor, is Pilgrim Hot Springs, the site of an old settlement including the former Our Lady of Lourdes chapel and orphanage for children during the 1918 influenza epidemic. And directly north of Nome is the beautiful village of Teller in Grantley Harbor, set on a buttonhook spit in a sheltered bay. Teller made the world news in 1926 when Roald Amundsen landed his zeppelin *Norge* here after the first successful flight over the North Pole.

Getting to these places means traversing unpaved roads that are mostly in good shape. You might see herds of reindeer (they like to use the road themselves since it's easier than running in tundra), musk oxen, grizzly bears, and moose, and a slew of different birds, like the long-tailed jaegers, yellow wagtails, and the bristle-thighed curlew, rarely seen in North America.

GETTING HERE AND AROUND

Just 165 miles from the coast of Siberia, Nome is considerably closer to Russia than to either Anchorage or Fairbanks. Though you'll find 300 miles of local road system branching out from the town, getting to Nome means flying or mushing a team of dogs.

Alaska Airlines flies to Utqiaġvik (formerly Barrow) and Nome. Local arrangements are taken care of by ground operators. The Alaska Travel Industry Association can give tips on air travel and flightseeing opportunities throughout the Bush. From

Nome, visitors can access Serpentine Hot Springs, in the Bering Land Bridge National Preserve, by charter plane. These hot springs are well maintained despite their location.

If you're set on doing your own driving while here, head to Stampede Ventures, which rents cars and vans of various types.

■ TIP➔ **Be sure to fill up with gas in Nome as there are no services once you leave town. And even if the gauge says the tank is full when you rent it, be sure to fill 'er up anyway—sometimes the gauge lies.**

ESSENTIALS

VEHICLE RENTAL Stampede Vehicle Rentals. ✉ *Aurora Inn and Suites, 302 Front St., Nome* ☏ *907/443–3838, 800/354–4606* ⊕ *www.aurorainnnome.com.*

VISITOR INFORMATION Nome Convention & Visitors Bureau. ✉ *301 Front St., Nome* ☏ *907/443–6555* ⊕ *www.visitnomealaska.com.*

⊙ Sights

Anvil Mountain

MOUNTAIN | Take a summer evening drive to the top of Anvil Mountain, near Nome, for a panoramic view of the old gold town and the Bering Sea. As this is the city's lone peak, anyone in town will be able to direct you there. Be sure to carry mosquito repellent. ✉ *Nome.*

Carrie M. McClain Memorial Museum

OTHER MUSEUM | FAMILY | This museum, located in the Richard Foster Building, holds the long-term exhibit *Nome: Hub of Cultures and Communities Across the Bering Strait*, which centers on five Arctic themes and involves interactive environments, such as an Iñupiat skin boat and miner's tent, along with hands-on technology to help engage the narratives. A second space contains a changing contemporary exhibit that typically features a regional artist or artists. ✉ *Richard Foster Bldg., 100 W. 7th Ave., Nome*

☎ *907/443–6630* 🌐 *www.nomealaska.org* 🎟 *$4* 🕒 *Closed Sun.*

Nome Convention & Visitors Bureau
VISITOR CENTER | Stop by the Nome Convention & Visitors Bureau for a historic-walking-tour map, a city map, and information on local activities. The offerings do a good job capturing Nome's historic and current role as a gateway to the vast expanses of western Alaska. ✉ *301 Front St., Nome* ☎ *907/443–6555* 🌐 *www.visitnomealaska.com.*

Activities

Iditarod Trail Sled Dog Race
LOCAL SPORTS | Travelers come from around the world to volunteer and to watch dog teams pass under the burled arch as they finish the 1,049 miles from Anchorage to Nome in the Iditarod, or what's billed as "The Last Great Race." Alaska's most well-known sled dog race pulls in spectators (and mushers) from around the world to brave the Alaska winter to witness or to participate as racers and volunteers in this massive feat of endurance. Many visitors watch the dog teams take off from the ceremonial start in Anchorage and then travel to Nome to celebrate as teams cross the finish line. For sled dog race dates, starting times, and viewing locations, and anything else relating to The Last Great Race, contact the Iditarod Trail Committee. ✉ *Iditirod Trail, Nome* ☎ *907/376–5155* 🌐 *www.iditarod.com.*

Restaurants

Bering Sea Bar & Grill
$$$ | **AMERICAN** | This old bar with a good selection of beers serves up seafood, steak, noodles, rolls, and sides ranging from onion rings to kimchi. It's a great place to sip wine or beer while enjoying fantastic views of the Bering Sea. **Known for:** old-school atmosphere; good bar food with an Asian flair; beautiful views. [$] *Average main: $25* ✉ *305 Front St., Nome* ☎ *907/443–4900* 🌐 *www.facebook.com/theBeringSea.*

★ **Bering Tea & Coffee**
$ | **CAFÉ** | This little coffee shop, in a repurposed old A-frame house, is an adorable place and the perfect spot for a breakfast sandwich or midday coffee. Tasty beverages and delicious homemade scones, cinnamon rolls, cupcakes, and muffins are a welcome respite from Nome's wind and the industrial surroundings. **Known for:** hip hangout atmosphere; fresh baked goods; good coffee and tea. [$] *Average main: $10* ✉ *301 Bering St., Nome* ☎ *907/387–0352* 🌐 *www.beringteacoffee.com* 🕒 *Closed Sun. year round and Mon. in winter.*

Milano's Pizzeria
$$ | **PIZZA** | **FAMILY** | This popular Front Street restaurant has a casual atmosphere and offers dine-in service as well as takeout from midmorning to late. They serve pizzas with a wide assortment of toppings, along with steak dinners and Japanese (including sushi), Korean, and Italian food. **Known for:** good value pizza; arguably the best sushi in town; lots of local customers. [$] *Average main: $20* ✉ *2824 Front St., Nome* ☎ *907/443–2924.*

Polar Café
$$ | **DINER** | **FAMILY** | If diner fare with a side of true Nome life is what you're after, this is the spot. Traditional hearty breakfast options are served all day, plus steak, chili, a modest salad bar, and unexpectedly delicious burgers, with everything clearly made to order. **Known for:** views of the Bering Sea; breakfast served all day; standard diner fare (with local clientele to match). [$] *Average main: $22* ✉ *224 Front St., Nome* ☎ *907/443–5191.*

Pingo Bakery-Seafood House
$$ | **AMERICAN** | **FAMILY** | Open early for breakfast and into the afternoon, Pingo serves up freshly made bread and fresh seafood meals Wednesday through

Gold Mining in Alaska

The Golden Era

The region's gold stampede began in 1898, when three prospectors—known as the "Lucky Swedes"—struck rich deposits on Anvil Creek, about 4 miles from what became Nome. Their good fortune was followed by the formation of the Cape Nome Mining District. More gold was found the following summer on the beaches of Nome, a place no one ever expected to find it. Ordinarily, placer gold sits on bedrock, but here thousands of winter melts washed it down to the sea.

Prospectors' Short-Lived Paradise

Word spread quickly to the south, right about the same time everybody was discovering that all the good spots for gold in the Klondike were staked. When the Bering Sea ice parted the next spring, ships from Puget Sound (in the Seattle area) arrived in Nome with eager stampeders, while miners who struck out in the Klondike arrived via the Yukon River to try again in Nome. An estimated 15,000 people landed in Nome between June and October 1900, bringing the area's population to more than 20,000. Dozens of gold dredges were hauled into the region to extract the metal from Seward Peninsula sands and gravels; more than 40 are still standing, though no longer operating (if you explore them, be sure to call out regularly, as warning to any bears that might have taken shelter inside). Among the gold-rush luminaries were Wyatt Earp, the old gunfighter from the O.K. Corral,

who mined the gold of Nome the easy way: by opening a posh saloon and serving drinks to thirsty diggers. Also in Nome were Tex Rickard, the boxing promoter, who operated another Nome saloon (money made there later helped him build the third incarnation of Madison Square Garden, and helped him found the New York Rangers hockey team); and Rex Beach, whose first novel, *The Spoilers*, was based on the true story of government officials stealing gold from the hardworking miners (it was a best seller, letting even people warm and cozy down south experience the stampede).

Incorporation of Nome

The city of Nome was incorporated in 1901, which means it is now Alaska's oldest first-class city, with the oldest continuously operating school district. But the community's heyday lasted less than a decade; by the early 1920s the bulk of the region's gold had been mined, and only 820 or so people continued to live in Nome.

Finding Gold Today

Although the city's gold boom ended long ago, gold mining still continues today. The size of the mines (and the number of offshore mini-dredges) fluctuates. Visitors are welcome to try their own luck by picking up a gold pan at one of Nome's stores and sifting through the beach sands along a 2-mile stretch of shoreline east of Nome. Visitors can also contact the **Nome Convention & Visitors Bureau** for information on tours that feature gold panning.

Sunday. The menu changes daily, with items like seafood omelets, waffles, breakfast sandwiches, and burritos often making an appearance, along with sandwiches, soups, noodles, and pizza, plus an assortment of fresh pastries. **Known for:** fresh bread and seafood; daily changing menu; catering to different dietery needs. $ *Average main: $18* ✉ *308 Bering St., Nome* ☎ *907/387–0654* ⊕ *www.pingobakery-seafoodhouse.com* ⊘ *Closed Mon. and Tues.*

Hotels

Aurora Inn & Suites
$$$ | HOTEL | Close to shops, eateries, and local watering holes, this inn offers more than 50 modern rooms within easy walking distance of Nome's historic district. **Pros:** some rooms have sea views; refreshingly clean; ideal location. **Cons:** no free Wi-Fi; proximity to the bars means it can get a little rowdy outside; noise carries easily. $ *Rooms from: $250* ✉ *302 E. Front St., Nome* ☎ *907/443–3838, 800/354–4606* ⊕ *www.aurorainnome. com* ❌ No Meals ❌ *54 rooms.*

Dredge Inn No. 7
$$$ | B&B/INN | This inn has a turn-of-the-century vibe with mining memorabilia and historical photos that pay homage to the city's mining past. **Pros:** cool mix of vintage and modern furnishings; kitchen spaces where you can actually cook; convenient location. **Cons:** only three people per room; limited amenities; downstairs rooms get some noise. $ *Rooms from: $235* ✉ *1700 Teller Hwy., Nome* ☎ *907/304–1270* ⊕ *www.dredge7inn. com* ❌ No Meals ❌ *35 rooms.*

Nome Nugget Inn
$$ | HOTEL | The architecture and kitschy interiors of the Nugget Inn combine every cliché of the Victorian gold-rush era—it's not very authentic, but it is quite fun. **Pros:** Bering Sea views; cool atmosphere in public areas; central location. **Cons:** bar noise; dated rooms; old hotel

idiosyncrasies. $ *Rooms from: $175* ✉ *315 Front St., Nome* ☎ *877/443–2323, 907/443–4189* ⊕ *www.nomenuggetinn-hotel.com* ❌ *47 rooms* ❌ No Meals.

Shopping

Nome is one of the best places to buy walrus ivory because many of the Indigenous carvers from outlying villages come to Nome first to sell their wares to dealers.

★ Maruskiyas of Nome
CRAFTS | Come to this shop for its selection of art and craft objects made by Iñupiaq, St. Lawrence Island Yupik, and Siberian Yup'ik Alaska artists. The shop buys items from these local artists daily and has been doing so for over 40 years. Items include dolls, baskets, jewelry, and masks along with ivory, baleen, and jade sculptures. ✉ *247 Front St., Nome* ☎ *907/980–9806* ⊕ *www.maruskiyas.com.*

Bering Land Bridge National Preserve

100 miles north of Nome.

This expanse of tundra contains coastal beach environments, sand dunes, mountains, and lakes created by ancient lava flows, along with a great diversity of animals, birds, and plants. Many of Alaska's iconic animals move through this landscape, like caribou, brown bears, and musk oxen, as well as marine animals, like polar bears, walruses, and ribbon seals. Travelers to the preserve need to be adventurous and self-reliant; only six cabins offer emergency shelter in an area of nearly 3 million acres.

GETTING HERE AND AROUND
The Bering Land Bridge National Preserve has no trails, campgrounds, or other visitor facilities. Access is largely by air taxi and sometimes by small boat, although there is a road leading from

Nome that passes within hiking distance. Winter access is possible by ski-plane, snowmachine, or dogsled.

AIR TAXI CONTACTS Bering Air.
☎ *907/443–5464 Nome, 800/478–5422 Nome, 907/478–3943 Kotzebue* ⊕ *www.beringair.com.*

ESSENTIALS

VISITOR INFORMATION Bering Land Bridge Visitor Center. ✉ *214 Front St., Nome* ☎ *800/471–2352* ⊕ *www.nps.gov/bela.*

Sights

Bering Land Bridge National Preserve
NATURE PRESERVE | The frozen ash and lava of the 2.8-million-acre Bering Land Bridge National Preserve lie between Nome and Kotzebue, immediately south of the Arctic Circle, one of the most remote parks in the world. The Lost Jim lava flow is the northernmost flow of major size in the United States, and the paired maars (clear volcanic lakes) are a geological rarity.

Of equal interest are the paleontological features of this preserve. Sealed into the permafrost are flora and fauna—bits of twigs and leaves, tiny insects, small mammals, even the fossilized remains of woolly mammoths—that flourished here when the Bering Land Bridge linked North America to what is now Russia. "Bridge" is something of a misnomer; essentially, the Bering Sea was dry at the time, and the intercontinental connection was as much as 600 miles wide in places. Early people wandered through this treeless landscape, perhaps following sources of food and materials, such as the musk ox, whose descendants still occupy this terrain, or the mammoths and steppe bison, which are both long gone. Flowering plants thrive in this seemingly barren region, about 250 species in all, and tens of thousands of migrating birds can be seen in season. More than 100 species, including ducks, geese, swans, sandhill cranes, and various shorebirds and songbirds, come

here from around the world each spring. ✉ *Bering Sea Land Bridge National Preserve* ⊕ *www.nps.gov/bela* ☜ *Free.*

Kotzebue

170 miles northeast of Nome.

Most of the 3,000 or so residents of this coastal village are Iñupiat, whose ancestors have lived and moved throughout the region for thousands of years, creating seasonal camps when following caribou, moose, and other wildlife. Today, the Iñupiat people continue to depend on whales, seals, fish, and a wide variety of berries and other plants for their food and culture.

Built on a 3-mile-long spit of land that juts into Kotzebue Sound, the village lies 33 miles above the Arctic Circle on Alaska's northwest coast. The Iñupiat name for the village is Kikiktagruk. The Europeans named the town after the German explorer Otto von Kotzebue, who passed through in 1818 while sailing for Russia.

Kotzebue is the region's economic and political hub and headquarters for both the Northwest Arctic Borough and the NANA Regional Corporation, one of 13 regional Native corporations formed when Congress enacted the Alaska Native Claims Settlement Act in 1971. Nearby villages also use Kotzebue as a hub for trade, travel, business, and other services.

Many people in Kotzebue still fish, hunt, and gather wild food as their main meal source. Some also fish commercially. The government and the Native corporation provide employment in education, health care, utilities, and other public services, while a smaller number of people work for small businesses and extraction industries like mining. As in many Bush villages, the local government here is a blend of tribal government and a borough system.

Kotzebue has dark, cold winters and short, cool summers. The average low temperature in January is –12°F, and mid-summer highs rarely reach the 70s. "We have four seasons—June, July, August, and winter," a tour guide might jest. But don't worry about the sometimes chilly weather—the local sightseeing company has snug, bright-color loaner parkas for visitors on package tours. And there's plenty of light in which to take in the village and surrounding landscape; in fact, the sun doesn't set for 36 days from June into July. One of summer's highlights is the Fourth of July parade and fair, with contests, food, and games, including a foot race, bike race, blanket toss, and other traditional games.

This is also a great place to buy Iñupiat art and crafts, including parkas, dolls, caribou-skin masks, birchbark baskets, and whalebone and walrus-ivory carvings.

Although most people come to Kotzebue on day trips or overnight package tours, the town also serves as a gateway for three exceptional national wilderness areas: Cape Krusenstern National Monument, Kobuk Valley National Park, and Noatak National Preserve.

GETTING HERE AND AROUND

As with pretty much everywhere else in the Bush, the main way to get to Kotzebue is via plane. Alaska Airlines offers regular flights. The major air-taxi services fly to Kotzebue too, offering daily flights from Anchorage. Once here, cab drivers will take you anywhere in town for reasonable fees, and you can get to most places by foot.

Sights

Brooks Range

MOUNTAIN | The most northern mountain range in North America stretches some 700 miles west to east across northern Alaska into Canada's Yukon Territory. Considered a subrange of the Rocky Mountains, the Brooks Range is the highest range above the Arctic Circle, with peaks of nearly 9,000 feet. Noatak National Preserve, Kobuk Valley National Park, and Gates of the Arctic National Park all lie within it. At the range's western end, the Baird Mountains, where Mt. Angayukaqsraq is the highest peak (4,700 feet), are in Kobuk Valley National Park. ⊠ *Kobuk Valley National Park*.

Permafrost

NATURE SIGHT | If you're hiking the wild-flower-carpeted tundra around Kotzebue, you are entering a living museum dedicated to permafrost, the permanently frozen ground that lies just a few inches below the spongy tundra. Even Kotzebue's 6,000-foot airport runway is built on permafrost—with an insulating layer between the frozen ground and the airfield surface to ensure that landings are smooth. These days, thawing permafrost can cause problems for communities like Kotzebue: as the ice that binds frozen ground melts due to warm temperatures, the ground collapses and splits, damaging buildings, roads, and other infrastructure. ⊠ *Kotzebue*.

Activities

Golden Eagle Outfitters

ADVENTURE TOURS | With this outfitter, you can fly out of Kotzebue and access six national parks and preserves; they also do custom charters for an array of Arctic adventures. Some of the standard trips include half-day flightseeing tours and full-day multipark flight tours with landings in each park. They also do fly-in fishing, birding, and multiday float trips, as well as drop-offs and pickups for remote hiking and camping. ⊠ *Kotzebue* ☎ *907/388–5968, 907/442–2315* ⊕ *www. alaskawildernessexpeditions.com* 🎫 *From $350 per hour.*

Kotzebue Sound Wild

BOAT TOURS | FAMILY | This boating outfitter offers tours and charters on a custom-built dory-style boat, along with

Did You Know?

The blanket toss is traditionally performed during Nalukataq, the spring Iñupiat whaling festival. It was originally used for hunters to get into the air to scout game. Now it's used more for community connection and entertainment at cultural gatherings and athletic events.

cabin packages and boating skills classes. Options include multiday stays in a cabin about a 90-minute boat ride from Kotzebue on a tree-lined creek within Cape Krusenstern National Monument. Other tour and fishing charter options abound. ✉ *Kotzebue* ☎ *907/712–4649* 🌐 *www.kotzebuesoundwild.com* 🎫 *From $200 per hour.*

🍴 Restaurants

Empress Restaurant
$$ | **CHINESE** | Look for mostly Thai, Chinese, and American dishes at this spot along the shore. It offers a simple but filling selection of tempura, rolls, burgers, and more, along with fast and friendly service. **Known for:** friendly, fast service; burgers and Philly cheesesteaks; good array of Chinese dishes. [$] *Average main: $19* ✉ *301 Shore Ave., Kotzebue* ☎ *907/442–4304* 🌐 *www.facebook.com/EmpressKotzebue* ⏲ *Closed Sun.*

Little Louie's
$$ | **AMERICAN** | This basic but cozy eatery offers a range of food from morning to night. The menu includes pizza, burgers, omelets, wraps, nacho burritos, milkshakes, barbeque, Asian fusion dishes, and even packaged candy to go. **Known for:** fair prices for good food; varied selection of menu items; vegetarian options. [$] *Average main: $18* ✉ *388 Third Ave., Kotzebue* ☎ *907/442–4400* ⏲ *Closed Sun.*

The Nullagvik Restaurant
$$ | **AMERICAN** | This restaurant within the Nullagvik Hotel serves classic American food for breakfast, lunch, and dinner. Choose from a decent selection of pizzas, sandwiches, burgers, and appetizers, along with dishes like caribou stew and goulash. **Known for:** delicious smoothies and coffees; beautiful views of Kotzebue Sound; unique caribou dishes. [$] *Average main: $18* ✉ *306 Shore Ave., Kotzebue* ☎ *907/442–1650* 🌐 *www.nullagvikhotel.com/dining.*

🛏 Hotels

Bibber's B&B
$$ | **B&B/INN** | This longtime B&B offers rooms with shared kitchens, a tasty continental breakfast, and an owner who can tell you just about anything you need to know about Kotzebue. **Pros:** friendly, knowledgeable owner; homey and affordable; great way to meet fellow travelers. **Cons:** no website or online booking; rooms are pretty basic; not always someone there to check you in. [$] *Rooms from: $150* ✉ *398 Lagoon St., Kotzebue* ☎ *907/442–2693* 🍽 *Free Breakfast* 🛏 *15 rooms.*

★ LaVonne's Fish Camp
$$$ | **HOUSE** | Sitting on an intimate beach on the Chukchi Sea seven miles outside Kotzebue, this is where Iñupiat families and locals come to fish, and visitors can spend time here in one of the four simple cabins, joining fish camp activities, sharing meals, and browsing locally made art and craft pieces and meeting the people who create them. **Pros:** off-the-beaten-path yet just miles from town; great introduction to local fishing; unique chance to meet and learn from locals about their way of life. **Cons:** shared shower; remote from the town center; only a beach outhouse for toilet facilities. [$] *Rooms from: $250* ✉ *Kotzebue* ☎ *907/995–6013 camp phone in July and August, 907/276–0976 winter number, 907/529–5928 summer number* 🌐 *www.fishcamp.org* ⏲ *Closed Sept.–mid-Jun.* 🍽 *All-Inclusive* 🛏 *4 cabins.*

Nullagvik Hotel
$$$ | **HOTEL** | Although it's been a Kotzebue fixture since 1975, the Nullagvik Hotel offers the most modern rooms in town, along with communal areas, like a meeting room for 100 and a third-floor observation lounge overlooking the Chukchi Sea. Amenities include Wi-Fi, televisions, microwaves, and mini-refrigerators, along with access to an exercise area and a restaurant on the first floor. **Pros:** nice amenities; great views;

comfortable rooms. **Cons:** generic room decor; the best lodging in town comes at a price; room windows too small to capture the vast views. 💲 *Rooms from: $279 ✉ 306 Shore Ave., Kotzebue* ☎ *907/442–3331 ⊕ www.nullagvikhotel. com* ⦿*No Meals ⇌ 78 rooms.*

Kobuk Valley National Park

65 miles east of Kotzebue.

Half a million caribou leave tracks on the vast Kobuk dunes every year, tracing their migration in the sandy remnants of retreating glaciers from the Pleistocene epoch. These dunes appear as a rivuleted sand sprawl in a park with broad wetlands, meandering rivers, boreal forests, and mountains rising from wide and wooded valleys. The Kobuk River bisects the park, with dunes situated in the lower reaches and rivers valleys and the Baird Mountains to the north. The boreal forest reaches its most northern limits in the valley, giving way to upland areas of tundra and scree. In summer, this Arctic landscape comes alive with insects and birds, bears and foxes, waterfowl and sheefish. The Western Arctic caribou herd—the largest in the United States—passes north in the spring and south in the fall, crossing Kobuk on the way. All this life has helped people survive in the region for thousands of years.

ESSENTIALS
Kobuk Valley National Park
✉ *Kobuk Valley National Park, Kotzebue* ☎ *907/442–3890 ⊕ www.nps.gov/kova.*

 Sights

Kobuk River and Valley
BODY OF WATER | The Kobuk Valley provides a glimpse into what the thousand-mile-wide grassland of Beringia, the land connecting Asia and North America

during the last ice age, looked like. The Kobuk River bisects the national park, with dunes to the south and broad wetlands leading to the Baird Mountains to the north. Running hundreds of miles (60 of them in the national park) from the Endicott Mountains to Kotzebue Sound, the generally wide river has been used for transportation for thousands of years. It also sustains a big population of sheefish, a large predatory whitefish in the salmon family that spawns in the river's upper reaches every fall. A portion of the vast Western Arctic caribou herd uses the Kobuk Valley as a winter range, and the boreal forest reaches its northernmost limits here. ✉ *Kobuk Valley National Park.*

Kobuk Valley Sand Dunes
NATURE SIGHT | South of the Kobuk River, the Great Kobuk (the largest active, high-altitude dune field on Earth), Little Kobuk, and Hunt River Sand Dunes—stabilized by small trees, shrubs, and the lichen that's typical of the tundra—cover much of the southern Kobuk Valley. They formed when glaciers slowly pulverized mountain rock into sand that washed into the valley during the last ice age. Of note, a flowering herb called the Kobuk locoweed is only found on the slopes of the Great Kobuk Sand Dunes. Most outfitters and air taxis that operate in the Arctic will take visitors to the sand dunes. ✉ *Kobuk Valley National Park.*

The Northwest Arctic Heritage Center
VISITOR CENTER | This facilty in Kotzebue serves as the visitor center for Kobuk Valley National Park, Cape Krusenstern National Monument, and Noatak National Preserve. Here you can find information and borrow bear-resistant containers on a first-come, first-served basis. ✉ *Kobuk Valley National Park, Kotzebue* ☎ *907/442–3890 ⊕ www.nps.gov/kova.*

Hotels

Kobuk River Lodge

$$ | B&B/INN | Located in Ambler, east of Kobuk Valley National Park, this lodge offers rooms for rent with meals included, as well as supplies, guided tours, and river transport services into the park on the Kobuk River. **Pros:** Wi-Fi and satellite TV; easy access to hiking, fishing, and sightseeing on the Kobuk River and in the valley; laundry facilities. **Cons:** limited room amenities; tight quarters; only one room has a double bed. $ *Rooms from: $200* ✉ *11 Ambler Ave., Ambler* ☎ *907/445–5235 tours and lodging reservations, 907/445–2166 store and restaurant* ⊕ *www.kobukriverlodge.com* ⇆ *3 rooms.*

Noatak National Preserve

20 miles northeast of Kotzebue.

For well-organized and self-reliant adventurers, Noatak National Preserve offers a stunning landscape for those who want to hike, paddle, fish, and view birds and wildlife. Bring bug spray, along with everything else you need to camp and explore. There are no visitor facilities.

👁 **Sights**

Noatak River

BODY OF WATER | Adjacent to Gates of the Arctic National Park and Preserve, 6.5-million-acre Noatak National Preserve encompasses much of the basin of the Noatak River. This is the largest mountain-ringed river basin in the country, and part of it is designated by the National Park Service as a Wild and Scenic River. The river carves out the "Grand Canyon of the Noatak" over 425 miles and serves as a migration route between arctic and subarctic ecosystems. Its importance to wildlife and plants has resulted in its designation as an International Biosphere Reserve. The Noatak River also serves as a natural highway for humans and has for thousands of years. These days, river runners head here because of its beauty, inviting tundra for camping, and good hiking in the nearby Poktovik Mountains and Igichuk Hills. Birding can be exceptional; horned grebes, gyrfalcons, golden eagles, parasitic jaegers, owls, terns, and loons are among the species you may see. You may also spot grizzly bears, Dall sheep, wolves, caribou, and lynx, as well as the occasional musk ox. The most frequently run part of the river, ending at Lake Machurak, is mostly an easy Class I–III paddle. As with other parks and preserves in this northwest corner of Alaska, no visitor facilities are available and you are expected to be self-sufficient. Do not forget first-aid supplies, clothing for all conditions, and precautions for being on the water and around wildlife. Most trips on the Noatak use the inland town of Bettles as a gateway. ✉ *Noatak River* ☎ *907/442–3890* ⊕ *www.nps.gov/noat* 🎫 *Free.*

Gates of the Arctic National Park and Preserve

180 miles east of Kotzebue.

The northernmost national park in the United States stands apart, with 8.4 million acres of truly epic scenery featuring endless, cragged peaks (once part of an ancient seabed), stunning river valleys, and six of Alaska's 13 Wild and Scenic Rivers: the Alatna, John, Kobuk, Noatak, and Tinayguk, and the North Fork of the Koyukuk. With a scant 10,000 visitors a year, Gates of the Arctic promises total solitude and immersion into a living Arctic landscape. On foot, the contours of the land will take you into terrain pock-marked with blue- and green-hued ponds and huge glacial lakes.

For a more intense experience (and bragging rights), hike the famed and arduous Anaktuvuk Pass, or backpack into the Arrigetch Peaks, massive granite pinnacles that rise thousands of feet from the surrounding uplands. Whether backpacking in for weeks or flying in for the day, you can count on walking away with stories and photos that will stay with you forever.

Sights

Anaktuvuk Pass

TRAIL | Anaktuvuk Pass lies on a divide between the Anaktuvuk and John Rivers in the central Brooks Range. A small Nunamuit Iñupiat village of the same name sits atop this 2,000-foot pass. The economy and traditions here center on the caribou herds that supply residents with most of their meat. Surrounded by mountains, rivers, and lakes, this is one of the North Slope's most scenic spots. Daily flights from Fairbanks travel to the village, and you can walk from there into the national park. You can also do backpacking trips that start or end at the pass. As elsewhere in Gates of the Arctic, some of the terrain here is on private or Native corporation land, so inquire at the ranger station about where it's best to hike and camp—and whether or not you need permission to do so. ⊠ *Gates of the Arctic National Park and Preserve* ☎ *907/661–3520 Anaktuvuk Pass Ranger Station (Apr.–Sept.)* ⊕ *https://www.nps. gov/gaar/index.htm.*

Brooks Range and Arrigetch Peaks

MOUNTAIN | The northernmost moun-tain range in North American stretches some 700 miles west to east across Alaska into Canada's Yukon Territory. The Brooks Range also forms the continent's

northernmost drainage divide, separating streams flowing into the Arctic Ocean and the Pacific. It also marks the northern extent of the tree line. The range is the highest to the east, with peaks of nearly 9,000 feet. Gates of the Arctic National Park lies in the center of the Brooks Range, with the Arrigetch Peaks as the showpiece. Designated a National Natural Landmark, the peaks draw hikers, flightse-ers, and even climbers intrepid enough to scale granite walls that rise thousands of feet. "Arrigetch" means "fingers of the out-stretched hand" in the Iñupiaq language, and the name truly conveys the sense of awe experienced by many of those who visit them. ⊠ *Gates of the Arctic National Park and Preserve.*

The Dalton Highway

SCENIC DRIVE | One of the most isolated roads in the country, the Dalton Highway (Alaska Route 11) consists mostly of loose-packed dirt and gravel that can put wear and tear on your vehicle, as well as your spine. It can also take you on a magical road trip with sublime views and remarkable experiences. If heading up the 400-plus-mile "haul road" toward the Arctic Ocean, start 80 miles north of Fairbanks at a tiny town called Livengood (population: a baker's dozen, more or less), and then keep heading north.

The Dalton was built to support con-struction of the Trans-Alaska Pipeline and the oil fields on the North Slope, so the pipeline and tinges of industrializa-tion parallel the road—and spellbinding beauty spreads out beyond it. The drive will take you through boreal forest, the Brooks Range, the Arctic foothills, the coastal plain tundra, and finally, a few miles short of the Arctic Ocean, to a town called Deadhorse, a place named exactly how it feels.

There's much to see along the way, yet many reasons to miss the show. The drive can be treacherous, with hazards ranging from speeding 18-wheelers to fog, snow, rain, potholes, and steep grades, with only a few services along the way. Plan ahead (spare tires, provisions, etc.), and take your time. Like all good road trips, there are things you won't want to miss, and a few you will.

Gates of the Arctic National Park Visitor Centers

VISITOR CENTER | Information is available at visitor centers in Fairbanks, Bettles, Coldfoot, and Anaktuvuk Pass. The Anaktuvuk Pass Ranger Station, Bettles Ranger Station, and Arctic Interagency Visitor Center in Coldfoot are open during the summer months and can provide info on hiking routes. They also loan bear-resistant food containers on a first-come, first-served basis. ☎ *907/459–3730 Fairbanks Alaska Public Lands Information Center, 907/692–5494 Bettles Ranger Station (July–Sept. only), 907/678–5209 Arctic Interagency Visitor Center (Coldfoot; July–Sept. only), 907/661–3520 Anaktuvuk Pass (Apr.–Sept. only)* ⊕ *www.nps. gov/gaar.*

National Wild and Scenic Rivers

BODY OF WATER | The Alatna, John, Kobuk, Noatak, and Tinayguk Rivers with the North Fork of the Koyukuk River make up six of the 13 National Wild and Scenic Rivers in Gates of the Arctic National Park. They have been byways for people and animals for thousands of years, and they support each summer's explosion of life. They're also navigable, with a variety of access points. Boating through the park reveals mountains, glacial valleys, and rolling tundra, plus glimpses of animals along the landscape.

Most people use rafts, inflatable canoes, packrafts, or other collapsible boats, as air taxis will not haul rigid vessels. Although the waters are generally Class I and II rapids, a few sections include Class II–IV rapids. The water is cold, and conditions constantly change, with levels fluctuating dramatically and the possibility of log jams and strainers. But when the going is good, boating can beat walking through thick tussocks and boggy

ground. Many outfitters offer paddling options. If you're heading out on your own, talk to your air-taxi operator or local guides about current conditions. ✉ *Gates of the Arctic National Park and Preserve* ☎ *907/459–3730 National Park Service in Fairbanks* ⊕ *www.nps.gov/gaar/learn/ nature/wildandscenicrivers.htm.*

Activities

Alaska Alpine Adventures

ADVENTURE TOURS | This family-friendly company out of Anchorage offers paddling, backpacking, and combination trips throughout Alaska. Scheduled trips include 10 days of hiking in the Arrigetch Peaks in Gates of the Arctic and 12 days of rafting the Noatak River and hiking the sand dunes in the Kobuk Valley. Custom trips are available, too. ✉ *Anchorage* ☎ *877/525–2577* ⊕ *www.alaskaalpineadventures.com* 🖃 *From $5195.*

Arctic Treks

ADVENTURE TOURS | Based in Fairbanks, this outfit offers hiking, boating, and base-camp trips of 7 to 12 days, including hiking in the Arrigetch Peaks, fall caribou-viewing in Gates of the Arctic, and hiking and camping trips that go to Gates of the Arctic and Kobuk Valley National Parks. The company offers other trips in the western Arctic and the Arctic National Wildlife Refuge, along with custom trips for groups of three to nine people. ✉ *Fairbanks* ☎ *907/455–6502* ⊕ *www. arctictreksadventures.com* 🖃 *From $4700.*

Hotels

Bettles Lodge

$$$$ | B&B/INN | Open year-round and offering an array of all-inclusive packages, the historic Bettles and its more modern Aurora Lodge together make a comfortable base camp for viewing the northern lights or exploring Gates of the Arctic and Kobuk Valley National Parks. **Pros:** sometimes accessible from Dalton

Highway via ice road in winter; lots of on-site services and amenities; tasty meals and to-die-for hot cocoa. **Cons:** weather and shoulder seasons may limit activities; shared baths; pricey for fairly basic accommodations. [$] *Rooms from: $1090* ✉ *1 Airline Dr.* ✈ *Short walk from the airport or Bettles Ranger Station* ☎ *907/692–5111* 🌐 *bettleslodge.com* 🍴 *All-Inclusive* 🛏 *14 rooms.*

Utqiaġvik

330 miles northeast of Kotzebue.

The northernmost community in the United States, Utqiaġvik—known previously as Barrow—sits 1,300 miles south of the North Pole, 10 miles south of the Beaufort Sea and Point Barrow, and about 350 miles north of the boundary of the Arctic Circle. In the Iñupiaq language, Utqiaġvik means a place for gathering wild roots and comes from the word now used for potato, "utqiq."

The Iñupiat and their ancestors have lived in the area for thousands of years. The town became officially known as Barrow in 1901 after being named Point Barrow in 1825 by British captain Frederick William Beechey, who'd been ordered by the British Navy to map the continent's northern coastline. Beechey wished to honor Sir John Barrow, a member of the British Admiralty involved in exploring the Arctic. The town voted to change its name in 2016 to better reflect its Indigenous heritage.

About 4,400 people reside in Utqiaġvik today, making it easily the largest community on the North Slope. Nearly two-thirds of the residents are Iñupiat, deeply rooted in their culture and homelands. The community has a public radio station, cable TV, and Internet access, along with a recreation center. In Utqiaġvik, as in much of Bush Alaska, basketball is a favorite sport, played year-round by people of all ages.

Utqiaġvik is the economic and administrative center of the **North Slope Borough,** which encompasses more than 88,000 square miles, making it the world's largest municipal government in terms of area. The village is also headquarters for the **Arctic Slope Regional Corporation,** formed in 1971 through the Alaska Native Claims Settlement Act, as well as the Ukpeagvik Inupiat Corporation, an economic and political entity. Several village councils are also headquartered in the town.

GETTING HERE AND AROUND

Alaska Airlines and several regional and charter airlines fly to Utqiaġvik. The Alaska Travel Industry Association can give tips on air travel and flightseeing opportunities throughout the Bush.

ESSENTIALS

CONTACTS Alaska Travel Industry Association. ✉ *2600 Cordova St., Suite 201, Anchorage* 🌐 *www.travelalaska.com.* **City of Utqiaġvik.** ✉ *2022 Ahkovak St., Barrow* ☎ *907/852–5211* 🌐 *www.utqiagvik.us.*

Sights

Colonial settlers established a presence at Utqiaġvik in the early 1880s, when the U.S. Army built a research station here. Drawn to the area by the Beaufort Sea's abundant whales, commercial whalers established the **Cape Smythe Whaling and Trading Station** in 1893; a cabin from that operation still stands and is the oldest frame building in Alaska's Arctic. The station is now listed on the National Register of Historic Places (as are the Birnirk dwelling mounds). By the early 1900s, both a Presbyterian church and a U.S. Post Office had been established here.

Oil and gas exploration later brought more people from the Lower 48 to the area; even more came as schools and other government agencies took root in the region. Eben Nanauq Hopson, the first mayor of Utqiaġvik and later a state senator, played a major role in the area's development, as he funneled millions of dollars in tax revenues into road building, sanitation and water services, and heath-care services.

Utqiaġvik has opened its annual spring-time whale festival to outsiders, and there are several historic sites, including a military installation, points of Native cultural importance, and a famous crash site. The Utqiaġvik airport is where you'll find the **Will Rogers– Wiley Post Monument,** marking the 1935 crash that killed the American humorist and his pilot 15 miles south of town.

While in town, visitors often take the informative bus tour of the town's dusty roads and major sights.

Activities

Tundra Tours

GUIDED TOURS | **FAMILY** | Winter tours offered from mid-September through mid-May feature visits to a traditional hunting camp, the whaling station, and the DEW site (Distant Early Warning, part of an Arctic radar system), plus opportunities to visit Point Barrow and watch the northern lights. The summer program takes visitors to local historic sites and lets them experience traditional cultural activities such as dances, sewing demonstrations, and the famous blanket toss. In both winter and summer, visitors can purchase locally made Iñupiat art and crafts. ✉ *3060 Eben Hopson St., Utqiaġvik* ☎ *907/852–3900* 🌐 *www.tundratoursinc.com.*

Restaurants

Arctic Pizza

$$ | **PIZZA** | Go to Arctic for good pies and huge calzones, plus Mexican and Italian entrées. Everything is made to order, and the wait is worth it. **Known for:** good views of the Arctic Ocean; tasty calzones; reasonable prices. [$] *Average main: $22* ✉ *125 Apayauk S, Utqiaġvik* ☎ *907/852–4222.*

Cruz's Mexican Grill

$$ | **MEXICAN** | Try the tamales and flan at this eatery specializing in authentic Mexican fare. The owners were born in Cuba and Mexico, met in Utqiaġvik, and teamed up to make the food they grew up eating. **Known for:** cozy space with a laid-back feel; great baked goods and desserts; large portions of authentic Mexican food. [$] *Average main: $22* ✉ *3210 Paneatak St., Utqiaġvik* ☎ *907/852–2253* 🕒 *Closed Sun.*

Niġġivikput

$$$ | **AMERICAN** | This restaurant within the Top of the World Hotel offers a range of American food for breakfast, lunch, and dinner, including reindeer sausage scrambles, chicken fajita salads, Philly cheesesteaks, and various burgers, along with entrées like steak and halibut. For a good start to the day, try the well-prepared egg dishes for breakfast, with diner-style hash browns. **Known for:** meat and seafood entrees; well-prepared breakfasts; great views by the windows. [$] *Average main: $27* ✉ *Top of the World Hotel, Eben Hopson St., Kotzebue* ☎ *907/852–9440* 🌐 *www.tundratoursinc.com/dining.*

Sam & Lee's Restaurant

$$ | **CHINESE** | **FAMILY** | Whether you're up early or late, Sam and Lee's has got you covered. They start with an excellent breakfast menu and stay open late with mostly Chinese fare, such as kung pao beef, almond chicken, and Szechwan chow mein. **Known for:** friendly staff; delicious kimchee; all day hours. [$] *Average main: $22* ✉ *1052 Kogiak St., Utqiaġvik* ☎ *907/852–5556.*

Hotels

King Eider Inn

$$ | **HOTEL** | At the King Eider Inn near the airport, you'll find comfortable rooms with simple furnishings and decor.

Pros: private sauna rooms; simple but lovely rooms; Internet and cable. **Cons:** some airport noise; pretty bare-bones; no on-site eatery. $ *Rooms from: $199* ✉ *1752 Ahkovak St., Barrow* ☎ *907/852–4700* ⊕ *www.kingeider.net* ⇄ *19 rooms* ⦿I *No Meals.*

Latitude 71 BnB

$$$ | **B&B/INN** | This B&B filled with ivory carvings and scrimshaw by local artists makes everyone feel welcome. **Pros:** peaceful atmosphere; delicious meals; great hospitality. **Cons:** not ideal for families; most rooms have shared bathrooms; room pricing is for singles. $ *Rooms from: $225* ✉ *5725 B Ave., Utqiaġvik* ☎ *907/301–6017* ⊕ *www.latitude71bnb. com* ⦿I *Free Breakfast* ⇄ *10 rooms.*

Top of the World Hotel

$$$ | **HOTEL** | On the shores of the Arctic Ocean, this tiered and multicolored hotel is minimalist but comes with the modern conveniences expected by most travelers. **Pros:** quick walk to the beach; modern rooms and conveniences; restaurant on-site. **Cons:** no alcohol allowed; no elevators (which means you're taking the stairs to the top of the world); no frills. $ *Rooms from: $280* ✉ *1200 Agviq St., Barrow* ☎ *907/852–3900* ⊕ *www.tundra-toursinc.com* ⇄ *44 rooms* ⦿I *No Meals.*

⊖ Shopping

AC Value Center

MARKET | Known by most as "Stuaqpak" ("Big Store" in Iñupiaq), this is the only major market in town. It primarily sells groceries, but it also has a hot-food court and stocks local crafts, including furs, parkas, mukluks, and ceremonial masks (sometimes the artists set up vendor tables outside). For many people, AC Value is a lifeline to the most basic food and clothing supplies that make the extreme reaches of Alaska habitable. If you have time to visit one, you should do so, if for no other reason than to see firsthand the prices of milk and bread this far north.

✉ *4725 Ahkovak St., Barrow* ☎ *907/852–6711* ⊕ *www.alaskacommercial.com.*

Prudhoe Bay

250 miles southeast ofUtqiaġvik.

Most towns have museums that chronicle local history and achievements. Deadhorse is a work camp catering to the oil industry in Prudhoe Bay, but it's also a living museum documenting humankind's thirst for energy via its modular, prefabricated structures.

Access to Prudhoe Bay and the Arctic Ocean is restricted to oil field workers and tour groups with special permits. When on tours, visitors can survey oil wells, stations, and oil company residential complexes that are small cities in themselves.

GETTING HERE AND AROUND
In the past, individual travelers rarely turned up in Prudhoe Bay, but once the Dalton Highway opened as far north as Deadhorse, people found their way. Still, rather than driving hundreds of miles of gravel road in varied conditions while grappling with fast-moving semi-trucks, most people head to Deadhorse on tours, which are recommended for exploring the area and in fact required to cross the oil fields to get to the Arctic Ocean.

Hotels

The Aurora Hotel

$$ | **HOTEL** | Like all lodging in Prudhoe Bay, the Aurora focuses on what oil workers need when rotating in and out of the area, so most of the rooms have one twin bed, while some have queens. **Pros:** good food and coffee 24/7; rate includes meals; library, rec room, and gym on-site. **Cons:** no alcohol allowed; private baths cost extra; thin walls. $ *Rooms from: $150* ✉ *123 E Lake Colleen Dr., Prudhoe Bay* ☎ *907/670–0600* ⊕ *www.theaurora-hotel.net* ⦿I *All-Inclusive* ⇄ *432 rooms.*

A hiker stands atop a rocky summit at the Arctic National Wildlife Refuge.

Deadhorse Camp

$$$ | HOTEL | This rustic space offers small rooms with two twin beds in a yellow industrial-looking building about 2 miles south of the Dalton Highway's northernmost point. **Pros:** good place to meet interesting people; hearty food; clean and comfortable rooms. **Cons:** meals not included in price; industrial ambience not very charming; no private baths and very small rooms. $ *Rooms from: $219* ⊠ *Mile 412.8 Dalton Highway, Prudhoe Bay* ☎ *907/474–3565* ⊕ *www.deadhorse-camp.com* ❑ *No Meals* ⇴ *50 rooms.*

Prudhoe Bay Hotel

$$ | B&B/INN | This hotel near the end of the road at Deadhorse primarily serves workers employed in the Prudhoe Bay oil fields, but tourists are also welcome. **Pros:** Wi-Fi and TVs provided; one of the few lodging options in the area; good food. **Cons:** industrial setting and feel; not all rooms have private bathrooms; rooms are dormitory-style. $ *Rooms from: $190* ⊠ *1 Deadhorse Dr., Prudhoe Bay* ☎ *907/659–2449* ❑ *All-Inclusive* ⇴ *200 rooms.*

Arctic National Wildlife Refuge

270 miles north of Fairbanks, 70 miles southeast of Prudhoe Bay.

Enormous even by Alaska standards, the Arctic National Wildlife Refuge (often referred to as ANWR) encompasses six different eco-zones that support a vast diversity of plants and animals, including the Porcupine caribou herd, polar bears, and migratory birds from around the world. In fact, the area supports the greatest variety of protected plant and animal life within the Arctic Circle.

The Iñupiat and Gwich'in have lived with and moved through these lands for thousands of years, and continue to fish, hunt, and practice their traditional cultural ways in the Arctic Refuge. Visitors often come to hike, backpack, bird-watch, view wildlife, and white-water raft. The northern side of the Arctic Refuge in particular lacks dense shrubbery and offers nice walking for hikers and backpackers.

Sights

Arctic National Wildlife Refuge (ANWR)

NATURE PRESERVE | The Arctic Refuge includes one of the few protected Arctic coastal lands in the United States, as well as millions of acres of mountains and alpine tundra in the easternmost portion of the Brooks Range. Hundreds of thousands of birds, caribou, and other animals move across the Arctic Refuge during their annual migrations, relying on the area to nurse and feed their young while finding refuge from insects and predators. The Iñupiat and Gwich'in peoples have also relied on the lands of the Arctic Refuge for their food and ways of life for thousands of years. The Gwich'in consider the coastal plain of the Arctic Refuge a sacred place because it feeds and protects the Porcupine caribou herd, which in turn feeds and provides the cultural foundation for the Gwich'in people. The quest for oil in the coastal plain has become a divisive issue that pits corporate interests and proponents of oil extraction against those seeking to protect traditional ways of life for generations to come. A lease sale of land in the coastal plan occurred in January 2021, but any further oil and gas activity or industrialization has been put on hold.

The coastal area of the Arctic Refuge also provides critical denning grounds for polar bears, which spend much of their year on the Arctic Ocean's pack ice. Other wildlife include grizzly bears, Dall sheep, wolves, musk ox, and dozens of varieties of birds, from snowy owls to geese and tiny songbirds. As in many of Alaska's more remote parks and refuges, there are no roads here, and no developed trails, campgrounds, or other visitor facilities. Counterintuitively, for such a notoriously brutal geography, the plants and permafrost are quite fragile. The ground can be soft and wet in summer months, so walk with care: footprints in the tundra can last 100 years. Plan for snow in almost any season, and anticipate subfreezing temperatures even in summer, particularly in the mountains. Many of the clear-flowing rivers are runnable, and tundra lakes are suitable for base camps (air taxis can drop you off and pick you up). ✉ *North Pole* ☎ *907/456–0250 Fairbanks office, 800/362–4546* ⊕ *www.fws.gov/refuge/arctic.*

★ Porcupine Caribou Herd

NATURE SIGHT | The Porcupine caribou herd, with nearly 200,000 animals, migrates through Alaska's Arctic and Canada's adjacent Vuntut and Ivvavik National Parks, flowing like a river of animals across the expansive coastal plain, through U-shape valleys and alpine meadows, and over high mountain passes. These migration routes demonstrate the interconnected nature of the region's lands and waters, and how arbitrary human boundaries seem. ✉ *Arctic National Wildlife Refuge.*

Index

Photo Credits

Front cover: Design Pics Inc/Alamy [Description: Scenic view of Lynn Canal and the Chilkat Mountains near Skagway at sunset, Southeast Alaska, Summer]. **Back cover, from left to right:** Izabela23/Shutterstock, Jef Wodniack/Shutterstock, emperorcosar/Shutterstock. **Spine:** CREATISTA/Shutterstock. **Interior, from left to right:** alaskarap (1). ursocalgirl (2-3). emperorcosar/Shutterstock (5). **Chapter 1: Experience Alaska:** Papilio/Alamy (6-7). emperorcosar/Shutterstock (8-9). Gleb Tarro/Shutterstock (9). Michael Turner/Dreamstime (9). Steve Boice/Shutterstock (10). Russ Heinl/Shutterstock (10). reisegraf.ch/Shutterstock (10). Michele Cornelius/Dreamstime (10). Jeanninebryan/Dreamstime (11). Darryl Brooks/Dreamstime (11). Paxson Woelber [CC BY 2.0]/Wikimedia Commons (12). Bob Pool/Shutterstock (12). artincamera/Shutterstock (12). Mikhail Varentsov/Shutterstock (12). Leieng/Dreamstime (13). FloridaStock/Shutterstock (14). Martin Schneiter/Dreamstime (14). u photostock/Shutterstock (14). takeshi82/Shutterstock (14). Surangaw/Dreamstime (15). Izabela 23/Dreamstime (15). Christophe Avril/Dreamstime (20). Kondor83/Shutterstock (20). Steve Cukrov/Shutterstock (20). Matyáš Havel [CC BY-SA 3.0]/Wikimedia Commons (21). hlphoto/Shutterstock (21). vitaliy_73/Shutterstock (22). Antonov Roman/Shutterstock (22). Khritthithat Weerasirirut/Shutterstock (22). Reinhardt/Dreamstime (23). The Kobuk Team (23). Chris McDaniel/Shutterstock (24). Bryan Brazil/Shutterstock (24). Chase Dekker/Shutterstock (24). Gary M. Karl (24). Tomas Kulaja/Shutterstock (25). Travis J. Camp/Shutterstock (25). Tyler Westhoff/Fly Denali Inc. (25). Haley Johnston/Alaska Alpine Adventures (25). Chase Dekker/Shutterstock (26). Major Marine Tours (26). John Coffey (26). Tory Kallman/Shutterstock (26). Wildnerdpix/Shutterstock (27). Lawrence Weslowski Jr/Dreamstime (27). Julien Schroder/Iditarod Trail Committee (27). Anastasiia Vereshchagina/Shutterstock (27). Michael Turner/Dreamstime (28). Ruth Peterkin/Shutterstock (29). VicPhotoria/Shutterstock (30). Hemuli/Shutterstock (31). **Chapter 3: Anchorage:** 2017 Daniel Case/Shutterstock (53). Jeff Schultz/agefotostock (65). Ha Mediagroup/Dreamstime (68). Jay Yuan/Shutterstock (82). **Chapter 4: Juneau, the Inside Passage, and Southeast Alaska:** crmarlow (87). Sandy1122 (107). Stephen Frink Collection/Alamy (129). ImageState/Alamy (129). Santiparp Wattanaporn/Shutterstock (130). Pieter Folkens (130). Pieter Folkens (131). A Henderson/Shutterstock (132). Pieter Folkens (132). Design Pics Inc/Alamy (136-137). John Baston/Mountain Travel Sobek (161). Everett Collection/Shutterstock (173). lembi/Shutterstock (174). P277-001-009 Alaska State Library James Wickersham/State Historic Sites Collection (175). Alaska Stock LLC/Alamy (177). Christian Racich (177). Pep Roig/Alamy (177). **Chapter 5: The Kenai Peninsula and Southcentral Alaska:** Izanbar/Dreamstime (183). Izanbar/Dreamstime (197). Sutthirat Wongsunkakorn/Dreamstime (205). Alyssand/Dreamstime.com (220). Nenad Basic/Shutterstock (221). Alaska Stock LLC/Alamy (223). emperorcosar/Shutterstock (223). bobby20/Dreamstime (241). **Chapter 6: Denali Park and the Preserve:** Tyler Westhoff/Fly Denali Inc. (261). Brett Baunton/Alamy (273). Alissa Crandall/CORBIS (274-275). John Schwieder/Alamy (275). Library of Congress Prints and Photographs Division (276). Ping Ye/Dreamstime (281). **Chapter 7: Fairbanks, the Yukon, and the Interior:** Eric Yeager/Bureau of Land Management (291). Patricia Fisher/Fisher Photography (305). Surangaw/Dreamstime (318). Bryan & Cherry Alexander Photography/Alamy (327). Walleyelj/Dreamstime.com (328). Sitka National Historical Park (329). Tracy Ferrero/Alamy (329). Alaska State Museum, Juneau (330, all). Alaska State Museum, Juneau (331, all). Pecold/Shutterstock (335). **Chapter 8: The Bush:** Peter Arnold, Inc./Alamy (343). Design Pics Inc/Alamy (381). WorldFoto/Alamy (390). **About Our Writers:** All photos are courtesy of the writers.

*Every effort has been made to trace the copyright holders, and we apologize in advance for any accidental errors. We would be happy to apply the corrections in the following edition of this publication.

Fodor's ALASKA

Publisher: Stephen Horowitz, *General Manager*

Editorial: Douglas Stallings, *Editorial Director*; Jill Fergus, Amanda Sadlowski, Caroline Trefler, *Senior Editors*; Kayla Becker, Alexis Kelly, *Editors*; Angelique Kennedy-Chavannes, *Assistant Editor*

Design: Tina Malaney, *Director of Design and Production*; Jessica Gonzalez, *Graphic Designer*

Production: Jennifer DePrima, *Editorial Production Manager*; Elyse Rozelle, *Senior Production Editor*; Monica White, *Production Editor*

Maps: Rebecca Baer, *Senior Map Editor*; Mark Stroud (Moon Street Cartography), David Lindroth, *Cartographers*

Photography: Viviane Teles, *Senior Photo Editor*; Namrata Aggarwal, Payal Gupta, Ashok Kumar, *Photo Editors*; Rebecca Rimmer, *Photo Production Associate*; Eddie Aldrete, *Photo Production Intern*

Business & Operations: Chuck Hoover, *Chief Marketing Officer*; Robert Ames, *Group General Manager*; Devin Duckworth, *Director of Print Publishing*

Public Relations and Marketing: Joe Ewaskiw, *Senior Director of Communications & Public Relations*

Fodors.com: Jeremy Tarr, *Editorial Director*; Rachael Levitt, *Managing Editor*

Technology: Jon Atkinson, *Director of Technology*; Rudresh Teotia, *Lead Developer*; Jacob Ashpis, *Content Operations Manager*

Writers: Teeka Ballas, J. Besl, David Cannamore, Amy Fletcher, Dawnell Smith

Editor: Amanda Sadlowski

Production Editor: Elyse Rozelle

37th Edition

ISBN 978-1-64097-475-3

ISSN 0271-2776

SPECIAL SALES

This book is available at special discounts for bulk purchases for sales promotions or premiums. For more information, e-mail SpecialMarkets@fodors.com.

PRINTED IN THE UNITED STATES OF AMERICA

10 9 8 7 6 5 4 3 2 1

About Our Writers

Based in Anchorage, **Teeka Ballas** is the publisher/editor of *F Magazine*, Alaska's only independent statewide arts magazine. For 13 years, she has worked as a freelance writer, staffer, and stringer for newspapers, international wire services, travel publications, and radio. In addition, Ballas is the director and events coordinator for four statewide arts and media competitions and directs teen musicals for Alaska Theatre of Youth. She worked on the Kenai Peninsula and Southcentral Alaska chapter this edition.

J. Besl is a university staff writer in Anchorage, where he shares the stories of students and faculty and their academic adventures in the north. He's also a freelance writer, and his stories have appeared in newspapers and magazines across the state. Originally from Cincinnati, you can now find him at the bus stops and bike lanes of Alaska's big city. He updated the Experience, Anchorage, and Fairbanks, the Yukon, and the Interior chapters.

A lifelong Alaskan, **David Cannamore** makes his home in the tiny town of Gustavus on the footsteps of Glacier Bay National Park. After updating the Denali National Park chapter this edition, David returned to his cabin, wife, cats, and summer occupation as a kayak guide. When not paddling, David can be found freelance writing, cobbling together a novel, or trying to make his tiny cabin more insulated.

The catalyst for **Amy Fletcher**'s initial visit to Alaska in 1992 was an enticing two-line description of Juneau's stunning natural beauty in a travel guide. She arrived to find the writer had not exaggerated, and two decades later she still calls the city home. She currently works as the arts editor for the *Juneau Empire*. She updated the Travel Smart and Juneau, the Inside Passage, and Southeast Alaska chapters for this guide.

Dawnell Smith has called Alaska home for over 30 years and currently resides in Anchorage. She makes a living in the nonprofit and gig economy and has previously worked as a brewer, journalist, nonprofit administrator, communications strategist, bookshop owner, and mom, among other things. She writes essays, poems, and other mixed-genre literary work and has been published in multiple newspapers, magazines, and literary journals. She updated the Bush chapter this edition.